First published in 2009 by
Amnesty International
Publications
International Secretariat
Peter Benenson House
1 Easton Street
London WC1X ODW
United Kingdom

© Copyright
Amnesty International
Publications 2009
Index: POL 10/001/2009

ISBN: 978-0-86210-444-3
ISSN: 0309-068X

A catalogue record for this
book is available from the
British Library.

Original language: English

Photographs:
All photographs appear with
full credits and captions
elsewhere in the report.

Printed on 100% recycled
post-consumer waste paper by
Pureprint Group
East Sussex
United Kingdom

Pureprint is a CarbonNeutral
company, and uses only
vegetable-oil-based inks.

www.amnesty.org

AMNESTY INTERNATIONAL REPORT 2009
THE STATE OF THE WORLD'S HUMAN RIGHTS

09

This report covers the period January to December 2008.

Overcrowding in the Pamandzi migration detention centre in Mayotte (a French overseas territory), December 2008. The UN Human Rights Committee has expressed concerns about the conditions in French detention centres.

PREFACE

'ALL PEOPLE ARE BORN FREE AND EQUAL, IN DIGNITY AND RIGHTS'

Universal Declaration of Human Rights, 1948

The *Amnesty International Report 2009* documents the state of human rights during 2008, in 157 countries and territories around the world. It reveals the systemic discrimination and insecurity that prevent progress in law from becoming a reality on the ground. Crucially, this report reveals a world where, time-and-again, states pick and choose the rights they are willing to uphold, and those they would rather suppress.

The report opens with five regional overviews that highlight the key events and trends that dominated the human rights agenda in each region in 2008.

The heart of the book is a country-by-country survey of human rights, from Afghanistan to Zimbabwe. Each entry begins with a summary of the human rights situation in the country. Amnesty International's concerns on various issues are then set out, highlighting individual cases where appropriate.

If an issue is not covered in a country entry, this should not be taken as a statement by Amnesty International that abuses within this category did not occur. Nor can the absence of an entry on a particular country or territory be taken to imply that no human rights abuses of concern to Amnesty International took place there during 2008. In particular, the length of individual entries cannot be used as the basis for a comparison of the extent and depth of Amnesty International's concerns.

AMNESTY INTERNATIONAL

Amnesty International is a worldwide movement of people who campaign for internationally recognized human rights to be respected and protected. Its vision is for every person to enjoy all of the human rights enshrined in the Universal Declaration of Human Rights and other international human rights standards.

Amnesty International's mission is to conduct research and take action to prevent and end grave abuses of all human rights — civil, political, social, cultural and economic. From freedom of expression and association to physical and mental integrity, from protection from discrimination to the right to shelter — these rights are indivisible.

Amnesty International is funded mainly by its membership and public donations. No funds are sought or accepted from governments for investigating and campaigning against human rights abuses. Amnesty International is independent of any government, political ideology, economic interest or religion.

Amnesty International is a democratic movement whose major policy decisions are taken by representatives from all national sections at International Council meetings held every two years. The members of the International Executive Committee, elected by the Council to carry out its decisions are Soledad García Muñoz (Argentina - Vice-Chair), Deborah Smith (Canada - Eng), Pietro Antonioli (Italy), Lilian Gonçalves-Ho Kang You (Netherlands), Vanushi Rajanayagam Walters (New Zealand), Christine Pamp (Sweden), Levent Korkut (Turkey), Peter Pack (UK - Chair), Imran Riffat (USA - co-opted member), David Stamps (USA - International Treasurer) and Tjalling J. S. Tiemstra (Netherlands - co-opted member). Amnesty International's Secretary General is Irene Khan (Bangladesh).

An overhead view of the remains of the burned-out village of Abu Suruj, Sudan, which was bombed on 8 February 2008 by the Sudanese army in an attempt to regain control of Western Darfur. Attacks on a number of villages in the area displaced an estimated 30,000 people.

COUNTRY DATA

The facts at the top of each individual country entry in this report have been drawn from the following sources:

All **Life expectancy** and **Adult literacy** figures are from the UN Development Programme's Human Development Index, found at http://hdr.undp.org/en/media/hdr_20072008_en_indicator_tables.pdf

The latest figures available were Life expectancy at birth (2005) and Adult literacy rate (percentage aged 15 and above, 1995-2005).

Data refer to national literacy estimates from censuses or surveys conducted between 1995 and 2005, unless otherwise specified. For more information see the UNDP website or www.uis.unesco.org

Some countries that fall into the UNDP's 'high human development' bracket have been assumed by the UNDP to have a literacy rate of 99 per cent for purposes of calculating the Human Development Index. Where this is the case, we have omitted the figure.

All **Population** and **Under-5 mortality** figures are for 2008 and are drawn from the UN Fund for Population Activities' Democratic, Social and Economic Indicators, found at www.unfpa.org/swp/2008/presskit/docs/en_indicators-sowp08.pdf

Population figures are there solely to indicate the number of people affected by the issues we describe. Amnesty International acknowledges the limitations of such figures, and takes no position on questions such as disputed territory or the inclusion or exclusion of certain population groups.

Some country entries in this report have no reference to some or all of the above categories. Such omissions are for a number of reasons, including the absence of the information in the UN lists cited above.

These are the latest available figures at the time of going to print, and are for context purposes only. Due to differences in methodology and timeliness of underlying data, comparisons across countries should be made with caution.

THE FOLLOWING ABBREVIATIONS ARE USED IN THIS REPORT:

ASEAN	Association of South East Asian Nations
AU	African Union
ECOWAS	Economic Community of West African States
European Committee for the Prevention of Torture	European Committee for the Prevention of Torture and Inhuman or Degrading Treatment or Punishment
European Convention on Human Rights	(European) Convention for the Protection of Human Rights and Fundamental Freedoms
EU	European Union
ICRC	International Committee of the Red Cross
ILO	International Labour Organization
NATO	North Atlantic Treaty Organization
NGO	Non-Governmental Organization
OAS	Organization of American States
OSCE	Organization for Security and Co-operation in Europe
UN	United Nations
UN Children's Convention	Convention on the Rights of the Child
UN Convention against Racism	International Convention on the Elimination of All Forms of Racial Discrimination
UN Convention against Torture	Convention against Torture and Other Cruel, Inhuman or Degrading Treatment or Punishment
UNHCR, the UN refugee agency	UN High Commissioner for Refugees
UNICEF	UN Children's Fund
UN Migrant Workers Convention	International Convention on the Protection of the Rights of All Migrant Workers and Members of Their Families
UN Refugee Convention	Convention relating to the Status of Refugees
UN Special Rapporteur on indigenous people	Special Rapporteur on the situation of human rights and fundamental freedoms of indigenous people
UN Special Rapporteur on racism	Special Rapporteur on contemporary forms of racism, racial discrimination, xenophobia and related intolerance
UN Women's Convention	Convention on the Elimination of All Forms of Discrimination against Women
WHO	World Health Organization

A police officer uses a Taser on a suspect following a chase at Huntington Beach, California, 13 April 2008. Since 2001, 346 people have died after being Tasered by police in the USA.

AMNESTY INTERNATIONAL REPORT 2009
PART ONE: REGIONAL OVERVIEWS

Kibera slum outside Nairobi, Kenya, is home to over one million people. Rapid urbanization and widespread poverty in many African countries means that large numbers of people find themselves without adequate housing, often living in slums.

AFRICA

Soldiers wearing red berets travelled 300 kilometres north from the Guinean capital Conakry, to Khoréra, near Boké. They were looking for Karamba Dramé, a youth leader in the town. When they found him, one of the soldiers shot him. He died before he reached hospital on 31 October 2008.

As in many countries across Africa, Guinea's population was hit hard by rising food and commodity prices during the year. Demonstrations erupted and the authorities believed that Karamba Dramé was one of the organizers of the protests. So they killed him.

The food crisis, which marked 2008 in Africa, had a disproportionate impact on vulnerable population groups, especially those already living in poverty. Across the Africa region, people demonstrated against the desperate social and economic situation and the sharp rise in living costs. While some demonstrations turned violent, leading to the destruction of private and public property, the authorities often repressed protests using excessive force. Security forces injured and killed numerous people who were claiming their right to an adequate standard of living, including the right to food. Protesters were arbitrarily arrested and detained. Some were ill-treated in detention or sentenced to prison terms after unfair trials. Most of the time, no investigations were carried out to identify those among the security forces responsible for the human rights violations committed while responding to the protests.

Deprivation

Millions across the region continued to be deprived of their basic needs in spite of the sustained economic growth in many countries in Africa during past years. People faced enormous challenges in securing a daily livelihood, often aggravated by marginalization or political repression, attempts to muffle their voices and render them powerless.

Despite such repression, demonstrators against the dire social and economic situation and the sharp rise in living costs took to the streets in numerous countries, including Benin, Burkina Faso, Cameroon, Côte d'Ivoire, Guinea, Mali, Mozambique, Senegal, Somalia and Zimbabwe. The demonstrations, sometimes violent themselves, were usually met with yet more violence by the state. In late February security forces in Cameroon killed up to 100 people in response to violent protests in various towns against the escalating cost of living and low wages. Some of those killed were apparently shot in the head at close range. In Mozambique, the police killed three people and injured 30 others in February when live ammunition was used against people protesting against an increase in transport costs.

In Mali, marches were organized against the rise in the price of basic commodities and against plans to privatize the supply of water in Lere, in the north-west of the country. At least six people were injured in November, one of whom died later in hospital, when security forces shot at the demonstrators. In Burkina Faso, security forces arrested several hundred people, after demonstrations against rising living costs in Ouagadougou and Bobo-Dioulasso erupted into violence. At least 80 of those arrested were sentenced to prison terms without having had access to a lawyer.

In Zimbabwe, hundreds of activists protesting against the dramatic decline in the economy and social infrastructure were arrested and detained without charge. Many protests were broken up by the police, often using excessive force. The government continued to manipulate access to food for political motives even though by the end of the year the UN estimated that about five million people were in need of food aid. Thousands of people, mostly in rural areas, became displaced as a result of the state-sponsored political violence and no longer had access to their food stocks, land or other forms of livelihood.

Thousands of people continued to migrate to other countries hoping to improve their families' lives. Many, in desperation, took to the sea, putting their lives in the hands of ruthless traffickers. Hundreds of people leaving the Horn of Africa across the Gulf of Aden, in an attempt to reach Yemen, died during the journey. In Mauritania, hundreds of migrants, believed to be heading to Europe, were arbitrarily arrested and detained in the country. Many were detained in inhuman conditions and ill-treated before being expelled, frequently not to their countries of origin and without being able to challenge the expulsion decision.

The rapid urbanization and prevailing poverty in many African countries means that many people find themselves without adequate housing, often living in slums. They are at risk of being forcibly evicted by the authorities and while living in the slums frequently have no access to basic facilities, such as water and sanitation. In Lagos, Nigeria, numerous people were forcibly evicted without due process and subsequently did not receive compensation or alternative housing. In Chad, a presidential decree, issued during the state of emergency early in 2008, ordered the demolition of thousands of homes in the capital N'Djamena, as the authorities considered they had been built on government land without authorization. Tens of thousands of people became homeless and had to seek alternative accommodation. In

Kenya, hundreds of families living close to the Nairobi River faced the threat of forced evictions after the government announced that people living in informal settlements close to the river needed to leave these areas.

Prison conditions in many countries remained well below international standards, often linked to overcrowding. As ever, prisoners from poor families were worst affected as they often lacked the resources to ensure their basic needs while in detention.

Insecurity

Armed conflict and insecurity in several African countries forced hundreds of thousands of people to flee from their homes, trying to find international protection across borders or some form of security within their own country. In some of the worst armed conflicts still affecting the region, government forces and armed groups completely disregarded the dignity and physical integrity of the population. The civilian population was routinely the object of attacks by parties to the conflict; rape and other forms of sexual violence remained widespread; children were often recruited to take part in hostilities; and humanitarian workers were targeted. Those responsible for crimes under international law, committed in the context of these armed conflicts, were hardly ever held to account.

The role of UN and regional peacekeeping missions in Africa increased during 2008, but failed to make a significant impact in terms of protecting the civilian population. This was partly, but not entirely, the result of inadequate resources. The UN and regional bodies, such as the African Union, made little progress in resolving the armed conflicts in Sudan (Darfur), Chad, Somalia and the Democratic Republic of the Congo (North Kivu).

The proliferation of small arms remained a significant contributing factor to the continuation of armed conflicts and to widespread human rights abuses. UN arms embargoes have not been effective.

The international community mobilized unprecedented resources to combat piracy off the coast of Somalia and to protect its commercial interests. It made no such efforts, however, to halt the flow of arms to Somalia – despite a UN embargo. Nor did it act effectively to stop the widespread violations of international humanitarian law by all parties to the conflict; nor to hold those responsible for crimes under international law accountable.

Hundreds of thousands of people were also newly displaced as a result of the conflict in Somalia. Fighting in and around the capital Mogadishu has led to 16,000 deaths, and undocumented numbers of wounded, among the civilian population since January 2007. The

WE HAVE BEEN HIT WITH A DOUBLE MISFORTUNE. FIRST WE HAD TO FLEE BECAUSE OUR CITY CAME UNDER ATTACK. NOW WE HAVE NOWHERE TO RETURN TO BECAUSE THE GOVERNMENT HAS DESTROYED OUR HOMES. WILL THE MISFORTUNE EVER END?

Chadian refugee, Maltam refugee camp, Cameroon, May 2008.

Transitional Federal Government was not able to establish its authority across south central Somalia and lost ground to armed opposition groups. Humanitarian organizations had only limited access to provide emergency assistance to an estimated 3.2 million people in need. Aid workers, as well as journalists and human rights defenders, were often targeted for political and criminal reasons.

The armed conflict in the eastern Democratic Republic of the Congo escalated again during the second half of 2008. Numerous human rights abuses were committed by all the parties to the conflict, including killings and abductions of civilians, rape and other forms of sexual violence, and the recruitment and use of children as armed fighters. Hundreds of thousands of people fled the fighting.

The armed conflict in Darfur intensified throughout the year with no political resolution in sight. Attacks against civilians continued, as well as rape, looting and the destruction of villages. Millions of people remained internally displaced and humanitarian organizations often had no access to those in need because of the overall insecurity and the attacks on humanitarian convoys. As a result, thousands of people remained beyond the reach of emergency aid. People lacked protection from violence, even in internally displaced sites. In just one example in August, the authorities surrounded Kalma camp in South Darfur, opened fire and reportedly shelled the camp, killing 47 people.

The armed opposition group, Justice and Equality Movement (JEM), launched an attack against Omdurman, on the outskirts of the capital Khartoum in May. In the aftermath of the attack, the Sudanese authorities persecuted people thought to be of Darfuri origin. Hundreds of people were arbitrarily arrested and detained – many were tortured or otherwise ill-treated. There were also reports of extrajudicial executions.

Fighting also erupted in Abyei, South Sudan, between the Sudanese Armed Forces and forces of the Sudan People's Liberation Movement (SPLM), resulting in the destruction of the town, the displacement of 50,000 people, and additional strains on the Comprehensive Peace Agreement between North and South Sudan.

Tensions between Chad and Sudan rose again during 2008, especially after an attack in early February by Chadian armed opposition groups on N'Djamena. After two days of intense fighting, Chadian government forces repelled the attack. Subsequently, the government declared a state of emergency and arrested various members of the opposition, one of whom has become a victim of enforced disappearance. There were also reports of extrajudicial executions immediately after the attack. An estimated 50,000 people

4

fled the violence in N'Djamena and sought refuge in neighbouring Cameroon.

Armed conflict was not the only source of widespread insecurity in the region in 2008. Political violence following elections also played its part in a number of countries. In Kenya, more than 1,000 people died as a result of politically motivated ethnic violence and associated police killings after the elections on 30 December 2007. Hundreds of thousands of people fled their areas of origin and some fled to neighbouring countries such as Uganda. In Zimbabwe, at least 180 people were killed and thousands injured as a result of state-sponsored political violence before and after the second round of presidential elections. Many continued to flee to neighbouring countries, particularly South Africa. In both Kenya and Zimbabwe, the violence and insecurity not only affected the people's physical security, but also their capacity to earn a livelihood as thousands lost their homes, food supplies, access to land and other sources of income. Hundreds of thousands of people became dependent on humanitarian assistance for their basic needs as a result of political violence.

Tens of thousands of people fleeing xenophobic attacks in South Africa in May also became dependent on humanitarian assistance as they had to flee from their homes and lost all their possessions. Over 60 people were killed and more than 600 were injured after people were beaten, sexually assaulted and killed in various provinces, often by people living in the same community. These xenophobic attacks against individuals, targeted because of their perceived nationality, ethnicity or migrant status, were fuelled partly by the deprivation in which many South Africans still live. Official investigations failed to bring the perpetrators to justice, or to clarify the causes of the violence.

Exclusion

Many groups in African societies continued to face discrimination and exclusion from protection or the means to get redress for the abuses they suffered. In Uganda, for example, victims of numerous human rights abuses during the armed conflict in the north of the country remained destitute and traumatized, often excluded from any means of redress.

Across the Africa region, people suffered discrimination within their families and communities because of their gender or their HIV status, exacerbated by their poverty. In South Africa for example, where 5.7 million people were living with HIV, poor rural women continued to face barriers in accessing health services for HIV and AIDS due to unmanageable distances from health facilities and

I WAS AT HOME WHEN A YOUNG FARDC SOLDIER CAME TO THE HOUSE... THEN HE RAPED ME... I WAS TOLD LATER THAT HE WAS WHIPPED AS A PUNISHMENT, BUT THE SOLDIER IS STILL AT THE CAMP AND I SEE HIM REGULARLY. WHEN I SEE HIM, HE TRIES TO JOKE WITH ME. HE FRIGHTENS ME. I FEEL VERY ANXIOUS AND DEPRESSED. I WOULD LIKE TO PRESS CHARGES, BUT WHAT COULD I REALLY DO TO A SOLDIER?

Venantie, a 56-year-old widowed farmer in Beni territory, North Kivu, DRC, was raped on 25 January 2008.

transport costs. Stigma and gender-based discrimination, including violence, also affected the women's ability to protect themselves against HIV infection and to seek health care and support.

Women were also discriminated against in various societies under customary laws and traditional practices. The customary laws of certain ethnic groups in Namibia, for example, discriminate against women and girls, specifically laws on marriage and inheritance.

In various countries, notably Tanzania, albino people were murdered in what were believed to be ritual killings. Although the government of Tanzania denounced the killings, nobody was prosecuted in relation to them during 2008, even though a number of people were arrested.

People were persecuted for their (perceived) sexual orientation in countries including Cameroon, Gambia, Nigeria, Rwanda, Senegal and Uganda. In various countries, same-sex sexual relationships were a criminal offence.

In many African countries the judicial system lacks independence. In addition, the justice system is often under-resourced, poorly equipped and understaffed, leading to excessive delays in hearing criminal cases. For those with little access to financial resources, negotiating the criminal justice system can prove a nightmare.

In Nigeria, for example, those who are poor face numerous obstacles to obtaining a fair trial within an acceptable period of time. Although some efforts have been made to provide legal aid, it is not nearly enough to grant legal representation for all who need it but cannot afford to pay for a lawyer – even in cases carrying the death penalty. The more than 700 people living on death row in Nigeria in 2008 all had one thing in common – they were poor.

However, in a landmark decision, the Community Court of Justice of the Economic Community of West African States (ECOWAS) ordered the government of Niger to pay reparations to a woman who had been held in domestic and sexual slavery for a decade, on the basis that the authorities had failed to implement existing laws against slavery.

Voice

Governments continued to restrict, without justification, the rights to freedom of expression, association and peaceful assembly. However, efforts by governments to control information were also countered by increasingly vibrant civil societies, often working in partnership with each other, and stronger independent media.

Legislation or other forms of regulation were frequently used to restrict the work of civil society and the media. In Ethiopia, the authorities prepared a draft bill that criminalizes human rights activities and gives authorities an excessive level of control over civil society organizations. In Swaziland, the new Suppression of Terrorism Act, with its impermissibly broad definitions of terrorism, had a chilling effect on the activities of civil society organizations and infringed the rights of freedom of expression, peaceful assembly and association. In Chad, a presidential decree to limit press freedom remained in place even after the state of emergency was lifted. In Sudan, censorship over privately owned media outlets was reinforced. In Rwanda, the space for independent media workers, including foreign journalists, remained restricted. In Lesotho, restrictive broadcasting regulations and the use of criminal defamation, sedition and similar charges continued to take their toll on individual media workers and infringed the right to freedom of expression. In Kenya, parliament passed a media bill, and in Uganda, the authorities were drafting legislation: both laws would further restrict press freedom. In Niger, the government imposed a media blackout on the conflict in the north of the country and banned journalists from travelling there.

In numerous countries, including Angola, Cameroon, Chad, Equatorial Guinea, Gambia, Niger, Nigeria, Senegal, Sudan, Tanzania and Togo, media outlets were suspended because the authorities disapproved of their stories. Journalists were routinely arrested and sometimes charged with criminal offences, purely for carrying out their work.

Political opponents of the government were arbitrarily arrested and detained in Burkina Faso, Burundi, Cameroon, Chad, Equatorial Guinea, Ethiopia, Gambia, Mauritania, Republic of Congo, Swaziland and Zimbabwe. In some cases members of the political opposition were subjected to enforced disappearance or unlawfully killed. In other countries the space for political opposition, free speech and civil society was non-existent, such as in Eritrea.

Human rights defenders remained at risk in various countries and were often harassed and sometimes arrested for defending their rights as well as the rights of others. Journalists and human rights activists regularly had to flee their country because of security risks.

In Zimbabwe, numerous human rights activists, trade union representatives and political opposition members were arrested. Some were abducted and killed by government security forces as well as non-state actors working on behalf of the authorities. In Cameroon, Central African Republic, Chad and Sudan, human rights defenders were also arrested. In some cases those detained were tortured or otherwise ill-treated. In a number of countries civil society organizations were closed down, or threatened with closure, by the authorities.

REGIONAL OVERVIEWS
AFRICA

I WANT TO BE COMPENSATED FOR THE INJURIES. I WANT TO TALK TO MY ATTACKERS AND BE TOLD THE TRUTH ABOUT WHY I WAS BEATEN. I ALSO WANT THEM TO BE BROUGHT TO JUSTICE.

Lyn, an 86-year-old woman victim of politically motivated violence, Zimbabwe, August 2008.

Accountability

Unless governments address impunity in a serious manner the widespread human rights violations across this region will continue. At the moment, those who abuse others' rights can continue to do so freely. Occasionally, after large-scale human rights violations, commissions of inquiry or other types of investigative panels are set up, but they are often more to appease public opinion than to establish the truth and identify those responsible.

In Chad, a national commission of inquiry into hundreds of killings and other human rights violations in February 2008 published its report in September – no action was taken by the government to implement its recommendations. A commission of inquiry set up in Guinea to investigate human rights violations committed in 2006 and 2007 did not conduct any investigations. In Liberia, the Truth and Reconciliation Commission concluded its public hearings and its findings were pending by the end of the year. The commission of inquiry in Kenya, set up to investigate the post-election violence, made its findings public in October. Even though the government pledged to implement the recommendations in the report it had not, by the end of the year, put in place a comprehensive plan of action to do so.

Unfortunately, governments often use commissions of inquiry, or truth and reconciliation, as surrogates for judicial inquiries, which are essential for establishing individual criminal responsibility.

The International Criminal Court (ICC) continued to pursue a number of cases from Africa. The application by the ICC Prosecutor for an arrest warrant to be issued against President Omar Al Bashir of Sudan for war crimes, crimes against humanity and genocide triggered efforts to undermine the work of the ICC by various states and regional bodies, including the African Union (AU). The AU, the League of Arab States and the Organization of the Islamic Conference called on the UN Security Council to defer the case. On the initiative of Rwanda, the AU adopted a decision criticizing what it called the abuse of universal jurisdiction.

While the ICC continued to pursue a number of cases from Africa, it can only prosecute a limited number of individuals. It is essential that national jurisdictions also investigate and prosecute those suspected of being responsible for crimes under international law, including by exercising universal jurisdiction. Regrettably, Senegal has only made limited progress in the case of former Chadian President Hissène Habré, indicating a lack of political will to initiate serious investigations.

On a more positive note, the AU adopted the Protocol on the

Statute of the African Court of Justice and Human Rights in July. Once operational, the Court could contribute to ending impunity in Africa if AU member states agree to allow victims of human rights violations to approach the Court directly for an effective remedy.

Conclusion

There is still an enormous gap between the rhetoric of African governments, which claim to protect and respect human rights, and the daily reality where human rights violations remain the norm.

In 2008, Africans deprived of their rights took to the streets. Protests often became violent, with resentment fuelled by the repressive attitudes of governments towards dissent and protest. These protests are likely to continue.

So many people are living in utter destitution; so few of them have any chance to free themselves from poverty. Their dire situation is exacerbated by the failure of governments in the Africa region to provide basic social services, ensure respect for the rule of law, address corruption and be accountable to their people.

As the global economic outlook appears more and more gloomy, hope lies in the continuing vitality of civil societies across the region, and the determination of human rights defenders willing to challenge entrenched interests despite the risks they face.

REGIONAL OVERVIEWS
AFRICA

EVEN THE SHORT MAN CAN SEE THE SKY. WHEN WILL THE INTERNATIONAL COMMUNITY SEE WHAT IS HAPPENING IN SOMALIA?

Somali human rights defender Abdullahi Alas Jumale, currently in exile, July 2008.

Women queuing outside a health centre in rural Huancavelica, Peru. Maternal mortality rates in Peru are among the worst in the region. They are disproportionately high among the country's poor and Indigenous rural communities.

AMERICAS

The Enxet Indigenous communities of Yakye Axa and Sawhoyamaxa in the Bajo Chaco region of Paraguay have been living at the side of the Pozo Colorado-Concepción highway for more than 15 years. Despite rulings in their favour by the Inter-American Court of Human Rights, they remain excluded from their lands. Deprived of their traditional livelihood and way of life, without adequate health care or sanitation, and dependent on irregular government food supplies, they face an insecure present and an uncertain future.

From the northernmost reaches of the Arctic, to the southern tip of Tierra del Fuego, Indigenous Peoples in the Americas have long experienced marginalization and discrimination. Denied a voice in decisions which affect their lands, lives and livelihoods, Indigenous Peoples are disproportionately affected by poverty, even when living in areas rich in minerals and other natural resources. Many still do not enjoy constitutional recognition and their rights to ancestral lands are ignored or dealt with in ways that fail to provide adequate protection to Indigenous economic and cultural traditions. Resource extraction, forestry, agro-industry and other development projects on Indigenous lands are often accompanied by harassment and violence as powerful corporations and private interests flout international and domestic laws in pursuit of profit. A persistent and entrenched cycle of deprivation and social exclusion puts Indigenous people, especially women, at increased risk of attack while helping ensure that their persecutors are rarely held to account.

Faced with this legacy of appalling human rights violations, Indigenous Peoples throughout the Americas region have mobilized to make themselves heard. Their demands for respect for their land rights and cultural identity, for their right not to face discrimination, indeed for their entitlement to all human rights, are increasingly being brought to the heart of, and reinvigorating, the human rights discourse in the region.

The Yakye Axa and Sawhoyamaxa communities were able to take their case to a regional court and were helped in doing so by a number of NGOs. This reflects the increasing collaboration and co-ordination of the Indigenous and human rights movement in the region, which allows defenders, campaigners and activists to draw strength, support and inspiration from each other's experiences and successes.

Insecurity

In Colombia, many of the human rights abuses committed in the internal armed conflict – including killings and enforced disappearances – are aimed at displacing civilian communities from areas of economic or strategic importance. Many Indigenous communities live in regions rich in mineral and other resources on lands legally and collectively owned by them. Such communities are often attacked in an effort to force them to flee so that the area can be opened up for large-scale economic development. Those communities that campaign against such development are accused of being "subversive" – an accusation which is often followed by paramilitary attacks. Guerrilla groups also threaten and kill members of Indigenous communities whom they accuse of siding with the enemy. However, Indigenous Peoples in Colombia are becoming increasingly militant in defence of their human rights. In the last few months of 2008, thousands of Indigenous people staged large-scale protests across various parts of the country, culminating in a march to the capital, Bogotá, in November to protest at continued human rights abuses and in support of their land rights.

In Mexico, members of the community of Huizopa, in the northern state of Chihuahua, which includes Pima and Raramuri Indigenous Peoples, demanded a mining company's operations on communal lands comply with agreements made with the community. Those supporting the protests faced threats and police operations to break up protests.

In Chile, the continuing expansion of the extractive and forestry industries combined with the slow progress in resolving land claims continued to provoke tensions between the authorities and Indigenous Peoples, particularly the Mapuche. In a worrying development in 2008, a regional prosecutor sought to use an anti-terrorism law against protesters supporting the Mapuche claims. The government had given repeated assurances that the law, which dates from the period of military government under General Augusto Pinochet, should not be used against Indigenous people seeking recognition of their rights.

In Bolivia, entrenched racism and discrimination persisted. Efforts by the government of President Evo Morales to promote the rights of Bolivia's Indigenous Peoples and other marginalized sectors of society met opposition from powerful landowning families and the business elite, fearful of losing long-held privileges. Tensions exploded into violence which culminated in the killing of 19 campesinos (peasant farmers) in Pando department in September. Investigations by the Union of South American Nations (UNASUR) and the Ombudsman's Office found that local officials were directly involved in the killings and that police had failed to protect the Indigenous and campesino protesters.

However, some states are increasingly having to recognize the legitimate claims of Indigenous Peoples and take steps to make them a reality. A Supreme Court decision in Brazil to recognize the constitutional rights to their ancestral lands of the Makuxi, Wapixana, Ingarikó, Taurepang and Patamona Peoples marked an important step in a 30-year battle and was widely seen as a landmark victory for the rights of Inidgenous Peoples in Raposa Serra do Sol state. However, positive outcomes remained an exception and many Indigenous Peoples continue the struggle for their land.

In Nicaragua the government finally recognized the land rights of the Awas Tingni Indigenous community, thereby complying with a 2001 decision of the Inter-American Court of Human Rights. In Suriname, the Saramaka People, descendants of escaped African slaves who established settlements in the rainforest interior in the 17th and 18th centuries won a judgment in their favour by the Inter-American Court of Human Rights. In a ruling by the Court regarding logging and mining concessions on the territory of the Saramaka People, the Court established that: "The State violated, to the detriment of the members of the Saramaka people, the right to property."

Violence against women and girls

Women's groups continue to demand action over an increasing number of homicides in the region. Many of the women's bodies bore marks of torture and in particular sexual violence. However, the response of many governments, particularly those in Central America, remains woefully inadequate and few of the killings have been properly investigated.

Laws to improve respect for women's rights and in particular the right to freedom from violence in the home, community and workplace, exist in most countries in the region, with the notable exceptions of Haiti and some other Caribbean countries. Nevertheless, progress on preventing violence against women and punishing those responsible remained limited. In Nicaragua, for example, specialist police investigation teams dealing with gender-based violence against women remain woefully under-resourced and in Venezuela specialist training for law enforcement officials on dealing with violence in the home has failed to materialize.

Nicaragua and Haiti stood out in the region as two countries where more than 50 per cent of all reported victims of sexual abuse were 18 years old or younger. In the vast majority of cases, the perpetrators were adult men, many holding positions of power. The sexual abuse of girls, some as young as nine or 10, was intrinsically linked to poverty, deprivation and exclusion which left the girls at risk of sexual exploitation as their only means of survival. Despite the widespread nature of the problem, the stigma associated with sexual violence condemned many survivors to silence.

BEING RAPED, IT MAKES YOU... A PERSON WITHOUT RIGHTS, A PERSON REJECTED FROM SOCIETY AND NOW, IN THE NEIGHBOURHOOD I LIVE IN, IT'S AS THOUGH I AM RAPED EVERY DAY BECAUSE EVERY DAY SOMEONE REMINDS ME THAT I SHOULD PUT MYSELF IN A CORNER, THAT I SHOULDN'T SPEAK, I SHOULD SAY NOTHING.

Rose (not her real name), interviewed by Amnesty International in Haiti, March 2008.

Given the high levels of sexual violence, it is particularly worrying that Nicaragua, along with Chile and El Salvador, continued a prohibition of abortion in all circumstances – even in cases where the pregnancy was the result of rape or where continued pregnancy could put the woman or girl's life at risk. There were reports of efforts by religious pressure groups in Peru and Ecuador to seek a similar ban. In Uruguay, despite widespread popular support for abortion to be decriminalized, President Tabaré Vázquez vetoed proposed reforms on the grounds of his personal religious beliefs. In contrast, in Mexico the Supreme Court voted to allow legislation decriminalizing abortion in the District of Mexico City.

Of the five countries in the Americas where a reduction in maternal mortality by 2015 is a government priority, national maternal mortality ratios (there is no disaggregated data for different maternal groups) decreased in Bolivia, Brazil, Mexico and Peru, but not in Haiti, where only 26 per cent of births were supported by a skilled attendant in 2008.

Deprivation

Many Latin American and Caribbean countries have made efforts in the last decade to reduce poverty. However, despite some progress, more than 70 million people were living on less than US$1 a day and levels of social inequality and disparities in wealth remained high. According to the UN Development Programme, Latin America remained the most unequal region in the world.

Marginalized and dispossessed communities in rural and urban settings in many countries continued to be denied their rights to health care, clean water, education and adequate housing. This already critical situation risked being exacerbated by the global economic crisis.

In relation to health indicators, figures published by the UN Population Fund showed that the Dominican Republic and Guatemala were among the countries with the lowest level of spending on public health care – a mere 1.7 per cent and 2 per cent of GDP respectively. This was in stark comparison with Cuba which spends 6.9 per cent of GDP on health and the USA where spending stood at 7.2 per cent of GDP. Nevertheless, thousands of people in the USA remained without health insurance, with many poor and marginalized people finding it difficult to access adequate health care.

Death penalty

Most countries in the region have abolished the death penalty either in law or in practice. However, in the USA, a notable exception in the region, the death penalty and deprivation remained inextricably interlinked; the vast majority of the more than 3,000 people on death row are too poor to pay for legal representation of their choice.

In April, the US Supreme Court issued a decision that execution by lethal injection did not violate the US Constitution. Executions resumed in May after a seven-month hiatus. By the end of the year, 37 prisoners had been put to death, bringing to 1,136 the number of executions since the USA resumed judicial killing in 1977.

The Supreme Court's decision is notable for the separate opinion by Justice John Paul Stevens, who has served on the Court since December 1975 and has therefore witnessed the entire "modern" era of the death penalty in the USA. He wrote that his experience had led him to the conclusion that "the imposition of the death penalty represents the pointless and needless extinction of life with only marginal contributions to any discernible social or public purposes. A penalty with such negligible returns to the State is patently excessive and cruel and unusual punishment". He added that racial discrimination continued "to play an unacceptable role in capital cases".

In December, Saint Kitts and Nevis carried out the first execution in the English-speaking Caribbean since 2000. Charles Elroy Laplace was hanged on 19 December 2008, ending a 10-year moratorium. He had been convicted of murder in 2006 and his appeal was dismissed in October 2008 for being filed out of time.

Exclusion

The trend towards improved political stability witnessed in the previous 10 years was overshadowed by the worsening crisis in public security.

Levels of police abuses and crime and gang violence were worse in areas where the state was largely absent, allowing criminal gangs to dominate much of the life of the community. In Brazil, for example, many impoverished urban communities continued to be denied basic services and state involvement remained largely limited to periodic military-style incursions by the police. These operations, often involving hundreds of officers in armoured vehicles and helicopters, were characterized by excessive use of force, extrajudicial executions, torture, and abusive behaviour towards residents. In Jamaica, the majority of police killings, many of which were unlawful, occurred in poor inner-city areas.

In Mexico, where criminal violence has spiralled, large numbers of military personnel have been deployed with police to combat crime. Few governments have made the connection between rising crime and abuses by state officials. However, ministers in some countries admitted publicly in 2008 that the quality of policing had fallen below both national and international standards. Mexico, the Dominican Republic, and Trinidad and Tobago all acknowledged significant failings

DOWN THERE, IN THE RICH PART OF TOWN, IT'S DIFFERENT. THEY THINK THAT THE POLICE REALLY HAVE TO INVADE, REALLY HAVE TO KILL, REALLY HAVE TO EXTERMINATE EVERYTHING THAT GOES ON HERE. THEY JUST DON'T SEE THAT THIS IS A COMMUNITY WITH PEOPLE WHO WORK AND CHILDREN THAT STUDY.

Lúcia Cabral, Complexo do Alemão, Brazil, April 2008.

in their police forces and their limited ability to offer reasonable levels of protection and effective law enforcement in many communities as a result. Nevertheless, the steps taken to remove officials responsible for human rights abuses or corruption in no way matched the magnitude of the problem and were bedevilled by procedural and administrative obstacles.

Too many governments have contributed to worsening standards of policing by closing their eyes to reports of torture or unlawful killings. Some have even sought to justify such abuses as necessary in the current public security climate. Independent police complaints commissions or police ombudsmen offices remained largely confined to the USA and Canada. In the few other countries where such bodies exist, they continued to be largely ineffective.

In some countries, such as Guatemala and Brazil, more evidence emerged during the year of the involvement of police officers and former officers in the killing of suspected criminals. In Pernambuco in Brazil, 70 per cent of all homicides in 2008 were attributed to death squads or so-called extermination groups mostly composed of agents of the state, particularly police. In Guatemala, the killing of hundreds of young men reminded many of the social cleansing campaigns of the 1990s when street children suspected of being petty thieves were tortured and killed. The targeting by police and others of groups of young men and boys from poor communities on the basis of their appearance and age aggravated feelings of exclusion from mainstream society.

In some instances, the disregard for life in excluded communities was particularly shocking. For example, dozens of young men from Soacha, near Bogotá, Colombia, were killed by members of the military in order to claim bonuses offered by the government for each "guerrilla" killed.

'War on terror'

There was continuing concern over the treatment of foreign nationals detained by US forces in the "war on terror"; more than 200 men were held in the US Naval Base at Guantánamo Bay in Cuba. However, there was some progress in 2008 in challenging the government's attempts to exclude them from the protections of the law. In June, in a landmark ruling, the US Supreme Court rejected the government's arguments that the Guantánamo detainees should be denied their right to habeas corpus on the grounds that they were non-US nationals captured and held outside US sovereign territory. In November, President-elect Barack Obama confirmed his commitment to take early action after taking office in January 2009 to close the Guantánamo detention facility and to ensure that the USA did not resort to torture.

Voice

Human rights defenders in Latin America remained in the forefront of efforts to make the voices of victims heard, often despite sustained efforts to silence them. On 4 February and 20 July, millions of people marched in Colombia and around the world in protest at kidnappings by the Revolutionary Armed Forces of Colombia (Fuerzas Armadas Revolucionarias de Colombia, FARC). Thousands of people had also taken to the streets in Colombia on 6 March to demand an end to human rights abuses by the security forces and paramilitary groups. Four months later, Jhon Fredy Correa Falla, a member of the National Movement of Victims of State Crimes (Movimiento Nacional de Víctimas de Crímenes de Estado), which organized the March protest, was shot dead by four gunmen on motorbikes. Several human rights defenders in Guatemala and Honduras were killed on account of their human rights work.

In several other countries, human rights defenders also faced increasingly hostile reactions from the authorities. In Venezuela, for example, the expulsion of the Director for the Americas of Human Rights Watch in September following publication of a critical report was followed by an upsurge in public statements accusing local NGOs and defenders of being "pro-Yankees", "anti-Bolivarian revolution" and "unpatriotic".

Some governments resorted to misuse of the criminal justice system to frustrate the work of human rights defenders. In Mexico, for example, five Indigenous leaders from the Me' phaa Indigenous People's Organization (Organización del Pueblo Indígena Me' phaa, OPIM) in Guerrero State, were detained in April and charged with murder. Despite a federal decision in October that there was no evidence implicating four of them and despite eyewitness testimonies that the fifth was elsewhere at the time of the murder, the five remained in detention at the end of 2008.

In Nicaragua, nine women human rights defenders faced legal proceedings for their involvement in the case of a nine-year-old Nicaraguan girl who obtained a legal abortion after she was raped in 2003. Although many professionals and officials were involved in the girl's case, the legal complaint focuses only on the women human rights defenders who have a background in promoting sexual health and women's rights.

Defenders promoting the rights of communities long consigned to the margins of society – Indigenous Peoples, Afro-descendant communities, and lesbian, gay, bisexual and transgender people – were often at particular risk. For example, in Honduras, leaders of the Afro-descendant Garifuna community in the village of San Juan Tela, were threatened and forced to sign over community land to a private

EDUCATION IS IMPORTANT SO THAT OUR CHILDREN CAN LEARN SKILLS, USE THE INTERNET, HAVE ACCESS TO THE SAME OPPORTUNITIES AS PARAGUAYANS, SO THEY STOP SAYING THAT THE INDIGENOUS PEOPLE ARE STUPID AND IGNORANT.

Florentín Jara, Sawhoyamaxa community, Paraguay, November 2008.

company at gunpoint. In Ecuador, Esther Landetta, a leading environmental and women's rights activist, was the target of repeated threats and intimidation because of her crucial role in voicing community concerns about the possible negative consequences of irregular mining activities in Guayas Province.

The repression and intimidation of human rights defenders in the region may have varied, but one aspect remained worryingly consistent – in almost all the cases investigated by Amnesty International, those responsible were not brought to justice.

However, justice for the long-silenced victims of gross human rights violations during the military regimes of the 1970s and 1980s moved several steps closer in a number of countries during 2008.

In Paraguay, President Fernando Lugo made a public apology to the victims of human rights violations under the military government of General Alfredo Stroessner. In December, the Truth and Justice Commission published its report and recommendations on human rights violations committed during the military government (1954-1989) and transition to democracy. It identified more than 20,000 victims and recommended that the Public Prosecutor investigate all cases.

In Uruguay, scores of former military officers were called to testify against General Gregorio Alvarez, head of the military government between 1981 and 1985, and Juan Larcebeau, a retired naval officer, accused of the enforced disappearance of more than 30 people.

In Argentina, in the first judgment of its kind, two people were convicted and sentenced to prison terms for the "appropriation" of the daughter of a couple who were the victims of enforced disappearance in 1977. The ex-army captain who stole the child and gave her to the couple was sentenced to 10 years' imprisonment in April.

In El Salvador, two human rights organizations filed a suit in a Spanish court in November against El Salvador's former President, Alfredo Cristiani(1989-1994), and 14 military officers in connection with the murder of six Jesuit priests, their housekeeper and her daughter in 1989.

Brazil stood out as one of the few countries in the region that had yet to confront the scars left by past abuses. By neglecting those who had suffered torture and other abuses, the Brazilian state had not only failed to respect the human rights of these victims, but had allowed abuses to become entrenched.

In Mexico, the 40th anniversary of the massacre of students in Tlateloco square, Mexico City, was commemorated but this was not accompanied by advances in bringing those responsible to justice.

In other cases, there was some progress in holding to account those responsible for more recent human rights violations. In Colombia, dozens of members of the armed forces, many of them senior officers, were dismissed for their alleged involvement in the extrajudicial execution of civilians. In Bolivia, the unprecedented speed with which the international community moved to ensure investigations into the killing of 19 campesinos in September raised hopes that those responsible would be brought to justice. In October, the Bolivian government filed an extradition request with the US government regarding former President Gonzalo Sánchez de Lozada and two former ministers who were accused of involvement in genocide for their role in the killing of 67 people during demonstrations in El Alto in 2003.

In the USA, a Senate committee concluded, after an 18-month inquiry into the treatment of detainees in US custody, that senior officials in the US government had "solicited information on how to use aggressive techniques, redefined the law to create the appearance of their legality, and authorized their use against detainees". Among other things, the committee found that the authorization by former Secretary of Defense Donald Rumsfeld of aggressive techniques for use in Guantánamo "was a direct cause of detainee abuse there" and had contributed to the abuse of detainees in US custody in Afghanistan and Iraq.

Conclusion

Throughout the Americas region, human rights defenders continue to work for a world where everyone is able to live with dignity and where all human rights are respected. To do this, defenders often have to challenge powerful social and economic elites, as well as the inertia and complicity of governments that are failing to honour their obligations to promote and defend human rights.

THE CANADIAN GOVERNMENT AND THE OIL COMPANIES... PERSIST IN THE DESTRUCTION OF OUR LAND AND OUR WAY OF LIFE. AT TIMES WE MAY SEEM DEFEATED AND INCAPABLE, BUT I ASSURE YOU WE ARE NOT. AS LONG AS THERE ARE LUBICON PEOPLE LEFT, WE WILL CONTINUE TO FIGHT FOR A FAIR AND JUST RELATIONSHIP WITH GOVERNMENTS AND CORPORATIONS ALIKE.

Cynthia Tomlinson, Lubicon Cree member, Alberta, Canada, April 2008.

Displaced civilians moving to safety in the Kilinochchi District, Wanni, Sri Lanka, September 2008. Hundreds of thousands of civilians displaced as a result of fighting lack access to adequate food, shelter, sanitation and medical care.

ASIA-PACIFIC

On 20 May, in Kawhmu township, near Yangon, the Myanmar authorities prevented desperate survivors of Cyclone Nargis from coming out onto the street to beg while punishing people who tried to help them – effectively cutting them off from any informal assistance. Almost three weeks earlier, the cyclone had devastated much of southern Myanmar, killing tens of thousands of people and displacing hundreds of thousands more from their homes and livelihoods.

The cyclone should have also wiped away any lingering doubts over whether repressive government policies can impoverish a population. The world watched in horror as Myanmar's government, the State Peace and Development Council (SPDC), refused to acknowledge the scope of the disaster and provided little assistance to the estimated 2.4 million survivors of the cyclone. For three weeks, the SPDC also rejected international assistance and blocked access to the Ayeyarwady delta when survivors most needed food, shelter and medicine. Instead, a week after the cyclone, as victims were still struggling to survive, the SPDC diverted crucial resources towards a rubber stamp referendum to approve a new and deeply flawed Constitution. By deliberately blocking vital aid while failing to provide adequate assistance itself the SPDC violated the rights of hundreds of thousands to life, food, and health.

In countries throughout the Asia-Pacific region, hundreds of millions of people suffered from government policies they were either unable or afraid to challenge. Millions more slid into poverty as the cost of food, fuel, and other commodities rose, in part as a result of a global financial crisis. Most of these people were denied the right to help shape an appropriate response to these crises by their own governments.

But the events around Cyclone Nargis were so extreme they elicited action from Myanmar's neighbours in the Association of South East Asian Nations (ASEAN), as well as from China, the country's chief international backer. Although these governments have previously claimed that international human rights clash with "Asian values", threaten national sovereignty, and deny the primacy of economic development, in the face of such large-scale disaster, ASEAN publicly called on the Myanmar authorities to provide access to aid, and went on to mediate between the SPDC and the international community.

Even more notably, the Chinese government responded to the scope of the catastrophe (and the desire to protect its image in the run-up to the 2008 Olympics in Beijing) by deviating from its long-held position of not interfering in the affairs of other sovereign states and seems to have used its significant influence to persuade the SPDC to cooperate with international offers of aid.

The Beijing Olympics, and China's resulting heightened sensitivity to its image, raised hopes for real and sustained improvements in the country's overall human rights situation. Indeed, this had been one of the reasons offered by the International Olympics Committee for awarding Beijing the Games. Instead, the run-up to the Olympics was marred by increased repression throughout the country as authorities tightened control over human rights defenders, religious practitioners, ethnic minorities, lawyers and journalists. The Chinese authorities forcibly evicted thousands of Beijing residents from their homes and punished those who dared challenge the government's actions.

As a sporting event, the Games were widely praised for their magnificence. They showed the government's ability to marshal massive resources and proved, as they were intended to, that China has assumed its position as one of the world's leading powers. But the Games also served to point out that a country capable of mounting such a spectacle cannot justify the failure to meet many of the human rights aspirations of its people, and in particular the rights of tens of millions of citizens who have not been allowed to share in the country's phenomenal economic development.

Deprivation

For years, the Chinese government advanced its economic policies upon the back of some 150 million migrant workers, most of whom flocked from the countryside into slums in China's rapidly growing cities. But with the end of the building boom associated with the Olympics, and the growing impact of the global economic crisis, China's millions of migrant workers faced an uncertain future as 2008 waned and they returned to their villages, without the promise of a constantly growing economy, and aware of how much their lives differed from those of China's increasingly affluent urban middle classes. The social tensions caused by this growing rift and awareness of the disparities between rich and poor, urban and rural, led to thousands of protests throughout China.

The Asia-Pacific region as a whole houses some of the world's wealthiest areas (in Australia, China, Japan, South Korea) next to some of the most impoverished populations (Afghanistan, Bangladesh, Laos, Myanmar, North Korea, Papua New Guinea). Throughout 2008, the differences in the wellbeing of these people seemed much more to do with government policy, than the distribution of natural resources.

Asia's other giant, India, has tried to achieve economic progress while maintaining a solid commitment to civil and political rights internally. But the Indian authorities have not managed to ensure the rights of the urban poor and already marginalized communities in rural areas, including landless farmers and adivasi communities who oppose exploitation of their land and other resources for industrial projects. In several states, authorities ignored existing constitutional provisions demarcating areas as exclusively adivasi territories and allotted them to mining and other industries. In Orissa, one of India's poorest states, the competition over limited resources was intertwined with political struggles about the rights of the adivasis, freedom of religion, and the government's development policies. The result was ongoing communal violence that led to at least 25 deaths and displaced at least 15,000 people, mostly Christians facing persecution – and prevented thousands of people from receiving adequate health care, education, and housing.

Indigenous communities in Bangladesh also suffered from government policies. While the political struggle between a military-backed caretaker government and veteran political leaders dominated the headlines, behind the scenes the government continued its steady support for the Bengali settlers seizing land from Jumma Indigenous inhabitants of the Chittagong Hill Tracts.

In October, the Asian Development Bank warned that 2 million Cambodians may have been thrust into poverty as the cost of food, fuel and other commodities rose amid the global financial crisis. This was in addition to the 4.5 million, around a third of the population, already living in poverty. More than 4,000 Phnom Penh families living around Boeung Kak Lake, many of them in basic housing, faced displacement as the lake was turned into a landfill site. Residents were given no notice before the landfill began on 26 August 2008, and protesters faced widespread threats from local authorities and company workers. Meanwhile, Phnom Penh's police increased night-time raids among those living in poverty and on the margins of society, arbitrarily arresting sex workers, homeless people and beggars.

In North Korea, millions of people experienced hunger on a scale not seen in a decade. Women, children and the elderly were the most vulnerable. Thousands continued to cross the border into China mainly for food and economic reasons. Those arrested and forcibly repatriated were subjected to forced labour, torture and other ill-treatment in prison camps. The North Korean government took no action to address the situation, and did not even request assistance from South Korea, one of the biggest donors of rice and fertilizer in previous years, due to strained relations.

REGIONAL OVERVIEWS
ASIA-PACIFIC

I WAS STILL A YOUNG LADY WHEN WE FIRST HAD TO EVACUATE. THEN WHEN I HAD YOUNG CHILDREN, WE HAD TO EVACUATE AGAIN. NOW, I HAVE THREE GRANDCHILDREN, BUT NOTHING HAS CHANGED.

A 63-year-old woman, one of the internally displaced people from North Cotabato province, Philippines, August 2008.

Insecurity

No countries in the Asia-Pacific region were officially at war with each other during 2008, but conflicts between governments and armed opposition groups threatened the lives of tens of thousands across Asia and prevented millions more from accessing health care, education, housing and food. These conflicts were at least partially based on ethnicity, with one group often taking up arms against another to demand equal, or greater, access to resources.

Regardless of the cause of the conflict, it was civilians, especially those already marginalized by gender, ethnicity, religion, caste or social class, who were particularly vulnerable in such conflicts.

Residents of Afghanistan, Pakistan, Sri Lanka, Myanmar, southern Thailand and the southern Philippines faced significant threats from armed forces – government and anti-government – that frequently trampled on even the basic laws of armed conflict.

Millions of Afghans living in southern and eastern Afghanistan, terrorized by the Taleban and other insurgent groups as well as local militias ostensibly allied with the government, faced persistent insecurity, further restricting their already limited access to food, health care, and schooling, especially for girls and women. The year set another bloody record of violence in Afghanistan – the death of around 1,400 civilians as a direct result of the fighting, while tens of thousands of people fled their homes to avoid it, many gravitating to the relative security and prosperity of major cities such as Kabul and Herat, huddling in new slums. The Taleban and other anti-government groups were responsible for most of the injuries to civilians, but the nearly 60,000 international troops in Afghanistan continued to carry out air strikes and night raids that harmed civilians and their property, predictably fostering tremendous popular anger.

The Afghan government failed to maintain the rule of law or to provide basic services to millions of Afghans even in areas under its control. The Taleban and other anti-government groups extended their sway over more than a third of the country, again barring girls from education and health care, and imposing their own brutal brand of justice, which frequently relied on public executions and flogging. As a result, despite some gains in terms of children's enrolment in school and basic health care, most Afghans lived short lives of great hardship. Life expectancy was just 42.9 years, the country again experienced one of the highest recorded levels of maternal mortality on the planet and the average per capita income was just US$350 per year – one of the lowest in the world.

The insecurity in Afghanistan overflowed the border and engulfed large parts of Pakistan; not just in the tribal areas bordering Afghanistan but increasingly in other areas of Pakistan, as members of the Pakistani Taleban took hostages, targeted and killed civilians, and committed acts of violence against women and girls. By the end of the year, Pakistani Taleban groups had entrenched their hold over large parts of the frontier tribal areas, as well as the Swat valley, a settled area outside the tribal territories and within easy distance of Islamabad. The Taleban shut down dozens of girls' schools, health clinics, and any business deemed insufficiently devout, such as music shops. Not surprisingly, people – especially women and girls – living in the tribal areas of Pakistan lived shorter lives than in other parts of Pakistan, suffered higher rates of infant and maternal mortality, and experienced significantly lower rates of education.

A newly elected civilian government came to power in Pakistan in February and made many promises to improve the country's human rights situation. The government of President Asif Ali Zardari followed through on some of those promises, but proved as hapless in addressing the country's growing crisis of insecurity as the military government of General Pervez Musharraf. By the end of the year, it was simply repeating the former's disastrous vacillation between abandoning significant portions of Pakistan's citizens to the rule of brutal insurgent groups, and pursuing a scorched earth policy – punishing the local populace without significantly diminishing the fighting ability of anti-government groups.

The pattern of civilians caught between pro- and anti-government forces disdainful of their wellbeing occurred throughout Asia. In southern Thailand, violence has simmered intermittently for a century, reflecting the long-standing disenfranchisement of the area's population, which is predominantly Malay in ethnicity and language, and Muslim in religion. The area is one of the poorest and least developed in Thailand, and the population has long resented efforts at assimilation by the country's Thai Buddhist central government and majority. Insurgent forces have resorted to brutal tactics, such as decapitating and otherwise targeting Buddhist citizens, and attacking schools. But the government's heavy-handed security response, including torture and other ill-treatment of Muslim suspects, has led to widespread human rights violations and has alienated the local population.

A somewhat similar dynamic fuelled the conflict in the southern Philippines island of Mindanao, where the Muslim population, feeling disenfranchised from the country's predominantly Christian population and leadership, suffered significantly lower rates of economic development. The failure of peace negotiations between the Philippine government and the Moro Islamic Liberation Front (MILF) led to a resumption of violence in August that continues to be accompanied by abuses by both sides. The number of civilians directly affected by this most recent escalation of hostilities has increased dramatically, with no

ARRESTING ONE MAN IS TO THREATEN HUNDREDS OF THOUSANDS OF PEOPLE, SCARING THEM FROM STRUGGLING AND ADVOCATING AGAIN... I SEE THIS AS AN INJUSTCE FOR THE CAMBODIAN PEOPLE.

Oeun Sarim, farmer and human rights defender, talking about the systematic arrest of land activists in Cambodia, February 2008.

clear end in sight. After attacks by the MILF on civilians in predominantly Christian and sometimes mixed Christian and Muslim neighbourhoods in August 2008, more than 610,000 people fled their villages to escape – both from MILF direct attacks and from fighting between the MILF and security forces. Around 240,000 of them have subsequently gone back to their homes after the Philippine military declared their villages safe. Many returned to find their houses burned and their livestock stolen, and they continue to live in fear.

In Myanmar, even as the government's policies pauperized the entire population, the SPDC acted with particular venom in its treatment of the country's 135 ethnic and religious minority groups – nearly a third of the entire population. The Myanmar army continued its offensive against the Karen civilians of Kayin (Karen) State and Bago (Pegu) Division. Since November 2005, when the current government offensive began, more than 140,000 Karen civilians have been killed, tortured, forcibly displaced, sexually violated, forced to work, including dangerous work related to military exercises, like clearing landmines, and otherwise subjected to widespread and systematic violations of their human rights. These violations amount to crimes against humanity.

Another 'forgotten conflict' of 2008 raged between the Sri Lankan government and the Liberation Tigers of Tamil Eelam (LTTE). The island's large Tamil population had long complained of political and economic discrimination by the ruling Sinhalese majority. The LTTE had used a range of brutal tactics, such as bomb attacks on civilians and forced recruitment of children as soldiers to carve out a de facto independent state in the north and east of the island for nearly a decade. But this hardly proved a haven for the Tamil population, as the LTTE brooked no opposition. As 2008 waned, the Sri Lankan government was on its way to overrunning this enclave in a series of military victories. Nearly the entire Tamil population of the northern area known as the Wanni, more than a quarter million, fled their homes in a search for safety. Many, if not most, of this population had already been displaced several times by the fighting, including in previous years, and some had survived the ravages of the 2004 Indian Ocean tsunami.

The Sri Lankan government prevented international aid workers or journalists from reaching the conflict zone to assist or witness the plight of those caught between the two sides. For their part, the beleaguered LTTE exploited this population as a ready source of forced labour, military personnel, and a buffer against approaching Sri Lankan troops.

Exclusion

Even where ethnic discrimination did not give rise to armed conflict, it remained a common feature of the social landscape in the Asia-Pacific region, from the wealthiest societies to the most impoverished. In February, the Australian government made an historic apology to the 'Stolen Generations': Aboriginal and Torres Strait Islander people who as children were forcibly removed from their families under government laws and policies. But the government announced it would not set up a compensation fund nor any other form of redress.

The government of the world's newest republic, Nepal, struggled to meet its promise to improve the lives of Nepalis who had suffered generations of officially sanctioned deprivation. The Maoists controlling the government had built much of their appeal on championing the rights of women, lower castes, and the poor. However, they met the most significant challenge to their rule from the country's large population of Madhesis, residents of the flat southern third of the country, who felt the new government did not sufficiently take account of their long-standing grievances.

China's large ethnic minorities in the west of the country, in Tibetan-populated areas and the predominantly Muslim province of the Xinjiang Uighur Autonomous Region, continued to suffer systematic discrimination. Both areas witnessed some of the worst unrest of recent years in 2008. Protests by Tibetan monks on 10 March and subsequent protests by more monks urged a halt to government-imposed political education campaigns and easing of restrictions on religious practice. Violence erupted as lay Tibetans joined the protests, expressing long-term grievances including perceived exclusion from the benefits of economic development and the weakening of Tibetan culture and ethnic identity through government policies. Some of the protesters attacked Han migrants and their businesses in Lhasa but protests continued largely peacefully throughout Tibetan areas. Chinese authorities ultimately reported that 21 people had been killed by violent protesters and that more than 1,000 individuals detained in the protests had been released, and overseas Tibetan organizations reported that more than 100 Tibetans had been killed, and estimated that at least several hundred remained in detention at the end of the year. Exact numbers were difficult to determine because the authorities denied access to media and independent monitors.

In Xinjiang, on 14 August, Wang Lequan, Secretary of the Communist Party in Xinjiang, announced a "life and death" struggle against Uighur Muslim "separatism". The authorities cited a series of violent incidents by alleged terrorists to justify a sweeping crackdown and continued their tight control over religious practice, including prohibiting all government employees and children from worshipping at mosques. The Chinese authorities reported that more than 1,300 people had been arrested during the year on charges of terrorism, religious extremism or other

WE ARE ALWAYS UNDER THREAT. WE WANT SUPPORT FROM THE STATE, SUPPORT FROM THE POLICE. IF WE CALL TO REPORT AN INCIDENT OF VIOLENCE WE WANT THE POLICE TO TAKE ACTION, NOT IGNORE US.

Mohna Answari, Muslim lawyer, woman human rights defender, Nepalgunj, Nepal, November 2008.

violations of state security laws, and 1,154 were formally charged or faced trials or administrative punishments.

Voice

As the year ended and the effects of a downturn in the global economy were manifested in lost jobs, less food on the table, and less income for necessities, such as housing, education, and health care, more people throughout the Asia-Pacific region demanded accountability from their governments. Rather than responding to their needs, their governments tried to silence them. This trend aggravated the long-standing, prevalent intolerance of free expression by many governments in the Asia-Pacific region, nowhere clearer than in North Korea and Myanmar, which have effectively banned freedom of expression absolutely for years.

Chinese authorities temporarily eased restrictions on freedom of the press in the run-up to the Olympics. They allowed foreign journalists unprecedented latitude to report and unblocked access to websites such as that of Amnesty International and the BBC. By the end of the year, however, with popular discontent on the rise, Chinese authorities reverted to silencing and intimidating critics. Signatories of Charter 08, which had called for fundamental legal and political reform, came under intense government scrutiny and several members of the group were harassed and subjected to ill-treatment. At least one signatory, Liu Xiaobo, remained in arbitrary detention at the end of the year. By the start of 2009, Amnesty International's website was one of many again banned.

Similarly, Viet Nam continued its crackdown of supporters of Bloc 8406, an Internet-based pro-democracy movement, as well as other unauthorized groups calling for democracy and human rights, many charged under Article 88 of the Penal Code, "conducting propaganda against the Socialist Republic of Viet Nam" or laws criminalizing "abusing democratic freedoms to infringe upon the interests of the State".

Assaults on free speech were not limited to socialist states. The government of Singapore continued its misuse of libel laws to silence criticism: the *Far Eastern Economic Review* was convicted of defaming Prime Minister Lee Hsieng Lee, while the *Wall Street Journal Asia* faced legal action in September for challenging the judiciary's independence. Some 19 anti-poverty campaigners faced charges for holding unauthorized public street gatherings.

In Thailand, there was a sharp increase in the number of people charged with lese-majesty, a law prohibiting any word or act that defames, insults or threatens the royal family. Fiji's interim government announced in August that it would establish a media tribunal to provide "stronger regulation" of the media.

In Sri Lanka, what was once a vibrant media environment suffered tremendously as the wave of attacks on journalists and media workers continued. At least 14 media workers have been unlawfully killed in Sri Lanka since the beginning of 2006. Others have been arbitrarily detained, tortured or reported to have become victims of enforced disappearance, while in the custody of security forces. More than 20 journalists have left the country in response to death threats.

Conclusion

Under increasing political and economic pressure, many people in the Asia-Pacific region turned to the international human rights framework to bolster their efforts to secure greater dignity for themselves and others.

Setting aside its historic reluctance to speak in the language of human rights, ASEAN's valuable efforts in the wake of Cyclone Nargis helped those devastated receive critical assistance. With longer-term effect, the ASEAN Charter came into force in November when it was ratified by all 10 ASEAN member states. The Charter asserts members' commitment to human rights and provides ASEAN with an unprecedented opportunity to create a strong human rights body. Parliamentarians at the Pacific Parliamentarians Conference in December unanimously supported moves to establish a Pacific regional human rights mechanism – a serious step forward for the Pacific Islands and for the Asia-Pacific region as a whole.

Both these initiatives are a credit to human rights activists in Asia and the Pacific, who have been at the forefront of pushing for such change. And despite heavy-handed responses by governments, placing human rights defenders at great personal risk, such individuals continued to work to secure the rights of people suffering deprivation and abuse. In many places, a growing number of activists and government critics began using the internet as a tool to voice dissent and mobilize support. In China, internet usage has grown tremendously, enabling people to share information about their government's actions and, in the case of a few, daring individuals, to call for reform. Similarly, in Viet Nam, brave activists increasingly took to blogs to call for change and voice dissent. In Malaysia and Singapore, countries where repression of free speech continues unabated, bloggers are the main source of independent information, analysis, and criticism – and pay the price for it.

At the root of all these efforts is the notion that all individuals have a claim to human rights and dignity. Although often honoured in the breach, the events of 2008 strongly indicated that this belief now has taken firm root among many communities in the Asia-Pacific region.

FOR US, RELIEF IS ONLY WHEN OUR LOVED ONE IS SAFE AND SOUND, STANDING FREED BEFORE US... I BELIEVE THAT MY HUSBAND IS HELD ONLY THREE KILOMETRES FROM MY HOME, YET HE CONTINUES TO SUFFER UNKNOWN ILL-TREATMENT.

Amina Masood Janjua, wife of Masood Janjua – a victim of enforced disappearance – Pakistan, July 2008.

Bombed building in Gori, 29 September 2008. The five-day conflict between Georgia and Russia and the subsequent pillage and arson of Georgian villages caused extensive damage to homes and displaced almost 200,000 people.

EUROPE AND
CENTRAL ASIA

*At the beginning of August 2008, two European states went to war for the
first time in almost a decade. Since the conflicts of the early 1990s,
Europe had assumed a degree of stability in terms of its economy, security
and embedding the rule of law, but these events showed how potentially
fragile the security assumptions underpinning post-Cold War Europe
could be. And how – as so often – civilians and their human rights pay the
price when such assumptions fail.*

The five-day conflict between Georgia and Russia over the disputed
region of South Ossetia resulted in hundreds of civilian deaths, thousands
of injuries and, at its peak, the displacement of almost 200,000
people. Georgian-Russian hostilities and subsequent pillage and arson
also caused extensive damage to civilian homes in South Ossetia and
adjacent areas. Cluster munitions, devastating to civilians' lives and
livelihoods both at the time of their use and after hostilities, were used.

By the end of the year, the global economic crisis had also shown
how the assumed stability of the region's economic architecture was
likewise subject to challenge. Several European states required
interventions from the International Monetary Fund to support their
economies, amid wider fears that the downturn would push more
people – particularly those already made vulnerable from conflict,
discrimination or insecurity – deeper into poverty.

Deprivation

Across Europe in 2008, those already in poverty continued to lack access
to many basic needs. Despite the festering economic crisis, Europe was
home to some of the wealthiest countries in the world in 2008. It also,
however, housed serious failings in the implementation of its inhabitants'
rights to education, health care, secure housing and livelihoods.
Across the region the divide between rich and poor remained gaping,
and from either side of that divide, the experience of accessing human
rights was markedly different. As it was for different groups within
countries – in Tajikistan, for example, poverty and unemployment
affected women disproportionately and made them more vulnerable to
human rights abuses.

When external events or internal mismanagement led to shortages, it was the poorest who felt them first and keenest. In Albania, for example, people living below the national poverty line – more than 18 per cent of the population – suffered most acutely from the country's already limited access to education, clean water, health and social care. One of the harshest winters to hit Central Asia in several decades beset vital infrastructure and left vast swathes of the region facing severe energy and food shortages, with the UN moved to launch emergency appeals for the inhabitants of Tajikistan and Kyrgyzstan.

Insecurity

As in previous years, the watchword of security was used to drive policies and practices that delivered the opposite – undermining human rights in the name of fighting terrorism, shrouding abuse with impunity, and fortifying barriers against those seeking to flee persecution, violence or poverty.

There continued to be a failure of political will to reveal the truth about the rendition of detainees by the USA to countries where they faced abuses, in spite of evidence that put the complicity of European states beyond doubt. The need for full, independent investigations into allegations of involvement in rendition flights was highlighted in February when the UK admitted that contrary to repeated assurances, the USA had used the UK overseas territory of Diego Garcia on at least two occasions in 2002 for the purposes of transferring detainees in its programme of rendition and secret detention.

States such as Denmark, Germany, Italy, Spain and the UK, were prepared to allow unenforceable "diplomatic assurances" as a justification to deport terrorism suspects to countries where there was a real risk of torture and other ill-treatment. In Turkey convictions under anti-terrorism laws were often based on insubstantial or unreliable evidence. Secrecy in the implementation of counter-terrorism measures in the UK led to unfair judicial proceedings.

In a landmark ruling in February, and an indication of the sort of leadership needed on other human rights concerns in the region, the European Court of Human Rights reaffirmed the absolute prohibition of torture and other inhuman or degrading treatment or punishment. The ruling forbids states to send anyone – including those suspected of terrorism and/or those who are alleged to pose a risk to national security – to countries where there is reason to believe they would face such violations.

Victims of torture and other ill-treatment, often race- or identity-based and frequently used to extract confessions, were likewise too often failed by justice systems which did not hold to account those charged with ensuring security and the rule of law. Obstacles to accountability included lack of prompt access to a lawyer, failure by prosecutors to vigorously pursue investigations, victims' fear of reprisals, low penalties imposed on convicted police officers, and the absence of properly resourced and independent systems for monitoring complaints. In countries such as Bosnia and Herzegovina, Greece, Kazakstan, Russia, Spain, Turkey, Ukraine and Uzbekistan, such failures perpetuated a culture of impunity.

Across the region, women faced personal insecurity, as states failed to protect them from the violence they faced in the home and from intimate partners. This abuse remained pervasive across the region for all ages and social groups, and was manifested through women enduring a range of verbal and psychological attacks, physical and sexual violence, economic control and even murder. There were gaps in protection, existing laws against such violence were often not fully implemented, and resources including for shelters and training of relevant law enforcement officials often remained woefully inadequate. The Council of Europe decided in December to draft one or more treaties setting binding standards for the prevention, protection and prosecution of violence against women and domestic violence against women.

Other marginalized groups also frequently found obstacles blocking their path to redress or to protection – as usual, it was groups such as Roma, migrants, women, those in poverty, who suffered the most insecurity.

Some people thrived on such insecurity, and made money in and across Europe by trafficking human beings. Feeding off those in poverty and exploiting corruption, lack of education and social breakdown, they forced men, women and children into domestic work, farming, manufacturing, construction, hospitality and sexual prostitution.

A major step forward in the protection of these individuals' rights came when the Council of Europe Convention on Action against Trafficking in Human Beings entered into force in February. By the end of the year 20 of the 47 member states had ratified the treaty and 20 more had signed it. Now states must implement its requirements and protections, so that in years to come this 'modern' form of slavery becomes history.

Refugees and migrants

There remained a consistent pattern of human rights violations linked to the interception, detention, and expulsion by states of foreign nationals, including those seeking international protection. In some

UNFORTUNATELY, MY RELEASE FROM PRISON DOESN'T SHOW PROGRESS... IN UZBEKISTAN. FIVE DAYS AFTER MY RELEASE THE JOURNALIST AND HUMAN RIGHTS ACTIVIST [SALIDZHON ABDARAKHMONOV] WAS DETAINED. A MONTH LATER ANOTHER COLLEAGUE, AGZAM TURGUNOV, WAS ALSO ARRESTED. BOTH OF THEM WERE SENTENCED TO 10 YEARS IN OCTOBER. I AM SURE THE NUMBER OF VICTIMS OF THE REGIME... IS FAR MORE.

Mutabar Tadzhibaeva, released from prison on 2 June, accepting the 2008 Martin Ennals Award for Human Rights Defenders, November 2008.

countries, people were denied the security of access to asylum procedures, and in others the level of protection given to Iraqi asylum-seekers was reduced, with some deported. Russia, Turkey and Ukraine, were among those that forcibly returned asylum-seekers to countries where they were at risk of serious human rights violations.

The UN's refugee agency (UNHCR) reported that 67,000 people made the perilous crossing by sea to Europe in 2008, with hundreds – the exact number is impossible to know – perishing along the way. Around 38,000 people arrived in Italy and Malta alone, mostly after transiting through Libya. The vast majority claimed asylum, and over half of those who did were granted international protection. Across the region, however, the signature response to the challenges of such large and mixed flows of irregular migration remained repressive.

In a deeply disappointing move, the European Union adopted a Directive on the return of irregular migrants. It instituted an excessive maximum period of detention for asylum-seekers and other irregular migrants of up to 18 months. The directive risks lowering existing standards in EU member states and setting a poor example to other regions in the world.

Exclusion and Discrimination

Many asylum-seekers and migrants were also subject to discrimination and exclusion from services and employment, and experienced extreme poverty. In some countries such as Switzerland, rejected asylum-seekers were excluded from the welfare system, resulting in marginalization and destitution. In Germany, migrants continued to suffer restricted access to health care and judicial remedies in cases of violation of their labour rights, and migrant children's access to education was limited.

Many countries routinely detained migrants and asylum-seekers, and in inappropriate conditions. The UN Human Rights Committee expressed its concern at conditions in French migration detention centres, which suffered from severe overcrowding and poor hygiene. In the Netherlands, alternatives to detention were used infrequently, even for unaccompanied minors and victims of trafficking or torture. Malta's policy of systematically detaining all migrants and asylum-seekers was linked by the European Commission against Racism and Intolerance with the rise of racism and intolerance on the island.

Others faced discrimination and exclusion on account of their legal status – or lack of it, including those displaced by conflicts in the former Yugoslavia and Soviet Union whose access to a range of rights was restricted or denied linked with issues of their registration and residency. The continuing use in some areas of the Soviet era system of *propiska* – registration in the place of permanent residence – was also a breeding ground for corruption and exploitation as many of its restrictive regulations could be overcome by paying bribes. The result of this was, of course, that those without the wealth to pay were excluded from the sinister system.

Many minority returnees to parts of the former Yugoslavia continued to face discrimination in accessing a number of services, finding employment – including in public institutions – and regaining their property or tenancy rights. In Turkmenistan the policy of checking people's Turkmen origin up to the third generation continued, and restricted access by ethnic minorities to work and higher education.

A climate of racism and intolerance in many countries helped to keep people excluded from society or government, and fostered further discrimination.

Migrants, Roma, Jews and Muslims were among those subjected to hate crimes by individuals or extremist groups. Often, a failure to acknowledge the gravity of racially motivated crimes and a lack of political will led to impunity for those responsible. Following the rise in anti-Roma sentiment and violent incidents in several European countries, such as the Czech Republic and Hungary, the UN Special Rapporteur on racism stated in November that "such actions reveal serious and deep-rooted problems of racism and discrimination against Roma at the heart of modern Europe that must be addressed in the most vigorous manner and through the rule of law."

Perhaps the most profound illustration of systematic discrimination in the region was against Roma, who remained largely excluded from public life in all countries. Roma families were unable to enjoy full access to housing, education, employment and health services. Many lived in what amounted to segregated ghettos, physically isolated from other parts of the community, and often with limited or no water or electrical supplies, sanitation systems, paved roads or other basic infrastructure. Unlawful forced evictions of Roma in places such as Italy drove them deeper into poverty. Some Roma remained displaced in camps in northern Kosovo where their health was seriously affected by lead contamination.

In some countries, the authorities failed to integrate Romani children fully into the education system, tolerating or promoting Roma-only schools, and placing Roma in special schools or classes for pupils with mental disabilities where a reduced curriculum was taught. In Bosnia and Herzegovina, according to the international NGO Save the Children, only 20 to 30 per cent of Romani children attended primary education,

I KNOW THAT THERE ARE MORE ROMANI CHILDREN WHO THINK THE SPECIAL SCHOOL IS VERY, VERY EASY; SOME OF THEM ARE VERY INTELLIGENT, BUT FOR SOME REASON THEY ARE STILL THERE... I DIDN'T LIKE IT BECAUSE I DIDN'T LEARN A LOT THERE. IN GRADE 7 OF THE SPECIAL SCHOOL I LEARNED THE SAME THINGS THAT I LEARNED IN GRADE 3 OF THE MAINSTREAM SCHOOL.

A 14-year-old Romani boy who spent six months at the special school of Pavlovce nad Uhom, because of an "administrative" error.

and only 0.5 to 3 per cent attended pre-school education.

Poor housing conditions, physical and cultural isolation, poverty and lack of transport also hindered Romani children's ability to attend school. Negative stereotyping likewise blighted their future prospects and led to further denial of rights.

The Albanian authorities again failed to implement legislation providing priority access to housing for orphans completing secondary education or reaching adulthood. Around 300 adults who were orphaned as children continued to share rooms in dilapidated and inadequate housing – conditions which aggravated their social exclusion. With few qualifications, they were often unemployed or undertook casual labour for low wages, surviving on minimal state assistance.

Recognizing the ongoing discrimination faced by many in the region, the European Union proposed in July to upgrade its anti-discrimination legislation.

Voice

In many ways, large areas of the region have traditionally been a beacon for free speech and participatory government. Human rights defenders, NGOs and local community activists have achieved many successes in Europe and Central Asia over the decades. But in 2008, in countries where the space for dissent was already small, those seeking to publicize abuses, articulate alternative views, or hold governments and others to account, remained unheard. Or repressed. Freedoms of expression and association remained under attack – as did human rights defenders themselves.

In Turkey, dissenting views were still met with prosecution and intimidation. The work of human rights defenders was hampered by unjustified prosecutions, some high-profile human rights defenders were subjected to regular criminal investigations, and others were threatened by unknown individuals or groups as a result of their work. Human rights NGOs also faced excessive administrative scrutiny of their work, and courts acted disproportionately when shutting down websites. Some demonstrations were banned without legitimate reason and those held without permission, particularly in the Kurdish-populated south-eastern region of Turkey – one of the poorest areas in the region – were dispersed with excessive force, often before peaceful methods had been tried.

In Belarus, the government continued to exert excessive control over civil society, denying freedom of association and expression. State control over the media increased, and restrictions on independent media continued. Some public events were banned; peaceful demonstrators were subjected to fines and to short periods of detention; and civil society activists and journalists were harassed.

There was little improvement in freedoms of expression and assembly in Uzbekistan. Human rights defenders, activists and independent journalists continued to be targeted for their work, despite claims to the contrary by the authorities. At least 10 human rights defenders remained in prison there in cruel, inhuman and degrading conditions, having been sentenced to long prison terms after unfair trials. They had limited access to relatives and legal representatives, and reportedly they had been tortured or otherwise ill-treated. Some were reported to be gravely ill in prison.

The authorities in Turkmenistan launched a new wave of repression against independent civil society activists and journalists. Independent journalists and media outlets in Armenia and Azerbaijan that covered opposition activities were harassed.

Libel and slander laws and legislation combating extremism were used in Russia to stifle dissent and to silence journalists and human rights activists. Independent journalists, media and NGOs were targeted by the authorities for reporting human rights violations in the volatile North Caucasus region. In a climate of growing intolerance towards independent views, several human rights defenders and supporters of opposition groups faced criminal charges for expressing dissenting views or criticizing government authorities.

Representatives of religious groups or confessions outside officially endorsed structures, or from non-traditional groups, continued to be harassed in Armenia, Azerbaijan, Kazakstan, Tajikistan and Uzbekistan.

Authorities in a number of countries continued to foster a climate of intolerance against the lesbian, gay, bisexual and transgender (LGBT) communities, making it harder for their voices to be heard and their rights to be protected. Authorities obstructed public events, failed to provide adequate protection to participants, and in some cases highly placed politicians used openly homophobic language. Public events in support of LGBT communities were banned in Belarus, Lithuania and Moldova. In Bosnia and Herzegovina the first such event closed earlier than planned owing to death threats against the organizers and physical attacks on participants. The festival had been surrounded by an atmosphere of intimidation as some politicians and media outlets ran a homophobic campaign. In Turkey discrimination based on sexual orientation and gender identity persisted, as did allegations of violence by law enforcement officials against transgender people. A court there also ordered the closure of an organization that supports LGBT rights, on the grounds that its objectives were "against moral values and family structure".

I PUT UP WITH HIS BEATINGS FOR 14 YEARS BECAUSE THAT'S WHAT'S EXPECTED HERE IN ARMENIA. IN THE ARMENIAN FAMILY THE WOMAN HAS TO PUT UP WITH EVERYTHING, SHE HAS TO KEEP SILENT.

D.M., a survivor of domestic violence, Yerevan, Armenia, 2008.

Conclusion

Despite worrying developments hindering the full realization of human rights for all Europe and Central Asia's people, 2008 saw some positive steps that must be built on in the coming years. In a continuing positive trend, Uzbekistan joined its neighbours in abolishing the death penalty – leaving Belarus as the lone, last executioner – not just in Europe, but now across the Central Asia region as well.

In the first such statement of its kind, the Turkish Justice Minister apologized in October to the family of a man who had died in custody, and acknowledged that the death may have been due to torture. A step towards accountability and redress that must be replicated by others.

Many abusers across the region continued to evade justice, but the arrest and transfer of former Bosnian Serb leader Radovan Karadžić to the institutions of international justice was a significant step in tackling impunity for war crimes committed in the former Yugoslavia. The challenge now is to replicate this at the local level, where insufficient or partial efforts by domestic courts were too often the cause or reason for continuing impunity in the successor Balkan states.

Europe too often lacked political leadership to ensure the protection of human rights in the region, with many of its states also lacking the political will to live up to their obligations.

Accountability systems must ensure effective protection of human rights. Together with the Council of Europe, the European Union must shoulder its responsibility in fighting against discrimination, poverty and insecurity.

The year ended on a high for accountability: it proved how individual struggles to be heard, to be counted, and to be included, can achieve success. On 25 December, the government of Montenegro officially recognized its responsibility for the "deportation" of Bosniak refugees in 1992.

The relatives of these refugees had filed lawsuits against the government, seeking compensation for the enforced disappearance of their loved ones, but the government had appealed against each decision by the courts to award compensation to the relatives. In effect it blocked the victims' right to access to redress and reparations. However, in December the government informed the lawyers representing the families that they would provide reparations for all 193 people affected by the enforced disappearances. They include nine survivors of the Bosnian Serb army concentration camp at Foča, 28 of their family members and 156 women and children, and the parents and siblings of 83 men who were killed after their enforced disappearance by the Montenegrin police, into the hands of Bosnian Serb military forces.

In a letter to Amnesty International, Dragan and Tea Prelevic, the lawyers who represent the families of 45 victims, said: "All families feel relieved from an enormous burden of a 16-year-long state denial, and they indeed finally feel some justice. A milestone has been moved and we expect it to have a positive effect on all victims of war crimes in Montenegro and the region … We are much aware that all those brave and devastated women, children and men would not have reached this day without your support."

WHAT THIS PRIDE DID WAS TO DRIVE BULGARIAN LGBT INTO THE PUBLIC AGENDA FOR THE WHOLE WEEK. IT OPENED DEBATE ABOUT THE... MEANING OF 'ACCEPTANCE'... THE PROCLAMATION OF FEAR AND HATRED FROM THE NATIONALISTS, THE THREATS THAT THEY WILL KILL US, THEY HAVE PREPARED BOMBS WITH NAILS AGAINST US... NEVERTHELESS, THE FEAR, THE FEELING OF COMMUNITY, OF SOLIDARITY, THE MEDIA, WHO WERE EVERYWHERE... WAS UNFORGETTABLE.

Aksinia Gencheva, Director of Bulgarian LGBT organization BGO Gemini, June 2008.

Women from surrounding towns and cities converge on Rabat, Morocco, to celebrate International Women's Day in March 2008. Despite some positive steps during the year, the authorities need to do more to address discrimination and violence against women.

MIDDLE EAST AND NORTH AFRICA

On 27 December, as 2008 drew to a close, Israeli jets launched an aerial bombardment of the Gaza Strip, where 1.5 million Palestinians live, crowded into one of the most densely populated areas of the planet. In the following three weeks, more than 1,400 Palestinians were killed, including some 300 children, and some 5,000 were wounded. Israeli forces repeatedly breached the laws of war, including by carrying out direct attacks on civilians and civilian buildings and attacks targeting Palestinian militants that caused a disproportionate toll among civilians.

Israel said it launched the attacks in order to stop Hamas and other Palestinian armed groups firing rockets at towns and villages in southern Israel. In 2008, seven Israeli civilians were killed by these mostly homemade, indiscriminate rockets or in other attacks by Palestinians from Gaza; three Israeli civilians were killed during the three-week conflict that began on 27 December.

The sudden conflict followed an 18-month period in which the Israeli army had subjected the inhabitants of Gaza to an unremitting blockade, preventing virtually all movement of people and goods in and out of the territory and stoking a growing humanitarian catastrophe. The blockade throttled almost all economic life and led growing numbers of Palestinians to become dependent on international food aid; even terminally ill patients were prevented from leaving to obtain medical care that could not be provided by Gaza's resource- and medicine-starved hospitals.

This latest round of bloodletting again underscored the high degree of insecurity in the region and the failure of military forces, on both sides, to abide by the basic requirements of distinction and proportionality that are fundamental to the principles of international humanitarian law. It underlined also the continuing failure of the two sides, and of the international community, to resolve the long, bitter conflict, to bring peace, justice and security to the region, and to enable all people in the region to live in the dignity that is their human right.

Insecurity

This continuing struggle between Israelis and Palestinians, together with the presence of US troops in Iraq, anxieties about Iran's nuclear intentions, evident divisions between Islamists and secularists, and the tension between some cultural traditions and rising popular aspirations, all contributed to a climate of political insecurity across the Middle East and North Africa region. Added to this in 2008 was growing economic and social insecurity as the global financial crisis took hold and rising food prices impacted those already living in or close to poverty. This was highlighted by a rash of strikes and other protests by workers in the private and public sectors, such as in Egypt, and months of unrest in Tunisia's phosphate-rich Gafsa region. In these countries and others, many people lived in extreme poverty, living on the margins as rural poor or in heavily congested urban slums, victims in practice of gross inequalities in access to basic rights – adequate housing and shelter, health care and education, work and the opportunity to secure a better, rights-rich life for themselves and their families.

In Iraq, a now much less reported war continued to blight the lives of millions, notwithstanding a welcome reduction in the number of attacks on civilians. The almost constant state of conflict in the country prevented many from pursuing their livelihoods and providing a secure future for their families. More than two million people were still internally displaced within Iraq while two million others were refugees abroad, principally in Syria and Jordan. Violent religious and ethnic sectarianism continued to divide communities and impact on daily life. Armed groups opposed to the government carried out suicide and other bomb attacks, often targeting places such as crowded markets. Meanwhile, thousands of Iraqis continued to be detained without charge or trial by US forces, some for more than five years. Thousands more were detained by Iraqi government forces; many were tortured, some were sentenced to death for alleged terrorist crimes, often after trials that were grossly unfair, including some who were executed. At the end of 2008, all detainees held by US forces were due to be handed over to Iraqi government custody under a joint agreement between the USA and Iraq. The agreement contains no human rights safeguards.

The death penalty was used extensively by the authorities in Iran, Iraq, Saudi Arabia and Yemen, but there were welcome signs of a growing repugnance of it among other Arab states. This was most evident in December when eight Arab states decided not to vote against a key UN General Assembly resolution calling for a worldwide moratorium on executions, helping secure its adoption by a large majority. Increasingly, the authorities in Iran, one of a tiny minority of states where juvenile offenders continue to be executed, and in Saudi

Arabia, where a discriminatory justice system resulted in the execution of a disproportionately high number of poor foreign nationals, appeared out of step with the views of the wider international community.

Violence against women and girls

Women within the region faced additional insecurity, through discrimination under the law and in practice, and violence, often at the hands of their male relatives. At its most acute, such violence saw women killed in so-called honour crimes, as in Iraq, Jordan, the Palestinian Authority and Syria. Women migrant domestic workers were particularly vulnerable to sexual and other abuse by employers as they were often unprotected by labour laws. In both Jordan and Lebanon women domestic workers died in suspicious circumstances amid speculation that some had been killed, had fallen to their deaths while attempting to escape their places of work, or had resorted to suicide in desperation. In the Kurdistan Region of northern Iraq, the high incidence of cases of women being burned to death, either at their own hand or others', suggested the same.

In other states there were positive developments reflecting growing appreciation among governments that women cannot continue to be relegated to a form of second-class status. The Egyptian authorities banned the practice of female genital mutilation; the governments of Oman and Qatar made legal changes to give women equal status with men in various housing and compensation matters; and the Tunisian government acceded to a key international treaty on women's rights and introduced a "hotline" for women facing domestic violence.

Asylum-seekers, refugees and irregular migrants

Nowhere in the region was insecurity more evident than among the communities of refugees and asylum-seekers who still had no permanent status or home – many after decades of waiting in poverty.

Thousands of Iraqi refugees lived a hand-to-mouth existence in Syria, Jordan, Lebanon and other countries, increasingly poverty stricken and desperate but threatened with deportation if they took paid work. In Iraq, the government demanded that 3,000 Iranian émigrés, long resident at Camp Ashraf, should leave the country, although it seemed unlikely that any country would be willing to receive them and that they would be at serious risk if forcibly returned to Iran. Some 80 Iraqi refugees who fled their country in 1991, at the time of the first Gulf War, spent a further year confined in a fenced and guarded camp established by the Saudi Arabian authorities, who continued to refuse them asylum. In Lebanon, around half of the hundreds of thousands of Palestinian refugees there remained in overcrowded camps dotted about the country

WHAT SHOULD WE DO? IF WE REBUILD THEY MAY DESTROY IT AGAIN. AND THERE IS NO CEMENT IN GAZA, NO BUILDING MATERIALS TO BE HAD.

A Palestinian man speaking to Amnesty International delegates in Gaza, January 2009.

60 years after they or their forebears first arrived. The government began action to rectify the status of the most vulnerable – those who exist without official papers and so are barred from legally marrying or registering their children's births – but there were continuing legal and other obstacles that prevented Palestinian refugees accessing their rights to health, work and adequate shelter.

In various states, authorities forcibly returned refugees and others, in breach of international law, to countries where they risked torture or execution. The Yemeni authorities returned hundreds of asylum-seekers and sent at least eight people back to Saudi Arabia despite fears for their safety. In January, the Libyan government announced its intention to deport all "illegal migrants" and later carried out mass expulsions of Nigerians, Ghanaians and others. In June, it was reported that the government had attempted to deport more than 200 Eritreans by informing them that they were to be flown to Italy, when the real intention was to return them to their own country, from which many had fled to avoid military conscription.

The Egyptian authorities also took abusive action. As well as mass deportations – summarily sending at least 1,200 asylum-seekers back to Eritrea – border guards shot dead at least 28 people who tried to cross from Egypt and seek sanctuary in Israel. Hundreds more were apprehended and jailed after trials before military courts. The Israeli authorities were no less uncompromising; they deported back to Egypt scores of asylum-seekers and migrants who did make it across the border, despite fears some of them would then be sent back to Sudan, Eritrea or other countries in which they could face torture or execution.

In Morocco/Western Sahara, the authorities rounded up and expelled thousands of suspected irregular migrants; some were reported to have been subjected to excessive force or other ill-treatment, and some to have been dumped without adequate food or water in inhospitable terrain close to the country's southern borders. The Algerian authorities tightened their controls on migrants, equipping themselves with new legal powers to summarily expel foreigners deemed to be in the country illegally.

Exclusion, discrimination and deprivation

In many countries, particular communities were excluded from accessing their human rights on an equitable basis with the mainstream population. Some of these communities comprised foreign nationals, refugees and asylum-seekers and legal and irregular migrants, exacerbating their insecurity – as illustrated above. Others were members of ethnic, religious or other minorities, stigmatized on account of their beliefs or identity.

In the Gulf, the Qatar government continued to deny nationality to hundreds of members of the al-Murra tribe, some of whom were involved in a failed coup attempt in 1996. As a consequence, they were barred from accessing social security, health care and employment rights. In Oman, people belonging to two tribes, Aal Tawayya and Aal Khalifayn, remained marginalized and were hampered from obtaining official identity documents, settling family matters such as divorce or inheritance, and registering businesses due to a government decision in 2006 to reduce their status to that of *akhdam*, servants.

In Iran, the authorities continued to prohibit the use of minority languages in schools and to crack down on minority activists – Ahwazi Arabs, Azerbaijani Iranians, Baluchis, Kurds and Turkmen – who campaigned for greater recognition of their rights, and to arbitrarily exclude members of suspect minorities from state employment. In Syria, the Kurdish minority, comprising up to 10 per cent of the population, was subject to continuing repression. Tens of thousands of Syrian Kurds continued to be rendered effectively stateless and so denied equal access to social and economic rights.

Personal religious beliefs that differed from the state were not tolerated in some countries, and their practitioners excluded from full participation in society, or physically punished. In Algeria, evangelical Christian converts from Islam were prosecuted although freedom of conscience is guaranteed by the Constitution; in Egypt, Christian converts from Islam and Baha'is were reported still to face difficulties in practice in obtaining official cards recognizing, or at least not misrepresenting, their faith, despite Supreme Administrative Court rulings; in Iran, the authorities continued to harass and persecute Baha'is and members of other religious minorities, detaining Sunni clerics and sentencing one Sufi religious leader to five years in prison and flogging for "spreading lies".

In the Gulf states, migrant workers from the Indian sub-continent and other parts of Asia were a mainstay of the oil-rich economies, providing labour and skills for construction and in the service industries. Often, however, such contract workers were required to live and work in grossly unsatisfactory conditions, excluded from any state protection against exploitation and abuse. If they protested against their conditions, as in Kuwait and the United Arab Emirates (UAE), the authorities' response was to round them up and deport them.

Homosexuality remained a taboo subject throughout most of the region and men suspected of being gay were targeted in several countries. In Egypt, men suspected of consensual sexual acts with other men were assaulted in detention, forced to undergo anal examinations and HIV-testing against their will. Some were chained to their beds when confined to hospital before being sentenced to prison terms on charges of debauchery. In Morocco/Western Sahara, six men

PLEASE DO NOT ABANDON US TO THE CLAWS OF TYRANNY AND BLIND POWER. I FEAR FOR MYSELF, MY CHILDREN AND ESPECIALLY MY HUSBAND, WHO IS IN DETENTION.

Woman in Saudi Arabia writing to Amnesty International, August 2008.

were imprisoned for "homosexual conduct" after being publicly accused of attending a "gay marriage" in 2007.

In September, a rockslide killed more than 100 residents of an informal settlement in Cairo, highlighting the precarious existence of the already deprived urban poor in cities across the region. The tragedy, it seems, was a predictable one. Water leaking from a nearby hillside had given warning of possible disaster – and in fact the area had experienced landslides before – but the authorities failed to take action until it was too late. Throughout the region, there were other communities of both urban and rural poor who appeared condemned to a cycle of deprivation – lacking adequate housing, health care or access to paid work – and disempowerment, with little or no say in the decisions that affected their lives. Certainly, they had no say in how to protect themselves from further impoverishment.

In the Israeli-occupied Palestinian territories, Palestinians already living in poverty were made homeless as a matter of deliberate policy. In the West Bank, including East Jerusalem, Israeli forces demolished many Palestinian homes on the grounds that they had been built without permits, while generally refusing to issue such permits to Palestinians, evicting hundreds of people. In the Jordan Valley, they brought in bulldozers to flatten villagers' homes and animal pens, depriving them of their livelihood, while elsewhere Palestinians were cut off from their agricultural lands by the construction of the fence/wall and were prevented from travelling to work, study or even to obtain hospital treatment by numerous Israeli army checkpoints and road-blocks. In the Gaza Strip, the three-week Israeli offensive that began on 27 December destroyed or badly damaged some 20,000 Palestinian homes and damaged schools and workplaces, as well as killing hundreds of Palestinian civilians. Meanwhile, Israeli settlements in the occupied West Bank continued to expand and develop, in breach of international law.

Voice

All across the region, those who spoke up in defence of their own or others' rights ran the risk of persecution at the hands of over-powerful secret police who were frequently allowed by their political masters to break the law with impunity. Governments generally were intolerant of dissent and appeared fearful of criticism and challenge, and the public exposure of corruption or other misdoings.

Throughout the region, state authorities used the need to be "secure" against "terrorism" as a means of sowing fear, insecurity and repression. Armed groups carried out violent attacks in several countries, including Algeria, Iraq, Lebanon, Syria and Yemen, but governments used often deliberately vague and sweeping counter-terrorism laws to clamp down on their political opponents and to stifle legitimate criticism and dissent. The overweening power of the Mukhabarat, security and intelligence services, permeated the region. Usually, these secret police reported directly to the heads of state or government and were allowed licence to arrest, detain and interrogate suspects, and often to torture and otherwise ill-treat them with impunity. Amnesty International received substantive reports of torture from several countries, including Bahrain, Egypt, Iran, Iraq, Jordan, Lebanon, Saudi Arabia, Syria, Tunisia, the UAE and Yemen. There were also reports of torture of Palestinians arrested by Israeli forces, and in the West Bank and Gaza respectively, of Palestinians being detained and tortured with impunity by rival Fatah and Hamas security forces.

One main purpose of torture was to obtain confessions for prosecutions before politically pliable courts, whose judges either feared or had no wish to check how evidence had been obtained. In a number of countries, trials of government opponents were held before "special" courts whose procedures failed to satisfy international fair trial standards. In Egypt, Muslim Brotherhood leaders, all civilians, were tried before a military court and international observers were excluded. Others accused were prosecuted before a court established under Egypt's long-running state of emergency. In Libya, 11 men arrested after they planned a peaceful protest to commemorate the killing of a dozen demonstrators by police were sentenced to imprisonment for up to 25 years by the State Security Court, although all but two were then released before the end of the year. In Syria, at least 300 people faced trial before the notoriously unfair Supreme State Security Court or other courts in which they would not receive fair trials, and 12 leading pro-democracy activists were sentenced to imprisonment on charges such as "weakening national sentiment". They complained they had been beaten in pre-trial detention to force them to sign "confessions" but the trial court took no steps to investigate. In other cases, a UN body ruled that prisoners were being detained arbitrarily as they had been convicted, in unfair trials, of acts that amounted to the legitimate exercise of their right to freedom of expression – the Syrian authorities took no action. The Saudi Arabian authorities detained hundreds of people on security grounds, including peaceful critics of the government, and thousands arrested in previous years remained in prison in virtual secrecy. In October, the government announced it would set up a special court to try more than 900 people accused of terrorist offences, but gave no details of the defendants, their trial dates, whether they would be allowed lawyers or whether the court would be open to international observers.

Everywhere, even in relatively more open states, journalists and

REGIONAL OVERVIEWS
MIDDLE EAST AND NORTH AFRICA

I BELIEVE THAT LASHING SENTENCES ARE A SOURCE OF SHAME AND CONSTITUTE DISPARAGEMENT FOR ALL IRANIANS WHO BELIEVE IN JUSTICE AND EQUALITY. FURTHER, THESE TYPES OF SENTENCES ARE A SIGN OF THE VIOLENCE WHICH IS PERPETUATED AGAINST WOMEN IN OUR SOCIETY.

Sussan Tahmasebi, a member of the Campaign for Equality in Iran, referring to punishments handed down to women's rights activists.

editors knew they had to operate within certain margins if they were not to place themselves at risk of prosecution, closure of their newspaper or worse. In Egypt, an editor was sentenced to imprisonment for commenting on the health of the President; in Algeria, journalists were prosecuted after reporting on alleged corruption in official circles and a leading human rights lawyer was harassed on a charge of bringing the judiciary into disrepute. In Libya, a political dissident detained in 2004 after calling for political reform in a media interview remained in custody. In Morocco/Western Sahara, where criticism of the monarchy remains taboo, human rights defenders were prosecuted for a peaceful protest deemed offensive to the King, although he subsequently issued them a royal pardon, and an 18-year-old student received a prison sentence after a slogan he wrote on a wall about his favourite football team was deemed to insult the monarchy. In Syria, where the government is intolerant of virtually any dissent, those targeted included bloggers accused of "spreading false news" or "weakening national sentiment", under catch-all laws designed to deter and suppress expression. The governments of Kuwait and Oman moved to tighten controls on expression through the internet, while the authorities in Iran, Tunisia and other states routinely blocked critical internet sites and cut internet connections between local human rights NGOs and the outside world.

In Egypt and Tunisia, the authorities' response to workers' protests about economic conditions was to put them down with excessive force and mass arrests. Similarly, Moroccan security forces broke up a protest blockade of the port of Sidi Ifni and launched a crackdown against those suspected of organizing or supporting it.

Human rights defenders and those advocating for greater rights – for women, minorities and others – or greater political freedom or access to social and economic rights, were very much in the frontline, all across the region. In most countries, however, human rights defenders continued to face major obstacles. In Syria and Tunisia, independent human rights organizations had to operate in a legal limbo, required by law to obtain an official registration that the state authorities, in practice, refused to allow. In Iran, a leading human rights NGO jointly founded by UN Peace Prize laureate Shirin Ebadi was closed down by government order, ironically as it was about to host an event commemorating the 60th anniversary of the Universal Declaration of Human Rights.

Conclusion

Accountability remained sorely lacking in the region for any of the human rights abuses people faced on a daily basis. Plunged further into insecurity, excluded from decision-making processes, ignored – or repressed – when attempting to be heard, people in the Middle East and North Africa saw their hardships perpetuated throughout 2008.

Impunity remained a cornerstone of policy in much of the region. In Morocco/Western Sahara, for example, the process of establishing the truth about enforced disappearances during the rule of King Hassan II appeared to have stalled. In Algeria, the authorities continued to block any investigation of the grave abuses committed during the internal conflict of the 1990s. In Iran, Lebanon, Libya and Syria, the authorities failed to take any effective steps to investigate or remedy gross abuses of the past. Unsurprisingly, these were also among a number of governments who failed to show any enthusiasm for investigating new allegations or incidents, such as the reported killing of 17 prisoners and others by Syrian security forces at Sednaya Military Prison.

But in the face of such varied, and often seemingly insurmountable problems, all across the region, many individuals – men, women and even children – worked to realize their and others' rights. Many were indomitable, even in the face of serious risks to their lives and livelihoods. In Algeria, relatives of victims of enforced disappearances during the country's "dirty war" of the 1990s continued to press for the truth and for justice in the face of unrelenting government obduracy and harassment. In Iran, women – and men – promoted a One Million Signatures petition to demand an end to legal discrimination against women, despite repeated harassment, arrests and assaults by state officials acting in breach of the law, while others campaigned for an end to executions of juvenile offenders.

In these countries and others, human rights defenders were in the vanguard of promoting change, but there were also signs that some of those holding political power also recognize the need for change, for reform, and for doing more to uphold human rights. The Bahrain government, for one, used the opportunity of the UN Universal Periodic Review process to kick start a programme of human rights reform that, if implemented, will stand as a powerful example to its neighbours. In Lebanon, the Minister of Justice promoted a law to abolish the death penalty, while the Algerian government was one of the key supporters of the call for a global moratorium on executions. Slowly but surely, there were signs in 2008 that a new generation is emerging, more aware of their rights and of what should be open to them, and with a growing resolve to achieve them.

REGIONAL OVERVIEWS
MIDDLE EAST AND NORTH AFRICA

WHEN I BECAME MORE INVOLVED IN HUMAN RIGHTS, I FOUND IT HAS A MUCH WIDER SCOPE THAN TORTURE, THOUGH ALL OF IT ARISES FROM THE ORIGINAL BASIC RULE, WHICH THE UNIVERSAL DECLARATION OF HUMAN RIGHTS ALSO UPHOLDS; AND THAT IS RESPECT FOR HUMAN DIGNITY.

Ahmed Seif El-Islam Hamad, speaking to Amnesty International in December 2008. An Egyptian lawyer and human rights activist, he was tortured and served five years in prison in the 1980s for his political beliefs.

A breach in the border barrier between the Gaza Strip and Egypt at Rafah, 25 January 2008. The blockade of the Gaza Strip imposed by the Israeli government stopped the flow of vital goods to the territory's 1.5 million residents.

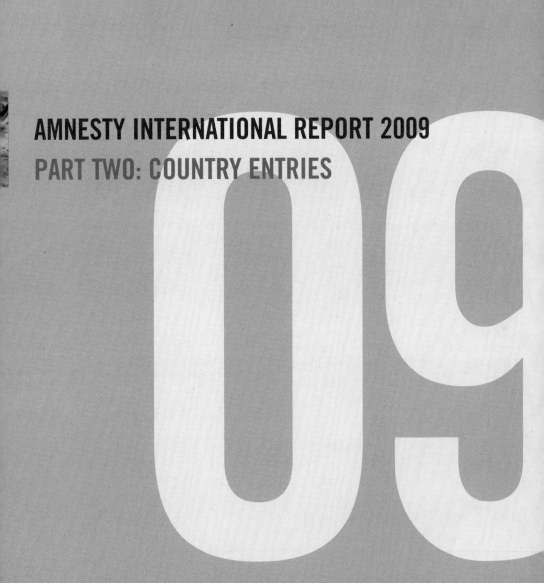

AMNESTY INTERNATIONAL REPORT 2009
PART TWO: COUNTRY ENTRIES

09

In August, a private company started turning Boeung Kak Lake, Phnom Penh, Cambodia, into a landfill. No prior notice was given to the 4,000 families who face displacement. Thousands of Cambodians were forcibly evicted in 2008 due to land disputes and commercial development projects.

AFGHANISTAN

ISLAMIC REPUBLIC OF AFGHANISTAN

Head of state and government:	**Hamid Karzai**
Death penalty:	**retentionist**
Population:	**28.2 million**
Life expectancy:	**42.9 years**
Under-5 mortality (m/f):	**232/237 per 1,000**
Adult literacy:	**28 per cent**

Millions of people living in southern and eastern Afghanistan were terrorized by the Taleban, other insurgent groups and local militias ostensibly allied with the government. Insecurity further restricted their already limited access to food, health care, and schooling. Indiscriminate attacks, abductions and the targeting of civilians reached unprecedented levels. The Taleban and other anti-government groups significantly expanded their attacks to cover more than a third of the country, including areas once considered relatively safe in the centre and the north. Increased military attacks between anti-government groups and US and NATO troops resulted in more than 2,000 civilian deaths. The government failed to maintain the rule of law or to provide basic services to millions of people even in areas under its control.

Background

In January, the Afghan-international Joint Co-ordination Monitoring Board (JCMB) acknowledged that little headway had been made in the implementation of the Action Plan on Peace, Justice and Reconciliation. The 2005 Action Plan called on the Afghan state to remove human rights abusers from positions of power, encourage institutional reform, and establish an accountability mechanism.

In its March annual review, the JCMB conceded that progress had been slow in the area of human rights. The JCMB also acknowledged that there was still insufficient civilian oversight of government security forces and law enforcement agencies, most notably the National Directorate of Security (NDS), Afghanistan's intelligence agency.

In June, the government launched the Afghanistan National Development Strategy (ANDS), a road map for development until 2013. The ANDS is counterpart to the 2006 Afghanistan Compact, a political agreement between the Afghan government and donor countries.

Justice system

Judicial and security sectors lacked the personnel, infrastructure, and political will to protect and promote human rights. The Ministry of Justice, which serves as the government's lead agency for the implementation and mainstreaming of human rights, did not sufficiently collaborate with the Afghanistan Independent Human Rights Commission (AIHRC). Without co-operation, recommendations by the AIHRC, including for investigations into military operations resulting in civilian casualties, were largely ineffective.

Working conditions including low wages and a lack of personal security are often cited as reasons for judges, prosecutors, and other civil servants working in the justice sector being susceptible to corruption, which is believed to be widespread. Citizens lacked confidence in the formal justice institutions and regarded them as slow, ineffective and often corrupt. Most people, and in particular women, had difficulty accessing courts and legal assistance; most could not afford court fees or travel costs. Traditional *jirgas* and *shuras* (informal tribal councils), which operate outside the formal justice system and have led to violations of the right to fair trial, continued to handle an estimated 80 per cent of all disputes, particularly in rural areas.

The trial proceedings continued of Afghan detainees from Guantánamo and Bagram transferred to the Afghan government for prosecution, but failed to meet national or international fair trial standards. The trials were undermined by serious flaws including lack of defence counsel and inadequate time to prepare a defence, the use of confessions obtained by torture and other ill-treatment and denial of the right to examine evidence and confront witnesses. A presidential committee was established in March to review trial complaints.

Impunity

Even in areas of the country under government control, impunity prevailed at all levels of administration. No effective accountability mechanism had been established and only a handful of those responsible for serious violations of human rights and international humanitarian law during three decades of conflict have been brought to justice, mostly in other states under the principle of universal jurisdiction. Many regional officials and

A

militia commanders continued to perpetrate human rights violations with impunity.

Arbitrary arrests and detentions

Arbitrary arrest and detention by the police and other official security agencies, as well as private militias working with Afghan and international security forces, were widespread.

The NDS continued to arbitrarily arrest and detain suspects without allowing access to defence lawyers, families, courts or other outside bodies. Scores of detainees were subjected to torture and other ill-treatment, including being whipped, exposed to extreme cold and deprived of food.

More than 600 detainees were being held at the US-run Bagram military airbase and other US military facilities outside the protection of international human rights laws and domestic laws. Some have been detained for several years and denied their right to due process, including access to lawyers and habeas corpus review.

Death penalty

Seventeen people were executed in 2008 and at least 111 others were on death row. The Supreme Court of Afghanistan upheld 131 death sentences issued by lower courts which await President Karzai's approval. The trial proceedings in most cases violated international standards of fairness, including providing inadequate time for the accused to prepare their defence, lack of legal representation, reliance on weak evidence and the denial of the defendants' right to call and examine witnesses.

■ On 22 January, Sayed Parwiz Kambaksh was sentenced to death for "blasphemy" in a grossly unfair trial. He was convicted of downloading material from the internet on the role of women in Islam, adding commentary and distributing it at Balkh University in northern Afghanistan. On 21 October, following an appeal hearing, the sentence was commuted to 20 years' imprisonment.

In December, Afghanistan voted against a UN General Assembly resolution calling for a worldwide moratorium on executions.

Abuses by Afghan and international forces

Civilian casualties have been increasing since 2001 and 2008 proved to be the bloodiest year yet. Most civilians were injured as a result of insurgent attacks but some 40 per cent (795) of civilian casualties were due to operations by Afghan and international security forces - a 30 per cent increase in the 559 reported in 2007.

Serious concerns about the indiscriminate and disproportionate use of air strikes were raised following several grave incidents. On 6 July US-led coalition air strikes in Deh Bala district in Nangahar Province reportedly killed 47 civilians, including 30 children; on 21-22 August air strikes carried out in Shindand district of Herat Province resulted in more than 90 civilian casualties, including 62 children.

In September 2008, responding to criticism regarding the high number of civilian deaths, NATO again revised its rules of engagement to limit the use of immediate air strikes if ground troops come under attack, giving more time to plan for an air strike and seek approval from higher levels of command.

Some families whose relatives were killed or injured and those who had property destroyed received financial compensation from governments involved in military operations. However, Afghan and international forces lack a systematic programme for assisting those injured by Afghan and international military forces.

NATO and US forces continued to hand over detainees to the NDS, Afghanistan's intelligence service, which perpetrates human rights violations including torture and arbitrary detention with impunity.

Abuses by armed groups

Criminal gangs and armed groups (some ostensibly allied to the government) abducted foreigners and attacked business owners, aid workers, teachers, education aid projects and schools to destabilize security and halt development efforts throughout the country. Seventy-eight employees of various NGOs were abducted and another 31 killed. The Taleban and other insurgent groups stepped up their "tactic" of deliberately targeting women, including kidnapping.

■ On 13 August, three international aid workers and an Afghan driver working for the International Rescue Committee were killed in Logar province by Taleban insurgents. A second Afghan driver was severely wounded.

■ On 20 October, a British Christian Aid organization worker was shot dead in broad daylight in Kabul by Taleban insurgents on a motorcycle.

Armed criminal groups kidnapped high-profile Afghans for ransom. Most abductions went unreported because victims and their families feared retaliation and corrupt police officials with ties to armed groups.

■ On 19 October, Humayun Shah Asefi, a relative of the late King Zahir Shah, was kidnapped by armed men from his home in Kabul. He was rescued a week later by Afghan police.

Suicide attacks

Suicide attacks resulted in 373 deaths. Taleban and other insurgent suicide attacks with military or police targets often resulted in high civilian deaths and injuries.

■ On 17 February, a suicide bomber blew himself up close to a crowd of around 500 people watching a dog fight in Arghandab, Kandahar Province. Around 100 civilians were killed and dozens were injured.

■ On 7 July, a suicide car bomb outside the Indian Embassy in Kabul killed 41 people and wounded nearly 150 others.

■ On 30 October, a Taleban suicide bomber targeted the Ministry of Information and Culture in central Kabul, killing five civilians and leaving more than 21 injured.

Freedom of expression

Freedom of expression, which flourished briefly after the fall of the Taleban in 2001, was eroded by threats and attacks from both state and non-state actors.

The Taleban and other anti-government groups targeted journalists and blocked nearly all reporting from areas under their control.

■ On 7 June, Abdul Samad Rohani, an Afghan journalist working for the BBC in Helmand province, was abducted; he was shot dead the next day, possibly in response to his investigation of the narcotics trade.

■ In May, journalist Nilofar Habibi was stabbed by a woman on the doorstep of her home in Herat reportedly for working as a television journalist.

The government, in particular the NDS, and the Ulema Council (council of religious scholars) attempted to curtail media independence.

■ In July, the NDS detained Mohammad Nasir Fayyaz, presenter of the TV programme *The Truth*, for "misrepresenting" government officials. Mohammad Nasir Fayyaz was released shortly after but reportedly remained under surveillance.

■ In September 2008, Ahmad Ghous Zalmai, a journalist and former spokesperson for the Attorney General, and Mullah Qari Mushtaq were each sentenced to 20 years' imprisonment for publishing a Dari translation of the Qur'an without the Arabic text alongside.

Discrimination and violence against women and girls

Although women increasingly participated in politics and public life, their rights remained constrained by social prejudice and violence within the home and by armed groups. The number of women holding senior ministerial positions decreased.

■ On 28 September, Malalai Kakar, the highest ranking policewoman in Afghanistan, was killed by Taleban gunmen near her home in Kandahar.

■ On 12 November, two men on a motorcycle used water pistols to spray acid on some 15 girls walking to school in Kandahar, blinding at least two of them and disfiguring several others. Ten Taleban insurgents were later arrested in connection with the attack.

Women suffered from high rates of domestic violence and had little, if any, recourse to legal protection. According to the AIHRC, 60 to 80 per cent of all marriages were forced and under-age marriages occurred in high numbers. Women who sought to flee abusive marriages were often detained and prosecuted for alleged offences such as "home escape" or "moral" crimes that are not provided for in the Penal Code.

Lack of humanitarian access

Insecurity caused by the Taleban and other insurgent groups in the south and east stopped many aid organizations from operating in these areas. In August, the International Rescue Committee halted all aid operations in Afghanistan after four workers were killed by militants in Logar province. In Kunar province, the significant Taliban presence prevented the UN High Commissioner for Refugees from directly providing supplies to Pakistani refugees who had fled fighting between the Pakistani security forces and pro-Taleban insurgents in Pakistan's Federally Administered Tribal Areas.

Right to health and education

The year saw increased attacks on schools, the intimidation of teachers and female students primarily by the Taleban, and greater disruption of classes because of armed conflict. In areas controlled by the Afghan government, both health and education systems suffered from inadequate funding, lack of qualified professionals, and security problems. Deteriorating security forced the Ministry of Public Health to shut down a significant number of health clinics, the only health services available to many people.

Internally displaced people and returnees

The Afghanistan internally displaced people task force, comprising international aid agencies and the government, estimated that more than 235,000 people were internally displaced. They faced desperate circumstances in conflict zones as international and local humanitarian agencies faced difficulties in reaching them.

More than 276,000 Afghan refugees living in Iran and Pakistan returned home in 2008 according to UNHCR. Many returnees faced destitution, with scarce job opportunities and lack of access to land, housing, water, heath care and education. Some returnees became internally displaced because their property had been appropriated by local power-holders.

In September, more than 20,000 people fled from Pakistan to eastern Afghanistan to avoid the fighting between the Pakistani security forces and pro-Taleban insurgents in Pakistan's Federally Administered Tribal Areas.

Amnesty International reports

📄 Afghanistan: Prisoner of conscience sentenced to death for downloading and distributing materials from the internet (ASA 11/001/2008)

📄 Afghanistan: Women human rights defenders continue to struggle for women's rights (ASA 11/003/2008)

📄 Afghanistan: Arms proliferation fuels further abuse (ASA 11/004/2008)

📄 Afghanistan: Death Penalty – Around 100 unnamed individuals sentenced to death (ASA 11/005/2008)

📄 Afghanistan: Civilians suffer the brunt of rising suicide attacks (ASA 11/006/2008)

📄 Afghanistan: No more empty promises in Paris (ASA 11/007/2008)

📄 Afghanistan: Further Information on Death Penalty – Sayed Perwiz Kambakhsh (ASA 11/013/2008)

📄 Afghanistan: Submission to the UN Universal Periodic Review – Fifth

Session of the UPR Working Group of the Human Rights Council, May 2009 (ASA 11/014/2008)

📄 Afghanistan: Stop Move Toward Wide Use of Executions, 12 November 2008

ALBANIA

REPUBLIC OF ALBANIA

Head of state:	Bamir Topi
Head of government:	Sali Berisha
Death penalty:	abolitionist for all crimes
Population:	3.2 million
Life expectancy:	76.2 years
Under-5 mortality (m/f):	24/20 per 1,000
Adult literacy:	98.7 per cent

Domestic violence was widespread. The trafficking of women and children for forced prostitution or other forms of exploitation continued. There were incidents of torture and other ill-treatment of detainees in police stations and prisons. Detention conditions for remand and convicted prisoners sometimes amounted to inhuman and degrading treatment. Adult orphans were denied their legal right to adequate housing.

Background

Unemployment levels remained high, despite continued economic progress. More than 18 per cent of the population were estimated to be living below the national poverty line. This sector of the population also suffered most acutely from limited access to education, water and health and social care.

Prosecutions for corruption increased, but mainly targeted low-level officials. Public confidence in the judicial system was low.

An investigation was initiated after an explosion in March at a depot where obsolete munitions were being dismantled. The Minister of Defence was dismissed and lost his immunity while several officials from the Ministry of Defence were arrested. The explosion resulted in 26 deaths, over 300 people injured and the destruction or damage of hundreds of houses. It also gave rise to allegations of corruption and irregular arms trading.

Legal, constitutional or institutional developments

In April, constitutional amendments were adopted, including changes to the electoral system. In November, a new electoral code was adopted. Amendments to the criminal code reinforcing protection for children and a law on gender equality aimed at increasing the representation of women in public life were also adopted.

Enforced disappearances

■ The trial of four former officers of the National Intelligence Service began in May on charges of the abduction and "torture with serious consequences" of three men in 1995. The fate of one of the victims, Remzi Hoxha, an ethnic Albanian from Macedonia, remained unknown. Ilir Kumbaro, one of the defendants, was being tried in his absence, but in September a man believed by the UK police to be Ilir Kumbaro was arrested in the UK, and Albania sought his extradition. He denied that he was Ilir Kumbaro; British court proceedings to establish his identity and rule on Albania's extradition request had not been concluded by the end of the year.

Violence against women and girls

Domestic violence was widespread, and was believed to affect about one in three women. In the first nine months of 2008 the police registered 612 incidents of domestic violence, although many others were believed to have gone unreported. The authorities took measures to increase protection for victims, the great majority of them women.

Few cases involving domestic violence were criminally prosecuted unless they involved threats to life, or resulted in serious injury or death. Nonetheless, victims increasingly sought protection from their abusers. Between January and September, police reportedly assisted 253 victims in applying to courts for protection orders under civil legislation adopted in 2007. However, courts often did not issue these orders because victims withdrew their complaints or failed to appear in court.

Trafficking in human beings

Women and girls continued to be trafficked for forced prostitution, and children for exploitation as beggars, generally to Greece and Italy. Victim protection remained weak, and police largely relied on the victims themselves to report trafficking. During the year, the Serious Crimes Court tried 30 defendants on charges of trafficking women for sexual exploitation and six defendants charged with trafficking children.

■ Allman Kera was sentenced in June to 15 years' imprisonment for trafficking his wife, a minor, to Kosovo where he forced her to work as a prostitute until she escaped and reported him.

■ K.D. was charged in November with trafficking a nine-year-old boy to Greece in 2002 and forcing him to work as a beggar. The boy's parents apparently reported him to the police when he failed to send them a monthly sum as agreed.

Torture and other ill-treatment

There were allegations that detainees had been tortured or otherwise ill-treated, usually immediately after arrest and during questioning. In October the Minister of Interior stated that, in the last three years, 128 police officers had been reported by the Internal Inspection Service to the prosecutor for "arbitrary acts" related to the use of violence.

However, very few of these cases went to court. In general, criminal proceedings were begun only if the victim filed a complaint or on the recommendation of the Ombudsperson. On one occasion, prosecutors and judges did not initiate investigations when a defendant bearing bruises was brought before them at a remand hearing. Prosecutors rarely, if ever, brought charges of torture, preferring to invoke lighter offences such as "arbitrary acts", which in practice are generally punished with fines.

In January, the functions of the national mechanism for the prevention of torture, under the Optional Protocol to the UN Convention against Torture, were entrusted to the Ombudsperson. In the course of unannounced inspections to police stations the Ombudsperson learned of, and made public, several instances of police ill-treatment. Following one such inspection in November, police in the town of Shkoder initiated criminal proceedings against the Ombudsperson, claiming that he had jeopardized an investigation by publicly referring to two judicial police officers and their alleged victim by their initials.

■ In November an inquiry was initiated against a judicial police officer in Saranda on charges of "using violence during an investigation". The officer was alleged to have beaten Aristil Gllучaj, aged 18, while interrogating him on 6 November, causing him to lose

A

consciousness. The young man was admitted to hospital the same day.

There were also allegations that detainees had been ill-treated by prison guards. In February the Ministry of Interior's Internal Inspection Service investigated complaints by prisoners at Peqin and Lezhë prisons that guards had ill-treated them. The investigation concluded that the complaints were well-founded and the guards were disciplined.

Prison conditions

Detention conditions amounted in some instances to inhuman and degrading treatment. Medical care was inadequate and prisoners with mental illnesses were generally not separated from other prisoners, and received little or no specialist treatment. Detainees, even after being remanded in custody or convicted, often remained in police stations where conditions were generally very poor. This was due to administrative delays and lack of prison capacity. Nonetheless, there were some improvements in detention conditions, and in legislation relating to prisoners' rights and prison monitoring.

Three new prisons were opened but overcrowding persisted; the national prison population in November stood at 4,666 – some 900 people above capacity. In June, the Ombudsperson concluded that the conditions of up to 120 detainees held in remand cells in the basement of Korça district police station amounted to inhuman and degrading treatment. The station had capacity for only 40 detainees.

In October a new prison was opened in Korça to which remand and convicted prisoners were transferred. In November, the Albanian Helsinki Committee (AHC) criticized conditions at the newly built prison in Fushë-Krujë, in particular damp in the ground floor cells, running water shortages and broken showers. The AHC also criticized the unhygienic conditions in which women were held in Tirana prisons 302 and 313.

Housing rights

The state again failed to implement domestic law which requires that orphans, on completing secondary education or reaching adulthood, should be given priority access to housing. Some 300 adults who were orphaned as children continued to share rooms in dilapidated and inadequate housing – conditions which aggravated their social exclusion.

With few qualifications, they were often unemployed or undertook casual labour for low wages, surviving on minimal state assistance. Under Albanian law, registered orphans up to the age of 30 are among the vulnerable groups to be prioritized when social housing is allocated. However, the very limited availability of social housing does not begin to meet the needs of the reportedly 45,000 families registered as homeless.

ALGERIA

PEOPLE'S DEMOCRATIC REPUBLIC OF ALGERIA

Head of state:	Abdelaziz Bouteflika
Head of government:	Ahmed Ouyahia (replaced Abdelaziz Belkhadem in June)
Death penalty:	abolitionist in practice
Population:	34.4 million
Life expectancy:	71.7 years
Under-5 mortality (m/f):	34/30 per 1,000
Adult literacy:	69.9 per cent

Terrorism suspects were detained incommunicado and subjected to unfair trials. The authorities continued to harass human rights defenders and journalists. Converts from Islam and individuals deemed to offend its tenets were prosecuted. Irregular migrants faced arrest, indefinite detention, ill-treatment and collective expulsion. Hundreds of people were sentenced to death but there were no executions. Impunity remained entrenched for members of armed groups and security forces who perpetrated grave abuses during the internal conflict of the 1990s.

Background

According to media reports, between 60 and 90 civilians were killed in continuing political violence, many of them in bomb attacks for which a group calling itself the Al-Qa'ida Organization in the Islamic Maghreb claimed responsibility. Dozens of suspected members of armed groups were killed in skirmishes and search operations by security forces; some may have been extrajudicially executed.

In May, the UN Committee against Torture (CAT)

recommended that the government take measures to combat impunity, investigate all past and present cases of torture, including enforced disappearance and rape, and ensure that Algeria's anti-terrorism measures comply with international human rights standards. However, the government took no steps in this regard.

On 12 November, parliament approved a constitutional amendment lifting the two-term limit on the presidency, paving the way for Abdelaziz Bouteflika, in power since 1999, to stand for a third term in presidential elections scheduled for April 2009.

Counter-terror and security

The authorities, including the Department for Information and Security (DRS) military intelligence agency, continued to detain terrorism suspects incommunicado, putting them at risk of torture and other ill-treatment. Those detained included several Algerian nationals returned from other states.
■ Rabah Kadri, an Algerian national returned from France in April, was reported to have been arrested on arrival and then held incommunicado by the DRS until he was released without charge 12 days later.
■ Seven former detainees held at the US naval base at Guantánamo Bay were returned to Algeria during 2008. All were arrested and detained incommunicado upon return for periods ranging from eight to 13 days. On release, they were placed under judicial control and faced charges of belonging to terrorist groups abroad. Fourteen Algerian nationals continued to be held at Guantánamo Bay.

People suspected of subversive activities or terrorism continued to face unfair trials. Some were denied access to legal counsel while held in pre-trial detention. The courts accepted as evidence, without investigation, "confessions" that defendants alleged had been obtained under torture or other duress.
■ In January, Blida military prison authorities acknowledged for the first time the detention of Mohamed Rahmouni, although he had by then been held for six months. Although a civilian, he was expected to be tried before a military court in Blida on terrorism-related charges. He was not allowed access to his lawyer, who had made at least six unsuccessful attempts to visit him.
■ The trial of Malik Mejnoun and Abdelhakim Chenoui

on charges of belonging to an armed terrorist group and of the murder of singer Lounes Matoub was postponed indefinitely in July. The two men, who had been held without trial for over nine years, partly in secret and incommunicado detention, remained in prison at the end of the year. Both alleged that they were tortured in detention but the authorities did not order an investigation, even though Abdelhakim Chenoui said that his "confession", which implicated Malik Mejnoun, was extracted under duress.
■ At least 30 detainees held on terrorism-related charges at the prison of El Harrach said they were severely beaten by prison guards in February after they refused to return to their prison ward in protest against the transformation of their prayer zone. No investigations were conducted into the allegations.

In May, the CAT urged the authorities to ensure that no detainees are held beyond the maximum period of pre-arraignment detention, to investigate reports of secret detention centres and to bring all DRS detention centres under the control of the civilian prison administration and judicial authorities.

Freedom of expression

Journalists and human rights defenders continued to face harassment. Some were prosecuted on defamation or other criminal charges for criticizing public officials or institutions.
■ Human rights lawyer Amine Sidhoum was convicted in April of bringing the judiciary into disrepute, in relation to comments attributed to him in a 2004 newspaper article. He was sentenced to a suspended six-month prison term and a fine. After an appeal court confirmed the conviction in November, the case was referred to the Supreme Court as a result of appeals by both the prosecution and Amine Sidhoum.
■ Hassan Bourras, a journalist for El Bilad newspaper, was sentenced to two months' imprisonment and fined in October after the Saida Court of Appeals upheld his conviction for defamation, imposed after he published an article about alleged corruption in the city of El-Bayadh. He remained at liberty pending a possible further appeal.
■ Hafnaoui Ghoul, a journalist and human rights activist with the Djelfa branch of the Algerian League for the Defence of Human Rights, faced four separate judicial proceedings for defamation and contempt after five Djelfa governorate officials complained about

A

articles he had published in *Wasat* newspaper about mismanagement and corruption. The charges also related to allegations he had made about secret detention centres and torture.

Freedom of religion

The Constitution makes Islam the state religion but guarantees freedom of conscience. Amid indications of an expansion of evangelical Christian churches in Algeria, the authorities were reported to have ordered the closure of dozens of churches of the Protestant Church of Algeria. The Minister of Religious Affairs and Endowments denied that any "authorized" churches had been closed.

At least 12 Christians and converts to Christianity from Islam were prosecuted on charges of breaching Ordinance 06-03, promulgated in February 2006, regulating faiths other than Islam. The Ordinance criminalizes incitement, coercion or other "seductive" means to convert a person of Muslim faith to another religion and religious activities that are not regulated by the state. Several of those prosecuted were reported to have been sentenced to suspended prison terms and fined.

■ Habiba Kouider, a Christian convert from Islam, was arrested in March after police found copies of the Bible in her bag. She was charged with "practising a faith other than Islam without authorization". Her trial was adjourned in May and she was reported to have been told by judicial officials that the prosecution would be dropped if she returned to Islam.

■ Six men were tried in June in Tiaret for allegedly breaching Ordinance 06-03. Two denied adherence to Christianity and were acquitted; the others were convicted and received suspended prison terms and were fined.

Other people were charged with "denigrating the dogma or precepts of Islam".

■ Ten men were tried in two separate cases in September for publicly breaking fast during the holy month of Ramadan. Six were acquitted on appeal, having been sentenced to four years' imprisonment and heavy fines by a lower court in Biskra. The others were sentenced to three years in prison and fined by a court in Beir Mourad Rais. The sentence was reduced to a two-month suspended prison term on appeal in November.

Migrants' rights

Thousands of Algerians and other nationals, mostly from sub-Saharan African countries, attempted to migrate to Europe from Algeria. Hundreds were intercepted at sea.

On 25 June, parliament passed Law 08-11, which regulates the entry, stay and movement of foreigners in Algeria. The law allows foreigners issued with expulsion orders by the Interior Ministry to have their removal stayed pending appeal, but empowers governors to order deportations without any right of appeal of foreigners deemed to have entered or to be residing in Algeria illegally. This increases the risk of arbitrary, collective expulsions. The law also provides for the establishment of "waiting" centres for irregular migrants where they may face indefinite detention, and prescribes severe penalties for smugglers and any other individuals who assist foreigners to enter or remain in Algeria irregularly.

In August, the Council of Ministers approved a draft law to amend the Penal Code in order to introduce heavier penalties for the smuggling of migrants and make it a criminal offence punishable by up to six months in prison to leave Algeria illegally.

Impunity

The government took no steps to address the gross and widespread human rights abuses committed by armed groups and state security forces during the internal conflict of the 1990s in which as many as 200,000 people are thought to have been killed.

In May, the CAT urged the government to amend Articles 45 and 46 of the 2006 Decree implementing the Charter for Peace and National Reconciliation (Law 06-01), which gives immunity to the security forces and allows for the punishment of victims and their families, human rights defenders and others who criticize the conduct of the security forces during the internal conflict.

Enforced disappearances

The authorities had still not investigated the fate of thousands of people subjected to enforced disappearance.

In May, a senior official stated that 5,500 families of victims of enforced disappearance had accepted compensation but that 600 others had refused, insisting that they be told the truth about the fate of their missing relatives. Later, the head of the National Advisory Commission for the Promotion and

Protection of Human Rights said that 96-97 per cent of the families of the disappeared had accepted compensation, but gave no details. Under Law 06-01, relatives can seek compensation if they obtain a death certificate from the authorities for the person who disappeared. Some families complained that they were put under pressure to seek such certificates.

Victims' families continued to be harassed when seeking truth and justice.

■ No progress was made in resolving the disappearance of Salah Saker, a teacher arrested by state agents in 1994. In August his wife, Louisa Saker, head of the Association of the Families of the Disappeared in Constantine, lost her appeal against a decision of the judicial authorities of the Tribunal of Constantine to dismiss her complaint regarding her husband's disappearance. In November, the Constantine Court of Appeals upheld the conviction against her for participating in an unauthorized "unarmed march" in connection with a peaceful demonstration in 2004 by families of victims of enforced disappearance. She had received a suspended fine. Louisa Saker appealed against the decision. Her two co-defendants, who were tried in their absence, were sentenced to one year in prison and fined.

Death penalty

Hundreds of people were sentenced to death, mostly on terrorism-related charges, but the authorities maintained a de facto moratorium on executions. Many of those sentenced were alleged members of armed groups who were tried and convicted in their absence.

In December, Algeria co-sponsored a resolution at the UN General Assembly calling for a worldwide moratorium on executions.

Violence against women

According to judicial police, 4,500 complaints of violence and harassment against women were received between January and June 2008. The actual number was believed to be much higher.

Constitutional changes passed in November included a provision calling for the promotion of women's political rights.

The 2008 report of the UN Special Rapporteur on violence against women commended advances in women's rights in Algeria, but criticized the failure of the authorities adequately to address violence and discrimination against women. The Special Rapporteur urged the authorities to investigate sexual violence committed during the internal conflict, to compensate the survivors and to bring perpetrators to justice.

Amnesty International reports

- Algeria: Briefing to the Committee against Torture (MDE 28/001/2008)
- Algeria: Amnesty International condemns bomb attacks in Issers and in Bouira (MDE 28/006/2008)

A

ANGOLA

REPUBLIC OF ANGOLA
Head of state:	José Eduardo dos Santos
Head of government:	António Paulo Kassoma (replaced Fernando da Piedade Dias dos Santos in September)
Death penalty:	abolitionist for all crimes
Population:	17.5 million
Life expectancy:	41.7 years
Under-5 mortality (m/f):	243/215 per 1,000
Adult literacy:	67.4 per cent

There were fewer reports of forced evictions and the government started to build social housing. Human rights violations by the police declined. Intimidation and harassment of human rights defenders continued: the authorities asked the UN office for human rights to close its office in Angola and sought to close down a local organization. Freedom of expression was restricted, with journalists facing harassment through defamation cases. A prisoner of conscience was sentenced to a long prison term.

Background

Heavy rains in the provinces of Cunene, Namibe and Huíla led to floods which forced more than 10,000 people from their homes in February. About 50 other families had their homes destroyed by heavy rains in Huambo in November.

Angola became the largest oil-producing country in sub-Saharan Africa in April, surpassing Nigeria. Despite this, 68 per cent of the population lived below the poverty line, of whom 28 per cent lived in extreme poverty.

In February Angola extradited Henry Himomotim Okah and Eduardo Atata to Nigeria. Both men were suspected of being involved in attacks in Nigeria's oil-rich Niger delta.

About 30 detainees, including 10 women and a child, died in March when the building of the National Directorate of Criminal Investigation (DNIC) collapsed. Another 145 detainees were hospitalized. Although an investigation was carried out to establish what caused the collapse, its findings were not made public.

In March a Portuguese employee of a Portuguese company was shot in the arm and leg while driving a company vehicle. The Armed Forces of Cabinda, the armed branch of the Front for the Liberation of the Cabinda State (FLEC), claimed responsibility for the attack, stating that they would target foreign companies working in Cabinda to stop them from supporting the economy of Angola.

The first legislative elections in 16 years were held in September. They were generally free from violence and other human rights violations, despite some isolated incidents of harassment of political activists in the pre-election period. The main opposition party, the National Union for the Total Independence of Angola (UNITA), initially demanded a re-run of the voting in the capital, Luanda, but eventually accepted the results which saw the ruling People's Movement for the Liberation for Angola (MPLA) win the elections with over 80 per cent of the votes.

Angola presented its combined initial, second and third report to the UN Committee on Economic, Social and Cultural Rights in November. During this session the Vice-Minister of Foreign Affairs acknowledged the importance of implementing economic, social and cultural rights in Angola.

Housing rights

The government started to build houses under the Angola Youth programme, which aims to build one million social housing units by 2012. Following the September elections, the Ministry of Urban Affairs and the Environment became the Ministry of Urban Affairs and Housing. In October the UN World Habitat Day celebrations were held in Luanda. During these celebrations the government undertook to commit more than 10 per cent of oil income to social housing.

There were fewer reports of forced evictions than in previous years. Some of those forcibly evicted were reportedly re-housed. There were also reports that the government planned to re-house the families forcibly evicted in previous years from their homes in Cambamba I, Cambamba II and Cidadania neighbourhoods, but this had not happened by the end of 2008.

■ In October at least 17 families were forcibly evicted and had their homes demolished by the Jardim do Éden (Garden of Eden) construction company in the Luanda neighbourhood of Iraque. The families claimed that they had had title to the land from the Kilamba Kiaxi municipality since 1989. Some residents reportedly received an amount between US$500 and US$2,500 as compensation. No alternative accommodation was offered to families who could not provide for themselves.

Police

There were improvements in police policy, including the approval of a model of policing which regulates the use of force. Police did not appear to behave in a partisan manner and there were few reports of violence or human rights violations during the elections. However, there were a few cases of unlawful killing by the police.

■ In July a group of about seven police officers went to the area of Largo da Frescura in a white, unmarked vehicle and opened fire on eight youths, killing them. The police officers claimed that they had responded to reports that a group of youths suspected of armed robbery were in the area and that the youths had fired shots at them. They claimed that they shot back in self-defence. None of the police officers was injured. Eye-witnesses stated that the police officers told the youths to lie on their stomachs, shot them while they were lying on the ground and then drove off. Seven police officers were arrested, but no trial had taken place by the end of 2008.

Human rights defenders

The environment for human rights defenders continued to be tense. In May the UN Office of the High Commissioner for Human Rights in Angola was closed at the request of the government. The authorities claimed that the Office did not have a legal mandate as it was a residue of the UN Observer Mission in Angola (MONUA), which had been allowed to remain in the country at the end of the peace-keeping mission in 2002.

A

In September, the Procurator General instituted a case in the Constitutional Court to close down the Association for Justice, Peace and Democracy, alleging that the association's founding documents include provisions that are contrary to Angolan law. No ruling was passed by the end of the year.

Freedom of expression – journalists

Restrictions on freedom of expression of journalists continued. A number of journalists faced harassment in the form of defamation cases.

In July the Ministry of Posts and Telecommunications and the Ministry of Media jointly ordered the private radio station Rádio Despertar to suspend its broadcasts for 180 days, on the grounds that the station's broadcasting range exceeded that stipulated in its licence.

Arbitrary arrests and detentions

People were arrested for exercising their rights to freedom of association and assembly.

■ In March police and members of the criminal investigative police stopped the annual pilgrimage celebration in Cabinda and refused to let more than 3,000 members of the Catholic Church continue with the pilgrimage. They were made to sit in the sun without water or food. Xavier Soca Tati and one other person were taken to the police station and questioned for several hours. They stated they had followed the necessary procedures before the pilgrimage but the police denied this. No charges were laid against any of the members of the Catholic Church.

■ Police arrested and detained members of the Angolan Teachers Trade Union in Caxito, Bengo Province in October. They were striking against low salaries and poor working conditions. Manuel Bento Azevedo, Gonçalves Ismael Lopes, Moniz Mujinga, César Gomes António and Almério Augusto Cristóvão were arrested at the Mission School 307, accused of coercing other teachers to join in the strike. Another five teachers were arrested that week in different schools in Bengo Province. On one occasion the police did not have arrest warrants, but said they were obeying orders. All 10 teachers were released without trial two days after the initial arrest, but about five days later Manuel Bento Azevedo and two other union members were once again arrested. At the end of October all three were acquitted by the Bengo Provincial Court.

Prisoner of conscience

In September, José Fernando Lelo, former correspondent of the Voice of America in Cabinda, was convicted by a military court in an unfair trial and sentenced to 12 years' imprisonment for crimes against the state and instigating a rebellion in Cabinda. He had been arrested in November 2007 and held without charge until March 2008. Five soldiers who were tried with him were convicted of attempted armed rebellion and other military crimes and sentenced to 13 years' imprisonment. A sixth soldier was acquitted.

Amnesty International visits/reports

🚌 In October Amnesty International delegates applied for visas to Angola but they had not received the visas by the end of the year. No reason was given for the delay nor was any indication given as to when the visas would be granted. Amnesty International's last visit to the country was in February 2007.

📃 Angola: Briefing for election monitors (AFR 12/002/2008)

📃 Angola: Briefing for the UN Committee on Economic, Social and Cultural Rights – 41st session, 3-21 November 2008 (AFR 12/010/2008)

ARGENTINA

ARGENTINE REPUBLIC

Head of state and government:	Cristina Fernández
Death penalty:	abolitionist for all crimes
Population:	39.9 million
Life expectancy:	74.8 years
Under-5 mortality (m/f):	17/13 per 1,000
Adult literacy:	97.2 per cent

Although there was some progress in bringing to justice those responsible for past human rights violations, there were also a number of setbacks during the year. Strikes and demonstrations were widespread. Several police officers were brought to trial for unlawful killings of demonstrators or criminal suspects. Conditions of detention, especially for young offenders, remained a concern.

Background

In March a government decree raising export tax on grains sparked nationwide strikes and highway blockades. In July, the Senate rejected a bill ratifying the measures and the government revoked the decree.

Forced evictions – Indigenous Peoples

Forced evictions of Indigenous Peoples in which both police and private security guards used excessive force were reported. Evictions continued despite an emergency law passed in 2006 on Indigenous land rights which called for eviction orders to be suspended pending a review and registration of Indigenous land tenure.

Freedom of association

In November the Supreme Court ruled unconstitutional an article of the trade union law that denied individuals who were not part of a trade union that had been granted union status by the government the right to represent workers. The decision emphasized the need to bring the trade union law into line with international human rights standards.

Death penalty

In August, the Senate abrogated the 1951 Military Code of Justice, creating a new system for prosecuting members of the military through the ordinary courts and abolishing the death penalty for all crimes. In September, Argentina ratified the Second Optional Protocol to the International Covenant on Civil and Political Rights, aiming at the abolition of the death penalty, and the Protocol to the American Convention on Human Rights to Abolish the Death Penalty.

Impunity – justice for past violations

The UN Working Group on Enforced or Involuntary Disappearances visited Argentina in July and noted that more than 20 judgments had been handed down on perpetrators of past human rights violations and that 1,000 criminal proceedings remained open. However, several suspects died before testifying in key cases, and threats against witnesses and human rights defenders were reported.

■ In April, in the first judgment of its kind, Osvaldo Rivas and María Cristina Gómez were sentenced to eight and seven years' imprisonment respectively for the "appropriation" of María Eugenia Sampallo, the daughter of a couple who were the victims of enforced

disappearance in 1977. The ex-army captain who stole the child and gave her to the couple was sentenced to 10 years' imprisonment in April.

■ In April, a court indicted seven military officers in connection with the "illegal appropriation" of babies from the military hospital in Campo de Mayo while their mothers were in detention. In July, Jorge Rafael Videla, former head of the military junta, was indicted on similar charges.

■ In April, Juan Evaristo Puthod, a survivor of clandestine detention centres, a trial witness and a human rights defender, was abducted by unidentified men in Buenos Aires. He was released 28 hours later, after being questioned about his human rights activities.

■ In July, five former officers, including former army general Luciano Benjamín Menéndez, received life sentences for the 1977 kidnapping, torture and murder of four political activists. Three others received shorter sentences. Luciano Menéndez was also tried, along with former provincial governor Domingo Antonio Bussi, on charges of being "co-authors" of the 1976 enforced disappearance of Tucumán senator Guillermo Vargas Aignasse. Both men received life sentences in August.

■ In July a court sentenced two former police officers to life in prison for their involvement in the August 1976 "Fátima massacre" in which 30 men and women were abducted and held in Buenos Aires before being extrajudicially executed.

■ Investigations continued in the cases of five former naval officers accused of involvement in the 1972 "Trelew massacre" in which 16 prisoners were gunned down after attempting to escape from the federal penitentiary in the city of Trelew.

■ Former naval officer Ricardo Antonio Cavallo was extradited to Argentina from Spain in March and indicted in July for the 1977 enforced disappearance of writer Rodolfo Walsh.

■ The whereabouts of Jorge Julio López, the main witness and complainant in the case against former Director of Investigations of the Buenos Aires Province Police Miguel Etchecolatz, remained unknown. He had not been seen since September 2006.

■ In December, forensic investigators announced the finding of thousands of bone fragments and a wall with 200 bullet holes in the Arana police detachment near Buenos Aires, the first time that a mass burial site has been found in a former clandestine detention centre. The process to identify the remains has been initiated.

Police and security forces

The police were accused of excessive use of force against demonstrators and during land disputes. Several officers were brought to trial on charges of unlawful killing.

■ In June and July, police officers were convicted of involvement in the unlawful killings of Jonathan Oros in Mendoza in January 2007 and of protester Carlos Fuentealba in April 2007 in Neuquén, Neuquén Province.

Prison conditions

Poor conditions, overcrowding, torture and other ill-treatment were reported in prisons and detention centres. In July, a judge ordered the immediate closure of two wings of the La Plata Detention Centre, which reportedly housed more than 50 young offenders, describing conditions there as "inhuman".

ARMENIA

REPUBLIC OF ARMENIA

Head of state:	**Serge Sargsian replaced Robert Kocharian in April**
Head of government:	**Tigran Sargsian (replaced Serge Sargsian in April)**
Death penalty:	**abolitionist for all crimes**
Population:	**3 million**
Life expectancy:	**71.7 years**
Under-5 mortality (m/f):	**36/31 per 1,000**
Adult literacy:	**99.4 per cent**

Mass protests over disputed presidential elections in February led to a 20-day state of emergency and a crackdown on civil and political rights evident throughout the year. Freedoms of assembly and expression were heavily restricted. Opposition and human rights activists were subjected to violent acts by unknown persons. Conscientious objectors continued to be imprisoned. Structures and resources to combat violence against women remained inadequate.

Freedom of assembly

Excessive use of force

On 1 March, police used force in the capital Yerevan to break up protests that had been ongoing since the results were published of the 19 February presidential election. Serge Sargsian, incumbent Prime Minister and close associate of outgoing President Robert Kocharian, had officially won. At least 10 people died, including two police officers, and over 350 were injured, including some 58 policemen. Police were reported as using truncheons, iron bars, tracer bullets, tear gas and conducted energy devices. The authorities declared a state of emergency on the same day.

In June a parliamentary commission was established for three months to investigate the March events. In mid-October, the commission requested a two-month extension in order to incorporate the findings of a second fact-finding group.

Arbitrary arrests and detentions

Dozens of opposition members were arrested in the aftermath of the 1 March violence, including many high-ranking figures associated with Levon Ter-Petrosian, the main rival to Serge Sargsian, and members of the opposition Republic party. Some of those arrested were reportedly beaten or ill-treated in police custody. Many of those arrested were still in pre-trial detention at the end of the year. The Council of Europe repeatedly expressed concern at the excessive length of the official inquiry into the March events, and the continued imprisonment, in some cases without trial, of dozens of opposition supporters. The trial of seven of those detained started on 19 December.

Legal, constitutional or institutional developments

On 17 March the National Assembly approved amendments to the law on public assembly giving local authorities the power to ban public meetings. After the lifting of the state of emergency there were continued reports of extensive detentions and harassment by security officials of citizens gathering in public places in central Yerevan. Concerns expressed by the OSCE and the Council of Europe led to the Armenian authorities agreeing on 22 April to the repeal or revision of the March amendments. Nonetheless, the Yerevan municipal authorities continued to ban some demonstrations by the opposition.

Freedom of expression

Journalists and media outlets that covered opposition activities were harassed. The vague wording of restrictions on freedom of expression gave the authorities broad powers to restrict opposition or independent media. Several opposition media outlets reported having websites closed, and newspaper editions were refused permission for publication. The Yerevan Press Club, the Committee to Protect Freedom of Expression, Internews, the Asparez Press Club of Giumri and the Femida public organization expressed concern that further delays to the government issuing broadcast licences would result in reduced media diversity.

■ In August *Haykakan Zhamanak* (Armenian Times) journalist Lusineh Barseghian was beaten by unknown men. Later that month, Hratch Melkumian, acting head of the Armenian Service of Radio Free Europe/Radio Liberty, was beaten in central Yerevan. There was reportedly no progress in the investigations into these assaults by the end of the year.

■ The independent Giumri-based television station Gala TV faced consistent harassment after it screened campaigning speeches by Levon Ter-Petrosian. On 19 March a fine of almost 27 million drams (about US$87,700) was imposed on Gala TV for alleged tax evasion; the sum was reportedly paid off by contributions from private donations. In April Gala TV was ordered to vacate its premises in Giumri's television tower, forcing it to temporarily cease broadcasting.

Impunity

A number of assaults on opposition and human rights activists were not investigated promptly or thoroughly. On 21 May, Mikael Danielian, a prominent human rights activist and director of the Armenian Helsinki Association, a human rights NGO, was shot at point-blank range with a pneumatic gun (a gun firing compressed air), reportedly by a former leader of a political party. Mikael Danielian was not seriously wounded. On 28 May Arsen Kharatian, a leader of the Armenian Democratic Youth Movement, was assaulted in Yerevan by unknown men. He was hospitalized with severe head injuries. On 25 June Narek Hovakimian, a member of the Hima youth movement and the opposition Alternative coalition, was assaulted in Yerevan by two unknown men. No one had been charged for these assaults by the end of the year.

Discrimination – Jehovah's Witnesses

Jehovah's Witnesses continued to face imprisonment because of their beliefs. As of 1 September, 77 young men were in prison for refusing on grounds of conscience to perform military service. The authorities still failed to introduce a genuinely civilian alternative service, in spite of previous commitments, with military supervision continuing over the alternative civilian service.

Jehovah's Witnesses reported further problems on release. The authorities refused to grant them certification of full service, without which important documents such as passports and internal residence permits were harder to obtain.

There were also reports of physical attacks on Jehovah's Witnesses, including allegedly by supporters of the country's dominant religious group. Investigation of these assaults was said to be slow or non-existent.

Violence against women and girls

Over a quarter of women in Armenia were said to have been hit by a family member and about two-thirds were said to have experienced psychological abuse, yet the authorities failed to prevent, investigate and punish violence against women. Adequate structures and resources to combat violence against women were lacking. Shelters previously operated by NGOs had closed due to lack of funding early in the year; one was able to reopen in September. A draft law on domestic violence, promoted by the Women's Rights Centre NGO, was made available for public discussion.

Amnesty International visits/reports

🚗 Amnesty International delegates visited Armenia in February, July and November.

📄 Armenia: Fear of the freedom of conscience and religion – violations of the rights of Jehovah's Witnesses (EUR 54/001/2008)

📄 Armenia: No pride in silence: countering violence in the family in Armenia (EUR 54/004/2008)

AUSTRALIA

AUSTRALIA
Head of state:	Queen Elizabeth II, represented by Quentin Bryce (replaced Michael Jeffery in September)
Head of government:	Kevin Rudd
Death penalty:	abolitionist for all crimes
Population:	21 million
Life expectancy:	80.9 years
Under-5 mortality (m/f):	6/5 per 1,000

The government apologized to the "Stolen Generations" of Indigenous Peoples who were removed from their families under government policy between 1910 and 1970. The Federal Race Discrimination Act remained suspended in the Northern Territory. A National Council to reduce violence against women and children was established. Temporary protection visas and mandatory detention were abolished but, in practice, asylum-seekers still faced detention.

Indigenous Peoples' rights

In February, the government made an historic apology to the "Stolen Generations" – Aboriginal and Torres Strait Islander people who as children were forcibly removed from their families. However, the government opposed compensation. The government pledged to "close the gap" between Indigenous Peoples and other Australians but opposed the UN Declaration on the Rights of Indigenous Peoples.

In October, a government-appointed Review Board recommended changes to the previous government's emergency response to protect children and make Aboriginal communities safe in the Northern Territory. The Board recommendations included increased engagement with Aboriginal communities, reinstatement of the Racial Discrimination Act and urgent action to address high levels of disadvantage and marginalization. The government agreed to reinstate the Racial Discrimination Act, but with a 12-month delay.

Violence against women

In May, the government established the National Council to Reduce Violence Against Women and their Children. In August, the High Court of Australia upheld the conviction of a Melbourne brothel owner, the first person convicted under anti-slavery laws introduced in 1999.

Refugees and asylum-seekers

In August, the government finalized the abolition of Temporary Protection Visas for asylum-seekers.

In January, the government closed its offshore detention facility on the island nation of Nauru. In May, the UN Committee against Torture expressed concern that the detention facility on Christmas Island was still in use. Despite this, Australia began use of a new high security facility on the Island in December.

In July, the government announced that asylum-seekers would be temporarily detained for identity, health and security checks, but only those who posed a risk to society would remain in detention. At the end of the year, this commitment had not been implemented.

Counter-terror and security

Australian law allowing pre-charge detention for terrorism suspects remained in force. The law remains incompatible with international law. However, in December the government agreed to reforms and established a National Security Legislation Monitor to review the operation of the legislation.

■ In October, Joseph "Jack" Thomas, the first person to be placed under a control order restricting movement, association and communication, was acquitted of terrorism-related offences after a retrial.

■ The control order imposed on former Guantánamo Bay detainee David Hicks ended in December.

Torture and other ill-treatment

The government announced its intention to ratify the Optional Protocol to the UN Convention against Torture and to introduce laws explicitly prohibiting torture.

Legal, constitutional or institutional developments

In July, Australia ratified the Convention on the Rights of Persons with Disabilities. In November, the government reformed legislation to remove discrimination against same-sex couples and their children, but did not include legal recognition of same-sex marriage.

Amnesty International report

📄 Setting the standard: International good practice to inform an Australian national plan of action to eliminate violence against women (Amnesty International Australia, 2008)

A

AUSTRIA

REPUBLIC OF AUSTRIA

Head of state:	**Heinz Fischer**
Head of government:	**Werner Faymann (replaced Alfred Gusenbauer in December)**
Death penalty:	**abolitionist for all crimes**
Population:	**8.4 million**
Life expectancy:	**79.4 years**
Under-5 mortality (m/f):	**6/5 per 1,000**

No progress was made on implementing safeguards against torture and other ill-treatment, as requested by regional and international human rights bodies. The authorities failed to protect the rights of asylum-seekers and migrants.

Torture and other ill-treatment

■ Torture victim Bakary J. had still not received compensation or any form of rehabilitation by the end of the year. He had been beaten and subjected to a mock execution after an aborted deportation on 7 April 2006. In September 2007 the appellate disciplinary authority had reduced the fines originally imposed on the four officers tried for the offences, and they remained on duty. On 18 September 2008, the Administrative Court declared that the decision of the appellate disciplinary authority was unlawful as it did not give due consideration to the "deliberate" and "brutal nature" of the conduct of the officers involved.

Police and security forces

Although in February the Ministry of Justice suspended the use of conducted energy devices (CEDs) in prisons in response to rising concerns about their use, the same month the Interior Ministry announced that, following a probation period, CEDs would be used by police in routine operations. The decree of the Interior Ministry governing use of CEDs classified them as harmless and non-lethal, and did not address the dangers of their disproportionate use.

■ Chechen asylum-seeker Ruslan A. was detained on 8 July in the local police station of Böheimkirchen with a view to securing his deportation to Poland, together with his wife and child, because he had applied for asylum in Poland prior to his arrival in Austria. He feared that if deported to Poland he would be at risk from members of Russian intelligence agents active there. He was severely traumatized and threatened to commit suicide unless he could see his psychotherapist. A short time later, masked special police officers shot him with a CED from outside his cell, following which he was taken to hospital. On 28 July, the Asylum Court overruled the decision to deport him and his family to Poland, and ruled that Austria had to consider his asylum request.

Refugees, asylum-seekers and migrants

The authorities continued to exploit loopholes in the law and expelled migrants and asylum-seekers without due consideration of their family ties and private lives.

In October, the Interior Ministry significantly reduced funding for legal advice for asylum-seekers, which is provided only by NGOs.

Justice system

■ Lawyers representing 10 animal rights activists reported they had been denied access to the case file necessary to effectively challenge the order to defer their clients' pending trial. The 10 activists had been arrested and detained on 21 May and charged with membership of a criminal organization that aimed to damage property. They remained in detention until 2 September, when they were released to await trial.

Amnesty International visits

🚍 Amnesty International delegates visited Austria in March, April and May.

AZERBAIJAN

REPUBLIC OF AZERBAIJAN

Head of state:	**Ilham Aliyev**
Head of government:	**Artur Rasizade**
Death penalty:	**abolitionist for all crimes**
Population:	**8.5 million**
Life expectancy:	**67.1 years**
Under-5 mortality (m/f):	**89/81 per 1,000**
Adult literacy:	**98.8 per cent**

Freedom of expression continued to be heavily restricted. Independent and opposition journalists were routinely harassed and some were imprisoned on disputed charges in trials failing to comply with international standards. Some religious groups faced continued harassment.

Freedom of expression – journalists

Opposition and independent journalists continued to face harassment, physical assault and intimidation on account of their journalistic activity. Although defamation and libel continued to be criminal offences, several journalists were imprisoned on other criminal charges ostensibly unrelated to their journalistic activity, such as "hooliganism" or "bribery". The trials of journalists facing such charges did not meet international fair trial standards, and they effectively silenced reporting critical of the government.

No significant progress was reported by the authorities in the investigations of numerous cases of assault against journalists. In the case of newspaper editor Elmar Hüseynov, shot dead in 2005, the authorities reported that they were engaged in "all possible measures" to extradite two ethnic Azeris of Georgian citizenship in connection with the crime; the Georgian government reportedly refused to extradite them on the grounds of their Georgian citizenship.

■ Faramaz Novruzoğlu and Sardar Alibeylı of the *Nota Bene* newspaper were sentenced to two years' imprisonment and 18 months' corrective labour respectively, after reporting on alleged corruption in the Ministry of Internal Affairs.

■ In March Qenimet Zahid, editor-in-chief of the opposition newspaper *Azadlıq* (Freedom), was sentenced to four years' imprisonment on charges of hooliganism and assault. His lawyer said that his trial was not conducted in accordance with international fair trial standards.

■ *Azadlıq* correspondent Aqil Xalil was physically assaulted in February, allegedly by local officials engaged in illegal tree felling, and then stabbed in an assault by unknown men in March. Aqil Xalil believed he was stabbed because of his investigation of alleged illegal land transactions. In April the Prosecutor General's Office claimed that he had been stabbed by a homosexual lover; these claims were refuted by Azerbaijani human rights NGOs.

■ In June Emin Hüseynov, director of the media watchdog the Institute for Reporters' Freedom and Safety (IRFS) and a prominent activist, was detained and allegedly beaten by police. He was hospitalized with severe head and neck pains.

■ In late August three journalists were allegedly beaten in Naxçıvan, an autonomous exclave situated between Iran and Armenia. Radio Liberty correspondents Malahet Nasibova and Ilgar Nasibov, and IRFS correspondent Elman Abbasov, were reportedly beaten up by members of the Nehram village local administration. The incident took place while the journalists were reporting on a confrontation between the Nehram village residents and local police, and their equipment was also taken and destroyed.

Freedom of religion

Representatives of religious groups or confessions outside officially endorsed structures continued to be harassed. In August the Abu Bekr mosque in Baku was bombed, resulting in three deaths. Following this incident, Muslims were banned from praying in public outside mosques. There were continued reports of the forcible shaving of beards by police.

■ In March Zaur Balaev, a Baptist pastor sentenced in August 2007 to two years' imprisonment on charges of resisting arrest and assault, was pardoned and released. In June another Baptist pastor, Hamid Şabanov, was arrested in Aliabad on charges of possessing a firearm. His family and Baptist community members said that the weapon was planted. His trial began in July and was still pending at the end of the year; he was transferred from prison to house arrest in November.

■ In August a Baku-based Protestant community had its place of worship confiscated without compensation, despite state-certified legal ownership of the site.

■ In September the Supreme Court rejected the appeal

of Said Dadaşbeyli, sentenced in December 2007 to 14 years' imprisonment on charges relating to terrorism. Said Dadaşbeyli had headed a religious organization called NIMA, accused by the authorities of co-operating with Iranian secret services but which his family and lawyer said was involved only in charitable activities.

Torture and other ill-treatment

In July the Baku Court of Appeals upheld the prison sentences of Dmitri Pavlov, Maksim Genashilkin and Ruslan Bessonov, aged between 15 and 16 at the time of detention and convicted in June 2007 on charges of the murder of another teenager. There was no investigation of the boys' allegations that they had confessed under torture.

Amnesty International reports

📖 Azerbaijan: Five journalists released (EUR 55/001/2008)

📖 Azerbaijan: Mixed messages on freedom of expression (EUR 55/002/2008)

📖 Azerbaijan: Persecution of opposition newspaper continues unabated (EUR 55/004/2008)

📖 Azerbaijan: Amnesty International condemns beating of media watchdog Emin Hüseynov (EUR 55/005/2008)

BAHAMAS

COMMONWEALTH OF THE BAHAMAS

Head of state:	Queen Elizabeth II, represented by Arthur Hanna
Head of government:	Hubert Ingraham
Death penalty:	retentionist
Population:	335,000
Life expectancy:	72.3 years
Under-5 mortality (m/f):	20/14 per 1,000
Adult literacy:	95.8 per cent

At least one person was sentenced to death; no executions were carried out. There were some reports of abuses by members of the security forces. Allegations of ill-treatment of and discrimination towards migrants continued to be reported.

Background

In December the Bahamas ratified the International Covenant on Civil and Political Rights and the International Covenant on Economic, Social and Cultural Rights.

Police and security forces

Several allegations of use of excessive force and one case of unlawful killing by the police were reported. The lack of an independent body to investigate allegations of ill-treatment involving police officers undermined confidence in due process.

■ Patrick Strachan was shot in the stomach by police on 27 February in Wilson Tract and died later in hospital. Local residents stated that he was not armed when police shot him. Police stated that the victim fired at the officers first. At the end of the year, Amnesty International was unaware of the status of the investigation into his death.

■ Emmanuel McKenzie, Chairman of an environmentalist organization, was harassed and ill-treated by the security forces in a joint army/police raid on a fundraising event on 19 April. He was handcuffed, dragged off to a clearing and had a gun pointed at his head. Some of those attending the event were also beaten and ill-treated. Although a formal complaint was lodged, no investigation had been initiated by the end of the year.

Asylum-seekers and migrants

Haitians living in the Bahamas appealed to the Haitian government to help them overcome the discrimination they face in the Bahamas. Some Cuban migrants also complained of discrimination and ill-treatment at the Carmichael Detention Center which houses foreign nationals accused of breaching immigration laws.

Violence against women

The Domestic Violence Protection Order Act came into force on 1 December, more than a year after it was passed by Parliament. Amendments to the Sexual Offences and Domestic Violence Act increasing the penalty for serious sexual crimes to life imprisonment were passed by Parliament in November.

Death penalty

According to the press, at least one person was sentenced to death during the year. A number of prisoners had their death sentences reviewed and commuted to life imprisonment; this followed a ruling in 2006 by the UK-based Judicial Committee of the Privy Council which abolished mandatory death sentences for murder. The national public debate on executions continued, with the Prime Minister, the President of the Bar Association and the Acting Commissioner of Police voicing support for resumption.

In December the Bahamas voted against a UN General Assembly resolution calling for a worldwide moratorium on executions.

Amnesty International report

📄 Bahamas: Submission to the UN Universal Periodic Review – Third Session of the UPR Working Group of the UN Human Rights Council, December 2008 (AMR 14/002/2008)

BAHRAIN

KINGDOM OF BAHRAIN

Head of state:	King Hamad bin 'Issa Al Khalifa
Head of government:	Shaikh Khalifa bin Salman Al Khalifa
Death penalty:	retentionist
Population:	766,000
Life expectancy:	75.2 years
Under-5 mortality (m/f):	14/14 per 1,000
Adult literacy:	86.5 per cent

The authorities failed adequately to investigate allegations of torture and other ill-treatment of detainees. Government critics were briefly detained and several websites were closed down. One person was executed. The government indicated it would decriminalize certain publishing offences, reduce legal discrimination against women and introduce other reforms.

Background

There were renewed, violent protests in March and April by members of the majority Shi'a population against what they alleged was discrimination, especially by the police and security forces, and the stalling of political reforms initiated by the King in 2001 and 2002. One policeman was killed and scores of people were arrested. Nineteen faced trial. Thirteen others who were charged with arson and

rioting were among a group pardoned by the King in July but still detained at the end of the year. They were reported to have refused to sign official documents authorizing their release because they considered that all charges against them should be dropped unconditionally.

International scrutiny and legal developments

Bahrain's human rights record was examined in April under the UN Human Rights Council's system of Universal Periodic Review.

The government made significant human rights commitments, including to establish a national human rights institution, withdraw reservations made when Bahrain ratified certain human rights treaties, reform family and nationality laws, and adopt new legislation to protect women domestic workers and lift restrictions on the press.

Torture and other ill-treatment

Detainees held in connection with violent protests in the villages of Karzakhan and Demestan in March and April alleged that they were tortured and otherwise ill-treated by police. They said they were held incommunicado for a week during which they were made to stand for excessive periods, blindfolded and beaten.

■ Fifteen people arrested in December 2007 and accused of burning a police car and stealing a weapon alleged that they were tortured. Five were sentenced to between five and seven years' imprisonment by the High Criminal Court in July; six were sentenced to one year in prison but were pardoned by the King; and four were acquitted. Among those acquitted was Mohammad Mekki Ahmad, aged 20, who was detained incommunicado for 12 days at the Criminal Investigations Department in Manama, where he alleges he was tortured by being suspended, beaten and subjected to electric shocks. A medical report, requested by the High Criminal Court and submitted to it in April, noted that some of the defendants had marks on their bodies which might have been caused by torture. The government failed to order an independent investigation into the torture allegations.

Freedom of expression

The government proposed to amend the 2002 Press and Publications Law to remove imprisonment as a

B

penalty for offences such as criticizing the King and "inciting hatred of the regime". The *Shura* (Consultative) Council added amendments in May. All the amendments were submitted to the House of Representatives.

In June, Abdullah Hassan Bu-Hassan was detained for three days in connection with his writings in *The Democrat*, published by the Democratic National Action Society. The same month, seven contributors to the Awal website and al-Wifaq Islamic Society's newsletter were briefly detained and accused of "inciting hatred and insulting the regime". A number of websites were closed because they contained articles criticizing the royal family and the government.

In November, the Interior Minister was reported to have announced that Bahraini nationals, including parliamentarians and NGO members, would be required to seek advance authorization before attending meetings abroad to discuss Bahrain's internal affairs, and that those who failed to do so could be imprisoned or fined.

Death penalty

A Bangladeshi national, Mizan Noor Al Rahman Ayoub Miyah, convicted of murdering his employer, was executed in August.

In December, Bahrain abstained on a UN General Assembly resolution calling for a worldwide moratorium on executions.

Amnesty International visits

🚗 An Amnesty International delegate visited Bahrain in October and met government officials, parliamentarians, human rights activists, journalists, former detainees and lawyers. In November an Amnesty International delegate attended a follow-up meeting hosted by the Bahraini government on the implementation of the recommendations of the UN Universal Periodic Review session in April.

BANGLADESH

PEOPLE'S REPUBLIC OF BANGLADESH

Head of state:	Iajuddin Ahmed
Head of government:	Fakhruddin Ahmed
Death penalty:	retentionist
Population:	161.3 million
Life expectancy:	63.1 years
Under-5 mortality (m/f):	68/67 per 1,000
Adult literacy:	47.5 per cent

In the first national parliamentary elections in seven years, the Awami League won a landslide victory in predominantly peaceful polls held on 29 December. Before the election, despite the relaxing of emergency measures and institutional reform, restrictions on freedom of assembly and association remained and tens of thousands of political activists reportedly attempting to gather peacefully in their party offices were detained throughout the country. Police used excessive force to disperse peaceful rallies, injuring participants. At least 54 people were estimated to have died in suspected extrajudicial executions by police and the Rapid Action Battalion (RAB) in the first half of the year alone. No one was held accountable for the deaths. At least 185 people were sentenced to death, and five men were executed. Throughout the year the caretaker government strengthened institutional reforms. In September, the ordinance establishing a national Human Rights Commission came into effect. The Right to Information Ordinance was enacted in October, under which citizens can request access to information held by public bodies. However, eight security agencies were exempt from the ordinance unless the information requested related to corruption and human rights violations.

Background

The year began with the caretaker government backed by the military, continuing the enforcement of restrictions under the state of emergency imposed on 11 January 2007. It ended with elections that delivered an overwhelming majority to the Awami League only weeks after the state of emergency was lifted on 17 December.

Uncertainties about the military authorities' commitment to allow the democratic process to resume were dispelled when parliamentary elections were held on 29 December. Two political alliances – one led by Sheikh Hasina of the Awami League and another by Begum Khaleda Zia of the Bangladesh Nationalist Party – contested the elections. It remained to be seen if the new government would use this unique opportunity to make good its election pledges and strengthen human rights protection.

Women continued to be discriminated against in law and in practice, and violence against women including beatings, acid attacks and dowry deaths, were reported. In March, the government announced amendments to the National Women Development Policy in order to further promote equality for women. However, the amendments were not implemented after the announcement met with fierce resistance from Islamist groups who rallied in protest saying the amendments defied the Islamic law of inheritance.

Bengali settlers continued to seize land from Jumma Indigenous inhabitants of Chittagong Hill Tracts. Three UN Special Rapporteurs – on the situation of human rights and fundamental freedoms of indigenous people, on adequate housing and on the right to food – expressed concern that there may be a systematic campaign to support the relocation of non-Indigenous peoples to the Chittagong Hill Tracts in order to outnumber the local Indigenous community.

Thousands of slum dwellers were forcibly evicted in Dhaka and other major cities. Their homes were demolished without any provision for compensation or alternative accommodation. Court orders were usually issued to evict people from land allocated to property development projects.

The Anti-Terrorism Ordinance came into effect. Its broadly formulated definition of acts of terror further eroded safeguards against arbitrary arrest and detention.

Fair trial standards continued to be undermined and were further exacerbated by emergency regulations as defendants' access to due process of law was limited.

The government continued to use the army, alongside the police, the RAB and other security forces to maintain law and order. The army, which had been deployed to maintain law and order since January 2007, was temporarily withdrawn in early November but redeployed on 18 December until after the elections.

Freedom of expression, assembly and association

Restrictions on freedom of expression were not strictly enforced and were eventually lifted in November. Although some restrictions on freedom of assembly and association were lifted in May and November, many restrictions remained under the state of emergency until it was lifted on 17 December.

The ban on indoor political meetings was lifted in May but some 30,000 political activists from various parties were arrested reportedly as they gathered in their party offices soon after the announcement. Police detained them for between several days and two months before releasing them, either without charge or on bail after charging them with apparently unrelated criminal offences.

On 3 November, the government announced the partial withdrawal of the ban on political rallies but this was not implemented until 12 December.

Excessive use of force

Police used excessive force against peaceful demonstrations on several occasions. On 6 July, police attacked several hundred Bangladesh Nationalist Party activists who had gathered peacefully on the premises of Bangabandhu Sheikh Mujib Medical University hospital to see a detained party leader being taken from hospital to a court hearing on corruption charges. At least 15 people were injured including a photojournalist who was covering the event.

On 11 November, police used sticks and rifle butts to disperse thousands of Jamaat-e-Islami activists at Baitul Mukarram Mosque in Dhaka. Despite the government announcement on 3 November that the ban on election-related political rallies was lifted, police told rally organizers that the lifting of the ban had not yet taken effect and forcibly dispersed the peaceful rally, injuring at least 30 demonstrators.

Extrajudicial executions and impunity

Police and RAB carried out at least 54 suspected extrajudicial executions during the first half of the year with scores more believed to have taken place in the second half of the year. No police or RAB personnel were prosecuted. According to the government, mandatory judicial inquiries were carried out into all fatal shootings by police and RAB, and found them to be justified. The number of judicial inquiries

B

conducted and the findings of such inquiries were not made public.

■ On 27 July, police announced the death of Dr Mizanur Rahman Tulul, leader of the outlawed Purbo Banglar Communist Party (Red Flag Faction) in a so-called "crossfire" incident – a term often used to describe extrajudicial executions. Dr Tulul's mother had reported his arrest to journalists on 26 July and publicly appealed to the authorities for his safety.

Past human rights abuses

In April, Foreign Adviser Iftehkar Ahmed Chowdhury discussed with the UN Secretary-General, Ban Ki-moon, the possibility of UN involvement in ending impunity for the 1971 violations. However, as in the past, no official Commission of Enquiry was established to investigate the war crimes, crimes against humanity and other serious violations of human rights and humanitarian law as a first step towards establishing truth, justice and full and effective reparations for victims. No concrete action was taken by the government to implement the 1973 International Crimes (tribunals) Act.

Death penalty

At least 185 people were sentenced to death, bringing the estimated number of prisoners on death row to at least 1,085. Five men convicted of murder were executed, one in June and four in December.

In December, Bangladesh voted against a UN General Assembly resolution calling for a worldwide moratorium on executions.

Amnesty International visit/reports

🚍 In January, Amnesty International's Secretary General Irene Khan visited Bangladesh and met with victims of human rights violations, civil society groups and political party officials.

📃 Bangladesh: Memorandum to the Caretaker Government of Bangladesh and political parties (ASA 13/001/2008)

📃 Bangladesh: Submission to the UN Universal Periodic Review – Fourth session of the UPR Working Group of the Human Rights Council, February 2009 (ASA 13/006/2008)

📃 Bangladesh: Elections present risks and opportunities for human rights (ASA 13/011/2008)

BELARUS

REPUBLIC OF BELARUS

Head of state:	Alyaksandr Lukashenka
Head of government:	Syarhey Sidorski
Death penalty:	retentionist
Population:	9.6 million
Life expectancy:	68.7 years
Under-5 mortality (m/f):	14/10 per 1,000
Adult literacy:	99.6 per cent

The government continued to exert excessive control over civil society. State control over the media increased, and restrictions on independent media continued. Some public events were banned; peaceful demonstrators were fined and detained for short periods; and civil society activists and journalists were harassed. Belarus continued to hand down death sentences and execute prisoners.

Background

The OSCE sent an observation mission to the parliamentary elections held on 28 September and found they fell short of OSCE standards. There were some improvements in access to the media for opposition candidates but the mission found that voters still could not make an informed choice. Article 193-1 of the criminal code continued to restrict rights to freedom of assembly and expression. A presidential decree in December 2005 had introduced this law – which penalizes membership and activities of civil society organizations – ahead of the presidential elections in March 2006.

There were signs of increased engagement with the EU. Following the release of a number of opposition prisoners in the course of the year, on 13 October the EU temporarily and partially lifted the travel ban that had been imposed on some leading government figures in 2006.

Freedom of assembly

The authorities continued to limit freedom of assembly by banning or using force to disperse demonstrations, detaining peaceful demonstrators, and harassing civil society activists and journalists.

■ On 10 and 21 January and 18 February, more than 40 people were detained and sentenced to maximum

sentences of 15 days or fines for taking part in demonstrations against Decree No. 760, which required small businesses to employ only family members or pay significantly higher business taxes.
■ On 25 March, security forces reportedly used excessive force against demonstrators who had gathered in the capital, Minsk, to commemorate Freedom Day (the anniversary of the creation of the Belarusian People's Republic in 1918). Around 100 demonstrators were detained and subsequently sentenced to a fine or held in administrative detention. The authorities took unprecedented action against journalists who were covering the demonstration.

Detainees included Andrey Lyankevich, a photo-journalist from the independent newspaper *Nasha Niva*, who reported he was beaten. He was charged with organizing and participating in an unsanctioned meeting. He was released on 27 March but the case remained under investigation at the end of the year. Two Lithuanian television reporters were allegedly beaten and their equipment damaged by police. On 27 March, the State Security Services – still named KGB – carried out nationwide searches in the homes of journalists who worked with foreign media. On 31 March, the EU expressed its "strong disappointment at the arrest of a large number of participants, especially young people" and condemned the use of violence in dispersing peaceful demonstrators.

Two opposition activists, Andrey Kim and Syarhey Parsyukhevich, were subsequently charged under Article 364 of the Criminal Code for assaulting police officers. Andrey Kim was sentenced to 18 months' imprisonment on this charge on 22 April. Witnesses claimed that it was he who was struck by a police officer, rather than the other way round. Syarhey Parsyukhevich, the leader of an organization of small entrepreneurs in Vitsyebsk, was placed under 15 days' administrative detention after the demonstration on 10 January. On 24 April he was sentenced to two and a half years' imprisonment for assaulting a police officer while in detention, although he alleges that he was taken out of his cell and beaten by two police officers. Local human rights groups claimed that the cases were fabricated, and that both men were being punished for the peaceful expression of their political views. Both were released in August by presidential decree.

Rights of lesbian, gay, bisexual and transgender people

Lesbian, gay, bisexual and transgender activists were denied permission to hold events. In Homyel and Minsk, groups applied for permission to hold small street actions on 4 and 10 May respectively, but both were refused permission by the city administrations. The Minsk activists were told that their action would block traffic. The Homyel activists were told that they had not proved that they would provide adequate medical assistance or stewarding for the event, or that they would clean up afterwards, although they had demonstrated this in their application.

Freedom of expression

■ On 7 August, the President signed a new law on mass media. The Belarusian Association of Journalists stated that the new law would considerably increase restrictions on freedom of expression and make it even more difficult for media outlets and journalists to work. In September no more than 30 independent social and political publications continued to print, and half of those had been excluded from the state-owned distribution systems. The OSCE representative on freedom of the media expressed concern that the law "extends the government's right to warn, suspend and close down media outlets." The new law further increased restrictions on registration, forbade any funding from abroad or from unacknowledged sources, and made it easier for state organs to close down media without a court order and with only one warning. The law applied to internet publications, and the Deputy Head of the Presidential Administration, Natalya Pyatkevich, stated that it would apply to websites because of the need to control "disinformation from foreign sites." She said the authorities had drawn on "the experience of China, which has closed access to such sites on its territory."

In September, an issue of the independent newspaper *Svaboda* (Freedom) and a number of video materials including the Polish documentary film *A Lesson in Belarusian* were classified as extremist by Kastrychnitski District Court of Hrodna, after an application by the Hrodna district department of the KGB. *Svaboda* had published a report on a demonstration by the youth opposition movement Malady Front (Young Front) against Russian military action in South Ossetia. The report fell foul of the Law to Counteract Extremism, ratified in 2007. This law ordered that any organizations found to promote the violent overthrow of the constitutional order, to promote terrorist activity or incite racial, national or religious hatred could be closed down and any publications classified as extremist could be destroyed. The decision against *Svaboda* was overruled on appeal. In November the same court refused to consider an application to classify the 2004 human rights report of the NGO Viasna (Spring) as extremist.

Prisoners of conscience

■ On 18 January, Alyaksandr Zdvizhkou, the former deputy editor of *Zhoda* (Unity) newspaper, was sentenced to three years' imprisonment by a Minsk city court for "inciting racial, national, or religious enmity or discord." He was sentenced for the publication in 2006 of the cartoons of the Prophet Muhammad, that some Muslims found offensive, originally published in a Danish newspaper in 2005. Criminal proceedings started on 22 February 2006, and the newspaper was closed down the following month. Alyaksandr Zdzvizhkou left Belarus to avoid prosecution, but was arrested on 18 November 2007 when he returned to visit his father's grave. The head of the Muslim community in Belarus reportedly opposed Alyaksandr Zdzvizhkou's sentence and the closing of the *Zhoda* newspaper. On 22 February, the Supreme Court of Belarus reduced his three-year prison sentence to three months. This decision resulted in his immediate release from the high security prison where he was being held.

■ Zmitser Dashkevich, a leader of Malady Front, was released on 23 January, two months early. He had been sentenced to 18 months' imprisonment in November 2006 for "participating in an activity of an unregistered non-governmental organization".

■ In August President Lukashenka released Alyaksandr Kazulin, presidential candidate during the March 2006 elections, who had been convicted of "hooliganism" and "organizing group activities that breach public order" and sentenced to five and a half years in prison in July 2006.

Death penalty

According to media reports, four people were executed during the year. On 5 February Valery Harbaty, Syarhey Marozaw and Ihar Danchanka were executed. The three men were convicted of a series of murders in the Homyel region between 1990 and 2004. All three were sentenced to death by shooting by the Supreme Court on 1 December 2006. On 9 October 2007, Syarhey Marozaw and Ihar Danchanka were tried for further murders and Syarhey Marozaw was sentenced again to death. According to press reports, all three men appealed to President Lukashenka for clemency. The Council of Europe Secretary General condemned the executions and accused the Belarusian authorities of a "blatant disregard" for human values.

On 6 October Pavel Lenny, who had been sentenced to death by Homyel district court for the rape and murder of a minor, was executed. At a press conference on 9 September, the Chair of the Supreme Court stated that only one person had been sentenced to death in 2008. The Ministry of the Interior stated in October that there was an "irreversible and gradual progress towards abolition."

In December, Belarus abstained on a UN General Assembly resolution calling for a worldwide moratorium on executions.

Amnesty International visit

🚗 An Amnesty International delegate visited Belarus in October to research the death penalty.

BELGIUM

KINGDOM OF BELGIUM

Head of state:	King Albert II
Head of government:	Herman Van Rompuy (replaced Yves Leterme in December, who replaced Guy Verhofstadt in March)
Death penalty:	abolitionist for all crimes
Population:	10.5 million
Life expectancy:	78.8 years
Under-5 mortality (m/f):	6/5 per 1,000

Incidents of ill-treatment and excessive use of force by law enforcement officials, particularly during expulsions of migrants and rejected asylum-seekers, were reported. The UN Committee on the Elimination of Racial Discrimination (CERD) severely criticized conditions in detention centres for migrants and asylum-seekers. The European Court of

Human Rights ruled that the prolonged detention of two asylum-seekers in an airport transit zone had constituted inhuman and degrading treatment. There were numerous hunger strikes by detained migrants in protest at their conditions of detention.

Torture and other ill-treatment

There were continued reports of ill-treatment by law enforcement officials, particularly during expulsions of undocumented migrants and asylum-seekers whose asylum claims had been rejected. In November, the UN Committee against Torture expressed concern at continuing allegations of ill-treatment, including ill-treatment with a racist element, by law enforcement officials. In February, the CERD had also expressed concern about racist ill-treatment and discrimination by law enforcement officials, including excessive use of force during expulsions.

■ On 26 April, Ebenizer Sontsa, a rejected asylum-seeker from Cameroon, was forcibly restrained by several law enforcement officials during an attempted deportation from Brussels Airport. Following protests by other passengers at his treatment, the deportation was abandoned and he was returned to the immigration detention centre of Merksplas where he made a complaint of ill-treatment. A new deportation was scheduled for 9 May, but on 1 May Ebenizer Sontsa committed suicide. In December, the Public Prosecutor closed the investigation into Ebenizer Sontsa's death.

■ Serge Fosso, one of the passengers who protested at the treatment of Ebenizer Sontsa, was forcibly removed from the flight with two other passengers who had also protested, and was detained for 10 hours in a cell at Brussels Airport where he said he was insulted and threatened by law enforcement officials, who then dragged him out of the cell in a headlock, resulting in injuries to his face, arms, fingers and back. He submitted a criminal complaint regarding the treatment he received, which was still under investigation at the end of the year.

Migrants and asylum-seekers

There were numerous public protests and hunger strikes by irregular migrants protesting at the continued lack of possibilities to regularize their migration status.

On 24 January the European Court of Human Rights ruled that the conditions of detention of two rejected Palestinian asylum-seekers who were held in

the transit zone of Brussels Airport in February 2003 for 11 days amounted to inhuman and degrading treatment. The Court also ruled that the repeated detention of the two men, in spite of judicial decisions ordering their release, constituted a violation of their right to liberty. The CERD expressed concern at the detention of asylum-seekers and the conditions of their detention.

In October the Minister for Asylum and Migration launched a pilot project in which families with children would no longer be held in closed detention centres while awaiting expulsion from Belgium; this measure applies to irregular migrants and rejected asylum-seekers. However, families who have applied for asylum upon arrival at an airport will continue to be detained.

Counter-terror and security

On 7 February the Court of Appeal in Antwerp acquitted Bahar Kimyongür, Sükriye Akar Özordulu, Dursun Karatas and Zerrin Sari. They had been charged with membership of or support for a terrorist organization because of their links with a Turkish opposition group, the Revolutionary People's Liberation Party-Front. The judge considered that there was no evidence linking them to terrorist plots, and that the group in Belgium was not a criminal or terrorist organization. Three others, including Fehriye Erdal, were acquitted of the terrorism-related charges but convicted of possessing firearms.

However, on 24 June, following an appeal by the Public Prosecutor, the Court of Cassation overruled the acquittal. At the end of the year the defendants were awaiting a fourth trial, to be held before the Court of Appeal in Brussels in May 2009.

B

BENIN

REPUBLIC OF BENIN

Head of state and government:	Thomas Boni Yayi
Death penalty:	abolitionist in practice
Population:	9.3 million
Life expectancy:	55.4 years
Under-5 mortality (m/f):	147/143 per 1,000
Adult literacy:	34.7 per cent

Prison conditions were very harsh and fell short of international standards. Security forces responsible for excessive use of force still enjoyed impunity.

Background

There were several demonstrations throughout the year against the high cost of living in Benin. People protested against the rise in price of basic necessities including maize and rice as well as cement and oil.

Prison conditions

Prison conditions were very harsh because of severe overcrowding in several prisons, largely because many detainees were awaiting trial for years. The conditions fell short of international standards, with several hundred children being held alongside adults.

Impunity

Members of the presidential guard considered responsible for killing two people and injuring at least five others in Ouidah, 35km west of the capital Cotonou, in May 2007 had still not been tried at the end of 2008. An investigation into the case was opened, but its results were not made public.

Death penalty

In May, Benin was examined under the UN Universal Periodic Review (UPR) and made a commitment to apply a moratorium on executions. The UPR Working Group recommended that Benin ratify the Second Optional Protocol to the International Covenant on Civil and Political Rights, aiming at the abolition of the death penalty.

Amnesty International visit

🚐 A representative of Amnesty International visited Benin in November.

BOLIVIA

REPUBLIC OF BOLIVIA

Head of state and government:	Evo Morales Ayma
Death penalty:	abolitionist for ordinary crimes
Population:	9.7 million
Life expectancy:	64.7 years
Under-5 mortality (m/f):	64/55 per 1,000
Adult literacy:	86.7 per cent

Tensions between the government and opposition over the introduction of a new constitution and its possible implications for the control of Bolivia's economic and natural resources led to further confrontations; most were violent and more than 20 people were killed. Journalists and media outlets were harassed and attacked. There were some positive developments in the area of economic, social and cultural rights.

Background

Civil unrest and regional and political tensions continued as several departments pursued an autonomist agenda and rejected the proposed new constitution. Four departmental referendums on autonomy were held in May and June, but were declared illegal by the Central Electoral Commission. In a recall referendum in August, 67.4 per cent of voters confirmed President Morales in his presidency. The outbreak of violence in Pando department in September (see below) led President Morales to declare a state of emergency which remained in place for more than two months.

The international community, in particular the newly formed Union of South American Nations (UNASUR), played an important role in efforts to find a peaceful solution to the political crisis. In October, Congress approved a revised text for the new constitution. The new text was due to be put to a nationwide referendum in January 2009.

Despite continuing high levels of poverty, particularly among Indigenous Peoples, there were positive developments in the area of economic, social and cultural rights. These included programmes to improve literacy and school attendance, to address malnutrition, to increase social housing and to provide retirement pensions. According to the United Nations Population Fund, Bolivia continued to have the highest incidence of maternal mortality in South America (approximately 290 per 100,000 live births).

Discrimination – Indigenous Peoples

Racially motivated attacks on organizations and individuals working for the rights of Bolivia's Indigenous Peoples and campesinos (peasant farmers) continued. The UN Special Rapporteur on indigenous people expressed concern about persistent racism in Bolivia. He observed that racist discourse, employed by some political parties, regional government officials and civic committee pressure groups and disseminated by some media outlets, was affecting Indigenous Peoples at all levels of society. Following its visit in June, the Inter-American Commission on Human Rights expressed concern regarding the large number of Indigenous Guaraní families in the Chaco region living in what the Commission described as a state of bondage analogous to slavery. More than 40 people were injured in February and April when landowners and groups of armed men attacked members of the Guaraní People in Santa Cruz during the process of clarifying title deeds to traditional lands of the Guaraní.

■ In May, Indigenous and campesino supporters of President Morales were marched by a group of opposition activists to Sucre's main square where they were beaten, their shirts were stripped off and they were forced to burn their traditional clothing and flags and to chant slogans critical of the President.

■ In September the offices of several NGOs working with Indigenous and campesino communities were attacked in several cities, notably Santa Cruz. Office equipment and documentation were destroyed.

Unlawful killings

Nineteen people, mostly campesinos, were shot and killed and 53 others were injured when violence escalated in Pando department in September. The violence occurred in the context of the mobilization of campesino groups on 11 September. Some prefecture and civic committee members were also allegedly detained temporarily by campesinos.

The results of detailed investigations by UNASUR and the national Ombudsman's Office into the killings were made public in November. They reported that the opposition prefecture and civic committees had directly participated in the killings, providing vehicles

and equipment to block the campesinos' path and bring in reinforcements. The investigations also highlighted the failure by police to protect the campesinos. The Ombudsman's Office and UNASUR concluded that the killings constituted crimes against humanity.

On 16 September, Leopoldo Fernández, Prefect of Pando department, was detained on the orders of the Ministers of Government and of National Defence. He remained in custody at the end of the year. Concerns were raised regarding the charges against Leopoldo Fernández, and the fact that no other individuals had been charged in connection with the killings.

Freedom of expression – journalists and media outlets

According to the National Press Association, between January and October there were 96 cases of physical and verbal aggression against the press. In September several pro-government media outlets were attacked by groups of university students and youths opposed to the government. Equipment was destroyed and several media outlets suspended.

■ In February, journalist Carlos Quispe Quispe from Radio Municipal Pucarani in La Paz died after being severely beaten by opponents of the pro-government mayor.

■ In October, approximately 200 members of the pro-government Popular Civic Committee and the radical Aymara group, the "ponchos rojos", attacked journalists outside the San Pedro prison in La Paz where the opposition member and former Prefect Leopoldo Fernández was being held in connection with the deaths in Pando in September. According to witnesses, the police failed to act to protect the journalists.

Impunity

In October, an extradition request was filed with the US government regarding former President Gonzalo Sánchez de Lozada and two former ministers, Carlos Sánchez Berzaín and Jorge Berindoague . All were accused of involvement in genocide for their role in the killings of 67 people during demonstrations in El Alto in 2003. In Bolivia, several former ministers and military officers were notified in November of charges in connection with the killings. However, there were concerns about delays in starting oral proceedings. In November, legislation was enacted which, in addition to recognizing state responsibility, provides for compensation for individuals injured during the confrontations and for the relatives of those killed.

Amnesty International report

📄 Bolivia: Respect for human rights is fundamental to stop escalation of violence (AMR 18/002/2008)

BOSNIA AND HERZEGOVINA

BOSNIA AND HERZEGOVINA

Head of state:	rotating presidency – Željko Komšić, Nebojša Radmanović, Haris Silajdžić
Head of government:	Nikola Špirić
Death penalty:	abolitionist for all crimes
Population:	3.9 million
Life expectancy:	74.5 years
Under-5 mortality (m/f):	15/13 per 1,000
Adult literacy:	96.7 per cent

The use of nationalist rhetoric increased in Bosnia and Herzegovina (BiH) and the country continued to be deeply divided along ethnic lines. Despite some progress, impunity for war crimes committed during the 1992-1995 war continued. Lesbian, gay, bisexual and transgender people were subjected to attacks and the measures undertaken by the authorities to respond to such attacks remained inadequate.

Background

Political disagreement between the nationalist parties representing the three constitutive nations - Bosnian Muslims (Bosniaks), Croats and Serbs - continued over the administrative division of the state. In October municipal elections were held and again brought nationalist parties to power.

The international community maintained a significant influence over political life in BiH. In June, the mandate of the Office of the High Representative was extended for an unspecified period. This office was set up as the chief civilian peace implementation agency in 1995, tasked by the Peace Implementation Council with the supervision of the Dayton Peace Agreement. The High Representative also acted as the EU Special Representative. An EU-led peacekeeping force (EUFOR) of approximately 2,200 troops remained stationed in the country. The EU also maintained its police mission in BiH.

In April, after several unsuccessful attempts, police reform legislation was introduced as one of the conditions of BiH's progress towards integration with the EU. As a result, a Stabilization and Association Agreement was signed with the EU in June.

International justice – war crimes

Senior politicians and military officers indicted for war crimes committed during the 1992-1995 war continued to be tried before the UN International Criminal Tribunal for the former Yugoslavia (Tribunal).

■ In April, the Appeal Chamber of the Tribunal reduced the sentences of Enver Hadžihasanović and Amir Kubura to three and a half years and two years respectively. In 2006 the accused had been convicted for having failed to take the necessary and reasonable measures to prevent or punish crimes committed by forces under their command, including by the El Mujahedin detachment of foreign Muslim volunteers of the Army of Bosnia and Herzegovina (ABiH). The Appeal Chamber found that they could not have been held responsible for the crimes committed by the detachment as they had not had effective control over it.

■ In July, the Appeal Chamber acquitted Naser Orić, a former commandant of ABiH in Srebrenica and surrounding areas, of all charges of war crimes. The Appeal Chamber stated that although there were no doubts that grave crimes were committed against Bosnian Serb detainees in the two detention facilities in Srebrenica between September 1992 and March 1993, the evidence presented was insufficient to attribute responsibility for those crimes to the accused.

■ Rasim Delić, a former ABiH general, was sentenced in September by the Trial Chamber to three years' imprisonment for crimes committed by the El Mujahedin detachment. He was found guilty of failing to take the necessary and reasonable measures to prevent and punish some crimes of cruel treatment committed by the detachment but acquitted of all other charges, including murder. He appealed in October.

■ In June, Stojan Župljanin, who had been indicted by the Tribunal for war crimes and crimes against humanity committed against Bosnian Croats and Bosniaks, was arrested in Belgrade and transferred to the custody of the Tribunal in The Hague.

■ In July, Radovan Karadžić, the war-time Bosnian Serb president, was arrested in Belgrade and transferred to the Tribunal's custody (see Serbia entry). He had been indicted by the Tribunal for, among other things, the siege of Sarajevo and murder of over 7,000 Bosniak men and boys in Srebrenica.

Justice system – war crimes

A large number of war crimes cases continued to be prosecuted by domestic courts throughout the country, including by the War Crimes Chamber (WCC) of the BiH State Court. The capacity of the domestic judiciary to deal with complex war crimes cases remained limited, especially taking into account the scale of yet unprosecuted cases.

■ The case of Mitar Rašević and Savo Todorović was transferred to the WCC from the Tribunal. Both the accused were convicted in February and sentenced to eight and half and twelve and a half years in prison respectively. They had been charged with participation in the establishment and maintenance of a system of punishment and mistreatment of Bosniak detainees in Foča detention facility during the 1992-1995 war and participation in the establishment of a forced labour system in the prison.

■ After a guilty plea agreement in April 2008, Dušan Fuštar was sentenced to nine years' imprisonment by the WCC for murder, torture and illegal detention of Bosnian Croat and Bosniak detainees in the detention camp Keraterm. The indictment against Dušan Fuštar had been transferred to the WCC from the Tribunal. Following an agreement with the BiH State Prosecutor, the indictment against Dušan Fuštar was modified and some charges dropped (he was initially included in the case against Željko Mejakić and others, below).

■ The remaining accused – Duško Knežević, Željko Mejakić and Momčilo Gruban – were sentenced in May to 31, 21 and 11 years' imprisonment respectively. They were charged with murder, rape, torture and unlawful detention of prisoners in the camps of Keraterm and Omarska.

■ Paško Ljubičić, the former commander of the Bosnian Croat military police, pleaded guilty as charged, and was sentenced to 10 years' imprisonment in April. Paško Ljubičić had ordered his subordinates to execute 27 Bosniak civilians in the town of Busovača.

He also conveyed orders to kill or expel all adult Bosniak men from the area of Ahmići in BiH in April 1993, which resulted in the murder of more than 100 civilians.

■ In May, Željko Lelek – a former Bosnian Serb police officer – was found guilty of taking part in "ethnic cleansing" operations in the Višegrad area in BiH during 1992. He was sentenced to 13 years' imprisonment on charges including unlawful imprisonment, torture and rape as well as participating in the forcible transfer of non-Serb civilians.

■ In July, seven out of 11 accused were found guilty of genocide committed at Kravica farm near Srebrenica in July 1995. They were convicted of killing more than 1,000 Bosniak men and sentenced to between 38 and 42 years' imprisonment. The remaining four accused were acquitted of all charges.

Courts in the two semi-autonomous entities of BiH (Republika Srpska, RS, and the Federation of Bosnia and Herzegovina, FBiH) continued to prosecute war crimes cases. A more proactive approach of the authorities in RS started to emerge with approximately 150 cases under investigation in this entity in 2008.

■ On 17 November, upon appeal the Supreme Court of RS convicted Milo Govedarica – a member of the White Eagles brigade – for war crimes against the civilian population of Gacko municipality.

Earlier, in July, Milo Govedarica was convicted and sentenced by the District Court in Trebinje to seven years and six months in prison for the rape of a Bosniak woman and for the killing of a civilian, Aziz Hasanbegović.

Enforced disappearances

Almost 13 years after the war ended an estimated 13,000 people still remained unaccounted for.

The Missing Persons Institute (Institut za Nestale Osobe, INO) started its work in full capacity in 2008.

In June, the ICRC donated its database of missing persons to the INO, facilitating the establishment of a centralized system of information on all missing people in the territory of BiH.

■ In May, the Constitutional Court of BiH delivered two verdicts in a hearing concerning 230 cases filed by the families of missing persons. It found the applicants' right to family and private life as well as their right to freedom from inhumane treatment had been violated because the state authorities had not opened

B

investigations into the enforced disappearance and deaths of their relatives.

Internally displaced people and refugees

People displaced during the 1992-1995 war continued to return to their homes but the scale of the return considerably decreased.

According to the BiH Ministry of Human Rights and Refugees, more than 1.2 million people had not yet returned to their homes. The ones that had come back were often faced with inadequate access to housing. About 2,700 families still lived in collective housing establishments. Some of the returnees were not able to repossess their property.

Minority returnees continued to face problems exercising their social and economic rights, including access to health services and education. Lack of access to employment, caused partly by the poor economic situation of the country as well as by discrimination, continued to be one of the main obstacles to return.

Counter-terror and security

On 20 November Judge Richard Leon of the US District Court for the District of Columbia ordered the release of five of a group of six men of Algerian origin who had been illegally arrested in BiH and transferred to US custody at Guantánamo Bay, Cuba, in 2002. The judge ruled there was enough evidence to keep the sixth man (Belkacem Bensayah) in detention. Despite the order, the authorities of BiH agreed to accept only three of the men (Mustafa Aït Idir, Boudella El Hadj and Mohammed Nechle) and failed to undertake diplomatic measures to release the remaining two detainees. The three men were released from Guantánamo and arrived in Sarajevo on 16 December.

In June the Sarajevo Canton Prosecutor's Office opened an investigation against Zlatko Lagumdžija (former Prime Minister of BiH) and Tomislav Limov (former Minister of Interior) as well as against some lower ranking public officials for their alleged role in the unlawful arrest and handover of the six men to US custody.

The State Commission for the Revision of Decisions on Naturalization of Foreign Citizens continued its work. Up to 1,500 individuals came to BiH during the 1992-1995 war in order to work for humanitarian NGOs or to join the ABiH and subsequently took BiH

citizenship. If their citizenship were to be revoked, these individuals could face deportation to their country of origin where they could be at risk of torture or the death penalty.

■ Imad al Husein appealed against the revocation of his citizenship and his case was pending before the BiH judiciary. In January, the European Court of Human Rights requested that the BiH authorities undertake temporary measures to stop his deportation to Syria pending the final decision of the Constitutional Court of BiH and for a period of seven days after the notification of its verdict. However, a deportation order was still issued. In October, the Constitutional Court asked for a re-trial at the BiH State Court. Despite this decision on 6 October Imad al Husein was placed in a deportation facility.

Torture and other ill-treatment

Ill-treatment by the police and in prisons continued. Impunity prevailed due to an ineffective complaints mechanism and lack of investigations by the prosecutors into allegations of ill-treatment.

Conditions of detention were below international standards. Of particular concern were conditions in the Zenica Prison Forensic Psychiatric Annexe, where patients with mental health problems lacked adequate medical assistance.

The police reform law passed in April failed to address the problem of police accountability.

Discrimination – Roma

Measures taken to combat discrimination and social exclusion of members of Romani communities remained insufficient and sporadic. The co-ordination of such steps undertaken by different authorities was very low.

According to the international NGO Save the Children, only 20 to 30 per cent of Romani children attended primary education, and only 0.5 to 3 per cent attended pre-school education.

The State Council of Ministers developed action plans for Roma integration in the areas of employment, health services and housing, and in September BiH joined the Decade of Roma Inclusion.

Freedom of assembly – Sarajevo Queer Festival

The authorities failed to protect the organizers and participants of the Sarajevo Queer Festival which was organized for the first time in BiH in September. The event was closed earlier than planned, due to death threats received by the organizers and physical attacks on participants. The festival was surrounded by an atmosphere of intimidation as some BiH politicians and some media ran a homophobic campaign.

In November the Sarajevo Canton Prosecutor's Office indicted two men for physical attacks against the participants of the festival.

Amnesty International visits/reports

🚌 Amnesty International delegates visited BiH in February and December.

📰 Bosnia and Herzegovina: "Better keep quiet" – ill-treatment by the police and in prisons (EUR 63/001/2008)

📰 State of denial – Europe's role in rendition and secret detention (EUR 01/003/2008)

BRAZIL

FEDERATIVE REPUBLIC OF BRAZIL

Head of state and government:	Luiz Inácio Lula da Silva
Death penalty:	abolitionist for ordinary crimes
Population:	194.2 million
Life expectancy:	71.7 years
Under-5 mortality (m/f):	32/24 per 1,000
Adult literacy:	88.6 per cent

Brazilian society remained deeply divided in terms of the enjoyment of human rights. Economic expansion and government-supported social projects contributed to some reductions in socio-economic disparities. However, despite modest improvements in poverty reduction, inequality in the distribution of income and wealth remained one of the highest in the region and human rights violations affecting millions of people living in poverty remained largely unaddressed. The poorest communities continued to be denied access to services, to experience high levels of gang violence, and to suffer systemic human rights violations by the police.

Marginalized urban communities continued to live with the consequences of inadequate social protection, discriminatory urban development policies, and a lack of any public security provision. As a result many were trapped in *favelas* (shanty towns) or substandard housing where they were caught between criminal violence and abuses by the police.

In rural areas, landless workers and Indigenous Peoples were intimidated and threatened with violence and forced evictions. Agro-industrial expansion and government and private development projects reinforced decades of social discrimination and poverty in rural communities. The constitutional and human rights of these communities were regularly flouted, be it through a lack of access to justice and social services, or violence and intimidation at the hands of irregular private security companies in the defence of powerful economic interests.

Many of those defending the human rights of marginalized communities, including lawyers, union leaders and community activists, were criminalized by the authorities, and threatened by those whose interests they challenged.

Background

Municipal elections were held in October throughout Brazil. The situation in Rio de Janeiro, where para-policing groups made up of off-duty or former police officers, firemen and soldiers (known as *milícias*) and drug gangs controlled large parts of the city, was considered so volatile that the army was deployed to safeguard candidates' security. In November, floods devastated parts of Santa Catarina state, killing over 100 and leaving more than 30,000 homeless.

Corruption continued to undermine both the provision of public services and access to justice. In May, a federal police investigation exposed a scheme involving the siphoning off of public funds from the Brazilian Development Bank for services contracted by local councils in São Paulo, Rio, Paraíba and Rio Grande do Norte states. In December, in a separate corruption investigation in Espírito Santo state, federal police arrested the president of the State Supreme Court, along with judges, lawyers and a member of the prosecution service, for alleged involvement in the selling of judicial decisions.

Brazil's long-standing record of impunity for crimes committed by the military regime (1964-1985) faced its first serious challenges. In July, Brazil's Minister of Justice, Tarso Genro, reopened the debate by stating that torture was not a political crime and therefore not covered by the 1979

Amnesty Law. His statements were dismissed by the Minister of Defence and members of the armed forces. In October, the Brazilian Bar Association petitioned the Supreme Court to rule on this interpretation of the Amnesty Law.

In October, retired army Colonel Carlos Alberto Brilhante Ustra, became the first person to be found guilty in a civil case of torture during the military government. Controversially, federal government lawyers announced they would defend Colonel Ustra and his co-defendant, former Colonel Audir dos Santos Maciel, in a separate civil case, brought by federal public prosecutors, on the grounds that the Amnesty Law should protect them from prosecution.

In the international arena, Brazil submitted a report to the UN Human Rights Council's new monitoring system, the Universal Periodic Review, in April. The federal government accepted the Council's recommendations, which included the adoption of measures to reduce excessive use of force by the police, improve conditions in the prison system, and guarantee the security of human rights defenders. A proposal to bring Brazilian legislation into line with the Rome Statute of the International Criminal Court was pending ratification in the Senate and the Chamber of Deputies at the end of the year.

Rural violence and forced evictions

Violence against landless workers continued, often carried out by unregulated or insufficiently regulated private security companies hired by landowners or illegal militias. Forced evictions persisted, in many instances with complete disregard for due process of law. There were attempts to criminalize movements that support landless people in their efforts to secure land and agrarian reform.

In Rio Grande do Sul state, prosecutors and military police built up a dossier of numerous allegations against members of the Landless Rural Workers Movement (Movimento dos Trabalhadores Rurais Sem Terra, MST) in what the MST described as an attempt to curtail their activities and criminalize members. The dossier, which included allegations of MST links with international terrorist groups, was used to support legal appeals for evictions, a number of which were carried out by police with excessive force.

In Paraná state, illegal armed militias linked to landowners continued to attack landless workers.

■ On 8 March, 15 gunmen invaded a settlement of 35 families in Terra Livre, Ortigueira, threatening children, beating men and women and burning their belongings. Seven of the gunmen were subsequently arrested. Three weeks later, two hooded men shot dead Terra Livre's local MST leader, Eli Dallemore, in front of his wife and children.

■ On 8 May, armed men invaded an encampment of 150 families near Cascavel with tractors, diggers and an armoured truck, firing shots and destroying crops, a school and a church. The armed men exchanged fire with the police before being subdued. Ten were arrested in connection with the attack.

Para state continued to record the highest numbers of threats and killings of land activists; few if any perpetrators were brought to justice.

■ In May, the retrial of Vitalmiro Bastos de Mouro for the killing of environmental and land activist Sister Dorothy Stang in February 2005 ended in his acquittal and release. An earlier trial had ended in conviction and a 30-year prison sentence. The acquittal was widely condemned by, among others, President Lula and other government officials. The Public Prosecution Service lodged an appeal, which was continuing at the end of the year.

Indigenous Peoples' rights

Indigenous Peoples fighting for their constitutional rights to ancestral lands continued to suffer killings, violence, intimidation, discrimination, forced evictions and other human rights violations, often pushing them into poverty. Delays in judicial decisions contributed to continuing violence against Indigenous Peoples. Following his visit to Brazil in August, the UN Special Rapporteur on indigenous people criticized "the persistent discrimination underlying the formation of policies, delivery of services, and administration of justice" which "has at times infested parts of society to result in violence."

In May, hooded men shot at and threw home-made incendiary bombs at a group of Indigenous people, in the Raposa Serra do Sol reservation in Rondônia state, injuring 10 of them. The attacks were attributed to large-scale rice farmers who remained illegally on indigenous land signed off on by President Lula in 2005. Federal police efforts to evict the farmers remained suspended pending a controversial appeal by the state government to the Supreme Court on the legality of the demarcation process. Although in

December eight out of 11 Supreme Court judges voted to maintain the original demarcation of the Reposa Serra do Sol, the final ruling was delayed until 2009 after one of the judges requested time for further consideration.

■ In Pernambuco state, Truká Indigenous leader Mozeni Araújo de Sá was shot dead in a crowded street in the city of Cabrobó in August. He was a key witness in the killings of two other Truká people, shot during community festivities in June 2005. He was also running for office in local elections. The gunman was detained and awaiting trial at the end of the year.

Human rights defenders

Human rights defenders across the country continued to be threatened, intimidated and attacked.

■ In Rio de Janeiro, João Tancredo, President of the Institute of Human Rights Defenders, survived an attempt on his life in January when his armoured car was hit by four bullets. He was returning from a meeting with residents of the favela Furquim Mendes, where he had heard allegations against a police officer known as "the predator", accused of killing five people in the community.

Pará remained the state with the most defenders under threat. According to the State Programme for the Protection of Human Rights Defenders in Pará, at least 50 defenders were at risk, with fewer than 10 receiving adequate protection.

Police and security forces

Brazil's criminal justice system continued to be characterized by negligence, discrimination and corruption. Although there was some reported decline in overall homicide rates, poor communities in urban centres and small towns in the interior continued to register high rates of violent crime and homicide. Elements within the law enforcement and security forces were found to be involved in death squads, milícias or criminal activity.

There was limited progress in the government's National Public Security and Citizenship Programme (Programa Nacional de Segurança Pública com Cidadania, PRONASCI) aimed at crime prevention and social inclusion in Brazil's most violent urban centres, with few states putting forward projects appropriate for funding.

Rio de Janeiro

State authorities continued to promote hardline policing exemplified by large-scale operations, involving scores of police officers, armoured vehicles and helicopters in incursions into the city's favelas. Six people were killed in an operation in the Jacarezinho and Mangueira favelas in January. In April, two operations, one in the Coréia and Vila Aliança favelas, the other in Vila Cruzeiro, left 20 people dead; at least seven residents were wounded by stray bullets. Another 10 people were killed in August during an operation in Duque de Caxias, in the Baixada Fluminense.

Although the number of homicides in the city of Rio de Janeiro dropped in comparison to 2007, police killings recorded as "acts of resistance" made up around one in seven of the total number of killings between January and October 2008. Off-duty killings by police persisted. Civil police investigations revealed 12 police officers, including two from the elite Special Operations Battalion (Batalhão de Operações Especiais, Bope), were operating as hired gunmen. Intimidation of those opposing organized crime continued. At least 17 public officials – including three judges, seven prosecutors, five police chiefs and a state deputy – received death threats from milícias and criminal gangs. Many were receiving police protection at the end of the year.

In June, parliament opened an inquiry into the role of milícias who were believed to control around 170 favelas. It followed the news that milícias controlling the Batan favela, in Rio de Janeiro's west zone, had abducted and tortured three reporters from the newspaper O Dia and a favela resident. The inquiry uncovered a web of protection rackets, electoral malpractice, violence and corruption, extending into the heart of state institutions, with extensive links between côrrupt police officers, milícias and state and municipal politicians. As a result of the inquiry several key milícia leaders were imprisoned, including a state deputy.

■ In August, masked men believed to be linked to the milícia shot dead seven residents of the Barbante favela, including a local shopkeeper who had refused to pay the milícia "tax".

São Paulo

Although overall homicide figures reportedly dropped, official statistics for killings by the military police in São Paulo state rose slightly during the period January to September 2008 to 353, compared with 325 over the same period in 2007. At the same time there were numerous reports of multiple homicides. Death squads with links to the police continued to operate in the periphery of São Paulo city.

■ Between April and October, five decapitated corpses were found dumped in Itapecerica da Serra. Civil police were investigating the possible involvement of a death squad known as "The Highlanders", allegedly made up of 10 military police officers.

The north-east

In his report on his visit to Brazil in November 2007, the UN Special Rapporteur on extrajudicial, summary or arbitrary executions stated that "the public prosecution service in Pernambuco estimated that approximately 70% of the homicides in Pernambuco are committed by death squads," and that according to a federal parliamentary commission of inquiry "80% of the crimes caused by extermination groups involve police or ex-police."

In Macéio, Alagoas state, communities were left at at the mercy of drug gangs.

■ In Benedito Bentes, a poor suburb in Macéio, community leaders and the mayor elect were repeatedly threatened by local drug gangs. In November, traffickers ordered a curfew, including the closure of the local school and the residents' association, after a shoot-out in which two people were killed and six wounded.

Torture and other ill-treatment

Despite several government initiatives, including the recent ratification of the Optional Protocol to the Convention against Torture, torture by law enforcement officials was still common at the point of arrest, during interrogation and in detention. Reporting, investigation and prosecution of such cases under the 1997 Torture Law were rare.

■ In Piauí state, two military police officers from the 4th Battalion in the city of Picos were accused of torturing two young men whom they had arrested in October on suspicion of theft. The men were beaten about the genitals and back. A medical examination revealed gross swelling of the testicles and extensive bruising. At the end of the year, two military police were on trial, and the commander of the battalion was removed from his post pending the outcome of investigations.

Many detention centres were dominated internally by criminal gangs, and detainees were frequently tortured, ill-treated and sometimes killed by guards or other detainees. Some states continued to adopt a system of extended solitary confinement in high security prisons, in contravention of international standards.

■ In September, three prisoners were found stabbed to death in the Paulo Sarasate detention centre, in Fortaleza, Ceará state. A further two were burned alive in their cell in November. This brought the total of prisoner killings in the detention centre in 2008 to 18. The authorities attributed these to gang conflicts within the prison.

In a landmark decision the Attorney General forwarded a petition to the Federal Supreme Court calling for federal intervention in Rondônia state to prevent systematic violations committed in the José Mário Alves prison, known as Urso Branco. The request came after eight years of reports – by national and local NGOs, Global Justice and The Peace and Justice Commission – of violations including summary executions and torture.

There were continuing reports of ill-treatment and abuses in the juvenile detention system.

■ In July, in São Paulo's Fundação CASA detention system (Centro de Atendimento Socioeducativo ao Adolescente) detainees in the Complexo de Franco da Rocha alleged that in the aftermath of a riot, they were locked in their cells and beaten with batons, bits of wood studded with nails, iron bars and the shaft of a hoe.

■ In November in Rio de Janeiro's DEGASE detention system (Departamento Geral de Ações Socioeducativas), a 17-year-old boy died of head injuries sustained in the Educandário Santo Expedito detention centre in Bangu. Witesses reported that the boy had been beaten by guards. A police inquiry was launched.

Women's rights

Women continued to experience violence and abuse. Survivors living in poor communities were not provided with basic services and had limited access to justice. Their contacts with the criminal justice system frequently resulted in ill-treatment and intimidation.

Women in communities dominated by criminal gangs or *milícias* faced abuse with little prospect of redress.

■ In August, a study on *milícias* by the State University of Rio de Janeiro reported on the treatment of a woman accused of infidelity in Bangu, a *milícia*-dominated community: she was stripped in front of her house, her head was shaved and she was forced to walk naked through the *favela*.

The number of women in prison continued to increase. Figures released by Depen, the National Prisons Department, showed an increase of 77 per cent in the women's prison population over the previous eight years – a higher rate of increase than for men. Women detained continued to face ill-treatment, overcrowding, inadequate support during childbirth and lack of childcare provision.

Amnesty International visits/report

🚐 Amnesty International delegates visited Brazil in May and November. In April they observed Brazil's submission to the Universal Periodic Review.

📃 Brazil: Picking up the pieces – Women's experience of urban violence in Brazil (AMR 19/001/2008)

BULGARIA

REPUBLIC OF BULGARIA

Head of state:	Georgi Parvanov
Head of government:	Sergey Stanishev
Death penalty:	abolitionist for all crimes
Population:	7.6 million
Life expectancy:	72.7 years
Under-5 mortality (m/f):	16/12 per 1,000
Adult literacy:	98.2 per cent

Asylum-seekers continued to be detained for months and even years, and were denied protection. Discrimination against minorities persisted. Lesbian, gay, bisexual and transgender (LGBT) people continued to experience violence and intolerance. Reports of ill-treatment by law enforcement officials were received throughout the year.

Political developments

The European Commission's progress report in July urged Bulgaria to increase efforts to combat corruption and criminality, following the country's accession to the EU. In the wake of a previous report by the anti-fraud EU agency OLAF, the Commission condemned the misuse of EU funds and adopted sanctions against Bulgaria.

Asylum-seekers and migrants

Refugees, asylum-seekers and migrants continued to be detained for months and even years awaiting expulsion. National NGOs continued to express concern that such detentions had become routine practice, contravening legislation that such a measure should be used only as a last resort.

In April, Iraqi asylum-seekers set light to furniture in the Special Centre for the Temporary Accommodation of Foreigners (SCTAF) in Busmantsi, near the capital, Sofia, in protest against a change of policy decreasing the level of protection in Bulgaria for Iraqi asylum-seekers. UNHCR, the UN refugee agency, had previously raised concerns about this change, which the authorities defended by alleging lack of space in the reception centres. The NGO Bulgarian Helsinki Committee (BHC) filed appeals in the courts against more than 40 decisions to reject applications between December 2007 and March 2008.

■ Said Kadzoev, a Russian national of Chechen origin, continued to face forcible return to the Russian Federation where he would be at serious risk of torture and other ill-treatment. He had been held in detention in the SCTAF in Busmantsi since 1 November 2006, and in solitary confinement for prolonged periods with no explanation from the authorities. The Head of the Migration Directorate of Bulgaria announced in May that a third safe country would be sought for Said Kadzoev's deportation. In October a complaint was filed with the European Court of Human Rights on the grounds that the rejection of his asylum claim, his administrative detention for more than two years and his arbitrary placement in solitary confinement for excessive periods, compounded by alleged physical ill-treatment during detention, constituted a violation of his rights.

Discrimination – minorities
Romani minority

The Romani minority continued to face discrimination at the hands of public officials and private individuals. The BHC reported cases of discrimination in access to housing, including forced evictions, and access to public services.

In June, the UN Committee on the Rights of the Child noted that despite government efforts to ensure equal enjoyment of rights for Romani children such as through the National Action Plan on the Decade of Roma Inclusion, concerns remained about the

B

negative attitudes and prejudices displayed towards Roma by the general population, as well as about the overall situation of children of minorities, particularly Roma. The Committee especially highlighted discrimination and disparities such as segregation in education, and unequal access to health care, housing, employment and an adequate standard of living.

Macedonian minority

In May, representatives of the OMO Ilinden PIRIN party, which represents the Macedonian minority in Bulgaria, reported on a campaign of harassment and intimidation by police officers against supporters of a new application for its registration. According to the party's allegations, police officers summoned supporters for interrogation at police stations without a written order and questioned them about the party. Its registration had been denied three times in 2007 despite a ruling by the European Court of Human Rights in 2005 and several calls by the EU.

Turkish minority

In April, the Sofia City Court ruled that Volen Siderov, leader of the far-right party Ataka (Attack), was guilty of using hostile and discriminatory language against the ethnic Turkish minority and of creating an atmosphere of animosity towards them. He was threatened with a fine if he ignored the ruling that he should stop using such language.

Rights of lesbian, gay, bisexual and transgender people

In June, the first LGBT Pride event to be held in Bulgaria was organized in Sofia by Gemini, a Bulgarian organization working for the rights of LGBT people. Increased intimidation of LGBT people in Bulgaria was reported in the run-up to the event, which was opposed by some religious authorities and far-right groups. Some 150 peaceful marchers faced violence from counter-demonstrators who threw stones, bottles and Molotov cocktails. More than 60 people were arrested by the police. The Prime Minister, although acknowledging the right to demonstrate peacefully, expressed his personal opposition to the march.

Torture and other ill-treatment

In February, the Council of Europe's Committee for the Prevention of Torture (CPT) issued a report on its visit to Bulgaria in September 2006 stating that efforts should be increased to combat ill-treatment of detainees and to improve detention facilities.

In April, the BHC denounced the non-compliance with international standards of legislation covering the use of firearms by law enforcement officials. The BHC also reported on cases of ill-treatment by police officials, in particular towards Roma, at the time of arrest or during detention. These were often not adequately investigated.

■ On 2 October, Sofia's Military Court sentenced five police officers to a total of 82 years' imprisonment after convicting them of beating 38-year-old Angel Dimitrov to death in 2005. His death was initially explained by the police as the result of a heart attack, but a second autopsy demanded by relatives showed that he had died from blows to the head. An appeal against the decision, to be reviewed by the Military Court of Appeals, was pending at the end of the year. Sofia's Military Court had previously issued a sentence against the five police officers in November 2007, but the decision was repealed by the Military Court of Appeals.

Ill-treatment in custody

In February the CPT reported overcrowding and verbal abuse against inmates in prison facilities visited in 2006, as well as allegations of physical ill-treatment by prison staff.

The BHC also reported that conditions in many prisons continued to be below those required by international standards.

■ On 6 March, Bulgaria was found by the European Court of Human Rights to be in violation of the prohibition of inhuman or degrading treatment. Nikolai Kirilov Gavazov, a prisoner accused of rape, spent nearly two years on remand in a tiny, windowless cell in Pazardjik prison, central Bulgaria. The Court also found that the seven-year length of the court case was excessive.

Mental health institutions

In February the CPT, following visits to mental health and social care institutions in 2006, raised serious concerns about admission procedures, ill-treatment and living conditions at the institutions visited.

The CPT highlighted the lack of staff, staff training and resources in such institutions, conditions which had led to violent incidents, limited therapeutic options and insufficient provision of rehabilitation programmes. Despite recommendations by the CPT in 2002 that attention be given to improving living conditions, these remained inadequate.

In February, following a BBC television documentary highlighting extremely poor conditions at the Mogilino childcare institution, the Minister of Labour and Social Policy announced that this and another six similar institutions would be closed down.

Amnesty International reports

📄 Bulgaria: Fear of forcible return/fear of torture or ill-treatment – Said Kadzoev (EUR 15/001/2008)

📄 Bulgaria: First Sofia Pride needs adequate protection (EUR 15/002/2008)

BURKINA FASO

BURKINA FASO
Head of state:	Blaise Compaoré
Head of government:	Tertius Zongo
Death penalty:	abolitionist in practice
Population:	15.2 million
Life expectancy:	51.4 years
Under-5 mortality (m/f):	183/176 per 1,000
Adult literacy:	23.6 per cent

More than 300 people were arrested during protests against rising living costs and more than 80 were sentenced to prison terms without having access to a lawyer.

Arbitrary arrests and detentions

In February, there were several demonstrations against rising living costs in the capital Ouagadougou and in Bobo-Dioulasso, the second largest town. The protests became violent, with demonstrators destroying property and hurling rocks at the police. The security forces arrested several hundred people and at least 80 of them were sentenced in March to prison terms without having access to a lawyer.

■ Nana Thibaut, leader of the opposition party, the Democratic and Popular Rally (Rassemblement démocratique et populaire, RDP) was sentenced to three years' imprisonment.

Impunity

No progress was reported in the investigation of the killing, in 1998, of the journalist Norbert Zongo.

Right to health

Despite some measures taken by the government in the past two years to improve access to maternal health services, including a reduction in fees for routine deliveries, the maternal mortality rate remained very high.

Death penalty

In February, one person was reportedly sentenced to death in Dédougou.

Amnesty International visit

🚌 An Amnesty International delegation visited Burkina Faso in July.

B

BURUNDI

REPUBLIC OF BURUNDI
Head of state:	Pierre Nkurunziza
Death penalty:	retentionist
Population:	8.9 million
Life expectancy:	48.5 years
Under-5 mortality (m/f):	178/156 per 1,000
Adult literacy:	59.3 per cent

Harassment and intimidation of political opponents, journalists and human rights defenders increased, often in violation of the right to freedom of expression. Soldiers were prosecuted for the killings of civilians in 2006, but other grave human rights violations committed in the past remained unaddressed and the government failed to break the cycle of impunity. Despite reforms to the judicial system, significant problems remained in the administration of justice. Rape and sexual violence, despite their prevalence, were rarely investigated and prosecuted. A large number of children were detained without trial.

Background

A political crisis started in February when opposition parties refused to attend the National Assembly following the dismissal of the First Vice-President, Alice Nzomukunda, by the ruling party, the National Council for the Defence of Democracy-Forces for the Defence of Democracy (CNDD-FDD). Divisions within the CNDD-FDD, leading to expulsions and defections, resulted in the party losing its majority in the National Assembly and paralysis in the government. In May the President of the National Assembly, a member of the CNDD-FDD, asked the Constitutional Court to remove 22 former CNDD-FDD members. The Court ruled that, according to the Constitution, the 22 could not sit in the National Assembly as "independent" members. The move was widely considered anti-constitutional and a serious breach of the judiciary's independence.

Negotiations on the ceasefire implementation between the government and the opposition National Liberation Forces (FNL) were slow. In April and May, renewed clashes between the FNL and the government took place on the outskirts of the capital, Bujumbura, and the surrounding western provinces.

On 10 June, the two sides signed the Magaliesberg Communiqué and jointly pledged to secure peace and negotiate the number of FNL positions in key state institutions. However, during the second half of 2008, the Joint Verification and Monitoring Mechanism, the body charged with implementing the September 2006 Comprehensive Ceasefire Agreement, made little progress. The government rejected the FNL's terms for the allocation of civil service and parliamentary positions. The FNL refused to omit the reference to ethnicity from the name of its political party (Palipehutu-FNL) ahead of elections in 2010, a reference which the government said violated the Constitution. Demobilization of FNL troops was behind schedule.

A draft revision of the criminal code, which included important provisions for the improvement of human rights – including addressing torture and sexual violence – was awaiting discussion at the National Assembly.

Poverty was exacerbated by high commodity prices and unemployment. The agricultural yield in certain rural areas was low and limited the local population's access to food. Returning refugees also placed an additional burden on limited resources. The prevalence of small arms, large numbers of newly demobilized fighters and a high crime rate all contributed to a prevailing sense of insecurity.

Unlawful killings

Security forces unlawfully killed civilians in the context of security operations against the FNL. Human rights abuses were also committed by the FNL, including unlawful killings and rape.

■ On 5 May, members of the army entered a family home in the commune of Muhuta, in Bujumbura Rural province, where they suspected FNL members were living. One of the soldiers reportedly opened fire, killing the mother of the household.

■ Three FNL soldiers went to the commune of Mutimbuzi, in Bujumbura Rural province, to search for new recruits in June. They reportedly visited a member of a local Hutu youth organization, but he refused to help them. The soldiers threw a grenade into his house, killing his wife.

Justice system

The government and the UN took steps to reform and strengthen the judicial system, including building and renovating magistrates' courts, training magistrates, addressing overcrowding in detention facilities and reducing the backlog of cases. However, significant problems remained. The judiciary lacked independence and was influenced by the executive. Corruption was reported. Judicial staff were inadequately trained and had on occasion little understanding of the law. The judicial system was ill-equipped and needed further financial and material resources. The local population had little confidence in the justice system and resorted to mob justice on numerous occasions.

Conditions of detention remained poor and prisons were overcrowded. Access to food and health care was severely limited and detainees were often kept in highly insanitary conditions. Personal and legal information on detainees was poorly managed by prison authorities.

Children were held in police detention facilities and prisons, in violation of arrest and detention procedures. They were held together with adult detainees and so exposed to sexual and physical abuse. Many juvenile detainees were held without trial, in conditions amounting to cruel, inhuman and degrading treatment and without access to health care or education. One international organization estimated that 80 per cent of juvenile detainees were awaiting trial.

Arbitrary arrests and detentions

The authorities frequently detained individuals without charge in violation of the legal maximum custody limit of 14 days. Officials without a working knowledge of the law frequently arrested people arbitrarily. Many of those arbitrarily arrested were suspected of supporting the FNL.

■ In April, 782 people were arbitrarily arrested following renewed clashes between the FNL and the National Defence Forces. The police arrested individuals whom they suspected of sympathizing with or supporting the FNL, often with no legal basis for the detention.

Torture and other ill-treatment

Human rights monitors reported that the National Police were responsible for beating detainees and other citizens. Members of the security forces had scant working knowledge of human rights despite on-going training provided by the UN and local human rights organizations.

■ Jean Claude Nkunzimana from Kinama commune, Bujumbura, was walking home on 1 July when he was stopped by five police officers drinking at a local bar. One officer asked him for a cigarette. When he refused, the five officers beat him severely.

■ A young man was arrested on 9 June for fraud in the Commune of Gisozi, Mwaro Province. When he was caught trying to escape, seven police officers reportedly beat him with the butts of their pistols and kicked him. He needed hospital treatment for his injuries.

Violence against women and girls

There was a high incidence of rape and other sexual violence against women and girls. For example, a centre run by the NGO Médecins sans Frontières in Bujumbura received an average of 131 rape victims a month in 2008. There was an increase in reports of rapes of girls, often by schoolteachers. By contrast, the UN reported a decrease in incidents of rape by members of the security forces.

Perpetrators – who were often known by the victim – did not fear prosecution and impunity remained the norm. Women survivors of sexual violence lacked confidence in the judicial system. The families of victims often reached an "amicable settlement" outside court with the suspected perpetrator.

■ A 15-year-old girl was raped by her schoolteacher on 20 March in the Commune of Kanyosha, Bujumbura. The teacher had asked her to take a mobile phone to his home. The girl pressed charges against the teacher who was detained.

Freedom of assembly

The government prevented opposition parties from holding meetings without prior authorization. The authorities enforced such decisions through local administrations, which were under increasingly tight control by the executive. On 6 October, the Interior Minister signed a ministerial decree which stipulated that opposition parties could only hold meetings at designated times. It also required opposition parties to formally ask, in writing, for permission from the local administration to hold meetings. The local administration was granted powers to reject such requests if they deemed the meetings would disturb "order and public security".

Two leading opposition parties, the National Council for the Defence of Democracy (CNDD) and Front for Democracy in Burundi (FRODEBU), publicly denounced the decree and asked for it to be withdrawn.

■ On 11 November, 21 members of the Union for Peace and Development (UPD-Zigamibanga) were arrested and detained by the local administration in the province of Ngozi. The detainees were accused of holding meetings without the authorization of the local authorities.

Freedom of expression

The authorities were increasingly intolerant of criticism, and relations between civil society and the government were tense.

■ Alexis Sinduhije, President of the political opposition group, Movement for Security and Democracy (Mouvement pour la Sécurité et la Démocratie), was arrested and detained on 3 November after holding a party meeting. On 11 November, he was charged with "contempt of the head of state" for calling into question the President's development policies.

■ Juvénal Rududura, Vice-President of the trade union of non-magistrate staff, was arrested on 15 September after a radio interview in which he accused staff at the Ministry of Justice of providing positions in return for bribes.

■ Journalist Jean-Claude Kavumbagu was arrested on 11 September and charged with defamation. He alleged in an article that the cost of President Nkurunziza's trip to see the opening ceremony of the Beijing Olympics caused some civil servants' salaries to be paid late.

B

Impunity – the Muyinga trial

On 23 October, the Muyinga military tribunal convicted 15 soldiers of killing 31 individuals between July and August 2006. The trial heard that they were first detained at Muyinga military camp and then taken to the banks of the Ruvubu River, where they were extrajudicially executed by members of the intelligence service. Fourteen soldiers received sentences varying from two years to life imprisonment. The former Commander of the Fourth Military Region, Colonel Vital Bangirinama, who reportedly gave the orders, had fled the country and did not attend the trial. He was found guilty in his absence and was sentenced to death. The outcome of the trial was welcomed by Burundian civil society and the international community as an important step in addressing impunity.

Transitional justice

The government, in conjunction with the international community and civil society, took few steps to establish a Truth and Reconciliation Commission and a Special Tribunal to investigate and prosecute the most serious crimes committed during Burundi's conflicts.

National consultations lasting 12 months were scheduled to start in June and funds from the UN Peacebuilding Commission were allocated for this purpose. However, meetings of the Tripartite Committee – established in November 2007 to oversee the process and made up of UN, government and civil society delegates – were postponed, mainly because members failed to attend and sessions were cancelled by the president of the committee. National consultations were rescheduled to start on 1 March 2009.

International scrutiny

On 24 September, the UN Human Rights Council extended the mandate of the Independent Expert on the Human Rights Situation in Burundi until a "national and independent human rights commission" was established. Concerns were raised by civil society about whether a future human rights commission would operate independently, without interference or intimidation from the authorities. There was no clear timeframe for the establishment of the human rights commission.

Refugees – returns

Between 1 January and 31 December, 95,050 Burundian refugees returned, principally from Tanzania, of whom 30,818 were refugees who had fled in 1972.

There was an increase in land disputes, especially involving returning refugees who left in 1972. Land disputes were highest in the south, especially in the provinces of Bururi and Makamba. The government set up a National Commission on land and other properties in 2006, but its work was hampered by its lack of legal jurisdiction over disputes and the number of complaints. By October 2008, the commission had recorded 11,200 land disputes and resolved 2,279.

Amnesty International visit/reports

An Amnesty International delegation visited Burundi in November for research.

Burundi: Submission to the UN Universal Periodic Review – Third Session of the UPR Working Group of the UN Human Rights Council (AFR 16/003/2008)

Rape in Burundi – demand justice now!, 21 July 2008

CAMBODIA

KINGDOM OF CAMBODIA

Head of state:	King Norodom Sihamoni
Head of government:	Hun Sen
Death penalty:	abolitionist for all crimes
Population:	14.7 million
Life expectancy:	58 years
Under-5 mortality (m/f):	92/84 per 1,000
Adult literacy:	73.6 per cent

Impunity, inadequate rule of law and serious shortcomings in the court system continued to cause a systemic lack of protection for human rights. Forced evictions, carried out with the direct involvement or complicity of government authorities, further impoverished thousands of marginalized Cambodians. Human rights defenders and community activists defending land and natural resources were imprisoned on baseless charges. Freedom of expression and assembly were restricted.

Background

In October, the Asian Development Bank warned that 2 million Cambodians may have slipped below the poverty line as the cost of food, fuel and other commodities rose amid the global financial crisis. This was in addition to the 4.5 million, around a third of the population, already living in poverty.

In July, the ruling Cambodian People's Party won National Assembly elections. The opposition had been weakened by internal and external political strife, and intimidation of voters, journalists and activists.

In September, the UN Human Rights Council replaced the Special Representative of the Secretary General for Human Rights in Cambodia with a Special Rapporteur of the Council for one year, retaining the mandate's functions. The mandate holder, Professor Yash Ghai, resigned deploring the government's refusal to co-operate with him.

In July, UNESCO listed the Preah Vihear Temple near the Thai border as a World Heritage Site. A territorial dispute with Thailand followed over ownership of land adjacent to the temple. Tension was periodically high as thousands of troops from both sides mobilized in the area. In October, two Cambodian soldiers were shot dead.

Forced evictions

Forced evictions continued in the wake of land disputes, land grabs, and agro-industrial and urban redevelopment projects. Thousands of forcibly evicted people did not receive an effective remedy, including restitution of housing, land or property. During the year, at least 27 forced evictions affected some 23,000 people. The government denied that forced evictions had taken place. The criminal justice system was increasingly used by the rich and powerful to silence those protecting their right to adequate housing and Indigenous Peoples protecting their land rights and way of life. Around 150 land activists and affected people were arrested during the year, many of them facing prosecution on spurious criminal charges.
■ Over 4,000 Phnom Penh families living around Boeung Kak Lake faced displacement as the lake was turned into a landfill site. Many of those affected lived in poverty in basic housing. Residents were given no notice before the landfill began on 26 August. Threats from local authorities and company workers against protesters were widespread.

Freedom of expression

Journalist Khim Sambor and his son were killed on 11 July during the election campaign. The killings followed an article by Khim Sambor in the opposition affiliated newspaper *Moneaksekar Khmer* (Khmer Conscience) alleging serious illegal actions by an unnamed senior government official. The killing spread fear among journalists. Nine journalists have been killed since 1994 – to date no-one has been brought to justice.

In the pre-election period, authorities closed down an independent radio station for allowing airtime to opposition parties, and the editor of *Moneaksekar Khmer (Khmer Conscience)* was briefly detained for reporting on a speech by the main opposition leader Sam Rainsy.

Impunity

The Supreme Court heard the appeal of Born Samnang and Sok Sam Oeun on 31 December and decided to send the case back to the Appeal Court for reinvestigation and to release the two men on bail. They had been convicted of the 2004 killing of union leader Chea Vichea. Both had alibis for the time of the killing.

In September, a Phnom Penh Court judge confirmed that the investigation into the 2007 killing of union leader Hy Vuthy had been closed due to lack of evidence.

In April, an International Labour Organization fact-finding mission to assess the progress of an investigation by authorities into the killing of three trade unionists concluded that the lack of an independent judiciary was a key factor behind the government's failure to stem violence and attacks against union members.

Breaking a cycle of impunity, five former Khmer Rouge soldiers were tried for their role in the 1996 abduction and killing of a British de-miner and his interpreter. Four of them were convicted and sentenced to long prison terms.

Detention without trial

Police in Phnom Penh increased night-time raids, arbitrarily arresting sex workers, homeless people and beggars. According to victims and witnesses, sex workers were routinely rounded up and forced – often with violence or threats – into trucks. Many arrests violated Cambodia's Criminal Procedure Code and international law. Some detainees were transferred to "education" or "rehabilitation" centres run by the municipal Social Affairs Department, where at least three detainees had been beaten to death, and women had been gang-raped by guards. The two centres remained operational at the end of the year, but the government issued assurances that those staying there did so voluntarily.

International justice
Several pre-trial hearings were held at the Extraordinary Chambers in the Courts of Cambodia (ECCC, the Khmer Rouge tribunal). However the first trial to take place, that of Kaing Guek Eav (also known as Duch), was postponed till 2009 following a decision by co-prosecutors to seek a broader indictment.

Amid continued corruption allegations both the UN and Cambodian sides of the Court agreed to establish an anti-corruption programme. This led a number of Cambodian staff to report they had to pay kickbacks to secure their jobs.

In September, a transgender woman submitted the first complaint to the ECCC about gender-related abuse under the Khmer Rouge, including sexual violence in the form of gang rape in detention, and forced marriage.

By year's end, the ECCC's Victims Unit had received over 1,100 civil party applications, 34 of which had been accepted, and about 1,700 complaints from victims.

Legal, constitutional or institutional developments
The new criminal code, which took 14 years to draft, was not passed; at the end of the year it was being reviewed by the Council of Ministers.

The anti-corruption law was not passed despite being a high priority for Cambodia's international donors. In May, a coalition of over 40 NGOs presented a petition signed and thumb-printed by over a million Cambodians calling on the National Assembly to adopt the law and take other steps to curb corruption.

In September, Prime Minister Hun Sen stated his intention to ensure a law on associations was passed, partly in order to increase control over NGO funding and objectives. NGOs countrywide expressed serious concern that the law would place further restrictions on their activities.

A new anti-trafficking law, adopted in March 2008, was criticized for focusing on the arrest and detention of sex workers instead of traffickers.

Amnesty International visits/reports
🚃 Amnesty International visited Cambodia in February/March and October.

📖 Cambodia: Release scapegoats for labor leader's murder (ASA 23/001/2008)

📖 Rights Razed – Forced evictions in Cambodia (ASA 23/002/2008)

📖 Cambodia: Ignoring the rights of Indigenous Peoples (ASA 23/008/2008)

📖 Cambodia: A risky business – defending the right to housing (ASA 23/014/2008)

CAMEROON

REPUBLIC OF CAMEROON

Head of state:	Paul Biya
Head of government:	Ephraim Inoni
Death penalty:	abolitionist in practice
Population:	18.9 million
Life expectancy:	49.8 years
Under-5 mortality (m/f):	150/136 per 1,000
Adult literacy:	67.9 per cent

In February the security forces killed as many as 100 people during protests against price rises and against a constitutional amendment that would extend the President's term of office. As part of a strategy to stifle opposition, the authorities perpetrated or condoned human rights violations including arbitrary arrests, unlawful detentions and restrictions on the rights to freedom of expression, association and assembly. Human rights defenders and journalists were harassed and threatened. Men and women were detained because of their sexual orientation.

Background
In late February, riots erupted in a number of towns, including the political capital, Yaoundé, and the economic capital, Douala. The protesters were demonstrating against the escalating cost of living, low wages and plans by the government to amend the Constitution to remove a provision barring President

Paul Biya from standing as a presidential candidate in 2011.

Tens of thousands of Chadians fled to northern Cameroon in February when armed political groups attacked Chad's capital, N'Djamena.

On 14 August, Nigeria handed over the oil-rich Bakassi peninsula to Cameroon, in accordance with a 10 October 2002 ruling by the International Court of Justice. Armed groups thought to originate in Nigeria launched several attacks on government and security installations in the peninsula, killing a number of members of the Cameroonian security forces and government officials.

Unlawful killings

The security forces routinely used excessive and unnecessary lethal force and no investigations were carried out into unlawful killings by members of the security forces.

■ In late February, the security forces killed as many as 100 people when repressing violent protests across the country. Some people were apparently shot in the head at point-blank range. In Douala, some were reported to have drowned after being forced to jump into the Wouri river under fire. Many people with gunshot wounds were denied medical care and some died as a result.

■ On 29 June, dozens of prisoners escaped from New Bell prison in Douala. Fifteen were reportedly shot dead by prison guards and other security forces in the ensuing manhunt. The next day René Mireille Bouyam, who lived beside the prison, was shot and fatally wounded when a prisoner was found hiding in his house. The prisoner was also shot dead.

Freedom of expression – journalists

Journalists reporting corruption or critical of the government faced arbitrary arrest and politically motivated defamation charges. The authorities shut down Equinoxe television station and two radio stations, Radio Equinoxe and Magic FM, in February. Several journalists covering the February protests were assaulted by the security forces. The government allowed the stations to resume broadcasting in July, but Magic FM was unable to do so because its equipment had been seized and apparently destroyed.

■ On 27 February, Eric Golf Kouatchou, a cameraman at the Canal 2 International television station, was arrested on his way to cover protests in Bonanjo near Douala. His equipment was confiscated and he and 36 other young men were detained and beaten before being released.

■ Marie Noëlle Guichi and Jean-François Channon of Le Messager were arrested on 3 June after reporting a corruption scandal linked to the purchase of a defective presidential jet. Although the two journalists were granted bail, they faced imprisonment if convicted.

■ On 15 October, police in Yaoundé arrested three newspaper editors who were planning to publish articles accusing the director of an educational institution of taking bribes. Max Mbida of Le Tenor de l'Info was reportedly held for a few days. Armand Ondoua of Le Régional and Zacharie Flash Diemo of Le Zénith were still held at the end of the year.

Human rights defenders

Human rights defenders who criticized the government's human rights record faced harassment and threats.

■ Alhadji Mey Ali, president of OS-Civile human rights group in Extreme-North Province, was arrested on 20 February and tried the following day. He was sentenced to one year's imprisonment and a fine of 1 million CFA francs (nearly US$2,000) after the High Court convicted him of criminal defamation.

■ Madeleine Afite of ACAT-Littoral (Actions des Chrétiens pour l'Abolition de la Torture, Christian Action for the Abolition of Torture) received death threats and her car was wrecked in early March after she denounced abuses during the February riots.

■ On 28 March, a procuracy official in Maroua reportedly telephoned and threatened Abdoulaye Math, president of the Movement for the Defence of Human Rights and Freedoms (MDDHL). On 3 April, guards at Maroua prison denied Abdoulaye Math access to detainees he had been asked by the Court of Appeal to represent in court.

Freedom of assembly

The security forces used violence, arbitrary arrests and unlawful detentions to prevent opposition political activists from holding meetings.

■ Mboua Massock ma Batalon was arrested on 16 February in Zoétélé to prevent him from holding a public rally to demand the President's resignation. During skirmishes at the rally, gendarmes and police arrested several people including Mboua Massock's son, Camille Massock, reportedly beating him severely. Those arrested were released without charge within a few days.

■ Paul Eric Kingué, mayor of Njombé-Penja county in Nkongsamba, Littoral Province, was arrested on 29 February and accused of involvement in the riots and inciting revolt. He claimed that he was arrested because he had challenged tax evasion by French farmers and powerful elements in the government.

Arbitrary arrests and detentions

Political opponents of the government were arbitrarily arrested and detained. Those targeted included members of the Social Democratic Front (SDF), the main opposition party, and the Southern Cameroons National Council (SCNC) – a group supporting independence for anglophone provinces.

■ At least 20 SCNC members, including Fidelis Chinkwo Ndeh, were arrested in Bamenda on 10 February and at least seven were arrested the following day. At the end of the year, nearly 40 members of the SCNC were awaiting trial on charges ranging from wearing SCNC T-shirts to agitating for secession.

■ At least 23 members of the main faction of the SDF were detained without trial for more than two and a half years, accused of killing Grégoire Diboulé, a member of a dissident SDF faction, in May 2006. In November, the High Court in Yaoundé ordered the unconditional release of one of the detainees and the provisional release of the others. The leader of the SDF, John Ni Fru Ndi, was also charged with the killing but had not been detained by the end of the year.

Unfair trials

More than 1,500 people arrested during the February protests were brought to trial unusually swiftly, with little or no time to prepare their defence. Many of the defendants had no legal counsel, while others were denied time to consult their lawyers. The trials were summary in nature. Hundreds of defendants were sentenced to between three months and two years in prison. Despite a presidential amnesty in June, hundreds remained in prison at the end of the year, either because they had appealed or because they could not afford to pay court-imposed fines.

■ Two musicians and political activists, Pierre Roger Lambo Sandjo (also known as Lapiro de Mbanga) and Joe de Vinci Kameni (also known as Joe La Conscience), were arrested in March and April respectively, after singing songs critical of the President. Joe de Vinci Kameni was convicted of inciting people to demonstrate and sentenced to six

months' imprisonment. Pierre Roger Lambo Sandjo was convicted of complicity in the riots and sentenced to three years' imprisonment and a large fine. Joe de Vinci Kameni was among 139 prisoners released in an amnesty on 16 June.

Rights of lesbian, gay, bisexual and transgender people

The Penal Code criminalizes same-sex sexual relations. Homophobia is endemic in Cameroonian society and prosecutions of suspected gay men leading to imprisonment continued on a regular basis.

■ Two men were convicted in March of same-sex acts and sentenced to six months' imprisonment and a fine. They were released because they had already spent more than six months in custody. The detainees had been subjected to humiliating anal examinations.

■ In May, police in Lomié, Eastern Province, arrested two young women on suspicion of same-sex acts. While in custody, the police reportedly forced the two women to denounce four others as their "accomplices".

Prison conditions

Prisons and other detention centres were habitually overcrowded and unhygienic. Medical care and food were often not provided. Children were held together with adults and, at times, men were held together with women. Disturbances and escape attempts were frequent. Prison guards were poorly trained and equipped.

■ At least 10 inmates died and as many as 78 sustained injuries after a fire broke out at New Bell prison on 20 August. New Bell prison was built in the 1930s for a prisoner population of 700 inmates but was holding nearly 4,000.

Death penalty

Courts continued to impose the death penalty, although no executions have been reported since 1997. On 20 May a presidential decree commuted an unspecified number of death sentences to life imprisonment.

In December Cameroon abstained on a UN General Assembly resolution calling for a worldwide moratorium on executions.

Amnesty International visits

🚗 The authorities did not grant Amnesty International access to the country.

CANADA

CANADA
Head of state: Queen Elizabeth II, represented by Governor
General Michaëlle Jean
Head of government: Stephen Harper
Death penalty: abolitionist for all crimes
Population: 33.2 million
Life expectancy: 80.3 years
Under-5 mortality (m/f): 6/6 per 1,000

Indigenous Peoples seeking to defend their land rights continued to face serious obstacles. The report of an inquiry into the role of Canadian officials in the detention and torture of detainees abroad found that they had contributed to violations of human rights.

Indigenous Peoples' rights

There were continuing concerns about the failure to ensure prompt and impartial resolution of disputes over land and resource rights. In August, the UN Committee on the Elimination of Racial Discrimination expressed concern about plans to construct a gas pipeline through lands in Alberta over which the Lubicon Cree continue to assert rights. The Alberta Utilities Commission ignored these concerns when it approved the project in October.

In September, the Canadian Human Rights Commission ordered an inquiry into a complaint about disparity in funding for Indigenous child protection agencies.

The government continued to assert that the UN Declaration on the Rights of Indigenous Peoples was not applicable in Canada because Canada had voted against its adoption.

In Ontario there was slow progress in implementing the 2007 report from the Ipperwash Inquiry into the circumstances surrounding the 1995 police shooting of Dudley George, an unarmed Indigenous man involved in a land protest.

Ontario Provincial Police used excessive force during land rights protests in and near Tyendinaga Mohawk Territory in 2007 and 2008.

Women's rights

In October, the UN Committee on the Elimination of All Forms of Discrimination against Women called on Canada to "take the necessary steps to remedy the deficiencies in the system" with respect to murdered or missing Indigenous women. The Committee also called for restrictions on funding the advocacy activities of women's groups to be lifted and for the establishment of an oversight mechanism for women prisoners.

Counter-terror and security

In February the government enacted reforms to the immigration security certificate system, following a 2007 Supreme Court of Canada decision, but the system remained unfair. Five men subject to certificates were released while court proceedings continued, some on very restrictive bail conditions. One man, Hassan Almrei, had been detained since October 2001.

In March, the Federal Court dismissed a challenge to the practice of transferring battlefield detainees in Afghanistan into Afghan custody where they were at serious risk of torture. This decision was upheld by the Federal Court of Appeal in December.

In October, a report was released of an inquiry into the role of Canadian officials in the cases of Abdullah Almalki, Ahmed El-Maati and Muayyed Nureddin, all Canadian citizens who were detained and tortured abroad. The report identified numerous ways in which the actions of Canadian officials contributed to violations of their rights.

The government continued to refuse to intervene with US officials regarding the case of Canadian citizen Omar Khadr, arrested in Afghanistan when he was 15 years old and held for more than six years at Guantánamo Bay.

Refugees and asylum-seekers

In June, the Federal Court of Appeal reversed, on procedural grounds, a 2007 Federal Court ruling that the Safe Third Country refugee agreement between Canada and the USA violated the Charter of Rights and international law.

Police and security forces

A provincial public inquiry was initiated into the October 2007 death of Polish national Robert Dziekanski at Vancouver International Airport after being Tasered by officers of the Royal Canadian Mounted Police (RCMP). The Office of the Commissioner for Public Complaints against the RCMP issued a report calling for restrictions on the

C

use of Tasers. Four people died during the year after being shocked by police with a Taser.

Death penalty

In September, the Federal Court heard an application by Canadian Ronald Smith, who was sentenced to death in the US state of Montana in 1983. Ronald Smith challenged the new policy of the Canadian government of not seeking clemency for Canadians sentenced to death in countries which it considered to be democratic and to adhere to the rule of law. The Court had not issued a decision by the end of the year.

Amnesty International reports

🗐 Canada: Amnesty International Submission to the UN Universal Periodic Review – Fourth session of the UPR Working Group of the Human Rights Council, February 2009 (AMR 20/004/2008)

🗐 Land and a way of life under threat – The Lubicon Cree of Canada (AMR 20/006/2008)

🗐 Canada: Unequal Rights – Ongoing concerns about Discrimination against Women in Canada (AMR 20/008/2008)

CENTRAL AFRICAN REPUBLIC

CENTRAL AFRICAN REPUBLIC

Head of state:	François Bozizé
Head of government:	Faustin Archange Touadéra (replaced Elie Doté in January)
Death penalty:	abolitionist in practice
Population:	4.4 million
Life expectancy:	43.7 years
Under-5 mortality (m/f):	178/145 per 1,000
Adult literacy:	48.6 per cent

Dozens of men, women and children were abducted by members of the Ugandan Lord's Resistance Army (LRA) armed group, who raped women and girls and ill-treated many other people. Government forces and armed political groups unlawfully killed civilians. Many detainees were ill-treated while being unlawfully held in life-threatening conditions, after arbitrary arrests. Human rights defenders and a journalist were threatened or detained for carrying out their professional activities. One person against whom an arrest warrant was issued by the International Criminal Court (ICC) was arrested and handed over to the court.

Background

Prime Minister Elie Doté resigned in January when the National Assembly threatened to censure him. He was replaced by Faustin Archange Touadéra.

The government signed peace agreements with several armed political groups as a prelude to a national conference, known as the National Inclusive Dialogue, to pave the way for national reconciliation, political stability and to create conditions for general elections in 2010. The agreements culminated in the signing of a comprehensive peace agreement in June. In February, the Benin government released two armed group leaders at the request of the Central African Republic (CAR) government. Abakar Sabone and Michel Djotodia had been detained without trial in the Benin capital, Cotonou, since November 2006. In October, the government released 12 suspected members of armed political groups.

Former President Ange-Félix Patassé, former Defence Minister Jean-Jacques Demafouth and several armed group leaders returned from exile in November and December to participate in the national conference which started on 8 December, chaired by former Burundian President Pierre Buyoya. The conference ended on 20 December with a resolution to form a government of national unity charged with preparing general elections.

Despite the peace agreements, sporadic clashes between government forces and armed political groups continued to be reported. Government and opposition forces attacked civilians suspected of supporting their opponents, killing and wounding many of them, as well as destroying or looting their property. Tens of thousands continued to be internally displaced as a result of the violence.

At least 200 members of the EU military force (EUFOR) and three military liaison officers of the UN Mission in Chad and the CAR (MINURCAT) were deployed in the CAR to protect civilians and humanitarian workers in north-eastern CAR. In September, the EUFOR and MINURCAT mandates were extended to March 2009. In July, the Economic Community of Central African States (CEEAC) replaced the Multinational Forces in CAR (FOMUC) with the Mission for the Consolidation of Peace in Central Africa (MICOPAX), led by a commander from the Democratic Republic of Congo (DRC). MICOPAX was joined by 120 Cameroonian soldiers.

Impunity

As part of the implementation of the comprehensive peace agreement, parliament adopted in September a general amnesty law. This covered crimes by government and armed political forces between 15 March 2005, when President François Bozizé came to power, and 13 October 2008, when the law was promulgated by the President. Although the amnesty was not supposed to cover crimes committed between October 2002 and March 2003, it granted immunity to several political and military leaders of the 2002-3 armed conflict. They included former President Ange-Félix Patassé who was in power during the period, his former Defence Minister Jean-Jacques Demafouth and former presidential security aide Martin Koumtamadji. Such an amnesty law would not preclude the ICC from pursuing prosecutions for crimes under international law.

Abuses by armed groups

In late February and early March, several hundred armed men, thought to be members of the LRA, abducted more than 100 men, women and children in eastern CAR. The gunmen, who were believed to have come from north-western DRC, also raped women and girls and destroyed or looted property. Although some of the victims were released or escaped, more than 100 were believed to be still held by the LRA in December. The female victims were feared to have been used in sexual slavery, while men and boys were turned into fighters.

In mid-December, the Ugandan authorities announced that their forces, supported by troops from the DRC and South Sudan, had launched military operations against the LRA. There were fears that many children and other civilians previously or newly abducted by the LRA would be killed during clashes.

International justice

Jean-Pierre Bemba, a former leader of an armed group and politician from the DRC, was arrested in Belgium on 24 May and transferred into the custody of the ICC. The pre-trial chamber of the ICC had issued a sealed arrest warrant for war crimes and crimes against humanity, including rape, committed in the CAR by members of his armed political group in late 2002 and early 2003. In December, the pre-trial chamber postponed to January 2009 the examination of the validity of the charges against Jean-Pierre Bemba and remanded him in custody.

Human rights defenders and journalists

Journalists and human rights defenders were arrested or threatened for their professional activities.

■ Faustin Bambou was arrested in January after his newspaper, *Les Collines de l'Oubangui*, published an article in December 2007 alleging that government ministers had embezzled funds intended to pay government employees' salary arrears. Following an unfair trial, he was sentenced on 28 January to six months' imprisonment. He was released on 23 February after being granted an amnesty by President Bozizé.

■ In June, an unidentified man who claimed to be a member of the security forces told Nganatoua Goungaye Wanfiyo, a lawyer and leader of the Central African Human Rights League, that he might be assaulted or even killed. The security forces reportedly suspected him of pursuing efforts to have President Bozizé investigated and prosecuted by the ICC. Nganatoua Goungaye Wanfiyo was arbitrarily arrested and detained for one day in September. He was accused of hindering a presidential convoy although he was not charged with any offence. He died in a traffic accident at the end of December.

Human rights activists Bernadette Sayo and Erick Kpakpo received anonymous death threats for their work in supporting victims of the 2002 and 2003 armed conflict atrocities seeking justice.

Torture and other ill-treatment

Detainees in various detention centres and prisons around the country were reported to have been subjected to torture and other forms of cruel, inhuman or degrading treatment. Some of the detainees, described by law enforcement and judicial officials as recalcitrant, were chained and deprived of food and water for several days at a time. Some detainees spent more than two weeks without being allowed to take a bath.

Detainees who became ill in custody or injured as a result of beatings were not allowed access to medical care. In at least one case in Bouar, detainees were held in a windowless and constantly locked cell where they used a bucket as a toilet which was emptied once every two days. Detention centres where these abuses took place included Bossangoa and Bouar in the north and the Central Office for the Repression of Banditry in the capital, Bangui.

Unlawful killings

Throughout the year, government forces and members of armed groups were reported to have unlawfully killed civilians suspected of supporting their respective opponents. Those responsible enjoyed impunity. In at least one case in March in Bouar, government forces paraded in the streets with freshly severed human heads which they claimed were of bandits. The authorities are not known to have taken action against government forces reported to have been involved in unlawful killings.

Arbitrary arrests and unlawful detentions

Government forces carried out arbitrary arrests without the authority of a judicial official and held detainees without charge beyond the 48 hours allowed by the country's Code of Penal Procedure.
■ On 12 January an officer of the Presidential Guard arrested Vincent Tolngar, mayor of the northern town of Markounda, on suspicion of warning the local population to flee before the arrival of the Presidential Guard. Vincent Tolngar was first detained in Bossangoa before being transferred to Bossembélé. He was released without charge or trial on 7 February.

Dozens of alleged sorcerers, most of them women, remained in custody with no prospect of being tried or released. Some were held in the Ngaragba and Bimbo prisons in Bangui. By the end of December, some had been detained for three or more years without trial.

CHAD

REPUBLIC OF CHAD
Head of state: Idriss Déby Itno
Head of government: Youssouf Saleh Abbas (replaced Nouradine Delwa Kassiré Koumakoye in April)
Death penalty: retentionist
Population: 11.1 million
Life expectancy: 50.4 years
Under-5 mortality (m/f): 195/180 per 1,000
Adult literacy: 25.7 per cent

Hundreds of civilians were killed and injured during two days of fighting in February between the Chadian army and a coalition of armed opposition groups. More than 50,000 civilians fled the country.

Civilians were victims of enforced disappearance, and some were unlawfully arrested, arbitrarily detained and tortured or otherwise ill-treated. Journalists and human rights defenders were intimidated and harassed. Children were abducted and recruited as soldiers. The security situation remained highly volatile in the east.

Thousands of people were forcibly evicted from their homes without prior consultation and no alternative accommodation or compensation was provided.

Background

On 14 February, President Déby declared a state of emergency, drastically restricting freedom of movement and expression. The decree was renewed on 29 February until 15 March. On 15 April, President Déby appointed a government led by Prime Minister Youssouf Saleh Abbas. On 23 April, four members of the opposition were appointed as ministers.

Chad and Sudan accused each other of supporting the other's opponents. In May Chad closed its border with Sudan, and Sudan then severed diplomatic relations with Chad. In November, after Libyan mediation, the two governments resumed diplomatic relations.

In the east, sporadic fighting continued between government forces and Chadian armed groups, as did intercommunal violence mainly between the Tama and Zaghawa ethnic groups. Insecurity – characterized by rape and killings – affected the population. International humanitarian personnel working in the region were at risk of banditry, notably carjacking and armed robbery.

Eastern Chad hosted more than 290,000 refugees from Sudan's Darfur region and more than 180,000 internally displaced people. Camps for refugees and the internally displaced were used by Chadian and Sudanese armed groups to recruit combatants. There were reports that weapons were being sold within refugee camps and internally displaced people's sites in the east.

The UN Security Council extended until 15 March 2009 the mandate of the UN Mission in the Central African Republic and Chad (MINURCAT). By the end of 2008, MINURCAT had representatives in N'Djamena, eastern Chad, and Bangui in the Central African Republic. Deployment of a Chadian contingent trained by MINURCAT started in September. The mandate of the European Union military operation known as EUFOR in eastern Chad and northern Central African Republic was extended to March 2009.

On 31 March, President Déby pardoned six members of the French charity L'Arche de Zoé (Zoe's Ark), who had been convicted in 2007 of abducting 103 children. A court in N'Djamena had sentenced them to eight years' imprisonment with hard labour. They were transferred to France, where a court ruled that a sentence of hard labour could not be enforced under French law and the sentence was replaced with eight years' imprisonment. In October, Chad demanded that France pay compensation to the children's families, but none had been paid by France by the end of 2008.

Armed conflict – attack on N'Djamena

On 31 January, armed opposition groups launched a major offensive on N'Djamena. For two days, heavy fighting racked the city. At least 700 civilians were killed and hundreds injured. More than 50,000 people fled to neighbouring Cameroon. The attack was carried out by a coalition of three armed groups: the Union of Forces for Democracy and Development (Union des forces pour la Démocratie et le Développement, UFDD), the Union of Forces for Democracy and Development-Fundamental (Union des forces pour la Démocratie et le Développement-Fondamentale, UFDD-Fondamentale), and the Rally of Forces for Change (Rassemblement des Forces pour le Changement, RFC).

The report of a government-appointed National Commission of Inquiry to investigate the violence was made public in September. It concluded that most human rights abuses were committed after armed groups had left the city and recommended the establishment of a follow-up committee to implement its recommendations. President Déby set up a follow-up committee composed only of government ministers in September. Civil society organizations called for a more independent committee.

Enforced disappearances

The authorities refused to disclose the whereabouts of men who disappeared after they were arrested by government forces.

■ The fate and whereabouts of more than 14 army officers and civilians arrested in April 2006 on suspicion of involvement in a 2006 attack on N'Djamena remained unknown.

■ Six members of the Tama ethnic group arrested in Guéréda in November 2007 remained disappeared. Harun Mahamat, the Sultan of Dar Tama Department, who had been arrested with the six men, was released on 3 May after being transferred to a N'Djamena military facility.

■ The National Commission of Inquiry failed to establish the whereabouts of opposition leader Ibni Oumar Mahamat Saleh who was arrested on 3 February by government forces. It suggested that he was probably dead.

Arbitrary arrests and detentions

Security personnel and soldiers arrested and detained civilians, particularly after the attack on N'Djamena.

■ Three opposition leaders – former President Lol Mahamat Choua, Ngarlegy Yorongar and Ibni Oumar Mahamat Saleh – were arrested by security forces on 3 February. Lol Mahamat was later released and Ngarlegy Yorongar resurfaced in Cameroon. Ibni Oumar Mahamat Saleh disappeared (see above).

Excessive use of force

The security forces used excessive and unnecessary lethal force against civilians.

■ At least 68 followers of Sheikh Ahmet Ismael Bichara and four gendarmes were killed on 29 June in Kouno, when gendarmes opened fire indiscriminately as they attempted to arrest the sheikh who had reportedly

C

threatened to launch a jihad. He was later arrested with five of his assistants and transferred to a detention centre in N'Djamena.

Extrajudicial executions

Government forces extrajudicially executed civilians in the wake of the attack on N'Djamena. A number of bodies, including that of Adam Bachir Abeldielil, were recovered along the banks of the Chari River. Similar killings were reported in the east. The government took no action to bring those suspected of the killings to justice.

■ Doungous Ngar was arrested by security forces on 5 February and the next day his body was found in a hospital mortuary in N'Djamena. He was arrested at his workplace by soldiers who accused him of stealing a motorbike, tied up his hands and feet and put him in a military vehicle.

■ Adam Hassan and Bineye Mahamat, two shopkeepers in Farcha, a suburb of N'Djamena, were arrested on 23 February by soldiers who accused them of supporting the armed opposition. They were beaten and thrown in the soldiers' vehicle. Their bodies were found on the banks of the Chari River.

Violence against women and girls

Girls and young women continued to be victims of rape and other forms of sexual violence. Displaced girls were raped when they ventured out of their camps. A number of rapes by Chadian soldiers were reported in the aftermath of the attack on N'Djamena, often in the context of house searches for arms and looted goods.

The practice of female genital mutilation continued and forced marriages were imposed, including in camps for refugees and the internally displaced.

■ On 21 May, a 55-year-old mother of five was raped by three government soldiers guarding a crossing point across a trench dug around N'Djamena to protect the city from armed attack. She later fled to Cameroon to escape social stigma.

Forced evictions

The government ordered the demolition of thousands of homes in N'Djamena, leaving tens of thousands homeless, following a 22 February presidential decree. The N'Djamena municipal council claimed that the destroyed houses had been built without authorization on government land. The government

failed to ensure prior consultation with the owners or to offer them alternative housing or compensation.

Refugees and internally displaced people

By the end of 2008, Chad was hosting nearly 250,000 refugees from Darfur in 12 camps. More than 13,000 refugees entered Chad during the year, fleeing fighting in Sudan. More than 180,000 Chadians were internally displaced. Around 50,000 refugees from the Central African Republic continued to live in southern Chad.

Death penalty

In August, a Chadian judge convicted and sentenced to death exiled former President Hissène Habré and 11 armed opposition leaders, including Timane Erdimi, leader of the Rally of Forces for Change, and Mahamat Nouri, leader of the National Alliance. The court convicted them in their absence for crimes against Chad's "constitutional order, territorial integrity and security."

Child soldiers

Both the Chadian army and armed groups continued to recruit and use child soldiers. According to the UN, there were between 7,000 and 10,000 children serving in armed groups and the Chadian army.

In the east, Sudanese armed groups – the Toro Boro and the Justice and Equality Movement – recruited children from refugee camps. The Chadian United Front for Democratic Change (Front uni pour le changement démocratique) also recruited children from refugee and internally displaced camps.

Freedom of expression – journalists

Journalists continued to be subjected to intimidation, harassment and arrest. Journalists reporting on the conflict in the east or on relations with Sudan were accused of being "enemies of the state".

No criticism of the authorities was tolerated, and a number of journalists were forced to flee the country. During the state of emergency, a presidential decree restricted press freedom and increased penalties that could be imposed on journalists. The decree remained in force after the end of the state of emergency in March.

■ On 16 January, police arrested Maji-maji Oudjitan, programme coordinator of FM Liberté, and shut the

C

radio station down. It reopened on 27 May on the orders of the new Prime Minister. The station's director, Djekourninga Kaoutar Lazare, was detained from 16 to 22 January.

■ On 16 February, Sonia Roley, correspondent for Radio France Internationale (RFI) and the only international journalist who remained in the country, had her accreditation withdrawn, forcing her to leave Chad.

Human rights defenders

Human rights defenders faced threats, attacks and arrests.

■ On 28 July, the Minister of Internal Affairs ordered the closure of the Chadian Association of Victims of Political Repression and Crime. On 31 July, the organization's president, Clément Abaïfouta, was arrested, accused of inciting ethnic hatred, forgery and use of forged documents. He was released on 1 August but continued to suffer harassment.

■ Deouzoumbé Daniel Passalet, President of Human Rights Without Borders, was arrested on 9 January after commenting on the enforced disappearance of a government official. In February, he went into hiding.

Abuses by armed groups

In eastern Chad, various Chadian and Sudanese armed groups subjected civilians to killings, rapes, child recruitment and kidnappings for ransom. They also attacked humanitarian workers.

Unlawful killings of civilians in the east by armed groups continued throughout 2008. People were also killed in intercommunal clashes, especially between members of the Tama and Zaghawa ethnic groups. Many of the killings occurred in April, particularly in Guéréda.

Violence broke out in July between the Moro and Dadjo ethnic groups in Kerfi, eastern Chad. A senior Moro official was killed in the clashes and thousands of Dadjo were forced to flee the area.

■ In April, Ramadan Djom, a driver for Save The Children UK, was killed by armed men near the Sudanese border. On 1 May, Pascal Marlinge, the organization's country director, was shot dead by gunmen between Farchana and Hajir Hadid, close to the Sudanese border.

Children were abducted by armed bandits for ransom, and were killed if their parents failed to pay.

Amnesty International visit/reports

🚌 Amnesty International delegates visited Chad in May.

📄 Double misfortune: The deepening human rights crisis in Chad (AFR 20/007/2008)

📄 Chad: Security forces shot 68 people in an attempt to arrest a Muslim spiritual leader (AFR 20/006/2008)

CHILE

REPUBLIC OF CHILE

Head of state and government:	Michelle Bachelet
Death penalty:	abolitionist for ordinary crimes
Population:	16.8 million
Life expectancy:	78.3 years
Under-5 mortality (m/f):	10/8 per 1,000
Adult literacy:	95.7 per cent

There was some progress in bringing perpetrators of human rights violations to justice. Indigenous Peoples and those defending their rights continued to face human rights violations. Social protests were increasingly criminalized, with police at times accused of excessive use of force against demonstrators.

Background

There were demonstrations, at times violent, throughout the year, on issues including education, Indigenous Peoples' rights and rising living costs.

A bill to bring domestic legislation into line with the Rome Statute of the International Criminal Court was before Congress at the end of the year.

The Inter-American Commission on Human Rights' Special Rapporteur on the Rights of Persons Deprived of Liberty visited prisons in Chile in August. The Rapporteur found some good practices, but condemned excessive use of force in punishment, an unprecedented level of overcrowding in state-run prisons and inadequate provision of basic services in juvenile detention centres.

On 15 September, Chile ratified International Labour Organization Convention 169 on Indigenous Peoples' rights after withdrawing a controversial interpretative declaration.

Indigenous Peoples' rights

Tensions between Indigenous Peoples – particularly the Mapuche – and the authorities remained high. The expansion of extractive and forestry industries continued and the resolution of land claims was slow. There were continuing allegations of human rights violations. In April, the government launched a policy framework for Indigenous Peoples' rights.

■ On 3 January, Matías Valentín Catrileo Quezada, a 23-year-old Mapuche student, died after being shot during a protest over land rights in Vilcún commune, Araucanía region. After initial inconsistencies in the autopsy and forensic investigations, it was confirmed that he had been shot in the back. A member of the Special Police Force (Fuerzas especiales de carabineros) was accused of the shooting and was on bail at the end of the year awaiting trial on charges of "unnecessary violence causing death".

■ In November, a regional prosecutor in Temuco charged three students linked to the Mapuche cause, one of whom was 16 years old, under an anti-terrorism law dating from the military government of Augusto Pinochet. The charge related to their alleged involvement in a Molotov bomb (home-made incendiary) attack on police. The government had given repeated assurances that it did not support the application of anti-terrorist legislation in cases involving Indigenous protests.

Justice and impunity

According to official figures, 1,125 cases of human rights violations committed during the military government of Augusto Pinochet (1973-1990) remained open; 3,195 had been subject to investigation. By the end of 2008, 245 members of the security forces had been convicted in connection with 115 cases.

There were important verdicts and developments in several high-profile cases.

■ In March, 24 retired senior military police officers were convicted of the kidnapping, murder and torture of 31 people in Osorno in October and November 1973. Sentences ranged from four years' imprisonment to life.

■ In June, Manuel Contreras, the former head of the National Intelligence Directorate (Dirección de Inteligencia Nacional, DINA) was found guilty of the 1974 car bomb killings of former army Commander-in-Chief Carlos Prats González and his wife in Argentina. The judge added two life sentences plus 20 years to the time Manuel Contreras was already serving in prison. Seven other former DINA agents and two civilians received sentences of up to 20 years' imprisonment.

■ In October, retired General Arellano Stark was sentenced to six years' imprisonment for his role in the killings of four political prisoners in 1973 as head of the Caravan of Death. Four other officers were given sentences of between four and six years. This was the first conviction in relation to the 72 killings carried out by the Caravan of Death in the north of Chile. In November it was confirmed that Arellano Stark would not be imprisoned for health reasons.

■ Nineteen navy officials, some still on active service, were charged in connection with the kidnapping of the priest Miguel Woodward. All were granted bail. Investigations confirmed that Miguel Woodward died under torture in 1973 and had been detained on the Navy ship *Esmeralda*, which remained in service as part of the Navy's fleet. The judge presiding over the case was threatened and witnesses were harassed as they entered the court.

■ In July, the former Temuco military prosecutor, Alfonso Podlech, was detained in Spain. An international arrest warrant had been issued in connection with his role in the disappearance of four Italian-Chilean citizens, including the priest Omar Venturelli in 1973. Alfonso Podlech was later extradited to Italy where he remained in preventive detention at the end of the year.

Police and security forces

Police were accused of ill-treating detainees and of using excessive force against demonstrators.

■ During a protest on 21 May in Valparaíso, an officer on horseback struck Victor Salas, a photographer, in the face with a metal baton. As a result Victor Salas suffered a severe loss of vision with long-term consequences. An internal inquiry failed to identify the perpetrator and subsequent investigations were not conclusive.

Amnesty International visit/reports

🚗 In November, Amnesty International's Secretary General visited Chile and met President Bachelet and other senior government officials.

▦ Memorandum to the Chilean Government (AMR 22/009/2008)

▦ Chile: Submission to the UN Universal Periodic Review – Fifth session of the UPR Working Group of the Human Rights Council, May 2009 (AMR 22/010/2008)

CHINA

PEOPLE'S REPUBLIC OF CHINA

Head of state:	Hu Jintao
Head of government:	Wen Jiabao
Death penalty:	retentionist
Population:	1,336.3 million
Life expectancy:	72.5 years
Under-5 mortality (m/f):	24/34 per 1,000
Adult literacy:	90.9 per cent

The Olympic Games in Beijing brought heightened repression throughout the country as authorities tightened control over human rights defenders, religious practitioners, ethnic minorities, lawyers and journalists. Following protests and unrest which began in March in Lhasa the government originally detained over 1,000 people. Hundreds remained in detention or were unaccounted for at year's end. The authorities used a series of violent incidents alleged to be linked to terrorists to launch a sweeping crackdown on the Uighur population in the Xinjiang Uighur Autonomous Region (XUAR). Torture and other ill-treatment remained widespread. The authorities maintained tight control over the flow of information, with many internet websites blocked, and journalists and internet users harassed and imprisoned for the peaceful expression of opinions. The authorities made increased use of punitive forms of administrative detention, notably the Re-education through Labour system, to silence critics in the lead-up to the Olympic Games.

Human rights defenders

Individuals who peacefully exercised their rights to freedom of expression, assembly and association remained at high risk of harassment, house arrest, arbitrary detention, and torture and other ill-treatment. Family members of human rights activists, including children, were increasingly targeted by the authorities, including being subjected to long-term house arrest and harassment by security forces. Lawyers who took on sensitive cases were also at risk; several had their licences suspended, and others lost their jobs. Some lawyers were specifically warned by the authorities not to take on sensitive cases, including cases of Tibetans arrested during the unrest in Tibetan areas and Falun Gong practitioners.

■ Chen Guangcheng, blind activist and legal adviser, continued to suffer ill-treatment in prison. He is serving a prison sentence of four years and three months after he tried to hold local officials in Shandong accountable for conducting forced abortions and sterilizations in order to enforce birth quotas. His wife, Yuan Weijing, continued to suffer police harassment, particularly in the lead-up to the Beijing Olympics, and remained under tight police surveillance.

Justice system and unfair trials

The criminal justice system remained highly vulnerable to political interference. The courts, the prosecuting organ (procuratorate) and the police remained under the supervision of the Chinese Communist Party. The authorities continued to use broad and vaguely defined provisions of the criminal law relating to state security and "state secrets" to silence dissent and punish human rights defenders. Many of those charged under "state secrets" provisions received unfair trials and, in accordance with criminal procedure law provisions, were not given the protections afforded to other criminal suspects regarding access to legal counsel and family, and open trials.

Arbitrary arrests and detentions

The authorities intensified their use of administrative forms of detention which allowed police to incarcerate individuals without trial. Hundreds of thousands of individuals were in administrative detention, including in Re-education through Labour camps, where they may be detained for up to four years without trial. Secret detention centres on the outskirts of Beijing, referred to as "black jails", reportedly detained thousands of petitioners – individuals seeking redress from central authorities for a wide variety of grievances they were unable to resolve locally – before they were forcibly returned to their home towns. Detainees in administrative detention remained at high risk of torture and other ill-treatment. In November, the UN Committee Against Torture (CAT) called upon China to "immediately abolish all forms of administrative detention".

■ In June, police detained Sichuan-based human rights activist Huang Qi on suspicion of "unlawful holding of documents classified as highly secret". The reason for his detention was unclear, but appeared to be connected to his work assisting the families of five

C

primary school pupils who died when their school buildings collapsed in the Sichuan earthquake in May. The families were seeking compensation from local officials because they believed corruption led to poor construction standards. Huang Qi was held incommunicado for over 100 days before his first meeting with a lawyer in September. In October, he refused the authorities' offer to release him on condition he gave up human rights work. He remained in detention without trial or access to his family.

Torture and other ill-treatment

Despite legal reforms, torture and other ill-treatment continued in prisons, police stations, Re-education through Labour camps, and other unofficial detention facilities. Human rights defenders, petitioners, Tibetans, Uighurs, Falun Gong practitioners, Christians, and others practising their religion in officially unsanctioned ways were at particular risk of torture and other ill-treatment by the authorities and unidentified individuals.

Death penalty

During the year, the authorities stated their intention to increase the use of lethal injection as a "more humane" method of execution than firing squad. Amnesty International estimates a minimum of 7,000 death sentences were handed down and 1,700 executions took place. However, the authorities refused to make public national statistics on death sentences and executions and the real figure is undoubtedly higher.

In December, China voted against a UN General Assembly resolution calling for a worldwide moratorium on executions.

Freedom of expression

The government maintained strict control on freedom of expression. Internet users and journalists were at risk of harassment and imprisonment for addressing politically sensitive topics. Approximately 30 journalists and 50 other individuals remained in prison for posting their views on the internet.

Two weeks prior to the Olympics, the authorities established "protest zones" in three Beijing parks where people were allowed to demonstrate. However, no individuals were known to have received official permission to protest and the zones remained empty.

Numerous people were detained and put under surveillance in connection with their applying for permission to protest.

The authorities unblocked a number of internet websites days before the Olympics. However, many more remained blocked. In October, the authorities announced that regulations put in place in January 2007 that eased controls over foreign journalists covering the Olympics would be extended indefinitely.

The authorities questioned and harassed numerous signatories of Charter 08, which proposed a blueprint for fundamental legal and political reform in China.
■ Signatory Liu Xiaobo remained in detention at year's end.

Freedom of religion

Individuals who practised their religion outside officially sanctioned channels, including Christians, Muslims, Buddhists and others, faced harassment and persecution. The authorities harassed, detained and often ill-treated members of unsanctioned Christian house-churches, and confiscated or destroyed their church property. Falun Gong practitioners were among those most harshly persecuted by the government. In the run-up to the Beijing Olympics, thousands were reported to have been arrested, with hundreds imprisoned or assigned to Re-education through Labour camps and other forms of administrative detention where they were at risk of torture and other ill-treatment sometimes leading to death.
■ On 25 January, Yu Zhou, a well-known folk singer, graduate of Beijing University, and reportedly a Falun Gong practitioner, was arrested in Tongzhou District, Beijing, along with his wife, Xu Na, a poet and painter. On 6 February, the authorities from the Qinghe District Emergency Centre told his family that Yu Zhou had died from either diabetes or from a hunger strike, although the family maintains he was healthy at the time of his arrest. The staff at the Emergency Centre refused the family's request to view the body and for an autopsy. On 25 November, Xu Na was sentenced to three years in prison for "using a heretical organization to undermine the implementation of the law". She appealed against the sentence and is at risk of torture and other ill-treatment in detention.

Tibet Autonomous Region and surrounding Tibetan areas

Tibetan-populated areas of China remained tightly

sealed off from outside scrutiny following unrest in March. After the initial few days, protests were largely peaceful. However, the authorities reported that 21 people had been killed by violent protesters and overseas Tibetan organizations reported that over 100 Tibetans had been killed. While Chinese authorities announced that over 1,000 individuals detained in the protests had been released, overseas Tibetan organizations estimated that at least several hundred remained in detention at year's end. Exact numbers were difficult to determine because the authorities denied access to media and independent monitors. There were reports of torture and other ill-treatment in detention, in some cases resulting in death. Major monasteries and nunneries were reported to remain under virtual lock-down. Local authorities renewed the "Patriotic Education" campaign which required Tibetans to participate in collective criticism sessions of the Dalai Lama and to sign written denunciations against him. Tibetan members of the Chinese Communist Party were also targeted by this campaign, including being forced to remove their children from Tibet exile community schools, where they were obtaining religious education.

■ Paltsal Kyab, a Tibetan from Sichuan province, died on 26 May, five weeks after he had been detained by police in connection with the protests. Aged around 45, Paltsal Kyab had been present at a protest march on 17 March in Charo township in Ngaba (Ch:Aba) county. His family was not given permission to visit him in detention and had no news of his situation until 26 May when two Charo township leaders informed them of his death. When family members went to claim his body, they found it bruised and covered with blister burns, discovering later that he had internal injuries. The police told them that he had died of an illness, although relatives claimed he was healthy when first detained.

Xinjiang Uighur Autonomous Region

The Uighur Muslim population in the Xinjiang Uighur Autonomous Region (XUAR) in northwest China faced intensified persecution. The authorities used a series of violent incidents, allegedly linked to terrorists, to launch a sweeping crackdown. According to official media, almost 1,300 people were arrested during the year on terrorism, religious extremism or other state security charges, and 1,154 were formally charged and faced trials or

administrative punishments. On 14 August, Wang Lequan, Party Secretary of the XUAR, announced a "life and death" struggle against Uighur "separatism".

■ Ablikim Abdiriyim, the son of exiled Uighur human rights activist, Rebiya Kadeer, remained in Baijiahu prison on a charge of "separatism", for which he was sentenced to nine years in prison in April 2007. On 6 December 2007, during the first permitted visit since his detention, his family found him to be in extremely poor health. Prison authorities attributed this to a heart condition, suggesting that it could deteriorate further if he refused to "cooperate" or "admit his guilt". Despite ongoing requests from his family, the authorities refused to grant him parole for medical treatment.

Local authorities maintained tight control over religious practice, including prohibiting all government employees and children under the age of 18 from worshipping at mosques.

■ One hundred and sixty Uighur children, aged between eight and 14, who had been living and studying in a Hui Muslim area of Yunnan province, were reportedly arrested by police sent by the Public Security Bureau in the XUAR. They were brought to Urumqi and held in Baijiahu prison. Ten of the children were reportedly released after their parents paid 20,000 Yuan ($3,140). Those who could not pay were told that their children would be charged with participating in "illegal religious activities".

According to reports, many people sentenced to death in the XUAR, some of whom had been given death sentences with two-year reprieves, were executed in 2008. Following domestic legal practice, death sentences with two-year reprieves can be commuted to life imprisonment if individuals exhibit good behaviour during the first two years. With the exception of one Tibetan case, the XUAR remains the only region in China where individuals are executed for political crimes.

Hong Kong Special Administrative Region

In July, tens of thousands of protesters marched to demand an improvement in human rights, people's livelihoods and meaningful political participation.

Freedom of expression and assembly
Dozens of activists, Tibetan Buddhist monks, and Falun Gong practitioners were denied entry to Hong Kong before the Olympic torch relay in May and before and during the Olympics. Government restrictions on protests at equestrian venues limited

C

freedom of expression and assembly.

Refugees and asylum-seekers

Despite co-operation between the government and UN High Commissioner for Refugees, immigration laws continued to permit the deportation of asylum-seekers, including unaccompanied minors, before asylum applications had been determined. In November, the CAT expressed concerns about the lack of legal measures governing asylum and a fair and efficient refugee status determination.

In July, the Court of Appeal ruled that placing individuals in administrative detention without clear explanation of the detention policy and process was in violation of Article 5 of the Hong Kong Bill of Rights Ordinance. This resulted in the release of hundreds of detainees, including asylum-seekers and individuals at risk of torture if returned to countries of origin.

Police and security forces

The CAT criticized the police practice of automatically body searching all detainees. Official figures showed police conducted more than 1,600 strip searches between July and September. The CAT urged limiting body searches strictly to cases where they are clearly justified.

Racism

Anti-race discrimination legislation passed in July fell short of guarantees provided for in the UN Convention on the Elimination of Racial Discrimination to which Hong Kong is a party. The legislation included exemptions for many government administrative measures, as well as exemptions for discrimination based on nationality, citizenship and residency status.

Violence against women

In June, the Domestic Violence Ordinance was expanded to include abuses at the hands of present or former cohabitants and relatives who do not live in the same premises. However, violence between same-sex couples and damage to property remained unprotected.

Macao Special Administrative Region

Between October and November, the authorities conducted a 40-day public consultation on a national security bill to prohibit acts of "treason", "secession", "sedition" and "subversion". In December, the government submitted the bill to the Legislative Assembly. Vague definitions of the crimes could lead to misuse of the legislation by the authorities to suppress rights to freedom of expression and association.

Amnesty International reports

- People's Republic of China: Legacy of the Beijing Olympics – Issues and facts: Stop Executions – China's choice (ASA 17/029/2008)
- People's Republic of China: Legacy of the Beijing Olympics - Issues and facts: Fair trials for all – China's choice (ASA 17/030/2008)
- People's Republic of China: Legacy of the Beijing Olympics - Issues and Facts: Respect the rights of rights defenders – China's choice (ASA 17/031/2008)
- People's Republic of China: Legacy of the Beijing Olympics - Issues and Facts: Freedom from censorship – China's choice (ASA 17/032/2008)
- People's Republic of China: The Olympics countdown – crackdown on activists threatens Olympics legacy (ASA 17/050/2008)
- People's Republic of China: The Olympics countdown – crackdown on Tibetan protesters (ASA 17/070/2008)
- People's Republic of China: Tibet Autonomous Region - Access Denied (ASA 17/085/2008)
- People's Republic of China: The Olympics countdown – broken promises (ASA 17/089/2008)
- People's Republic of China: Briefing for the Committee against Torture in advance of their consideration of China's fourth periodic report, 3-21 November 2008 (ASA 17/094/2008)
- People's Republic of China: Submission to the UN Universal Periodic Review – Fourth session of the UPR Working Group of the Human Rights Council, February 2009 (ASA 17/097/2008)

COLOMBIA

REPUBLIC OF COLOMBIA

Head of state and government:	Álvaro Uribe Vélez
Death penalty:	abolitionist for all crimes
Population:	46.7 million
Life expectancy:	72.3 years
Under-5 mortality (m/f):	29/22 per 1,000
Adult literacy:	92.8 per cent

Many hundreds of thousands of people continued to be affected by the ongoing armed conflict. Civilians were the main victims of the conflict, with Indigenous Peoples, Afro-descendants and campesinos (peasant farmers) most at risk; many lived in areas of economic and strategic interest to the warring parties. All parties to the conflict – the security forces, paramilitaries and guerrilla groups – were responsible for widespread and systematic human rights abuses and violations of international humanitarian law (IHL). While some indicators of conflict-related violence, such as kidnapping and hostage-taking, continued to improve, others deteriorated. There was an increase in internal displacement and an upsurge in threats against human rights defenders and in killings of trade unionists. Killings of civilians by the security forces remained high. Paramilitaries continued to operate, despite government claims to the contrary. The killing of dozens of youths by the army led to the sacking of senior members of the military and forced the resignation of the head of the army, General Mario Montoya. Several high-profile hostages regained their freedom after years of captivity at the hands of the Revolutionary Armed Forces of Colombia (Fuerzas Armadas Revolucionarias de Colombia, FARC), but hundreds of people were still being held hostage by the FARC and the National Liberation Army (Ejército de Liberación Nacional, ELN). The FARC were again thought to have been responsible for bomb attacks in urban areas. There was some progress in judicial investigations into emblematic human rights cases, although impunity remained a serious problem. The extradition of paramilitary leaders to the USA on drugs-trafficking charges undermined human rights investigations in Colombia.

Internal armed conflict

In the 12-month period ending in June 2008, more than 1,492 civilians were killed in the conflict, compared to at least 1,348 in the previous 12-month period. More than 182 people were the victim of enforced disappearance during the 12-month period ending in June 2008, compared to 119 in the previous 12-month period.

■ On 26 May, an Indigenous man, Oscar Dogirama Tequia, was killed by the FARC in Ríosucio Municipality, Chocó Department. He was accused of being an army informant.

In October, mass demonstrations by Indigenous people in Cauca Department, which were part of nationwide protests in support of land rights and against human rights abuses, led to claims that the anti-riot police (ESMAD) used excessive force and that some of the protesters were violent. Dozens of demonstrators and members of the security forces were injured and there were reports that several protesters were killed. There was a spate of killings of

and threats against leaders of Indigenous, Afro-descendant and campesino communites around the country, some of whom were active in campaigns on land rights.

■ On 16 December, army troops fatally shot Edwin Legarda, the husband of Indigenous leader Aída Quilcué, in controversial circumstances. At the time, Edwin Legarda was travelling by car to the city of Popayán, Cauca Department, to pick up his wife, who was returning from Geneva where she had attended a session on Colombia at the UN Human Rights Council.

■ On 14 October, Walberto Hoyos Rivas, a leader of the Afro-descendant community of the Curvaradó River Basin in Chocó Department, was killed by paramilitaries in the Humanitarian Zone of Caño Manso, one of several communities set up by local people to assert their right as civilians not to be drawn into the conflict. He had been active in seeking the protection of the right of Afro-descendant communities to collective ownership of lands in the Curvaradó River Basin, and had survived an attempt on his life in 2007. He was due to give testimony in the trial of two paramilitaries implicated in the killing of another community leader when he was shot.

There was a significant rise in new cases of forced displacement, from 191,000 in the first half of 2007, to 270,000 in the same period in 2008. The south of the country was particularly badly affected because of ongoing combat between the security forces and paramilitary and guerrilla groups. Those displaced by the conflict faced deeply entrenched discrimination and marginalization, making it even more difficult for them to access basic services, such as health and education.

Guerrilla and paramilitary groups forcibly recruited children. The security forces used children as informants, contrary to a 2007 Directive issued by the Ministry of Defence which prohibits the use of children for intelligence purposes. On 12 February, the government finally accepted the reporting and monitoring mechanisms under UN Security Council Resolution 1612 (2005) on children and armed conflict, but expressed reservations about extending it to cover acts of sexual violence.

In April, the government issued Decree 1290, which created a programme to allow victims of abuses by guerrilla and paramilitary groups to receive monetary compensation from the state. However, it did not address the issue of restitution of stolen lands

C

or other forms of reparation, or of reparation for victims of violations by the security forces.

A bill on reparations for victims of human rights abuses, approved by a congressional committee in November, had not been voted on by Congress by the end of the year. The Office of the UN High Commissioner for Human Rights in Colombia said that, as it stood, the bill, which was weakened significantly by the pro-government majority on the committee, was discriminatory.

Extrajudicial executions by the security forces

The killings of dozens of young men from Soacha, near the capital Bogotá, forced the government to finally acknowledge that the security forces were responsible for extrajudicial executions. The killings, which had been falsely presented by the military as "guerrillas killed in combat", were reportedly carried out in collusion with paramilitary groups or criminal gangs. In October, the scandal led to the sacking of 27 army officers, including three generals, and in November forced the resignation of the head of the army, General Mario Montoya, who had been linked to human rights violations. President Uribe said the Soacha killings would be investigated by the civilian courts rather than by the military justice system, which often claims jurisdiction in such cases and then closes them without any serious investigation.

At least 296 people were extrajudicially executed by the security forces in the 12-month period ending in June 2008, compared to 287 in the previous 12-month period. The military justice system claimed jurisdiction over many of these cases.

In November, during a visit to Colombia, the UN High Commissioner for Human Rights said extrajudicial executions in Colombia appeared to be systematic and widespread.

Paramilitary groups

Paramilitary groups remained active, despite claims by the government that all paramilitaries had demobilized in a government-sponsored process that began in 2003. Paramilitaries continued to kill civilians and to commit other human rights violations, sometimes with the support or acquiescence of the security forces. Some 461 killings were attributed to paramilitaries in the 12-month period ending in June 2008, compared to 233 in the previous 12-month period.

■ On 14 June, members of the paramilitary Peasant Self-Defence Forces of Nariño entered San José de la Turbia in Olaya Herrera Municipality, Nariño Department. They warned the community that the navy was nearby and that they were working together. They called out the name of Tailor Ortiz. When he raised his hand, the paramilitaries said, "We're going to kill this one right away". They tied him up and shot him in the head. They then said: "Each time we come, we'll come for someone else".

Some 1,778 bodies of victims of enforced disappearance by paramilitaries were exhumed by the authorities from 1,441 graves between 2006 and 2008. By the end of 2008 the remains of only around 300 victims had been identified and returned to their families. The exhumations were dogged by serious deficiencies, making it more difficult to identify both the victims and the perpetrators.

The security forces continued to use supposedly demobilized paramilitaries in military and intelligence operations despite a ban, introduced in 2007, on such deployments.

The Justice and Peace process

More than 130,000 victims of paramilitary violence made official claims for reparation under the Justice and Peace process. This process allows paramilitaries who have laid down their arms to benefit from significantly reduced prison sentences in return for confessions about human rights violations and reparations for their victims. However, 90 per cent of paramilitaries were not eligible for inclusion in the process and thus evaded justice. Threats against and killings of victims testifying in the process continued, while many paramilitaries failed to collaborate fully with the Justice and Peace tribunals, in particular failing to return land misappropriated by them. This continued to undermine the right of victims to truth, justice and reparation.

In May, 15 national paramilitary leaders were extradited to the USA to face drugs-related charges. Their extradition followed claims by the Colombian government that they had failed to abide by the terms of the Justice and Peace process. The US government maintained that Colombian investigators would have access to the extradited paramilitaries. However, concerns remained that the extradition had undermined investigations in Colombia into human rights violations committed by the paramilitaries and into the links these may have had with Colombian politicians and other state officials.

In May the Constitutional Court ruled that the government's protection programme for victims and witnesses participating in the Justice and Peace process was in breach of the state's constitutional and international obligation to prevent discrimination and violence against women.

'Para-political' scandal

Around 70 members of Congress were still being investigated for alleged links to paramilitary groups. However, many legislators resigned from their posts, thereby ensuring that responsibility for investigations was transferred from the Supreme Court of Justice to local units of the Office of the Attorney General, increasing the risk of possible political manipulation. While cases against some legislators were dropped, others were found guilty by the Supreme Court and sentenced to terms of imprisonment.

Tensions increased between the government and the Supreme Court over the scandal, with the former claiming the Supreme Court was politically motivated and the latter accusing the government of seeking to undermine the investigations. Most of the legislators implicated in the scandal were members of the pro-government coalition.

In December, the Inter-American Commission on Human Rights granted precautionary measures on behalf of the Supreme Court judge co-ordinating the para-political investigation, Iván Velásquez. These imposed certain obligations on the government regarding the judge's security.

Guerrilla groups

The FARC and the ELN continued to kill civilians and carry out kidnappings. More than 166 killings of civilians were attributed to guerrilla groups in the 12-month period to June 2008, compared to 214 in the previous 12-month period.

■ On 16 January, two boys aged 12 and 14 were killed, allegedly by the FARC, in La Hormiga Municipality, Putumayo Department. Their families' homes were burned down. The killings were apparently in reprisal for the boys' refusal to join the FARC.

The use of landmines by guerrilla groups was widespread. In 2008, more than 45 civilians and 102 members of the security forces were killed and 160 and 404 injured, respectively.

■ On 27 June, three Indigenous children from the Las Planadas Telembí reservation in Samaniego Municipality, Nariño Department, were killed after they stepped on mines placed by guerrillas.

There were a series of bomb attacks in urban centres, some of which the authorities blamed on the FARC, and in which civilians were the main victims.

■ The Colombian authorities blamed the FARC for detonating an explosive device in Ituango, Antioquia Department, on 14 August. The explosion killed seven people and injured more than 50 in an area of the town where a fiesta was being held. The FARC denied responsibility for the attack.

In March, Colombian troops attacked a FARC base in Ecuador killing the group's second-in-command, "Raúl Reyes". The operation led to a deterioration in relations between Colombia and neighbouring countries.

The Colombian government claimed that information recovered from the computer of "Raúl Reyes" following the raid revealed the existence of a FARC "support network" in several European countries, as well as the names of Colombian politicians with links to the FARC. FARC leader "Manuel Marulanda" also died in March, albeit of natural causes.

Impunity

Impunity remained the norm in most cases of human rights abuses. However, there was continued progress in several high-profile investigations, mainly as a result of international pressure. Among those cases where some progress was made were the killing by the army and paramilitaries of eight members of the Peace Community of San José de Apartadó, Apartadó Municipality, Antioquia Department, in February 2005; and the killing by the army of 10 officers from the judicial police, a police informer and a civilian, in May 2006 in Jamundí, Valle del Cauca Department.

However, in most of these cases there were very few, if any, advances in identifying chain-of-command responsibility.

Human rights defenders and trade unionists

There was an increase in threats against human rights defenders and killings of trade unionists, especially around the time of the 6 March demonstrations in Colombia and abroad in protest at human rights violations by paramilitaries and the security forces. Responsibility for these attacks was attributed to paramilitaries.

At least 46 trade union members were killed in 2008, compared to 39 in 2007. Some 12 human rights defenders were killed in 2008, similar to the figure recorded in 2007.

■ On 20 September, two gunmen on a motorbike shot and killed Ever González in Bolívar Municipality, Cauca Department. Ever González, a campesino leader from the NGO CIMA, had drawn public attention to extrajudicial executions in Cauca.

President Uribe again made statements undermining the legitimacy of human rights work.

■ In November, following the publication of reports on Colombia by Amnesty International and Human Rights Watch (HRW), he accused Amnesty International of "blindness", "fanaticism" and "dogmatism". He also publicly accused HRW's Americas Director of being a "supporter" and an "accomplice" of the FARC.

Kidnapping and hostage-taking

Former presidential candidate Ingrid Betancourt was the most high-profile of a number of hostages who regained their freedom in 2008 after years of captivity at the hands of the FARC. Ingrid Betancourt and 14 other hostages were freed following a military operation on 2 July. The operation proved controversial as one of the soldiers involved wore a Red Cross emblem, in violation of IHL.

On 4 February and 20 July, millions of people marched in Colombia and around the world in protest at FARC kidnappings. The FARC and ELN continued to hold hundreds of hostages.

The number of kidnappings continued to fall; 437 were recorded in 2008 as compared with 521 in 2007. Criminal gangs were responsible for most of the kidnappings carried out during the year. Of those kidnappings which were specifically conflict-related, guerrilla groups were responsible for the vast majority.

Violence against women and girls

All the parties to the conflict continued to subject women and girls to sexual abuse and other forms of violence. Guerrilla groups also reportedly forced women combatants to have abortions or take contraceptives, in violation of their reproductive rights.

■ On 24 September, gunmen shot and killed Olga Marina Vergara, a leader of the women's coalition Ruta Pacífica de Mujeres, at her home in the city of Medellín.

Her son, daughter-in-law and a five-year-old grandson were also killed in the attack. The killings coincided with the launch of a new report by the Ruta Pacífica on violence against women in the context of the armed conflict.

On 14 April, the Constitutional Court issued a judicial decree on the rights of women displaced by the conflict. The decree made an explicit link between displacement and sexual violence, and concluded that the conflict had a disproportionate impact on women. It called on the government to establish 13 specific programmes to protect women displaced by the conflict.

US military aid

In 2008, US assistance to Colombia amounted to around US$669.5 million. This included some US$543 million from the Foreign Operations funding bill, of which US$235 million was allocated for social and economic projects. The remaining US$307 million was earmarked for the security forces, and 30 per cent of this was conditional on the Colombian authorities meeting certain human rights conditions. This marked a continuation of the trend towards redressing the imbalance in US assistance between security and socio-economic concerns. In August, Congress released the last portion of the US$55 million military funding for the Fiscal Year 2006 that it put on hold in April 2007 because of concerns over extrajudicial executions by the security forces. Also in August, Congress put a hold on an additional US$72 million for military funding in Fiscal Years 2007 and 2008 for the same reasons.

Reportedly in response to the Soacha killings, the US State Department vetoed three military units, which meant they became ineligible to receive US military assistance.

International scrutiny

The report on Colombia of the Office of the UN High Commissioner for Human Rights, published in February, stated that although there had been some improvements "the situation of human rights and international humanitarian law remains a matter of concern". In terms of the fight against impunity the report claimed that "structural problems persist in the administration of justice". The report also expressed concern about the persistence of extrajudicial executions by the security forces and about grave and systematic violations of IHL by guerrilla groups. It also noted the links between certain members of the armed forces and what the report termed "new illegal armed groups".

The Representative of the UN Secretary General on the Human Rights of Internally Displaced Persons visited Colombia in November, and the UN Working Group on Arbitrary Detention did so in October.

In December, Colombia's human rights record came under scrutiny at the UN Human Rights Council under the Universal Periodic Review mechanism.

Amnesty International visits/reports

🚗 Amnesty International delegates visited the country in February, March, April, June, July and October.

📄 "Leave us in Peace!" – Targeting civilians in Colombia's internal armed conflict (AMR 23/023/2008)

📄 Colombia: Ingrid Betancourt gains her freedom (AMR 23/024/2008)

📄 Colombia: Amnesty International condemns bomb attack (AMR 23/030/2008)

📄 Colombia: Killings of Indigenous and Afro-descendant land right activists must stop (AMR 23/038/2008)

CONGO (REPUBLIC OF)

REPUBLIC OF CONGO

Head of state:	Denis Sassou-Nguesso
Head of government:	Isidore Mvouba
Death penalty:	abolitionist in practice
Population:	3.8 million
Life expectancy:	54 years
Under-5 mortality (m/f):	112/89 per 1,000
Adult literacy:	84.7 per cent

Human rights defenders and journalists faced threats, arrests and detention. More than 30 people were arrested after a disturbance in July, some of whom were tortured or otherwise ill-treated. They were released without trial in December. Three asylum-seekers arrested in 2004 remained in custody without charge or trial. More than 30

people charged with endangering the security of the state after their arrest in 2005 were tried in June.

Background

More than five political parties declared their intention to field presidential candidates for the general elections scheduled for 2009. President Denis Sassou-Nguesso who returned to power in October 1997 was widely expected to be the candidate for a ruling coalition led by the Congolese Workers Party (Parti congolais du travail, PCT). Opposition political parties called for an independent electoral commission but their demand was not granted by the end of the year. In August, several opposition political parties withdrew from the National Commission for the Organization of Elections. They demanded guarantees that the elections in 2009 would be fair, that all political parties would have equal access to the media, that public bodies charged with organizing the elections would be impartial and that a new law setting up an independent electoral commission would be passed.

The ruling coalition won an overwhelming majority of seats during local and municipal elections in June. However, government critics accused the government of organizing the elections poorly, amid reports that voter turn-out was as low as 25 per cent.

The government announced a programme for the demobilization, disarmament and reintegration of fighters belonging to the former armed group, the National Resistance Council. In September the government announced that it had destroyed 500 weapons and tens of thousands of rounds of ammunition and explosives captured from or handed over by former armed opposition fighters.

There was civil unrest in Pointe-Noire in July during the funeral of Thystère Tchicaya, leader of the Rally for Democracy and Social Progress. Some protesters damaged private and public property and shouted insults against President Nguesso. Several dozen people were arrested and at least 35 were detained until December.

Nearly 40 former members of the security forces and civilians were tried in June on the charge of endangering the security of the state. Most of them had been arrested in early 2005 after a group of gendarmes were accused of stealing weapons from Bifouiti gendarmerie south of Brazzaville. Others, including civilians and a retired army colonel, had been arrested

C

in Pointe-Noire in connection with an alleged coup plot. Ten of the defendants were not in court – some because they were living abroad and others because they had been granted provisional release and had not been informed of the trial date. When the trial ended on 27 June, the court found most of the defendants guilty of endangering the state and sentenced them to prison terms of up to three and a half years, which coincided with the period they had spent in custody or on provisional release. Those who had been in custody, including the alleged plot leader, Captain Bertin Pandi Ngouari, and retired army colonel Serge André Mpassi, were released immediately after the trial. Some of those tried and released claimed that they had been subjected to torture and other forms of ill-treatment during the months after their arrest in 2005.

Freedom of expression and association

Human rights defenders and journalists were threatened or arrested and detained for carrying out their professional activities.

In January, police in Brazzaville threatened the human rights group Observatoire congolais des droits de l'homme (OCDH) with closure if it did not desist from making public statements which the authorities deemed political. OCDH had earlier called for a postponement of local elections until an independent electoral commission had been set up and a reliable electoral register had been established.

■ Christian Perrin, a journalist and head of news at Télé pour tous television station in Pointe-Noire, was arrested on 21 July and detained for 24 hours. He was subsequently charged with inciting violence. The charge related to the station's coverage of riots on 7 July and criticism of the government by members of an opposition political party during a television programme. The High Court in Pointe-Noire found him guilty and sentenced him to a fine in August.

■ Gilbert Tsonguissa Moulangou, a member of the Pan-African Union for Social Democracy (UPADS) political party, was arrested and detained in December after he addressed a meeting in Brazzaville. During the meeting, he had shown a video message by a UPADS leader living in exile after he was sentenced to 20 years' imprisonment in 2001. The message criticized the government and factions of the UPADS. Gilbert Moulangou was charged with endangering the security of the state and issuing false information. He was still held without trial at the end of the year.

Arrest, detention and ill-treatment of alleged rioters

Several dozen people, most of them youths, were arrested on and soon after 7 July following riots in Pointe-Noire during the funeral of Thystère Tchicaya. Some of those arrested and initially detained by members of the security forces were reportedly beaten and subjected to other forms of ill-treatment. One of those arrested, Sylvestre Guy Poaty, was reportedly beaten in police custody and died in hospital on 19 July. Another detainee, Sita Ndombet, a national of the Democratic Republic of Congo (DRC), reportedly became a victim of enforced disappearance after he was removed from prison by members of the security forces. Government officials claimed that he had escaped. His whereabouts remained unknown at the end of the year.

After numerous calls by opposition political leaders and human rights defenders for the release of the alleged rioters, the Minister of Justice said on television on 16 December that the state had lost interest in prosecuting them. At least 35 who were still being held were released without trial on 18 December.

Long-term detention without trial of asylum-seekers

Three asylum-seekers from the DRC arrested in March 2004 remained in the custody of the military security service without charge or trial. Germain Ndabamenya Etikilome, Médard Mabwaka Egbonde and Bosch Ndala Umba were accused of spying for the DRC at the time of their arrest but were never charged with any offence. The authorities did not reveal why the three men continued to be held without charge or trial.

Amnesty International visit

🚌 Amnesty International delegates visited the country in July.

CÔTE D'IVOIRE

REPUBLIC OF CÔTE D'IVOIRE

Head of state:	Laurent Gbagbo
Head of government:	Guillaume Soro
Death penalty:	abolitionist for all crimes
Population:	19.6 million
Life expectancy:	47.4 years
Under-5 mortality (m/f):	192/173 per 1,000
Adult literacy:	48.7 per cent

Presidential elections originally due to take place in 2005 were again postponed due to delays in registering voters and disarming fighters. The UN Security Council decided that international peacekeeping forces would remain in the country until after presidential elections and extended an arms embargo and targeted sanctions. Security forces used excessive force to disperse people demonstrating against rising living costs. Human rights abuses continued to be committed by both government and opposition forces, particularly against women, and harassment and physical assault remained widespread, notably at roadblocks.

Background

The coalition government remained in place, composed of supporters of President Laurent Gbagbo and led by Guillaume Soro, Secretary General of the New Forces (Forces Nouvelles), the coalition of armed groups in control of the north since September 2002. However, the main objectives set out in the 2007 Ouagadougou peace agreement were not achieved. Despite some efforts, the process of disarming members of the New Forces and creating an integrated army was not completed. In addition, the identification and voter registration processes were hampered by attacks launched by a student organization linked to President Gbagbo. The students ransacked registration centres, stole computer equipment and seized birth certificates. In October, the presidential elections were again postponed for a fourth year.

In October, two people were convicted of dumping deadly toxic waste in Abidjan in 2006 and sentenced to 20 and five years' imprisonment. Officials from Trafigura, the Dutch multinational company which operated the ship that brought the waste to the country, escaped prosecution after reaching a financial settlement with the Ivorian government, apparently in return for immunity from prosecution.

In October, the UN Security Council renewed for a further year the embargo on arms and diamond exports as well as sanctions on individuals seen as obstacles to peace such as travel bans and asset freezes. The Security Council stressed that these measures would be reviewed after free, fair and transparent presidential elections.

Excessive use of force

In March and April, riot police dispersed several hundred demonstrators who had blocked roads and burned tyres in Abidjan, the economic capital, to protest against the rising cost of staple foods. The police used tear gas grenades and live ammunition. Two people were killed and more than 10 people, including women traders, were wounded.

■ A 16-year-old school student died after being hit on the head by a tear gas canister in Yopougon commune, Abidjan. A 24-year-old man was reportedly shot three times in the head in Port-Bouet commune, near Abidjan. The Ministry of Interior said that investigations had been launched into the killings, but by the end of 2008 no member of the security forces appeared to have been charged or prosecuted.

Violence against women and girls

Acts of sexual violence against women and girls continued in both the area held by government forces and in the northern area controlled by the New Forces. Most of the alleged perpetrators were never brought to trial or were released shortly after arrest.

■ In April, a 14-year-old girl was raped and killed by four members of the New Forces in the town of Katiola, an area held by the New Forces. No-one was held to account for this crime. A few days later, in the same town, a woman was sexually assaulted and then raped by a member of the New Forces who was arrested, held for a few days and then released.

■ In September, two young girls were raped in Duekoué (in the west of the country) by six men who were part of an armed group carrying guns, suspected to be members of a pro-government militia. None of the perpetrators had been arrested by the end of 2008.

No measures were taken to provide reparation or access to health care for the countless women and

C

girls subjected to rape and sexual assault by fighters and civilians linked to them since 2002, when armed conflict broke out.

Police and security forces
The security forces frequently committed abuses to extort money at checkpoints and during inspections of identity documents.
■ In February, Lanciné Bamba, a bus driver, was shot dead by a member of the Command Centre for Security Operations (Centre de commandement des Opérations de Sécurité, CECOS) after he had refused to hand over money at a checkpoint. In October, a member of the CECOS was convicted of the murder and sentenced to three years' imprisonment.

Abuses by armed groups
Combatants and supporters of the New Forces were responsible for human rights abuses including torture and other ill-treatment, arbitrary detention and widespread extortion. A climate of impunity prevailed due to the absence of a functioning judicial system in the north.
■ In September, more than 50 people were arrested in the area of Vavoua and Séguéla reportedly because they objected to the dismissal of Zakaria Koné, a military leader of the New Forces. Those arrested were sent to Bouaké, the stronghold of the New Forces, where they were reportedly detained unlawfully.

Amnesty International report
📄 Côte d'Ivoire. Silence and Impunity: the only response to sexual violence against women (AFR 31/002/2008)

CROATIA

REPUBLIC OF CROATIA

Head of state:	Stjepan Mesić
Head of government:	Ivo Sanader
Death penalty:	abolitionist for all crimes
Population:	4.6 million
Life expectancy:	75.3 years
Under-5 mortality (m/f):	8/7 per 1,000
Adult literacy:	98.1 per cent

Despite slow progress in prosecution of war crimes committed by members of the Croatian Army and police forces against Croatian Serbs and other minorities during the 1991-1995 war, the country continued to move towards full integration with the EU. Physical attacks and intimidation of journalists increased.

Background
The November European Commission Progress Report asserted that Croatia would be able to complete the accession negotiations by the end of 2009, and that EU membership would follow by 2011 at the latest.

Following the November 2007 elections, in January the Croatian Democratic Union formed a coalition government with the support of the Croatian Peasant Party, the Croatian Social Liberal Party and the Independent Serbian Democratic Party. A parliamentary representative of the Roma community joined the governing coalition.

In July Croatia signed accession protocols with NATO and the ratification process continued.

In January the OSCE office in Zagreb was established, replacing the OSCE Mission to Croatia which had operated since 1996. It monitors war crimes trials and reports on the implementation of housing care programmes for returnees.

International justice – war crimes
The International Criminal Tribunal for the former Yugoslavia (Tribunal) continued to prosecute high-profile cases of war crimes and crimes against humanity committed during the 1991-1995 war in Croatia.

The trial of three Croatian Army generals – Ante Gotovina, Ivan Čermak and Mladen Markač – started in March. They were charged with command responsibility for war crimes and crimes against humanity committed during Operation Storm between August and November 1995. Serious concerns were expressed by the Tribunal's Prosecutor concerning the lack of co-operation by the Croatian authorities, including their intentional concealment of the military documents concerning Operation Storm.

Vladimir Gojanović, a prosecution witness in the case against the three Croatian Army generals, was threatened on his return to Croatia in May, allegedly by members of veterans' associations. On 28 May, a group of 20 men tried to assault him in front of Šibenik University but were prevented by the police.

A visit by the Deputy Prime Minister to the three Croatian Army generals at the Tribunal's detention centre in February was viewed by some as tacit government support for them.

Justice system – war crimes

A number of war crimes cases against lower-ranking perpetrators were prosecuted by the domestic judiciary. However, according to a report by the OSCE Office in Zagreb, the ethnicity of victims and perpetrators continued to affect the prosecution of war crimes cases. In the vast majority of prosecutions, the victims were ethnic Croats, and the perpetrators members of the Yugoslav Peoples Army (JNA) or Serbian paramilitary groups. There was a continuing failure to investigate most war crimes committed by the Croatian Army and police forces, and impunity for the perpetrators prevailed.

Despite the fact that specialized war crimes chambers had been created in four county courts in 2003, they prosecuted only two cases in 2008, both for war crimes committed against Croatian Serbs. The vast majority of war crimes cases continued to be prosecuted by the local courts in the communities where the alleged crimes had been committed. In some cases witnesses refused to testify as they feared for their safety.

Proceedings against Branimir Glavaš – currently a member of parliament – and six others continued at the Zagreb County Court. The accused were charged with the unlawful arrest, torture and killing of Croatian Serb civilians in Osijek in 1991. Branimir Glavaš was also charged with having failed to prevent his subordinates from detaining, ill-treating

and killing civilians and of having directly participated in some of the crimes, in his capacity as local military leader in 1991.

The trial restarted several times from the beginning, most recently in November 2008 following the judge's failure to hold a hearing in the case for more than three months. On other occasions, hearings were adjourned after the accused or their legal representatives had not appeared in court, on grounds of ill-health or because of dissatisfaction with the way the judge was handling the case. On 24 November, one of the accused, Ivica Krnjak, left the courtroom in protest against the court's decision that he was fit to stand trial. As a result the hearing was adjourned. In June, Branimir Glavaš publicly disclosed on local television in Osijek the identity of one of the protected witnesses.

Two former Croatian Army generals, Mirko Norac and Rahim Ademi, were tried by the Zagreb County Court. In May the court acquitted Rahim Ademi of all charges whereas Mirko Norac was found guilty of some of the charges and sentenced to seven years' imprisonment. The case had been transferred to the Croatian judiciary by the Tribunal in 2005. The accused were indicted for war crimes, including murders, inhumane treatment, plunder and wanton destruction of property, against Croatian Serb civilians and prisoners of war during military operations in 1993. There were serious concerns about the number of witnesses who refused to testify, some of them because they feared for their safety. In October, the State Prosecutor's Office appealed against the judgment in relation to both of the accused.

Enforced disappearances

Little progress was made in establishing the whereabouts of more than 2,000 people still unaccounted for since the 1991-1995 war, although the Croatian authorities had assumed full responsibility from the ICRC in 2007 for investigating these disappearances.

Impunity for enforced disappearances remained a serious problem due to the failure of the Croatian authorities to conduct thorough investigations and bring perpetrators to justice.

Freedom of expression – journalists

There was an increase in the number of physical attacks on, and murders of, journalists. The majority

C

of such incidents were perpetrated against journalists investigating war crimes and organized crime.

■ Ivo Pukanić, owner of the Croatian weekly *Nacional*, and his colleague Niko Franjić were killed in October by a car bomb in Zagreb. The killing was reportedly due to the investigation undertaken by his newspaper into organized crime activities in the former Yugoslavia. An investigation was opened and the government announced special measures to fight organized crime structures.

■ In February and November journalist Drago Hedl, a prosecution witness in the Branimir Glavaš trial, received death threats following his reports about the role of Branimir Glavaš in the murders of Croatian Serbs in the Osijek area during the 1991-1995 war. The alleged perpetrator of the November incident was identified and the investigation against him was ongoing at the end of the year.

■ In November a fake car bomb was planted under journalist Hrvoje Appelt's car. This was believed to be related to his investigation of oil smuggling involving organized crime structures from other countries in south-east Europe.

■ Dušan Miljuš, a journalist for the newspaper *Jutarnji List*, was severely beaten in June by unknown individuals in front of his house in Zagreb following his reports on links between politicians and illegal business activities.

■ In April a freelance journalist Željko Peratović received two death threats posted on his blog. One of the threats was investigated by the police and the State Prosecutor's Office, but the results were not made public. It is alleged that the other death threat was not investigated.

Discrimination
Returnees
Croatian authorities failed to address the problem of people who had occupied socially owned apartments, and had lost their tenancy rights during the war (many of them Croatian Serbs). In June, an Action Plan on implementation of the housing care programmes was adopted but Croatian Serb NGOs disputed official statistics on the number of people included in the programmes. Reportedly, many of the potential applicants were not able to register their claims due to short deadlines.

Croatian Serb returnees faced problems accessing employment, including in public institutions.

Roma
Romani children continued to suffer discrimination in education as the authorities failed to develop and implement a meaningful strategy to address their access to education. Roma segregation in some schools remained a problem.

The authorities failed to provide teaching in Romani languages which limited the progress of some Romani students. The use of Romani teaching assistants was sporadic. Attendance in pre-school programmes was low amongst Roma.

Violence against women and girls
Croatia continued to be a source and transit country for women trafficked for the purpose of sexual exploitation. Increasingly, during the summer months, it was a destination for women trafficked from other south-east European countries to service the tourist industry.

In January, a new Law on Foreigners entered into force, enabling temporary residence permits based on humanitarian grounds to be granted for trafficked persons, and providing adults and children with a reflection period of 30 days and 90 days respectively.

Amnesty International visits/report
Amnesty International delegates visited Croatia in February, and a high-level delegation visited in April.

Croatia: Set of recommendations to combat impunity for war crimes (EUR 64/004/2008)

CUBA

REPUBLIC OF CUBA

Head of state and government:	Raúl Castro Ruz
Death penalty:	retentionist
Population:	11.3 million
Life expectancy:	77.7 years
Under-5 mortality (m/f):	7/6 per 1,000
Adult literacy:	99.8 per cent

Restrictions on freedom of expression, association and assembly persisted. Journalists and political dissidents faced harassment and intimidation by security officials. Four prisoners of conscience were released early in the year; 58 remained

imprisoned. **Cubans continued to feel the negative impact of the US embargo particularly in relation to the right to food.**

Background

In February, parliament named Raúl Castro President of the Council of State, making him the country's head of state and government. Cuba signed the International Covenant on Civil and Political Rights, and the International Covenant on Economic, Social and Cultural Rights; no date was set for ratification.

Cuba and the EU officially renewed ties, five years after the EU imposed sanctions following the arrest and sentencing of 75 prisoners of conscience in March 2003. The EU lifted its diplomatic sanctions and initiated a dialogue with the authorities on various issues, including human rights.

Economic reforms in the agricultural sector began to be introduced during the first half of the year. However, the devastation caused by several hurricanes hampered the government's reform initiatives. According to official sources, tens of thousands of people were rendered homeless as a result of hurricanes and the country suffered losses in agricultural production of nearly US$1 billion.

Cubans were allowed for the first time to buy mobile phones and computers for personal use, but access to the internet remained restricted. In October, for the 17th consecutive year, the UN General Assembly passed a resolution, supported by 185 countries, calling on the USA to end its embargo on Cuba.

Impact of the US embargo

The US embargo and related measures continued to have a negative effect on the exercise of human rights. Freedom of movement between Cuba and the USA and family reunification remained severely limited. Also the extra-territorial application of US legislation limited the Cuban government's capacity to buy, among other things, food, medical supplies and construction materials from Cuba's trading partners. However, Cuba was allowed to buy staple foods from the USA worth more than US$530 million, which had to be paid for in cash and in advance.

Freedom of expression and association

Freedom of expression remained limited, with all mass media outlets remaining under state control. Journalists working for independent and alternative news agencies continued to face harassment and intimidation in the form of short-term detention and monitoring by security officers. Opposition political groups and many civil and professional associations continued to be barred from gaining legal status. In December, more than 30 people were briefly detained by the Cuban authorities, preventing them from celebrating International Human Rights Day in Havana.

■ Journalist Carlos Serpa Maceira, of the Sindical Press news agency, was arrested at his home in Havana in June 2008. He was charged with engaging in "provocative and mercenary acts under the guidance of the United States Interests Section in Cuba." Officials ordered Carlos Serpa Maceira to stop working as a journalist or face a forcible return to his home town. He was later released.

■ In July, the authorities prevented scores of dissidents from participating in several events in Havana, including the civil society meeting "Agenda for Transition" and an event organized by the United States Interests Section to celebrate US Independence Day. Some were prevented from travelling to the capital, others in Havana were prevented from leaving their homes, and around 30 were detained by police and then released a few hours later or the following day.

Prisoners of conscience

At the end of the year, 58 prisoners of conscience continued to be held solely for the expression of their political views. In February, four prisoners of conscience were released on health grounds, but were ordered to leave the country. There were reports of harassment and intimidation against prisoners of conscience and political prisoners by other prisoners and prison guards.

Justice system

The justice system continued to be used to harass political dissidents opposed to the Cuban government, in particular using charges of "dangerousness". Journalists, political dissidents and critics of the government were often detained for 24 or 48 hours and then released without charge.

■ Gorki Águila, a musician in the band Porno Para Ricardo, was arrested and charged with "dangerousness" in Havana in August because his

C

lyrics were critical of the government. On 29 August the court dropped the charge of "dangerousness", but convicted him of the lesser offence of civil disobedience, for which he was fined.

Death penalty

In April, President Raúl Castro announced that nearly all death sentences were to be commuted to life sentences. There were no executions in 2008.

In December, Cuba abstained for the second time in the vote on a UN General Assembly resolution calling for a worldwide moratorium on executions.

Amnesty International reports

📰 Cuba: Submission to the UN Universal Periodic Review – Fourth session of the UPR Working Group of the Human Rights Council, February 2009 (AMR 25/002/2008)

📰 Cuba: Five years too many, new government must release jailed dissidents, 18 March 2008

CYPRUS

REPUBLIC OF CYPRUS

Head of state and government:	**Demetris Christofias**
	(replaced Tassos Papadopoulos in February)
Death penalty:	**abolitionist for all crimes**
Population:	**864,000**
Life expectancy:	**79 years**
Under-5 mortality (m/f):	**8/6 per 1,000**
Adult literacy:	**96.8 per cent**

A new government elected in February pledged a series of policy changes aimed at strengthening respect for human rights. Migrants' rights and anti-trafficking policies were two areas highlighted for improvement. The UN Committee on Missing Persons continued its work to exhume and identify victims of the inter-ethnic conflict who have been missing since 1963. Concerns remained in two cases regarding the authorities' failure to carry out effective, thorough and impartial investigations.

Background

The first President of Cyprus from the Communist Party took office following elections in February.

Demetris Christofias was elected on a pledge to solve the Cyprus conflict within his five-year term and to improve social conditions. Negotiations at leadership level between the Greek Cypriot and Turkish Cypriot sides began in September. Human rights issues were expected to be among the focal points discussed.

Missing persons

The UN-backed Committee on Missing Persons continued its work of overseeing the exhumation, identification and return of remains of missing persons. The remains of 93 individuals were exhumed during the year, and the remains of 39 were identified and returned to their families. Since 2004 these brought the total number of exhumations to 466, and the total number of identified and returned remains to 110.

Refugees' and migrants' rights

In September, the government announced plans to revise its immigration policy, putting more emphasis on the integration of migrants. The proposed new policy also included establishing a maximum length for detention pending deportation.

Releases

Detainees held in Nicosia Central Prison for periods exceeding 18 months while awaiting deportation were released throughout the year.

Racist violence

On 18 December, 40 teenagers attacked a 14-year-old Cypriot girl whose family had repatriated from Sudan, after her team won a volleyball match. The youths reportedly punched and kicked her repeatedly while shouting racist abuse, and she was hospitalized with serious injuries as a result. The attack was strongly criticized by politicians and the Minister of Education, while local NGOs reported failures in the police investigation of the incident.

Violence against women and girls

In November, the government abolished its practice of granting artists' visas to foreign nationals employed in dancing and musical entertainment. The policy had been criticized over several years by a number of local and international organizations, as well as the UN Committee on the Elimination of Discrimination against Women, as a measure facilitating trafficking for sexual exploitation.

Police and security forces

■ In May, an inquest into the 2006 death of Athanasios Nicolaou, a soldier with the National Guard, returned a verdict of suicide. The family lodged an application for re-examination of the case, which was heard by the Supreme Court in October. On 31 December the Court ruled that the case should be re-opened. Amnesty International had expressed concerns in 2007 that the authorities had failed to investigate the death in a thorough, impartial and effective manner.

■ The trial opened in October of 10 police officers accused of using excessive force against two handcuffed students in December 2005. Six of the officers had faced charges of torture and grievous bodily harm, of which they were cleared – but they continued to face charges of cruel, inhuman or degrading treatment among a total of 34 charges. Another officer was accused of neglect of duty and the other three officers of acquiescence.

CZECH REPUBLIC

CZECH REPUBLIC

Head of state:	Václav Klaus
Head of government:	Mirek Topolánek
Death penalty:	abolitionist for all crimes
Population:	10.2 million
Life expectancy:	75.9 years
Under-5 mortality (m/f):	5/4 per 1,000

The government again failed to implement adequate anti-discrimination provisions. The Roma continued to experience discrimination, particularly in accessing education, housing and health, as well as threats of attacks by far-right groups. There were concerns over inhuman and degrading treatment of people with mental disabilities.

Legal, constitutional or institutional developments

Comprehensive anti-discrimination legislation providing legal aid for victims and effective monitoring mechanisms was not enacted. In May the President vetoed anti-discrimination legislation alleging, according to news reports, that it was "unnecessary,

counter-productive and of a poor quality, and its impact ... very questionable". This was despite a government pledge to introduce a law safeguarding the right to equal treatment and protection against discrimination, in line with EU directives.

Discrimination – Roma

Roma continued to suffer discrimination from public officials and private individuals in education, housing, health and employment. Localities with marginalized Romani communities became targets of far-right groups; public officials continued to use racist language against the Roma.

■ In August, four Romani clients and non-Romani staff of a bar in the town of Rokycany were assaulted by a group of approximately 15 young people. Staff at the bar were attacked allegedly because they served Romani customers. Czech police denied the attack had been racially motivated. Five men were prosecuted for lesser crimes of disorderly conduct, delinquency and intention to cause bodily harm. Romani local residents rejected the outcome as openly racist. Anti-Roma leaflets appeared on the streets in the following days. The tense situation in Rokycany led some Roma to seek asylum outside the country.

■ On 17 November, demonstrators linked to the far-right Czech Workers Party (CWP) chanted anti-Roma slogans at a rally in Litvínov. About 500 demonstrators armed with stones, firecrackers and petrol bombs were reported to have clashed with police while attempting to reach the mainly Roma neighbourhood of Janov. Twelve people were arrested. The CWP had previously tried to organize similar demonstrations against the Romani community in Litvínov on 4 and 18 October, and again on 29 November, but had been banned by local authorities. The Minister of Interior submitted a proposal to outlaw the CWP in November which was approved by the government. On 24 November the Supreme Administrative Court was asked to dissolve the CWP. Following the events in Litvínov, the UN Special Rapporteur on racism stated on 20 November that "such actions reveal serious and deep-rooted problems of racism and discrimination against Roma at the heart of modern Europe that must be addressed in the most vigorous manner and through the rule of law." On 13 December, another rally was organized by the CWP in Litvínov. About 100 far-right demonstrators, including locals, were eventually dispersed by mounted and anti-riot police.

C

■ In April, the Ostrava state attorney's office brought defamation charges against Jiří Jizerský, Ostrava's former deputy mayor, and Liana Janáčková, a member of the Senate and former mayor of the district, for racist statements regarding Roma in 2006. However, as the Senate did not strip Liana Janáčková of parliamentary immunity, her prosecution was impeded.

Education

The practice of segregating Romani children in Czech schools for children with mental disabilities continued despite a European Court of Human Rights ruling in November 2007 that it amounted to unlawful discrimination. Two NGOs – the European Roma Rights Centre and the Roma Education Fund – reported in November that many Romani children continued to attend segregated schools with inferior curriculums. The report demonstrated that legal changes from 2005, where the category of "special schools" for children with minor mental disabilities had been replaced by "practical schools", offered students the same restricted curriculums and so limited their educational and employment opportunities. The report also showed that Romani children continued to be over-represented in these schools.

The Ministry of Education acknowledged during the year the system's shortcomings and took some preliminary steps to address them.

Housing

Roma suffered from racial discrimination and deliberate segregation policies within some municipalities. In their submission to the UN Human Rights Council (UNHRC) for the Universal Periodic Review (UPR) in April, the Czech NGOs Centre on Housing Rights and Evictions, Life Together, and the Peacework Development Fund reported that "Roma are frequently forced to reside in segregated ghettos, which constitute substandard and inadequate housing." The review pointed out that discriminatory practices in public and private rental markets meant that Roma frequently could not obtain housing, even when they were able to present financial guarantees.

In January, the Agency for Social Inclusion of Roma Communities was established to pilot projects in 12 localities in order to improve the situation in socially excluded Romani communities.

Forced sterilization of Romani women

In March, in the national report prepared for the UPR, the Czech authorities acknowledged that some cases of sterilization of Romani women had in the past not strictly complied with Ministry of Health law and guidelines. However, they did not regard them as "motivated by a racial or national bias".

■ Iveta Červeňáková, now 32, was illegally sterilized without her consent in 1997 after she gave birth to her second daughter by caesarean section. In November the Olomouc High Court overturned a 2007 decision by the Ostrava Regional Court ordering the Ostrava municipal hospital to pay compensation of 500,000 korunas (20,460 euros) and to apologize for violating her rights. The judgement was overturned because the case's three-year statute of limitations had expired, and the hospital was only required to apologize.

Torture and other ill-treatment – mental health

In January, the UK television channel BBC One broadcast secret footage of the use of "cage beds" for young people with severe mental and physical disabilities in several social care homes. The use of enclosed restraint beds for psychiatric patients continued. By the end of 2008 the authorities had still not announced any intention to discontinue the use of "net beds", despite calls from the UNHRC in April for them to be abolished. The National Defender of Rights (Ombudsperson) made unannounced visits to psychiatric institutions in the first half of the year. The visits revealed that restraint beds were being used in geriatric psychiatric units, not only in situations of acute endangerment but also as long-term solutions.

Rights of lesbian, gay, bisexual and transgender people

On 28 June, in Brno, around 500 lesbian, gay, bisexual and transgender activists took part in the first Pride parade in the Czech Republic. Despite two counter-demonstrations being banned by the city authorities, an estimated 150 far-right demonstrators gathered to protest against the parade. Several counter-demonstrators were arrested.

International justice

In October, the Czech parliament recognized the International Criminal Court. The decision followed formal approval by the Czech Senate in July, 10 years after it was originally agreed. The Czech Republic was the only EU member state not to have approved the Rome Statute although representatives had signed it

C

in April 1999. The parliamentary decision had yet to be ratified by the President.

Amnesty International visit/reports

🚌 Amnesty International visited the Czech Republic in November.

📄 Eastern Europe: Eighth session of the UN Human Rights Council, 2-20 June 2008: Review of the Czech Republic, Poland and Romania under the Universal Periodic Review – Amnesty International's reflections on the outcome (EUR 02/001/2008)

📄 Oral statement on the outcome on the Czech Republic under the Universal Periodic Review (IOR 41/025/2008)

📄 UN Human Rights Council Eighth Session, 2-18 June 2008: Compilation of statements by Amnesty International (including joint statements and public statements) (IOR 41/034/2008)

DEMOCRATIC REPUBLIC OF THE CONGO

DEMOCRATIC REPUBLIC OF THE CONGO

Head of state:	Joseph Kabila
Head of government:	Adolphe Muzito (replaced Antoine Gizenga in October)
Death penalty:	retentionist
Population:	64.7 million
Life expectancy:	45.8 years
Under-5 mortality (m /f):	205/184 per 1,000
Adult literacy:	67.2 per cent

An upsurge of armed conflict deepened the human rights and humanitarian crisis in North Kivu province, eastern Democratic Republic of the Congo (DRC). The violence was marked by war crimes and other serious human rights violations by armed groups and government forces. These included the killing and abduction of civilians, widespread rape and other forms of sexual violence, and the recruitment and use of children as armed group fighters. By the end of the year, one in four of the population of North Kivu was displaced by conflict.

Ethnic and inter-communal tensions rose in other areas. Army, police and intelligence services across the country were responsible for serious and often politically motivated human rights violations. Little progress was made by the government to alleviate severe poverty or to rehabilitate the country's ruined infrastructure.

Background

Health professionals, teachers and civil servants staged lengthy strikes in protest at low pay and non-payment of salaries.

There was violent unrest in several parts of the country, including Bas-Congo province, where around 100 people were killed in the course of police operations in February and March.

In April the government signed a US$9 billion mining and infrastructure deal with a consortium of Chinese companies. Accusations that the state was selling off the DRC's mineral assets cheaply provoked a parliamentary walkout in May. The sharp fall of world mineral prices, however, threatened to leave tens of thousands working in the DRC's mining zones without income.

There were some positive developments, including a large release of political detainees in July and the adoption of a national law on child protection in June.

Armed conflict

Despite a January peace agreement, heavy fighting resumed in August in North Kivu between the National Congress for the Defence of the People (CNDP) armed group and the national army (FARDC).

In a major offensive in October, the CNDP captured large areas of the province and advanced to within a few kilometres of the provincial capital, Goma. The bulk of FARDC forces fled and went on sprees of killing, rape and looting, notably around the town of Kanyabayonga. By the end of the year, armed resistance to the CNDP was offered mainly by generally pro-government *mayi-mayi* militia groups, sometimes acting in collusion with the Rwandan insurgent group, the Democratic Liberation Forces of Rwanda (FDLR).

The fighting led to a fresh breakdown in relations between the governments of the DRC and Rwanda. The DRC government accused Rwanda of providing support to the CNDP; the Rwandan government accused the DRC army of collaborating with the FDLR. A December report by the UN Group of Experts largely confirmed both sets of allegations.

In Ituri district, Orientale province, a new armed group, the Popular Front for Justice in the Congo

D

(FPJC), launched attacks in October against army positions and villages close to the district capital, Bunia. The FPJC claimed to unite within its ranks members of former Ituri armed groups whom it said were disaffected by unfulfilled government promises on demobilization and reintegration.

In Haut-Uélé district, Orientale province, attacks on civilian centres by the Ugandan Lord's Resistance Army (LRA) intensified throughout 2008. The LRA was responsible for unlawful killings, rapes, the systematic abduction of hundreds of children, and the burning of homes in Dungu territory. A military offensive by government forces of Uganda, DRC and South Sudan against LRA positions in the DRC began in mid-December. In apparent retaliation, the LRA attacked several towns and villages in the region in late December, unlawfully killing around 500 civilians, abducting hundreds of others, and forcing the displacement of approximately 50,000 people.

Government security forces failed to protect civilians in the conflict zones and were themselves responsible for many human rights violations, including killings of civilians, rape and torture. Civilian protection in the east remained wholly dependent on the overstretched UN (MONUC) peacekeeping force, with a strength of around 17,000. Although regularly intervening to protect civilian life, MONUC was incapable of protecting civilians in all circumstances and failed to intervene to halt a massacre in Kiwanja, North Kivu, in November. On 20 November, the UN Security Council authorized the temporary reinforcement of MONUC by an additional 3,000 peacekeepers. By the year's end, there were mounting calls for the deployment of an EU military force to North Kivu.

Unlawful killings

State security forces as well as Congolese and foreign armed groups committed hundreds of unlawful killings. All forces deliberately targeted civilians. A number of possible political killings were reported, often perpetrated by men in military uniform. These included Aimée Kabila, repudiated half-sister of President Joseph Kabila, shot dead at her home in Kinshasa in January, and opposition politician Daniel Botheti, murdered in Kinshasa in July.

A UN investigation concluded that around 100 people, mainly members of the *Bunda dia Kongo* politico-religious group, were killed during police operations in Bas-Congo province in February and March. The investigation blamed the high death toll on excessive use of force and in some cases extrajudicial executions by the police. The government, claiming that only 27 people died, failed to investigate the allegations or initiate criminal proceedings against those allegedly responsible.

Another UN investigation found that on 16/17 January, CNDP forces unlawfully killed at least 30 civilians around Kalonge in North Kivu.

■ On the night of 5/6 November CNDP forces allegedly killed scores of civilians, mainly adult males, in house-to-house searches in Kiwanja, North Kivu. Eyewitnesses said that victims, described as "young fathers and newly-weds", were pulled from their homes and shot or stabbed to death. The killings appeared to be in reprisal for an earlier attack on the town by *mayi-mayi* forces.

Violence against women and girls

High levels of rape and other forms of sexual violence continued throughout the country, with a concentration in eastern DRC, where armed group fighters and government soldiers were the principal perpetrators. Many women and girls suffered gang rape, were raped more than once or were held in sexual slavery. Most victims did not receive medical or psycho-social care. The majority of rapists went unpunished and women and girls lived in fear of reprisals if they reported the rape or even sought medical treatment.

■ A 16-year-old girl was held captive in an army camp in North Kivu for several days in February and raped nightly by an officer. Her mother came to the camp gate to beg for her release, but was turned away by the soldiers.

Child soldiers

An estimated 3,000 to 4,000 children were still serving with armed groups in 2008. Many children reportedly also still served with the army, although the FARDC formally ended the recruitment of children in 2004. UN and NGO child protection and community reintegration programmes for former child soldiers remained under-resourced.

There were new recruitments of children by armed groups in North Kivu and some other areas. Children were sometimes forcibly recruited in groups. Demobilized children were also targeted. The army also used children as porters during combat operations in North Kivu in September and October. The LRA reportedly abducted at least 160 children from several villages in Dungu territory.

■ According to a former child soldier, two youths who had attempted to escape from an armed group in North Kivu in early 2008 were beaten to death in front of other child recruits. They were taken out of a pit in the ground and the commander then gave the order to beat them. Two soldiers and a captain pushed them down into the mud, kicked them and beat them with wooden sticks until they died.

Internally displaced people and refugees
More than 1.4 million people were internally displaced by conflict in North Kivu at the year's end, and a further 30,000 were forced to flee to Uganda. Most displaced people moved to areas close to Goma under government control. However, tens of thousands in less secure areas remained outside the reach of humanitarian assistance at the year's end. Many of those displaced were in extremely poor health following days or weeks of flight.

Outbreaks of cholera and other infectious diseases were reported in several camps for internally displaced people (IDPs). Standards of protection in the camps were often poor, with rape, shootings and robberies reported in a number of IDP sites. Belligerent forces failed to respect the civilian character of IDP camps.

■ On 4 June, an attack allegedly by the FDLR on an IDP camp at Kinyandoni, North Kivu, resulted in at least three civilian deaths.

■ A 16-year-old boy said he was forcibly recruited to fight for the CNDP from inside in IDP camp in Masisi territory in early 2008.

The CNDP reportedly destroyed IDP camps around the town of Rutshuru in October, and forced the camps' residents to leave.

Torture, other ill-treatment and arbitrary detention
Torture and ill-treatment were routinely committed by government security services and armed groups, directed particularly against perceived political opponents. Methods included beatings, stabbings, suspension from grilles or window bars and rape in custody.

There were regular arbitrary arrests by state security forces, especially of military or police officers

with suspected affiliations to the Mouvement de Libération du Congo (MLC) political opposition and its leader, Jean-Pierre Bemba Gombo, or of individuals suspected of supporting the CNDP. Many detainees were held incommunicado for weeks or months in unofficial military or intelligence service detention.

Conditions in most detention centres and prisons were poor and constituted cruel, inhuman or degrading treatment. Deaths of prisoners from malnutrition or treatable illnesses were regularly reported.

Prisoner releases
In July the government ordered the release of 258 military and civilian detainees from Kinshasa's central prison. The detainees had been held unlawfully without trial for long periods, some since 2004, on suspicion of crimes against state security. While welcome, the releases appeared to follow no organized or transparent judicial process. A large number of political prisoners remained in detention.

Human rights defenders
Human rights defenders were physically attacked, abducted, and subjected to death threats and other forms of intimidation by government security forces and armed groups. Many defenders were forced into hiding or to flee by the conflict in North Kivu. Others were targeted because of their involvement in high-profile human rights cases.

Impunity
Impunity for human rights crimes persisted in the vast majority of cases, with only small numbers of low-ranking military personnel brought to justice. Prosecutions were undermined by frequent escapes from prisons and detention centres (at least 250 in 2008).

International justice
Four Congolese former armed group commanders or leaders were in International Criminal Court (ICC) custody, awaiting trial. A fifth was the subject of an ICC arrest warrant.

Mathieu Ngudjolo Chui was arrested by the DRC authorities and surrendered to the ICC in February. He was accused with Germain Katanga, detained in 2007, of war crimes and crimes against humanity committed during and after an armed group attack in February 2003 on the village of Bogoro in Ituri.

D

Jean-Pierre Bemba Gombo, DRC Senator, President of the MLC and former Vice-President of the DRC, was arrested in Belgium in May under an ICC arrest warrant and transferred to the ICC. He was charged with crimes committed in the Central African Republic between October 2002 and March 2003, when MLC armed group forces allegedly carried out systematic rape and other abuses against civilians.

A temporary stay of proceedings against a fourth detainee, Thomas Lubanga Dyilo, the first person to be detained by the ICC in March 2006, was lifted in November. The stay was imposed in June after the trial chamber of the ICC held that the withholding of potentially exculpatory evidence by the prosecution violated the right of the accused to a fair trial.

In April, the Court unsealed an arrest warrant issued in August 2006 against Bosco Ntaganda for the war crimes of recruitment and use in hostilities of children under the age of 15 between July 2002 and December 2003, while he was a senior commander of an Ituri armed group. Bosco Ntaganda remained at large and Chief of Staff of the CNDP in North Kivu.

Death penalty

Military courts sentenced at least 50 people to death during the year, including civilians. No executions were reported.

Amnesty International visits/reports

🚐 Amnesty International delegates visited the country in February and November.

📄 Democratic Republic of Congo: Open Letter to the Minister of Defence and Minister of Justice and Human Rights. Death in detention of Major Yawa Gomonza (AFR 62/004/2008)

📄 Democratic Republic of Congo: North Kivu – No end to war on women and children (AFR 62/005/2008)

📄 Democratic Republic of Congo: Crisis in North Kivu (AFR 62/014/2008)

📄 Democratic Republic of Congo: Open Letter to the United Nations Security Council on strengthening the arms embargo (AFR 62/016/2008)

DENMARK

KINGDOM OF DENMARK

Head of state:	Queen Margrethe II
Head of government:	Anders Fogh Rasmussen
Death penalty:	abolitionist for all crimes
Population:	5.5 million
Life expectancy:	77.9 years
Under-5 mortality (m/f):	6/6 per 1,000

The government indicated that it would consider relying on diplomatic assurances to deport people to countries where they could be at risk of human rights violations. The system for investigating complaints against the police failed to ensure a remedy for ill-treatment. Discriminatory legislation and practice led to a lack of protection for survivors of rape.

Torture and other ill-treatment – deportation with assurances

In April the Minister for Refugees, Immigrants and Integration commissioned a working group to consider ways of deporting foreign nationals believed to pose a threat to national security. The working group was asked to consider whether Denmark should seek and rely on "diplomatic assurances" to deport people to countries where they would be at risk of grave human rights violations, including torture or other ill-treatment.

The working group was established in response to the cases of K.S. and S.C., two Tunisian nationals resident in Denmark who were arrested in February, along with a Danish national. The three men were suspected of involvement in an alleged conspiracy to kill one of the cartoonists responsible for controversial cartoons of the Prophet Muhammad which appeared in a Danish newspaper in September 2005. The Danish national was released shortly after his arrest. The residence permits of the two Tunisian nationals were revoked, and an order was made for their expulsion on the grounds that they were considered a threat to national security. The men were detained pending the execution of the expulsion order. In August, K.S. was reported to have left Denmark voluntarily and travelled to an unknown destination.

In October, the Refugee Appeals Board found that S.C. would face a real risk of torture or other ill-treatment if deported to Tunisia, and ruled that the expulsion could not go ahead. As a result S.C. was released from detention. The government indicated that it would continue its efforts to deport him, including by seeking and relying on assurances from the Tunisian authorities as to his treatment on return, if this was recommended by the working group.

Police and security forces
The system for resolving complaints against the police failed to ensure an effective remedy for allegations of ill-treatment. Very few complaints – between five and eight out of every 1,000 – were upheld by regional public prosecutors, and even fewer resulted in criminal charges being brought against the police.

In 2006 the Minister of Justice had commissioned a committee to examine the current complaints system and suggest possible changes. The committee had not published its report by the end of 2008.

Refugees and asylum-seekers
In November, new legislation imposed further restrictions on the "tolerated residency" status given to foreign nationals against whom an expulsion order has been made but cannot be carried out. This includes people whose return to their country of origin has been ruled to be unsafe by the Refugee Appeals Board. In November there were believed to be 18 people with a "tolerated residency" status, including the Tunisian national referred to as S.C. The new legislation required these people to live in designated centres for asylum-seekers and to report daily to the police, in all but exceptional cases. The legislation increased to one year the maximum period of imprisonment which can be imposed for failure to comply with these requirements.

At least 11 Iraqis were forcibly returned to Iraq, contrary to the recommendations of the UNHCR, the UN refugee agency.

Some asylum-seekers who had been subjected to torture or other ill-treatment did not receive adequate medical treatment in Denmark.

Violence against women and girls
There was a lack of legal protection and redress for survivors of rape. Only one in five rapes reported to the police resulted in a conviction. Sixty per cent of cases where charges were brought did not reach court due to lack of evidence.

Legislation provides for a possible reduction in the sentence for rape if the victim and the perpetrator subsequently marry or enter into a civil partnership. Non-consensual sex with a victim who is in a vulnerable state, for instance as a result of illness or intoxication, is not categorized as rape unless the perpetrator can be shown to have been directly responsible for the victim's condition.

Amnesty International report
🗐 Police accountability mechanisms in Denmark (EUR 18/001/2008)

DOMINICAN REPUBLIC

DOMINICAN REPUBLIC
Head of state and government:	Leonel Fernández Reyna
Death penalty:	abolitionist for all crimes
Population:	9.9 million
Life expectancy:	71.5 years
Under-5 mortality (m/f):	37/28 per 1,000
Adult literacy:	87 per cent

The number of alleged unlawful killings by security forces increased in 2008. Haitians and Dominico-Haitians faced serious discrimination. High levels of domestic violence were reported.

Right to health – HIV/AIDS
In July the Joint United Nations Programme on HIV/AIDS stated that the epidemic had stabilized in the Dominican Republic. However, it warned that the country was over-dependent on external funding for its response to HIV/AIDS. It stated that HIV incidence remained high among residents of *bateyes* (communities of sugar plantation workers). National civil society organizations continued to denounce discrimination in the workplace against people living with HIV/AIDS.

Police and security forces
There were widespread concerns about the escalating level of violent crime and the government's inability to combat it effectively.

According to figures from the General Prosecutor's

Office, 298 people were killed by the police between January and August, an increase of 72 per cent over the same period in 2007. There were concerns that a number of these fatal shootings may have been unlawful. In October the Dominican Interior and Police Minister described the levels of fatal police shootings as "alarming" and called for corrupt officers to be expelled from the force and for improved police training. With no independent body to investigate allegations of abuse by members of the security forces, impunity remained the norm.

■ On 12 February, five criminal suspects were killed by a police patrol during an "exchange of fire" in the district of Ensanche Isabelita, in eastern Santo Domingo. Eyewitnesses claimed that two of the individuals had surrendered before they were shot by police.

Discrimination – Haitian migrants and Dominico-Haitians

Reports by the UN Independent Expert on minority issues, the Special Rapporteur on racism, the Committee on the Rights of the Child and the Committee on the Elimination of Racial Discrimination, all highlighted the discrimination faced by Haitian migrants and Dominico-Haitians.

Access to nationality

A 2007 directive issued by the Dominican Electoral Board continued to be used as a pretext to seize the identity documents of thousands of black Dominicans. The directive instructs government officials to examine closely any identity documents presented for renewal or registration, on the grounds that such documents had been wrongly issued in the past. In May, the Committee on the Elimination of Racial Discrimination urged the Dominican authorities to take immediate steps to issue all Dominicans of Haitian descent with identity documents.

Expulsions

According to local human rights organizations, more than 6,000 Haitians were deported in the first six months of the year. Many of these deportations were arbitrary and did not comply with international human rights standards. There were reports of ill-treatment of deportees by migration officials and members of the security forces.

Lynchings

There were continued reports of mob attacks against Haitian migrants in apparent reprisal for killings of Dominican citizens attributed to Haitians.

■ A Dominico-Haitian and a Haitian national were murdered by a mob on 27 October in the south-western municipality of Neiba. The attack followed the murder of a Dominican, allegedly by a Haitian. The local authorities reportedly intervened swiftly and an investigation was under way at the end of the year.

Trafficking in human beings

Human rights organizations working on both sides of the border between the Dominican Republic and Haiti reported that during the first six months of 2008, 1,353 Haitian children were trafficked into the Dominican Republic where they were exploited for agricultural and domestic work, begging, street-vending and prostitution.

Freedom of expression – journalists

Media workers were harassed and intimidated. In October the Dominican National Union of Press Workers announced that between January and September, 32 journalists had been physically attacked or threatened and that 21 others had been subjected to spurious judicial proceedings because of their work.

■ On 7 August Normando García, a cameraman and producer with the local television station Teleunión, was shot dead in Santiago. Prior to his killing, his car had been set on fire and he had received anonymous threats following the broadcast of various programmes investigating crime in the local area.

Violence against women and girls

Violence against women continued to be widespread. In July the Public Prosecutor of Santo Domingo Province called the level of domestic violence in the Dominican Republic "alarming". According to official statistics, between January and August, 133 women were killed by their current or former partners. A report entitled *Critical Path of Dominican Women Survivors of Gender Violence,* issued in June jointly by several Dominican women's rights NGOs, found that the great majority of survivors of gender-based violence were re-victimized by the justice system. It found that a high percentage of victims abandon the legal process and highlighted the lack of judicial personnel trained to deal with the issue.

Amnesty International report

🗋 Challenging discrimination in the Dominican Republic – Protecting and promoting the rights of Haitian migrant workers and their descendants (AMR 27/003/2008)

ECUADOR

REPUBLIC OF ECUADOR
Head of state and government: **Rafael Vicente Correa Delgado**
Death penalty: **abolitionist for all crimes**
Population: **13.5 million**
Life expectancy: **74.7 years**
Under-5 mortality (m/f):   **29/21 per 1,000**
Adult literacy: **91 per cent**

A new Constitution was approved in a referendum held in September. In June the Truth Commission into past human rights violations presented an initial report. Prison reforms announced in 2007, and reiterated at Ecuador's UN Universal Periodic Review in April, remained pending. Reports of violations against Indigenous and environmental activists continued, and critics accused the government of a growing intolerance of dissent.

Background

The Constituent Assembly, which opened the reform process in November 2007, approved a draft Constitution in July. It increased presidential powers and gave government more control over extractive industries and land distribution. It recognized the multi-ethnic and multicultural nature of Ecuador and gave local communities the right to consultation over mining and oil extraction projects. A bill on mining was still under discussion at the end of the year, amid protests from civil society groups who feared it would give too much control to large mining companies, to the detriment of local communities and the environment.

The Truth Commission, set up in May 2007 to investigate human rights violations committed under the government of León Febres Cordero (1984-1988), began receiving testimonies in February 2008; an interim report was issued in September. Former President Febres Cordero died in December.

In March, the Revolutionary Armed Forces of Colombia's second-in-command, Raúl Reyes, was among those killed during a military operation by the Colombian security forces within Ecuadorean territory (see Colombia entry).

Extractive industries and human rights

In a report released in August, the UN Special Rapporteur on indigenous people expressed concern about reported violations and indicated that he would continue monitoring conflicts between transnational petroleum companies and Indigenous or other local communities.

■ Esther Landetta Chica, an environmental and women's activist, received a series of anonymous death threats between May and July because she had voiced community concerns about the possible negative consequences of irregular mining activities in Guayas Province.

In March the Constituent Assembly amnestied several hundred detainees, most of whom had been arrested in the context of environmental protests. They included 37 people arrested in the town of Dayuma, Orellana Province, in December 2007, after the government declared a state of emergency in response to protests against oil operations. A number of the detainees who had been charged with terrorism had their charges dropped, including Provincial Prefect Guadalupe Llori. However, she remained imprisoned charged with fraud for almost 10 months. She was acquitted of all charges and released in September.

In November the government withdrew the controversial mining concession from the Canadian mining company Copper Mesa Mining Corporation (formerly Ascendant Copper). This, and a number of other decisions to withdraw mining concessions, followed the approval by the National and Constitutional Assemblies of a Mining Mandate in April, which aimed to protect the environment and local populations from the negative impacts of mining.

Violence against women and girls

In its concluding observations on Ecuador, issued in November, the UN Committee on the Elimination of Discrimination against Women expressed concerns about violence against girls in schools. It also highlighted the persistence of high levels of poverty and social exclusion among Indigenous women and women of African descent who faced obstacles in

E

accessing education and health care and in participating in decision-making processes. The Committee urged Ecuador to design and implement a comprehensive strategy, with dedicated appropriate resources, to combat and eradicate all forms of violence against women and girls. The Committee also expressed concern about the high incidence of maternal mortality. It noted that the second leading cause of maternal mortality was abortion and that the magnitude of unsafe abortion in the country and its effects on maternal mortality were under-recorded and unknown.

Freedom of expression

Tensions between the government and some sectors of the media increased. In July, two television stations were among businesses seized by the state to collect debts resulting from a banking scandal. The news directors of the television stations were sacked and replaced by government appointees, leading to concerns about the imposition of state editorial control.

In June, a judge ordered the closure of a case against Francisco Vivanco Riofrío, editor of the newspaper La Hora, for "disrespect" against President Correa, stemming from publication of a March 2007 editorial critical of the government.

Police and security forces

Police at times used excessive force against demonstrators. Cases of arbitrary arrest and ill-treatment were reported, particularly against Indigenous people and members of ethnic minority groups.

■ On 13 April, police detained 23 Ecuadoreans of African descent in La Carolina Park in Quito, reportedly because they were thought to be acting "suspiciously". Several were held for a few days before being released without charge. The Minister of the Interior subsequently apologized. Following its July review, the UN Committee for the Elimination of Racial Discrimination expressed concern at the events.

■ In February, three Quito police officers accused of killing 17-year-old Paúl Alejandro Guañuna Sanguña in January 2007 were each sentenced to 20 years in prison.

EGYPT

ARAB REPUBLIC OF EGYPT

Head of state:	Muhammad Hosni Mubarak
Head of government:	Ahmed Nazif
Death penalty:	retentionist
Population:	76.8 million
Life expectancy:	70.7 years
Under-5 mortality (m/f):	37/29 per 1,000
Adult literacy:	71.4 per cent

The renewal of the state of emergency for a further two years caused widespread discontent. Rising food prices and growing poverty fuelled a wave of strikes by private and public sector workers. Some protests led to violent clashes between police and demonstrators, and some protesters were prosecuted, including before emergency courts. A rockslide in Al-Duwayqah slum in September killed at least 100 people and highlighted the plight of slum dwellers in Cairo, believed to comprise nearly a third of the capital's population. Journalists remained under threat of imprisonment for defamation and on other charges. Hundreds of political activists, mainly from the Muslim Brotherhood, were arrested, including in the run-up to local elections in April. While a new anti-terrorism law was still being prepared, thousands of political prisoners continued to be held in administrative detention under emergency legislation, many of them for more than a decade. Torture and other ill-treatment were widespread. Migrants were killed by Egyptian security forces when attempting to cross into Israel, and around 1,200 Eritrean asylum-seekers were forcibly returned to Eritrea despite fears for their safety there. The practice of female genital mutilation (FGM) was banned by law.

Legal developments

A law passed in April banned demonstrations inside places of worship and prescribed up to one year in prison for offenders. Amendments to the Child Law in June banned FGM and marriage under 18, allowed women to register children under their own family name and prescribed prison terms for the sale, sexual molestation and exploitation of children.

Several draft laws threatened human rights. Draft legislation on audio-visual media, which would further curtail freedom of expression, was widely debated. Journalists found to have damaged "social peace", "national unity", "public order" and "public values" could face up to three years' imprisonment.

The state of emergency, in force continuously since 1981, was renewed in May, pending the introduction of a new anti-terrorism law that was expected to equip the authorities permanently with emergency-style powers similar to those which currently facilitate serious human rights violations.

Justice system
Military and special courts
Grossly unfair trials continued before military and special courts. Defendants tried before military courts included civilians, in breach of international fair trial standards.

■ Twenty-five members of the Muslim Brotherhood were sentenced in April to up to 10 years in prison by the Haikstep military court, including seven who were tried in their absence. Khairat al-Shatir, a Muslim Brotherhood leader, was jailed for seven years. Fifteen defendants were acquitted and released but banned from travel abroad. All were tried on terrorism-related and money laundering charges, which they denied. They appealed. Amnesty International observers were denied access to the trial.

■ The trial began in August before the (Emergency) Supreme State Security Court in Tanta of 49 people accused of involvement in violent protests on 6 April (see below). The defendants said they were blindfolded for nine days and tortured by State Security Investigation (SSI) officials in Mahalla and at Lazoghly Square, Cairo, after their arrests. Methods alleged included beatings, electric shocks and threats that their female relatives would be sexually abused. The authorities failed to order an independent investigation into their complaints, and confessions allegedly obtained through torture comprised the main evidence against the defendants. Twenty-two of the defendants were sentenced in December to up to five years in prison.

Administrative detention
The Interior Ministry stated in January that the number of administrative detainees did not exceed 1,500. Unofficial sources suggested, however, that the real figure was considerably higher, possibly up to 10,000, and included people who had been held continuously without charge or trial for years.

Administrative detainees, held on the orders of the Interior Minister, were kept in conditions that amounted to cruel, inhuman or degrading treatment, and some were reported to be ill as a result. Many remained in prison despite repeated court orders for their release. In August, the Interior Ministry agreed to pay a total of 10 million Egyptian pounds (US$1.87 million) in compensation to around 1,000 Islamists who had been detained without trial or kept in jail despite release orders during the 1990s.

■ Musaad Suliman Hassan (known as Musaad Abu Fagr), a novelist and founder of the Sinai-based movement Wedna Na'ish (We Want to Live), was detained in Borg Al-Arab Prison, Alexandria, and later in Abu Zaabal Prison in Cairo, on the authority of the Interior Minister despite several court orders for his release. The Minister ordered his detention in February after a court in El-Arish acquitted him of charges of inciting protests and resisting the authorities. He was arrested in December 2007 after demonstrations in July and December 2007 calling for the economic, social and cultural rights of the Sinai Bedouins to be respected.

Counter-terror and security
An unknown number of Egyptians who were considered terrorism suspects and forcibly returned by the US and other governments in previous years continued to be detained; some were reported to have been tortured by Egyptian security forces.

Torture and other ill-treatment
Torture and other ill-treatment were systematic in police stations, prisons and SSI detention centres. Impunity continued for most perpetrators, exacerbated by police threatening victims with re-arrest or the arrest of relatives if they lodged complaints. However, some alleged torturers were brought to trial during the year.

■ In October, Mervat Abdel Salam died after police officers raided her home in Samalut, Minya Governorate, and beat her during a robbery inquiry. Although she was pregnant and bleeding, police officers were reported to have locked her in the house, delaying medical assistance. Her family complained to the Public Prosecutor, who ordered an investigation, but the initial forensic medical report concluded that there were no external signs of violence despite injuries visible to her family. Lawyers for the family requested

E

an independent medical report, which later confirmed that there were signs of violence on her body. Police detained several members of Mervat Abdel Salam's family apparently to pressure them into withdrawing the complaint.

Deaths in custody

A number of deaths in custody, apparently as a result of torture and other ill-treatment, were reported.

■ Ali Muhammad Muhammad Abd-al-Salam died in Asyut Prison in Upper Egypt on 8 September. Fellow prisoners said a prison guard had assaulted and killed him. The Interior Ministry said he had died while held in solitary confinement following a quarrel with other prisoners.

Freedom of assembly and association

The government clampdown on political opposition groups, particularly the Muslim Brotherhood, intensified in April. On 5 April, three days before local elections and a day before a planned general strike, the government banned all demonstrations. Protests were nevertheless held in Mahalla, north of Cairo, which were violently suppressed, and in other cities. At least three people were shot dead and dozens wounded as a result of excessive use of force by the security forces.

■ On 23 July, 14 members of the "6 April Youth" group – a collection of bloggers, activists and others who called for a general strike on 6 April to support striking textile workers in Mahalla – were arrested during a peaceful protest in Alexandria. Some of those detained were ill-treated in police custody. All were released without charge in late July and early August.

Freedom of expression

The authorities used repressive laws to clamp down on criticism and dissent. They prosecuted journalists for defamation and other offences, censored books and editions of foreign newspapers, and imposed restrictions on the Egyptian media. Some internet websites were blocked and bloggers and others who criticized the government were arrested. Several foreign satellite television stations were ordered to close their offices in Cairo or had their transmission suspended in Egypt. The Cairo News company director was fined 150,000 Egyptian pounds (US$27,000) and its broadcasting equipment seized for broadcasting footage of protesters destroying a poster showing President Mubarak during the

demonstrations in April in Mahalla.

■ In March, Ibrahim Eissa, editor of *Al-Dustour* daily newspaper, was sentenced to six months in prison, reduced to two months on appeal in September, for writing an article that questioned the President's health. He was charged under the Penal Code for publishing information considered damaging to the public interest and national stability. He was pardoned by the President in October. In August, an edition of *Al-Dustour* was censored.

Human rights defenders

Human rights defenders, including lawyers, who sought to expose abuses or defend torture victims were harassed and prosecuted by the authorities. However, in March the Centre for Trade Union and Workers' Services, closed by the authorities in 2007, was allowed to register as an NGO and to resume its work. In October, the Association for Human Rights and Legal Aid won a court case against closure.

■ On 30 April, Magda Adly, director of the Nadim Centre, which provides vital services for torture victims, sustained fractures and other injuries when she was assaulted inside the Kafr Dawwar court building. Her assailant was apprehended by the public; he said he carried out the assault on the orders of a local police officer.

Violence against women and girls

Amendments to the Child Law passed in June outlawed female genital cutting except when "medically necessary", a qualification that many feared could undermine the ban. Those who break the law face up to two years in jail or a substantial fine.

In October a Cairo court sentenced a man to three years in prison for repeatedly groping a woman from his car as he drove slowly alongside her as she walked down the street.

Discrimination – suspected gay men

In a police crackdown begun in October 2007, 24 men were arrested in Cairo and Alexandria on charges of the "habitual practice of debauchery", a criminal charge used to prosecute consensual sexual acts between men. Twelve who were suspected of being HIV-positive were arrested in Cairo, then tortured and otherwise ill-treated by police, including with beatings, and tested for HIV/AIDS without their consent. Those testing positive were kept chained to their hospital beds until February, when the Ministry of Health and Population ordered them to be unchained after international protests. Most of the men were forcibly subjected to anal examinations to "prove" that they had engaged in homosexual conduct; such examinations conducted without consent constitute torture. Nine of the men were later sentenced to between one and three years in prison; charges against three others were dropped. Four of those sentenced to one year in prison were granted an early release in September after serving three-quarters of their sentence.

Eleven of the 12 arrested in Alexandria in April had their two-year prison sentences upheld by an Alexandria Appeals Court in August. They had all been subjected to forcible anal examinations.

Discrimination – religious minorities

The Supreme Administrative Court overturned government policy in January by ruling that Baha'is, whose religion is not recognized by the state, could obtain identity (ID) documents without stating their faith. In February the court ruled that Coptic Christians who had converted to Islam could convert back to Christianity and have this recognized on their ID cards. Despite this, the authorities remained reluctant to comply with the court's orders. ID cards are essential to access basic services.

Sectarian attacks on the Coptic Christian community, comprising between 6 and 8 million people in Egypt, increased, according to reports. Sporadic clashes between Coptic Christians and Muslims left eight people dead.

Death penalty

At least 87 death sentences were passed and at least two people were executed. There was increasing debate on the use of the death penalty; a conference of judges and jurists agreed to campaign for its scope to be limited.

In December Egypt voted against a UN General Assembly resolution calling for a worldwide moratorium on executions.

Migrants, refugees and asylum-seekers

Security forces used excessive lethal force against migrants, possibly including refugees and asylum-seekers and most of whom were from Sudan and Eritrea, who attempted to cross the border from Egypt into Israel; 28 people were shot dead and scores were injured. Hundreds of migrants were tried before a military court for "attempting to exit unlawfully the Egyptian eastern border"; none was allowed access to UNHCR representatives in Egypt to seek asylum. Many migrants, including from Eritrea and Sudan, were forcibly returned to countries where they were at risk of serious human rights violations.

■ In June, up to 1,200 Eritrean asylum-seekers were forcibly returned to Eritrea where they faced the risk of torture and other serious human rights violations. Most were immediately detained by the Eritrean authorities in military training camps.

Housing rights – slums/informal settlements

More than 100 residents of Al-Duwayqah were killed by a rockslide on 6 September. Water leaking from Al-Moqattam hill had given warning of a possible disaster, but the authorities did not take appropriate action. After a similar tragedy at the nearby Zabaleen slum in 1993, the government ordered the clearance of Al-Duwayqah in 1999, but many residents refused to leave because the authorities reportedly failed to provide them with adequate alternative housing.

Police cordoned off the disaster scene and restricted access to journalists and humanitarian organizations, although camps for survivors were established by the army and the Egyptian Red Crescent. Survivors held protests and most but not all were provided with alternative housing. The Public Prosecutor was reported to have opened an investigation into the cause of the deaths.

The tragedy provided a stark reminder of the risks facing many of Egypt's slum-dwellers, who number between 5 and 11 million people, according to official estimates, and live in around 1,000 overcrowded informal settlements (*ashwaiyyat*) that lack adequate basic services.

Right to health

On 4 September, a Cairo administrative court found the Prime Minister's transfer under a 2007 decree of the health care facilities of the public non-profit-making Health Insurance Organization, plus its assets and affiliated companies, to the Egyptian Healthcare Holding Company to be in violation of the state's duty to guarantee the right to health. It also found the

E

transfer in breach of the Constitution and Egypt's obligations under the International Covenant on Economic, Social and Cultural Rights. The court reasoned that people who cannot afford health care would be deprived of it. The court also stated that the right to medical care at a reasonable price should govern a government's right to introduce new administrative methods.

Amnesty International visits/reports

🚌 Amnesty International delegates visited Egypt in February in an unsuccessful attempt to observe a trial before the military court, as well as in May and July to participate in conferences and workshops.

📄 Egypt: 117 NGOs slam HIV-based arrests and trials – doctors helping police denounced for breaching medical ethics, human rights, 7 April 2008

📄 Egypt: Sentences against Muslim Brothers a perversion of justice, 15 April 2008

📄 Egypt: Deadly journeys through the desert (MDE 12/015/2008)

📄 Egypt: No justice for 49 facing trial before emergency court (MDE 12/019/2008)

📄 Egypt: Amnesty International voices concern over pattern of reckless policing (MDE 12/023/2008)

EL SALVADOR

REPUBLIC OF EL SALVADOR

Head of state and government:	**Elías Antonio Saca**
Death penalty:	**abolitionist for ordinary crimes**
Population:	**7 million**
Life expectancy:	**71.3 years**
Under-5 mortality (m/f):	**32/26 per 1,000**
Adult literacy:	**80.6 per cent**

Levels of violence remained high and there was widespread concern about public insecurity. The authorities were criticized for misusing the 2006 Special Law against Acts of Terrorism. Widespread human rights violations committed during the internal armed conflict (1980-1992) remained unpunished and the 1993 Amnesty Law remained in place.

Background

In February charges were dropped against 13 representatives of local social organizations in Suchitoto detained in July 2007. The 13 had been

arrested following clashes with police during a protest about government policy on access to clean water, and were charged under the 2006 anti-terrorism law.

Indigenous Peoples' rights

In May, four groups of Indigenous Peoples, the Lenca, Nahuat, Kakawira and Maya, lobbied the legislative assembly to ratify ILO Convention 169 on Indigenous and Tribal Peoples. They also requested that the legislative assembly carry out reforms to ensure the identity and collective rights of Indigenous Peoples were recognized in national law in order to enable them to own land and have access to clean water. By the end of the year El Salvador had not ratified ILO Convention 169 or legally recognized the rights of its Indigenous Peoples.

Impunity

In September, the mandate of the Inter-Institutional Commission for the Search for Disappeared Children was extended, although the extension was only granted until 31 May 2009. The Commission was established in 2004 to clarify the whereabouts of some 700 children who were the victims of enforced disappearance during the internal armed conflict (1980-1992). The Commission has been criticized for inefficiency and lack of independence; only 30 of the disappeared children have been located by the Commission.

■ In June, former army General Rafael Flores was summonsed to testify before the Attorney General of Chalatenango regarding the Serrano Cruz case. This was the first time a high-ranking military officer had been called to provide information on serious human rights violations that occurred during the conflict. Two sisters, seven-year-old Ernestina and three-year-old Erlinda Serrano Cruz, disappeared in June 1982 during a military campaign in Chalatenango. As the case did not progress through the domestic courts, the Inter-American Court of Human Rights requested in a 2005 judgment that the authorities carry out an investigation. At the end of the year, the investigation had yet to begin and the whereabouts of the sisters remained unknown.

■ In November, a complaint was filed with the Spanish courts against 14 members of the El Salvadoran army and former President Alfredo Cristiani Burkard for the murder of six Jesuit priests, their housekeeper and her

16-year-old daughter at the Central American University (UCA) in November 1989.

Violence against women and girls

In May, a formal request was made by women's organizations to the Attorney General calling for the investigation into the rape and murder of nine-year-old Katya Miranda in April 1999 to be re-opened immediately. The organizations claimed that new evidence had been found and feared that the statute of limitations could prevent any further proceedings being opened after April 2009. No formal response to the request had been made by the Attorney General by the end of 2008. Several women's organizations also expressed concern at the high number of women killed in the first five months of the year.

EQUATORIAL GUINEA

REPUBLIC OF EQUATORIAL GUINEA

Head of state:	Teodoro Obiang Nguema Mbasogo
Head of government:	Ignacio Milán Tang (replaced Ricardo Mangue Obama Nfube in July)
Death penalty:	retentionist
Population:	520,000
Life expectancy:	50.4 years
Under-5 mortality (m/f):	162/145 per 1,000
Adult literacy:	87 per cent

Poverty remained widespread – 60 per cent of the population lived on US$1 a day – despite high levels of economic growth and oil production, and one of the highest per capita incomes in the world. According to UNICEF, more than half of the population had no access to clean drinking water and 20 per cent of children died before the age of five.

There were fewer arrests of political opponents than in previous years despite an upsurge in the run-up to elections. Some people were briefly detained and released uncharged; others were sentenced to prison terms after unfair trials. Most appeared to be prisoners of conscience. In June the President pardoned about 30 political prisoners, including prisoners of

conscience. There were fewer reports of torture. Prisoners were held incommunicado; some were held in isolation in shackles and handcuffs. A former army officer was a victim of enforced disappearance. Scores of families were forcibly evicted from their homes and hundreds more remained at risk of eviction.

Background

In February parliament approved the National Development Plan aimed at eradicating poverty within the next 12 years.

In May the ruling Democratic Party of Equatorial Guinea won municipal and parliamentary elections, taking 99 of 100 parliamentary seats and all the municipalities. The opposition Convergence for Social Democracy (CPDS) won one parliamentary seat. Election rigging and harassment of voters and opposition candidates were reported. A new government was appointed in July.

In September the government signed the Revised Cotonou Agreement, under which the EU will finance good governance, human rights and social projects and provide support to civil society groups. A law to regulate land ownership was tabled in parliament.

The UN Special Rapporteur on torture visited Equatorial Guinea in November. The Special Rapporteur visited the country's prisons and other detention centres and was able to speak to most prisoners. However, access was denied to three prisoners who were abducted from Nigeria in 2005 and whose imprisonment the authorities denied, despite credible evidence of their being held in Black Beach prison in the capital, Malabo.

Housing rights – forced evictions

Regeneration of the main cities continued and led to forced evictions. Scores of families were forcibly evicted from their homes to make room for roads and luxury housing developments, especially in the capital, Malabo, and Bata. Hundreds of other families remained at risk of eviction. Families forcibly evicted in previous years were not compensated or rehoused.

Arbitrary arrests and detentions

Although the number of politically motivated arrests decreased compared to previous years, there was an upsurge in the first quarter of the year. Some of those arrested were released without charge after being held for varying periods. Most of them appeared to be prisoners of conscience. Dozens of prisoners, including possible prisoners of conscience, remained in detention.

■ Brigida Asongsua Elo, the wife of prisoner of conscience Guillermo Nguema Ela released in June, was held without charge or trial at the Central Police Station in Malabo for over four months. She had been arrested without a warrant in December 2007, the day after visiting her husband in Black Beach prison. The authorities accused her of receiving a map from her husband that was to be used to plan an attack on the prison. She was held in degrading and inhumane conditions in a cell with up to 100 other detainees, mainly men. The police ignored a court order to bring her to court.

Prisoner releases

On the occasion of his birthday in June, President Obiang Nguema pardoned about 30 prisoners. They included 13 prisoners of conscience convicted after an unfair trial in June 2002 of plotting to overthrow the government, and Reverend Bienvenido Samba Momesori, who had been held without charge or trial since October 2003. However, the released prisoners were ordered to return to their places of origin within a week and told they needed permission to leave these places.

Torture and other ill-treatment

There were fewer reports of torture and other ill-treatment of political detainees. However, suspected criminals continued to be tortured or otherwise ill-treated with impunity in police stations.

A female police officer arrested in November 2007 in connection with the death in Nsuemang, Ebebiyin district, of Lázaro Ondo Obiang on 29 September 2007, was tried before a military court in Bata in February. Lázaro Ondo Obiang died as a result of beatings by four police officers, who apparently acted on her orders. She was convicted and sentenced to six months' imprisonment. A senior police officer who had been accused of torturing other detainees in Bata police station and had reportedly been arrested in November 2007 was one of the judges.

Two soldiers arrested in November 2007 in connection with the death of Salvador Ndong Nguema in Evinayong prison in 2007 were released untried in February and resumed their duties.

■ Saturnino Ncogo, a former member of the banned Progress Party of Equatorial Guinea (PPGE), died in Black Beach prison on 12 March. He had been arrested a few hours earlier after three weapons were found hidden in his house. The authorities claimed he committed suicide by throwing himself from the top of a bunk bed. There was no investigation and an autopsy was not carried out. His relatives said that the body was in an advanced state of decomposition by the time they received it, three days later, and that he had a fractured skull.

Prison conditions

Although prison facilities improved, prisoners were held incommunicado throughout the year after the authorities suspended all prison visits in January. The provision of food and medicines remained inadequate, although a doctor reportedly visited on a regular basis. At least eight prisoners in Black Beach prison remained permanently handcuffed and shackled in isolation cells.

Enforced disappearances

On 8 October, two Cameroonian police officers, who reportedly had been paid by Equatorial Guinean security personnel, unlawfully arrested former Equatorial Guinean army colonel Cipriano Nguema Mba, a refugee in Cameroon, and handed him over to the Equatorial Guinea embassy in Yaoundé. He was transferred to Black Beach prison and held incommunicado. Although he was seen by the UN Special Rapporteur on torture, his whereabouts remained unacknowledged by the government at the end of the year.

The authorities still failed to acknowledge the detention of three people abducted by security personnel in Nigeria in July 2005, although they were known to be held in Black Beach prison. Information received in July indicated that former Lieutenant-Colonel Florencio Bibang Ela, Felipe Esono Ntutumu and Antimo Edu were held incommunicado in hand and leg cuffs. Juan Ondo Abaga, who was also abducted from Nigeria in February 2005, was among the prisoners released in June. Until his release, he was held in an isolation cell in leg chains and handcuffs.

Unfair trial

Six former members of the PPGE were convicted in June of possession of arms and ammunition and sentenced to between one and six years in prison, although no weapons or ammunition had been found in their possession. Cruz Obiang Ebele, Emiliano Esono Michá, Gerardo Angüe Mangue, Gumersindo Ramírez Faustino, Juan Ecomo Ndong and Bonifacio Nguema Ndong were arrested without a warrant in Malabo in March and April. Their arrests followed that of Saturnino Ncogo (see above), whom they knew. They were held at the Central Police Station for about two months. At least two claimed they had been ill-treated. Their trial was unfair; no evidence was presented in court to substantiate the charges other than the three weapons found in Saturnino Ncogo's house and the defendants' statements that they knew about the weapons. In court they claimed that their statements had been altered and that they had been made to sign different statements under duress. However, the court dismissed this claim. They had no access to a defence lawyer until three days before the trial started.

The six men were tried alongside Simon Mann, a UK national accused of an attempted coup in March 2004, even though the charges against the six were unrelated to the alleged coup attempt. Simon Mann was convicted as charged and sentenced to 34 years' imprisonment. He had been extradited from Zimbabwe in February. Mohamed Salaam, a Lebanese businessman and long-term resident in Equatorial Guinea, was convicted of the same offences and sentenced to 18 years in prison.

Freedom of expression

In September the authorities threatened CPDS leaders for attempting to set up a radio station. After weeks of negotiations with the authorities, the day after the CPDS formally requested a licence police raided the party's headquarters in Malabo and demanded the radio transmitter, which the CPDS refused to hand over. No licence had been granted by the end of the year.

Amnesty International report

📄 Equatorial Guinea: Opposition under threat (AFR 24/011/2008)

ERITREA

STATE OF ERITREA

Head of state and government:	Issayas Afewerki
Death penalty:	abolitionist in practice
Population:	5 million
Life expectancy:	56.6 years
Under-5 mortality (m/f):	79/72 per 1,000
Adult literacy:	60.5 per cent

The government prohibited independent journalism, opposition parties, unregistered religious organizations, and virtually all civil society activity. Up to 1,200 Eritrean asylum-seekers forcibly returned from Egypt and other countries were detained upon arrival in Eritrea. Separately, thousands of prisoners of conscience and political prisoners remained in detention after years in prison. Prison conditions were harsh. Perceived dissidents, deserters and those evading mandatory military conscription and other critics of the government and their families were punished and harassed. The government reacted dismissively to any criticism on human rights grounds.

E

Background

Close to half the population remained under-nourished and dependent on international food aid, including more than 85,000 children with malnutrition.

The Eritrea-Ethiopia Boundary Commission completed its mandate in October despite Ethiopia failing to apply its ruling, and the UN Security Council withdrew the UN Mission in Ethiopia and Eritrea (UNMEE) in the wake of Eritrean obstruction of its operations along the Eritrea/Ethiopia border.

From February to April, Eritrea built up its forces in the long-disputed Ras Doumeira area along the Eritrea/Djibouti border, with Djibouti claiming that Eritrea had encroached on its territory. Small-scale armed conflict between the two countries erupted in June. At least 35 soldiers were reported killed and 50 injured.

Eritrea hosted the Asmara wing of the Alliance for the Re-Liberation of Somalia (ARS), which split off from a Djibouti-based ARS wing. Eritrea provided and served as a transit point for weapons and ammunition sold in weapons markets in Somalia.

Eritrean opposition parties in exile remained active in Ethiopia and other countries in Africa, Europe and North America.

Freedom of religion

More than 2,000 members of unregistered minority religions, including Pentecostal and evangelical denominations, which were banned by the government in 2002, remained in incommunicado detention without charge or trial. Many were arrested in 2008. Some government critics from registered religions, including Islam and the Eritrean Orthodox Church, also remained in detention. Amnesty International considers all who are detained solely on the basis of their religious affiliation or practice prisoners of conscience.

■ Abune Antonios, Patriarch of the Eritrean Orthodox Church, arrested in January 2006, remained in secret detention, after a period of house arrest, for criticizing government intervention in church affairs and the detention of three Orthodox priests. He was earlier replaced by a government-appointed Patriarch. His health remained poor and he was reportedly refused adequate medical care for diabetes.

■ On 13 and 14 August, at least 40 Muslim clerics and scholars from the Saho ethnic group were arrested by soldiers in Asmara and other towns. They were held incommunicado in undisclosed locations without charge and at risk of torture.

■ Pastor Ogbamichael Teklehaimanot of the Kale Hiwot Church, arrested in October 2007, remained in detention. He had previously been subjected to 10 months of solitary confinement and hard labour at Sawa military camp.

■ In February, 10 members of the Full Gospel Church who had been imprisoned for five years were released.

Prisoners of conscience and other political prisoners

The government was intolerant of peaceful dissent and restricted freedom of expression, assembly and association. Family members of detainees said that no form of international communication was safe from government monitoring and subsequent reprisal, adding to the difficulties of monitoring individual detainees, especially those who are believed to be held in secret detention.

Political prisoners, some held since 2001 or earlier, accused of support for armed opposition groups in exile, including Eritrean Liberation Front (ELF) factions, were presumed to be still detained without charge or trial. Prisoners of conscience included draft evaders, military deserters and failed asylum-seekers who had been returned to Eritrea.

■ Hundreds of former officials, independent journalists and civil servants arrested in September 2001 were believed to still be held in incommunicado detention after more than seven years. Among them were 11 former government ministers and veterans arrested after calling for government reform. Some were reported to have died in detention as a result of harsh conditions.

■ Aster Yohannes, wife of prisoner of conscience Petros Solomon, was still held in incommunicado detention without charge. She was detained in 2003 when she returned from the USA to visit her children.

Freedom of expression – journalists

The government prohibited all independent and private journalism. There has been no functioning private press in Eritrea since 2001.

■ Ten journalists detained in 2001 were still held incommunicado without charge. At least one, Fessahaye Yohannes (known as "Joshua"), was reported to have died in prison in January 2007. The government did not respond to questions about him.

■ Daniel Kibrom, a journalist for state-owned Eri TV, was serving a sentence of five years' forced labour for trying to cross the border into Ethiopia. He had been detained in a prison camp since October 2006.

Refugees and asylum-seekers

Egypt, Sudan, Germany, Sweden and the UK forcibly returned Eritrean refugees and asylum-seekers from November 2007 onwards. These forced returns disregarded the fate of earlier returnees who had been arbitrarily detained and tortured, and ignored UNHCR guidelines which strongly recommend against any forced returns to Eritrea because of Eritrea's poor human rights record.

■ The Egyptian authorities carried out a mass forced return of Eritreans from Egypt to Eritrea in the first half of 2008. Up to 1,200 asylum-seekers from Egypt were returned to Eritrea and were arrested and detained upon arrival. They were at grave risk of torture and other ill-treatment. While some pregnant women and women with children were released after weeks in detention, the majority of those returned were transferred to the remote Wia prison and other military facilities and were still held there at the end of the year. Egyptian authorities returned more than 20 additional Eritrean asylum-seekers in late December, while hundreds more remained at risk of return from Egypt.

■ On 14 May German immigration authorities forcibly returned asylum-seekers Yonas Haile Mehari and Petros Aforki Mulugeta to Eritrea. Both were arrested upon arrival and remained in detention, Yonas Haile Mehari was held incommunicado, and both were at grave risk of torture and other ill-treatment.

■ Some 700 Eritrean nationals, including 60 women and 30 children, who had fled from Eritrea to Sudan and then to Libya, were held in detention facilities in Mistarah, Libya, and other locations under threat of forcible return to Eritrea.

Military conscription

National service was mandatory for men aged 18 to 40 and women aged 18 to at least 27. Initially 18 months long, it included six months' military service and frequent forced labour, could be extended indefinitely, and was followed by reserve duties. Much of the adult population was engaged in mandatory service.

Some young people aged 17 were required to register for national service for the following year and were refused exit permits so that they could not leave the country.

The standard punishment for evading military service has been detention and being tied in painful positions. Imprisonment, ordered by military commanders, could be extended indefinitely. There was no exemption from military service for conscientious objectors.

Torture and other ill-treatment

Conditions of detention in Eritrea remained harsh and prisoners were regularly tortured or otherwise ill-treated. A common reported method of punishment over recent years has been tying detainees in painful positions known as the "helicopter" and the "eight". Prisoners have also frequently been left exposed to the sun for extended periods, or locked in metal shipping containers which magnify extremes of heat and cold. Many detainees were held in secret prisons and some in security prisons such as Karchele in Asmara. Many prisoners were held in crowded

underground cells without access to daylight. Conditions were unhygienic and damp, with no water for washing or cleaning. Prisoners were underfed and received unclean drinking water. There was almost no medical assistance available.

■ In February local sources reported the death in prison of Muslim leader Taha Mohammed Nur, co-founder of the ELF.

■ Teklesenbet Gebreab Kiflom, a member of the evangelical Full Gospel Church, reportedly died in Wia military prison in October after being denied treatment for malaria. Another evangelical Christian, Azib Simon, was reported to have died in similar circumstances in June.

Amnesty International reports

▤ Egypt: Deadly Journey through the Desert (MDE 12/015/2008)

▤ Eritrea: Prisoners of conscience remembered on 7th anniversary of mass detentions (AFR 64/007/2008)

▤ Egypt: Amnesty International calls for President to stop flights to possible torture in Eritrea (MDE 12/014/2008)

▤ Libya: Amnesty International warns against deportations of Eritreans (MDE 19/007/2008)

E

ESTONIA

REPUBLIC OF ESTONIA

Head of state:	**Toomas Hendrik Ilves**
Head of government:	**Andrus Ansip**
Death penalty:	**abolitionist for all crimes**
Population:	**1.3 million**
Life expectancy:	**71.2 years**
Under-5 mortality (m/f):	**11/8 per 1,000**
Adult literacy:	**99.8 per cent**

Linguistic minorities continued to face discrimination in a number of areas, particularly in the fields of employment and education. Migrants were exposed to harassment by state officials and attacks by extremist groups. Criminal investigations into allegations of excessive use of force by law enforcement officials were dismissed. A human rights organization continued to be harassed by the government.

Discrimination – ethnic minorities

In March, the UN Special Rapporteur on racism, reporting on a visit in September 2007, expressed his concern at the conditions of the Russian-speaking minority. The Rapporteur noted a high level of discrimination particularly in the field of employment, where Russian speakers suffer unemployment rates almost twice as high as among ethnic Estonians. The Rapporteur urged the government to take measures to facilitate the naturalization process of stateless people.

The government started to implement the "New Strategy for Integration of Society (2008-2013)", which aims at improving knowledge of the Estonian language among those who do not speak it as a first language, providing free language courses for citizenship applicants and for a number of different groups of workers.

Workers from minority groups faced regular monitoring of their Estonian language proficiency by the Language Inspectorate, a state agency charged with overseeing the implementation of the Language Act. According to the data made public in 2008, and referring to 2007, around 97 per cent of the teachers in Russian schools and kindergartens checked by the Inspectorate failed the controls. Local media and organizations raised concerns about the discriminatory character of the linguistic requirements.

In June, the government introduced new language requirements for some professions in the private sector.

Racism and discrimination – migrants

In his March report the UN Special Rapporteur on racism noted that migrants were subject to discrimination and exposed to racially motivated attacks, particularly by members of extremist organizations, including neo-Nazi groups. The Rapporteur raised concerns about cases of harassment of migrants by law enforcement officials, particularly by border guards.

In December, the Equal Treatment Act was introduced which included provisions against discrimination in several fields, among them employment and education. In 2007 the EU had formally requested that Estonia reflect the EU Racial Equality Directive in its national legislation.

Excessive use of force

By mid 2008, criminal investigations into allegations of ill-treatment of protesters and other people by law enforcement officials at a demonstration in the capital, Tallinn, in April 2007 were dismissed for lack of evidence by the police and the prosecutor's office. However, in at least one case the investigation ascertained that people had been ill-treated, but no action was taken as the perpetrators were not identified.

In February, seven people filed a complaint with the European Court of Human Rights on the grounds that they were unlawfully arrested and detained and subjected to inhuman and degrading treatment, and that the Estonian authorities refused to initiate an investigation into their unlawful arrest and detention.

Human rights defenders

In June, the Estonian Security Police Board published its annual report which made serious allegations against the Legal Information Centre for Human Rights (LICHR), an NGO promoting and defending the rights of those belonging to linguistic minorities. The report stated that the LICHR was used by the Russian Federation to carry out scientific research for propaganda purposes, and accused the LICHR of trying to conceal the specific sources of funding it received from the Russian Federation. These allegations were widely seen as an attempt by the government to misrepresent the LICHR and to undermine its attempts to secure the necessary financial and social support to carry out its work.

E

ETHIOPIA

FEDERAL DEMOCRATIC REPUBLIC OF ETHIOPIA

Head of state:	Girma Wolde-Giorgis
Head of government:	Meles Zenawi
Death penalty:	retentionist
Population:	85.2 million
Life expectancy:	51.8 years
Under-5 mortality (m/f):	151/136 per 1,000
Adult literacy:	35.9 per cent

Restrictions on humanitarian assistance to the Somali Region (known as the Ogaden) continued. The government engaged in sporadic armed conflict against the Ogaden National Liberation Front (ONLF) and both forces perpetrated human rights abuses against civilians. Ethiopian troops fighting insurgents in Somalia in support of the Transitional Federal Government (TFG) committed human rights abuses and were reported to have committed war crimes. Security forces arrested members of the Oromo ethnic group in Addis Ababa and in the Oromo Region towards the end of the year. Independent journalists continued to face harassment and arrest. A number of political prisoners were believed to remain in detention and opposition party leader Birtukan Mideksa, who was pardoned in 2007, was rearrested. A draft law restricting the activities of Ethiopian and international organizations working on human rights was expected to be passed by parliament in 2009. Ethiopia remained one of the world's poorest countries with some 6.4 million people suffering acute food insecurity, including 1.9 million in the Somali Region.

Background

The Eritrea-Ethiopia Boundary Commission completed its mandate in October, despite Ethiopia failing to implement its ruling, and the UN Security Council withdrew the UN Mission in Ethiopia and Eritrea (UNMEE) in the wake of Eritrean obstruction of its operations along the Eritrea/Ethiopia border.

Thousands of Ethiopian armed forces remained in Somalia to support the TFG in armed conflict against insurgents throughout most of the year. Accusations of human rights violations committed by Ethiopian forces continued in 2008. Insurgent factions stated that they were fighting to force Ethiopia's withdrawal from Somalia. A phased plan for Ethiopian withdrawal was included in a peace agreement signed by the Alliance for the Re-Liberation of Somalia-Djibouti and TFG representatives in late October. Ethiopian forces began to withdraw late in the year, but had not withdrawn from Somalia completely by the end of the year.

The government faced sporadic armed conflict in the Oromo and Somali regions, with ONLF members also implicated in human rights abuses against civilians. Ethiopian opposition parties in exile remained active in Eritrea and in other countries in Africa and Europe.

Divisions split the opposition Coalition for Unity and Democracy (CUD) party, leading to the emergence of new opposition parties, including the Unity for Democracy and Justice Party (UDJP) led by former judge Birtukan Mideksa. She was one of more than 70 CUD leaders, journalists and civil society activists convicted, then pardoned and released in 2007.

Suicide bombers attacked Ethiopia's trade mission in Hargeisa, Somaliland, on 29 October killing several Ethiopian and Somali civilians.

Prisoners of conscience and other political prisoners

A number of political prisoners, detained in previous years in the context of internal armed conflicts or following contested elections in 2005, remained in detention.

■ Bekele Jirata, General Secretary of the Oromo Federalist Democratic Movement party, Asefa Tefera Dibaba, a lecturer at Addis Ababa University and dozens of others from the Oromo ethnic group were arrested in Addis Ababa and parts of the Oromo Region from 30 October onwards. Some of those detained were accused of financially supporting the Oromo Liberation Front (OLF).

■ Sultan Fowsi Mohamed Ali, an independent mediator, who was arrested in Jijiga in August 2007 reportedly to prevent him from giving evidence to a UN fact-finding mission, remained in detention. Tried for alleged involvement in two hand grenade attacks in 2007, he was sentenced to 22 years' imprisonment in May 2008.

■ On 15 January Birtukan Mideksa, Gizachew Shiferaw and Alemayehu Yeneneh, then senior members of the CUD, were briefly detained by police after holding party meetings in southern Ethiopia. Birtukan Mideksa was rearrested on 28 December after she issued a public statement regarding the negotiations that led to her 2007 pardon. Her pardon was revoked and the sentence of life imprisonment reinstated.

Prisoner releases

Many released prisoners faced harassment and intimidation, with some choosing to leave the country.
■ Human rights defenders and lawyers Daniel Bekele and Netsanet Demissie were released on 28 March. They had been detained since November 2005 together with hundreds of opposition parliamentarians, CUD members and journalists. Unlike their co-defendants in the trial who were pardoned and released in 2007, Daniel Bekele and Netsanet Demissie remained in detention, having refused to sign a document negotiated by local elders. They mounted a defence and were convicted by the Federal High Court of criminal incitement (although the presiding judge dissented) and sentenced to 30 months' imprisonment. When it became evident they would not be released, even after they appealed, they chose to sign the negotiated document, and were subsequently pardoned and released after serving 29 months of their sentence.
■ Charges of conspiring to commit "outrages against the Constitution" faced by Yalemzewd Bekele, a human rights lawyer who had been working for the European Commission in Addis Ababa, were dropped, without prejudice, before trial.
■ Abdirahman Mohamed Qani, chief of the Tolomoge sub-clan of the Ogaden clan in the Somali Region, was detained on 13 July after receiving a large public welcome when he returned from two years abroad. He was released on 7 October, and his relatives who had also been detained were reportedly released several days later.
■ CUD activist Alemayehu Mesele, who had suffered harassment since his release from prison in 2007, fled Ethiopia in early May after he was severely beaten by unknown assailants.
■ The editor of the *Reporter* newspaper Amare Aregawi was severely beaten by unknown assailants on 31 October in Addis Ababa. He had previously been detained by security officers in August.

In September, the government announced that it had released 394 prisoners and commuted one death sentence to life imprisonment to mark the Ethiopian New Year.

Freedom of expression

Independent journalists continued to face harassment and arrest.

At least 13 newspapers shut down by the government in 2005 were still closed. Independent journalists were reportedly denied licences to operate, although others did receive licences. Serkalem Fasil, Eskinder Nega and Sisay Agena, former publishers of Ethiopia's largest circulation independent newspapers, who had been detained with CUD members, were denied licences to open two new newspapers.

In February the Supreme Court upheld a decision to dissolve the Ethiopian Teachers Association (ETA) and hand over its assets to a rival union formed by the government, also known as the Ethiopian Teachers Association. This action followed years of harassment and detention of union members. In December the union, under its new name, the National Teachers' Association, had its application for registration as a professional organization rejected.
■ On World Press Freedom Day (3 May) Alemayehu Mahtemework, publisher of the monthly *Enku*, was detained and 10,000 copies of his publication impounded. He was released after five days without charge and copies of the magazine were later returned to him.
■ In November a Federal High Court judge convicted editor-in-chief of the weekly *Enbilta,* Tsion Girma, of "inciting the public through false rumours" after a reporting mistake. She reportedly paid a fine and was released.

Human rights defenders

A draft Charities and Societies Proclamation was revised several times by the government in 2008, but remained threatening to the rights of freedom of assembly, association and expression.

Its provisions included severe restrictions on the amount of foreign funding Ethiopian civil society organizations working on human rights-related issues could receive from abroad (no more than 10 per cent of total revenues). It would also establish a Civil Societies Agency with sweeping authority over organizations carrying out work on human rights and

E

conflict resolution in Ethiopia. It was expected to be passed into law by Parliament in early 2009.

Ethiopian troops in Somalia

Ethiopia maintained a significant troop presence in Somalia which supported the TFG until the end of the year. Ethiopian forces committed human rights abuses and were reported to have committed war crimes. Ethiopian forces attacked the al-Hidya mosque in Mogadishu killing 21 men, some inside the mosque, on 19 April. More than 40 children were held for some days after the mosque raid before being released .

Many attacks by Ethiopian forces in response to armed insurgents were reported to have been indiscriminate and disproportionate, often occurring in densely civilian-populated areas.

Internal armed conflict

The government continued counter-insurgency operations in the Somali Region, which increased after attacks by the ONLF on an oil installation in Obole in April 2007. These included restrictions on humanitarian aid which have had a serious impact on conflict-affected districts of the region. The government did not allow unhindered independent access for human rights monitoring.

Reports, dating back to 2007, of beatings, rape and other forms of torture, forcible conscription and extrajudicial executions in the Somali Region were investigated by a government-contracted body but not by an independent international body.

Torture and other ill-treatment

Reports of torture made by defendants in the trial of elected parliamentarian Kifle Tigeneh and others, one of several CUD trials, were not investigated.

Conditions in Kaliti prison and other detention facilities were harsh – overcrowded, unhygienic and lacking adequate medical care. Among those detained in such conditions were long-term political prisoners held without charge or trial, particularly those accused of links to the OLF.

■ Mulatu Aberra, a trader of the Oromo ethnic group accused of supporting the OLF, was released on 1 July on bail and fled the country. He had been arrested in November 2007 and reportedly tortured and denied medical treatment for resulting injuries while in detention.

Death penalty

While a number of death sentences were imposed by courts in 2008, no executions were reported.

■ In May the Federal Supreme Court overturned earlier rulings and sentenced to death former President Mengistu Haile Mariam (in exile in Zimbabwe) and 18 senior officials of his *Dergue* government. The prosecution had appealed against life imprisonment sentences passed in 2007, after they were convicted by the Federal High Court of genocide and crimes against humanity perpetrated between 1974 and 1991.

■ On 6 April a court sentenced to death five military officers in absentia. They served under Mengistu Haile Mariam, and were held responsible for air raids in Hawzen, in the Tigray Region, which killed hundreds in a market in June 1980.

■ On 8 May a court in Tigray Region found six people guilty of a bus bombing in northern Ethiopia between Humora and Shira on 13 March and sentenced three of them to death.

■ On 21 May the Federal Supreme Court sentenced eight men to death for a 28 May 2007 bombing in Jijiga in the Somali Region.

■ On 22 May a military tribunal sentenced to death in absentia four Ethiopian pilots , who sought asylum while training in Israel in 2007.

Amnesty International reports

▒ Ethiopia: Government Prepares Assault on Civil Society (AFR 25/006/2008)

▒ Ethiopia: Comments on the Draft Charities and Societies Proclamation (AFR 25/008/2008)

▒ Ethiopia: Draft Law would Wreck Civil Society (AFR 25/009/2008)

▒ Ethiopia: Arbitrary detention/torture or other ill-treatment (AFR 25/012/2008)

▒ Routinely Targeted: Attacks on Civilians in Somalia (AFR 52/006/2008)

E

FIJI

REPUBLIC OF THE FIJI ISLANDS

Head of state:	Ratu Josefa Iloilovatu Uluivuda
Head of government:	Commodore Josaia Voreqe Bainimarama
Death penalty:	abolitionist for ordinary crimes
Population:	844,000
Life expectancy:	68.3 years
Under-5 mortality (m/f):	24/24 per 1,000
Adult literacy:	94.4 per cent

The interim, military-supported government continued to violate freedom of expression and intimidate journalists and members of the public. The Fiji Human Rights Commission supported the expulsion of senior media figures from the country and attacked the role played by human rights NGOs in Fiji civil society. Reports of violence against women continued.

Freedom of expression

■ In February, Minister of Defence Epeli Ganilau ordered Russell Hunter, publisher of the *Fiji Sun*, to be deported to Australia after a series of articles were published alleging that a senior cabinet minister had evaded tax.

The deportation was carried out by immigration officials despite the seven-day notice and appeal period given in Minister Ganilau's order. Hunter had no opportunity to challenge the Minister's decision.

■ In May, Immigration officials deported Evan Hannah, publisher of the *Fiji Times*, to Australia after a number of articles critical of the interim government were published.

During his arrest and detention, Evan Hannah had no opportunity to appeal against the decision to deport him, nor did he have access to his lawyer once he was removed from his home.

Government officials ignored a court order instructing immigration and police officials to produce Evan Hannah in the Suva High Court on 2 May.

■ In August, journalist Serafina Silaitoga was subjected to threats and intimidation by police officers in Labasa, after her article criticizing a senior Cabinet Minister was published in the *Fiji Times* on 9 August. Police officers tried to force her to make a statement on her article and when she refused to do so without legal representation, threatened to lock her in a police cell.

In February, a report commissioned by the Fiji Human Rights Commission (FHRC) called for greater regulation of the media, including the setting up of a media tribunal. In August, the interim government announced that it would establish a tribunal to provide stronger regulation of the media.

In June, an FHRC report on the deportation of the two above newspaper publishers attacked NGOs and called for increased government scrutiny of their activities and funding. The report also published confidential emails between NGO representatives and the newspaper publishers discussing the political situation in Fiji.

The ousted leader of the opposition, Mick Beddoes, raised a concern that the Commission was able to access private and confidential emails between human rights defenders and other individuals working for human rights NGOs.

Torture and other ill-treatment

■ In July, escaped prisoner Josefa Baleiloa was severely beaten by police officers during and following his recapture in Suva. Josefa Baleiloa was in a coma for two weeks and died as a result of his injuries in September.

According to television news reports, Josefa Baleiloa was beaten by more than 10 police officers long after he had been subdued. Witnesses reported that officers dragged Josefa Baleiloa, beat him with pieces of timber and stones, jumped on him after he lost consciousness and continued to do so as he was taken away in a police vehicle.

No investigation into his death has been carried out.

Violence against women and girls

Levels of violence against women remained high. Reports of sexual violence against women and girls increased.

FINLAND

REPUBLIC OF FINLAND
Head of state: Tarja Halonen
Head of government: Matti Vanhanen
Death penalty: abolitionist for all crimes
Population: 5.3 million
Life expectancy: 78.9 years
Under-5 mortality (m/f): 5/4 per 1,000

Women were not adequately protected in law or practice against violence. Asylum-seekers were sent back to EU countries where they were less likely to be offered some form of protection than if their claim had been considered in Finland. Conscientious objectors to military service were imprisoned.

Violence against women and girls

Less than 10 per cent of rapes in Finland were reported to the police, according to Amnesty International findings, and only one in seven of those reported resulted in a conviction.

The Penal Code continues to differentiate between categories of rape according to the degree of physical violence used or threatened by the perpetrator. This fails to address the psychological harm done to survivors and protect adequately their right to sexual self-determination.

Sexual intercourse when the victim is incapable of giving genuine consent, for instance because of illness or intoxication, is categorized not as rape but as "sexual abuse", a less serious offence. In addition, certain categories of rape and "sexual abuse" are only investigated and prosecuted if the victim so requests.

The government did not establish a comprehensive action plan to combat violence against women.

In September the government launched a National Action Plan for implementing UN Security Council Resolution 1325 on Women, Peace and Security.

Refugees and asylum-seekers

The strict application of the "Dublin II" EU regulations saw asylum-seekers returned to the EU member state in which they first arrived for determination of their asylum claim, even when those states were less likely to provide some form of protection than Finland. The total number of "Dublin returns" from Finland increased from 320 in 2007 to at least 430 in 2008.

Returns of asylum-seekers to Greece were halted during the second half of the year after the European Court of Human Rights and Helsinki Administrative Court expressed concern about the asylum determination procedure in Greece. Courts in Finland adopted exceptional procedures to process appeals from asylum-seekers who had travelled through Greece on their way to Finland.

At least 22 asylum-seeking children were detained, including seven who were unaccompanied.

International justice

The police continued to investigate the case of a Rwandan national suspected of crimes of genocide, who had been in pre-trial detention since his arrest in Finland in April 2007. The Rwandan government filed an extradition request in April 2008. If extradited he would be at risk of an unfair trial.

Prisoners of conscience – conscientious objectors to military service

A new law governing the length of the civilian alternative to military service came into force in January. The length of the civilian alternative remained punitive and discriminatory; it was shortened from 395 to 362 days but was still more than twice as long as the most common length of military service – 180 days.

■ Eighteen prisoners of conscience, all conscientious objectors to military service, were jailed; most were serving sentences of 181 days for refusing to perform alternative civilian service.

F

FRANCE

FRENCH REPUBLIC
Head of state:	**Nicolas Sarkozy**
Head of government:	**François Fillon**
Death penalty:	**abolitionist for all crimes**
Population:	**61.9 million**
Life expectancy:	**80.2 years**
Under-5 mortality (m/f):	**6/5 per 1,000**

Allegations of ill-treatment by law enforcement officials, including at least one fatal incident, continued to be made. Procedures for investigating such incidents and bringing those responsible to justice continued to fall short of international standards. Conditions in detention centres for irregular migrants were criticized by the UN Human Rights Committee. Individuals having their asylum claim examined under the accelerated procedure remained at risk of forcible deportation while waiting for a decision. Despite the risk of serious human rights violations, France forcibly returned one man to Algeria and attempted to return another. New legislation authorizing indefinitely renewable "preventive detention" and a decree authorizing police to collect broad personal information on individuals believed to be a possible threat to public order, undermined the principle of the presumption of innocence.

Police and security forces

Allegations of ill-treatment by law enforcement officials continued. Law enforcement bodies and judicial authorities failed to investigate such allegations in line with international standards, leading to a climate of effective impunity. The UN Human Rights Committee expressed concern at allegations of ill-treatment by law enforcement officials against irregular migrants and asylum-seekers held in detention centres, and the lack of adequate investigation and punishment of such human rights violations.

On 22 September the Minister of Interior authorized municipal police officers to use conducted energy devices. Previously, only police officers of the national police force were authorized to use this type of weapon.

Unlawful killing

■ On 9 May Abdelhakim Ajimi died during arrest in Grasse. Police officers arrested and restrained Abdelhakim Ajimi after an altercation in a bank where he was trying to withdraw money. A judicial investigation into the incident was opened and was still in progress at the end of the year. According to the autopsy report, Abdelhakim Ajimi died as a result of asphyxiation caused by the restraint techniques used against him. Several witnesses to the event reported an excessive use of force by the police. The officers involved remained on active duty at the end of the year.

Impunity

■ In July, the public prosecutor closed the investigation into allegations of ill-treatment made by Josiane Ngo. Josiane Ngo was allegedly punched, kicked and dragged along the ground by police officers in July 2007, when she was eight months pregnant. The incident took place in a street, in front of a large number of witnesses. She was held in police custody overnight but released the following day without charge. Following a medical examination she was signed off work for 10 days as a result of her injuries.

Migrants, refugees and asylum-seekers

The UN Human Rights Committee expressed concern at reports of overcrowding and inadequate hygiene, food and medical care for irregular migrants and asylum-seekers – including unaccompanied minors – held in detention. It called on France to review its detention policy and improve living conditions in detention centres, especially those in the Overseas Departments and Territories. In December, photographs and a video documenting the inhuman conditions in the migration detention centre in the French overseas territory of Mayotte were sent anonymously to Amnesty International and a French media outlet. The footage revealed severe overcrowding and poor hygiene and medical facilities.

In April, the government agency that determines the status of refugees (OFPRA) reported that the rate of recognition of asylum claims reached almost 30 per cent in 2007, one of the highest rates in recent years. In contrast, the number of new asylum requests continued to decrease, falling from 26,269 to 23,804 between 2006 and 2007.

On 3 July, a bill was presented by several members of parliament to amend the right of appeal before the National Court on Asylum for asylum-seekers whose claims were being examined under the accelerated procedure. Under the new proposal asylum-seekers who were appealing against an accelerated decision could not be forcibly returned to their country of origin while their appeal was still in progress. The bill was not supported by the government.

Counter-terror and security

In July, the UN Human Rights Committee expressed concern at anti-terrorism legislation adopted in 2006 and called on France to ensure all detainees were brought promptly before a judge, and had prompt access to a lawyer. The French authorities continued to forcibly return individuals to countries where they faced a risk of torture or other serious human rights violations.

■ On 14 April Rabah Kadri, an Algerian national, was released from Val de Reuil prison. He had completed the sentence imposed on him on 16 December 2004 by the Paris Criminal Court for involvement in a terrorist plot to bomb the Strasbourg Christmas market in 2000. He had been sentenced to six years' imprisonment, followed by a permanent prohibition from French territory. Immediately upon his release from prison, Rabah Kadri was taken into police custody and subsequently returned to Algeria by sea on 15 April. Rabah Kadri arrived in Algiers on 16 April and was handed over to the Algerian authorities, who detained him incommunicado for 12 days at an undisclosed location.

■ On 21 April, Kamel Daoudi was released from La Santé prison after serving his sentence and immediately taken into custody pending expulsion to Algeria. In 2005, he was convicted of "criminal association in relation to a terrorist enterprise" and falsification of official documents and sentenced to six years' imprisonment and permanent prohibition from French territory. Originally an Algerian national, Kamel Daoudi had acquired French citizenship but in 2002 he was stripped of his French nationality due to the allegations of his involvement in terrorist groups, even though the criminal case against him was still in progress at the time. Following a request by Kamel Daoudi's lawyer, on 23 April the European Court of Human Rights ordered the French authorities to suspend the deportation procedure while it considered whether Kamel Daoudi would be at risk of torture or other ill-treatment if returned to Algeria. At the end of the year Kamel Daoudi was living under a "compulsory

residence order" (which restricted his movements to certain areas of France and required him to report regularly to a police station) while awaiting the decision of the European Court.

Legal, constitutional or institutional developments

Preventive detention

On 7 February new legislation was passed on "preventive detention". This allows individuals convicted of certain crimes to be detained after completing their prison sentence for indefinitely renewable periods of one year, if they are considered to be dangerous and to present a high risk of recidivism. In effect, it allows the custodial sentence imposed at trial to be extended indefinitely, in violation of the right to liberty, the prohibition of arbitrary detention and the presumption of innocence. The UN Human Rights Committee called for this legislation to be reviewed.

Police files on individuals

A decree published on 1 July, linked to the creation of the Public Security Central Directorate, authorized the collection of new data on individuals by police and security services in the form of the so-called "EDVIGE file". These files would collect and store information on individuals aged 13 and above believed to be "likely to disturb public order" and would include, among other things, information on an individual's health and sexual orientation. Following widespread public protests and hearings of the parliamentary law commission, the Minister of Interior proposed a revised version of the text which, in December, was still being examined by the National Commission on Data and Freedom.

Inspector general of detention centres

On 11 June, the Council of Ministers named Jean-Marie Delarue as inspector general of detention centres, in line with the requirements of the Optional Protocol to the Convention against Torture and Other Cruel, Inhuman or Degrading Treatment or Punishment. In July parliament adopted legislation to allow France to ratify the Optional Protocol.

Defender of rights

On 21 July a new constitutional law was adopted with the aim of reforming certain aspects of the political system and public administration. The legislation created a new national institution for the protection of human rights, known as the "Defender of rights". The precise mandate of this institution was still to be

F

determined at the end of the year, but it was expected to replace some existing bodies, including the institution responsible for the independent oversight of the law enforcement agencies, the National Commission on Ethics in Security (CNDS). There was concern that this could lead to a loss of the specialization, expertise, and resources for the work carried out by the CNDS, and might even restrict its capacities, leading to a negative impact on the effective independent oversight of the law enforcement agencies.

Amnesty International visits/reports

🚌 Amnesty International delegates visited France in March and May.

📃 France: Recording interrogations is not enough – more safeguards needed for rights of detainees (EUR 21/004/2008)

📃 France: Briefing to the Human Rights Committee (EUR 21/005/2008)

GAMBIA

REPUBLIC OF THE GAMBIA

Head of state and government:	Yahya Jammeh
Death penalty:	abolitionist in practice
Population:	1.8 million
Life expectancy:	58.8 years
Under-5 mortality (m/f):	129/124 per 1,000
Adult literacy:	42.5 per cent

Members of the National Intelligence Agency (NIA), army, military police and police unlawfully arrested and detained suspected opponents of the government. Among those unlawfully held were human rights defenders, journalists, former security personnel and opposition leaders. At least two journalists were forced to flee the country. Three judges were unconstitutionally removed by the President and then later reinstated. The government ignored a ruling by a regional court to release the missing journalist, Chief Ebrima Manneh.

Enforced disappearances and unlawful killings

■ In July the ECOWAS Community Court of Justice (CCJ) ordered the Gambian government to release Chief Ebrima Manneh, a former reporter from the *Daily*

Observer arrested in 2006, and pay him US$100,000. The government ignored the ruling and continued to deny that he was in their custody.

■ The fate of Kanyiba Kanyie, an opposition supporter arrested in September 2006, remained unknown as the government continued to deny knowledge of his whereabouts. A former detainee who was held with Kanyiba Kanyie in Mile 2 prison in 2007 stated that he was released in early 2007, but there was no further news of him.

Six other people remained disappeared, and it was feared that they may have been extrajudicially executed. They were Momodou Lamin Nyassi, Ndongo Mboob and Buba Sanyang, arrested in 2006, and Marcia Jammeh, Haruna Jammeh and Jisacha Kujabi, arrested in 2005.

There was no investigation during 2008 into the fate of five men, including former NIA Director General Daba Marena, initially arrested in connection with the March 2006 foiled coup plot. The men were alleged to have escaped during a prison transfer in April 2006. It was suspected that they had been extrajudicially executed.

ECOWAS and the UN formed a team to investigate the deaths of 55 foreigners allegedly killed unlawfully by Gambian security forces in 2005. The victims were 40 Ghanaians, 10 Nigerians, two Senegalese, one Togolese, one Congolese and one Ivorian. No results emerged by the end of 2008 and no suspects were brought to justice.

Detention without trial

A number of people were held in long-term detention without trial.

■ At least two people arrested in connection with the March 2006 coup plot remained in detention. Neither Alieu Lowe, held without charge, nor Hamadi Sowe, charged with concealment of treason, had been tried by the end of the year.

■ At least six other people were held in detention without charge, some for more than four years: Ismaila Bajinka and Kebba Secka (former members of the NIA), army sergeant Sam Kambai, army corporal Ebrima Joof, presidential cook Ebou Jarju, and police officer Alfusainey Jammeh.

At least 19 other people, including some foreign nationals from Senegal and Nigeria, were held without charge in Mile 2 prison maximum security cell, one for at least 12 years.

Freedom of expression – journalists

At least two journalists – Momodou Justice Darboe and Lamin Fatty – left the country following intimidation by the NIA and other government personnel. Journalists Yahya Dampha, Omar Bah, Pa Ousman Darboe, Musa Saidykhan, and Sulayman Makalo, previously in hiding in other West African countries, were granted asylum in Europe and the USA. Several journalists were arrested and detained without charge for longer than the 72 hours allowed by Gambian law, including journalists Dida Halake, Sam Obi, and Abdulgafari Oladimeji.

■ Journalist Mam Ceit Ceesay was released in February after being held for four months without charge.

■ In August, Fatou Jaw Manneh, a US-based Gambian journalist, was convicted of sedition in a trial that began in March 2007. She was sentenced to four years' imprisonment with hard labour, but was allowed to pay a fine of 250,000 Dalasis (US$12,000) in lieu of imprisonment. Afterwards she left the country.

■ The *Today* newspaper stopped publishing after the editor, Abdulhamid Adiamoh, a Nigerian, was convicted of failing to pay tax. He was also charged with sedition for writing about social conditions for children in Gambia. At the end of 2008 the trial was continuing.

■ In December a British couple, David and Fiona Fulton, who had been living in Gambia for nine years, were arrested and charged with sedition.

The Independent newspaper's premises remained under police surveillance and did not open for a second consecutive year.

Justice system

Three judges were unconstitutionally removed from office. High Court Justice B.Y. Camara and Justice Haddy Roche were dismissed in July by an order of the President, and Justice Naceesay Sallah-Wadda in September. No official reason was given for the removal of the judges and no consultation took place with the Judicial Service Commission. All three judges were reinstated before the end of the year.

There were no developments in the unsolved murder of prominent journalist Deydra Hydara, killed in 2005.

Death penalty

At the end of 2008, there were 15 people on death row. The 1997 Constitution required the National Assembly to carry out a constitutional review of the death penalty within 10 years, with a view to abolishing it. The National Assembly again failed to carry out this review.

■ Tambara Samba, a Senegalese woman sentenced to death for murder, lost her case on appeal in October.

■ In November a police officer on trial since 2007 was convicted of murder and sentenced to death.

Rights of lesbian, gay, bisexual and transgender people

In a speech in May, President Yahya Jammeh threatened to expel or kill lesbian and gay people. After that speech, at least three Gambian and two Spanish men were arrested on suspicion of same-sex sexual conduct. The government later retracted the President's statement.

Article 144 of Gambia's 1965 Criminal Code criminalizes homosexual conduct as an "unnatural offence" and provides for a prison sentence of up to 14 years, contrary to Gambia's international human rights obligations.

Amnesty International visit/report

🚍 In September Amnesty International delegates visited Gambia.

📓 Gambia: Fear Rules (AFR 27/003/2008)

GEORGIA

GEORGIA	
Head of state:	Mikheil Saakashvili (replaced Nino Burdzhanadze in January)
Head of government:	Grigol Mgaloblishvili (replaced Vladimer "Lado" Gurgenidze in November)
Death penalty:	abolitionist for all crimes
Population:	4.4 million
Life expectancy:	70.7 years
Under-5 mortality (m/f):	45/37 per 1,000

Georgian forces did not appear to take necessary measures to protect civilians during armed conflict with Russia in South Ossetia. In the conflict's aftermath, South Ossetian militia groups engaged in the pillaging and arson of several Georgian-majority settlements in South Ossetia. Nearly 200,000

people were displaced, although a majority had returned by the end of the year. There were reports of harassment of opposition activists and media.

Background

On 5 January Mikheil Saakashvili was narrowly re-elected President in pre-term elections resulting from mass protests in November 2007. The results of the inquiry into the violent dispersal of those protests had not been published by the end of 2008. The ruling party, the United National Movement, won parliamentary elections in May. Tensions in the conflict zones in Abkhazia and South Ossetia heightened from April, with increasing reports of bombing and shelling incidents and alleged airspace violations. Large-scale hostilities broke out in South Ossetia on 7 August, resulting in a five-day war between Georgian and Russian forces in which over 600 people, more than half of them civilians, died. Russian forces rapidly pushed Georgian forces out of South Ossetia and further occupied areas of undisputed Georgian territory, referred to as the "buffer zone", until early October. On 26 August the Russian Federation recognized the independence of Abkhazia and South Ossetia; by the end of the year Nicaragua was the only other state to have done so.

In April, NATO decided not to offer membership to Georgia, but in December, agreed to intensify co-operation, using the existing framework of the NATO-Georgia Commission, to review Georgia's progress towards a Membership Action Plan.

Armed conflict

Georgian armed forces did not appear to take appropriate precautionary measures to protect civilians in their assault on the South Ossetian capital Tskhinvali on the night of 7-8 August. Dozens of civilians were killed during the assault, which also caused extensive damage to civilian infrastructure. Much of the damage was caused by GRAD rockets, a weapon known to be difficult to direct accurately and therefore not suitable for use in densely populated civilian areas. The Georgian government later admitted the use of cluster munitions against military targets. As a result of their high dud rate, cluster munitions continue to indiscriminately injure and maim after a conflict has ended.

In September, the Georgian Parliament established a commission to investigate all aspects of the war; the Office of the Prosecutor also launched an investigation into the conduct of hostilities by all sides.

Abuses by armed groups

In the aftermath of the Georgian withdrawal from South Ossetia, militia groups loyal to the de facto South Ossetian authorities carried out the large-scale pillaging and arson of several Georgian-majority settlements in South Ossetia. These settlements were under Russian military control at the time, although the Russian military did not take action to stop the activities of militia groups. There were also reports of the killing and beating of ethnic Georgians. Pillaging and arson did not extend to all Georgian settlements in South Ossetia, but was concentrated in those areas previously associated with the alternative administration headed by Dmitri Sanakoev and backed by the Georgian authorities. Satellite imagery confirmed the large-scale destruction in these settlements reported by eyewitnesses. The South Ossetian authorities impeded humanitarian access to areas under their control in the aftermath of the conflict.

Internally displaced people

At the peak of the conflict, over 190,000 people were internally displaced or (in the case of Ossetians displaced to the Russian Federation) became refugees, although the majority were able to return in the aftermath. Those displaced included some 2,000 people from Upper Abkhazia, previously the only part of Abkhazia under Georgian control, following hostilities between Abkhazian and Georgian forces in the area simultaneous to the Georgian-Russian hostilities in South Ossetia. The Georgian authorities stated that up to 25,000 internally displaced people from South Ossetia faced long-term displacement, adding to the approximately 220,000 people internally displaced by the conflicts of the early 1990s. Some 10,000 people were also not able to return to homes in the former buffer zone – some of which was under Russian military control until October – due to damaged homes or the ongoing risk of shooting and abduction.

Repression of dissent

A number of opposition members and activists were assaulted by unknown, in some cases masked, men in late May and early June. The victims included members of the United Opposition coalition of parties, and in particular the Republican and New Rights parties. According to the Public Defender, 12 assaults took place in the aftermath of the May parliamentary election. The assaults were mainly in the capital Tbilisi, and some were reported in Gori. There was no progress in investigations into these assaults by the end of the year.

Freedom of expression

On 30 May, the directors of Imedi TV, a channel broadcast nationally and known for commentary critical of government not available on other channels, were sacked following changes in the company's ownership. Imedi TV had resumed partial broadcasting in May after its offices were taken over by riot police in November 2007 and the channel was taken off air.

Maestro TV, a regional channel serving the capital and three other cities in eastern Georgia, was refused a licence for political programming on 4 April by the Georgian National Communications Commission.

International scrutiny

On 24 January, the Parliamentary Assembly of the Council of Europe (PACE) passed a resolution on the honouring of Georgia's commitments and obligations. PACE noted that "[o]n a formal level, a significant number of commitments… have been fulfilled, even if several important shortcomings still persist." The resolution highlighted for continuing concern the conditions of detention, prevention of torture, and respect for minority, religious or property rights. On 2 October, PACE issued a resolution addressing the consequences of the Georgia/Russia war, which described the Georgian assault on Tskhinvali as "a disproportionate use of armed force".

Amnesty International visits/report

🚌 Amnesty International delegates visited Georgia in July, August and October.

📘 Civilians in the line of fire: the Georgia/Russia conflict (EUR 04/005/2008)

GERMANY

FEDERAL REPUBLIC OF GERMANY

Head of state:	Horst Köhler
Head of government:	Angela Merkel
Death penalty:	abolitionist for all crimes
Population:	82.5 million
Life expectancy:	79.1 years
Under-5 mortality (m/f):	5/5 per 1,000

As in previous years, Germany failed to address human rights violations committed in the context of the US-led "war on terror", including its involvement in renditions (unlawful transfers of suspects between countries). Germany again referred to diplomatic assurances as appropriate means in deportation cases where individuals may be at risk of serious human rights abuses, in violation of its obligations under international law. Irregular migrants continued to be deprived of their economic, social and cultural rights.

Counter-terror and security

The Federal Prosecutor stated in September that evidence obtained through "dubious circumstances" in a foreign country may be used – although carefully – in a criminal procedure, especially to prevent terrorist attacks. As well as stating that the burden of proof lies fully with the defendant, the Federal Prosecutor also argued that evidence obtained in a manner which violated German standards could be used to initiate a criminal investigation. He did not exclude evidence obtained through torture.

Draft regulatory rules governing the Aliens Act were proposed by the Ministry of Interior in October. The rules anticipated the use of diplomatic assurances to eliminate the danger of torture or other cruel, inhuman or degrading treatment faced by those returned to their country of origin. Amnesty International and other human rights organizations considered such assurances in contravention of international obligations against torture.

Two Tunisian nationals continued to be at risk of expulsion on the basis that the Federal Ministry of Interior considered that assurances from the Tunisian government were sufficient to eliminate the risk the men would face on return. The judicial review of the

G

cases was still pending at the end of the year. Criminal investigations to prove the involvement of one of the Tunisians in terrorism-related activities were closed in March.

In June the parliamentary committee of inquiry concluded its preliminary investigations into involvement by the German authorities in the US-led rendition programme. Government and intelligence officials were not willing to co-operate with the committee effectively. Delays and failures by the authorities to provide some of the files requested by the committee severely impeded its investigations.

The committee's Special Prosecutor revealed that Egyptian nationals Ahmed Agiza and Mohammed El Zari were subject to rendition to Egypt in December 2001 through German airspace and that one CIA rendition flight, carrying the Egyptian national Abu Omar who was abducted in Italy in February 2003, had landed at Ramstein airbase en route to Egypt. The German authorities failed to introduce measures to prevent future renditions through its territory, including its air space.

In June, the Tübingen Public Prosecutor terminated investigations into the alleged ill-treatment of Murat Kurnaz by members of the German Special Forces Command (Kommando Spezialkräfte, KSK) while in US custody in Afghanistan in 2002 for lack of evidence, although he accepted Murat Kurnaz' testimony as credible. A request to hear US Army personnel as witnesses had been turned down by the US authorities. The parliamentary inquiry into the same allegations was closed in September for the same reason. However, members of opposition parties spoke of strong evidence supporting Murat Kurnaz' allegations against the German soldiers.

In June, German national Khaled el-Masri filed a legal complaint to force the government to pursue the extradition of 13 US citizens suspected of transferring him illegally to Afghanistan. Extradition warrants were issued by a Munich court in January 2007 but not handed over to the US government.

Refugees and asylum-seekers

In an accelerated asylum procedure at Frankfurt Airport on 14 May, immigration authorities forcibly returned Eritrean nationals Yonas Haile Mehari and Petros Aforki Mulugeta after their asylum claims were rejected as manifestly unfounded. Both men

were arrested upon arrival in Eritrea. On 20 July they were transferred to Adi Abeto prison. On 30 July, Petros Aforki Mulugeta was transferred to Wia prison. Yonas Haile Mehari, classified as a military deserter by the authorities, was transferred to his military unit where he was at risk of torture and other ill-treatment.

Amnesty International criticized the government's discriminatory approach on the admission of Iraqi refugees. The Minister of Interior had provoked controversy in April when he announced that only Iraqi Christians would be admitted. After a public debate the policy was modified to apply to religious minorities in general and other vulnerable Iraqi refugees. However, in July Chancellor Merkel, on the request of the Iraqi Prime Minister, halted preparations for the admission of Iraqi refugees as well as for reaching a resettlement decision within the EU. Following the conclusions of the EU Justice and Home Affairs Council in November, the German Minister of Interior agreed in December that 2,500 Iraqi refugees from particularly vulnerable groups in Jordan and Syria would be admitted to Germany.

Migrants' rights

All public institutions, including those that provide social services, are required by law to report the identity of any irregular migrant to the authorities. This provision restricts migrants' access to health care and access to judicial remedies in case of violation of their labour rights, and children's access to education.

Police and security forces

■ A man, A.Ö., died in hospital on 5 March after falling into a coma while in police custody in Hagen on 17 February where he had been bound face-down. The Office of the Public Prosecutor terminated its investigations and found that the force used by the police was proportionate, despite the fact that since 2000, police officers have been trained not to restrain a person face-down because of the danger of asphyxia.

In December, the regional court of Dessau acquitted two police officers of killing Oury Jalloh as a result of negligence. Oury Jalloh had died in 2005 from heat shock caused by a fire in his cell while in police custody. In its oral reasons for the judgment, the court strongly criticized the testimonies of most of the police officers who were witnesses in the court case.

Legal developments – economic, social and cultural rights

Contrary to previous years, the government actively supported the draft optional protocol of the Covenant on Economic, Social and Cultural Rights, and voted in favour of its adoption by the UN General Assembly on 10 December 2008.

Amnesty International reports

▣ State of denial: Europe's role in rendition and secret detention (EUR 01/003/2008)

▣ Germany: Submission to the UN Universal Periodic Review - Fourth session of the UPR Working Group of the Human Rights Council, February 2009 (EUR 23/004/2008)

GHANA

REPUBLIC OF GHANA

Head of state and government:	John Agyekum Kufuor
Death penalty:	abolitionist in practice
Population:	23.9 million
Life expectancy:	59.1 years
Under-5 mortality (m/f):	90/86 per 1,000
Adult literacy:	57.9 per cent

The criminal justice system was slow, prisons were overcrowded and poorly resourced, and no steps were taken to abolish the death penalty. Violence against women continued to be pervasive, despite new laws.

Background

Presidential and parliamentary elections were held on 7 December. After a second round of presidential elections on 28 December, John Evans Atta Mills was declared President-elect. Pre-election violence led to clashes in Tamale (capital of the Northern Region) and Ho (capital of the Volta Region).

At the end of 2008, the Freedom of Information Bill, first introduced in 2002, was still not passed into law.

Criminal justice system

The police often failed to bring suspects before a court within a reasonable time. Some police officers signed remand warrants themselves and took suspects directly to prison.

A Justice for all Programme, initiated in 2007 by the Ministry of Justice and the judiciary to speed up the trials of those remanded in prison, had not had a significant effect by the end of the year.

Prison conditions

Prisons were overcrowded and under-resourced, with poor medical and sanitary facilities and not enough beds or bedding. Many inmates slept on bare floors and were forced to sleep in turns. According to official figures, prisons with a capacity for about 8,000 prisoners were holding approximately 14,000. Almost one third were awaiting trial.

■ At the end of 2008, Nsawam Medium Security Prison, built for 800 inmates, incarcerated approximately 3,000 people, more than 60 per cent of whom were awaiting trial. The files of about 300 prisoners awaiting trial were reportedly lost, and another 300 prisoners were still being held after the expiry of their court warrant.

During a visit to Ghana in March 2008, the government refused Amnesty International's request to visit prisons.

Death penalty

No steps were taken to abolish the death penalty. There were 104 prisoners on death row, including three women. In 2008, two men and one woman were sentenced to death. No executions were carried out.

Housing rights

Forced evictions and resulting internal displacement, particularly of marginalized people, continued throughout 2008.

Violence against women and girls

Violence against women continued to be widespread, with violence in the family thought to affect one in three women. The impact of the Domestic Violence Act passed in 2007 had yet to be seen.

Unlawful killings

The media reported several killings of suspected thieves and others during 2008 in "mob violence". According to reports, there were no investigations into these killings.

G

Amnesty International visits/reports

🚌 Amnesty International delegates visited Ghana in March and July.

📘 Ghana: Submission to the UN Universal Periodic Review (AFR 28/001/2008)

📘 Ghana: What's happening in the prisons? (AFR 28/002/2008)

📘 Ghana: Review of Ghana under the Universal Periodic Review - Amnesty International's reflections on the outcome (AFR 28/003/2008)

GREECE

HELLENIC REPUBLIC

Head of state:	Karolos Papoulias
Head of government:	Kostas Karamanlis
Death penalty:	abolitionist for all crimes
Population:	11.2 million
Life expectancy:	78.9 years
Under-5 mortality (m/f):	8/8 per 1,000
Adult literacy:	96 per cent

After police shot dead a 15-year-old boy in December, police reportedly used excessive force against demonstrators as protests, including violent riots, spread across the country. Despite new legislation on the asylum process and conditions of reception of migrants, the treatment of irregular migrants and asylum-seekers continued to violate international standards. Thousands of prisoners went on hunger strike to protest against their treatment in prison. A conscientious objector was sentenced to a term in jail.

Alexis Gregoropoulos killing – excessive use of force

On 6 December, 15-year-old Alexis Gregoropoulos was killed by a police officer serving as a "special guard" in central Athens. Accounts of events leading up to the killing varied. According to the police, two police officers in a vehicle were attacked by a group of 20 to 30 youths. In a second encounter, one of the officers threw a flash grenade while the other fired two shots in the air and one towards the ground; one shot ricocheted and fatally wounded Alexis Gregoropoulos. According to bystanders, two police officers in a vehicle approached Alexis Gregoropoulos and his group of friends at around 9pm and verbally abused

them. As the officers left, someone in the group threw a bottle towards the police vehicle. The vehicle stopped and the officers returned on foot and verbally abused the youths. During this exchange, an officer fired three shots, one of which killed Alexis Gregoropoulos. Within days, both officers had been suspended. The officer who fired the shot was charged with unlawful use of firearms and manslaughter with intent; the other was charged with complicity.

The shooting sparked widespread anti-government protests throughout the country that were continuing at the end of the year. Police reportedly used excessive force and punitive violence against peaceful demonstrators rather than targeting rioters who were destroying property. Among those beaten by police were two Amnesty International members. The police also carried out many arbitrary arrests.

Refugees and asylum-seekers

Two presidential decrees were announced in July relating to the procedures for determining refugee status and the criteria for refugee qualification. Both failed to address fully the concerns raised by human rights and other organizations. Presidential Decree 90/2008 makes legal aid available only at the appeal stage after the asylum application has been rejected. The review process for rejected applications lacks independence as the Appeals Committee retains the status of an advisory body to the Interior Minister. Lawyers' access to case files and clients in detention is limited. Asylum applications must be filed in person, putting some asylum-seekers at risk of arrest. Applications must be filed immediately on entry into the country, without specific provisions ensuring access to the procedure for people detained on arrival. Detention of asylum applicants is allowed for up to 60 days. Presidential Decree 96/2008 sets out the criteria for qualification for refugee protection and protection on humanitarian grounds. Grounds of exclusion from subsidiary humanitarian protection include misdemeanours punishable by three months' imprisonment.

In April the local office of UNHCR, the UN refugee agency, reported that minors' access to refugee protection was arbitrary and that information provided about the asylum process was inadequate. It also found that age rarely played a role in the prioritization of applications. The UNHCR's report called for an end to the administrative detention of minors.

■ In October, 160 unaccompanied migrant children, some of whom were probably asylum-seekers, were reported to be in Pagani detention centre on Lesvos island, in degrading, inhumane and unsanitary conditions. Detainees slept on floors, which were permanently flooded due to faulty plumbing, and were rarely allowed outside for exercise. The centre, built to hold 300, accommodated 830 detainees, including mothers with babies and at least one pregnant woman. Access to lawyers and NGOs was limited.

Torture and other ill-treatment

Ill-treatment by police of detainees, particularly migrants and members of marginalized groups, was reported throughout the year.

■ Migrants arriving on the island of Samos were reported to have been ill-treated by coastguard officers after their arrest on 7 July. The migrants said they were slapped, punched and kicked on the coastguards' boat. A guard allegedly poured sun-protecting lotion down a man's throat, while another migrant was grabbed by the hair and his head knocked against the side of the boat. A third male migrant was reported to have suffered a ruptured eardrum after being slapped. An investigation into the allegations had not been concluded by the end of the year. An investigation into ill-treatment of migrants on Chios island ordered in October 2007 had also not been concluded.

■ On 26 October police officers outside the Aliens Directorate in Athens attacked a crowd of asylum-seekers waiting to file applications, killing one man and injuring several others, according to the Athens-based Group of Lawyers for the Rights of Migrants and Refugees. The Directorate had reportedly been refusing to accept new applications for the previous two months.

■ A Romani man detained on 19 June said he was beaten at Aharnon police station for several hours after arrest.

■ On 16 October, three police officers were fined and suspended from duty for up to six months by the police Appeals Disciplinary Council for their part in the beating of a Cypriot student, Avgoustinos Demetriou, on 17 November 2006 in Thessaloniki. Avgoustinos Demetriou was seriously injured as a result of the beating. Four police officers present during the incident but who had not taken part in the beating were acquitted.

In February the report was published of the European Committee for the Prevention of Torture's (CPT) 2007 visit to the country. The report noted a serious breach of Articles 3 and 8 of the European Convention on Human Rights (ECHR) relating to the prohibition of torture and respect for privacy. The CPT reported inhuman and degrading conditions in some border guard stations and numerous allegations of ill-treatment. It noted that the rights of detained migrants to have access to a lawyer and to inform their families about their detention were not effective in practice, while access to medical care was limited. The CPT made a second ad hoc visit to Greece from 23 to 29 September.

Trafficking in human beings

On 23 May, the Athens Appeals Court reduced the sentence of a man accused of trafficking from 19 to seven years' imprisonment for people smuggling, after overturning convictions for trafficking and blackmail. This was one of the first cases brought under a new law on trafficking. Trial observers expressed concern about the court's lenience towards racist and demeaning remarks by the defence lawyer as well as the failure of translators to communicate accurately statements by the victims, including testimony about torture by their traffickers.

There was a mounting campaign to protect the rights of victims of trafficking, including lobbying of the government to ratify the Council of Europe Anti-Trafficking Convention and amend legislation to ensure that victims not be criminalized.

Workers' rights

■ On 23 December the Secretary General of the Attica Union of Cleaners and Domestic Workers, Konstantina Kouneva, a Bulgarian national, was attacked in Athens with sulphuric acid by unknown persons. She sustained multiple serious injuries and remained in intensive care in hospital at the end of the year. The police investigation was alleged to have been ineffective, focusing on Konstantina Kouneva's private life and failing to take into account her trade union activities.

Prison conditions

In October and November prisoners around the country held protests against conditions in prison, including overcrowding, inadequate sanitary facilities,

G

ill-treatment, ineffective investigations of deaths in custody, punitive disciplinary measures, and restrictions on the rights to freedom of expression and communication. On 3 November prisoners began hunger strikes across the country. A week later the Initiative for Prisoners' Rights reported that 3,311 prisoners were on hunger strike and thousands of others had refused meals. Among the hunger strikers were 17 prisoners held in the town of Trikala who had sewn their lips together as well as children held in juvenile detention centres. The Initiative for Prisoners' Rights reported complaints of intimidation against the hunger strikers by prison guards.

Conscientious objector to military service

■ On 20 May, conscientious objector Lazaros Petromelidis was sentenced in his absence to three years' imprisonment on two charges of insubordination by the Naval Court of Piraeus. This was his 15th trial on the same charges. An arrest warrant was issued, putting him in danger of imprisonment for his beliefs.

Freedom of expression

In March, the European Court of Human Rights found that there had been violations of Article 11 of the ECHR pertaining to freedom of assembly and association in two cases, *Emin and Others v Greece* and *Tourkiki Enosi Xanthis and Others v Greece,* involving associations founded by members of a minority community. The Cultural Association of Turkish Women of the Region of Rodopi had been refused registration because its name included the word "Turkish". The Turkish Association of Xanthi had been dissolved in 1986 on the same grounds. In *Alexandridis v Greece* and *I Avgi Publishing and Press Agency S.A. & Karis v Greece,* the European Court found in February and June respectively that there had been violations of the rights of freedom of thought, conscience and religion (Article 9) and freedom of expression (Article 10).

Rights of lesbian, gay, bisexual and transgender people

On 3 June, the first same-sex marriages were performed by the Mayor of the island of Tilos. The marriages were declared invalid by the Minister of Justice and the government filed a motion to have the marriages annulled. This sparked protests in September.

Amnesty International reports

▤ Greece: Lazaros Petromelidis repeatedly convicted for his beliefs (EUR 25/003/2008)

▤ Greece: Failing system of police accountability, 9 December 2008

▤ Greek police use punitive violence against peaceful demonstrators, 11 December 2008

GUATEMALA

REPUBLIC OF GUATEMALA

Head of state and government:	Álvaro Colom Caballeros
	(replaced Óscar Berger Perdomo in January)
Death penalty:	retentionist
Population:	13.7 million
Life expectancy:	69.7 years
Under-5 mortality (m/f):	44/33 per 1,000
Adult literacy:	69.1 per cent

Human rights defenders continued to face threats, harassment and attacks. The government failed to fulfil its commitment to release previously classified military documents that could assist the prosecution of those responsible for committing grave human rights violations during the internal armed conflict (1960-1996). Little improvement was seen in public security.

Background

In September, hidden listening devices were found in the President's office and private residence. The heads of the two agencies responsible for providing the President with security and intelligence resigned. Arrest warrants were subsequently issued. At the end of the year, one was under house arrest; the other was being sought by the police.

The UN-sponsored International Commission Against Impunity in Guatemala completed its first year of operations, reporting that it was assisting in the prosecution of two cases and investigating another 15.

Land disputes – forced evictions

In February, the police arrested rural activist Ramiro Choc in the context of land disputes in the area of Izabal, on the Atlantic coast. Communities protesting against his arrest retaliated by holding four Belgian tourists. However, police action connected to the incident resulted in the death of rural worker Mario Caal. An investigation by the Guatemalan Human Rights Ombudsman's Office alleged that Mario Caal had been extrajudicially executed.

Police recorded 22 forced evictions during the year.

Human rights defenders

Local human rights organizations reported scores of attacks against human rights defenders, in which a few human rights defenders were killed.
■ In July, Antonio Morales was shot dead. His body was found in the street in his home town of Tixel, Huehuetenango department. He was a member of a local community development committee which had been seeking to reclaim land for the community, and was active in rural workers and Indigenous rights campaigns. He had reported receiving threats one week before his killing.

Trade unionists

Several trade unionists were killed during the year.
■ In March, two armed men shot Miguel Ángel Ramírez Enríquez, one of the founders of the Union of Banana Workers of the South (Sindicato de Trabajadores Bananeros del Sur, SITRABANSUR), as he was returning home. He died later in hospital. His relatives stated that he had received death threats and been pressured to stop his trade union activities.

Police and security forces

Various initiatives were announced by the new government, but by the end of the year there were no visible results in reducing violent crime including homicide. Members of the security forces, either on or off duty, were believed to be implicated in many killings.
■ In January, the bodies of two men aged 17 and 23 were found by a roadside to the south of Guatemala City. They had been strangled with ropes and then shot in the head at close range. Although there was reportedly some evidence that the two were killed by members of the security forces, no significant investigation had taken place by the end of the year.

Violence against women and girls

The police reported that 687 women were the victims of homicide in 2008; their bodies frequently showed signs of rape and other torture. The Office of the UN High Commissioner for Human Rights reported in January that discriminatory practices by the authorities persisted, resulting in a failure to investigate killings of women and a tendency to blame the victim. In April, Congress passed a new Law Against Femicide. The law received a mixed response from civil society organizations.

Impunity

In February, the President announced that all military archives relating to human rights violations committed during the internal armed conflict would be made public, but the army refused to comply. In March, in a case brought against former high ranking army officers for alleged crimes against humanity, the Constitutional Court ruled that classified military documents be made public. At year end, the documents had still not been released.
■ Six members of the former civil defence patrols, paramilitary groups set up to support the army in counterinsurgency operations during the internal armed conflict, were found guilty of killing 26 people in a massacre in Río Negro, Baja Verapaz department, in March 1982; 177 people were killed in this massacre, 70 women and 107 children.
■ In July, the Inter-American Commission on Human Rights again referred to the Inter-American Court of Human Rights the case of a massacre committed in Dos Erres, Petén department in December 1982, on the grounds that the government had not complied with the first ruling. At least 251 people were killed in the massacre.

A draft law to establish a commission to find victims of the estimated 45,000 enforced disappearances carried out during the internal armed conflict was still awaiting approval by Congress.

Death penalty

During the year four people had their death sentences commuted and none were sentenced to death. Fifteen people remained on death row at the end of the year. There were no executions.

In February, Congress passed a decree that could have led to the resumption of executions. The President vetoed the decree in March. In December, Guatemala abstained on a UN General Assembly resolution calling for a worldwide moratorium on executions.

G

Amnesty International reports

📄 Guatemala: Submission to the UN Universal Periodic Review: Second session of the UPR Working Group, 5-16 May 2008 (AMR 34/001/2008)

📄 Guatemala: The refusal to grant the extraditions requested by Spain for crimes under international law (AMR 34/013/2008)

GUINEA

REPUBLIC OF GUINEA

Head of state:	**Moussa Dadis Camara (replaced Lansana Conté in December)**
Head of government:	**Kabiné Komara (replaced Ahmed Tidiane Souaré in December, who replaced Lansana Kouyaté in May)**
Death penalty:	**retentionist**
Population:	**9.6 million**
Life expectancy:	**54.8 years**
Under-5 mortality (m/f):	**163/144 per 1,000**
Adult literacy:	**29.5 per cent**

There were protests against shortages in water and electricity, the rise in prices of basic commodities, and the lack of education and health care facilities. Security forces used excessive force against protesters. Revolts erupted, led by unpaid soldiers and police, and several civilians were killed in clashes between mutinous soldiers and presidential guards.

Torture and other ill-treatment continued to be widespread. The Commission of Inquiry set up to investigate grave human rights violations was not able to operate. Independent journalists were subject to intimidation, harassment and arbitrary arrest.

Background

President Lansana Conté, who had ruled Guinea for more than 24 years, died on 22 December. Immediately after his death, a military junta led by Moussa Dadis Camara seized power and promised to organize a presidential election in 2010. Under the Constitution, the President of the National Assembly assumes power until elections, to be held within 60 days. The coup was welcomed by most Guineans, including members of civil society, but was condemned by the international community,

including the African Union which suspended Guinea. The military junta appointed Kabiné Komara as Prime Minister.

In May and June, armed revolts led by soldiers and police demanding payment erupted in the capital city of Conakry, in Nzérékoré and in Kindia. Mutinous soldiers clashed with presidential guards and soldiers detained the deputy army chief when he tried to negotiate. During the protests, several people were killed by stray bullets and dozens were wounded. Most of the victims were civilians, including one woman in Kindia. No official inquiry was opened into the killings. In June, police demanding back pay fired into the air and took at least 10 police chiefs hostage. They were subsequently released.

Commission of Inquiry

The Commission of Inquiry set up in 2007 to investigate grave human rights violations committed in 2006 and 2007 did not conduct any investigations. In May, the Commission's President accused the government of freezing its financial support. In a statement at the UN in October, the Special Rapporteur on extrajudicial, summary or arbitrary executions expressed concern at the lack of progress and the failure to assure funding or to put in place a witness protection mechanism. He stated that the situation had all the hallmarks of a Commission being used to distract attention and promote impunity.

Excessive use of force

The security forces used excessive force against demonstrators in and around Conakry and in Boké who were protesting against the high cost of basic commodities, including rice. At least five people were killed and around 20 injured after the security forces clamped down on demonstrations.

■ In October, Abdoulaye Cissé, a 13-year-old boy, and one other person were killed by the security forces during demonstrations.

■ Two people were killed and seven others were seriously injured when security forces broke up demonstrations in Mambya, near Kindia in October. The demonstrators were protesting against the lack of electricity, water, schools and health centres.

■ In October, security forces extrajudicially executed one of the suspected organizers of demonstrations in Boké. Karamba Dramé, President of a youth group in Khoréra, near Boké, was shot dead in Khoréra by soldiers wearing red berets. They had come especially from Conakry, after they had identified him through his mobile phone.

No official inquiry was opened into the killings during the year.

Arbitrary arrests, torture and other ill-treatment

Torture and other ill-treatment continued to be widespread and systematic during and after arrests. In September and October, shortly after the demonstrations in Conakry and Boké, more than 10 people were arrested and held for a few days without charge. During their detention in Boké, the detainees were held in a tiny cell, surrounded by excrement and urine, and were lashed with rubber straps by soldiers. The detainees were forced to count, and if they made a mistake, to resume at zero. Aboubakar Fofana, a student, fell into a coma as a result of lashings by soldiers and was admitted to hospital in Boké.

Freedom of expression – the media

Independent journalists were subject to intimidation, harassment and arbitrary arrest. There were restrictions on freedom of speech and of the press, particularly when the authorities were criticized.

■ In August, Lansana Babara Camara, a journalist with *La Guinée Actuelle*, a privately owned newspaper, was assaulted by a member of the Autonomous Presidential Security Battalion while inquiring about a visit by President Conté to Kindia.

■ In October, Facely Traoré, a reporter for Familia FM, a privately owned radio station, was arrested and briefly held in the police Criminal Investigation Department. The journalist was arrested while investigating the arrest of two policemen accused of stealing two bags of rice.

In October, the National Communication Council lifted all penalties on newspapers. The only newspaper banned at that time was *La Vérité* which had published an article critical of an unnamed government minister.

Death penalty

More than 26 prisoners remained on death row in Conakry civil prison and Kindia high security prison, east of Conakry.

Three people – Boubacar Sidy Diallo, Moustapha Bangoura and Naby Camara – were sentenced to death during the assize court session in Conakry in November and December.

In December, Guinea abstained on a UN General Assembly resolution calling for a worldwide moratorium on executions.

Amnesty International report

Guinea: Excessive use of force and torture following demonstrations against the high cost of living (AFR 29/001/2008)

GUINEA-BISSAU

REPUBLIC OF GUINEA-BISSAU

Head of state:	João Bernardo "Nino" Vieira
Head of government:	Carlos Gomes Júnior (replaced Carlos Correia in December, who replaced Martinho Ndafa Cabi in August)
Death penalty:	abolitionist for all crimes
Population:	1.7 million
Life expectancy:	45.8 years
Under-5 mortality (m/f):	204/181 per 1,000
Adult literacy:	44.8 per cent

G

Dire economic conditions and drug trafficking continued to threaten the country's fragile political and social stability. There were reports of attempted coups. Journalists and judicial officials received death threats in connection with their work. Efforts were made to combat child trafficking.

Background

Poverty remained widespread. In February the authorities said they needed 20,000 tonnes of food aid. However, the country remained politically unstable and donors were reluctant to grant aid for food and social projects, or for much needed reforms of the armed forces and security sector.

There were frequent strikes throughout 2008 by civil servants and others over non-payment of salaries. A cholera epidemic broke out in April which spread to the whole country, killing more than 200 people by November, when the epidemic was brought under control. According to a UNICEF report in May, the country had the world's sixth highest child mortality rate.

In August, President João Bernardo "Nino" Vieira dismissed parliament and appointed a new government.

Parliamentary elections were held in November and were won by the African Party for the Independence of Guinea-Bissau and Cape Verde, PAIGC. The leader of the Social Renewal Party, PRS, claimed that the results were rigged. Although a new Prime Minister was appointed in late December, no new government had been established by the end of the year.

There were sketchy and unverified reports of a coup attempt in August. In November a group of soldiers attacked the Presidential Palace, two days after the results of the elections were announced. The authorities disagreed as to whether this was an attempted coup or a mutiny. One soldier died in the attack and several Presidential Guards were reportedly injured. Seven soldiers were arrested and the alleged leader of the attack, a nephew of the PRS leader, fled to Senegal where he was reportedly arrested.

Drug trafficking continued to be a major destabilizing factor and allegations persisted that members of the armed forces were involved in the trafficking. In July a private plane containing drugs was seized at Bissau airport. However, soldiers obstructed investigations by the judicial police and prevented them from entering the plane. Five Latin American crew members and a Guinean air traffic controller were arrested but were released on bail. The foreign nationals fled the country.

Four soldiers were arrested and remained in detention at the end of the year, after reportedly being accused of involvement in an alleged coup attempt in August. The alleged leader of the coup attempt, the former Chief of Staff of the Navy, fled the country, although the authorities claimed that he had been placed under house arrest. He had been persistently linked to drug trafficking.

In August Guinea-Bissau ratified the ILO Convention on the Worst Forms of Child Labour.

Freedom of expression

Freedom of expression was curtailed and journalists who reported on drug trafficking received death threats.

■ In January, journalist Alberto Dabo received anonymous telephone death threats, a few days after he met the then Chief of Staff of the Navy in the street. Alberto Dabo claimed that the naval officer brandished his fist at him in a threatening manner. Alberto Dabo first received threats in June 2007 after he accused the naval officer of involvement in drug trafficking. In

August 2007 the officer filed a case against him, but the trial was still pending at the end of 2008.

■ Journalist Athizar Mendes Pereira was arrested and interrogated for several hours by the Intelligence Services of the Ministry of Interior in March. He had written an article in which he said that the Chief of Staff of the Armed Forces had taken it upon himself to promote police officers. He was released uncharged six hours later.

Death threats against judicial officials

In July the Attorney General and the Minister of Justice said they received death threats to force them to stop their investigation into a cocaine haul. Both had publicly accused high ranking political, military and security service figures of involvement in the trafficking, and of obstructing their investigations.

Trafficking in human beings – children

Reports of child trafficking decreased by about 45 per cent, as there were better co-ordinated efforts to end it. Surveillance committees were set up along the border between Guinea-Bissau and Senegal with the participation of local residents, NGOs, lorry drivers and the authorities. Nine children from Guinea-Bissau were reportedly rescued from the streets in Dakar, Senegal, in April.

HAITI

REPUBLIC OF HAITI

Head of state:	René García Préval
Head of government:	Michèle D. Pierre-Louis (replaced Jacques-Édouard Alexis in July)
Death penalty:	abolitionist for all crimes
Population:	9.8 million
Life expectancy:	59.5 years
Under-5 mortality (m/f):	82/59 per 1,000
Adult literacy:	54.8 per cent

Food shortages, chronic unemployment and natural disasters exacerbated poverty and marginalization, jeopardizing minimal essential levels of access to health care, adequate housing, education, water and sanitation. Ill-treatment and excessive use of force

by police officers were reported. Sexual violence against women was pervasive; girls under 18 were at particular risk. Thousands of people remained in detention awaiting trial in severely overcrowded conditions. Trafficking in persons into the Dominican Republic continued unabated.

Background

In April, amid demonstrations against the rising cost of staple foods, Prime Minister Jacques-Édouard Alexis was forced to resign following a vote of no confidence in the Senate. Violence and looting accompanying the demonstrations forced businesses and schools to close. The country was without a functioning government for four months, paralysing essential development projects and preventing the adoption of the national budget.

In July, the Senate and Parliament ratified Michèle D. Pierre-Louis as Prime Minister. Elections to renew one third of the Senate, due in the first quarter of the year, were postponed until 2009, compromising the state's capacity to legislate as the Senate was inquorate during many sessions.

In October, the UN Security Council renewed the mandate of the UN Stabilization Mission in Haiti (MINUSTAH) for a fifth year.

Public security concerns persisted and, according to UNICEF, children were at increased risk of kidnapping, compared with previous years. The involvement of corrupt police officers in kidnappings intensified calls for comprehensive vetting of the Haitian National Police.

Children's rights

Food shortages and spiralling food prices put children's lives at risk. In November, 26 children from the South-East Department were hospitalized suffering from acute malnutrition. In the wake of the hurricanes, organizations involved in humanitarian assistance reported that dozens of children died of hunger.

Access to education remained a concern. According to UNICEF, an estimated 500,000 school-age children were not in education.

Child offenders were frequently sentenced outside juvenile courts and detained in cells shared with adults.

Right to health

Efforts were made to remove the barriers facing pregnant women in accessing health care in public institutions. However, some hospitals continued to impose arbitrary charges for obstetric care.

Reports indicated that anti-retroviral kits for victims of rape were not available outside the capital, Port-au-Prince.

Lack of access to clean water and sanitation continued to affect 40 per cent of the population across the country, according to the UN and official sources.

Violence against women and girls

Reports of intimate partner and sexual violence increased compared with 2007. Haitian women's organizations recorded at least 110 rapes of girls under 18 in 2008, a number that was believed to represent a very small fraction of the overall problem. Specific legal measures to protect women and girls, such as legislation on domestic violence and marital rape, were still lacking in Haiti. Women and girls who experienced rape or other forms of sexual violence faced discrimination in seeking justice and redress. Lack of political will, widespread prejudice and an ineffective criminal justice system were among the factors which contributed to the failure to take effective steps to end violence against women. In March, the Haitian government submitted its first report to the UN Committee on the Elimination of Discrimination against Women.

Trafficking in human beings

Thousands of Haitians, including women and children, continued to be trafficked into the Dominican Republic despite increased surveillance along the border. The authorities failed to implement anti-trafficking legislation and to investigate those suspected of trafficking. People deported from the Dominican Republic to Haiti did not receive any assistance from the Haitian authorities.

Justice system

The vast majority of prisoners faced prolonged pre-trial detention because of the lack of capacity and resources to speed up judicial procedures. According to the Human Rights Section of MINUSTAH, prison conditions were extremely poor with only 0.55m^2 of cell space per prisoner. Some judicial authorities, such as justices of the peace, exceeded their powers and acted outside their jurisdiction by conducting trials in criminal cases and ordering the arrest of people for acts that were not offences under national law.

The Inter-American Court of Human Rights ruled in August that the arrest in 2004 of former Prime Minister Yvon Neptune and his imprisonment for 23 months without trial had violated his right to a fair trial and to be free from political persecution.

Impunity

No progress was made in investigating cases of past human rights violations.

■ Father Jean Pierre-Louis, known as "Ti Jean", was killed on 3 August 1998 in Port-au-Prince. More than 10 years later, those responsible for his murder had not been brought to justice. Father Pierre-Louis was an advocate for the human rights of Haitian migrants. He was also one of the co-founders of the Ecumenical Service for Development and Popular Education (Service Œcuménique pour le Développement et l'Education Populaire, SEDEP).

Police and security forces

Overall the number of reports of abuses by the police appeared to decline. However, there were some reports of excessive use of force during demonstrations and arrests; fatal shootings and ill-treatment of detainees. At least two people died in police custody. Arbitrary arrests without warrants and the filing of charges without evidence were common throughout the country.

Amnesty International visits/report

🚌 Amnesty International delegates visited Haiti in March and November.

📰 Don't turn your back on girls – Sexual violence against girls in Haiti (AMR 36/004/2008)

HONDURAS

REPUBLIC OF HONDURAS

Head of state and government:	Manuel Zelaya Rosales
Death penalty:	abolitionist for all crimes
Population:	7.2 million
Life expectancy:	69.4 years
Under-5 mortality:	46/36 per 1,000
Adult literacy:	80 per cent

Human rights defenders and trade unionists were attacked and threatened throughout the year. In most cases the perpetrators of attacks and threats were not held accountable. At least 27 prisoners were killed during different episodes of prison violence.

Background

Several prosecutors and others went on hunger strike in April and May, demanding the resignation of the Attorney General whom they accused of corruption and of blocking several important anti-corruption cases. In September, one of the prosecutors on hunger strike, Luis Santos, who had been granted state protection, was shot and seriously wounded by an unidentified attacker/gunman. At the request of the Inter-American Commission on Human Rights, protection measures were strengthened. The Attorney General remained in post at the end of the year.

UNAIDS reported that the national prevalence for HIV infection was 0.7 per cent. In a report to the UN General Assembly in February, the government reported a reduction in HIV prevalence among the Garifuna communities. Despite recent evidence of a decline in HIV prevalence among women sex workers, UNAIDS reported that the infection rate stood at 10 per cent.

In December, the President issued a decree setting up a compensation programme for victims of human rights violations and crimes against humanity committed between 1980 and 1993.

Human rights defenders

At least three human rights defenders were killed; many others were attacked and threatened.

In September, two plain-clothes police officers were detained by university staff after they were seen taking photographs. The officers were found to be carrying a list entitled "pressure groups" with the details of approximately 135 human rights defenders, trade unionists, religious leaders and some government officials. The two police officers were arrested and the deputy director of the Information and Analysis Unit of the police was suspended. In October, the officers were released and charges against them dropped; the deputy director remained suspended at the end of the year.

■ In June, Irene Ramírez, leader of a rural workers' organization, was shot and killed in the city of Trujillo, Colón department. He had been leading a dispute over land. The day before his death he had given a radio interview calling for recently approved land reform legislation to be implemented by the authorities. At the end of the year, two men were on trial for his killing.

Workers' rights – trade unionists

Trade unionists were threatened and attacked; at least three were killed.

■ Altagracia Fuentes, Virginia García de Sánchez and Juan Bautista – general secretary, first officer and driver respectively of the Confederation of Workers of Honduras – were shot and killed as they drove towards the town of El Progreso, Yoro department, in April. Witness reports indicated that the perpetrators, wearing balaclavas, drove up beside the car and machine-gunned the occupants. In June, the authorities issued arrest warrants for 11 individuals, none of whom had been captured by the end of the year. Members of the Public Prosecutor's Office claimed that the motive for the killings had been robbery; others believed they were killed for trying to form trade unions in assembly factories.

■ Lorna Redell Jackson and Juana Maldonado Gutiérrez, leaders of the trade union at the Alcoa Fujukura Company (Sindicato de Trabajadores de la empresa Alcoa Fujukura Limitada, SITRAFL) were shot and injured by two unidentified individuals on a motorcycle in September in the town of El Progreso, Yoro department. In October, Lorna Redell Jackson received telephone death threats. SITRAFL had exposed violations of labour rights in the context of a company closure.

Violence against women and girls

According to the Public Prosecutor's Office 312 women were killed in 2008. Various women's rights organizations launched a campaign in November calling on the authorities to do more to stop the rising number of killings of women. They demanded that the authorities dedicate more resources to the investigation and prosecution of cases, introduce legislative changes, and make public more information about the killing of women. In addition, women's organizations called for more government action to combat the high levels of domestic violence recorded.

Impunity

The principal recommendation of the UN Working Group on Enforced or Involuntary Disappearances, which called on the government to carry out a comprehensive investigation to clarify cases of enforced disappearances during the 1980s and 1990s, had not been implemented by the end of the year. The Working Group reported in 2007 on 125 cases of disappearance that remained to be clarified.

In July, four policemen were found guilty of the killing in 2006 of Heraldo Zuñiga and Roger Iván Cartagena, both members of the Environmentalist Movement of Olancho. Three weeks after being sentenced, two of the police officers escaped, and another escaped a few days later. At the end of the year the three men were still on the run.

The investigation into the beating and rape of Donny Reyes, treasurer of the Rainbow Association (Fundacion Arcoiris), a lesbian, gay, bisexual and transgender rights organization, did not progress. In 2007, Donny Reyes was arbitrarily detained by police officers, and taken to a police station where an officer told other inmates "look, I'm bringing you a little princess, you know what to do". Other inmates repeatedly beat and raped him. One police officer was punished with one month's suspension from duty without pay.

Prison conditions

Nine inmates were killed in a single incident in April in a San Pedro Sula prison, Cortés department, and a further 18 prisoners were killed in May in a Tegucigalpa prison, Francisco Morazán department. Conflicts between rival gangs were alleged to be the cause of the deaths.

In June, 21 prison officials of different ranks were found guilty of causing the deaths of 68 inmates in a fire in the El Porvenir prison farm, in Atlántida

H

department in 2003. Their sentences varied from three years to life imprisonment.

Amnesty International reports

📄 Honduras: Open letter to the President of Honduras on the situation of human rights defenders and the recent escape of three men convicted in the case of the killing of two environmentalists (AMR 37/002/2008)

📄 Honduras: Open letter to the President of Honduras about human rights defenders (AMR 37/004/2008)

HUNGARY

REPUBLIC OF HUNGARY
Head of state:	László Sólyom
Head of government:	Ferenc Gyurcsány
Death penalty:	abolitionist for all crimes
Population:	10 million
Life expectancy:	72.9 years
Under-5 mortality (m/f):	9/8 per 1,000

The Romani community continued to face discrimination in all aspects of life and Romani individuals were victims of allegedly racially motivated attacks. Lesbian, gay, bisexual and transgender people continued to experience intolerance from violent groups.

Background

There was a rise in support for the Magyar Gárda (Hungarian Guard), a radical right-wing organization, which is primarily anti-Roma and has demonstrated against what they describe as "Roma criminality". In December, the Municipal Court of Budapest ruled that this group should be disbanded as it "means to create a climate of fear, while its activities – the marching of its members in Roma-populated settlements and the speeches of its leaders – constitute a breach of the rights of other citizens". The organization's leader announced they would appeal against the decision.

Legal, constitutional or institutional developments

In June, the Constitutional Court rejected amendments to the civil code and penal code passed by parliament in November 2007 and February 2008 respectively. The amendments represented the fourth attempt by parliament since 1992 to change the law on hate speech. They would have criminalized incitement targeted against a minority group and allowed a maximum two-year prison sentence for anyone using inflammatory expressions about specific ethnic groups or offending their dignity. The Court considered these amendments to be unconstitutional as they would curtail freedom of expression.

Discrimination – Roma

The Roma continued to face discrimination, including in lack of access to education, health services, housing and employment. In July the NGO Decade Watch, reporting on Hungary's progress in the Decade of Roma Inclusion, stated that "measures to eliminate segregated education of Roma have been met with resistance by some local authorities, and funding available for such measures has been underused or misused due to the lack of interest in promoting the integrated education of Roma by educational institutions at a local level." Although the Supreme Court on 19 November ruled that a municipality and two schools were practising segregated education, Decade Watch found that de facto segregated Roma-only schools continued to exist in 170 localities.

A 50-member investigation team was set up by the police to focus on assaults against Roma after the growing number of cases of violent assaults against them reported during the year. Such assaults included attacks with petrol bombs, hand grenades and other weapons.

■ A Romani couple were killed in Pecs on 18 November by a grenade thrown at their house, which also injured two of their three children. According to press reports, initial remarks by local police denied any racial motivation behind the killings. However, the Chief of National Police, speaking to the media on 20 November, stated that in all cases when the victims of assaults were Roma, the possibility of ethnic motivation could not and must not be dismissed until there was clear-cut evidence to prove otherwise.

Rights of lesbian, gay, bisexual and transgender people

On 11 June, the Budapest Chief of Police decided to ban the lesbian, gay, bisexual and transgender

(LGBT) pride parade scheduled for the beginning of July, alleging security concerns after violent incidents with counter-demonstrators in 2007. Amid international and national pressure he reversed his decision on 13 June.

On 5 July, around 450 people took part in the parade during which explosive devices were thrown at police by hundreds of violent far-right demonstrators chanting threatening slogans. The following day, Prime Minister Ferenc Gyurcsány condemned violence against LGBT rights marchers and called for decisive action against extremism and intolerance.

On 8 July, four counter-demonstrators received minor fines and three were acquitted by Budapest's Central District Court, after they were taken into custody for throwing eggs and disobeying police orders during the parade. All seven were tried for misconduct, which can be either a minor or a major offence. If violent misconduct threatens others or causes mass disagreement, or is perpetrated in groups it qualifies as a major offence. In this case it was considered a minor offence.

On 17 July, the Budapest Central District Court gave an 18-month suspended prison sentence to a man who attacked police by throwing stones at least three times during the parade.

Police and security forces

The individual law enforcement officers responsible for ill-treatment and excessive use of force during policing of demonstrations in Budapest in 2006 were still not identified. The National Prosecutor's Office reported that following 200 complaints filed against the police, 174 were dismissed, 24 were still pending, and in only two cases had the court delivered sentences.

■ In February, the Metropolitan Court of Budapest acquitted one police officer in the case of alleged ill-treatment of Ángel Mendoza during his detention in a Budapest police station after the September 2006 demonstrations. However, in June, the Court of Appeals repealed the judgement and ordered the retrial of the acquitted officer. The case of Ángel Mendoza, who was represented by the NGO Hungarian Helsinki Committee, was still pending at the end of the year.

■ Two police officers were found guilty of ill-treating Imre Török by the Metropolitan Court of Budapest in March. The police officers received suspended sentences of 14 and 16 months respectively. The Court

of Appeals in November reduced the sentence on the first officer to nine months, but upheld that passed on the second, who had a previous conviction for ill-treatment during official procedure. Imre Török was represented by the NGO Hungarian Helsinki Committee.

Violence against women and girls

In April, the NGO initiative, Hungary Rape and Sexual Violence Working Group, became an official sub-committee of the Council on Social Equality between Men and Women of Hungary within the Ministry of Social Affairs and Labour.

■ There were no major positive developments in the highly publicized case of 22-year-old Zsanett E., who was allegedly raped by two police officers in May 2007. In December 2007, the Budapest Prosecutor's Office dropped the investigation stating that no crime had been committed. In February, Zsanett E.'s lawyer filed a substitute civil action. The first court hearing took place on 17 November, and proceedings were still pending at the end of the year.

INDIA

REPUBLIC OF INDIA

Head of state:	Pratibha Patil
Head of government:	Manmohan Singh
Death penalty:	retentionist
Population:	1,186.2 million
Life expectancy:	63.7 years
Under-5 mortality (m/f):	73/83 per 1,000
Adult literacy:	61 per cent

Police were either inactive or responded with excessive force in the face of sectarian violence against religious and linguistic minorities and ethnic clashes. *Adivasis* (indigenous communities) and small farmers continued to protest their exclusion from government decision-making on new development projects which could threaten their livelihoods and result in forced evictions. The low-level conflict continued between Maoists and the government and militia widely believed to be supported by the government. Both sides committed

abuses including targeting civilians. Bomb-blasts in various parts of the country killed hundreds of people. In response the government arbitrarily detained and tortured suspects. Following the November Mumbai attacks in which more than 170 people were killed, the government tightened security legislation and set up a federal agency to investigate terrorist attacks. Judicial processes failed to ensure justice for many victims of communal violence. The courts sentenced at least 70 people to death. No executions took place.

Background

In addition to the 170 killed in the November Mumbai attacks, more than 400 people were killed in bomb attacks in the cities of Jaipur, Ahmedabad, Bangalore, Malegaon, Delhi and Imphal and in the states of Tripura and Assam.

India-Pakistan ties deteriorated following allegations by the Indian authorities that the November Mumbai attacks had been carried out by people or groups based in Pakistan. India-Pakistan peace initiatives including talks on Kashmir failed to make progress.

The government's response to widespread violence against women remained inadequate.

While India continued to experience economic growth, a quarter of the population, approximately 300 million people, 70 per cent of whom lived in rural areas, remained in poverty. Indian authorities had not managed to ensure the rights of already marginalized communities, such as landless farmers and *adivasi* communities, who oppose exploitation of their land and other resources for industrial projects.

Violence against minorities

In August, a prominent local Hindu leader and four of his associates who campaigned against conversion to Christianity were killed in the state of Orissa, sparking two months of attacks against Christian minorities. The attacks, which resulted in at least 25 deaths, were led by supporters of Hindu nationalist organizations reportedly allied to the Bharatiya Janata Party – part of Orissa's ruling coalition – and included arson, looting and sexual assault of women. Police either failed to act or used excessive force resulting in the fatal shooting of 15 people. At least 15,000 people, mostly Christians, were displaced by the violence. In at least two camps for the displaced, Christians continued to be subjected to violent attacks

by supporters of Hindu nationalist organizations. During the two months of violence, more than 250 people were arrested in connection with the attacks. However, no judicial inquiries had been completed at the end of the year.

In September, supporters of Hindu nationalist organizations damaged about 30 Christian places of worship in Karnataka. The suspected perpetrators were arrested only after opposition party protests.

In Mumbai city and other places in Maharashtra, linguistic minorities from northern states were subjected to repeated attacks by supporters of the Maharashtra Navnirman Sena, resulting in around 1,000 migrant workers fleeing the state. Police were slow to stop the attacks and arrest suspected perpetrators.

More than 50 people were killed in intra-ethnic clashes between members of the Muslim community and the Bodo community in the predominantly Bodo districts of Assam. The authorities failed to take timely action to prevent the violence.

During July and August, communal protests in Jammu and Kashmir rose to levels unseen in recent years and erupted into violence on several occasions. Police used excessive force to deal with the violence and shot dead more than 60 people.

Members of Dalit communities in several states continued to face attacks and discrimination. The authorities failed to use existing special laws enacted to prosecute perpetrators of ethnic violence.

Human rights defenders working on minority rights including rights of Dalits and *adivasis* in Chhattisgarh continued to face harassment, including arbitrary detention by state police.

Legislation introduced in 2005 to address communal violence was still pending before parliament at the end of the year.

Forced evictions

Local authorities forcibly displaced or evicted marginalized communities in rural areas, including landless farmers and *adivasis* to make way for mining, irrigation, power, urban infrastructure and other industrial projects. In several states, authorities evicted *adivasis* from land demarcated as exclusively *adivasi* by constitutional provision. Authorities failed to comply with new legislation guaranteeing access to information by denying affected communities information on planned development projects. In most cases communities were excluded from decision-making processes. Legislation containing improvements in land acquisition procedures and rehabilitation and resettlement policies was pending before parliament.

Local community protests continued over land acquisition and forced evictions. In some cases, police responded by baton-charging peaceful protesters and detaining them without charge for up to one week. Police failed to protect protesters when private militias, reportedly allied with ruling political parties, violently suppressed the protests. Authorities did not carry out timely or impartial inquiries into several of these incidents.

■ In May, private militia reportedly shot dead Amin Banra, an *adivasi* leader, during a protest against forced displacement in Kalinganagar steel city complex, Orissa. The authorities arrested two people but failed to investigate reports that they were part of a large private militia.

■ In August, members of the endangered *Dongria Khond adivasi* in Orissa resumed protests after the Supreme Court permitted a joint venture between Vedanta, a multinational company, and the government to open a bauxite mine in protected forest areas on *Dongria Khond* land.

■ At least 30 people were injured in six-month-long protests by farmers and opposition parties in Singur, West Bengal, against acquisition of their lands for an automobile manufacturing plant without the farmers' prior and informed consent. Subsequent negotiations between the protesters and the state authorities failed, forcing the project to relocate to Gujarat.

Human rights defenders

Human rights defenders campaigning for land and environmental rights of rural communities were subjected to harassment, torture and other ill-treatment by police and to violent attacks by private militias, sometimes resulting in death.

Ongoing monitoring by local communities and human rights defenders ensured that new legislation guaranteeing the rural poor a right to work for at least 100 days per year was implemented in a few states.

Violence between security forces, militia and Maoists

In Chhattisgarh, clashes continued between Maoist armed groups and state forces supported by Salwa Judum, a militia widely believed to be state-sponsored. Both sides targeted civilians, mainly *adivasis* who reported killings, abductions and torture and other ill-treatment. Around 40,000 *adivasis* continued to be internally displaced, of whom 20,000 lived in camps in Chhattisgarh and 20,000 were scattered in neighbouring Andhra Pradesh.

In November, India's National Human Rights Commission (NHRC) submitted its findings of a month-long inquiry to verify reports of human rights abuses by Salwa Judum and the Maoist armed groups. The NHRC found that both sides were responsible for abuses. Human rights organizations criticized the findings, stating that the NHRC had failed to fully investigate abuses committed by the Salwa Judum.

Violence escalated between Maoist armed groups and police in Orissa and Jharkhand.

■ On 15 February, more than 500 armed Maoists raided the Nayagarh district police armoury in Orissa, killing 16 police. In a combing operation following the raid, the Orissa police shot dead 20 people in nearby forests claiming them to be Maoists and their supporters.

Human rights defenders in Orissa and Jharkhand who exposed abuses by the parties to the conflict continued to be at risk of harassment by state authorities.

■ Dr Binayak Sen, who worked for the rights of *adivasis* and contract labourers and had been critical of the Salwa Judum militia, remained in Chhattisgarh prison while his trial continued. He was imprisoned in May 2007 on charges relating to aiding Maoists. Human rights organizations expressed fair trial concerns.

Security and human rights

The authorities responded to the November Mumbai attacks by tightening security legislation and setting up a federal investigating agency. The amended legislation includes sweeping and broad definitions of "acts of terrorism" and of membership of terrorist organizations and extends the minimum and maximum detention periods for terrorism suspects before they are charged.

More than 70 people were detained without charge, for periods ranging from one week to two months in connection with bomb-blasts in several states throughout the year. Reports of torture and other ill-treatment of suspects led to protests from both Muslim and Hindu organizations.

- In November, the authorities in Andhra Pradesh announced cash compensation for 21 Muslims who had been detained without charge for five to ten days and tortured in the wake of multiple bomb-blasts in Hyderabad in August last year. No criminal proceedings were initiated against those responsible for their torture.
- In January, Abujam Shidam, a college teacher and member of the opposition Manipur People's Party, was arrested and tortured in police custody for four days following the December 2007 bomb-blast that killed seven people in Manipur. No action was taken against those responsible for his torture.

Despite ongoing protests, the authorities refused to repeal the Armed Forces Special Powers Act, 1958. The UN Special Rapporteur on extrajudicial, summary or arbitrary executions stated that the Act could facilitate extrajudicial executions by giving security forces the power to shoot to kill in circumstances where they are not necessarily at imminent risk.

Gujarat, Rajasthan and Madhya Pradesh joined the list of states that enacted special security legislation meant to control organized criminal activity. The legislation provided for detention without charge for periods ranging from six months to one year. Uttar Pradesh repealed a similar law.

Jammu and Kashmir

Between June and August, central security forces shot and killed at least 40 people who defied curfew restrictions. The curfew had been imposed during demonstrations and counter-demonstrations over a proposal to transfer forest land to the Amarnath Shrine Board.

Impunity continued for past offences including enforced disappearances of thousands of people during the armed conflict in Kashmir since 1989.

Impunity

Impunity continued to be widespread.

Gujarat

Those responsible for the violence in 2002 in which thousands of Muslims were attacked and more than 2000 killed largely continued to evade justice. The Mumbai High Court made limited progress towards accountability by convicting 12 people in January for one incident of sexual assault.

Punjab

Many of the police officers responsible for serious human rights violations between 1984 and 1994 were not brought to justice. Findings of a Central Bureau of Investigation inquiry into allegations of unlawful killings of 2,097 people cremated by police has not been made fully public.

Assam

No action was taken on the Commission of Inquiry findings published in 2007 that found the unlawful killings of 35 individuals between 1998 and 2001 were carried out at the behest of a former chief minister and the state police.

Death penalty

The authorities failed to make public information detailing the number of executions and people on death row. However, no executions were known to have taken place during the year. Despite government claims that the death penalty was used only in the "rarest of cases", the courts sentenced at least 70 people to death. The NHRC began conducting a study into the application of the death penalty.

In December, India voted against the UN General Assembly resolution calling for a worldwide moratorium on executions.

Amnesty International visits/reports

- Amnesty International delegates visited India in May, July-August and December and met government officials and civil society organizations.
- India: Concern over human rights violations during "recapture" of Nandigram by ruling CPI(M) supporters in West Bengal (ASA 20/001/2008)
- India: Lethal Lottery – The death penalty in India: A study of Supreme Court judgments in death penalty cases 1950-2006 (ASA 20/007/2008)
- India: Serious concerns over fair trial of human rights defender Dr Binayak Sen in Chhattisgarh (ASA 20/013/2008)
- India: Indigenous communities at risk of forced eviction in Orissa (ASA 20/017/2008)
- India: Government should match its words with action and halt violence against Christian minorities in Orissa (ASA 20/021/2008)
- India: Act with restraint during elections in Jammu & Kashmir (ASA 20/028/2008)
- India: New threshold of violence in India, attacks an outrage (ASA 20/030/2008)
- India: New anti-terror laws must meet international human rights standards (ASA 20/031/2008)
- India: Repeal shoot on sight orders in Jammu & Kashmir, 13 August 2008

INDONESIA

REPUBLIC OF INDONESIA

Head of state and government:	**Susilo Bambang Yudhoyono**
Death penalty:	**retentionist**
Population:	**234.3 million**
Life expectancy:	**69.7 years**
Under-5 mortality (m/f):	**36/26 per 1,000**
Adult literacy:	**90.4 per cent**

The situations in Papua and Maluku continued to deteriorate, including continued attacks on freedom of expression. The number of prisoners of conscience rose sharply to 117. Attacks against minority religious groups and their leaders increased across the archipelago. Torture, excessive use of force and unlawful killings by police and security forces continued. No progress was made in bringing the perpetrators of past gross human rights violations in Nanggroe Aceh Darussalam (NAD), Papua and Timor-Leste to justice. Indonesia resumed executions in June, executing 10 people in total. Maternal deaths remained the highest recorded in South East Asia.

Freedom of expression

The government continued to severely restrict freedom of expression. The number of people arrested and detained for peacefully expressing their views rose to at least 32. An additional 85 people imprisoned in previous years remained in jail.

It remained a criminal offence to raise the "Morning Star" flag in Papua, the "Benang Raja" flag in Maluku, and the "Crescent Moon" flag in NAD.

Papua

Low-level conflict between the security forces and pro-independence insurgents in Papua continued. Local community leaders were intimidated and threatened by the military and police. There were reports of torture and other ill-treatment, excessive use of force and extrajudicial executions by security forces.

■ In August, at a rally celebrating World Indigenous Day, police opened fire into a crowd of people after some of them had raised the banned "Morning Star" flag. One peaceful demonstrator, Opinus Tabuni, was found dead following the event.

■ Filep Karma, sentenced to 15 years, and Yusak Pakage, sentenced to ten years, remained in jail. The two men were convicted in 2005 for raising the "Morning Star" flag.

Maluku

Twenty-one men who performed a traditional war dance in front of the President culminating in the unfurling of the banned "Benang Raja" flag were sentenced to between seven and 20 years' imprisonment for "rebellion" in trials throughout 2008.

Freedom of religion

The Ahmadiyya religious minority continued to face discrimination, intimidation and violence. At an interfaith rally in June, Ahmadiyya demonstrators were attacked by sections of the Front Pembela Islam (FPI). Police who were monitoring the rally did not intervene. In response, the Indonesian government announced a joint ministerial decree "freezing" the activities of Ahmadiyya, effectively outlawing its followers. In October, Munarman, a commander of the Islamic Defender Squad, and Rizieq Shihab, leader of the Islamic Defenders' Front, were jailed for 18 months for inciting violence at the rally.

Attacks on Christian leaders and the closure of church buildings in Papua continued.

■ In August, three unknown assailants beat unconscious Catholic priest and human rights defender Father Benny Susetyo in South Jakarta.

Police and security forces

Human rights violations by police and military personnel included excessive use of force during arrest sometimes resulting in death, torture and other ill-treatment of detainees, failure to protect demonstrators during peaceful demonstrations and endemic corruption.

In April, the UN Committee against Torture examined Indonesia's second periodic report. While commending certain legislative developments, the Committee expressed deep concern about the numerous, reliable reports of "routine and widespread use of torture and ill-treatment of suspects in police custody", as well as torture during military operations.

Impunity

In January, the Supreme Court sentenced Pollycarpus Priyanto, a former pilot, to 20 years in prison for poisoning human rights activist Munir Said

Thalib on a Garuda airlines flight from Indonesia to the Netherlands in 2004. In February, Indra Setiawan, a former boss of Garuda, was sentenced to one year's imprisonment for falsifying documents that allowed Pollycarpus Priyanto to travel on Munir Said Thalib's flight. In December, Muchdi Purwoprandjono, a former deputy chief of Indonesia's Intelligence Agency (BIN), was acquitted of masterminding Munir Said Thalib's murder due to lack of evidence. There were fears that the trial was obstructed after three prosecution witnesses, all former BIN members, retracted their testimony in September.

In July, the Commission of Truth and Friendship (CTF), established to document crimes committed in Timor-Leste in 1999 and promote reconciliation, submitted its findings to the Timor-Leste government and the Indonesian government. It allocated institutional responsibility for gross human rights violations to pro-autonomy militia groups, Indonesia's military, civilian government and police. The Indonesian government welcomed the report and expressed its regret over the events of 1999, but stopped short of offering an apology.

The CTF's mandate prevented it from pursuing its own prosecutions, and it did not name violators. Concerns about impunity led the UN to boycott the CTF's investigations and instead resume prosecutions through the Serious Crime Unit and Timor-Leste prosecutors, specifically to probe the 1999 violence.

■ In April, Indonesia's Supreme Court overturned on appeal the conviction and 10-year sentence of former militia leader Eurico Guterres for crimes against humanity in Timor-Leste. He was the only defendant out of the six originally found guilty, whose conviction had been upheld and who was serving a prison sentence.

Death penalty

Executions resumed in June, ending a 14-month hiatus. Ten people were executed in 2008, compared to 11 recorded in the entire preceding decade. At least 10 people were sentenced to death, and at least 116 people remained on death row.

■ On 8 November, Amrozi bin H. Nurhasyim, his brother Ali Ghufron and Imam Samudera were executed. The three men had been convicted of involvement in the Bali bombings on 12 October 2002, in which 202 people died.

In December, Indonesia voted against a UN General Assembly resolution calling for a worldwide moratorium on executions.

Right to health

Indonesia had the highest recorded maternal deaths in South East Asia, with an estimated 19,000 deaths every year. Rates of maternal mortality in remote areas and among Indigenous Peoples far exceeded those within more central and developed areas.

Amnesty International visits/reports

🚍 Amnesty International delegates visited Indonesia in March, July, August and November.

▨ Indonesia: Briefing to the UN Committee against Torture (ASA 21/003/2008)

▨ Indonesia: Investigate ill-treatment of Papuan prisoner (ASA 21/019/2008)

▨ Indonesia: Crackdown on freedom of expression in Maluku (ASA 21/021/2008)

IRAN

ISLAMIC REPUBLIC OF IRAN

Head of state:	Leader of the Islamic Republic of Iran: Ayatollah Sayed 'Ali Khamenei
Head of government:	President: Dr Mahmoud Ahmadinejad
Death penalty:	retentionist
Population:	72.2 million
Life expectancy:	70.2 years
Under-5 mortality (m/f):	35/34 per 1,000
Adult literacy:	82.4 per cent

The authorities maintained tight restrictions on freedom of expression, association and assembly. They cracked down on civil society activists, including women's rights and other human rights defenders and minority rights advocates. Activists were arrested, detained and prosecuted, often in unfair trials, banned from travelling abroad, and had their meetings disrupted. Torture and other ill-treatment of detainees were common and committed with impunity. Sentences of flogging and amputation were reported. At least 346 people were known to have been executed, but the actual number was probably higher. Two men were executed by stoning. Those executed included eight juvenile offenders.

Background

There was continuing unrest among Iran's main ethnic minorities, notably the Azerbaijani, Baluchi and Kurdish communities, over their perceived marginalization and the government's failure to uphold their economic, social and cultural rights as well as their civil and political rights.

The government proposed changes to the Penal Code and other laws that, if ratified, would further erode human rights.

International tension persisted over Iran's nuclear enrichment programme. In March the UN Security Council voted to extend economic and political sanctions imposed in previous years.

International criticism of human rights violations continued. In an October report, UN Secretary-General Ban Ki-moon urged the government to ensure Iran's laws complied with international standards and end discrimination against women and ethnic and religious minorities. In November the UN General Assembly called on the government to end the harassment, intimidation and persecution of political opponents and human rights defenders; to uphold the rights to due process; and to end impunity for human rights violations. It also called on the government to facilitate visits by UN human rights bodies.

Human rights defenders

Human rights defenders were harassed and intimidated but continued to press for greater respect for the rights of women and ethnic minorities and for an end to executions of juvenile offenders. Some were arrested and imprisoned, with prosecutions brought on vague charges; others were banned from travelling abroad.

■ Shirin Ebadi, Nobel Peace Prize laureate and co-founder of the Tehran-based Centre for Human Rights Defenders (CHRD), faced increasing harassment, threats and intimidation by state organs. On 29 December officials claiming to be tax inspectors raided her offices and removed clients' confidential files.

■ In December the CHRD was forcibly closed by security officials shortly before the centre was to hold an event commemorating the 60th anniversary of the Universal Declaration of Human Rights.

■ Emadeddin Baghi, head of the Association for the Defence of Prisoners' Rights (ADPR), was released in October, after serving a sentence imposed unfairly in 2003 for "undermining national security", following criticisms he made about the use of the death penalty. The sentence had initially been suspended. Prison officials delayed urgently needed medical treatment, although he was granted medical leave. He and members of his family were cleared by an appeal court of further charges related to their human rights work, but the judiciary reportedly referred the case to another court for further investigation. In November the trial began of Emadeddin Baghi on charges related to his work with ADPR.

Discrimination against women

Women faced continuing discrimination in law and in practice, and those campaigning for women's rights were targeted for state repression. Parliament debated legislation that, if implemented, would limit women's access to university education of their choice by imposing new residency restrictions. Controversial articles relating to marriage in draft legislation were dropped under pressure from women's rights campaigners. The authorities closed the journal Zanan (Women), blocked women's rights websites and disrupted peaceful gatherings of women's rights activists, such as members of the Campaign for Equality which demands an end to legal discrimination against women.

In February the UN Special Rapporteur on violence against women, its causes and consequences reported that the government had not responded to a single communication made in 2007. In November the Rapporteur criticized Iran for its repression of women's rights defenders.

Dozens of women's rights campaigners were detained, interrogated and some tried for their peaceful activities, including up to 10 who were sentenced by lower courts to prison terms and, in at least two cases, flogging.

■ Maryam Hosseinkhah, Parvin Ardalan, Jelveh Javaheri and Nahid Kesharvarz were sentenced to six-month prison terms in September. Convicted of "spreading propaganda against the state", they remained at liberty awaiting appeals. They were charged for articles they had written for the Campaign for Equality's website and for Zanestan, a women's rights website closed down by the authorities in 2007.

Freedom of expression and association

The authorities continued to repress dissent by restricting access to the internet, banning newspapers and student journals, and prosecuting journalists whose reporting they deemed critical. Officials harassed, intimidated and detained university teachers, trade unionists and students who advocated reform.

Scores of students were suspended or expelled from university for supporting pro-reform groups and the rights of suspended students. Others were arrested and detained, possibly as prisoners of conscience, for participating in demonstrations.

The authorities harassed and intimidated people on account of their appearance. Thousands of prospective candidates were barred from standing in parliamentary elections in March under the discriminatory practice of *gozinesh*, or selection, which impairs – on grounds of political opinion or religious affiliation – equality of opportunity to those who seek employment in the public sector.

■ In August security forces forcibly prevented a peaceful gathering at an unmarked graveyard in Tehran to mark the 20th anniversary of mass executions starting in 1988 for which no one was held to account. At least three people were subsequently sentenced to prison terms for participating in the commemoration, or planning to do so.

Discrimination – repression of minorities

The use of minority languages in schools and government offices continued to be prohibited. Those who campaigned for greater political participation or recognition of minorities' economic, social and cultural rights faced threats, arrest and imprisonment. Members of minorities were denied access to employment in the public sector under *gozinesh* legislation. Many women were doubly disadvantaged, as members of a marginalized minority ethnic or religious group and because of the subordinate status accorded to women in some communities, such as the Baluchi and Kurdish communities.

Arabs

Members of the Ahwazi Arab community continued to protest against perceived discrimination, notably in relation to access to resources.

■ Ma'soumeh Ka'bi and her five children were immediately detained after they were forcibly returned to Iran from Syria in October, apparently to put pressure on her husband, an Ahwazi Arab activist, to return to Iran from Europe and surrender himself to the authorities.

Azerbaijanis

Activists continued to call for the Azerbaijani Turkic language to be used in schools and government services in the areas where Azerbaijani Iranians mainly live. Dozens of activists were arrested in February in connection with demonstrations on International Mother Language Day.

■ Four activists were held in solitary confinement between September and November, accused of "acting against national security". They were among 18 people arrested apparently to prevent a symbolic one-day boycott of schools and universities in protest against the lack of teaching in Azerbaijani Turkic. Their fate was not known.

■ Asgar Akbarzadeh was sentenced by a court in Ardebil in December to five years' imprisonment, to be served in the province of Sistan-Baluchistan, on charges of forming an illegal political party; preparing and distributing "Pan-Turkist" documents; taking part in gatherings associated with Azerbaijani culture, including Azerbaijani folk dancing; and sending information to human rights websites.

Baluchis

In Baluchi areas, the People's Resistance Movement of Iran (PRMI), an armed group also known as Jondallah, sporadically clashed with government forces. In June the group took 15 or 16 Iranian border guards prisoner. One was released but the PRMI killed the rest by October. The authorities took harsh measures against suspected PRMI members and supporters.

■ Ya'qub Mehrnehad, a Baluchi cultural and civil rights activist and member of the Voice of Justice Young People's Society, was executed in August after a grossly unfair trial. He was arrested after criticizing local authorities. He was reported to have been tortured, denied a lawyer and convicted of links with Jondallah by a court in Zahedan.

Kurds

Members of the armed group, Party for a Free Life in Kurdistan, known by its Kurdish acronym PJAK, continued to attack Iranian forces. Many Kurds who were detained faced charges of membership or support of PJAK or other groups. Some, like teacher Farzad Kamangar, who denied the charge and was tortured, were sentenced to death following unfair trials.

Proponents of greater recognition of the Kurdish language and cultural and other rights were arrested and imprisoned after unfair trials.

The authorities failed to take adequate steps to address the longstanding problem of protecting women from violence within the family, despite a continuing high incidence of cases in which women set themselves alight, often fatally, apparently because they were subject to such violence.

More than 50 prisoners went on hunger strike between August and October to protest against the use of the death penalty on Kurdish political prisoners and to demand respect for the civil rights of Kurdish prisoners.

■ Mohammad Sadiq Kabudvand, founder and Chair of the Human Rights Organization of Kurdistan, detained since July 2007, was sentenced to 11 years' imprisonment in May following conviction after an unfair trial of "propaganda against the system" and "acting against state security by establishing the Human Rights Organization of Kurdistan". An appeal court overturned the one-year sentence for "propaganda against the system" and confirmed the 10-year sentence. He was denied visits by his family and lawyer for a prolonged period, and medical treatment that he required was delayed.

Turkmen

Hundreds of members of the Turkmen minority were detained in January in the wake of protests against the killing of a young Turkmen fisherman by maritime security forces in late 2007 near Bandar-e-Torkman. The killers did not appear to have been brought to justice by the end of the year. At least six school children aged under 15 were held for up to 12 days and reportedly tortured, including with beatings, rape with an object and electric shocks.

Religious minorities

Members of some religious minorities continued to suffer discrimination, harassment, arbitrary arrest and damage to community property. Some converts from Islam were arrested. Others detained before 2008 faced trial; at least two were acquitted of "apostasy" and all were eventually released. Adherents of the Baha'i faith continued to be denied access to higher education and some sites considered sacred by them were destroyed. Leaders and other members of the Gonabad Sufi order were harassed and arrested. At least three Sunni clerics were killed in suspicious circumstances; others were detained and two

executed. A Sunni seminary in Baluchistan was destroyed in August. School administrators were required to report to local security offices the presence in their schools of members of "subversive sects" such as the Baha'i, Ali-Ellahi and Ahl-e Haq.

■ In March and May, seven Baha'i community leaders were arrested by Ministry of Intelligence officials. In August they were charged with vaguely worded national security offences. All were prisoners of conscience.

■ Ayatollah Hossein Kazemeyni Boroujerdi, a cleric opposed to the government, remained in prison in poor health serving an 11-year prison term imposed after an unfair trial by the Special Court for the Clergy (SCC) in August 2007. The sentence included internal exile and in November he was moved from Tehran to Yazd.

Justice system

Scores of government critics were arrested, often by plain-clothes officials who did not show any form of identification. Some were detained without trial for long periods beyond the control of the judiciary and were reported to have been tortured or otherwise ill-treated and denied access to medical care, lawyers and their families. Others were sentenced to prison terms after unfair trials or were serving sentences imposed in previous years.

■ Brothers Arash and Kamiar Alaei, both medical doctors specializing in HIV and AIDS prevention and treatment, were arrested in June and detained without charge possibly because of their links with US-based NGOs and their criticism of government policy towards HIV and AIDs programmes. They faced an unfair trial on 31 December, accused of having "co-operated" with an "enemy government" and seeking to overthrow the Iranian government. During the trial, the prosecutor told the court of additional, secret evidence which the brothers' attorney had no opportunity to refute because the prosecutor did not disclose it.

■ Mansour Ossanlu, President of the unrecognized Tehran Bus Workers' Union, continued to serve a five-year prison sentence upheld by an appeal court in October 2007 because of his peaceful trade union activities. A prisoner of conscience and in poor health, he faced delays to necessary medical treatment.

Torture and other ill-treatment

Torture and ill-treatment of detainees were common, facilitated by prolonged pre-charge detention, denial of access to lawyers and family, and a longstanding pattern of impunity for perpetrators. At least four deaths in custody were reported. No independent investigations were known to have been held into these cases or two others in 2007.

■ Abdolreza Rajabi, a supporter of the proscribed People's Mojahedin Organization of Iran who had been imprisoned since 2001, died in custody in October. There were reports that he may have been tortured.

Cruel, inhuman and degrading punishments

Sentences of flogging and judicial amputation were imposed and carried out.

■ Amir Ali Mohammad Labaf, a Gonabad Sufi leader, was said to have been sentenced in November by a court in Qom to five years in prison, flogging and exile to Babak for "spreading lies".

Death penalty

At least 346 people were executed, including at least eight juvenile offenders sentenced for crimes committed when they were under 18. The actual totals were likely to have been higher, as the authorities restricted reporting of executions. Executions were carried out for a wide range of offences, including murder, rape, drug smuggling and corruption. At least 133 juvenile offenders faced execution in contravention of international law. Many Iranian human rights defenders campaigned to end this practice. The authorities sought to justify executions for murder on the grounds that they were qesas (retribution), rather than 'edam (execution), a distinction not recognized by international human rights law. In January, new legislation prescribed the death penalty or flogging for producing pornographic videos, and a proposal to prescribe the death penalty for "apostasy" was discussed in the parliament, but had not been enacted by the end of 2008.

In January, the Head of the Judiciary ordered an end to public executions in most cases and in August judicial officials said that executions by stoning had been suspended, although at least 10 people sentenced to die by stoning were still on death row at the end of the year and two men were executed by stoning in December.

In December, Iran voted against a UN General Assembly resolution calling for a moratorium on executions.

Refugees and asylum-seekers

Iran continued to host almost 1 million refugees, most of them from Afghanistan. According to the government, up to an estimated 1 million other people were in Iran illegally.

■ At least 12 Afghan nationals, apparently returning to Afghanistan from Iran, were shot dead by Iranian border police in April in unclear circumstances.

Amnesty International visits/reports

🚌 The authorities did not reply to over 50 letters sent by Amnesty International and refused to discuss the possibility of Amnesty International visiting the country.

📄 Iran: End executions by stoning (MDE 13/001/2008)

📄 Iran: Women's rights defenders defy repression (MDE 13/018/2008)

📄 Iran: Human rights abuses against the Kurdish minority (MDE 13/088/2008)

IRAQ

REPUBLIC OF IRAQ

Head of state:	Jalal Talabani
Head of government:	Nuri al-Maliki
Death penalty:	retentionist
Population:	29.5 million
Life expectancy:	57.7 years
Under-5 mortality (m/f):	105/98 per 1,000
Adult literacy:	74.1 per cent

The year saw a marked reduction in violence, but all sides to the continuing conflict committed gross human rights abuses. Thousand of civilians, including children, were killed or injured, mostly in suicide and other bomb attacks carried out by armed groups opposed to the government and the US-led Multinational Force (MNF). Civilians were also killed by MNF and Iraqi government forces. The MNF and the Iraqi authorities both held thousands of detainees; most were held without charge or trial, some for up to five years. Government security forces, including prison guards, were reported to have committed torture, including rape, and unlawful killings. The authorities made extensive use of the death penalty. More than 4 million Iraqis were displaced; 2 million were refugees abroad and others were internally displaced within Iraq. The Kurdistan region remained less affected by the conflict but there were continuing reports of abuses by the security forces and violence against women.

Background

Shi'a religious leader Moqtada al-Sadr announced a six-month extension to the ceasefire by the Mahdi Army in February, which was then extended indefinitely in August.

In October the Iraqi authorities assumed responsibility for funding the Sunni-dominated Awakening Councils, formed with the assistance of the US military to fight against the armed opposition group, al-Qa'ida in Iraq.

In November parliament approved the Status of Forces Agreement (SOFA) between the Iraqi and US governments, to take effect after the UN mandate providing for the presence of US troops in Iraq expired on 31 December 2008. Under the SOFA, US troops are to pull back from urban areas before July 2009, withdraw completely from Iraq by the end of 2011, obtain Iraqi government permission for military operations that they mount, and hand over to Iraqi custody all detainees that they hold. The Iraqi authorities will have jurisdiction over US soldiers and civilians who commit "grave premeditated felonies" outside agreed facilities and "duty status", although the US authorities will determine when these conditions apply. Contractors employed by the US Department of Defense will lose their immunity from prosecution in Iraq but the SOFA is silent on other contractors, such as private military and security contractors employed by the US State Department who have been accused of unlawful killings of civilians and other serious abuses.

The humanitarian situation remained alarming. According to the UN, at least 4 million Iraqis still did not have enough food, around 40 per cent of the population did not have access to clean drinking water, and 30 per cent did not have access to adequate health care services. The education system was near collapse with schools and universities lacking essential materials such as books, and teachers and students terrorized by violence. Many schools were bombed. The unemployment rate remained extremely high at 50 per cent or even higher.

In August, Iraq ratified the UN Convention against Torture and in November parliament passed a law establishing a High Commission for Human Rights.

Abuses by armed groups

Armed groups fighting against the government and US-led forces committed numerous gross human rights abuses, as did militia groups affiliated to Shi'a religious groups and political parties represented in the Iraqi parliament. The abuses included kidnapping, torture and murder. The groups also carried out bombings and other indiscriminate attacks against civilians, causing numerous deaths and injuries. Many attacks were apparently carried out by al-Qa'ida in Iraq. Those targeted for kidnapping or killing included members of religious and ethnic minorities, such as Christians and Palestinians; members of professional associations, such as doctors, lawyers and journalists; and women.

■ On 1 February at least 99 civilians, including children, were killed when two women suicide bombers blew themselves up at crowded markets in Baghdad.

■ On 23 February Shihab al-Tamimi, a journalist and head of the Iraqi Journalists' Syndicate, was fatally shot by armed men in Baghdad's al-Waziriya district. He had been a strong critic of sectarian violence.

■ On 14 August suicide bombers killed at least 19 Shi'a pilgrims in Iskandariya who were making their way to Karbala for a religious festival.

■ At least 28 people, including five children, were killed on 10 November, and some 70 others were injured, in bomb attacks in al-Adhamiya, a Sunni district of Baghdad.

Death penalty

At least 275 men and 10 women were sentenced to death. There were at least 34 executions, including at least three carried out in the Kurdistan region (see below). The true totals may have been higher. Most death sentences were passed by the Central Criminal Court of Iraq, whose procedures do not satisfy international standards for fair trial. Defendants complained that "confessions" used as evidence against them had been obtained under torture or other duress. The courts failed adequately to investigate such complaints.

■ In April a senior Interior Ministry official stated that 28 people from Basra had been executed in Baghdad after being convicted of multiple murders and kidnappings.

In December Iraq voted against a UN General Assembly resolution calling for a worldwide moratorium on executions.

Trials of former officials

The Supreme Iraqi Criminal Tribunal (SICT) continued to try former senior officials, Ba'ath party members, military officers and others associated with the former presidency of Saddam Hussein. Trials have been marred by political interference undermining the independence and impartiality of the tribunal. It was reported in September that the Iraq government had engineered the dismissal of one of the judges who had tried former President Saddam Hussein shortly before the year-long trial ended in 2006, replacing the judge with one considered more likely to support the imposition of the death penalty.

■ On 2 December, the SICT imposed death sentences on 'Ali Hassan al-Majid and 'Abdul Ghani 'Abdul Ghafour, both senior officials under Saddam Hussein, after convicting them of involvement in thousands of killings during the 1991 uprising in southern Iraq. Ten other defendants received prison sentences ranging from 15 years to life, and three were acquitted. 'Ali Hassan al-Majid and two of those who received prison terms had already been sentenced to death after a previous trial in 2007; in February, the Presidential Council approved the death sentence on 'Ali Hassan al-Majid but was reported to have ruled that the other two should not be executed as they were serving military officers and following orders at the time the crimes were committed. All three were still in US military custody at the end of the year.

Abuses by private military and security contractors

Employees of foreign security firms remained immune from prosecution for crimes committed in Iraq. The government proposed legislation in October 2007 to revoke this immunity but it was not passed by parliament. In April the US authorities renewed the US company Blackwater's contract to guard US diplomats despite the controversy caused by the killing of Iraqi civilians by Blackwater security guards in September 2007.

■ On 15 January, five schoolchildren were killed when they were struck by a security contractor's car in a convoy accompanying a senior Iraqi judicial official in al-Salihiya, Baghdad. The convoy was reported to have failed to stop at a checkpoint, prompting a gun battle between private security guards and police.

■ On 7 December, five Blackwater security guards were charged in the USA with killing 14 Iraqi civilians and wounding 18 others in September 2007.

Arbitrary arrests and detentions

Thousands of people continued to be detained without charge or trial. US forces of the MNF held some 15,500 detainees, mostly without charge or trial, at Camp Bucca, near Basra; Camp Cropper, near Baghdad airport; and other locations. Some had been held for five years. The Iraqi authorities were reported to be holding at least 26,000 detainees, many without charge or trial. Some were believed to be held incommunicado in secret detention facilities.

Releases

An Amnesty Law came into effect on 27 February and it was expected that most uncharged detainees and those suspected of lesser offences would be freed. Several thousand detainees were released by the MNF and the Iraqi authorities during 2008, far fewer than the 23,000 that the Supreme Judicial Council recommended should be freed.

Human rights violations by Iraqi security forces

Government forces committed gross human rights violations, including torture and extrajudicial executions. Prison guards and security forces were reported to have tortured and otherwise ill-treated detainees, including juveniles. Methods alleged included beating with cables and hosepipes, prolonged suspension by the limbs, electric shock torture, breaking of limbs, removal of toenails with pliers, and piercing the body with drills. Detainees held by Interior Ministry officials were particularly at risk of torture.

■ Male juveniles were reported to have been physically and sexually assaulted by guards at the Tobchi juvenile detention facility in West Baghdad. US investigators found clear evidence that two Sunni juveniles had been killed by prison guards at the beginning of 2008.

■ Allegations of rape and other torture were made by male juveniles held in al-Karkh juvenile prison in Baghdad.

Human rights violations by the Multinational Force

US forces committed serious human rights violations, including unlawful killings of civilians and arbitrary arrests. Several US soldiers were tried before military tribunals in the USA for crimes committed in Iraq; those convicted mostly received lenient sentences not commensurate with the gravity of the crimes.

■ On 4 February a missile fired from a US helicopter killed nine Iraqi civilians, including a child, and injured three others. The missile was reported to have been fired by mistake at a crowd near a military checkpoint manned by government supporters and MNF troops. The US military stated that the incident was under investigation.

■ On 19 September, three women and five men from one family were killed by a US air strike in the village of al-Dawr near Tikrit. The US authorities confirmed the attack, stating that four of those killed were "terrorist suspects".

■ Michael C. Behenna, a US soldier accused of shooting dead 'Ali Mansour Mohammad, a detainee, on 16 May near Beiji, north of Baghdad, was charged with premeditated murder. Michael Behenna was alleged to have detained 'Ali Mansour Mohammad 11 days earlier and assaulted him.

■ Christopher Shore, a US soldier accused of killing an unarmed Iraqi man in June 2007 near Tikrit, was acquitted of murder by a US military tribunal in February but sentenced to 120 days' imprisonment for aggravated assault. This was later reduced to assault, a misdemeanour, and 70 days' imprisonment.

Violence against women and girls

Women were threatened and attacked for not complying with strict codes of behaviour, including dress codes, and the authorities did not afford women adequate protection against violence, including by other family members. Some women were killed apparently by male relatives whom the authorities failed to bring to justice.

■ Leila Hussein was shot dead on 17 May in Basra while walking with two other women, who were injured. Her life was known to be in peril because she had denounced and parted from her husband after he allegedly killed their teenage daughter, Rand Abd al-Qader, in March because of her friendship with a British soldier. No prosecutions for either murder were known to have been initiated.

Refugees and internally displaced people

Several million Iraqis remained displaced, including some 2 million who were refugees in Syria, Jordan and other countries. Some 2.77 million others were internally displaced within Iraq, according to UNHCR, the UN refugee agency. Hundreds of refugees returned, many with the assistance of the government; some said their return was due to improved security conditions in Iraq and others said their return was due to deteriorating living conditions in their countries of refuge.

■ In October, some 13,000 Christians fled Mosul after acts of violence against the city's Christian minority. Most took refuge in nearby villages or in Dohuk, Erbil or Kirkuk, but some 400 fled to Syria. A third of those displaced were reported to have returned to Mosul by the end of 2008.

Kurdistan region

The Kurdistan region of Iraq, administered by the semi-autonomous Kurdistan Regional Government (KRG), remained much less affected by the continuing conflict than other parts of Iraq and saw several positive developments. Hundreds of political prisoners, including many who had been detained without trial for years, were released. A new press law adopted in September abolished imprisonment as a penalty for defamation. Amendments to the Personal Status Law, including restrictions on polygamy, were passed in October.

There were, however, continuing reports of human rights violations: the KRG's security police, the Asayish, operated with virtual impunity; there were new reports of arbitrary arrests; and the authorities failed to clarify the fate of victims of enforced disappearance.

Torture and other ill-treatment

Torture and other ill-treatment by the Asayish were reported.

■ Melko 'Abbas Mohammad and his 60-year-old mother Akhtar Ahmad Mostafa were detained in solitary confinement for 19 days after their arrest in March as suspects in a bomb attack. While held at the Asayish Gishti prison in Sulaimaniya, Melko 'Abbas Mohammad was reported to have been tortured by being suspended by his limbs, beaten with a cable and subjected to electric shocks. He and his mother were acquitted of all charges in November by a court which ordered their release, but the Asayish continued to detain them.

Violence against women and girls

There were reports of domestic violence and burnings and killings of women, including killings by male relatives. Women human rights defenders were threatened because of their work, including by male relatives of women they were assisting. In some cases the authorities failed to identify or arrest perpetrators of violence against women.

■ On 11 May, a woman being protected at the shelter run by the women's rights organization Asuda in Sulaimaniya was seriously injured when gunmen, believed to be her relatives, fired into the shelter.

Death penalty

At least nine people were sentenced to death and at least three executions took place. At least 84 people were on death row, including 33 in Erbil and 47 in Sulaimaniya. In June, the Kurdish parliament extended the application of the 2006 Anti-terrorism Law, which increased the number of capital offences, for a further two years.

■ Two men were executed in April after being convicted in connection with a car bomb explosion in May 2005 in Erbil which killed 48 people.

Freedom of expression

Several journalists and writers who wrote about corruption or criticized the policies of the KRG and the two leading Kurdish political parties received death threats or faced prosecution. One journalist was murdered.

■ Souran Mama Hama was shot dead on 21 July outside his parents' home in Kirkuk, effectively under the security control of the KRG, by men in a car wearing plain clothes. He had published articles critical of corruption and nepotism within the two main Kurdish political parties.

■ 'Adil Hussain, a medical doctor, was sentenced to six months in prison and fined in November after an article he wrote about sex and homosexuality from a medical perspective was published in *Hawlati* newspaper. He was released on 7 December following international protests.

Amnesty International visit/reports

🚗 Amnesty International delegates visited the Kurdistan region of Iraq in May/June.

📓 Carnage and despair – Iraq five years on (MDE 14/008/2008)

📓 Iraqi refugees in Syria (MDE 14/010/2008)

📓 Rhetoric and reality – the Iraqi refugee crisis (MDE 14/011/2008)

📓 Al-Tanf camp – Trauma continues for Palestinians fleeing Iraq (MDE 14/012/2008)

IRELAND

REPUBLIC OF IRELAND

Head of state:	Mary McAleese
Head of government:	Brian Cowen (replaced Bertie Ahern in May)
Death penalty:	abolitionist for all crimes
Population:	4.4 million
Life expectancy:	78.4 years
Under-5 mortality (m/f):	6/6 per 1,000

The use, production and transfer of cluster munitions were banned. Concerns were expressed about overcrowding in prisons and the inadequate provision of children's mental health services. Proposed reductions in government spending threatened to undermine the protection of human rights.

Arms trade

The Control of Exports Act, which came into force in May, tightened controls over the export of goods, technology and technical assistance for military use. However, gaps remained, including in the control of overseas licensed production agreements, and in the transit and transhipment of military and security goods.

In December, Ireland ratified the Convention on Cluster Munitions. The same month the Oireachtas (parliament) enacted the Cluster Munitions and Anti-Personnel Mines Act, outlawing the use, development, production, acquisition, possession, retention and transfer of cluster munitions and explosive bomblets. The Act also prohibits investment of public money in any company that produces cluster munitions or anti-personnel mines.

Children's rights

A referendum on the incorporation of a range of children's rights into the Irish Constitution, promised in 2007, had not been scheduled by the end of 2008.

In April, in a report of his visit to Ireland in November 2007, the Council of Europe Commissioner for Human Rights noted high levels of child poverty in Ireland, and called on the authorities to promote equal opportunities in order to protect children against the negative impact of economic hardship.

The UN Human Rights Committee (HRC) expressed concern in July at the inadequate availability of non-denominational primary education in Ireland.

Child protection guidelines were not made statutory, contrary to recommendations by the UN Committee on the Rights of the Child in 2006. In April, a report of an inquiry by the Health Services Executive into a child protection incident in 2004 exposed serious gaps in child protection policies and procedures.

Police and security forces

In July, the HRC expressed regret at the backlog in cases lodged with the Garda Síochána Ombudsman Commission, and concern that this had led to a number of complaints involving allegedly criminal conduct by police officers being assigned to the Garda Commissioner (the head of the police force) for investigation.

The HRC also expressed concern that access to a lawyer during police interrogation was not prescribed by law, and that the right of an accused person to remain silent was restricted.

In April, a Garda Emergency Response Unit used an electro-shock stun gun for the first time in Ireland during an arrest.

Prison conditions

In July, the HRC noted the persistence of overcrowding in a number of prisons, and expressed concern at a shortage of mental health care for detainees and the high level of inter-prisoner violence.

Discrimination - Travellers

In July, the HRC expressed concern that Ireland did not "intend to recognize the Traveller community as an ethnic minority", and that "the criminalization of trespassing on land in the 2002 Housing Act... disproportionately affects Travellers".

Refugees and asylum-seekers

The Immigration, Residence and Protection Bill 2008 was published in January, aiming at consolidating and updating all immigration and asylum legislation. The UN High Commissioner for Refugees and the HRC expressed concern about aspects of the Bill, while welcoming the creation of a single procedure for reviewing applications for refugee status and subsidiary protection. The HRC called for the Bill to be amended to provide for an independent appeals procedure to review all immigration-related decisions, and noted concerns about the "alleged lack of independence" of the new Protection Review Tribunal which would be created by the Bill, to replace the Refugee Appeals Tribunal. The Bill would allow a government minister to appoint Tribunal members.

In April, the Council of Europe Commissioner for Human Rights expressed concern about conditions in accommodation centres for asylum-seekers, including overcrowding and problems of safety.

Legal and institutional developments

Drastic cuts to the funding for 2009 for the Irish Human Rights Commission and the Equality Authority, announced in October, threatened to prevent these bodies from carrying out their work.

In July, the HRC had called on the government to "strengthen the independence and the capacity of the Irish Human Rights Commission... by endowing it with adequate and sufficient resources".

Right to health – mental health

In April, the Council of Europe Commissioner for Human Rights noted concerns at the lack of implementation of the 2006 mental health strategy. Particular concern was expressed about the 3,000 children on waiting lists for mental health assessment, and at the continued treatment of children in adult facilities.

Counter-terror and security

In November, the government established a Cabinet Committee on Aspects of International Human Rights. Its remit included reviewing, and making recommendations to strengthen, the statutory powers of the police and civil authorities regarding the search and inspection of aircraft potentially engaged in renditions.

Violence against women and girls

In July, the HRC expressed concern about continuing impunity for domestic violence, "due to high withdrawal rates of complaints and few convictions".

Trafficking in human beings

In June, the Criminal Law (Human Trafficking) Act 2008 came into force, creating an offence of trafficking. The Act criminalized the use of services of victims of trafficking, and abolished any defence based on the victim's consent for such offences.

The Immigration, Residence and Protection Bill 2008 would, if enacted, provide for a 45-day recovery and reflection period for victims of trafficking. It would also provide for a six-month temporary residence permit for victims, but this would be conditional on the victim's co-operation with a criminal investigation.

ISRAEL AND THE OCCUPIED PALESTINIAN TERRITORIES

STATE OF ISRAEL

Head of state:	Shimon Peres
Head of government:	Ehud Olmert
Death penalty:	abolitionist for ordinary crimes
Population:	7 million (Israel); 4.1 million (OPT)
Life expectancy:	80.3 years (Israel); 72.9 years (OPT)
Under-5 mortality (m/f):	6/5 per 1,000 (Israel); 22/17 per 1,000 (OPT)
Adult literacy:	97.1 per cent (Israel); 92.4 per cent (OPT)

Israeli forces launched a military offensive on an unprecedented scale – code-named "Operation Cast Lead" – on 27 December in the Gaza Strip, killing many civilians and destroying homes and other civilian property. Earlier in the year there had been a marked upsurge in killings of civilians and others by both Israeli forces and Palestinian armed groups in Israel and the Occupied Palestinian Territories (OPT) before a ceasefire was agreed in June (see Palestinian Authority entry). Some 70 children were among the 425 Palestinians killed in the first half of the year. In addition to the large-scale destruction of homes and property in the Gaza Strip, Israeli forces also destroyed scores of Palestinian homes in the West Bank and in Bedouin villages in the south of Israel. Throughout the year, the Israeli army maintained stringent restrictions on the movement

of Palestinians in the OPT, including a blockade on the Gaza Strip, which caused an unprecedented level of humanitarian hardship and virtually imprisoned the entire population of 1.5 million. This was further exacerbated by the Israeli offensive launched on 27 December. Hundreds of patients with serious medical conditions requiring treatment not available in local hospitals were refused passage out of Gaza; several died. Hundreds of students could not travel to their universities abroad because they could not leave Gaza, where many fields of study are not available. Most of Gaza's inhabitants depended on international aid, but the Israeli blockade hampered the ability of UN agencies to provide assistance and services. In the West Bank the movement of Palestinians was severely curtailed by some 600 Israeli checkpoints and barriers, and by the 700km fence/wall which the Israeli army continued to build mostly inside the West Bank. The expansion of illegal Israeli settlements on seized Palestinian land increased to a level not seen since 2001. Israeli soldiers and settlers who committed serious abuses against Palestinians, including unlawful killings, assaults and attacks against property, enjoyed impunity in most cases. Hundreds of Palestinians were arrested by Israeli forces; reports of torture and other ill-treatment were frequent, but investigations were rare. Some 8,000 Palestinians remained in Israeli prisons, many after unfair military trials.

Background

Prime Minister Ehud Olmert resigned in September because of a police investigation into his alleged involvement in corruption and fraud, but remained in office pending legislative elections scheduled for February 2009. Peace talks between the Israeli government and the Palestinian Authority (PA) continued, but neither the peace agreement that US President George W. Bush had undertaken to broker before the end of the year, nor any other concrete progress was achieved by the end of 2008. On the contrary, at the end of the year the Gaza Strip was under an unprecedented level of bombardment – by air, land and sea – by Israeli forces. In addition, the Israeli authorities did not fulfil their undertakings to ease restrictions on the movement of Palestinians in the OPT and to remove illegal Israeli settlements established in recent years. A ceasefire agreed in June between Israel and Palestinian armed groups in

Gaza held for four and a half months, but broke down after Israeli forces killed six Palestinian militants in air strikes and other attacks on 4 November.

Gaza blockade and other restrictions fuelling humanitarian hardship

The continuing Israeli military blockade of the Gaza Strip exacerbated an already dire humanitarian situation, health and sanitation problems, poverty and malnutrition for the 1.5 million residents. The Israeli military offensive launched in late December brought conditions to the brink of human catastrophe. Even before it began, the local economy was paralysed by the lack of imports and a ban on exports. Shortages of most basic necessities fuelled price increases, causing some 80 per cent of the population to become dependent on international assistance. UN and other aid and humanitarian organizations faced additional restrictions which hindered their ability to provide assistance and services to Gaza's people and increased their operational costs. UN reconstruction projects to provide housing for families whose homes had been destroyed by the Israeli army in previous years were suspended due to a lack of construction material. Seriously ill patients in need of medical care not available in Gaza and hundreds of students and workers wishing to study or travel to jobs abroad were among those trapped in Gaza by the blockade; only relatively few were allowed to leave the area by the Israeli authorities. Several patients who were denied passage out of Gaza later died.

■ Mohammed Abu 'Amro, a 58-year-old cancer patient, died in October. He had sought a permit to leave Gaza since March. The permit was denied on unspecified "security grounds" but was finally granted a week after his death.

■ Karima Abu Dalal, a 34-year-old mother of five who suffered from Hodgkin's lymphoma, died in November due to lack of treatment. The Israeli authorities had repeatedly refused her a permit to travel to the hospital in Nablus, in the West Bank, since November 2007.

In the West Bank, some 600 Israeli military checkpoints and barriers restricted the movement of Palestinians, hindered their access to workplaces, education and health facilities and other services. The Israeli army continued its construction of a 700km fence/wall, mostly within the territory of the West Bank. This separated tens of thousands of Palestinian farmers from their land; they were required to obtain permits to

access their land but these were frequently denied.

Palestinians were also denied access to large areas of the West Bank close to Israeli settlements established and maintained in breach of international law, and were barred from or had only restricted access to more than 300km of roads used by Israeli settlers.

■ In February, Fawziyah al-Dark, aged 66, was denied passage through an Israeli military checkpoint to access Tulkarem hospital after suffering a heart attack. She died shortly after.

■ In September, Israeli soldiers refused to allow Naheel Abu Rideh to pass through the Huwara checkpoint and travel to Nablus hospital although she was in labour. She gave birth in her husband's car at the checkpoint; her baby boy died.

Killings of unarmed Palestinian civilians

Some 450 Palestinians were killed and thousands of others were injured by Israeli forces in air strikes and other attacks, most of them in the first half of the year in the Gaza Strip. Up to half of those killed were civilians, including some 70 children. The rest were armed group members killed in armed confrontations or in targeted air strikes. Hundreds of other Palestinian civilians were killed and injured in the last five days of the year in the Israeli military offensive, some as a result of direct attacks on civilians or civilian buildings, others in indiscriminate and disproportionate attacks.

Many killings of Palestinian civilians in the first half of the year and during the December military offensive were in response to indiscriminate rocket and mortar attacks launched by Palestinian armed groups from the Gaza Strip against nearby Israeli towns and villages and against Israeli army positions along the perimeter of the Gaza Strip. Six Israeli civilians and several soldiers were killed in such attacks and 14 other Israeli civilians, including four 17-year-olds, were killed in shooting and other attacks by Palestinians in Jerusalem and elsewhere in the country.

■ During a four-day military incursion into the Gaza Strip in late February Israeli forces killed more than 100 Palestinians, about half of whom were civilians not involved in fighting, including some 25 children. Among the victims were 16-year-old Jackline Abu Shbak and her 15-year-old brother Iyad. They were both shot dead with a single bullet to the head in front of their mother and younger siblings, in their home north of Gaza City on 29 February. The shots were fired from a house which had been taken over by Israeli soldiers opposite the children's home.

■ On 16 April, Israeli forces killed 15 Palestinian civilians, including 10 children aged between 13 and 17 and a journalist, in three separate attacks, which also injured dozens of other civilians, in the Jouhr al-Dik area in the south-east of the Gaza Strip. First, Israeli tank fire killed six children – 'Abdullah Maher Abu Khalil, Tareq Farid Abu Taqiyah, Islam Hussam al-'Issawi, Talha Hani Abu 'Ali, Bayan Sameer al-Khaldi and Mohammed al-'Assar. Then, Israeli soldiers in a tank fired a flechette shell at Fadel Shana', a Reuters cameraman, killing him, as he was filming the tank. A further tank shell fired immediately after killed two more children, Ahmad 'Aref Frajallah and Ghassan Khaled Abu 'Ateiwi, and injured five others. Two of them, Ahmad 'Abd al-Majid al-Najjar and Bilal Sa'id 'Ali al-Dhini, died three days later.

Military justice system

Detentions

Hundreds of Palestinians, including scores of children, were detained by Israeli forces in the OPT and many were held incommunicado for prolonged periods. Most were later released without charge, but hundreds were charged with security-related offences and tried before military courts, whose procedures often failed to meet international standards for fair trial. Some 8,000 Palestinians arrested in 2008 or in previous years were still imprisoned at the end of the year. They included some 300 children and 550 people who were held without charge or trial under military administrative detention orders, including some who had been held for up to six years.

■ Salwa Salah and Sara Siureh, two 16-year-old girls, were arrested at night from their homes in June and were still held in administrative detention at the end of 2008.

■ Mohammed Khawajah, aged 12, was arrested by Israeli soldiers at his home in Ni'lin village at 3am on 11 September. He was beaten and detained with adults in an army detention camp until 15 September, when he was released on bail. He was charged with throwing stones at soldiers and sent for trial before a military court.

■ Dozens of Hamas members of the Palestinian parliament and ministers in the former Hamas-led PA

government remained detained without trial, up to two years after their arrest. The Israeli authorities held them apparently to exert pressure on Hamas to release an Israeli soldier held in the Gaza Strip by Hamas' armed wing since 2006.

Almost all Palestinian detainees were held in prisons in Israel in violation of international humanitarian law, which prohibits the removal of detainees to the territory of the occupying power. This made it difficult or impossible in practice for detainees to receive family visits.

Denial of family visits

Some 900 Palestinian prisoners from the Gaza Strip were denied any family visits for a second year. Many relatives of Palestinian detainees from the West Bank were also denied visiting permits on unspecified "security" grounds. Many parents, spouses and children of detainees had not been allowed visits to their detained relatives for more than five years. No Israeli prisoners were subject to such restrictions.

Prisoner releases

In July, the Israeli authorities released five Lebanese prisoners, one of them held since 1979 and four captured during the 2006 war. They also gave back the bodies of 199 other Lebanese and Palestinians killed by Israeli forces in previous years in exchange for the bodies of two Israeli soldiers killed by Hizbullah in July 2006. In August and December, the Israeli authorities released some 430 Palestinian detainees, in what were described as goodwill gestures to PA President Mahmoud Abbas.

Torture and other ill-treatment

Reports of torture and other ill-treatment by the Israeli General Security Service (GSS) increased, especially during interrogation of Palestinians suspected of planning or involvement in armed attacks. Methods reported included prolonged tying in painful stress positions, sleep deprivation and threats to harm detainees' families. Beatings and other ill-treatment of detainees were common during and following arrest and during transfer from one location to another.

Increase in violence by settlers

Violent attacks by Israeli settlers against Palestinians and their property throughout the West Bank increased markedly in the last quarter of the year, especially during the olive harvest and when the army attempted to evacuate a house which had been taken over by settlers in Hebron. Settlers who carried out the attacks were often armed. In Hebron in December a settler shot and injured two Palestinians.

Impunity

Israeli military judges rarely ordered investigations into allegations of torture and other ill-treatment made by Palestinian defendants during their trials before military courts, and no GSS officers were known to have been prosecuted for torturing Palestinians. In October, two Israeli human rights groups filed a court petition requiring the Justice Ministry to disclose information about its handling of complaints of torture and other ill-treatment made by Palestinian detainees against the GSS.

Impunity remained the norm for Israeli soldiers and members of other security forces and for Israeli settlers who committed serious human rights abuses against Palestinians, including unlawful killings, physical assaults and attacks on their property. Few investigations were carried out into such abuses and most were closed for "lack of evidence". Prosecutions were rare and usually limited to cases publicized by human rights organizations and the media; in such cases, soldiers accused of killing Palestinians unlawfully were charged with manslaughter, not murder, and soldiers and settlers who were convicted of abuses against Palestinians generally received relatively lenient sentences.

■ A soldier who shot a Palestinian demonstrator in the foot while the latter was blindfolded, handcuffed and held by the soldier's commander in July was charged with the minor offence of "improper conduct". In September, the army's chief prosecutor rejected a recommendation by the High Court to add more serious charges.

Forced evictions, destruction of Palestinian homes and expansion of illegal Israeli settlements

Israeli forces destroyed many Palestinian homes as well as factories and other civilian buildings in Gaza in the first days of the military offensive launched on 27 December, razing entire neighbourhoods. In the West Bank, including in East Jerusalem, Israeli forces demolished scores of Palestinian homes, forcibly evicting families and leaving hundreds of people homeless. The targeted homes lacked building permits, which were systematically denied to

Palestinians. At the same time, the authorities sharply increased the expansion of Israeli settlements on illegally confiscated Palestinian land, in violation of international law.

■ In February and March, Israeli forces destroyed several homes and animal pens in Hadidiya, a small village in the Jordan Valley area of the West Bank. Some 65 members of the Bisharat and Bani Odeh families, 45 of them children, were made homeless.

■ In March, Israeli soldiers demolished the homes of several families in the Southern Hebron Hills villages of Qawawis, Imneizil, al-Dairat and Umm Lasafa. Most of those rendered homeless were children. Those who lost their homes included three brothers, Yasser, Jihad Mohammed and Isma'il al-'Adra, their wives and their 14 children.

■ In nearby Umm al-Khair, Israeli forces destroyed the homes of 45 members of the al-Hathaleen family, most of them children, in October.

Refugees, asylum-seekers and migrants

In August, the Israeli army forcibly returned scores of refugees, asylum-seekers and migrants to Egypt without allowing them an opportunity to challenge the decision and despite the risk that they could be exposed to serious human rights violations in Egypt or their home countries, including Eritrea, Somalia and Sudan.

Prisoners of conscience – Israeli conscientious objectors

In the latter part of the year there was a marked increase in the number of Israeli conscientious objectors imprisoned for refusing to serve in the Israeli army because of their opposition to the Israeli military occupation of the Palestinian Territories. At least seven teenagers were repeatedly imprisoned for short periods. At least two were still detained at the end of the year. Most of the others were eventually classified as "unfit for service" and exempted.

Amnesty International visits/reports

🚗 Amnesty International delegations visited Israel and the OPT from February to May.

📄 Israel/Occupied Palestinian Territories: Punitive restrictions – families of Palestinian detainees denied visits (MDE 15/006/2008)

📄 Israel/Occupied Palestinian Territories: Gaza blockade – collective punishment (MDE 15/021/2008)

📄 Israel/Occupied Palestinian Territories: Under threat – the West Bank village of 'Aqaba (MDE 15/022/2008)

Israel/Occupied Palestinian Territories: Submission to the UN Universal
Periodic Review (MDE 15/029/2008)

Israel/Occupied Palestinian Territories: Briefing to the Committee
against Torture (MDE 15/040/2008)

Israel/Occupied Palestinian Territories: Health Professional Action –
Crushing the right to health: Gaza (MDE 15/044/2008)

ITALY

ITALIAN REPUBLIC

Head of state:	Giorgio Napolitano
Head of government:	Silvio Berlusconi
	(replaced Romano Prodi in May)
Death penalty:	abolitionist for all crimes
Population:	58.9 million
Life expectancy:	80.3 years
Under-5 mortality (m/f):	6/6 per 1,000
Adult literacy:	98.4 per cent

Roma were subjected to serious attacks throughout
the year, and there was little available information on
effective investigations into these incidents. Forced
evictions against Roma drove them deeper into
poverty. Several people were given deportation
orders and at least two people were deported to
Tunisia where they were at risk of serious human
rights violations. Italy still lacked comprehensive
legislation for the protection of asylum-seekers.
However, a more extensive set of rules, including
some improvements in the asylum procedure,
entered into force following the implementation of
EU legislation. Investigations into allegations of ill-
treatment by law enforcement officials were
inadequate.

Racism and discrimination – Roma

Racially motivated attacks took place against Roma,
who were unprotected by the authorities. Unlawful
forced evictions continued, and special powers were
granted to prefects to control Romani settlements.
Roma and Sinti were still not recognized as a
national minority.

Attacks on Romani settlements

Romani communities were frequently attacked, and
the authorities often failed to stop the violence.

In May, the UN Committee on the Elimination of
Racial Discrimination (CERD) expressed its concern
about "reported instances of hate speech, including
statements targeting nationals and Roma, attributed
to politicians."

In July, a group of UN experts said they were
"dismayed at the aggressive and discriminatory
rhetoric used by political leaders, including Cabinet
members, when referring to the Roma community"
and stated that the "climate of anti-Roma sentiment
has served to mobilize extremist groups, which have
recently launched a series of attacks against Roma
camps and individuals."

■ On 13 May, up to 100 people, reportedly armed with
sticks and Molotov cocktails, set fire to parts of a
Romani settlement in the suburb of Ponticelli in
Naples. One Molotov cocktail was thrown at a trailer
housing a number of children, who only just managed
to escape being burnt alive. In total, around 800
Romani people were forced to flee the settlement. On
the same day, several Romani people were also
physically attacked in the surrounding area.

■ On 6 June, a Romani woman who was six months
pregnant was kicked repeatedly in the back outside a
bar in Rimini.

■ Other arson attacks were also reported during the
year in Naples, Novara, Pisa, Rome and Venice.

Forced evictions

Unlawful forced evictions of Romani communities
continued throughout the year.

■ In April, around 800 Roma were evicted from the
settlement of Via Bovisasca in Milan. No alternative
accommodation was provided and no provision was
made for pregnant women, elderly people and children
who were made homeless.

■ In June, the settlement of Campo Boario in Rome,
home to 130 Italian Roma, was destroyed by law
enforcement officers. The community was moved to a
temporary settlement in the Tor Vergata
neighbourhood, where they lacked basic facilities such
as water and electricity. In October, the community was
moved to another temporary settlement in a car park a
few kilometres away.

New legislation targeting Romani communities

On 26 May, the Prime Minister declared a state of
emergency targeting Romani communities in the
regions of Lazio, Campania and Lombardia until May
2009. The prefects in these regions gained powers to
carry out censuses of people living in settlements,

carry out evictions, derogate from a series of national laws and fingerprint people, including children.

Following widespread criticism by human rights organizations, people have only been fingerprinted in exceptional situations, when no other means of identification were available.

Racism

Racially motivated attacks continued, including physical assaults, verbal abuse and the destruction of property. Both the EU Commissioner for Human Rights and the CERD commented that racist statements by politicians and the adoption of legislation targeting migrants contributed to a hostile environment against non-nationals. They urged the authorities to take action against hate speech and introduce more severe sentences for racially motivated crimes.

Migrants' and asylum-seekers' rights

Migrants and asylum-seekers without valid documentation, including pregnant women and families with children, were routinely detained upon arrival in detention centres before having the chance to apply for international protection. Migrants and asylum-seekers detained in some centres were not granted the right to appeal in court against the lawfulness or conditions of their detention.
■ In Cassabile detention centre, asylum-seekers were detained for up to five weeks before being given the chance to apply for asylum.

There were reports of the deaths of migrants in detention centres due to delays in medical help.
■ On 24 May, Hassan Nejl, a Moroccan national, died in the Turin Temporary Stay Centre after being taken ill. According to other detainees, he was not given prompt or adequate medical care. A judicial investigation was launched, but no results were available at the end of the year.

A decree adopted on 3 October suspended the deportation of asylum-seekers appealing against rejection of their asylum claim. The decree also gave local prefects the power to limit the movements of migrants and asylum-seekers to a specified area.

Several measures were adopted by municipal authorities against migrants. On 11 February, a court in Milan cancelled a circular issued by Milan City Council because of its discriminatory nature. The circular restricted kindergarten enrolment of the children of migrants without a residence permit.

The European Commissioner for Human Rights and the UN Working Group on Arbitrary Detention raised concerns after a set of legislative proposals known as the "security package" was adopted on 21 May to tackle irregular migration. One decree which was converted into Law 125/08 on 24 July ruled that if a migrant committed an offence, their irregular status would be added to the list of aggravated circumstances as set out in the Penal Code, which could result in the imposition of a more severe punishment.

Counter-terror and security

Italy failed to address human rights violations committed in the context of the US-led programme of renditions.

Complicity in renditions

■ On 3 December, the trial of seven Italian nationals, primarily members of the Italian Military Security Service Agency, in connection with the abduction of Abu Omar was suspended again. (Abu Omar, an Egyptian refugee with Italian residency, was abducted in Milan in February 2003 and flown to Egypt where he was subsequently detained and reportedly tortured. He was released in February 2007 without charge.)

In November the Prime Minister declared that the use of evidence relating to contacts with the CIA would be a threat to state secrecy. The judge decided to suspend the trial as it was impossible to proceed given that the majority of the evidence related to contacts with the CIA. The suspension of the trial was pending a decision by the Constitutional Court in March 2009.

By the end of the year the Minister of Justice had not forwarded to the US authorities the extradition requests, issued by a Milan court, of 26 US citizens, including consular staff, CIA agents and an air force colonel.

Counter-terrorism legislation

Italy retained the so-called Pisanu Law, Law 155/05, which provides for expulsion orders of terrorist suspects. The expulsion can be ordered by the Minister of Interior or by a prefect when there is a presumption of terrorist connections. The Law does not provide for judicial confirmation or authorization of the expulsion decision and does not guarantee effective protection against forcible return to countries where there might be a risk of torture or other ill-treatment.

On 28 February, the European Court of Human Rights ruled against the 2006 decision by the Minister of Interior to deport Nassim Saadi to Tunisia, following his conviction in Italy for criminal conspiracy. Despite diplomatic assurances, he would have been at risk of human rights violations had he been returned to Tunisia.

On 4 June, Sami Ben Khemais Essid, a Tunisian national, was deported to Tunisia under an expedited procedure for removal of those considered a risk to national security, despite a request by the European Court of Human Rights for Italy to suspend his transfer to Tunisia pending their review of the case.

On 13 December, Mourad Trabelsi, a Tunisian national, was deported to Tunisia despite a request by the European Court of Human Rights to suspend his expulsion due to the risk of torture and other ill-treatment he would face in Tunisia. Neither Mourad Trabelsi's family nor his lawyer knew of his whereabouts at the end of the year.

Torture and other ill-treatment

The authorities failed to include torture as a crime in its Criminal Code or to introduce an effective police accountability mechanism. There were continued allegations of torture and other ill-treatment by law enforcement officials, particularly towards migrants.

The trial in the case of the death of Federico Aldrovandi continued. Federico Aldrovandi died on 25 September 2005 after being stopped by four police officers, who were subsequently accused of voluntary manslaughter. On 25 November, new evidence appeared suggesting Federico Aldrovandi's death was caused by the method of restraint used by the police, which restricted his breathing and led to cardiorespiratory arrest.

There were developments in the case of Aldo Bianzino, who died in October 2007 in prison in Perugia two days after his arrest. A medical check just after his arrest had revealed that he was in perfect health. An autopsy revealed a brain haemorrhage and ruptured liver. The Public Prosecutor initiated legal proceedings against unidentified people for manslaughter and against a prison guard for failing to come to Aldo Bianzino's help. His family was convinced that he died because of ill-treatment while in detention. In February 2008, further forensic tests ordered by the Public Prosecutor concluded that he had died of natural causes – a brain aneurysm. The Public

Prosecutor asked for the manslaughter case to be closed, which was opposed by Aldo Bianzino's family. In October 2008, the judge ruled that the case should not be closed.

On 29 September, Emmanuel Bonsu, a Ghanaian citizen, was arrested and reportedly beaten by municipal police officers in Parma, resulting in damage to his eye. He was released after four hours. Ten police officers were charged with kidnapping, ill-treatment and abuse of power, among other things.

G8 trials

Trials against demonstrators and law enforcement officials involved in the policing of the G8 summit in Genoa in 2001 continued.

In January, the Ministry of Interior was ordered to pay €35,000 to M.P., a doctor who was severely beaten by law enforcement officers in Genoa in 2001.

Fifteen people, including police officers, prison guards and doctors, were sentenced to prison terms of up to five years after being found guilty on 14 July of abuse of office and ill-treating protesters detained in Bolzaneto prison. In November, the judge admitted that he could only sentence the accused on lesser charges, since torture is not a criminal offence in the penal code. It was unlikely that any of those sentenced would actually serve time in prison because their offences would expire under Italy's statute of limitations before the completion of the appeal process.

Thirteen law enforcement officials were found guilty on 13 November of ill-treating protesters staying at the Armando Diaz School, defamation and planting evidence, among other charges. Those found guilty, along with the Ministry of Interior, would be responsible for paying reparations to the victims. The sentences handed down by the Italian court ranged from one month to four years' imprisonment.

Amnesty International reports

Italy: the witch-hunt against Roma people must end (EUR 30/006/2008)

State of denial – Europe's role in rendition and secret detention (EUR 01/003/2008)

JAMAICA

JAMAICA
Head of state: Queen Elizabeth II, represented by
                         Kenneth Hall
Head of government: Bruce Golding
Death penalty: retentionist
Population: 2.7 million
Life expectancy: 72.2 years
Under-5 mortality (m/f):   18/16 per 1,000
Adult literacy: 79.9 per cent

There were high rates of murder and police killings in socially excluded inner-city communities. The government initiated some reforms to the police and justice system to tackle the security crisis. Discrimination and violence against women and people in same-sex relationships were widespread. At least one person was sentenced to death; there were no executions.

Background

In the context of the public security crisis, a reported 1,611 people were murdered. The majority of victims were from marginalized inner-city communities. A raft of so-called "anti-crime" bills – including extension of police powers of arrest, increases in bail periods and minimum sentences for gun-related crimes – remained before Parliament at the end of the year. National human rights organizations questioned the constitutionality of some of the bills' provisions and expressed concerns that the proposed extra police and judicial powers could lead to abuse. The Inter-American Commission on Human Rights visited Jamaica in December. In its preliminary observations the Commission stated it had witnessed an "alarming level of violence" which affected all sectors of society, and pointed to continued shortcomings in the security forces and justice system as well as widespread corruption and poverty as the principal causes for the deteriorating public security situation.

Police and security forces

The rate of police killings fell but remained high with 222 people allegedly killed by police. Many occurred in circumstances suggesting that they were unlawful, despite frequent police claims that they were a result of shoot-outs with criminal gangs.

Government efforts to address police impunity and lack of accountability included parliamentary discussions on a draft bill to create an independent commission to investigate abuses by the security forces. These were still ongoing at the end of the year.

A report emerging from the strategic review of the Jamaica Constabulary Force (JCF) was issued in June. The vast majority of its 124 recommendations were approved by the government.

Although training in crime scene investigation and new forensic equipment for the JCF were introduced, failure to protect crime scenes and poor quality of forensic investigations continued to severely hamper effective police work.

■ Seventeen-year-old Carlton Grant was shot dead by police on 23 August in downtown Kingston. The two police officers involved stated that Carlton Grant and a friend had shot at them after they were stopped by police in the street and that officers returned fire. Eyewitnesses claimed Carlton Grant and his friend were unarmed and were shot as they attempted to surrender to police. In November, the Director of Public Prosecutions ruled that the two officers should be charged with murder.

■ Thirteen-year-old Jevaughn Robinson was fatally shot in the head by members of a police patrol on 22 September in Spanish Town, St Catherine. The police stated he was killed in a shoot-out and claimed they retrieved a gun from the crime scene. Local residents refuted this, alleging that when the police entered the community, men close to Jevaughn Robinson started to run for cover towards nearby bushes and he did the same. Witnesses stated that police officers chased him, accosted him and, without making any effort to restrain or detain him, shot him in the head. An investigation was ongoing at the end of the year.

Justice system

Some progress was made in implementing recommendations from a June 2007 report by the Justice System Reform Task Force, including appointment of additional court staff, but the majority remained to be implemented. At the end of the year, legislation to create a special coroner's office to expedite investigations into new cases of fatal police shootings and address the backlog of cases was still in discussion as was a bill to establish a special prosecutor to investigate corruption by state officials. In September, Parliament passed bills to increase the

J

number of judges in the Supreme Court and Appeal Court. Despite these moves, national human rights organizations pointed to continued chronic problems with the judiciary, including severe delays in cases being heard, unavailability of jurors, witness absenteeism and sporadic court scheduling.

Violence against women and girls

Sexual violence against women and girls remained widespread. According to police statistics, 655 women were raped between January and October. A Sexual Offences Bill, which would offer greater legal protection to women and children victims of sexual violence, had still not been presented to Parliament by the end of the year. The Bill was finalized in 2007, and was the culmination of attempts, which began in 1995, to reframe existing gender-discriminatory legislation.

Discrimination – lesbian, gay, bisexual and transgender people

There were continuing reports of mob violence against people, mostly men, perceived to be involved in same-sex relationships. The true extent of attacks on gay men was unknown as the subject is taboo and people do not report attacks for fear of exposure.
■ In August, a Molotov cocktail (petrol bomb) was thrown into a house in Clarendon, south central Jamaica, occupied by two men who were alleged to be gay. As the emergency services arrived, a small jeering crowd assembled outside the house. One of the men received burns covering 60 per cent of his body and was hospitalized for three weeks.

Death penalty

At least one new death sentence was handed down, but no executions were carried out. There were nine people on death row at the end of the year. At the end of the year the Jamaican Parliament voted to retain the death penalty.

In December, Jamaica voted against a UN General Assembly resolution calling for a worldwide moratorium on executions.

Amnesty International visit/report

🚌 Amnesty International delegates visited Jamaica in March/April.
📃 "Let them kill each other" – Public security in Jamaica's inner-cities (AMR 38/001/2008)

JAPAN

JAPAN
Head of government: Aso Taro (replaced Fukuda Yasuo in September)
Death penalty: retentionist
Population: 127.9 million
Life expectancy: 82.3 years
Under-5 mortality (m/f): 5/4 per 1,000

The number of executions increased. Prisoners continued to face prolonged periods of solitary confinement and inadequate access to medical care. Under the *daiyo kangoku* pre-trial detention system, police interrogated suspects without lawyers and often in the absence of electronic recording. Despite international pressure, the Japanese government failed to accept full responsibility or provide adequate reparations to the survivors of Japan's World War II military sexual slavery system.

Background

In September, a deadlock in the Diet (parliament) between the ruling Liberal Democratic Party and the opposition led to the resignation of Prime Minister Fukuda Yasuo, who had been in the post for less than a year.

Death penalty

Fifteen executions were carried out in 2008, the highest number since 1975. One hundred prisoners remained on death row.
■ In June, Japan executed three men, including Miyazaki Tsutomu. According to his lawyer, he was mentally ill and had been receiving psychiatric medical treatment in the detention centre for more than a decade.

Death row inmates continued to be confined to single cells, day and night, with limited opportunity to exercise or socialize. They were typically notified of their execution only on the morning of their execution, and their families were informed only after the execution had taken place.

In December, Japan voted against a UN General Assembly resolution calling for a worldwide moratorium on executions.

Prison conditions

Under new prison rules introduced by the Ministry of Justice, the number of prisoners in solitary confinement increased. Those categorized as high security, exempt from time limits on solitary confinement and access to complaints mechanisms, could remain in solitary confinement indefinitely. Prisoners in solitary confinement remained in single cells, day and night, had no communication with other prisoners and were permitted only 15 minutes' exercise a day.

Prisoners continued to have inadequate access to medical care. Due to a shortage of doctors, prisoners were often examined and given medication by nurses. Reports indicated that it was difficult for prisoners to obtain permission from wardens to visit medical specialists outside the prison due to a shortage of prison guards. Prison authorities prevented prisoners from accessing their medical records.

■ In February, a group of about 20 inmates and former inmates at Tokushima Prison filed a criminal complaint against a prison doctor who allegedly abused them from May 2004 to November 2007. One of the prisoners, who came to the doctor about dizzy spells, alleged that the doctor treated him by pinching his inner thighs, stepping on his ankle and giving him a rectal examination. He subsequently developed an infection from the examination and had to undergo surgery at a private hospital.

Pre-trial detention

In October, the UN Human Rights Committee examined Japan's report under the International Covenant on Civil and Political Rights. The Committee reiterated concerns raised in 2007 by the Committee against Torture that the *daiyo kangoku* (a system of pre-trial detention) did not comply with international standards.

The Human Rights Committee expressed concern that a system which allowed for the detention of suspects for 23 days with limited access to a lawyer increased the risk of abusive interrogation methods to obtain confessions.

Refugees and asylum-seekers

The government continued to deport failed asylum applicants to countries where they faced a risk of torture or other ill-treatment. There were also cases where the government deported failed asylum-seekers immediately after the conclusion of the administrative proceedings and before they could appeal against the decision in the courts. In December, the government suspended financial assistance for asylum-seekers during the determination process.

Violence against women and girls

Parliaments in Taiwan and South Korea passed resolutions calling for justice for the survivors of Japan's military sexual slavery system during World War II. The UN Human Rights Committee recommended that Japan apologize and accept legal responsibility for the "comfort women" system. The city councils of Takarazuka, Kiyose and Sapporo passed resolutions calling on the Japanese government to resolve this issue.

Amnesty International visits/reports

🚌 Amnesty International delegates visited Japan in February and March.

📄 Japan: New executions emphasize need for death penalty moratorium in Japan (ASA 22/008/2008)

📄 Japan: Fear of imminent execution – Makino Tadashi (ASA 22/010/2008)

📄 Japan: Amnesty International Submission to the UN Human Rights Committee, September 2008 (ASA 22/012/2008)

J

JORDAN

HASHEMITE KINGDOM OF JORDAN

Head of state:	King Abdullah II bin al-Hussein
Head of government:	Nader al-Dahabi
Death penalty:	retentionist
Population:	6.1 million
Life expectancy:	71.9 years
Under-5 mortality (m/f):	23/19 per 1,000
Adult literacy:	91.1 per cent

Prisoners were reported to have been tortured and otherwise ill-treated. Thousands of people were held without charge or trial under a sweeping provision allowing administrative detention. Procedures in trials before the State Security Court (SSC) breached international standards for fair trial. New restrictions on freedom of expression, association and assembly

were approved by the parliament. Women faced discrimination and were inadequately protected against domestic violence. Migrant domestic workers were exploited and abused, and inadequately protected under the law. At least 14 people were sentenced to death but there were no executions.

Counter-terror and security

Two security suspects were released after being held in prolonged detention without trial in the General Intelligence Department in Amman.

■ 'Isam al-'Utaibi, also known as Sheikh Abu Muhammad al-Maqdisi, was freed on 12 March after nearly three years in solitary confinement. In January the UN Working Group on Arbitrary Detention declared that his detention was arbitrary.

■ Samer Helmi al-Barq was released in January, having been detained since October 2003 when he was unlawfully transferred to Jordan by US authorities. Arrested in Pakistan, he had been detained there for 14 days then handed over to the US authorities, who held him in a secret prison until transferring him to Jordan.

Justice system – administrative detention

Thousands of people were held under the Law on Crime Prevention of 1954, which empowers provincial governors to authorize the detention without charge or trial of anyone suspected of committing a crime or "deemed to be a danger to society". Such detention orders can be imposed for one year and are renewable. In March the government-funded National Centre for Human Rights called for the abolition of the law and noted that in 2007 some 12,178 men and 81 women were detained under the law.

Torture and other ill-treatment

There were new reports of torture and other ill-treatment of prisoners. In October, Human Rights Watch reported that more than half of 110 prisoners it had interviewed during visits to seven prisons said they had been tortured or ill-treated, some citing prison directors. The authorities dismissed the organization's findings.

■ Firas al-'Utti, Hazim Ziyada and Ibrahim al-'Ulayan were reported to have died in a fire on 14 April when guards at Muwaqqar Prison forced them to remain in their cell. Two of them had allegedly been tortured by being beaten and suspended from a wall with their hands tied behind their back. The Public Security

Department was reported to have held an investigation into the deaths but its outcome was not disclosed and no prosecutions were known to have been initiated.

■ Two prison officers were each sentenced to 30 months in prison by a police court in May for beating Firas Zaidan to death in May 2007 in Aqaba Prison. A third prison officer was acquitted.

In February, the UN Special Rapporteur on torture reported that the authorities had failed to implement "effective mechanisms" to prevent torture and other ill-treatment or to ensure prosecution of perpetrators, which he had called for following his visit to Jordan in 2006.

Unfair trials – State Security Court

Procedures in trials before the SSC continued to breach international standards for fair trial. In particular, the court, which has jurisdiction to try cases involving offences against state security, including sedition and armed insurrection, and financial and drugs-related crimes, continued to accept "confessions" allegedly obtained under torture in pre-trial detention as evidence against defendants without adequate investigation.

■ In May, the SSC sentenced Nidal Momani, Sattam Zawahra and Tharwat 'Ali Draz to death and then immediately commuted their sentences to 15 years' imprisonment after convicting them of planning to attack US President George W. Bush when he visited Jordan in 2006. The defendants denied the charges and alleged that their "confessions" were false and had been obtained under torture.

Freedom of expression, association and assembly

New legislation was proposed that would further restrict the rights to freedom of expression, association and assembly. The Societies Law and the Law on Public Gatherings were passed by the parliament and were awaiting approval by the King. The first would increase government control over NGOs, requiring them to provide their work plans on demand and obtain official approval before receiving funds from abroad. It would also empower the authorities to order their closure even for minor infractions or appoint a state employee as their temporary president. The second law would relax some controls, allowing NGOs to hold general assembly meetings without prior approval, but those planning public gatherings would be required first to obtain the approval of the administrative governor, who would be able to terminate or disperse meetings or rallies by force if they contravened their agreed purpose.

Journalists and others continued to face prosecution for exercising their right to freedom of expression.

■ Fayez al-Ajrashi, editor of *El-Ekhbariya*, a weekly newspaper, was arrested and detained for several days before being charged with "inciting sectarian strife" and "sowing national discord". The case arose from articles he wrote that criticized the governor of Amman and dealt with corruption in the capital. He was released on bail. He was due to be tried before the SSC; if convicted, he could be sentenced to three years in prison.

Violence and discrimination against women

In January, the Protection from Family Violence Law was approved by the parliament. This makes provision for the reporting of domestic violence, including sexual violence and harassment, and for victim compensation. The new law fails to explicitly criminalize domestic violence or provide adequately for the prosecution of those who perpetrate it.

Temporary amendments to legislation that would give women the right to divorce without their husband's consent and establish penalties for perpetrators of family killings remained pending before parliament for the seventh year.

During the year at least 16 women were killed in the name of so-called honour. Article 98 of the Penal Code continued to be invoked in defence of men who had killed female relatives. It allows for reduced sentences where the killing is deemed to be committed in a "fit of rage caused by an unlawful or dangerous act on the part of the victim".

■ In March, the Criminal Court imposed a three-month prison sentence on a man who had shot dead his married sister in 2007 because of what he considered her "immoral behaviour", which included leaving home without her husband's consent and speaking to other men on her mobile phone.

Tens of women were reportedly administratively detained without charge or trial. Some, including rape victims, women who had become pregnant outside marriage and women accused of extramarital sexual

relations or of being prostitutes, were believed to be held to protect them from their family and community members. A government-run shelter for women in need of protection from domestic violence became operational but few women were in the shelter by the end of the year.

Migrants' rights – domestic workers

Tens of thousands of women migrant domestic workers faced economic, physical and psychological abuse with little or no protection from the state. Many worked up to 19 hours a day with no days off and were denied some or all of their wages. Many were effectively imprisoned in their employers' home. Many were beaten by their employers and representatives of recruitment agencies. Few perpetrators of abuse were prosecuted or otherwise punished.

In July, parliament approved various amendments to the Labour Law as a result of which domestic workers will no longer be explicitly excluded from its scope. A separate regulation will be issued to regulate the conditions of employment of migrant domestic workers.

■ A 22-year-old Indonesian worker attempted suicide after being raped three times by her employer's son and being sexually abused twice by her employer. When the wife of her employer found out, she beat the young woman.

Refugees and asylum-seekers

Jordan continued to host as many as 500,000 Iraqi refugees, most of whom fled Iraq after the US-led invasion in 2003. Most had no legal status as they were unable to meet the narrow criteria for obtaining residence permits and so were not legally entitled to work. Access to Jordan for Iraqis seeking international protection remained very restricted and in May the government introduced new visa requirements obliging Iraqis to obtain visas in Iraq before seeking to enter Jordan.

Death penalty

At least 14 people were sentenced to death but there were no executions. Draft law changes proposed in 2006 which would reduce the number of capital offences remained pending before the parliament.

In December, Jordan abstained on a UN General Assembly resolution calling for a worldwide moratorium on executions.

Amnesty International visits/reports

🚌 Amnesty International delegates visited Jordan in March and October.

📋 Isolated and abused – Women migrant domestic workers in Jordan denied their rights (MDE 16/002/2008)

📋 Lenient sentences for perpetrators of "honour killings" a step backwards for protection of women in Jordan (MDE 16/001/2008)

KAZAKSTAN

REPUBLIC OF KAZAKSTAN

Head of state:	**Nursultan Nazarbaev**
Head of government:	**Karim Massimov**
Death penalty:	**abolitionist for ordinary crimes**
Population:	**15.5 million**
Life expectancy:	**65.9 years**
Under-5 mortality (m/f):	**33/23 per 1,000**
Adult literacy:	**99.5 per cent**

Torture and other ill-treatment by members of the security forces remained widespread and continued to be committed with virtual impunity, despite stated efforts by the authorities to introduce safeguards. Refugees and asylum-seekers from Uzbekistan and China were at risk of abduction and forcible return. Members of religious minorities came under increasing pressure from the authorities.

Background

In January, Rakhat Aliev, President Nursultan Nazarbaev's exiled former son-in-law, was sentenced in his absence to 20 years' imprisonment on charges including kidnapping, money laundering, assault and murder. A military tribunal in March found him guilty of planning to overthrow the President and of disclosing state secrets and sentenced him to a further 20 years in prison. Rakhat Aliev claimed that the charges were politically motivated.

Domestic and international organizations were monitoring the authorities' preparations to assume the rotating chairmanship of the OSCE in 2010. The OSCE took the decision that Kazakstan should assume the Chair at the end of 2007 after Kazakstan agreed to carry out reforms to meet OSCE commitments on democratization and human rights.

Torture and other ill-treatment

In February, Kazakstan made declarations under the UN Convention against Torture allowing individual complaints to be lodged with the UN Committee against Torture. In June, Kazakstan ratified the Optional Protocol to the Convention against Torture.

In November, the Committee against Torture called on the authorities "to apply a zero-tolerance approach to the persistent problem of torture". The Committee also urged the authorities to "promptly implement effective measures to ensure that a person is not subject in practice to unacknowledged detention and that all detained suspects are afforded, in practice, all fundamental legal safeguards during their detention".

Police and security forces

Despite the authorities' declarations, torture and other ill-treatment remained widespread and such acts were committed with impunity. Beatings by law enforcement officers were routine, especially in temporary pre-charge detention centres, in the street or during transfer to detention centres. Few law enforcement officers were brought to trial and held accountable for violations, including torture, despite scores of people alleging that they were tortured in custody in order to extract a confession. Evidence based on such confessions was still routinely admitted in court.

The National Security Service (NSS) was reported to have used counter-terrorism operations to target vulnerable groups and groups perceived as a threat to national and regional security, such as asylum-seekers from Uzbekistan and China and members or suspected members of banned Islamic groups or Islamist parties.

■ In February, a court in Shimkent sentenced 14 men to long terms of imprisonment – up to 19 years – for planning a terrorist attack on the local NSS department. Most of the accused had been held in NSS detention facilities with very little access to lawyers, relatives or medical assistance. Claims of torture and other ill-treatment to extract confessions were not investigated. Information extracted as a result of these confessions allegedly extracted under torture was admitted as evidence by the trial judge.

Legal developments

A law introducing judicial review of the decision to detain a person entered into legal force in August. While a positive measure, it still does not allow the detainee or their representative to challenge the lawfulness of their detention as required by international standards.

Refugees and asylum-seekers

The authorities continued to co-operate with Uzbekistan, Russia and China in the name of regional security and the "war on terror" in ways that breached their obligations under international human rights and refugee law.

Kazakstani migration police continued to co-operate with their Uzbekistani counterparts and transmitted information on asylum-seekers and refugees to them. Uzbekistani authorities then exerted pressure on relatives in Uzbekistan to get those seeking protection to return voluntarily, in some cases even paying for relatives to travel to Kazakstan to trace the refugees and convince them to return.

■ In May, three Uzbekistani asylum-seekers were detained by Kazakstani police officers after they left the office of UNHCR, the UN refugee agency, in the centre of Almaty. They were interrogated by Kazakstani and Uzbekistani officers and threatened with forcible return to Uzbekistan. They were only released after the joint intervention of representatives of the office of the UNHCR and the Kazakstan International Bureau of Human Rights.

Freedom of religion

In January, President Nazarbaev attacked religious minorities as a threat to national security and values. He alleged that thousands of missionaries and extremists were threatening the fabric of society. Law enforcement officials, especially the NSS, stepped up their harassment of non-traditional groups such as the Hare Krishna community, Jehovah's Witnesses, and Evangelist and Protestant churches.

In November, parliament rushed through a controversial draft law on freedom of conscience which would, among other restrictions, ban all unregistered religious activity and require all religious communities to re-register.

Amnesty International visit/reports

🚗 Amnesty International delegates visited Kazakstan in February.

📄 Central Asia: Summary of human rights concerns, March 2007-March 2008 (EUR 04/001/2008)

📄 Kazakstan: Summary of concerns on torture and ill-treatment – a briefing to the United Nations Committee against Torture (EUR 57/001/2008)

KENYA

REPUBLIC OF KENYA

Head of state and government:	Mwai Kibaki
Death penalty:	abolitionist in practice
Population:	38.6 million
Life expectancy:	52.1 years
Under-5 mortality (m/f):	111/95 per 1,000
Adult literacy:	73.6 per cent

The government failed to put in place a plan to bring to justice those responsible for human rights abuses committed during post-election violence, which subsided early in 2008, or to guarantee reparations. State security officials continued to torture and kill suspects with impunity. Violence against women and girls was widespread. The government did not impose a moratorium on forced evictions. Public health facilities were poorly funded, equipped and maintained.

Background

The post-election violence abated following political mediation supported by the UN and the African Union that led to the signing, in February, of a power-sharing agreement between the main parties – President Kibaki's Party of National Unity and the Raila Odinga-led Orange Democratic Movement. The parties also signed an agreement aimed at achieving "sustainable peace, stability and justice in Kenya through the rule of law and respect of human rights". Further agreements committed the parties to short and long term constitutional, land, legal and electoral reforms.

Unemployment, crime and poverty were widespread, and millions of people were highly vulnerable to frequent droughts.

Insecurity – post-election violence

More than 1,000 people were killed as a result of politically motivated ethnic violence and associated police killings following the December 2007 disputed presidential and parliamentary elections. Over 300,000 people were estimated to have been displaced from their homes. About 12,000 crossed into neighbouring Uganda as refugees.

In addition, thousands suffered serious injuries. Other abuses recorded included sexual violence against girls and women, the burning of homes and widespread forced relocation.

K

A Commission of Inquiry on Post Election Violence (CIPEV) was formed following political mediation with a mandate to investigate the facts and the conduct of state security agencies, and to make recommendations. In October, the Commission submitted its report to the government. The Commission's recommendations covered individual criminal responsibility of alleged perpetrators of the violence, police reform, the incorporation into domestic legislation of the Rome Statute of the International Criminal Court (ICC) and constitutional reforms. The Commission's key recommendation was for the government to establish a Special Tribunal to investigate and prosecute perpetrators of the violence. If the government failed to do this, the Commission recommended that the cases be referred to the ICC for investigation and possible indictments in relation to alleged crimes against humanity committed during the post-election violence.

In November the government announced its support for implementation of the report and formed a cabinet committee headed by the President and Prime Minister to recommend action. In December the government announced that the committee would prepare a draft Bill to establish a Special Tribunal to investigate and prosecute alleged perpetrators of the post-election violence. Parliament also enacted the International Crimes Act, 2008, to incorporate the Rome Statute of the International Criminal Court into domestic law. However, by the end of 2008 the government had not announced a comprehensive plan of action to implement the report or guarantees that victims of human rights abuses would receive reparations.

Internally displaced people

In May the government launched "Operation Rudi Nyumbani" ("Operation go back home"), a programme of government assistance to help more than 300,000 people displaced by the post-election violence to return home. Although the government regularly stated that the programme was a success, a research report released in late October by the non-governmental Kenya Human Rights Commission found that most internally displaced people (IDPs) had not returned to their original homes. They were still living in tents in hundreds of transit IDP camps that emerged when the main IDP camps were closed after the launch of the programme.

Local civil society groups also documented complaints by IDPs that the government did not consult them while devising the programme. There were numerous complaints of forcible returns in some areas – sometimes including the use of force by government security personnel. Many IDPs complained that they could not freely choose between return, resettlement or integration at the site of displacement, as these options were not all meaningfully available to them. In particular many expressed the view that the areas where they originally lived remained insecure. There were also complaints of inadequate humanitarian assistance and that the cash sums meant to assist them in return were too low.

Thousands of people remained internally displaced in the Mount Elgon area near the Kenya-Uganda border following clashes over land.

By the end of 2008 there was neither a legal framework for the displaced nor a national strategy to deal with the long-standing issue of forced displacement in Kenya. This was despite recommendations to this effect from a UN fact-finding mission and CIPEV.

Truth, Justice and Reconciliation Commission

In October Parliament passed a law establishing a Truth, Justice and Reconciliation Commission (TJRC), in line with the political mediation agreement signed in March. The TJRC's mandate would be to investigate human rights violations, including those committed by the state, groups or individuals, between 12 December 1963 and 28 February 2008.

The law governing the TJRC contained a number of provisions which breached international law and best practice standards. These included provisions allowing the TJRC to recommend amnesty for crimes under international law such as torture, enforced disappearance and extrajudicial executions, and provisions creating obstacles to prosecutions of crimes under international law. The law would not guarantee a comprehensive protection programme for victims and witnesses, and fell short of ensuring a broad range of reparations for victims of human rights violations.

By the end of the year, the TJRC had not been formed.

Impunity

Allegations of human rights violations, including torture and unlawful killings, by state security officials persisted.

In March (after complaints of government inertia for many months), the government launched a joint police-military operation called "Operation Okoa Maisha" ("Operation Save Life") in the Mount Elgon area in western Kenya. The operation was targeted against members of the Sabaot Land Defence Forces – an armed militia blamed for unlawful killings, forced displacement and other human rights abuses in the area. The local media and local and international organizations documented cases of human rights violations by the military and police during the operation. These included arbitrary and unlawful arrests of hundreds of civilians, arbitrary detentions, and torture in military camps and police custody. There were reports of unlawful killings of dozens of individuals by military personnel and cases of families complaining that their relatives had disappeared. The government denied these reports but failed to ensure an independent investigation into the allegations.

In November, dozens of residents of Mandera district in northern Kenya complained of rape, torture, beatings and the use of excessive force by government security personnel involved in a joint police-military operation to curb the influx of illegal arms from the Horn of Africa. The government denied these allegations but had not instituted independent and impartial investigations by the end of the year.

The government failed to investigate allegations of torture and unlawful killings committed by the police in 2007, including the shooting and killing of hundreds of people in the course of security operations against members of the banned Mungiki group.

Violence against women and girls

Women and girls continued to face widespread violence. During the post-election violence and in the conflict in the Mount Elgon area, women and girls were subjected to rape and other forms of sexual violence. Alleged perpetrators of gender-based violence, including the police and other law enforcement officials, were hardly ever brought to justice.

Right to health

Public health facilities remained poorly funded, equipped and maintained, leading to a high rate of maternal mortality and other nationwide health problems. The effect of under-funding of the health sector was particularly evident in public maternity hospitals. Most low-income women who used these facilities received a low standard of health care.

Forced evictions

The government announced, in July 2008, the formation of a Task Force on the Mau Forest complex, following its promise in October 2007 that it would compensate and resettle thousands of people who were forcibly evicted from the Mau Forest complex in 2006. The Task Force was to deal with the demarcation of the Forest complex; identification of Forest residents with ownership documents; and compensation and resettlement of identified residents. By the end of the year, the Task Force had not completed its work.

In November, hundreds of families living in informal settlements close to the Nairobi River were living under the threat of forced evictions by the government.

By the end of 2008, the government had not fulfilled its 2006 pledge to release national guidelines on evictions. It also failed to impose a moratorium on forced evictions until the guidelines were in place.

Refugees and asylum-seekers

The government did not reverse its decision of January 2007 to close the Kenya/Somali border. However, due to ongoing fighting and a significant escalation of the conflict in Somalia, refugees and asylum-seekers continued to cross the border into Kenya. Between January and September, more than 38,000 new refugees and asylum-seekers had been registered by UNHCR. In October alone, more than 8,000 refugees and asylum-seekers were reported to have crossed the border. Humanitarian agencies reported poor and deteriorating conditions in camps housing new refugees and asylum-seekers and called for more humanitarian assistance from the Kenyan government and the international community.

Refugees and asylum-seekers fleeing into Kenya faced harassment by Kenyan security personnel at the border; many were arrested, beaten and forced back into Somalia. Some had to pay bribes to security

K

officials (partly as a result of the official decision to maintain the formal closure of the border) in order to gain access into Kenya.

Counter-terror and security

Some of the more than 40 victims of unlawful transfers from Kenya to Somalia and Ethiopia, who were held in secret and incommunicado detention in Ethiopia at the end of 2007, were released. Those released included at least eight Kenyans, despite the continued denial of the Kenyan government that no Kenyans were part of the unlawful transfers.

■ Mohamed Abdulmalik, a Kenyan national, was arrested by Kenyan police in February 2007 and unlawfully transferred to US custody in Guantánamo Bay, Cuba, where he was believed to be held at the end of 2008. He was not charged with any offence, nor was he able to exercise his right under international law to challenge the lawfulness of his detention.

By the end of 2008 the government had taken no action in response to calls for a thorough and independent investigation into the arrests, detention and transfer of these individuals, and their treatment during detention.

Freedom of expression

In February, the government formally lifted the ban on live broadcasts that it had imposed in December 2007 at the start of the post-election violence.

Between January and March, a number of human rights defenders and journalists were subjected to threats, including death threats, by armed groups which accused them of "betraying the tribal cause" for commenting on the elections and speaking out against some of the post-election violence.

In March military personnel involved in the joint police-military operation in the Mount Elgon area arbitrarily arrested, harassed and physically ill-treated journalists reporting on events.

In December, parliament passed the government-sponsored Kenya Communication (Amendment) Bill 2008 into law. The new law could lead to an unjustified restriction on the right to freedom of expression. It grants broad powers to the minister in charge of internal security to ban media coverage and seize broadcast equipment on grounds of national security and gives a government-controlled Communications Commission the power to license and regulate broadcasting services and to prescribe the nature and content of media broadcasts. The new law was awaiting presidential assent at the end of the year.

■ In September, Andrew Mwangura, a former journalist and a Seafarers Assistance Programme official, was arrested by police. He was charged with "spreading false information" after he gave press interviews contradicting the official government version of the destination of a Ukrainian cargo ship seized by pirates off the Somali coast in September. At the end of the year, the trial was ongoing.

Death penalty

Courts continued to impose the death penalty, although no executions were reported. There was no progress towards the abolition of the death penalty.

Amnesty International visits/reports

🚍 Amnesty International delegates visited Kenya in February, March, September and December.

▤ Kenya: Amnesty International's Recommendations to the African Union Peace and Security Council (AFR 32/007/2008)

▤ Kenya: Concerns about the Truth, Justice and Reconciliation Commission Bill (AFR 32/009/2008)

▤ Kenya: Unlawful transfers of "terror suspects" must be investigated (AFR 32/010/2008)

▤ Amnesty International's Recommendations to the African Union Assembly (IOR 63/001/2008)

▤ Kenya: New government must ensure justice for victims of post-election violence, 18 April 2008

▤ Kenya: Amnesty International calls on government and the African Commission to act, 15 February 2008

▤ Kenya: Government must protect people from politically-motivated and ethnic attacks, 25 January 2008

▤ Kenya: Amnesty International condemns excessive use of force by police, 18 January 2008

▤ Kenya: Kenyan election sparks political killings, 4 January 2008

KOREA
(DEMOCRATIC PEOPLE'S REPUBLIC OF)

DEMOCRATIC PEOPLE'S REPUBLIC OF KOREA

Head of state:	Kim Jong-il
Head of government:	Kim Yong-il
Death penalty:	retentionist
Population:	23.9 million
Life expectancy:	66.8 years
Under-5 mortality (m/f):	62/62 per 1,000

Millions of people faced the worst food shortages since the late 1990s. Thousands continued to cross the border into China, mainly for food and economic reasons. Those arrested and forcibly repatriated were subjected to forced labour, torture and other ill-treatment in prison camps. Other widespread violations of human rights persisted, including politically motivated and arbitrary use of detention and executions, and severe restrictions on freedoms of expression and movement. Independent human rights monitors continued to be denied access to the country.

Background

In June, North Korea submitted a list of its nuclear assets to the Chinese Foreign Ministry, as part of the process to denuclearize the Korean peninsula. In October, the US government removed North Korea from its list of countries sponsoring terrorism after it agreed to provide full access to its nuclear facilities.

In November, the UN General Assembly adopted a resolution expressing very serious concern about human rights violations in North Korea.

Right to food

According to the World Food Programme (WFP), millions of people experienced hunger on a scale not seen in a decade with women, children and the elderly being the most vulnerable. Food production dropped sharply and food imports declined. Long-distance telephone calls were reportedly blocked to prevent news of food shortages from spreading.

In June, a WFP and Food and Agriculture Organization (FAO) survey covering 53 counties in eight provinces indicated that almost three quarters of North Korean households had reduced their food intake. The majority of families stopped eating protein-rich foods and were living on cereals and vegetables. Many people were forced to scavenge for wild foods which are poor in nutrition and cause digestive problems. According to the WFP and FAO, one of the leading causes of malnutrition among children under the age of five was diarrhoea caused by increased consumption of wild foods.

Despite the food shortage reaching critical levels, the government failed to ensure minimum essential levels of food. Due to strained relations, North Korea did not request assistance from South Korea, one of the biggest donors of rice and fertilizer in previous years.

Migrants, refugees and asylum-seekers

Thousands of people crossed into China, mainly in search of food and economic opportunities but also because of political oppression. Some stayed on a short-term basis gathering food and other essential supplies before returning home. Others, mostly women, stayed for the long-term and often married Chinese farmers. Some brokers took advantage of their vulnerability by trafficking them into forced marriages. The majority of North Koreans in China lived in fear of arrest and forcible return. Virtually all those forcibly returned to North Korea faced up to three years in a prison camp where they were subjected to forced labour, torture and other ill-treatment.

Hundreds of North Koreans travelled through China to Thailand where they were able to seek settlement in a third country. The majority went on to South Korea where they were granted citizenship but significant numbers faced difficulty in adapting to life in South Korea and some reportedly suffered from post traumatic stress disorder. A growing number migrated to other countries, mainly in Europe.

■ On 2 December, the Myanmar authorities arrested 19 North Koreans, including one seven-year-old boy, for illegal entry as they were attempting to cross into Thailand. There were fears that the Myanmar government may deport them back to North Korea.

Prison conditions

Prisoners in camps and detention centres were forced to undertake physically demanding work which included mountain logging and stone quarrying, often for 10 hours or more per day, with no rest days.

Guards beat prisoners suspected of lying, not working fast enough or for forgetting the words to patriotic songs. Forms of punishment included forced exercise, sitting without moving for prolonged periods of time and humiliating public criticism.

Prisoners fell ill or died in custody, or soon after release, due to the combination of forced hard labour, inadequate food, beatings, lack of medical care and unhygienic living conditions.

Death penalty

The government continued to execute people by hanging or firing squad. There were reports that the authorities executed individuals to deter political and economic crimes. In February, North Korean authorities executed 15 people in public for illegally crossing the border with China, reportedly as a warning to others.

In December, North Korea voted against a UN General Assembly resolution calling for a worldwide moratorium on executions.

Enforced disappearances

North Korea's widespread policy of enforced disappearance practised since the Korean War (1950-53) continued. North Korean family members of suspected dissidents disappeared under the principle of "guilt by association".

The authorities continued to refuse to acknowledge the use of enforced disappearances. However in August, North Korean officials agreed to re-open investigations into the fate and whereabouts of several Japanese nationals who had been disappeared since the 1970s.

Freedom of expression

The government rigidly controlled the media and severely restricted religious practice. There were reports that local authorities arrested individuals who watched South Korean videos or were in possession of unauthorized mobile phones.

International scrutiny

The government continued to deny access to independent human rights monitors. In December, the UN General Assembly expressed serious concern at the refusal of North Korea to recognize the mandate of the UN Special Rapporteur on the human rights situation in North Korea.

KOREA
(REPUBLIC OF)

REPUBLIC OF KOREA
Head of state:	Lee Myung-bak
	(replaced Roh Moo-hyun in February)
Head of government:	Han Seung-soo
	(replaced Han Duck-soo in February)
Death penalty:	abolitionist in practice
Population:	48.4 million
Life expectancy:	77.9 years
Under-5 mortality (m/f):	5/5 per 1,000

Riot police used excessive force when dispersing largely peaceful protesters demonstrating against US beef imports. Large numbers of irregular migrants were deported amid reports of cruel, inhuman and degrading treatment during arrest. There was heightened concern about freedoms of expression, assembly and association of protesters, unionists and journalists. No executions took place but 58 people remained on death row. The Special Bill to Abolish the Death Penalty lapsed in March.

Excessive use of force

Candlelight protests against the resumption of US beef imports attracted tens of thousands of people and took place almost daily from May to early July. During the largely peaceful protests some police beat protesters with shields and batons, fired water cannons at close range and denied medical care to protesters in detention. Protesters suffered injuries such as broken bones, concussion, temporary blindness and punctured eardrums.

Migrants' rights

In September, the government announced its intention to deport approximately half of irregular migrant workers, an estimated 220,000 people, by 2012. There was a growing number of cases of cruel, inhuman and degrading treatment of migrant workers during arrests in the ongoing crackdown.

■ In November, about 280 immigration officials and police raided factories and dormitories in Maseok, Gyeonggi province, where at least 110 regular and irregular migrant workers were indiscriminately apprehended en masse. One female migrant worker

K

was not permitted to go to the toilet, but was instead forced to urinate in public. One male migrant worker broke his leg when he tried to escape, after which he was handcuffed and made to wait five hours before being allowed to go to hospital.

■ In May, the government deported Torna Limbu, a Nepalese national, and Abdus Sabur, a Bangladeshi national, president and vice-president respectively of the Seoul-Gyeonggi-Incheon Migrants' Trade Union (MTU), despite a call from the National Human Rights Commission for a stay of deportation until it could investigate allegations of beatings by immigration officials during their arrests. There were concerns that the two men were targeted specifically because of their union activities.

Freedom of expression, assembly and association

Labour movement

According to the Korean Confederation of Trade Unions, irregular employment protests occurred at more than 30 different factories. Security forces used excessive force against striking irregular workers, who were protesting because they received less pay than regular workers for equal work. They also faced losing their jobs after two years so that their employers could avoid regularizing their status in line with the 2007 Contract Based Employment Law.

Media independence

The chief executives and presidents of the Korean Broadcasting System (KBS), Korean Broadcasting Advertising Corporation, Arirang TV, Sky Life and Yonhap Television Network (YTN) were replaced by supporters of the government.

■ Protests against the appointment of the new YTN president Ku Bon-hong, a former aide to President Lee Myung-bak, resulted in Ku Bon-hong suing 12 trade union journalists and firing six journalists for "interfering with business".

Conscientious objectors

Police imprisoned at least 408 conscientious objectors, mostly Jehovah's Witnesses, for refusing compulsory military service. This significant drop in numbers compared to the 733 imprisoned in 2007 was largely because cases were not heard ahead of plans to introduce an alternative to military service in 2009. However, in December the Ministry of Defence put the plans on hold due to lack of public support.

■ Lee Gil-joon, a conscripted riot police officer was sentenced to one and a half years in prison for failure to return to duty and disobeying orders because he opposed using violence to disperse demonstrators during the candlelight protests.

Arbitrary arrests and detentions – National Security Law

2008 marked 60 years since the National Security Law (NSL) was introduced. As of December, there were at least nine detained individuals charged under the vague provisions of the NSL.

■ On 26 August, police arrested seven activists from the Socialist Workers League of Korea, including a university professor, Oh Se-chul, for violating article three (forming anti-state groups) and article seven (praising or sympathizing with anti-state groups) of the NSL. Seoul Central District Court rejected the arrest warrants submitted by the prosecutor's office on grounds of insufficient evidence. On 14 October, police re-submitted the arrest warrant for Professor Oh, but it was again rejected by the court due to lack of evidence.

Refugees and asylum-seekers

A total of 364 applications for refugee status were submitted in 2008. Thirty-six people were granted refugee status and 22 were given humanitarian protection. Seventy-nine applications were rejected. Serious concerns were raised about the lack of resources in immigration offices as the backlog of asylum claims reached over 1,200 cases.

Violence against women and girls

In January, President-elect Lee Myung-bak said he would not call on Japan to apologize for its wartime atrocities.

In October, the South Korean parliament passed a resolution calling for justice for the survivors of Japan's military sexual slavery system during World War II.

Death penalty

South Korea's unofficial moratorium on executions continued. Fifty-eight prisoners were on death row at the end of the year. The Special Bill to Abolish the Death Penalty lapsed in March. Two new bills on the abolition of the death penalty were introduced in the National Assembly.

K

Amnesty International visits/report

Amnesty International delegates visited South Korea in March, July and October/November.

Policing the candlelight protests in South Korea (ASA 25/008/2008)

KUWAIT

STATE OF KUWAIT
Head of state: **al-Shaikh Sabah al-Ahmad al-Jaber al-Sabah**
Head of government: **al-Shaikh Nasser Mohammad al-Ahmad**
al-Sabah

Death penalty:	**retentionist**
Population:	**2.9 million**
Life expectancy:	**77.3 years**
Under-5 mortality (m/f):	**11/9 per 1,000**
Adult literacy:	**93.3 per cent**

Migrant workers continued to experience exploitation and abuse, and to demand protection of their rights. Some were deported after participating in mass protests. The government promised to improve conditions. Several journalists were prosecuted. One case of torture was reported. At least 12 people were under sentence of death but no executions were known to have been carried out.

Migrants' rights

In July, thousands of migrant workers, mostly Bangladeshis, held mass protests to demand better pay and working conditions. Police used batons and tear gas to disperse the protests, and as many as 1,000 workers were reported to have been rounded up and deported. Some alleged that they had been beaten and otherwise ill-treated by police at the time of arrest and while detained.

Following the unrest the government introduced a minimum monthly wage for cleaners and security guards employed by companies on government contracts but not for other workers. On 8 September, the parliamentary Human Rights Committee called for a review of the system under which foreign workers must be sponsored by a Kuwaiti employer.

Thousands of women domestic workers were especially vulnerable to abuse by employers. In August, the parliamentary Human Rights Committee proposed a new bill stipulating jail terms of up to 15 years for offences including forced labour, abusing workers and sexually exploiting domestic workers.

Counter-terror and security

Four Kuwaiti men continued to be held at the US detention facility in Guantánamo Bay. On 22 October, US military prosecutors filed war crimes charges against two of them, Fouad al-Rabia and Faiz al-Kandari. If convicted of conspiracy and supporting terrorism, they could be sentenced to life imprisonment.

■ On 22 May, masked State Security officials detained Adel Abdul Salam al-Dhofairi, blindfolded, handcuffed and shackled him, and interrogated him over three days. They asked him to identify an Afghan man suspected of sending people to Afghanistan, and accused him of passing a small amount of money for families in need to this man, which he denied. The officials beat Adel al-Dhofairi severely, plunged him in freezing water and made him run blindfolded and handcuffed along a corridor. He was then taken before the prosecutor, who authorized his further detention for 15 days and fined him. He was released without charge after 18 days in detention. Adel al-Dhofairi's attempt to lodge a complaint to the authorities was refused and no investigation was carried out.

Freedom of expression

An independent journalists' union was formed in July, four years after its establishment had been rejected by a court. However, several journalists were prosecuted on defamation and other charges although these no longer incur prison sentences.

■ On 8 March, two editors were fined by the Criminal Court in Kuwait City and their newspaper licences were withdrawn. Mansur Ahmad Muhareb al-Hayni, editor of the weekly *al-Abraj* newspaper, was convicted of defaming the Prime Minister, and Hamed Turki Abu Yabes, editor of the weekly *al-Shaab*, was convicted of publishing political articles (his newspaper is licensed only to report on arts and culture).

A proposed new law to punish "internet offenders" would, according to reports, prescribe imprisonment and fines for a range of online offences, including promoting immoral conduct, encouraging anti-government sentiments, divulging state secrets, and insulting Islam.

Death penalty

At least 12 people were on death row, including six who were sentenced in 2008, but no executions were known to have been carried out. Two of four death sentences confirmed by the Supreme Court were later commuted by the Amir, the Head of State.

In December, Kuwait voted against a UN General Assembly resolution calling for a worldwide moratorium on executions.

■ On 24 June, the Supreme Court confirmed the death sentence imposed on Sheikh Talal bin Nasser al-Sabah, a member of the royal family, in December 2007 for drug smuggling.

■ On 8 July, the Amir commuted the death sentence imposed on May Membriri Vecina, a domestic worker from the Philippines, after she was convicted of murdering one of her employer's children and attempting to murder two others. At her trial, she alleged that her employer had physically and mentally abused her, causing her to become mentally incapable.

KYRGYZSTAN

KYRGYZ REPUBLIC
Head of state:	Kurmanbek Bakiev
Head of government:	Igor Chudinov
Death penalty:	abolitionist for ordinary crimes
Population:	5.4 million
Life expectancy:	65.6 years
Under-5 mortality (m/f):	69/58 per 1,000
Adult literacy:	98.7 per cent

New legislation severely restricted the rights to freedom of religion and assembly. Refugees and asylum-seekers from Uzbekistan continued to be at risk of abduction and forcible return.

Background

One of the harshest winters to hit Central Asia for several decades beset vital infrastructure and left vast swathes of the country facing severe energy and food shortages. In November the UN launched a US$20 million emergency appeal to provide food, shelter and additional energy supplies.

Freedom of religion

In November parliament approved a restrictive new law on religion. It bans all unregistered religious activity and makes it very difficult for religious minorities to seek official registration. A national programme of action to combat the "spread of religious extremism" launched in January appeared to be targeting members of the banned Islamist party Hizb-ut-Tahrir.

■ In November a court convicted 32 people, including a 17-year-old boy and two women, of calling for the overthrow of the constitutional order, and sentenced them to prison terms of between nine and 20 years. Allegations that they were tortured to force them to confess were not taken into consideration by the court. They were accused of being members of Hizb-ut-Tahrir and of participation in violent protests in the town of Nookat on 1 October. Scores of villagers had reportedly clashed with police when traditional Muslim celebrations of *Eid-al-fitr* were cancelled. Relatives claimed that the 32 were not members of Hizb-ut-Tahrir, and that police officers had used excessive force to disperse villagers, including by beating women and children with batons. Protesters reportedly threw stones and bricks at police officers.

Freedom of assembly

In July the Constitutional Court ruled that restrictions placed on the right to demonstrate in a draft law approved by parliament in June were unconstitutional. Despite this, President Bakiev signed it into law in August. The new legislation gives local authorities the right to refuse permission for a demonstration on an extensive number of grounds. One human rights activist was repeatedly detained during the year for staging peaceful protest actions outside government offices in Bishkek.

Refugees and asylum-seekers

Refugees and asylum-seekers from Uzbekistan continued to be at risk of forcible return or abduction by the Uzbekistani security service operating sometimes in co-operation with their Kyrgyzstani counterparts. Those fleeing faced serious human rights violations in Uzbekistan. At least one asylum-seeker was feared to have been abducted. The Migration Service persisted in not giving refugee status to asylum-seekers.

K

■ In July the UN Human Rights Committee found that Kyrgyzstan had committed grave breaches of its international obligations under the Optional Protocol to the International Covenant on Civil and Political Rights by forcibly returning four asylum-seekers to Uzbekistan in 2006 in disregard of the Committee's request for interim measures of protection for the four men.

■ Erkin Kholikov, an Uzbekistani asylum-seeker, was extradited to Uzbekistan in May even though his asylum application was pending before a court. He had been detained in Kyrgyzstan in August 2007 and was sentenced to four years' imprisonment in March 2008 for concealing a crime and illegally crossing the border.

Freedom of expression – killing of journalist

■ There was no substantive progress in the investigation into the murder of independent ethnic Uzbek journalist and editor Alisher Saipov in October 2007. In June, Alisher Saipov's family publicly urged President Bakiev to keep his promise to personally supervise the investigation and ensure that the suspected perpetrators were brought to justice without delay. In November the Ministry of Internal Affairs stated that Alisher Saipov's murder was not connected to his journalism. Alisher Saipov had often covered sensitive subjects, including the situation in Uzbekistan, and had reportedly received anonymous threats. Parts of the Uzbekistani media had conducted a campaign denouncing his reporting as an attack on the Uzbekistani state.

Amnesty International reports

📄 Summary of Human Rights Concerns in Central Asia, March 2007-March 2008: (EUR 04/001/2008)

📄 Kyrgyzstan: A year after the murder of Alisher Saipov – no closer to the truth (EUR 58/001/2008)

LAOS

LAO PEOPLE'S DEMOCRATIC REPUBLIC

Head of state:	Choummaly Sayasone
Head of government:	Bouasone Bouphavanh
Death penalty:	abolitionist in practice
Population:	6 million
Life expectancy:	63.2 years
Under-5 mortality (m/f):	69/62 per 1,000
Adult literacy:	68.7 per cent

Religious persecution increased in rural areas, where evangelical Christians came under attack. Pressures on land and natural resources continued to increase, with a rise in land and property disputes. Over 1,700 Hmong people were returned to Laos from Thailand; some were forcibly returned. No independent monitoring was allowed to assess their well-being.

Background

Thousands of people, in particular ethnic minorities, faced displacement, including forced evictions, as a result of seven new large dams and other development projects. Some affected communities experienced food insecurity and child malnutrition as a result of resettlement. A further dozen dams were being designed, and discussions were ongoing about 65 hydropower projects. A new media law passed by the National Assembly in July failed to alleviate harsh restrictions on freedom of expression.

Freedom of religion

Christians, from mainly evangelical congregations, faced increased persecution. Between July and September at least 90 Christians, including pastors, were arrested and detained without charge or trial. Some were held for several weeks. At least two people were released after being forced to renounce their faith.

■ On 8 September, police and district authorities arrested a teacher in Phonthong District, Champassak Province, for converting to Christianity. He was detained in a "re-education centre" in deplorable conditions and told he would only be released if he recanted his faith. He was released about a week later following intervention by provincial authorities. Although he was able to return to teaching, he was threatened with re-arrest if he continued to practise his religion.

L

Death penalty

At least two people were sentenced to death during the year for offences related to drug trafficking. The government publicly defended its use of the death penalty, claiming it was needed to deter drug trafficking within the country and across its borders. No executions were believed to have taken place. However, information about the application of the death penalty, including conditions in prison, was not made public despite repeated calls by the UN.

Discrimination – Hmong

At least 1,700 Hmong people were returned from Thailand, among them were an unknown number who had been seeking asylum. Many returnees went through a transit centre in the town of Paksan, Borikhamsay Province. According to state-controlled media, authorities "educated" the returning Hmong in the ideology of the Communist Party. Many were resettled in the newly constructed Phalak village, Kasi District in Vientiane Province. Others were sent back to their home provinces. It was unclear whether the choice of resettlement site was voluntary. No independent monitoring was allowed.

At least four returnees were arbitrarily detained upon return to Laos and were reportedly held without charge in a prison in Attapeu Province. The true number of detained returnees was believed to be higher. Authorities failed to account for six individuals from a group of 27 ethnic Hmong Protestants who were forcibly returned to Laos from Thailand in December 2005.

Amnesty International visit/reports

🚍 An Amnesty International delegation visited Thailand in October to gather information about Laos.

📄 Laos: Official moratorium on the death penalty – an opportunity for Laos (ASA 26/001/2008)

📄 Thailand/Laos: Forcible return/fear for safety (ASA 39/005/2008)

LATVIA

REPUBLIC OF LATVIA

Head of state:	Valdis Zatlers
Head of government:	Ivars Godmanis
Death penalty:	abolitionist for ordinary crimes
Population:	2.3 million
Life expectancy:	72 years
Under-5 mortality (m/f):	16/11 per 1,000
Adult literacy:	99.7 per cent

About 400,000 people remained stateless, leaving them exposed to various forms of discrimination. Migrants and Roma were victims of discrimination and racially motivated attacks. Lesbian, gay, bisexual and transgender (LGBT) people faced discrimination. The authorities called for a review of the law on the abolition of the death penalty.

Discrimination – stateless persons

The Latvian authorities were criticized by the UN and the Council of Europe about the treatment of non-citizens, including stateless persons, the majority of whom were born in Latvia or had lived there for almost their entire lives.

Stateless people continued to suffer from limited or no access to a broad range of rights, including the right to participate in political processes, and the right to employment in the civil service and private sector. Restrictions on property ownership also negatively impacted on their ability to access other rights.

The European Commission against Racism and Intolerance (ECRI), in its third report published in February, noted that "the number of differences between Latvian citizens and non-citizens remains significant as far as some political, civil, social and other rights are concerned."

In March, the UN Special Rapporteur on racism, reporting on a visit in September 2007, expressed concern about the large number of non-citizens living in Latvia. He urged the government to revisit the existing requirements for naturalization, especially for children of non-citizens who were born in Latvia and elderly people who could enjoy easier access to citizenship.

L

Racism and discrimination – migrants and Roma

Racially motivated attacks continued and the authorities failed to respond adequately. Roma citizens and visible minority migrants faced mounting racist violence, leaving them under constant fear of attacks.

ECRI and the UN Special Rapporteur on racism expressed concern at the lack of comprehensive national legislation dealing with all forms of discrimination. Law enforcement officials tended to prosecute racist aggression as acts of hooliganism or vandalism, disregarding the racial connotations of the crime.

Both ECRI and the Special Rapporteur noted the use of racist discourse by some politicians and the media, and urged the government to adopt legislation that unambiguously criminalizes all types of hate crimes.

Rights of lesbian, gay, bisexual and transgender people

On 31 May, a Pride march was held in Riga to celebrate the rights of LGBT people. The march was protected by law enforcement officials and no major attacks were mounted against participants. However, a large number of counter-demonstrators engaged in verbal abuse. Prior to the event, derogatory statements were reportedly made against LGBT people by an official in the Mayor of Riga's office.

Torture and other ill-treatment

In March, the European Committee for the Prevention of Torture, reporting on a visit in December 2007, strongly criticized the authorities for failing to investigate fully allegations of ill-treatment of detainees by law enforcement officials and prison staff, and improve detention conditions in police stations and prisons. Conditions had been found on some occasions to be inhuman and degrading.

The Committee reported allegations of deliberate physical ill-treatment of detainees by prison staff at Daugavpils Prison and Riga Central Prison. The Committee also received reports of psychological ill-treatment, such as prison staff verbally abusing detainees and threatening to put inmates in cells with other inmates prone to violence.

The Committee expressed particular concern at the allegations of frequent and severe inter-prisoner violence in various prisons. These included severe beating, sexual assault (including rape) and threats. The Committee highlighted the case of a juvenile prisoner in the Šķirotava Prison in Riga who had been repeatedly raped by fellow inmates. The Committee expressed concern that the staff had apparently been aware of the situation, but had failed to take effective steps to protect the minor.

Death penalty

In September several politicians, including the head of the parliamentary Human Rights Committee, the Justice Minister and the Interior Minister, called for a review of domestic law on the abolition of the death penalty with a view to reintroducing it. The President of the Parliamentary Assembly of the Council of Europe expressed his concern about such statements.

Amnesty International report

📄 Latvia and Lithuania: Human rights on the march (EUR 53/001/2008)

LEBANON

LEBANESE REPUBLIC

Head of state:	Michel Suleiman (from May)
Head of government:	Fouad Siniora
Death penalty:	retentionist
Population:	4.1 million
Life expectancy:	71.5 years
Under-5 mortality (m/f):	30/20 per 1,000
Adult literacy:	88.3 per cent

At least 30 civilians were killed in political violence. Torture and other ill-treatment of detainees were reported. Women faced discrimination and were inadequately protected against violence. Migrant domestic workers were exploited and abused. Palestinian refugees faced continuing discrimination although steps were taken to alleviate conditions for some of the most vulnerable. The Minister of Justice proposed a law to abolish the death penalty.

Background

Following renewed political violence between supporters of the government and Hizbullah and

L

other parties, the two sides agreed an accord on 21 May in Qatar which ended an 18-month political stalemate. Parliament then elected a new President. In July, a national unity government was formed and a new electoral law was passed in September. A Human Rights Action Plan was in development. On 15 October, Lebanon and Syria agreed to establish diplomatic relations.

At least 30 civilians were among around 160 people killed in political violence. More than half died as a result of armed clashes between pro-government forces and the Hizbullah-led opposition in May, when about 70 people were killed, and fighting between rival groups in Tripoli in June and July.

■ On 13 August, five civilians and 10 soldiers were killed in a bomb attack on a bus in Tripoli.

■ On 10 September, Saleh Aridi, a leading member of the Democratic Party, which advocates close ties with Syria, was killed by a car bomb.

Impunity

Little action was taken to address impunity for political killings, enforced disappearances, torture and other abuses committed during the civil war (1975-1990) and since then. The Lebanese authorities said in 1992 that more than 17,000 people had disappeared in the custody of the parties to the conflict.

In March, Milad Barakat was returned to Lebanon after 16 years in prison in Syria. Lebanese security officials had detained him in 1992 and handed him over to the Syrian authorities, who sentenced him to 15 years' imprisonment for fighting against the Syrian army. There was no new information, however, about some 650 Lebanese and other nationals reported to have disappeared in the custody of the Syrian authorities after they were abducted or detained in Lebanon. In August, the authorities said they were "committed to pursuing the issue of Lebanese citizens who are missing or detained in Syria".

No participants from either side of the 2006 war between Israel and Hizbullah were brought to justice for serious violations of international humanitarian law.

Rafiq al-Hariri case

On 2 December, the 11th report was issued of the UN International Independent Investigation Commission on its investigations into the killing of former Prime Minister Rafiq al-Hariri and 22 others in February 2005 and 20 other bombings and assassinations. The Special Tribunal for Lebanon, which will further investigate and prosecute the cases, was scheduled to begin functioning on 1 March 2009.

■ In August, Ayman Tarabay and Moustapha Talal Mesto, two of nine men detained without charge since 2005 in connection with the investigation into the killing of Rafiq al-Hariri, were released on bail. The seven others continued to be detained without charge or trial even though the UN Working Group on Arbitrary Detention ruled in November 2007 that six of them were arbitrarily detained.

Aftermath of the 2006 war

One person was killed and seven others working with clearance teams were injured, as well as 22 civilians, by unexploded cluster bombs fired by Israeli armed forces during the 2006 war. The Israeli authorities continued to refuse to provide the data to assist clearance of unexploded munitions and were still occupying the border village of Ghajar at the end of the year.

On 16 July, the bodies of two Israeli soldiers captured by Hizbullah from northern Israel in July 2006 were handed to Israel in exchange for five Lebanese prisoners, four of them Hizbullah members, and the human remains of almost 200 Arab nationals.

Torture and other ill-treatment

Allegations of torture and other ill-treatment in custody were not independently investigated, and "confessions" allegedly given under torture were used in trials as evidence. On 7 October, a group of human rights organizations listed 27 deaths in custody since 2007, 15 of them in 2008.

In December, Lebanon ratified the Optional Protocol to the UN Convention against Torture.

■ On 5 June, the trial began before the Military Court in Beirut of Hassan Naba' and 12 others referred to as the "Net of 13". Detained in December 2005 and January 2006, they were charged with "plotting to commit terrorist acts". In court, several of the defendants repudiated "confessions" made while held in pre-trial detention at the Information Branch of the Internal Security Department in Beirut and alleged that they were given under "police brutality and torture", but the court failed to investigate their claims. Three of the defendants were released on bail on 25 September.

L

No investigations were carried out into credible reports that the majority of 316 suspected Fatah al-Islam members or sympathizers arrested in the wake of the May to September 2007 clashes in the Nahr al-Bared Palestinian refugee camp were tortured in detention. Methods alleged included the *ballanco* (hanging by the wrists tied behind the back), electrocution, having a glass bottle forced into the anus, beatings and religious insults. Tens of detainees said that they gave "confessions" as a result.

Excessive use of force

Seven protesters were killed, reportedly by Lebanese army soldiers and unidentified individuals, on 27 January during demonstrations against power cuts affecting Beirut's largely Shi'a southern suburbs. Eleven soldiers and two army officers charged with "involuntary manslaughter" were among more than 70 people charged in connection with the events.

Violence and discrimination against women

Women migrant domestic workers continued to receive inadequate protection against workplace exploitation and physical, sexual and psychological abuse. At least 45 died from unnatural causes, many apparently as a result of suicide or falling to their deaths while trying to escape from high buildings in which they worked. The authorities generally did not adequately investigate the deaths or any abuse that may have preceded them. On 4 September, Shi'a cleric Sayyed Muhammad Hussein Fadlallah urged employers not to abuse migrant domestic workers and called on the authorities to provide better protection.
■ On 17 January, the body of Ethiopian domestic worker Enate Belachew was found in her employer's house in south Beirut; she had apparently hanged herself.

In February, the UN Committee on the Elimination of Discrimination against Women recommended that the Lebanese authorities enact legislation to criminalize violence against women, ensure that women and girls subject to violence have immediate access to protection, prosecute and punish perpetrators, and amend the Penal Code to ensure that perpetrators of so-called "honour crimes" do not escape punishment. The Committee also called for marital rape to be criminalized, for enactment of a draft law regulating the employment of domestic

workers, who are excluded from the Labour Law, and for women domestic workers to be protected from exploitation and abuse.

Refugees and asylum-seekers

Several hundred thousand Palestinian refugees continued to suffer from discriminatory restrictions affecting their economic and social rights, notably their access to employment, health care, social security, education and housing.

On 19 August, it was announced that some 2,500 "non-ID" Palestinian refugees, who are not registered with the Lebanese authorities or the UN Relief and Works Agency for Palestine Refugees in the Near East (UNRWA) and consequently face more restrictions of their human rights than registered Palestinian refugees, had been issued with official temporary ID cards that would enable them to access rights and services previously denied them. A similar number of "non-ID" Palestinians were yet to approach the authorities for the ID cards, apparently fearing arrest.

Only a small minority of the 27,000 Palestinian refugees displaced from Nahr al-Bared camp by fighting there between May and September 2007 were able to return home.

On 21 February, UNHCR, the UN refugee agency, welcomed the government's steps to issue work and residency papers to some 50,000 Iraqi would-be refugees, previously considered illegal and subject to imprisonment and deportation.

Arbitrary detention

The authorities failed to rectify the situation of Nehmet Na'im al-Haj and Yusef Cha'ban, who remained in detention even though the UN Working Group on Arbitrary Detention declared in 2007 that they were arbitrarily detained.

Human rights defenders

Human rights organizations were generally able to operate without undue interference from the authorities. However, lawyer Muhamad Mugraby was harassed. On 27 November, he was cleared by a criminal court in Beirut of slander of a public official, relating to a speech on human rights he made at the European Parliament in November 2003. However, the court's decision was appealed in December by the Public Prosecutor. In April 2006, the Military Court of Cassation had dismissed the same charge against him.

Death penalty

At least 40 prisoners were on death row but no new death sentences were imposed and there were no executions.

In October, the Justice Minister announced that he had submitted to the Council of Ministers a law to abolish the death penalty.

In December, Lebanon abstained on a UN General Assembly resolution calling for a worldwide moratorium on executions.

Amnesty International visits

🚗 Amnesty International's Secretary General met President Michel Suleiman, Prime Minister Fouad Siniora and Speaker of the National Assembly Nabih Berri in Beirut in July. Amnesty International delegates visited Lebanon in October and November to attend meetings.

LIBERIA

REPUBLIC OF LIBERIA

Head of state and government:	Ellen Johnson-Sirleaf
Death penalty:	abolitionist in practice
Population:	3.9 million
Life expectancy:	44.7 years
Under-5 mortality (m/f):	212/194 per 1,000
Adult literacy:	51.9 per cent

President Ellen Johnson Sirleaf signed into law an Act that reintroduced the death penalty for murder committed during armed robbery. The judiciary continued to be hampered by lack of personnel. High rates of rape and other forms of sexual violence were reported. Efforts to address the increase in rape and sexual violence included a government decision to establish a special court to deal with these particular crimes. No progress was made in appointing commissioners to the Independent National Commission on Human Rights.

The work of the Truth and Reconciliation Commission (TRC) made significant progress, with individual hearings concluded by the end of the year. The trial of former President Charles Taylor resumed in January in The Hague. Chuckie Taylor, son of Charles Taylor, on trial in the USA under the 1994 torture act, was convicted for crimes he committed in Liberia in the late 1990s while serving as the head of the Anti-Terrorist Unit under former President Charles Taylor.

Background

In December the final phase of the disarmament, demobilization, rehabilitation and reintegration programme concluded with 7,251 ex-combatants, of whom 40 per cent were female.

Treason trials of former Armed Forces of Liberia (AFL) General Charles Julu and Colonel Andrew Dorbor resulted in acquittals in May. Former Acting Speaker of the National Transitional Legislative Assembly George Koukou, charged with treason, was pardoned by the President in January.

The trial on corruption charges of former Chairman of the National Transitional Government of Liberia (NTGL) Charles Gyude Bryant was discontinued, and he agreed to return misappropriated funds. The trial of Edwin Snowe, former Speaker of the House of Representatives, indicted for theft of public funds, continued.

During the year Liberia received US$15 million from the UN Peacebuilding Fund to foster reconciliation and conflict resolution. In April, Paris Club creditors agreed on US$254 million debt relief for Liberia, conditional on International Monetary Fund reforms. A poverty reduction strategy was finalized in June in Berlin in a meeting that brought together members of government and donors.

In February the first all-female peacekeeping unit from India was deployed as part of the United Nations Mission in Liberia (UNMIL). The mandate for UNMIL was renewed until September 2009 with troop strength at 11,000 by the end of the year.

The UN Independent Expert on Liberia visited Liberia in July.

Violent crime, especially armed robbery, was on the increase throughout the year, fuelled by high unemployment, disputes over land ownership, poverty and readily available small arms. The activities of ex-combatants continued to be a source of instability, particularly in the context of illicit mining activities.

The UN extended the arms embargo on Liberia for another year.

L

Land disputes

A survey released by the TRC in September showed that land disputes were the biggest threat to peace in Liberia.

■ In May at least 19 farm workers were allegedly killed and at least 21 others went missing on the border between Margibi and Grand Bassa Counties as a result of a land dispute between Senator Roland Kaine, formerly of the National Patriotic Front of Liberia (NPFL), and Commerce Secretary Charles Bennie, formerly with the Liberians United for Reconciliation and Democracy (LURD). Roland Kaine allegedly ordered the killing of farm workers hired by Charles Bennie. The style of killing was reminiscent of the Liberian conflict with evidence that victims had their hands tied behind their backs and were then thrown in a river to drown. The trial of Roland Kaine and 15 others started in November.

Death penalty

In May the House of Representatives passed a Bill that retained the death penalty for murder committed during armed robbery, terrorism or hijacking. In July the Act was signed into law by the President, in contravention of Liberia's obligations under the Second Optional Protocol of the International Covenant on Civil and Political Rights, aiming at the abolition of the death penalty, to which Liberia acceded in 2005.

In December Liberia abstained on a UN General Assembly resolution calling for a worldwide moratorium on executions.

Transitional justice

Individual public hearings of the TRC began in January and concluded by September. One session took place in the USA, the first time TRC hearings have been held outside the country where the violations occurred. They were followed by institutional and thematic hearings that were continuing at the end of the year.

The UN and other international bodies expressed concern about the lack of adequate witness protection. The mandate of the TRC was extended for three months, with its report likely to come out in 2009. In September the TRC made a request to the Special Court for Sierra Leone for former President Charles Taylor to testify. In December, in an effort to call on alleged perpetrators to attend hearings, the

TRC published a list of 198 names of alleged perpetrators who refused to appear before it to respond to allegations against them.

The Independent National Commission on Human Rights was still not operational because of delays in the appointment of commissioners. In June amendments to some provisions of the Act governing the Commission were submitted to the legislature.

Impunity

The government failed to take any steps to investigate and prosecute those responsible for crimes under international law committed during the 14-year conflict.

Roy M. Belfast Jr (known as Charles McArthur Emmanuel or Charles "Chuckie" Taylor Jr), the son of Charles Taylor, was convicted at the end of October in a US court for torture and related crimes while serving as the head of the Anti Terrorist Unit in Liberia. This was the first ever conviction under the US Torture Victim Protection Act, which was enacted in 1994. Chuckie Taylor was also the first person to be tried and convicted for crimes under international law committed during the Liberian conflict. Sentencing was due in early 2009.

In March an appeal court in the Netherlands overturned the conviction of Gus Kouwenhoven who had been convicted of breaking a UN arms embargo by supplying weapons for Charles Taylor during Liberia's conflict. The appeals court followed the district court by acquitting Gus Kouwenhoven on charges of war crimes.

Violence against women and children

Rape and other forms of sexual violence remained among the most frequently committed crimes. According to the UN there were 349 rapes reported between January and June 2008, a significant increase over the previous year. Access to health facilities to address emergency needs and psychological care continued to be inadequate.

Crimes against children, including rape, sexual violence, physical violence, trafficking and neglect, remained of serious concern.

There were some positive developments in addressing rape and other forms of sexual violence. In May, the government decided to establish a special court dedicated to hearing gender and sexual violence cases. In June, a safe house for survivors of sexual violence, supported by UNMIL and run by a local NGO, opened in Monrovia. During 2008 a national action plan on gender-based violence was adopted and funds were provided by the UN to implement the plan. In July Liberia ratified the Protocol to the African Charter on Human and Peoples' Rights on the Rights of Women in Africa.

Administration of justice

There was some progress in training police officers. Between 2004 and the end of 2008, at least 3,661 officers, including 344 women, received basic training and over 1,000 received specialist training. However, the police continued to suffer from inadequate resources, including delays in payment of salaries, leading to corrupt practices and limiting their ability to work effectively and to ensure a presence throughout the country.

The justice sector continued to suffer from a shortage of qualified judges, lack of infrastructure, archaic rules of procedure, and too few legal officers. Only one public defender was deployed in the entire country.

The problems in the judicial system resulted in overcrowding at Monrovia Central Prison. Approximately 95 per cent of those detained in Monrovia Central Prison were held without charge, some for as long as two years. In February efforts by a local organization facilitated the release from Monrovia Central Prison and Kakata prison of 36 prisoners who had been held for more than 180 days without charge. In November and again in early December more than 50 and 100 people respectively escaped from Monrovia Central Prison. The police responded by arresting some of the escaped prisoners, and also some bystanders.

Amnesty International visits/reports

🚍 Amnesty International delegates visited Liberia in January to make a film and in March to launch a report.

📄 Liberia: Towards the final phase of the Truth and Reconciliation Commission (AFR 34/002/2008)

📄 Liberia: A flawed process discriminates against women and girls (AFR 34/004/2008)

📄 Film: Women of Liberia fighting for Peace

LIBYA

SOCIALIST PEOPLE'S LIBYAN ARAB JAMAHIRIYA
Head of state:	Mu'ammar al-Gaddafi
Head of government:	al-Baghdadi Ali al-Mahmudi
Death penalty:	retentionist
Population:	6.3 million
Life expectancy:	73.4 years
Under-5 mortality (m/f):	20/19 per 1,000
Adult literacy:	84.2 per cent

Libya's human rights record and continuing violations cast a shadow over its improved international diplomatic standing. Freedom of expression, association and assembly remained severely restricted in a climate characterized by the repression of dissident voices and the absence of independent human rights NGOs. Refugees, asylum-seekers and migrants continued to be detained indefinitely and ill-treated. At least eight foreign nationals were executed. The legacy of past human rights violations remained unaddressed.

Background

2008 saw a further improvement in diplomatic relations between Libya and the USA and European countries. In September, US Secretary of State Condoleezza Rice visited Tripoli after the two states agreed a claims settlement in August relating to the Lockerbie aircraft bombing, among other issues. In August, the government agreed a Treaty of Friendship, Partnership and Co-operation with Italy, including provision for bilateral efforts to combat "illegal migration". In November, negotiations started with the EU over a Framework Agreement covering issues such as economic co-operation and migration policy. The same month the government held high-level negotiations with Russia on energy co-operation, civilian nuclear development and foreign policy.

The government failed to extend invitations to the UN Special Rapporteur on torture and the UN Working Group on Arbitrary Detention despite pending requests.

Repression of dissent

The government did not tolerate criticism or dissent and maintained draconian legislation to deter it.

L

Under the Penal Code and Law No. 71 of 1972 on the Criminalization of Parties, independent political expression and group activity is banned and those who peacefully exercise their rights to freedom of expression and association may face the death penalty. The authorities continued to take action against anyone who openly addressed such taboo topics as Libya's poor human rights record or the leadership of Mu'ammar al-Gaddafi.

■ Prisoner of conscience Fathi el-Jahmi continued to be held at the Tripoli Medical Centre. Arrested in March 2004 after he called for political reform and criticized the Libyan leader in international media interviews, he was declared mentally unfit when taken before a court in September 2006. In March 2008 he was examined by an independent medical doctor on behalf of the US-based NGO Physicians for Human Rights, who assessed him as showing no signs of mental incapacity but found him to be in poor health and in need of surgery.

■ Idriss Boufayed and 11 others were tried before the State Security Court, a court created in August 2007 to try individuals accused of unauthorized political activity and offences against state security and whose proceedings do not conform to international fair trial standards. Idriss Boufayed and 10 others were sentenced to prison terms of up to 25 years after being convicted on vaguely worded charges, including "attempting to overthrow the political system", "spreading false rumours about the Libyan regime" and "communication with enemy powers". The 12th defendant was acquitted. The defendants did not have access to court-appointed counsel outside the courtroom and all but one were not allowed to appoint counsel of their choosing. Idriss Boufayed and his co-accused were arrested in February 2007 after he and three others issued a statement about a planned peaceful protest to commemorate the killing of at least 12 people during a demonstration in February 2006 in Benghazi. Two other people detained at the same time were not brought to trial: Jum'a Boufayed was released from Ain Zara Prison on 27 May after more than a year in incommunicado detention without trial; the fate and whereabouts of Abdelrahman al-Qateewy were unknown. Idriss Boufayed was released in October, and eight of his co-defendants were released in November. No explanation was given for the releases. Two men sentenced with them remained in prison.

Freedom of association

The right to freedom of association was severely curtailed and the government did not allow independent human rights NGOs. The only organization permitted to address human rights was the Society of Human Rights of the Gaddafi International Charity and Development Foundation (GDF), headed by Saif al-Islam al-Gaddafi, a son of Mu'ammar al-Gaddafi. In July, the GDF launched "al-Gaddafi Call", an initiative encouraging people to submit information and complaints about human rights violations.

■ In March, a group of lawyers, journalists and writers applied to register a new NGO, the Centre for Democracy, to work towards "the dissemination of democratic values and human rights and the rule of law in Libya", but then dropped the proposal. According to the chairperson of its founding committee, this was because the authorities objected to 12 of those named as founders of the organization and because of an attack on Dhow Al Mansouri, who headed the founding committee of the Justice Association for Human Rights within the Centre for Democracy. He was abducted and assaulted in June by three unidentified assailants who warned him against the establishment of the NGO.

Counter-terror and security

In April, the GDF announced that 90 members of the Libyan Islamic Fighting Group had been released from prison following negotiations led by the GDF with the group's leaders. The GDF stated that this represented a third of the group's membership.

The authorities did not disclose any information about two Libyan nationals, Abdesalam Safrani and Abu Sufian Ibrahim Ahmed Hamuda, who were detained when they were returned from US custody in Guantánamo Bay in December 2006 and September 2007 respectively. The lack of information raised fears for their safety and that of other Libyans who might be returned under similar circumstances. At least seven other Libyans continued to be held by the US authorities at Guantánamo Bay.

Impunity

The authorities failed to address the long-standing pattern of impunity for perpetrators of gross human rights violations. No public information was made available about the investigation into events in 1996 at Tripoli's Abu Salim Prison in which hundreds of prisoners were allegedly killed. The GDF announced that a preliminary report establishing criminal and legal responsibility for the incident would be submitted to the judicial authorities, but gave no date. In June it was reported that the North Benghazi court ordered the authorities to disclose the fate of some 30 prisoners who were feared to have died in detention during the events at Abu Salim, but they failed to provide any public information. Some reports suggested that the authorities had agreed to pay financial compensation to about 35 families of prisoners who died in return for their agreement not to seek judicial redress.

The authorities took no steps to address the legacy of gross human rights violations committed in earlier years, notably the 1970s, 1980s and 1990s, including the enforced disappearance of hundreds of critics and opponents of the government. Many are feared to have died or been killed in custody.

The authorities also failed to investigate properly a death in detention in suspicious circumstances in 2008.
■ In May, Mohammed Adel Abu-Ali was reported to have died in custody following his deportation from Sweden earlier that month. He was arrested upon arrival in Libya. The authorities said that he committed suicide; an investigation conducted by the Swedish Ministry of Foreign Affairs concluded that it was impossible to establish the cause of death.

Refugees, asylum-seekers and migrants

There were persistent reports of torture and other ill-treatment of detained migrants, refugees and asylum-seekers; the latter were not afforded protection, as required by international refugee law. On 15 January, the authorities announced their intention to deport all "illegal migrants", and subsequently carried out mass expulsions of Ghanaians, Malians, Nigerians and nationals of other countries. At least 700 Eritrean men, women and children were detained and were at risk of forcible return despite fears that they would be subjected to serious human rights abuses in Eritrea.
■ On 21 June, the authorities informed some 230 Eritreans held at a detention centre in Misratah, 200km east of Tripoli, that they were to be flown to Italy later that day for resettlement and told them to be prepared for medical examinations and transportation to the airport. However, it appeared that this was a ruse and that the authorities intended to forcibly return them to

Eritrea. None of the Eritreans was known to have been deported by the end of the year, apparently because UNHCR intervened. Many were believed to have fled Eritrea to seek refuge abroad.

Amnesty International visits/reports
🚌 The authorities did not permit Amnesty International to visit the country.
📄 Libya: Mass expulsion of irregular migrants would be a violation of human rights, 18 January 2008
📄 Libya: Prisoner of conscience Idriss Boufayed released (MDE 19/008/2008)

LITHUANIA

REPUBLIC OF LITHUANIA

Head of state:	Valdas Adamkus
Head of government:	Andrius Kubilius (replaced Gediminas Kirkilas in December)
Death penalty:	abolitionist for all crimes
Population:	3.4 million
Life expectancy:	72.5 years
Under-5 mortality (m/f):	13/9 per 1,000
Adult literacy:	99.6 per cent

Racist attacks and discrimination persisted against non-European migrants and the Roma minority. There still was no specific law addressing domestic violence against women. The authorities failed to respect the rights of lesbian, gay, bisexual and transgender (LGBT) people and to condemn acts that restricted, and in some cases denied, their right to freedom of expression, peaceful assembly and association.

Racism and discrimination – migrants and Roma

In February the UN Special Rapporteur on racism, reporting on a visit in September 2007, expressed concern about the situation of minorities in Lithuania, noting the profound discrimination faced by Roma in the fields of employment and housing.

Unemployment rates among Roma remained several times higher than among ethnic Lithuanians, and living conditions in Roma settlements were

L

sometimes below minimum standards, lacking electricity and heating as well as drinking water and sanitation facilities.

The Special Rapporteur expressed concern about the increase in racially motivated attacks against migrants, especially of non-European descent, and in hate speech. Despite a clear constitutional prohibition on incitement to racial hatred, in practice very few cases were brought to justice.

The Special Rapporteur urged the Lithuanian authorities to recognize in the criminal code racism as an aggravating factor.

Violence against women and girls

In its concluding observations, published in July, the UN Committee on the Elimination of Discrimination against Women (CEDAW) expressed concern at the lack of a specific law on domestic violence, especially considering the high level of violence against women. CEDAW noted that the lack of legislation on this issue may lead "to such violence being considered a private matter, in which the consequences of the relationship between the victim and the perpetrator are not fully understood by police and health officers, the relevant authorities and society at large." CEDAW observed that the authorities contributed to the perpetuation of patriarchal attitudes and stereotypes regarding the roles and responsibility of women and men through the State Family Policy Concept adopted in June.

Rights of lesbian, gay, bisexual and transgender people

Municipal authorities in Lithuania issued derogatory statements against LGBT people. An EU initiative, the "For Diversity, Against Discrimination" touring truck, aimed at raising awareness about EU legislation prohibiting discrimination on the grounds of gender, disability, age, religion and belief, race and ethnicity, and sexual orientation, was banned in August for the second consecutive year by the city authorities in Vilnius. The Mayor refused permission for the truck to enter the city centre for the event on 20 August, claiming that participation of LGBT activists would be "propaganda of homosexuality". The Mayor of Kaunas also banned the EU initiative, saying that "[the] homosexual festival may cause many negative emotions".

Amnesty International report

Latvia and Lithuania: Human rights on the march (EUR 53/001/2008)

MACEDONIA

THE FORMER YUGOSLAV REPUBLIC OF MACEDONIA

Head of state:	Branko Crvenkovski
Head of government:	Nikola Gruevski
Death penalty:	abolitionist for all crimes
Population:	2 million
Life expectancy:	73.8 years
Under-5 mortality (m/f):	17/16 per 1,000
Adult literacy:	96.1 per cent

War crimes cases relating to the 2001 internal conflict were returned to Macedonia for prosecution. The general elections in June saw violent confrontations between different political parties. Serious concerns were expressed by international organizations about prison conditions and impunity for ill-treatment by the police. Little progress was made to address discrimination against Roma.

Background

Following elections in June, the ruling Internal Macedonian Revolutionary Organization-Democratic Party for Macedonian National Unity was returned to power, and in July formed a coalition with the ethnic Albanian Democratic Union for Integration (DUI).

The run-up to the elections on 1 June was characterized by rivalry between the two ethnic Albanian parties which often resulted in violence. In May, a member of the ethnic Albanian Democratic Party of Albanians (DPA) was killed, while DUI members alleged that they, their offices or their homes had been attacked by members of the DPA, including an attempt on 13 May to assassinate their leader, Ali Ahmeti.

On election day, Naser Ajvazi was killed in Aračinovo after the special police unit "Alfa" allegedly returned fire on unidentified armed individuals. Voting was suspended in several cities and election results subsequently annulled in 187 polling stations, necessitating a re-run in several major cities.

M

Some 164 people were arrested in connection with election violations, including fraud and intimidation. Twenty-eight police officers were suspended and 11 of them charged with election fraud.

■ In October, Agim Krasniqi and eight others were convicted for possession of firearms, being part of a criminal gang and causing public disorder. They received sentences of between five and six years' imprisonment.

In November the European Commission reported that Macedonia had not yet met the criteria for membership of the EU. Reforms, including on the conduct of elections, independence of the judiciary, police accountability and prison conditions, as set out in a Stabilization and Association Agreement, were not fully implemented. Consequently no date was set for accession talks.

International justice – war crimes

■ In July, at the International Criminal Tribunal for the former Yugoslavia (Tribunal), Johan Tarčulovski, an Escort Inspector in the President's Security Unit, was convicted on three counts of war crimes and sentenced to 12 years' imprisonment. He was responsible for the deaths of seven ethnic Albanians and the detention and cruel treatment of over 100 others in Ljuboten in August 2001. Former Minister of the Interior Ljube Boškovski, indicted for superior responsibility for crimes committed by Johan Tarčulovski, was acquitted.

Justice system – war crimes

In September, proceedings opened in the "Mavrovo" road workers' case, one of four cases returned for prosecution to Macedonia from the Tribunal in February. The road workers had been abducted in August 2001, allegedly physically ill-treated, sexually violated and threatened with death before being released some hours later.

Ethnic Albanians had argued that the cases returned from the Tribunal should be subject to the Amnesty Law adopted in March 2002, which applied to all those involved in the 2001 armed conflict, except in cases of war crimes taken under the jurisdiction of the Tribunal. As this case had been returned by the Tribunal some argued that the amnesty law should apply. However, Skopje Criminal Court requested that DUI assembly member Hisen Xhemaili be stripped of his immunity from prosecution in order to face trial.

No progress was made in resolving the fate of three ethnic Albanians and 13 Macedonians who were victims of enforced disappearance and abduction in 2001.

Torture and other ill-treatment

In the absence of an independent oversight mechanism, allegations of torture and other ill-treatment were subject to internal investigations by the Interior Ministry, which failed to be independent or impartial. In February, for example, national television showed mobile phone footage, apparently taken by a police officer, of the bruised and bloody face of a man detained in Brodec in November 2007 during Operation Mountain Storm. While police officers responsible for the footage were suspended pending investigation, the Interior Minister refused to re-open an internal investigation into the incident, in which six people were killed and others allegedly ill-treated by the police.

■ In July, 17 men, including 13 of those arrested in Brodec, were convicted of armed attacks against the police, preparation of a terrorist act and weapons possession.

The European Court of Human Rights in April found Macedonia in violation of Article 3 of the European Convention on Human Rights (freedom from torture) for failing to investigate the claim of five Romani applicants that they had been ill-treated by police in 1998 in a restaurant in Štip and subsequently in detention.

In May the UN Committee against Torture highlighted concerns about the failure of the authorities to investigate allegations of torture and other ill-treatment; the continued absence of an independent external oversight mechanism to investigate and monitor alleged police misconduct; and the low penalties imposed on police officers convicted of torture and other ill-treatment. In April the UN Human Rights Committee (HRC) had also expressed concerns about police violence against minorities, in particular Roma, and the lack of effective investigation. The Council of Europe's Committee for the Prevention of Torture (CPT) noted similar concerns in its reports in February and September.

Prison conditions

The CPT expressed serious concerns about the lack of co-operation by the Ministry of Justice, its failure

M

to remedy "glaring deficiencies" in prison conditions identified in 2006, including the use of chains as punitive restraints, and accommodation amounting to inhuman and degrading conditions in Idrizovo prison.

Counter-terror and security

The HRC in April and the UN Committee against Torture in May recommended that the authorities open a new investigation into their part in the detention for 23 days in 2003 of Khaled el-Masri in a Skopje hotel. He was subsequently unlawfully transferred to the US authorities and flown to Afghanistan, where he was tortured. In October Khaled el-Masri filed a complaint against unknown police officers.

Discrimination – Roma

In April the HRC raised concerns about the authorities' failure both to guarantee Romani children education in their own language, and to prevent the continued high drop-out rate, segregation and harassment of Romani school children.

Local NGOs reported that their contribution to a consultation process on legislation on discrimination failed to be included in a draft law prepared for presentation to the parliament. The draft law failed to establish an independent anti-discrimination body to provide effective remedies against, or protect people from, discrimination.

The government adopted a national action plan for the advancement of Romani women based on recommendations by Romani women's NGOs. Little was achieved in implementing the national action plans for the Decade of Roma Inclusion, which were revised but had not received ministerial approval by the end of the year.

Refugees

An estimated 1,883 predominantly Roma and Ashkalia refugees from Kosovo remained in Macedonia under temporary humanitarian protection. The state failed to guarantee them access to social and economic rights.

In May the UN Committee against Torture expressed concerns about the failures of the system for determining refugee status and the absence of effective remedies by which decisions might be challenged.

Violence against women and girls

Macedonia prepared legislative amendments, but had still to ratify the Council of Europe Convention on Action against Trafficking in Human Beings by the end of the year. The Ministries of Interior and of Labour and Social Policy established protocols for the protection of trafficked children. The authorities reported increasing numbers of internally trafficked people.

In April the HRC expressed concerns about the undue burden of proof imposed on victims of rape, which created impunity for perpetrators. It urged that the definition of rape in the Criminal Code be amended.

Amnesty International reports

Former Yugoslav Republic of Macedonia: Submission to the UN Universal Periodic Review (EUR 65/001/2008)

State of denial – Europe's role in rendition and secret detention (EUR 01/003/2008)

MALAWI

REPUBLIC OF MALAWI

Head of state and government:	Bingu wa Mutharika
Death penalty:	abolitionist in practice
Population:	14.3 million
Life expectancy:	46.3 years
Under-5 mortality (m/f):	134/125 per 1,000
Adult literacy:	64.1 per cent

Journalists working for the privately owned media and opposition party politicians were at risk of arrest. Prisons were overcrowded and lacked adequate facilities.

Background

The political wrangling that started in 2004 when President Bingu wa Mutharika broke away from the United Democratic Front (UDF) party continued to affect government programmes that required parliamentary approval. Approval of the national budget by parliament was held up by political party agendas.

The prevalence of HIV/AIDS remained high, significantly affecting farming and leading to a

M

reduction in food production. Food security in Malawi continued to deteriorate as a result of declining productivity, rising population and the high prevalence of HIV/AIDS. More than 86 per cent of the population had limited access to basic health and education services.

Prison conditions

Prisons were overcrowded and lacked adequate facilities. For example, Kachere prison, in which about 170 juveniles were detained at the beginning of December, only had one toilet and one bathroom. Maula prison, built to accommodate 700 detainees, housed about 1,800 at the beginning of December.

Prisons faced food shortages, leading to high levels of malnutrition. Although prisoners suffering from HIV/AIDS received anti-retroviral treatment, they were not given the necessary supplementary diet.

Freedom of expression – journalists

■ In February police charged journalist Mike Chipalasa and editor James Mphande of the privately owned *Daily Times* with "publishing false news likely to lead to a breach of public order", an offence carrying up to six months' imprisonment. This followed the publication of an article on 14 January which quoted the leader of the opposition Malawi Congress Party, John Tembo, accusing the government of working with foreign experts to manipulate the 2009 elections in favour of the President's Democratic Progressive Party. The two journalists were released on bail.

Arrest of opposition politicians

Several key opposition politicians were arrested and opposition parties faced harassment.
■ Former President Bakili Muluzi, a presidential candidate for the UDF in elections scheduled for 2009, was arrested in Lilongwe on 25 May and accused of involvement in a coup plot. He was charged with treason and placed under house arrest. Before Bakili Muluzi's arrest, eight former senior security officials and politicians who served under him were arrested on similar allegations. All were granted bail.
■ The trial of Vice-President Cassim Chilumpha, who was arrested on treason charges in April 2006, continued. The prosecution produced no evidence that he had attempted to assassinate the President. He remained on bail.

MALAYSIA

MALAYSIA
Head of state: Yang di-Pertuan Agong Tuanku Mizan Zainal Abidin
Head of government: Abdullah Ahmad Badawi
Death penalty: retentionist
Population: 27 million
Life expectancy: 73.7 years
Under-5 mortality (m/f):   12/10 per 1,000
Adult literacy: 88.7 per cent

The government tightened control of dissent and curtailed the right to freedom of expression and religion. Bloggers were arrested under the Sedition Act, and the Printing Press and Publications Act (PPPA) was used to control newspaper content. Ten people were arbitrarily arrested and detained under the Internal Security Act (ISA). Security forces continued to use excessive force while the establishment of an independent police complaints misconduct commission was postponed. Immigration personnel and volunteers conducted mass arrests of migrant workers. At least 22 people were sentenced to death. The number executed was unknown.

Background

During March elections, the opposition won control of five of Malaysia's 13 states and 82 of the 222 parliamentary seats, ending the overwhelming majority held by the Barisan Nasional (National Front) coalition. In August, opposition leader and former ISA detainee Anwar Ibrahim was elected to Parliament.

Freedom of expression

Authorities suspended or threatened to cancel publishing permits under the PPPA, and arrested bloggers under the Sedition Act.
■ In April, authorities suspended the publishing permit of Tamil daily *Makkal Osai*, allegedly for giving extensive coverage to the opposition coalition in the run-up to the elections.
■ In May, authorities threatened to revoke the publishing licence of the Catholic newspaper *The Herald* for using the word "Allah" as a synonym for "God".

M

- In September, blogger Syed Azidi Syed was arrested and detained for three days under the Sedition Act allegedly for posting an article that called on people to fly the Malaysian flag upside down as a protest against certain government policies.
- In May, blogger Raja Petra Kamarudin was charged under the Sedition Act for an article in which he allegedly implied the involvement of the Deputy Prime Minister in the murder of a Mongolian woman. In September, he was arbitrarily arrested and detained under the ISA. Six days before his arrest, the Home Minister was quoted as saying that he could be arrested under the ISA for insulting Muslims and degrading Islam in articles that appeared on his website. The Home Minister issued a two-year detention order, which is renewable indefinitely. In November, after much public discussion, the High Court ruled that he be released.

Detention without trial

Ten people were arrested under the ISA in 2008. At year's end, there were at least 50 ISA detainees, including 17 who had been detained for between four and eight years without charge or trial. Thirty-one detainees were known to have been released, including four Indonesian nationals who were deported.
- Mechanic Sanjeev Kumar, who became paralyzed and mentally unstable, allegedly as a result of torture while in detention, was released in September. At the end of the year he was under restricted residence orders.
- Five leaders of the Hindu Rights Action Force remained detained for organizing rallies against the marginalization of ethnic Indian Malaysians. In March, while in detention, Manoharan Malayalam was elected to the state assembly. In May, the Federal Court dismissed their appeal for habeas corpus saying that their arrest had been lawful. They have since appealed against the decision to the Federal Court. Amnesty International considers them to be prisoners of conscience.

Excessive use of force

- In May, opposition MP Lim Lip Eng was beaten by security personnel believed to be from the Federal Reserve Unit (FRU) after he attempted to mediate in a stand-off between police and residents in a road access dispute.
- In May, at least 10 uniformed men allegedly from the FRU forcibly dragged mechanic Chang Jium Haur from

his car and beat him until he lost consciousness. To date, no one has been prosecuted for the incident.

Parliament postponed discussion on the Special Complaints Commission Bill, a proposal from government to monitor police misconduct that was highly criticized by local and international human rights groups.

Migrants' rights, refugees and asylum-seekers

One third of Malaysia's three million migrants remained at risk of arrest and deportation due to their irregular status, including unknown numbers who feared persecution if returned to their home country. The government makes no distinction between migrant workers and asylum-seekers and refugees. The UN High Commissioner for Refugees had registered 41,405 people of concern as of August, of whom 11,172 were children. Eighty-eight per cent were from Myanmar.

In March, the Prisons Department completed the handover of 11 immigration detention centres to the Immigration Department. The 480,000 untrained volunteers from the Relawan Ikatan Rakyat (Rela, People's Volunteer Corps) took over management of the centres. Reports of serious abuses against detainees by Rela members increased.
- In April, a riot broke out in Lenggeng Immigration Detention Centre in protest against the severe beating of some detainees and the deplorable conditions in the immigration centre.

Rela members, who can make arrests without a warrant or assistance from police or immigration officers, failed to distinguish between asylum-seekers, refugees, stateless persons, and migrant workers during their immigration operations. In one operation in August, Rela arrested some 11,600 people, to find out after processing that only 500 did not have a regular immigration status.

In June, the Home Minister announced a crackdown that aimed to deport 200,000 irregular migrants, mainly Filipinos. Philippine government figures suggested that 35,000 had been deported as of August. Thousands more had been deported by the end of the year. The Philippines Human Rights Commission was investigating allegations of beatings and overcrowded conditions of detention during the operation.

Freedom of religion

The politicization of religion markedly increased in 2008. People continued to face barriers to conversion from Islam.

■ In March, Muslim-born woman Kamariah Ali was sentenced by a Shari'a court to two years' imprisonment for renouncing Islam.

■ In August, a Bar Council forum into legal conflicts faced by Malaysian families if a spouse converts to Islam was forced to stop midway through the event by police and Islamist protesters because the protesters were threatening to forcibly enter the venue. No action was taken against the protesters.

Discrimination

Racial discrimination remained institutionalized in Malaysia, particularly in government-backed "affirmative action policies" for Bumiputeras (Malays and Indigenous Peoples from Sabah and Sarawak) in land ownership, employment and education, which in some cases resulted in the complete exclusion of other groups.

■ There was a public outcry in August after a state official proposed that the University Teknologi Mara (UITM) allocate 10 per cent of university places to non-Malays. The university, home to 120,000 students, has been open only to Malays for the last five decades. The Prime Minister and the Minister of Higher Education rejected the proposal.

Death penalty

In January, the NGO Malaysians Against the Death Penalty estimated the number of inmates on death row to be as high as 300, mostly for drug offences. Amnesty International is aware of 22 people sentenced to death by the High Courts in 2008, while the number of those executed was unknown.

In December, Malaysia voted against a UN General Assembly resolution calling for a worldwide moratorium on executions.

Cruel, inhuman and degrading punishments

Caning continued to be used to punish many offences, including immigration offences.

MALDIVES

REPUBLIC OF MALDIVES

Head of state and government:	Mohamed Nasheed (replaced Maumoon Abdul Gayoom in November)
Death penalty:	abolitionist in practice
Population:	311,000
Life expectancy:	67 years
Under-5 mortality (m/f):	41/41 per 1,000
Adult literacy:	96.3 per cent

A new constitution, with positive legislative developments, was followed two months later by the election of the country's first new president for 30 years. Some administrative and justice issues remained unresolved at year's end, and a severe lack of adequate housing remained a problem.

Background

In October, former prisoner of conscience Mohamed Nasheed was elected president in the country's first ever multi-party presidential elections; he took office in November. A coalition of political parties, led by his party the Maldivian Democratic Party, defeated another coalition led by the Dhivehi Rayyithunge (Maldivian Peoples) Party of President Maumoon Abdul Gayoom.

Legal and constitutional developments

A new constitution was ratified in August, which provided for greater independence of the judiciary, reduced executive powers vested in the president and strengthened the role of parliament. However, it barred non-Muslims from obtaining Maldivian citizenship.

To implement the new constitution, the first prosecutor-general was appointed in September. Five judges were also sworn in to the first Supreme Court, the final court of appeal, the same month. However, an acute shortage of qualified lawyers and judges made it hard to guarantee fair and prompt trials, thus hampering the full and adequate functioning of the criminal justice system.

Parliament enacted the Anti-Corruption Commission Act in September, but the commission was not fully functional by the end of the year.

President Nasheed pledged to uphold the rule of law, promote human rights, and strengthen the

M

political and administrative process. Much of the new draft penal code, submitted to the Majlis (parliament) in 2007, remained to be adopted by the end of the year.

Housing rights

The Maldives Human Rights Commission reported in November that there was a severe lack of adequate housing amid continuing reports of significant overcrowding especially in the capital Malé. The Maldives remained at risk of rising global sea levels, and erosion continued to encroach on some islands.

Amnesty International report

📄 Maldives: New president must ensure continued protection of human rights (ASA 29/001/2008)

MALI

REPUBLIC OF MALI

Head of state:	Amadou Toumani Touré
Head of government:	Modibo Sidibé
Death penalty:	abolitionist in practice
Population:	12.7 million
Life expectancy:	53.1 years
Under-5 mortality (m/f):	206/189 per 1,000
Adult literacy:	24 per cent

At least 10 people were killed when conflict intensified in the north of the country. One person died when the security forces used excessive force against demonstrators protesting over water privatization plans. Two Mauritanian detainees said they were tortured in detention. Lawmakers postponed a bill to abolish the death penalty.

Background

Peaceful marches were organized against rising prices for basic commodities and against plans to privatize the supply of water in the north-west of the country.

At least 250 migrants arrested in Spain were sent back to Bamako, the capital, during 2008. More than 100 migrants arrested and held for months in Libya were also sent back to Mali. Some of them

complained that they had been beaten by Spanish and Libyan security forces.

The conflict in the north-western region of Kidal intensified, particularly in March and April.

Excessive use of force

In November, the security forces used excessive force against people protesting over plans to privatize water in Léré, in the north-west of the country. At least six people were wounded, one of whom, Kassim Sidibé, later died.

Armed conflict – Kidal region

Continuing conflict between a Tuareg armed group led by Ibrahim Ag Bahanga and the army resulted in at least five civilian deaths, some in landmine explosions, and casualties among Tuareg civilians crossing into Burkina Faso.

In March, the Tuareg armed group again broke a six-month ceasefire. On two occasions in March and September, more than 30 people, both civilians and soldiers, were abducted by the group and held in the desert. Others had been detained since 2007. All were released following mediation by Libya, and Ibrahim Ag Bahanga went into exile to Libya.

Two Austrian tourists taken hostage in Tunisia by a group close to al-Qa'ida in the Maghreb were transferred to Mali in March and released in October.

In September, an armed self-defence group, "Ganda Izo", led by a former soldier, was allegedly responsible for killing four Tuaregs. The group's leader and at least 30 of its members were later arrested.

Torture and other ill-treatment

During a mission to Mauritania, Amnesty International delegates met two Mauritanian citizens, who were arrested in Mali in late November 2007 and accused of being members of al-Qa'ida in the Maghreb. They were transferred to Mauritania in February 2008 where they remained in detention. The two men told Amnesty International that they had been tortured in a secret detention centre in Bamako. Methods used included kicking, beating, electric shocks, suspension by the arms and sleep deprivation.

Death penalty

The draft bill to abolish the death penalty was not examined at the parliamentary session which ended in July. The members of parliament postponed the reading and adoption of the bill to a later session. In May, when Mali was examined under the Universal Periodic Review at the UN, a Malian representative stated that his country was committed to abolition and that the abolition bill would be adopted before 2012.

At least 15 people were sentenced to death.

■ In Segou, in July, an assize court sentenced Broulaye Bagayogo to death for attempted murder and sentenced Najim Lakhal Aly to death for conspiracy, kidnapping, robbery and illegal possession of weapons.

No executions were carried out.

MALTA

REPUBLIC OF MALTA

Head of state:	Edward Fenech-Adami
Head of government:	Lawrence Gonzi
Death penalty:	abolitionist for all crimes
Population:	408,000
Life expectancy:	79.1 years
Under-5 mortality (m/f):	8/7 per 1,000
Adult literacy:	87.9 per cent

Migrants and asylum-seekers continued to be detained on arrival, in contravention of international laws and standards. The policies of the Maltese authorities were of concern to the European Commission against Racism and Intolerance (ECRI), which linked detention procedures towards migrants with the rise of racism and intolerance in the country.

Migrants, refugees and asylum-seekers

International scrutiny

A report by ECRI, published in April, highlighted the lack of legal aid and information available to asylum-seekers upon arrival in Malta; asylum-seekers were denied access to free legal aid for their initial asylum claim, and were only entitled to legal representation if they paid the costs themselves.

ECRI also pointed out that irregular migrants, asylum-seekers, people under humanitarian protection and refugees faced racial discrimination in accessing various services and exploitation in the labour market.

Detention

The authorities implemented a policy of systematically detaining all irregular migrants and asylum-seekers.

At the end of the year, around 2,050 migrants were detained in closed detention centres. A further 2,100 were accommodated in open centres, where they were free to come and go. Vulnerable groups such as families with minors, unaccompanied minors, pregnant women, people with disabilities and the elderly were among those detained for several weeks or months in closed detention centres while waiting for the identification process to be completed. Only then were they transferred to open centres. Asylum-seekers were kept in closed detention centres and transferred to open centres only after filing their asylum applications, which often took several weeks.

No automatic judicial review of detention was provided, in contravention of Article 5(4) of the European Convention on Human Rights.

Some conditions of detention were very poor. In a study commissioned by the European Parliament Committee on Civil Liberties, Justice and Home Affairs and published in January, detention centres were described as overcrowded, and characterized by poor hygiene and inadequate health care.

In Hal Far Open Centre, more than 1,000 people were accommodated in tents and mobile containers and exposed to the cold and the rain. The government had not earmarked funds to improve living conditions in the Centre by the end of the year.

Racism

ECRI expressed concern at Malta's practice of detaining migrants, saying it affected their rights and noting that the policies put in place by the authorities to respond to the challenges of irregular immigration were "seriously reinforcing perceptions of immigrants as criminals and increasing the levels of racism and xenophobia among the general population."

ECRI also noted that the legal provisions against racist expression, racially motivated offences and racial discrimination were not yet fully applied, and there was still little awareness of the need to actively monitor racism and racial discrimination in order to properly identify and address these concerns.

M

MAURITANIA

ISLAMIC REPUBLIC OF MAURITANIA

Head of state:	General Mohamed Ould Abdel Aziz (replaced Sidi Mohamed Ould Cheikh Abdallahi in August)
Head of government:	Moulaye Ould Mohamed Laghdaf (replaced Yahya Ould Mohamed El Waghef in August, who replaced Zeine Ould Zeidane in May)
Death penalty:	abolitionist in practice
Population:	3.2 million
Life expectancy:	63.2 years
Under-5 mortality (m/f):	98/85 per 1,000
Adult literacy:	51.2 per cent

A military coup overturned the elected government, and several former officials were held as prisoners of conscience. Torture and other ill-treatment were reported throughout the year. Suspected Islamist activists were held in prolonged incommunicado detention under counter-terror measures. Hundreds of migrants were detained and expelled with no opportunity to challenge the legality of their detention or collective expulsion. Prison conditions were harsh.

Background

In August, a group of army officers overthrew and arrested President Sidi Mohamed Ould Cheikh Abdallahi, in office since the presidential election of March 2007, which had restored civilian government to the country.

The August 2008 coup was preceded by disagreements between the President and some army officers, especially regarding the dismissal of the Chief of Staff. A High State Council comprising 11 members of the armed forces was established by General Mohamed Ould Abdel Aziz, who led the coup. The High State Council promised to organize elections as soon as possible.

The international community called for the release of the President and a return to constitutional order. The EU and the USA froze their non-humanitarian aid and the AU suspended Mauritania. A number of peaceful demonstrations called for the release of the President and the restoration of constitutional order. Following a decision in September by the governor of the capital Nouakchott to suspend all political demonstrations, some demonstrations were forcibly broken up or prevented.

Arbitrary detention

The UN Working Group on Arbitrary Detention expressed concern about the lack of effective control by the prosecutor over police action and over the situation of individuals in custody. Many detainees told the Working Group that abuse of power, corruption, torture and other ill-treatment were common in detention and that often detainees were coerced into confessions. Complaints against the police were reportedly investigated only in exceptional cases.

Counter-terror and security – incommunicado detention

Scores of people, mostly suspected Islamist activists, were arrested in the context of counter-terror measures. Among them were the men charged with killing four French tourists in Aleg in December 2007, and those charged with attacking the Israeli Embassy in Nouakchott in February. Others were suspected of having participated directly or indirectly in terrorist acts. Among those arrested were relatives of suspected Islamist activists. Some were released within two weeks, but at the end of 2008 many were still held without trial.

Many detainees, including those accused of belonging to al-Qa'ida in Maghreb, were detained incommunicado for prolonged periods, exceeding the 15 days allowed by law. Security forces and prison officers refused to allow some judicially authorized family visits.

■ The mother of an alleged Islamist activist, arrested at his home on 30 April and detained at the Army Chief of Staff headquarters, was refused access to her son despite obtaining authorization for a visit from a magistrate.

Prisoners of conscience

Following the August coup, President Sidi, the Prime Minister Yahya Ould Mohamed El Waghef, the Interior Minister and two other senior officials were arrested. Some were released a few days later. President Sidi was detained until 13 November when he was transferred to his home village of Lemdem and held under house arrest. He was finally released on 22 December. In September, Isselmou Ould Abdelkhader, a former Minister of Health, was arrested for criticizing the August coup.

M

Torture and other ill-treatment

Torture and other ill-treatment continued to be reported throughout 2008 in a wide variety of detention centres including the first police brigade and private villas in Nouakchott. Common methods included kicking, beating, electric shocks, cigarette burns, sexual violence, suspension by the arms, shackling in painful positions, and deprivation of sleep and food.

Restricted access to the outside world and failure to establish effective mechanisms for complaint and investigation continued to be key factors allowing torture to persist.

Allegations of torture and other ill-treatment were recorded from scores of people including detainees at Dar Naïm prison. Some detainees, especially alleged Islamist activists, reported that they had been tortured with electric shocks. One said that he was given electric shocks on the soles of his feet. Another said that he was blindfolded, his hands and feet were tied behind his back and he was given electric shocks. A third told Amnesty International that the security forces urinated on him and inserted a truncheon in his anus.

Prison conditions

Hundreds of detainees continued to be held in overcrowded conditions with inadequate sanitation and health care, and poor quality food.

Detainees in Dar Naïm and Nouadhibou prisons were pressed up against one another in stifling heat and were rarely allowed to leave their cells.

Prison officials confirmed that the prisons in Dar Naïm and in Nouadhibou did not meet national standards. In particular, they stressed inadequacies in the water disposal system, damp and the lack of ventilation in cells.

Around 30 prisoners with mental health problems were left to wander around the cells with no medical care in Dar Naïm prison. Detainees in Nouadhibou, Dar Naïm and Nouakchott civil prison complained about brutality and corporal punishment. Prisoners were regularly beaten by guards if they asked to see the prison administrator or sought medical care. One prisoner alleged that he was beaten and left tied up for two weeks after a group of prisoners complained about the lack of food and medical care. At least eight Islamist detainees held in Nouakchott civil prison were beaten by guards in October.

Migrants' rights

Hundreds of people suspected of trying to reach European countries were arbitrarily arrested during the year, without evidence of their intentions and even though it is not an offence to leave Mauritania irregularly. Many were expelled from Mauritania, not necessarily to their home countries, and often in large groups. They had no opportunity to challenge the legality of their detention or their collective expulsion. These measures appeared to be a consequence of pressure from the EU, particularly Spain, to control migration to Europe.

Many migrants were held in a detention centre at Nouadhibou, northern Mauritania, known locally as Guantanamito, where some were ill-treated. This former school received up to 300 people a month but was not subject to any judicial control.

Refugees and asylum-seekers

Some refugees and asylum-seekers were denied their rights. Most came from West Africa, particularly Liberia and Sierra Leone.

Death penalty

According to official figures, there were 37 prisoners under sentence of death, held together with other prisoners in six prisons, including Dar Naïm and Nouadhibou prisons.

A number claimed that their trials had been unfair, asserting that they were not allowed to defend themselves properly or that they did not have a lawyer. One prisoner alleged he was sentenced solely on the basis of confessions obtained under torture. Another claimed that he was sentenced after he was forced to sign a police statement in a language he could not read.

Slavery

Although slavery was officially abolished in 1981 and made a criminal offence in 2007, evidence indicated the continued existence of the practice. People were believed to be held in forced labour or slavery in the regions of Tiris Zemour and Nema. In September a former slave wrote to the authorities asking them to look for 14 members of his family still held in slavery in Tiris Zemour.

Amnesty International visits/reports

🚌 Amnesty International delegates visited Mauritania in January, February, July and November.

M

📖 Mauritania: "Nobody wants to have anything to do with us" – arrests
and collective expulsions of migrants denied entry into Europe
(AFR 38/001/2008)

📖 Mauritania: Amnesty International calls for the release of the President
of the Republic and respect for fundamental freedoms (AFR 38/007/2008)

📖 Mauritania: Peaceful demonstrations demanding restoration of the rule
of law violently repressed (AFR 38/008/2008)

📖 Mauritania: Torture at the heart of the state (AFR 38/009/2008)

MEXICO

UNITED MEXICAN STATES

Head of state and government:	Felipe Calderón Hinojosa
Death penalty:	abolitionist for all crimes
Population:	107.8 million
Life expectancy:	75.6 years
Under-5 mortality (m/f):	22/17 per 1,000
Adult literacy:	91.6 per cent

Serious human rights violations committed by members of the military and police included unlawful killings, excessive use of force, torture and arbitrary detention. Several journalists were killed. Human rights defenders faced threats, fabricated criminal charges and unfair judicial proceedings. People protesting against economic development projects faced harassment. The Supreme Court rejected a constitutional challenge to Mexico City's law decriminalizing abortion. Reforms to the criminal justice system were initiated. Violence against women remained widespread.

Background

Public security and reform of the energy sector dominated political debate. Thousands of federal police and 45,000 military personnel were deployed in operations targeting organized crime. However, levels of violence attributed to these networks increased; media reports indicated that more than 6,000 people were killed in such violent incidents during the year. Scores of security force personnel were also killed or injured in the line of duty.

■ In September, the bodies of 24 murdered men were found in La Marquesa National Park, Mexico State. In an alleged reprisal attack by a drug gang, two grenades were thrown into crowds celebrating Mexico's Independence Day in Morelia, Michoacán State, killing eight people and wounding many others. In October federal police arrested three men in connection with the grenade attack. The men confessed, although they filed a legal complaint for torture while in pre-charge detention.

Measures adopted to combat crime included harsher sentencing and the incorporation of 80-day pre-charge detention (*arraigo*) into the Constitution. In September, federal and state institutions signed the National Accord for Security, Justice and Legality to improve co-ordination of policing and other security measures. In December, public security legislation regulating police forces was approved by Congress, but human rights safeguards were not strengthened.

In June, the US Congress approved the Merida Initiative which provides for US$400 million in funding for Mexico. The package included the provision of equipment and training to the Mexican police and army as well as justice and immigration officials. Fifteen per cent of the funding for the military was withheld pending US Secretary of State reports that Mexico had met human rights conditions. These included credible investigations to identify those responsible for the killing of US video-journalist Bradley Roland Will during political disturbances in Oaxaca in 2006. In October, Juan Manuel Martínez Moreno, a member of a political opposition group, was detained and charged by the Federal Attorney General's Office with the murder of Bradley Will. Many, including independent forensic experts and the National Human Rights Commission, criticized the basis of the detention, fearing that those charged in the case may have been scapegoated to demonstrate compliance with Merida Initiative conditions.

In August the government published its National Human Rights Programme but this did not make clear how or when the broad commitments would be delivered. Many civil society organizations criticized the government's failure to maintain a dialogue with them in order to develop a substantive human rights agenda. The government and the UN High Commissioner for Human Rights renewed the agreement to maintain an office in Mexico.

Human rights defenders

Human rights defenders continued to face threats, attacks, politically motivated criminal charges and

M

imprisonment for leading protests or promoting respect for human rights. The government agreed to provide the protection measures ordered by the Inter-American Commission on Human Rights to several human rights defenders. However, some defenders reported that no substantial efforts were made to investigate their cases or provide effective protection.

■ In April, five members of the Me' phaa Indigenous People's Organization (Organización de Pueblos Indigenas Me' phaa, OPIM) from the municipality of Ayutla, Guerrero State were detained and accused of the murder of Alejandro Feliciano García on 1 January. OPIM has consistently campaigned against the marginalization of the Me' phaa community and promoted Indigenous Peoples' rights. Despite a federal injunction in favour of four of the detainees and compelling evidence that the case was politically motivated, all five remained in custody at the end of the year. They were prisoners of conscience.

Several economic development and investment projects gave rise to protests by local communities over the lack of adequate consultation and the potential negative impact on social, environmental and other rights. Indigenous communities faced a particularly high number of reprisals.

■ In the community of Huizopa, Madera municipality, Chihuahua State, inhabitants demanding that mining operations on communal lands comply with agreements made with the community, faced threats and police operations to break up their legal demonstrations.

Police and security forces
Military

There were increasing reports implicating military personnel in unlawful killings, torture, ill-treatment, arbitrary detention and illegal house searches. The military justice system retained jurisdiction to investigate and prosecute military personnel accused of human rights violations. The National Human Rights Commission issued nine recommendations regarding serious abuses committed by soldiers during 2008.

■ In March, military personnel opened fire on a vehicle in Santiago de los Caballeros, Badiraguato municipality, Sinaloa State, killing four men and wounding two others. There was no evidence that the victims were armed or posed a threat. Five soldiers were in military custody under investigation at the end of the year. A petition for an injunction filed by relatives

to prevent the military claiming jurisdiction in the case remained pending at the end of the year.

Police

Unlawful killings, torture, excessive use of force and arbitrary detention by police remained widespread. Measures were initiated to create a single federal police force with strengthened investigative powers. However, there were no major initiatives to strengthen police accountability for human rights violations and at state and municipal level police forces remained unreformed.

■ In September, Federal Preventive Police reportedly shot and killed a 17-year-old passer-by when they unnecessarily and without warning fired several rounds of bullets at a car in Matamoros, Tamaulipas State. The car's occupants, Carlos Solis and Luis Alberto Salas, were arrested and accused of the killing, despite witnesses stating that police fired the only shots. The two men were reportedly tortured in custody and were awaiting trial on charges of possessing arms at the end of the year.

■ In October, six members of the Indigenous community of Miguel Hidalgo, La Trinitaria municipality, Chiapas State, were shot and killed by state police. At least four were killed in circumstances which suggested that they were executed. Several officers were arrested and 26 were reportedly under investigation at the end of the year.

■ More than 30 prisoners died during riots at La Mesa state prison in Tijuana, Baja California, in September. The director of the Baja California Human Rights Commission concluded some of the deaths were the result of excessive use of force and other human rights violations committed by the security forces responsible for the operation.

Torture and other ill-treatment

Torture and other ill-treatment remained widespread. Despite various initiatives, there was little improvement in the effective prosecution of perpetrators. In August, the UN Subcommittee on Prevention of Torture visited detention facilities in several states and received information on numerous cases of torture. The findings of the Subcommittee remained confidential.

■ In February, Eliseo Silvano Espinoza and Eliseo Silvano Jiménez, two Tzeltal Indigenous men, were detained in Chilón, Chiapas State, by the State Highway Police. They were reportedly shot at, beaten, almost

M

suffocated, threatened and sprayed with tear gas to try to extract a confession. The two men were subsequently released without charge. Two police officers were in custody under investigation at the end of the year.

■ In October, teachers and community supporters held protests in Morelos State. In the town of Xoxocotla federal police broke up protests on a main highway. Many of those detained alleged they had been arrested in their homes, beaten and some forced to walk barefoot on hot cinders.

Freedom of expression – journalists

At least five media workers were killed and the whereabouts of at least one other who was abducted remained unknown. Impunity for these crimes and other attacks on journalists attributed to criminal gangs persisted.

■ In April, two Indigenous women, Felícitas Martínez and Teresa Bautista, working with a community radio station in the Triqui region of Oaxaca State, were killed when armed men fired on the car they were travelling in. The authorities denied their murder was related to their media work, but failed to conduct a full investigation.

Impunity

Impunity for past and recent human rights violations persisted. The lack of effective institutions to investigate and prosecute human rights violations at federal or state level seriously restricted accountability and access to justice.

■ On the 40th anniversary of the Tlatelolco Square massacre, when government forces gunned down protesters in Mexico City in circumstances that have never been clarified, those responsible were no closer to being held to account. A federal court review of a previous ruling that former President Echeverría should not stand trial for genocide in connection with the Tlatelolco massacre was pending at the end of the year.

There were no judicial advances or government commitments to hold to account those responsible for hundreds of cases of extrajudicial killings, enforced disappearances and torture committed during the 1960s, 1970s and 1980s.

■ The case of Rosendo Radilla, who was forcibly disappeared by the security forces in 1976 and whose whereabouts have never been established, was presented to the Inter-American Court of Human Rights in June.

Investigations into recent emblematic cases, such as torture and other ill-treatment of scores of protesters in Guadalajara in 2004; the torture, including rape, of at least 26 women detainees in San Salvador Atenco in May 2006; and dozens of cases of torture, arbitrary detention and unlawful killing, during the political crisis in Oaxaca in 2006 and 2007, produced almost no positive results. The results of National Supreme Court enquiries into abuses in San Salvador Atenco and Oaxaca remained pending at the end of the year.

■ The whereabouts of Edmundo Reyes Amaya and Gabriel Alberto Cruz Sánchez, two members of the Popular Revolutionary Army (Ejército Popular Revolucionario, EPR), who were feared to have been forcibly disappeared in May 2007, remained unknown after the federal investigation failed to make progress.

Violence against women and girls

In August, the National Supreme Court rejected constitutional challenges to reforms made in 2007 to Mexico City's legislation decriminalizing abortion in the first 12 weeks of pregnancy.

Violence against women in the home, community and workplace remained pervasive. The government again failed to publish new procedures for medical professionals to attend to women survivors of violence.

Twenty-eight states enacted legislation on women's access to a life free from violence, but only the federal authorities and three state governments issued executive regulations to implement this new legislation. Funding commitments for many women's refuges were delayed, placing severe strain on the network of services.

■ In the context of spiralling violent crime, more than 75 women were murdered in Ciudad Juárez, Chihuahua State. Human rights defenders pressing for justice on cases of murdered or abducted women and girls faced threats and intimidation.

■ Three of the cases of eight women found murdered in Campo Algodonero, Ciudad Juárez, in 2001 were brought before the Inter-American Court of Human Rights.

Migrants

The number of migrants crossing the border into the USA reportedly declined, while deportations to Mexico increased. Irregular migrants in Mexico faced abuses such as extortion, beatings, kidnap, rape and murder by officials or criminal gangs that often operated with

M

the complicity of local authorities. Those responsible for these crimes were virtually never held to account. Federal legislative reforms reduced the punishment for the offence of illegal presence in Mexico from imprisonment to a fine. Detention prior to repatriation remained the norm for almost all migrants. Training for migrant officials on child protection rights was increased. The UN Special Rapporteur on the human rights of migrants visited Mexico in March and expressed grave concern at the treatment of Central American migrants.

■ In April, photos taken of a joint migration services and navy operation to detain irregular migrants in Las Palmas, Niltepec municipality, Oaxaca State, were published in the media. The images, which showed migrants being subject to beatings and humiliation, were confirmed by eyewitness testimony. Nevertheless, migration services and the navy denied that abuses took place.

■ Father Alejandro Solalinde and co-workers at the hostel in Ciudad Ixtepec, Oaxaca, which provides migrants with humanitarian assistance and documents abuses against them, faced repeated threats in reprisal for their work.

Legal, constitutional or institutional developments

Major reforms were made to the Federal Constitution affecting public security and the criminal justice system, including the introduction of oral trials and improvements to due process for ordinary crimes, such as the presumption of innocence. However, reforms increased the powers of prosecutors investigating serious federal offences without ensuring adequate controls. An eight-year period was established for introducing reforms, and a special governmental committee was established to develop legislative proposals to implement reforms at federal level. Reforms in most states had not begun.

Reforms to incorporate international human rights treaties explicitly into the Constitution were blocked.

Amnesty international reports

📄 Women's struggle for Justice and safety – Violence in the family in Mexico (AMR 41/021/2008)

📄 Amnesty International Submission to the UN Universal Periodic Review (AMR 41/038/2008)

📄 Promoting Indigenous Rights in Mexico: Me' phaa Indigenous People's Organization (AMR 41/040/2008)

MOLDOVA

REPUBLIC OF MOLDOVA

Head of state:	Vladimir Voronin
Head of government:	Zinaida Greceanîi (replaced Vasile Tarlev in March)
Death penalty:	abolitionist for all crimes
Population:	3.8 million
Life expectancy:	68.4 years
Under-5 mortality (m/f):	21/17 per 1,000
Adult literacy:	99.1 per cent

There were continuing reports of torture and other ill-treatment and the perpetrators continued to enjoy impunity. A progressive new law on freedom of expression was introduced, but practice and attitudes failed to keep pace with these changes. International bodies commented that certain groups suffered discrimination, and acts of racial discrimination were not prosecuted effectively.

Torture and other ill-treatment

On 14 March, the parliament passed a law which could help to prevent torture and reduce impunity for torture and other ill-treatment. Among the changes, the Criminal Procedural Code was amended so that the institution in which the alleged victim was detained had to prove that the torture and other ill-treatment did not occur. Previously, the burden of proof had lain with the victims, who had to prove that they were tortured or otherwise ill-treated.

The Consultative Council within the Parliamentary Ombudsman's office, which is intended to monitor places of detention in accordance with Moldova's obligations under the Optional Protocol to the UN Convention against Torture, was functional by March. However, concerns remained that the Council was not adequately funded or sufficiently independent from the Parliamentary Ombudsman's office. There were continued reports of torture and other ill-treatment in police custody.

■ In February, brothers Vasiliu and Petru Livadari were allegedly beaten by staff in Cricova prison because of their complaints about their treatment and conditions in prison. After they complained to the Ombudsman they were reportedly threatened that they would be beaten to death. On the insistence of the Ombudsman, the two prisoners were moved, but the prosecutors who

M

arrived at Cricova prison to investigate the allegations tried to dissuade the brothers from making a complaint. On 6 March, the Ministry of Justice, which has jurisdiction over the prison service in Moldova, stated that Vasiliu and Petru Livadari had been transferred to a prison hospital where they were receiving medical treatment, but that there was no evidence that they had been ill-treated. However, the Prosecutor General's office announced on 4 April that two prison officers had been charged with torture under Article 309/1 of the Criminal Code. The case was ongoing at the end of the year.

Impunity

Perpetrators of torture and other ill-treatment continued to enjoy impunity because of a flawed and ineffective system of investigations, and a lack of political will to prosecute the perpetrators.

■ In February, Viorica Plate informed Amnesty International that she and her lawyer had been harassed by police. Viorica Plate had been tortured by police officers in Chişinău in May 2007, and on 1 November 2007 two of the officers were sentenced to six years' imprisonment and one was given a suspended sentence. She accused the police officers who had been convicted of torturing her of harassment, and said that two of the officers had not been detained. On 6 March, the Prosecutor General's Office said that the officers in question had not been detained because they were appealing against their sentence, and that it was not considered necessary to take protective measures on behalf of Viorica Plate.

■ On 23 June, the Chişinău Prosecutor's Office again refused a request to open a criminal case concerning the allegations of torture made by Sergei Gurgurov. Sergei Gurgurov allegedly sustained head and spinal injuries at the hands of the police in Chişinău in October 2005 and had been left permanently disabled.

Freedom of expression

On 22 February, the Moldovan parliament passed a new law on assembly which came into force on 22 April. The new law, drafted after extensive consultation with civil society, was a significant step towards greater freedom of expression in Moldova. Organizers of public events have to inform local authorities of the event, but are no longer required to seek permission, and assemblies of fewer than 50 individuals can meet spontaneously without notification. The law also stipulates that assemblies can only be prohibited by a court. However, despite these progressive provisions, police and local authorities continued to restrict freedom of expression. According to monitoring carried out by a local NGO, the Resource Centre for Human Rights, police presence at demonstrations, the number of detentions and the use of force by police had increased since the new law came into force. People were prevented from demonstrating peacefully or detained for short periods if they did, although most prosecutions brought by the police were not upheld by the courts.

■ On 8 May, the Chişinău Mayor's Office banned a demonstration by lesbian, gay, bisexual and transgender (LGBT) activists. The NGO Genderdoc-M had informed the Mayor's office about its intention to demonstrate outside parliament in favour of the new anti-discrimination law. In a written notification the Mayor's Office stated that religious organizations, school students and residents of the capital had reacted negatively to the planned demonstration and "accused sexual minorities of aggressiveness and violation of spiritual and moral values". Therefore, to "avoid any tension in society", it was necessary to prohibit the planned public meeting for the protection of the demonstrators. When the activists arrived at parliament by bus on 11 May, they were surrounded by approximately 300 aggressive counter-demonstrators, who prevented them from leaving the bus. Onlookers reported that there were very few police officers present at the scene, and despite the rising tension they took no action to protect the LGBT activists, who were forced to leave the area. Nobody was injured.

■ On 30 April, Oleg Brega of the freedom of expression organization Hyde Park was detained by police for protesting peacefully and alone in the centre of Chişinău on the anniversary of the founding of the state broadcasting company. Police tried to prevent him protesting and charged him with hooliganism. On 8 May, the court sentenced him to three days' detention for swearing in public. His brother Ghenadie Brega was fined for protesting in public against Oleg Brega's detention. Oleg Brega was acquitted by the Court of Appeal on 27 May.

Discrimination

On 29 April, the European Commission against Racism and Intolerance published its third report on Moldova, and on 16 May the UN Committee on the Elimination of all Forms of Racial Discrimination published its concluding observations on the fifth to seventh periodic reports of Moldova. Both bodies expressed concern that existing legislation banning the incitement of racial, national and religious hatred was not being implemented, that Muslim ethnic minority organizations were being denied registration, and that acts of discrimination including racial discrimination by the police were not being prosecuted effectively.

In June, the Ministry of Justice circulated a draft Law on Preventing and Combating Discrimination for comment by civil society. The new law was based on international standards and was progressive in its inclusion of civil society in the drafting of the law. However, it concentrated on the negative obligation not to discriminate and did not include the positive duty to promote equality.

International justice

On 11 February, President Voronin submitted a bill for the ratification of the Rome Statute of the International Criminal Court to parliament. However, progress towards ratification continued to be slow. Moldova signed the Rome Statute in 2000, but it was not until 2006 that the Ministry of Justice drafted the ratification law. On 2 October 2007, the Constitutional Court ruled that Moldova could ratify the Rome Statute without requiring a change in the Constitution.

MONGOLIA

MONGOLIA

Head of state:	Nambaryn Enkhbayar
Head of government:	Sanjaagiin Bayar
Death penalty:	Retentionist
Population:	2.7 million
Life expectancy:	65.9 years
Under-5 mortality (m/f):	57/49 per 1,000
Adult literacy:	97.8 per cent

In July, riots broke out in the capital, Ulaanbaatar, amid allegations of widespread electoral fraud – five people were killed and hundreds injured. Police arrested more than 700 people and denied them access to a lawyer, relatives and medical care. There were reports of detainees being beaten by police while in custody. The death penalty continued to be carried out in secret.

Background

Parliamentary elections were held on 29 June. A coalition government was formed by the majority Mongolian People's Revolutionary Party and the minority Democratic Party.

Suppression of violent protests

On 1 July, following allegations of electoral fraud, protesters in Ulaanbaatar set fire to the Mongolian People's Revolutionary Party headquarters and looted commercial offices. On 2 July, a state of emergency was declared for four days. Hundreds of people, including police officers, were injured. Local media reported that police used tear gas, rubber bullets and live ammunition to suppress the rioters. Five people died, four from gunshot wounds. Ten police officers were arrested in relation to the shootings. The Chief of Police was removed from his position. The heads of the Ulaanbaatar Police, the Security Police and the Patrol Police were moved to positions in the Police Academy. A State General Prosecutor's Office investigation into the shootings was ongoing at the end of the year.

■ On 2 July, police shot Enkhbayar Dorjsuren, aged 24, in the neck in Ulaanbaatar. When he failed to report for work the next day, his family searched for him and discovered his body in the morgue. An autopsy had been performed without their knowledge. No information about the investigation into the killing was made available.

Arbitrary arrests, detention and ill-treatment

In the early hours of 2 July, police arrested more than 700 people in the vicinity of the riots. Two hundred and fifty-nine people, including 27 children, were charged with crimes such as organizing chaos, theft and robbery. In some cases children were held with adults. Access to a lawyer and medical care was denied in the early weeks of detention. There were reports of police beating detainees, sometimes in order to obtain confessions, and in some cases detainees reported being beaten by other detainees.

■ On 3 July, the police arrested Davaasuren Batzaya, aged 23, for inciting public disorder and looting. He

M

was taken to Chingeltei Detention Centre. Despite being deaf, Davaasuren Batzaya was not given access to an interpreter or a lawyer. According to his family, he was beaten by police and other detainees. On 6 July, he was transferred to Gants Khudag Detention Centre before being released on bail on 10 July.

■ On 5 July, police arrested Jalbasuren Batzandan, Chairperson of the Civil Movement Party. On 7 July, Vice Chairperson Otgonjargal Magnai was also arrested. According to family members, they both gave speeches at the protests in which they discussed the allegations of electoral fraud and urged non-violent protest. Jalbasuren Batzandan was released on bail on 19 August. Otgonjargal Magnai was released on bail on 28 August. Both men are facing charges of "banditry" and "creating mass disorder". Otgonjargal Magnai is also facing a charge of assault. The crime of "banditry" carries a minimum sentence of 20-25 years' imprisonment or the death penalty.

Freedom of expression

The authorities arrested or fined people who were critical of the government's handling of the riots. Only the state-funded television channel was permitted to broadcast during the state of emergency.

Death penalty

Executions were carried out in secret and no official statistics on death sentences or executions were available. Conditions of detention for prisoners on death row were reported to be poor. Prisoners were typically on death row for 12 months, but some were on death row for more than 24 months.

In December, Mongolia voted against a UN General Assembly resolution calling for a worldwide moratorium on executions.

Legal developments

Mongolia acceded to the Protocol to Prevent, Suppress and Punish Trafficking in Persons, Especially Women and Children, Supplementing the UN Convention against Transnational Organized Crime (Palermo Protocol).

MONTENEGRO

REPUBLIC OF MONTENEGRO

Head of state:	Filip Vujanović
Head of government:	Milo Đukanović (replaced Željko Šturanović in February)
Death penalty:	abolitionist for all crimes
Population:	0.6 million
Life expectancy:	74.1 years
Under-5 mortality (m/f):	25/23 per 1,000
Adult literacy:	96.4 per cent

The authorities did not resolve impunity for cases of enforced disappearances, alleged political killings and police ill-treatment. Journalists were denied freedom of expression. Roma, including refugees from Kosovo, were denied access to basic rights.

Background

Milo Đukanović was elected Prime Minister for the third time. In March he was questioned by the Italian authorities in connection with an investigation into money laundering and cigarette smuggling between Montenegro and Italy between 1994 and 2002; charges were filed against six of his close associates in October.

International justice – war crimes

In July, the Appeals Panel at the International Criminal Tribunal for the former Yugoslavia decided that former Yugoslav National Army (JNA) commander Pavle Strugar should be convicted on two further counts, in addition to his conviction in 2005 for failing to prevent the 1991 attack on Dubrovnik launched from Montenegro. However, his original eight-year sentence was reduced by six months due to his ill-health.

Justice system – war crimes

In August, four former JNA Montenegrin reservists indicted by the Montenegrin courts were arrested for the torture and inhumane treatment of 169 Croatian civilians and prisoners of war at Morinj camp between 1991 and 1992. Seven former JNA soldiers were also arrested for the murder of 23 Kosovo Albanian civilians near Rozaje in April 1999.

M

Enforced disappearances

Judicial investigations proceeded slowly into the enforced disappearance in 1992 of 83 Bosnian Muslims (Bosniaks) who had fled to Montenegro from the then Republic of Bosnia and Herzegovina (RBiH). In May, a retired senior police officer testified that the then Minister of Interior Pavel Bulatović had ordered that the Bosniaks be detained and handed over to the Bosnian Serb Army. In June, Milo Đukanović, also Prime Minister in 1992, denied knowledge of the "deportations".

On 25 December, the government recognized the state's responsibility for the enforced disappearances. In this unprecedented decision, they agreed to provide reparations to nine survivors and their families, and to the relatives of those who were killed as a result of their unlawful "deportation" by the Montenegrin police to Bosnian Serb military forces.

Torture and other ill-treatment

There was no progress in the bringing to justice of those responsible for the alleged torture of some members of a group of ethnic Albanians arrested in September 2006 during Operation Orlov let (Eagle's flight).

Proceedings against the group of 12 men, including four US citizens, and five others had opened in May 2007 at Podgorica District Court. The case was not conducted in accordance with international standards as the evidence against them included testimonies extracted under duress or unlawfully obtained. In August, 12 out of the 17 men were convicted of association for the purposes of terrorism and sentenced to prison terms of up to six and a half years. The others were convicted of possessing firearms and received suspended sentences, although the court subsequently ordered their detention.

In October, five members of the Special Anti-Terrorist Unit involved in Operation Orlov let were convicted and sentenced to three months' imprisonment for the ill-treatment of Peter Sinistaj, father of one of the detainees.

Allegations of ill-treatment followed the arrest of more than 100 people involved in demonstrations in October against Montenegro's recognition of Kosovo; investigations were opened, including into allegations by Aleksandar Pejanović that he had been beaten with sticks by masked police officers.

Unlawful killings

■ Proceedings opened on 9 September against Damir Mandić, after the Appeals Court overturned his acquittal in December 2006 for the murder of Duško Jovanović, editor-in-chief of the newspaper *Dan,* in 2004.

Freedom of expression – journalists

Journalists critical of the government were criminally indicted for defamation.

■ In May, Željko Ivanović, managing editor of the newspaper *Vijesti* who had accused the Prime Minister Milo Đukanović of complicity in an assault on him in 2007, was convicted of inflicting mental suffering on the Prime Minister and fined €20,000.

■ In May, sports journalist Mladen Stojović, a contributor to Belgrade-radio B92's investigation into the football mafia, was seriously assaulted in his apartment in the town of Bar.

Discrimination – Roma and Roma refugees

The authorities failed to address discrimination against Roma, the majority of whom were denied access to citizenship due to a lack of personal documentation, and consequently excluded from access to basic rights. An estimated 60 per cent of Romani children were denied education and some 82 per cent of adults were unemployed.

UNHCR, the UN refugee agency, reported that 4,458 Roma, Ashkali and Egyptian refugees from Kosovo remained in Montenegro; defined as internally displaced persons and denied refugee status, they remained at risk of statelessness.

Violence against women and girls

In July, Montenegro ratified the Council of Europe Convention on Action against Trafficking in Human Beings. In June, the authorities arrested a group responsible for trafficking, via Montenegro, two Ukrainian women for the purposes of sexual exploitation in Kosovo.

Despite an increase in the number of domestic violence incidents reported to the police, arrest, prosecution and conviction rates remained low.

Amnesty International report

📃 Montenegro: Submission to the UN Universal Periodic Review, (EUR 66/001/2008)

MOROCCO/ WESTERN SAHARA

KINGDOM OF MOROCCO

Head of state:	King Mohamed VI
Head of government:	Abbas El Fassi
Death penalty:	abolitionist in practice
Population:	31.6 million
Life expectancy:	70.4 years
Under-5 mortality (m/f):	42/28 per 1,000
Adult literacy:	52.3 per cent

The rights to freedom of expression, association and assembly continued to be restricted. Criticism of the monarchy or views contradicting the official position on other politically sensitive issues were penalized. The authorities used excessive force to break up anti-government protests. Proponents of self-determination for the people of Western Sahara were harassed and prosecuted. Allegations of torture were not investigated, and victims of past human rights violations were not granted effective access to justice. The authorities continued to arrest, detain and collectively deport thousands of foreign nationals. At least four people were sentenced to death, but the government maintained a de facto moratorium on executions.

Background

In March, UN-mediated talks on the Western Sahara between the Moroccan government and the Polisario Front, which calls for an independent state in Western Sahara and runs a self-proclaimed government-in-exile in refugee camps in south-western Algeria, ended in stalemate. Morocco insisted on an autonomy plan for the territory annexed in 1975, while the Polisario Front called for a referendum on self-determination, as agreed in previous UN Security Council resolutions. The UN Security Council extended the mandate of the UN Mission for the Referendum in Western Sahara until 30 April 2009. The mandate makes no provision for human rights monitoring.

In October, the EU and Morocco agreed an "ambitious roadmap" towards granting Morocco "advanced status" with the EU, including closer security, political, trade and other co-operation.

Among recommendations made by several states when Morocco was considered under the Universal Periodic Review process in April were harmonization of national law with international standards and respect for migrants' rights. However, the issue of impunity for torturers was not raised.

Repression of dissent

Critics of the monarchy

Criticism of the monarchy remained taboo. Human rights defenders, journalists and others were prosecuted for expressing views that the authorities deemed offensive to the King and the royal family.

■ In February, the Court of Cassation confirmed prison terms imposed on three members of the Moroccan Association for Human Rights (AMDH) for "undermining the monarchy" by participating in a peaceful protest in June 2007. In April, they and 14 other AMDH members accused on similar grounds were granted a royal pardon.

■ In September, the Court of Appeal in Agadir overturned on procedural grounds the two-year prison sentence against blogger Mohamed Erraji. He had been convicted of "lack of respect due to the King" after writing an online article suggesting that the King encouraged a culture of economic dependence.

■ In November, the Court of Appeals in Marrakesh upheld the conviction of Yassine Bellasal, aged 18, for insulting the King but suspended the one-year prison sentence imposed by a lower court. He had written on a school wall "God, the Nation, Barça" – the last a reference to the Barcelona football team – in a play on words of the country's motto "God, the Nation, the King".

Sahrawi activists

Sahrawi human rights activists continued to face harassment, including politically motivated charges, restrictions on movement and administrative obstruction to prevent their organizations' legal registration.

■ Ennaâma Asfari, co-President of the Committee for the Respect of Freedoms and Human Rights in Western Sahara, who lives in France, alleged that he was tortured by Moroccan security forces when he was detained while visiting the region in April. The authorities did not investigate his allegations and he was convicted of violent conduct and jailed for two months.

■ Brahim Sabbar, head of the Sahrawi Association of Victims of Grave Human Rights Violations Committed by the Moroccan State (ASVDH), was told by the security authorities that he should not visit areas in Laayoune in which other ASVDH members live after he was released from prison in June.

Hundreds of Sahrawis suspected of demonstrating against Moroccan rule or distributing pro-Polisario Front materials were arrested. Some were released after questioning; others were tried on charges of violent conduct in proceedings that were reported not to have complied with international standards of fair trial. Many complained that they were tortured or otherwise ill-treated by security forces during questioning and that information allegedly obtained under torture was used as evidence in convictions.

■ In October, Yahya Mohamed Elhafed Iaazza, a member of the Collective of Sahrawi Human Rights Defenders, was found guilty of violent conduct and sentenced to 15 years' imprisonment in connection with his participation in a protest in Tan Tan against Moroccan rule. Eight other defendants received sentences of up to four years in prison. Allegations that they were tortured during questioning were not investigated.

Al-Adl wal-Ihsan activists

Hundreds of members of the unauthorized political organization Al-Adl wal-Ihsan were questioned by police and at least 188 were charged with participating in unauthorized meetings or belonging to an unauthorized organization. The trial of the group's spokesperson, Nadia Yassine, charged in 2005 with defaming the monarchy, was postponed.

Excessive use of force

Security forces used excessive force to disperse anti-government demonstrations, highlighting the failure of the authorities to implement a key recommendation of the Equity and Reconciliation Commission (IER). Established in 2004 to look into grave human rights violations committed between 1956 and 1999, the IER called in 2006 for improved regulation of the state's security organs.

■ On 7 June, security forces were reported to have used excessive force to end a blockade of the port of Sidi Ifni established by protesters on 30 May. The security forces reportedly fired rubber bullets and tear gas, and used batons and police dogs. They also conducted unauthorized raids on homes, confiscated property, verbally and sexually harassed people, and carried out arbitrary arrests and detentions.

Subsequently, 21 people, including four members of the Moroccan Centre for Human Rights (CMDH), were charged with violent conduct. A report by the parliamentary commission established on 18 June to investigate the Sidi Ifni events was made public in December. While affirming that the security intervention was justified, the report outlined a number of abuses committed by law enforcement forces, including violence against individuals. It called on the authorities to identify and bring to justice all citizens and members of the security forces responsible for illegal conduct and human rights abuses. To Amnesty International's knowledge, no law enforcement officer had been charged by the end of the year.

■ In July, Brahim Sabbaa Al-Layl, a CMDH member, was imprisoned for six months after stating in an interview with Al Jazeera television that people had been killed and raped in Sidi Ifni. The journalist who interviewed him had his press accreditation withdrawn by the authorities and was ordered by a court to pay a heavy fine.

■ Security forces were reported to have used excessive force to prevent a planned student protest march at Cadi Ayyad Marrakesh University in May. They raided the university campus, assaulting and arbitrarily detaining students, and confiscating personal belongings. Eighteen members of the National Union of Moroccan Students were arrested, including supporters of the leftist Democratic Path student movement. In June, seven people were sentenced to one-year prison terms for violent conduct; the remainder were awaiting trial at the end of the year. All alleged that they were tortured and otherwise ill-treated in police custody.

Counter-terror and security

Some 190 suspected Islamist militants were convicted of terrorism-related offences and sentenced to prison terms ranging from six months to life. According to reports, they included a Moroccan national who had been forcibly returned from Spain.

In February, the authorities said they had broken up a terrorist network led by Abdelkader Belliraj, a Belgian-Moroccan dual national. Some 35 people were arrested, including the leaders of three political parties – Al-Badil al-Hadari, the Oumma and the Party of Justice and Development. The Prime Minister then issued a decree dissolving Al-Badil al-Hadari, and a court rejected the Oumma party's application for legal registration. The 35 faced a range of charges,

M

including attempted murder, money laundering and financing terrorism. Their trial began in October and had not been completed by the end of the year. Some defence lawyers complained that the authorities failed to provide them with complete case files, others reported that their clients were tortured in custody.

Hundreds of Islamist prisoners convicted after the 2003 Casablanca bombing continued to call for judicial review of their trials, many of which were tainted with unexamined claims of confessions extracted under torture.

Transitional justice

The Human Rights Advisory Board, charged with continuing the work of the IER, had still not published the list of all cases of enforced disappearances investigated by the IER. The IER's final report, published in January 2006, recommended measures to ensure non-repetition of grave human rights violations through a comprehensive programme of judicial and institutional reforms, but these had not yet been implemented. Nor was any progress made towards providing victims with effective access to justice or holding individual perpetrators to account, issues that were excluded from the remit of the IER.

In June, a court ordered *Al-Jarida Al-Oula* newspaper to stop publishing testimonies made by senior public officials to the IER, following a complaint by the President of the Human Rights Advisory Board. This intervention was widely criticized by local human rights organizations.

Discrimination and violence against women

In January the UN Committee on the Elimination of Discrimination against Women considered Morocco's third and fourth periodic reports on its application of the Convention on the Elimination of All Forms of Discrimination against Women. It welcomed positive steps taken by the government to address discrimination against women but called for the legal criminalization of violence against women and active measures to combat it. In November the Ministry of Social Development, Family and Solidarity announced that such a law was being developed.

In December, in a further welcome move, King Mohamed VI announced that Morocco would withdraw reservations it made when ratifying the Convention.

Discrimination – imprisonment for 'homosexual conduct'

In January an appeal court upheld prison terms of up to 10 months against six men convicted of "homosexual conduct" in Ksar El-Kebir, north-western Morocco. They were arrested in November 2007 after public denunciations that a private party they had held was a "gay marriage". Same-sex sexual relations between consenting adults are criminalized under Moroccan law.

In November, an appeal court upheld the conviction and heavy fine imposed by a lower court on the editor-in-chief of *Al-Massaa* for defamation of assistant Crown Prosecutors in Ksar el-Kebir, for having suggested that a Crown Prosecutor was present at the alleged "gay marriage". It appeared that the fine might cause the newspaper to cease publication.

Refugees, asylum-seekers and migrants

Thousands of people suspected of being irregular migrants were arrested and collectively expelled, mostly without any consideration of their protection needs and their right under Moroccan law to contest the decision to deport them or examine the grounds on which it was made. The authorities said they prevented 10,235 immigration attempts between January and November. Some migrants were reported to have been subjected to excessive force and other ill-treatment at the time of arrest or during their detention or expulsion; some were reported to have been dumped at the border with Algeria or Mauritania without adequate food and water.

■ At least 28 migrants, including four children, drowned in the sea off Al Hoceima on 28 April. Survivors alleged that Moroccan officials who intercepted their inflatable boat punctured and shook it when the migrants refused to stop. The authorities denied that their officials were responsible but did not carry out an investigation. The survivors were transported to the city of Oujda in eastern Morocco and left at the frontier with Algeria.

Polisario camps

Little independent information was available about conditions in the refugee camps run by the Polisario Front in Algeria. No steps were known to have been taken to address the impunity of those accused of committing human rights abuses in the camps in the 1970s and 1980s.

M

Amnesty International visit/report

🚗 An Amnesty International delegation visited Morocco and the Western Sahara in February/March.

📄 Morocco/Western Sahara: Investigate allegations of torture and grant detainees a fair trial (MDE 29/013/2008)

MOZAMBIQUE

REPUBLIC OF MOZAMBIQUE
Head of state:	Armando Guebuza
Head of government:	Luisa Diogo
Death penalty:	abolitionist for all crimes
Population:	21.8 million
Life expectancy:	42.8 years
Under-5 mortality (m/f):	170/153 per 1,000
Adult literacy:	38.7 per cent

Police continued to unlawfully kill suspects, possibly carrying out extrajudicial executions. At least six police officers were tried for human rights violations committed in previous years. Police used excessive force during demonstrations, killing at least three people and injuring more than 30. Freedom of expression was suppressed and journalists were increasingly harassed.

Background

Mozambique enacted three new laws in April relating to children: the Law on Child Protection; the Law on Trafficking of Persons, especially Women and Children; and the Law on Juvenile Justice.

The fight against corruption suffered a setback in January when the Anti-Corruption Forum was abolished on the grounds that the presidential decree establishing it was unconstitutional.

In September, the former Minister of the Interior, Almerino Manhenje, was arrested in connection with the disappearance of about US$8.8 million from the Ministry of Interior when he was the Minister between 1999 and 2005.

Between January and May, at least 22 prisoners died in the Chimoio Agricultural Penitentiary in Manica province. However, according to the Mozambican Human Rights League, prison conditions had improved.

At least 14 criminal suspects died after being lynched by mobs in the provinces of Maputo, Manica and Sofala between February and April. In Chimoio 29 people were arrested in connection with the lynching, three of whom were charged and found guilty of inciting violence. They were sentenced to six months' imprisonment.

At least 72 people died of cholera and other diseases brought on by floods that ravaged central Mozambique in early 2008, displacing more than 100,000 people from their homes.

Unlawful killings

Police continued to unlawfully kill criminal suspects and other people. They usually alleged that the victims were behaving in a suspicious manner or were criminals trying to escape. Some officers were reportedly arrested but were not brought to trial. In July, three police officers were sentenced to 21 years' imprisonment for the murder of three men at a football field in Costa do Sol in 2007. They were also ordered to pay US$25,000 compensation to the families of the victims. A member of the Presidential Guard was sentenced to 18 years' imprisonment for killing a man in the same area in 2006. However, the majority of police officers were not prosecuted for human rights violations.

■ Police shot and killed three alleged robbers in the Baixa area of Maputo in February. According to the police, the men were about to rob a bank and a factory. There were conflicting reports about what happened. An eyewitness said that one of the alleged robbers got out of the car, ran towards a nearby hotel and was shot dead. The other two were shot at by the car. According to other reports, one man was arrested when he got out of a parked vehicle. The police stated that he tried to escape while being taken to a police station and was shot dead. The other two were shot dead on the street corner near the factory.

Excessive use of force

Police used excessive force during demonstrations, killing several people.

■ In February, police fired what they claimed were rubber bullets at demonstrators in Maputo city who were protesting against an increase in transport fares. However, at least three people were killed and 30 injured by stray, live ammunition. Police also used live ammunition during related demonstrations in the

M

province of Gaza. A police spokesperson stated that live ammunition was used because some officers were caught by surprise by the rioters. No investigation was carried out into these incidents.

■ In March, police shot Celsio João Daimon in his home in Beira. The police, who were looking for an escaped prisoner and who were reportedly drunk, shot him with AKM rifles at close range when he emerged from a friend's room. He was hit in the thigh by three bullets. When the officers realized he was not the man they were looking for, they took his phone and left him. Celsio João Daimon's brother took him to the police station to report the incident. Members of the Rapid Intervention Force arrived and started beating him, apparently believing him to be the escaped prisoner. When they realized he was not, they took him to hospital, where he had to have his leg amputated. Three police officers were arrested and convicted in connection with this crime – two were fined and one sentenced to a four-year prison term. However, no action was taken against any member of the Rapid Intervention Force.

Freedom of expression

Freedom of expression was suppressed. In September, police stopped a demonstration called by war veterans demanding better living conditions. Nineteen were arrested and held for a few days before being released pending trial.

There was increasing harassment of journalists with defamation and criminal charges being used to suppress freedom of the press. Journalists were summoned for questioning by procurators to explain their work.

■ Three *Zambeze* newspaper journalists were tried in August on charges of defamation and threatening state security over an article questioning the Prime Minister's nationality. They were convicted and sentenced to six months' imprisonment, converted to a fine of 30 meticais (US$1.20).

Amnesty International visit/report

🚌 Amnesty International delegates visited Mozambique in May.

📖 Licence to Kill: Police accountability in Mozambique (AFR 41/001/2008)

MYANMAR

UNION OF MYANMAR

Head of state:	Senior General Than Shwe
Head of government:	General Thein Sein
Death penalty:	abolitionist in practice
Population:	49.2 million
Life expectancy:	60.8 years
Under-5 mortality (m/f):	105/87 per 1,000
Adult literacy:	89.9 per cent

In February, the government announced that a referendum would be held later in the year on a draft constitution, followed by elections in 2010. In May – only a week before the scheduled day for the referendum – Cyclone Nargis devastated parts of southern Myanmar, affecting approximately 2.4 million people. More than 84,500 people died and more than 19,000 were injured, while nearly 54,000 remained unaccounted for. In its aftermath the government delayed or placed conditions on aid delivery, and refused international donors permission to provide humanitarian assistance. Following a visit by the UN Secretary-General in late May, access improved, but the government continued to obstruct aid and forcibly evict survivors from shelters.

Also in May the government extended the house arrest of Daw Aung San Suu Kyi, General Secretary of the National League for Democracy (NLD), the main opposition party. By the end of the year there were more than 2,100 other political prisoners. Many were given sentences relating to the 2007 mass demonstrations after unfair trials. In eastern Myanmar, a military offensive targeting ethnic Karen civilians, amounting to crimes against humanity, continued into its fourth year. The government's development of oil, natural gas and hydropower projects in partnership with private and state-owned firms led to a range of human rights abuses.

Background

The commission established at the end of 2007 to draft a new constitution – the guidelines for which were 14 years in the making – completed its work in February. This marked the fourth step in the government's seven-step "Roadmap to Democracy", to be followed by the referendum, elections, and the

M

formation of a new government. The NLD had not participated in the process since 1995. In January, Daw Aung San Suu Kyi met with the government liaison official for the second time since the 2007 crackdown and with her own party leaders in November.

At year's end, there were more long-standing political prisoners behind bars in Myanmar than at any other time since the mass pro-democracy uprising in 1988, and nearly double the number in 2007. More than 2,100 political prisoners - many of them prisoners of conscience - remained behind bars.

Forced evictions

Within days of Cyclone Nargis, the government began to forcibly evict cyclone survivors from government and unofficial resettlement sites where they had fled after their homes were destroyed and their villages flooded. Amnesty International confirmed over 30 instances of forcible eviction by the government in the month following the cyclone alone. In many cases, assistance was either entirely lacking or inadequate. In addition, authorities evicted survivors taking emergency shelter in schools and monasteries in order to hold the constitutional referendum.

■ On 19 May in Bogale and Labutta in Ayeyarwady Division, local authorities forced large numbers of people onto boats in an effort to return them to their villages in Myaungmya and Maubin townships and elsewhere. By 25 May, only an estimated 10 per cent of the people originally displaced to Bogale remained there.

■ On 23 May, authorities in Yangon forcibly removed more than 3,000 cyclone survivors from an official camp in Shwebaukan township and from an unofficial camp in a State High School in Dala, both in Yangon Division.

■ On or just before 25 May, the authorities forcibly relocated around 600 people from an unofficial site at a State High School in Myaungmya to Labutta.

Forced evictions by local authorities were also linked to natural gas development and the South Korean-led Shwe Gas Project in western Rakhine State, and local authorities arrested and detained local residents who expressed opposition to the project. Other local residents fled into hiding. Elsewhere in Rakhine State, local authorities confiscated land from residents living near a Chinese-led onshore oil project to make way for the project.

Lack of humanitarian access

For three weeks after Cyclone Nargis struck Myanmar on 2-3 May, the government rejected offers of international assistance and blocked access to the Ayeyarwady delta at the time when survivors most needed food, shelter and access to medicine. Government officials also blocked private domestic donors from distributing aid in the delta. Some authorities conditioned aid and assistance on survivors' voting in favour of the government's draft constitution on 24 May, and on their willingness to work or join the army. Some soldiers and local government officials confiscated, diverted or otherwise misused aid intended for cyclone survivors.

Political prisoners

The government detained people for campaigning against the constitution, assisting cyclone survivors, and carrying out human rights and pro-democracy work. Ethnic minority leaders and activists were also detained for expressing concern about the status and role of their states and interests under the new constitution. In September, the government released 10 political prisoners. However, one of the released, prominent journalist and senior NLD official, U Win Htein, was rearrested a day later.

■ The government arrested at least 16 members of the protest group Generation Wave, many for their opposition to the constitutional referendum. In November, 10 of those arrested, including hip-hop star Zayar Thaw, were sentenced to up to seven and a half years' imprisonment for their peaceful political activities.

■ Elderly prisoner of conscience U Khun Htun Oo, the most senior political representative of the Shan ethnic minority, was in poor health. He was sentenced to 93 years' imprisonment in 2005 for taking part in a private discussion of official plans for political transition.

■ Comedian and director Zarganar was arrested on 4 June for criticizing the government's handling of Cyclone Nargis. In the aftermath of the cyclone, he led the private donor movement for humanitarian assistance and provided information about the crisis. In October, he was sentenced to 45 years' imprisonment under vaguely worded provisions of laws that criminalize peaceful dissent.

Armed conflict

In eastern Myanmar, a military offensive by the *tatmadaw* (Myanmar army) continued against ethnic

M

Karen civilians. Government forces engaged in widespread and systematic violations of international human rights and humanitarian law, amounting to crimes against humanity. Violations included extrajudicial executions, torture, forced labour, forced displacement and enforced disappearances.

Freedom of expression

In February, the government issued the Referendum Law for the Approval of the Draft Constitution, which provided for a prison term of up to three years and/or a substantial fine for anyone caught campaigning against the referendum. The government used the law to detain many activists peacefully campaigning against the constitution or calling for a boycott. Over 70 were arrested in late April for trying to stage a peaceful demonstration. Journalists and human rights defenders were particularly targeted for their work throughout the year.

■ Saw Wai, a poet, was arrested in January for inserting a concealed message in a Valentine's Day poem. He was sentenced to two years in prison.

■ Nay Phone Latt, a blogger, was detained in January for images and cartoons that appeared in his blogs. He was sentenced to 20 years and six months in prison.

Unfair trials

In November, there was a spate of summary and grossly unfair trials often held inside prisons, resulting in long prison sentences. The government consistently interfered with defendants' rights to mount a defence, including through harassing legal counsel, and other due process rights. The courts accepted blatantly non-credible evidence from the prosecution and forced confessions. Some 215 sentences were handed down during the month. Most trials involved charges relating to the 2007 protests.

■ In November, 23 people, including 88 Generation Student Group leaders Min Ko Naing, Ko Ko Gyi and Htay Kywe, received prison sentences of 65 years each.

■ In September, U Thet Wai, an NLD chairperson in Yangon who helped supply the ILO with information on forced labour and the recruitment of child soldiers, was sentenced to two years' imprisonment with hard labour.

■ In November, Aung Thein, a lawyer defending U Gambira, a monk who led the 2007 protests, and U Khin Maung Shein, a fellow lawyer, were both sentenced to four months in prison for contempt of court. They had submitted a letter withdrawing their legal representation, stating that their clients had no confidence in the judicial process and no longer wanted to be represented.

■ In November, Su Su Nway, an activist against forced labour, was sentenced to 12 years and six months in a trial in Insein Prison.

Internally displaced people

More than 500,000 people were internally displaced in Myanmar at the end of 2008, the majority in Shan and Kayin States. Others were in Kayah and Mon States and Bago and Tanintharyi Divisions.

Legal, constitutional or institutional developments

In February, the government agreed to extend a Supplementary Understanding with the ILO that allows for complaints of forced labour to be made without fear of official retribution, and requires the government to investigate the complaints. A number of cases of children allegedly forced to serve as soldiers were under investigation.

In May, the government claimed that 98.1 per cent of eligible voters had voted during the constitutional referendum and that 92.4 per cent of these were in favour of the draft constitution. Earlier in the year, the government had refused the UN's recommendation and offer of international monitors.

The constitution ensured impunity for past human rights violations. It granted the army power to suspend all fundamental rights during an emergency, and reserved the army 25 per cent of both houses of parliament and significant parts of the executive and judiciary. There were no provisions for freedom from torture and other ill-treatment, and crucial fair trial safeguards were missing. Provisions on freedom of expression, association and assembly were severely restricted by vague provisos or were discriminatory. The constitution itself was published only in the majority Burmese language prior to the referendum.

International scrutiny

In March and August, Ibrahim Gambari, the UN Secretary-General's Special Advisor, visited Myanmar. In March, Paulo Sérgio Pinheiro presented his final comprehensive report to the UN Human Rights Council before his term as Special Rapporteur on the situation of human rights in Myanmar expired. Tomás

Ojea Quintana, appointed the new Special Rapporteur after the position's mandate was renewed by the Human Rights Council, made his initial visit to the country in August, and presented his first report to the General Assembly in September. The Human Rights Council also adopted a resolution on Myanmar in March.

In May, the UN Security Council issued its second Presidential Statement on Myanmar since the 2007 crackdown. In the wake of Cyclone Nargis in May, the UN Under-Secretary-General for Humanitarian Affairs and Emergency Relief Coordinator and the UN Secretary-General visited Myanmar. The latter presented a report to the UN General Assembly in September. In November, the UN General Assembly adopted a resolution on Myanmar. The "Group of Friends", established by the UN Secretary-General to discuss Myanmar and comprising 14 nations and the EU, met five times during the year.

Dr Surin Pitsuwan, ASEAN Secretary-General, visited Myanmar in May and helped establish a Tripartite Core Group comprising the government, the UN, and ASEAN, to oversee the cyclone relief operation. International reactions to the constitutional referendum were mixed – some nations criticized the process and the constitution while others saw it as a potentially positive step. The USA, the EU and Australia further tightened economic sanctions against Myanmar.

Amnesty International reports

- Myanmar: Crimes against humanity in eastern Myanmar (ASA 16/011/2008)
- Myanmar: Human rights concerns a month after Cyclone Nargis (ASA 16/013/2008)
- Myanmar: Constitutional referendum flouts human rights, 9 May 2008

NAMIBIA

REPUBLIC OF NAMIBIA

Head of state and government:	**Hifikepunye Pohamba**
Death penalty:	**abolitionist for all crimes**
Population:	**2.1 million**
Life expectancy:	**51.6 years**
Under-5 mortality (m/f):	**70/58 per 1,000**
Adult literacy:	**85 per cent**

A long-running treason trial showed no sign of coming to a conclusion. Women and girls faced systemic discrimination and Indigenous communities continued to live in extreme poverty. Mass graves were found in the north of the country.

Background

Government officials from the ruling South West Africa People's Organization (SWAPO) repeatedly accused the opposition Rally for Democracy and Progress (RDP), a political party founded in late 2007, of promoting tribalism. The RDP was the most significant political challenge to SWAPO since Namibia's independence in 1990.

Caprivi treason trial

There was no end in sight for the Caprivi treason trial, which started in 2004 following attacks carried out in the Caprivi Strip in 1999 by a secessionist group, the Caprivi Liberation Army. Most of the 117 people on trial spent their ninth year in detention. By the end of 2008, the prosecution had still not closed its case.

None of the police officers accused of torturing suspects detained in the wake of the Caprivi uprising faced any formal charges or disciplinary action. Three civil claims against the Minister of Home Affairs and the Minister of Defence were settled out of court in October. Derick Ndala, Sylvester Ngalaule and Herbert Mutahane said they had been assaulted, tortured and unlawfully detained after attacks at Katima Mulilo on 2 August 1999.

Discrimination

The UN Committee on the Elimination of Racial Discrimination reiterated its concern that aspects of the customary laws of certain ethnic groups discriminated against women and girls, including laws pertaining to marriage and inheritance. It also expressed concern about discrimination in access to education, as well as the high illiteracy rate among marginalized parts of the population. The Committee was also concerned about the extreme poverty of the Indigenous communities.

Prison conditions

Prison conditions fell below international standards. Prisons were overcrowded, juveniles were held together with adult offenders, and inmates lacked access to hygiene products and nutritious food. The prevalence of HIV/AIDS in prisons was estimated to be at least as high as the national rate of 29 per cent. This was attributed to inadequate access to health care, including HIV/AIDS testing and counselling and anti-retroviral treatment. The Namibian Parliament has dismissed several proposals to allow condoms in prisons.

Discovery of mass graves

Mass graves were reportedly discovered in northern Namibia and southern Angola, apparently containing the bodies of people unlawfully killed between 1994 and 2002 by Namibian and Angolan security forces. Suspected supporters of the Angolan armed group the National Union for the Total Independence of Angola (UNITA), were allegedly targeted by the security forces, particularly in the late 1990s and in early 2000.

The existence of the graves was reported in September by the National Society for Human Rights (NSHR). On 1 October, the Minister of Safety and Security said that the government already knew about the graves. A police investigation launched by the government in October was criticized by the NSHR for its alleged lack of independence and failure to include independent forensic experts.

NEPAL

FEDERAL DEMOCRATIC REPUBLIC OF NEPAL

Head of state:	**Ram Baran Yadav**
	(replaced caretaker Girija Prasad Koirala in July)
Head of government:	**Pushpa Kamal Dahal**
	(replaced Girija Prasad Koirala in August)
Death penalty:	**abolitionist for all crimes**
Population:	**28.8 million**
Life expectancy:	**62.6 years**
Under-5 mortality (m/f):	**68/72 per 1,000**
Adult literacy:	**48.6 per cent**

Nepal continued to consolidate its peace process following the end of the 10-year conflict between the government and the Communist Party of Nepal-Maoist (CPN-M) in 2006. Commitments made in the November 2006 Comprehensive Peace Accord to uphold civil, political and economic rights, including ending discrimination, remained unfulfilled. The process of delivering truth, justice and reparations for violations committed during the conflict did not progress and a climate of impunity persisted. Lack of police capacity led to public insecurity as armed groups continued to operate in the Southern Terai region and the number of armed youth groups affiliated to the main political parties increased. The Armed Police Force used excessive force on a number of occasions, including while policing the many rights based demonstrations that took place across the country.

Background

Elections on 10 April for a new Constituent Assembly (CA) brought long excluded groups such as Dalits, Janajatis and Madhesis into mainstream politics. On 28 May, the CA declared Nepal a Federal Democratic Republic and formally announced the abolition of the monarchy. On 15 August, Pushpa Kamal Dahal (Prachanda), chairman of the CPN-M, was elected the first Prime Minister of the Federal Democratic Republic of Nepal by a huge majority. The CA started drafting a new Constitution.

Despite the measures taken by the state, discrimination against marginalized groups, including women, persisted with impunity, particularly with regard to accessing justice.

Transitional justice

Local and international NGOs continued to raise concerns that a draft bill establishing a Truth and Reconciliation Commission contained a proposal to grant the power to recommend amnesty for perpetrators of serious human rights violations.

Enforced disappearances

In early 2008, the ICRC listed more than 800 people who had disappeared at the hands of the government and the CPN-M and whose fate and whereabouts remained unknown.

The government conducted consultations on a draft bill which would make enforced disappearance a criminal offence under Nepalese law. However, the June 2007 Supreme Court order that the government form a commission to investigate cases of enforced disappearances during the 1996-2006 conflict remained in limbo due to lack of political will. In November, the government released a draft of the Disappearances (Crime and Punishment) Bill.

Impunity

Impunity continued for perpetrators of human rights abuses during the conflict – no cases had been tried before a civilian court. Survivors of sexual violence reported that the police refused to file their complaint.

Police

Police used excessive force during demonstrations in the southern Terai area in early 2008, as several Madhesi communities protested against discrimination. In February, police shot and killed at least six men during protests in the Nepalgunj and Siraha districts.

Between 10 March and 18 July, the police arrested at least 8,000 Tibetans and other human rights activists, including staff of Amnesty International Nepal, as they demonstrated peacefully in the lead-up to the Beijing Olympics. Many demonstrators reported that the police beat them with lathis (long wooden sticks) during the demonstration and while in custody.

Abuses by armed groups

A number of armed groups in the Terai region, including the Janatantrik Terai Mukti Morcha (JTMM-J); the Madhesi Mukti Tigers and Terai Cobras, committed human rights abuses including abductions

of members of the Pahadi (hill) community and bomb attacks on local administration buildings.

The Young Communist League (YCL), the youth wing of the CPN-M, committed a number of human rights abuses including abductions. In May, The National Human Rights Commission of Nepal expressed serious concern about the activities of the YCL. Instead of condemning their activities, other political parties formed armed youth groups, including the "Youth Force" associated with the Nepal Communist Party (UML).

Child soldiers

Over 2,500 child soldiers remained in cantonments (military areas where, under the Comprehensive Peace Accord, the CPN-M had agreed to be quartered). In August, the UN Special Representative for Children and Armed Conflict, Radhika Coomaraswamy, called upon the Nepal government and the CPN-M to immediately free all children previously associated with the Maoist forces.

Torture and other ill-treatment

Police routinely used torture and other ill-treatment against suspects. National laws providing safeguards against torture fell short of international standards, and remained inadequately implemented.

More than 1,300 new cases of torture had been recorded since April 2006.

■ Police arrested Sumitra Khawas on 9 September near her home in the Morang District, and detained her at the Belbari police station. She said that during her interrogation she was beaten repeatedly with the inner tube of a car tyre and punched all over her body. On 15 October, lawyers representing her filed a compensation claim for torture in custody but, at the end of the year no action had been taken against the perpetrators. Although she had been tried, no final verdict was given by the court and Sumitra Khawas remained in police custody.

Violence against women and girls

Women continued to face widespread discrimination and violence in public and private life. In June, the National Human Rights Commission reported that cases of dowry deaths and sexual violence had increased. Legislative weakness and inadequate policing continued to make prosecutions for domestic and sexual violence against women difficult. Police refused to provide information to women human rights defenders on the status of investigations into cases of sexual violence.

Women human rights defenders were harassed and killed.

■ Rita Mahato is a 30-year-old health counsellor with the Women's Rehabilitation Centre (WOREC) in Nepal, an organization defending the rights of women and Dalits. In June 2007, men from her community objected to WOREC's work, attacked the office in Siraha and threatened Rita Mahato with rape and death. Police failed to investigate the incident. She continued to face death threats in 2008.

Legal and institutional developments

A third of seats (191 out of 575) were filled by women in the newly formed Constituent Assembly.

In November, the Nepalese Supreme Court passed a judgement giving rights and protection to Nepal's lesbian, gay, bisexual, transgender, and intersex population.

Amnesty International visits/reports

🚌 Amnesty International delegates visited Nepal in March and November.

▦ Nepal: Need for respect for human rights in policing, 20 February 2008

▦ Nepal: Clampdown on Tibet demonstrators must stop immediately and protesters released, 24 March 2008

▦ Nepal: Overturning the Legacy of War – priorities for effective human rights protection, 12 May 2008

NETHERLANDS

KINGDOM OF THE NETHERLANDS

Head of state:	Queen Beatrix
Head of government:	Jan Peter Balkenende
Death penalty:	abolitionist for all crimes
Population:	16.5 million
Life expectancy:	79.2 years
Under-5 mortality (m/f):	6/6 per 1,000

Proposals to process all asylum applications through accelerated procedures led to fears that well-founded claims for protection would be rejected. Asylum-seekers were detained for excessive periods, in inappropriate conditions.

Refugees and asylum-seekers

In June the government announced plans to reform asylum-determination procedures. The accelerated procedure would be reformed so that applications would be determined within eight days, rather than five. The reformed accelerated process would then become the standard procedure for all asylum applications, including complex cases. There were concerns that this would lead to inadequate scrutiny of asylum applications and the rejection of well-founded claims for protection.

The State Secretary of Justice announced in September that asylum-seekers from central and southern Iraq would no longer be automatically entitled to protection in the Netherlands. Residence permits previously issued to Iraqis from central and southern Iraq would be withdrawn and each case would be made subject to individual review, to determine whether the individual was a refugee or otherwise in need of international protection.

At least five people were forcibly returned to northern Iraq, at least five to central Iraq and at least one to southern Iraq. Rejected asylum-seekers from Iraq were told that they were expected to return to Iraq, that they had no right to remain in the Netherlands and that they were not entitled to any support from the state, beyond the most basic emergency health care. Many, therefore, were faced with a choice between returning "voluntarily" to Iraq, despite real risks of human rights violations there, or being made forcibly destitute in the Netherlands.

Detention of irregular migrants and asylum-seekers

According to government figures, around 4,500 irregular migrants and asylum-seekers were subject to administrative detention in the first half of 2008. They were held in detention centres under a regime designed for remand prisoners. Some were detained for excessive periods, in some cases more than a year. Alternatives to detention were used infrequently, even for people belonging to vulnerable groups, such as unaccompanied minors and victims of trafficking or torture.

Not all allegations of ill-treatment in immigration detention were followed by prompt, impartial and thorough investigations.

Although the regimes for immigration detention

were under review, few concrete proposals for improvement were made. The supervision and complaints mechanisms were under review, but few measures for improvement were announced, apart from the creation of a mechanism to investigate complaints of ill-treatment by officers of the Transport and Support Service, which is responsible for the transport of detained individuals.

In January the government announced reforms to the policy governing the detention of asylum-seeking families with children, including the introduction of a maximum detention period for families of two weeks prior to expulsion, and the improvement of detention conditions. However, the government indicated it would continue to detain unaccompanied minors in juvenile justice institutions.

Legal, constitutional or institutional developments

In July the government committed itself to establishing a national human rights institution for the Netherlands.

Amnesty International report

📋 The Netherlands: The detention of irregular migrants and asylum-seekers (EUR 35/002/2008)

NEW ZEALAND

NEW ZEALAND

Head of state:	Queen Elizabeth II represented by Anand Satyanand
Head of government:	John Key (replaced Helen Clark in November)
Death penalty:	abolitionist for all crimes
Population:	4.2 million
Life expectancy:	79.8 years
Under-5 mortality (m/f):	6/6 per 1,000

In August, the police introduced Taser stun guns despite growing opposition to their use. The government attempted to introduce immigration legislation which could expose asylum-seekers to danger and raised concerns of prolonged and arbitrary detention. The Solicitor-General did not authorize a prosecution of domestic terrorism suspects using new anti-terrorism laws instead the suspects were charged under ordinary criminal law.

Taser stun guns

In August, the police commissioner approved the introduction of Taser stun guns to be used by the police in situations where they fear physical injury to themselves or others. This approval was given without an independent and impartial inquiry and despite concerns raised by civil society organizations and the objections to the use of Taser stun guns of the UN Committee against Torture. In August, the New Zealand Mental Health Foundation stated that the use of Tasers would "raise the possibility of additional trauma for people in mental health crisis". According to the Foundation's analysis of the use of Tasers from September 2006 to August 2007, Tasers were fired in 50 per cent of cases involving mental health emergencies, but only in 11 per cent of criminal cases.

Refugees and asylum-seekers

In July, the government tabled an Immigration Bill which had provisions for passenger screening at the point of departure to New Zealand. The Bill would allow withholding of reasons for denial of entry, and would deny the applicant access to judicial review.

Concern was expressed that the passenger screening process outlined in the Bill could expose asylum-seekers to harm if they were denied permission to board an aircraft when they were facing persecution, including possibly torture or death, in their own countries. The Bill also contained provisions that raised concerns about the possibility of prolonged and arbitrary detention.

Counter-terror and security

In October, the Solicitor-General, who is required to authorize prosecutions under the Terrorism Suppression Act, decided there was not enough evidence to prosecute in the case of 12 domestic terrorism suspects. The 12 suspects, plus six others suspected of related incidents, were instead charged with firearms offences under criminal law. In November, five of them were also charged with participating in a criminal gang.

Legal developments

In August, the government initiated a review of sexual violence legislation to improve the criminal justice response to sex offending. From 1997 to 2005, 19 per cent of women and five per cent of men reported being subjected to sexual violence. Maori women were at a greater risk of sexual violence than non-Maori women.

NICARAGUA

REPUBLIC OF NICARAGUA

Head of state and government:	**Daniel Ortega Saavedra**
Death penalty:	**abolitionist for all crimes**
Population:	**5.7 million**
Life expectancy:	**71.9 years**
Under-5 mortality (m/f):	**28/22 per 1,000**
Adult literacy:	**76.7 per cent**

Women human rights defenders were intimidated and harassed because of their work defending sexual and reproductive rights. The law criminalizing all forms of abortion, including in cases where the woman's life is at risk or where the pregnancy is a result of rape, came into effect. Allegations of electoral fraud and excessive controls over civil society organizations raised concerns about curbs on freedom of expression and association. The government formally recognized the rights to their ancestral land of the Awas Tingni community.

Background

In June 2008, the Nicaraguan Supreme Electoral Council announced that two opposition parties, the Sandinista Reformist Movement (Movimiento Renovador Sandinista) and the Conservative Party (Partido Conservador), were no longer legally registered and could not nominate candidates for election. In October, the government also refused to allow national or international observers to monitor the November municipal elections.

The Liberal Constitutional Party (Partido Liberal Constitucionalista) rejected the announcement that the ruling Sandinista National Liberation Front (Frente Sandinista de Liberación Nacional, FSLN) had won the elections, alleging fraud and a lack of transparency. FSLN and opposition supporters clashed violently in Managua in the weeks following the elections. Many people were wounded, but no official figures were available. The Inter-American Commission on Human Rights expressed concern at the violence and requested permission from the Nicaraguan authorities to send a Rapporteur to investigate. By the end of the year the government had not responded to the Commission's request.

Sexual and reproductive rights

Nine women human rights defenders remained at risk of legal proceedings. The accusations against them included incitement to commit a crime and concealment of a crime, and were believed to have been brought because of their human rights work and campaigning activities on the right of women to access safe and effective sexual and reproductive health services. By the end of the year, the Attorney General had yet to rule on whether the complaint, brought in November 2007, would be dropped or whether charges would be formalized.

■ In September, a government publication carried an article making a series of allegations against several female journalists, human rights defenders and political activists, including claims that they practised "black magic". The article criticized the women for supporting sexual and reproductive rights. Among those named in the publication was Patricia Orozco, a journalist and women's human rights defender. Following the publication of the article, Patricia Orozco received death threats and threats of sexual violence by phone and text (SMS) message.

The revised Criminal Code came into effect in July, criminalizing abortion and providing for lengthy prison sentences for women and health professionals convicted of carrying out or assisting women to have an abortion, even in cases where continued pregnancy endangered the life of the woman or where the pregnancy was the result of rape. No one was prosecuted under this legislation during 2008.

The UN Human Rights Committee and the UN Committee on Economic, Social and Cultural Rights, in October and November respectively, recommended that the Nicaraguan government reform its laws on abortion.

Violence against women and girls

Some 30 per cent of all criminal complaints filed with the police in the first three months of the year were of sexual violence. According to police figures, the vast majority of the victims of sexual violence were girls aged 18 or under, although in many cases the abuse had not come to light for several years.

■ A teenage girl interviewed by Amnesty International said that she had been raped by her uncle when she was nine. She told her mother, who advised her she had to keep quiet because the family was economically dependent on the uncle. Feeling unsafe in her home, the girl left, dropped out of school and turned to prostitution at the age of 14 in order to survive. The rejection by her community and prevailing social attitudes which blame the victim rather than the perpetrator had a profound effect on her ability to deal with her experience and on the possibility of bringing her attacker to justice. The uncle has never been prosecuted for this crime.

Freedom of expression and association

In the weeks following the municipal elections, at least 20 journalists were physically attacked; many were beaten. The majority of the attacks were carried out by groups of FSLN supporters. The premises of at least five independent media outlets were vandalized.

The documents of several national and international organizations working on issues ranging from development to governance and transparency were seized by police, apparently pending an investigation into their financial management. By the end of the year, the organizations had not been told the nature of the investigation or when their documentation would be returned.

■ In October, police raided the offices of the Autónomous Women's Movement (Movimiento Autonomo de Mujeres, MAM), an organization which had been involved in promoting women's rights and sexual and reproductive rights for more than 10 years. Documents and computers were taken. By the end of the year, MAM had not been informed of the legal reasons for the investigation and the documents taken had not been returned, seriously hampering their work.

Indigenous Peoples' rights

In 2001, the Inter-American Court of Human Rights had demanded that the Nicaraguan government legally recognize the land rights of the Awas Tingni Indigenous community. In a welcome move in December 2008, the community formally received legal recognition of their rights to land, in accordance with the judgement.

Amnesty International visits/reports

🚌 Amnesty International delegates visited the country in June and November.

📄 Defending women's right to life and health – Women human rights defenders in Nicaragua (AMR 43/001/2008)

📄 Nicaragua: Submission to the United Nations Committee on Economic Social and Cultural Rights 41st Session, 3-21 November 2008 (AMR 43/002/2008)

NIGER

REPUBLIC OF NIGER

Head of state:	Mamadou Tandja
Head of government:	Seyni Oumarou
Death penalty:	abolitionist in practice
Population:	14.7 million
Life expectancy:	55.8 years
Under-5 mortality (m/f):	183/188 per 1,000
Adult literacy:	28.7 per cent

The government blocked some humanitarian efforts despite widespread hunger and a growing threat of famine. Civilians suspected of supporting a Tuareg-led armed opposition group were unlawfully killed by security forces. A number of soldiers and civilians were abducted by this group. Several journalists were detained in an attempt to muzzle the press.

Background

Armed conflict between government forces and a Tuareg-led armed opposition movement, the Niger People's Movement for Justice (Mouvement des Nigériens pour la justice, MNJ), based in the Agadez region in the north, continued throughout the year. Despite calls by civil society and political parties to engage in talks with the MNJ, the Nigerien President ruled out any dialogue, describing the MNJ as "bandits" and "drugs dealers". The government renewed several times the state of emergency in the

Agadez region which gave additional powers to the security forces.

In December, Robert Fowler, UN special envoy to Niger and a fellow UN official Louis Guay, both Canadian nationals, disappeared with their driver while travelling in a car 40km from Niamey, the capital. There were allegations that they had been abducted, but despite the opening of an inquiry by the authorities, no further news of them had emerged by the end of the year.

In June, former prime minister Hama Amadou was arrested on corruption and embezzlement charges. Local human rights organizations called for a prompt and fair trial. His supporters claimed that the charges were politically motivated to prevent him from running in the 2009 presidential elections. Hama Amadou was still detained without trial at the end of the year.

Food insecurity

Despite many independent reports indicating serious risks of famine, the government suspended in July authorization for the activities of Médecins sans Frontières (MSF)-France in the south-central region of Maradi, forcing the NGO to leave the country. The government accused MSF of exaggerating the number of malnourished children in the Maradi region in order to raise funds. The government stated that the situation was not "dramatic" and that Niger could handle it without international assistance. The government's action threatened to undermine the obligation to ensure freedom from hunger and to seek international assistance where necessary.

Arbitrary arrests and detentions, torture and unlawful killings

Tens of civilians were arrested by the security forces in the Agadez region and some were allegedly tortured. Many were detained after attacks launched by the MNJ. Most were released after days or weeks of detention without charge or trial. Several enforced disappearances were also reported.

■ A tradesman, Aboubakar Attoulèle, was arrested by the military on 26 March. He reportedly had his ears cut off and his hair set on fire before being stabbed to death.

■ Four men, including Al Wali, village chief of Tourayat, were arrested by government soldiers on 30 March. Their families were unable to obtain any news about their whereabouts.

Abuses by armed groups

The MNJ abducted and held hostage a number of soldiers and civilians, including a senior government official, an imam and a teacher. Some of them were handed to the International Committee of the Red Cross, but others remained held at the end of the year.

■ In January, during an MNJ attack, Abdou Garba Kona, prefect of Tanout, a city 1,000km north-west of Niamey, was kidnapped with several members of military forces. He was released in March with 25 others.

■ In May, the MNJ abducted near Tanout the vice president of the National Commission on Human Rights, Ahmadou Ahellawey, while he was raising awareness about human rights. He was released a week later.

Freedom of expression

The government imposed a media blackout on the conflict in the north. The authorities banned journalists from travelling to the area and arrested or arbitrarily detained several journalists accused of links with the MNJ. In March, the Superior Council of Communication suspended Radio France International (RFI) for three months after accusing the station of "discrediting the Nigerien institutions" and in April ordered the indefinite closure of Sahara FM, the main private radio station in Agadez.

■ In October, prisoner of conscience Moussa Kaka, director of the privately owned Radio Saraouniya station and RFI correspondent in Niger, was provisionally released after more than a year in detention. The original charge of "complicity in undermining the state's authority" was replaced by the less serious charge of "actions liable to harm national defence". His trial had not taken place by the end of the year.

Slavery

In October, the Community Court of Justice of the Economic Community of West African States (ECOWAS) ordered the Niger government to pay reparations to a woman who had been kept as a domestic and sexual slave for a decade. The woman had lodged a complaint against the government for failing to implement existing laws against slavery.

The landmark decision corroborated denunciations by several international and national NGOs who had said that there were still slaves in Niger despite the criminalization of this practice in 2003.

Amnesty International reports

▥ Niger: Le mouvement d'opposition armé touareg doit cesser de prendre en otage des civils (24 January 2008)

▥ Niger: Executions and forced disappearances follow army reprisals (3 April 2008)

NIGERIA

FEDERAL REPUBLIC OF NIGERIA

Head of state and government:	Umaru Musa Yar'Adua
Death penalty:	retentionist
Population:	151.5 million
Life expectancy:	46.5 years
Under-5 mortality (m/f):	190/182 per 1,000
Adult literacy:	69.1 per cent

The situation in the Niger Delta deteriorated further, with clashes between armed groups and the security forces, inter-communal violence and violent crime including hostage-taking. Widespread pollution associated with the oil industry undermined human rights, including the right to an adequate standard of living and the right to health.

Human rights violations by the police included extrajudicial executions of detainees and people unable or unwilling to pay bribes and the frequent use of torture when interrogating suspects. More than 700 prisoners were on death row, hundreds of whom were sentenced after unfair trials. The justice system was in urgent need of reform, with detainees imprisoned in appalling conditions for many years awaiting trial.

The widespread poverty in Nigeria was attributed in large part to corruption. The maternal mortality rate was extremely high at about 1 per 100 live births. The right to adequate housing was also violated on a large scale with more than two million people forcibly evicted from their homes since 2000.

Background

In February an election tribunal upheld the 2007 election of President Umaru Musa Yar'Adua. An appeal was lodged against the tribunal's decision and in December the Supreme Court upheld Yar'Adua's election. Four state governors were removed by election tribunals and fresh governorship elections were ordered in six states due to irregularities during the 2007 elections.

In April President Yar'Adua gave assurances that his government would address impunity in relation to corruption. A New Partnership for African Development (NEPAD) report stated that poverty in Nigeria was primarily explained by corruption, and warned that Nigeria was unlikely to meet the Millennium Development Goals.

In August, the Nigeria Police Force demoted 140 police officers, including the former chairman of the Economic and Financial Crimes Commission (EFCC), Nuhu Ribadu. He had been effectively removed from the EFCC in December 2007, after the EFCC arrested and charged an influential former governor. Nuhu Ribadu was sent on one year's training. In September shots were fired at his car and he received death threats. In December he was dismissed from the Nigeria Police Force. During 2008, the EFCC prosecuted three former governors on corruption charges.

In November up to 400 people died in Jos, Plateau State, in three days of riots which broke out following local government elections. Before the elections, civil society groups had written to the Plateau State authorities expressing concern that violence could erupt. The State Governor issued a "shoot on sight" order to the security forces.

A Freedom of Information Bill, first presented in 1999 and passed by the previous National Assembly but not signed into law, was still pending before the National Assembly.

The Niger Delta

The situation in the Niger Delta deteriorated further in 2008. The inflow of weapons went virtually unchecked, fuelled by massive revenues generated from oil theft. The weapons were used by armed militias in clashes with the security forces, in inter-communal disputes, and for criminal activities. In 2008, dozens of oil workers and their relatives, including children, were kidnapped by armed groups and gangs; oil installations were also attacked.

The security forces, including the military, continued to commit human rights violations, including unlawful killings, torture and other ill-

N

treatment, and destruction of homes. The Joint Task Force (JTF) frequently raided communities, particularly following clashes with armed militias, often resulting in the death of bystanders.

■ In August, four people – two elderly men, a young woman and an elderly woman – were reportedly killed when the military raided the village of Agge, Bayelsa State. According to the JTF, the action followed an armed militia attack.

In Port Harcourt, Rivers State, gang clashes resulted in the deaths of at least 15 people in July and August.

The Niger Delta Summit, intended to bring together all stakeholders to address the violence, was postponed several times then replaced in September by a Niger Delta Technical Committee. In November the Committee presented its findings. Its recommendations to the Federal Government included the payment of the outstanding funds to the Niger Delta Development Commission, an increase in funds paid to the Niger Delta states and the disarmament and rehabilitation of militants.

No known action was taken to bring to justice members of the security forces suspected of grave human rights violations. Two judicial commissions of inquiry examined events in February 2005 – a raid by members of the JTF in Odioma, in which at least 17 people were killed, and a protest at the Escravosoil terminal, when soldiers fired on protesters. The commission reports were not made public.

People living in the Niger Delta lacked adequate drinking water and electricity, and had few functioning schools and health care centres. Widespread pollution associated with the oil industry in the Delta undermined human rights, including the right to an adequate standard of living and the right to health.

Between January and June 2008, 418 oil spills were reported to the authorities. Despite a Federal High Court order to stop gas flaring in the Iwerekhan community, the practice continued unabated.

Unlawful killings and extrajudicial executions

There were consistent reports of the police unlawfully killing detainees, people unable or unwilling to pay bribes and people stopped during road checks. Some or all of these killings may have been extrajudicial executions. In May, the NGO LEDAP (Legal Defence

and Assistance Project) estimated that in 2007 at least 241 people had been extrajudicially executed by state agents.

■ On 25 February, officers from the Police Mobile Force attacked Ogaminana community, in Kogi State, reportedly after a policeman was killed. According to witnesses, 15 people were killed, including two children, and cars, motorcycles and houses were burned. Following the attack, the Assistant Commissioner of Police, who reportedly directed the operation, was transferred. By the end of 2008, no investigation had been carried out.

Torture and other ill-treatment

The police frequently used torture and other ill-treatment when interrogating suspects and there was no standardized mechanism to prevent such practices. Confessions extracted under torture continued to be used as evidence in court, contrary to international law.

■ In Owerri prison, a 68-year-old man said that police had shot him in the leg, flogged him with electric cables and put a powdery substance in his eyes. He had been in prison awaiting trial for 10 years, despite a medical report confirming his allegations of torture, which were not investigated.

Justice system

Three out of five inmates in Nigeria's prisons were untried. Many awaited trial for years in appalling conditions. Few could afford a lawyer and the government-funded Legal Aid Council had only 91 lawyers for the whole country.

In July, both the Federal Ministry of Justice and the Prison Service assured Amnesty International that improvements had been made. The Federal Ministry of Justice claimed to have asked 2,000 lawyers to take up the cases of prisoners without legal representation. However, by the end of 2008 the impact of the scheme was not evident and prison congestion had not improved. The scheme did not address the causes of delay in the criminal justice system and the budget for the Legal Aid Council was not increased.

By the end of 2008, most justice sector reform bills were still pending before the National Assembly.

At state level, there were some improvements. In March, Lagos state amended its Criminal Procedures Act, prohibiting the arrest of third parties in lieu of suspects and requiring police interviews of suspects to be videotaped or conducted in the presence of a lawyer.

Several states set up legal aid services, such as the Ogun State Citizens' Rights Department and the Lagos State Office of the Public Defender. However, the capacity of such services was limited, funding was restricted and their independence was questionable.

■ At the end of 2008 Patrick Okoroafor was still imprisoned "during the pleasure of the governor of Imo State" in Aba prison, Abia State, despite a High Court judgement on 18 October 2001 which pronounced the death sentence against him to be illegal, null and void. He was 16 when he was sentenced to death by a Robbery and Firearms Tribunal in May 1997. He did not have the right to appeal and said he was tortured in police detention.

Death penalty

At the end of 2008, at least 735 prisoners were on death row, including 11 women. Hundreds did not have a fair trial. Approximately 140 had been on death row for longer than 10 years; some for over 20 years. Around 80 never had an appeal because they were sentenced to death before 1999 by a Robbery and Firearms Tribunal which denied defendants the right to appeal. Approximately 40 were under the age of 18 at the time of the offence and should not have been sentenced to death.

The Federal Government ignored the recommendation of the National Study Group on the Death Penalty (2004) and the Presidential Commission on Reform of the Administration of Justice (2007) to adopt a moratorium. In July 2008, a bill to abolish the mandatory death penalty under the Robbery and Firearms Act and replace it with life imprisonment was defeated in the House of Representatives.

By the end of 2008, most prisoners whose forthcoming release was announced by the Federal Minister of Information in May 2007 were still on death row.

In 2008 at least 40 death sentences were handed down. Five men had their sentences commuted by the Ogun State governor. In November, the President pardoned a man who had spent 22 years on death row. No confirmed executions were carried out in 2008.

In December Nigeria voted against a UN General Assembly resolution calling for a worldwide moratorium on executions.

Prison conditions

Living conditions in prisons were appalling. Overcrowding, poor sanitation, lack of food and medicines and denial of contact with families and friends were damaging to the physical and mental well-being of inmates. Many inmates slept two to a bed or on the bare floor. In some prisons, no beds were provided, toilets were blocked or non-existent, and there was no running water. Disease was widespread. Children as young as 12 were held together with adults.

Violence against women and girls

Violence against women remained pervasive, including domestic violence and rape and other forms of sexual violence by state officials and private individuals. The authorities consistently failed to exercise due diligence in preventing and addressing sexual violence by both state and non-state actors, leading to an entrenched culture of impunity.

With approximately 59,000 maternal deaths a year, Nigeria had the second largest number in the world. Nigeria's maternal mortality ratio was approximately one in every 100 live births. Contributing factors included lack of access to and ineffective health services, corruption, unsafe abortions, and diseases such as eclampsia and malaria.

In July, a Bill to Prohibit and Punish Public Nudity, Sexual Intimidation and Other Related Offences, which specified the appropriate length of women's clothing and gave wide powers of enforcement to the police, failed to pass its third reading in the National Assembly.

In January, Jigawa State passed a law prohibiting domestic violence. A similar bill remained before the Plateau state House of Assembly.

Freedom of expression

Human rights defenders and journalists critical of the government continued to face intimidation and harassment, and official intolerance of the media increased. At least eight journalists were arrested by the State Security Service (SSS) or police. Some were released after a few hours while others were detained incommunicado for up to 10 days. In addition, media offices were raided, Channels TV station was shut down and journalists were threatened and beaten by police and security forces. At least two journalists were killed in suspicious circumstances.

In the Niger Delta, there were at least three incidents in which foreign journalists or film-makers were arrested by the SSS and detained before being released without charge after some days.

Housing rights

Nigeria continued to violate the right to adequate housing. More than one million people were living in slums in Lagos alone.

No compensation or alternative housing was provided by the authorities to people forcibly evicted from their homes. Some communities were facing their third forced eviction. In Lagos widespread forced evictions were carried out without following due process. Between May and July they took place on an almost weekly basis. Mass demolitions were carried out in communities in Gosa, along the Nnamdi Azikiwe airport road, Federal Capital Territory, in May and June. In Port Harcourt forced evictions were carried out along the waterfront despite earlier state government promises that no evictions would take place.

■ Emeka, his wife and their three children were forcibly evicted from an informal settlement in Lagos and were left stranded without any compensation or alternative accommodation. All the property they had was destroyed in this eviction. Emeka and his family settled in Makoko, another informal settlement.

Rights of lesbian, gay, bisexual and transgender people

Human rights abuses against individuals suspected of same-sex sexual conduct continued throughout 2008. Nigeria's Criminal Code penalizes consensual same-sex sexual conduct between adults with 14 years' imprisonment. Shari'a penal codes criminalize "sodomy", in some states with the death penalty.

In 2008, several men and women were detained on charges of engaging in consensual same-sex sexual practices. Homophobia regularly resulted in violence against lesbian, gay, bisexual and transgender people and the authorities proved unable or unwilling to provide sufficient protection.

In December, a bill providing criminal penalties for marriage ceremonies between people of the same sex, as well as for anyone witnessing or helping to formalize such a marriage, was introduced by members of the House of Representatives.

Amnesty International visits/reports

Amnesty International delegates visited Nigeria in February/March, July and October/November.

📄 Nigeria: 'Waiting for the hangman' (AFR 44/020/2008)

📄 Nigeria: Open Letter to His Excellency President Alhaji Umaru Musa Yar'adua, President of the Federal Republic of Nigeria (AFR 44/007/2008)

📄 Nigeria: Amnesty International Submission to the UN Universal Periodic Review: Fourth session of the UPR Working Group of the Human Rights Council, February 2009 (AFR 44/016/2008)

📄 Nigeria: Nigerian police and security forces: Failure to protect and respect human rights (AFR 44/006/2008)

📄 Nigeria: Detention "during the pleasure of the governor" – NBA, Nigerian NGOs and Amnesty International urge the immediate release of Patrick Okoroafor (AFR 44/005/2008)

📄 Nigeria: Prisoners' rights systematically flouted (AFR 44/001/2008)

OMAN

SULTANATE OF OMAN

Head of state and government:	**Sultan Qaboos bin Said**
Death penalty:	**retentionist**
Population:	**2.7 million**
Life expectancy:	**75 years**
Under-5 mortality (m/f):	**14/13 per 1,000**
Adult literacy:	**81.4 per cent**

Members of two tribes continued to be denied equal access to economic and social rights. New restrictions on freedom of expression were introduced and several journalists and writers were harassed by the authorities. Women were subject to discrimination in law and practice.

Background

In November, Sultan Qaboos issued Decree No. 124/2008 to provide for the establishment of a National Human Rights Commission, which would exercise its functions independently of but be affiliated to the Majlis al-Dawla, the upper legislative house. The Commission had not commenced operation by the end of the year.

In December, Oman abstained on a UN General Assembly resolution calling for a worldwide moratorium on executions.

Discrimination – Aal Tawayya and Aal Khalifayn tribes

People belonging to the Aal Tawayya and Aal Khalifayn tribes continued to suffer adverse economic and social consequences following the Interior Ministry's 2006 decision to change the name of the tribes and affiliate them to al-Harithi, another tribe, effectively reducing their status to that of *akhdam*, or servants, of the main tribe. The two tribes sought to overturn the Ministry's decision but the Court of Administrative Judiciary held that it was a sovereign act beyond judicial scrutiny. In October, the government said that it had addressed the two tribes' grievances but no changes were known to have been made. Members of both tribes continued to face problems when seeking to renew identity cards, which are essential for registering businesses, obtaining travel documents and settling matters such as divorce and inheritance.

Freedom of expression

New measures were introduced which further restricted freedom of expression. Several journalists and writers were harassed for criticizing government policies and public services. Article 61 of the Communications Law, previously amended in 2007, was again amended in April to tighten restrictions on the use of means of communication for certain activities, including some which could constitute legitimate exercise of freedom of expression. The new amendments also extended criminal liability to those operating communication facilities and services, such as websites. Confidential government instructions relating to a popular phone-in radio programme, which were leaked and widely publicized, included directives to move from live to pre-recorded broadcasting and exclude calls about military, security or judicial matters or concerning the head of state.

Several journalists and writers were questioned by the Public Prosecution or harassed for criticizing the government, including the role of the Ministry of Labour in seeking wage cuts and deteriorating conditions for workers employed at the port of Salala.

■ 'Ali al-Zuwaydi, a writer for the *Sublat Oman* forums news website, was questioned by the Public Prosecution about an article which accused the main state-owned telecommunications company of administrative and financial mismanagement. He was released after questioning.

Women's rights

Women continued to face discrimination in law and practice, including in relation to personal status, employment and their subordination to male guardians. In November, however, the government announced that it had amended the law on acquisition of government-owned land for housing to give women equal rights with men.

PAKISTAN

ISLAMIC REPUBLIC OF PAKISTAN

Head of state:	Asif Ali Zardari (replaced Pervez Musharraf in September)
Head of government:	Yousuf Raza Gilani (replaced caretaker prime minister Muhammadmian Soomro in March)
Death penalty:	retentionist
Population:	167 million
Life expectancy:	64.6 years
Under-5 mortality (m/f):	89/99 per 1,000
Adult literacy:	49.9 per cent

A civilian government was elected in February. The new government released prisoners detained during the November 2007 state of emergency but failed to fulfil many of its promises to ensure human rights protection. Torture, deaths in custody, attacks on minorities, enforced disappearances, "honour" killings and domestic violence persisted. After the new government announced that it would commute death sentences to life imprisonment, it executed at least 16 people; at least 36 were executed throughout the year. Violence in the tribal areas bordering Afghanistan spilled over into other areas of Pakistan, as members of the Pakistani Taleban took hostages, targeted and killed civilians, and committed acts of violence against women and girls.

Background

Following general elections on 18 February, a civilian government took office on 31 March. However, the ruling coalition began to split when the parties could not reach agreement on how to reinstate the judges who had been unlawfully dismissed during the state of emergency in November 2007. President Musharraf resigned in August under threat of impeachment for violation of the constitution and misconduct. On 6 September, Asif Ali Zardari, Benazir Bhutto's widower and Pakistan People's Party leader, was elected President.

The majority of the deposed judges resumed office after taking a new oath. The lawyers' movement objected stating that reappointment, under a new oath, amounted to endorsing the illegal imposition of the emergency and dismissal of judges in November 2007.

Faced with an escalation of armed attacks, including suicide bombings, the new government vacillated between military operations and accommodating tribal armed groups and Pakistani Taleban. On 22 October, both houses of parliament unanimously passed a resolution urging the government to replace military operations with civilian law in border areas with Afghanistan and to initiate dialogue with Taleban who are willing to forgo violence. On 9 December, President Zardari stated that 1,400 civilians, 600 security personnel and 600 militants were killed in military operations in the border areas over the past five years.

The Afghan and US governments repeatedly called on Pakistan to destroy bases from which the Taleban launch attacks in Afghanistan. Despite strong protest from Pakistan, US forces operating in Afghanistan increasingly fired missiles across the border into Pakistan.

India-Pakistan relations deteriorated after allegations by the Indian authorities that the November Mumbai attacks had been carried out by people or groups based in Pakistan.

Legal and constitutional developments

Despite some positive efforts, Pakistan's new civilian government failed to fulfil many of its promises to protect human rights. In March, the government released scores of political activists detained during the state of emergency and freed judges held under illegal

house arrest. In April, Pakistan ratified the International Covenant on Economic, Social and Cultural Rights and signed the International Covenant on Civil and Political Rights as well as the UN Convention against Torture. In May, the government announced that Pakistan would accede to the International Convention on the Protection of all Persons from Enforced Disappearance but it did not do so by year end.

In November, a separate Human Rights Ministry was established. On 15 October, the cabinet approved a draft bill to set up a national human rights commission but parliament did not pass it by year end.

Arbitrary arrests and detentions

Police continued holding detainees for long periods of time without bringing them before a magistrate as required by law.

In the wake of attacks in November on civilian targets in Mumbai, India, the UN Security Council imposed sanctions against the organization Jamaat-ud-Dawa and its leaders, leading to the detention of hundreds of its workers under preventive detention legislation in December.

Torture and other ill-treatment

Law enforcement and security agencies routinely used torture and other ill-treatment, including beating, prolonged standing, hanging by the ankles and rape. Several deaths in custody were reported.

Enforced disappearances

In April, Law Minister Farooq Naik promised the government would trace all people subjected to enforced disappearance. According to the government's own figures, 1,102 people have disappeared in Balochistan province alone. In May, the government set up two committees to trace disappeared people. In June, the government stated that 43 disappeared persons had been traced in Balochistan, and had either been released or detained in an official place of detention. Petitions relating to hundreds of cases of disappearances remained pending before the Supreme Court.

On 21 November, Human Rights Minister Mumtaz Alam Gilani announced that a new law was being prepared to facilitate the recovery of disappeared people and stated that his ministry had 567 documented cases of enforced disappearance.

On 25 November, the Senate Standing Committee on Interior reportedly acknowledged that intelligence agencies maintained "countless hidden torture cells" across the country. Despite these initiatives, new cases of enforced disappearance were reported.

■ Aafia Siddiqui, a neuroscientist, and her three small children were reportedly apprehended in Karachi by Pakistani intelligence in March 2003. However, according to US sources she was not apprehended until 17 July 2008 along with her 11-year-old son Mohammed Ahmed by Afghan police in Ghazni, Afghanistan. According to the US government, US officials shot her allegedly in self-defence as they took custody of her from Afghan officials on 18 July. She was transferred to a detention facility in New York, and charged with the attempted murder of US officials and employees in September, charges unrelated to the previous suggestion that she had allegedly collaborated with al-Qa'ida. Her son was returned to his family in Pakistan. US authorities repeatedly stated that her other children were not in their custody. Her fate and whereabouts between 2003 and July 2008 and that of her two younger children remained unclear. In December, a US federal court ordered further psychiatric evaluation of her competence to stand trial and postponed hearings to 23 February 2009.

■ On 22 September, Dr Abdur Razaq was apprehended in Rawalpindi on his return from hospital. His wife filed a habeas corpus petition in the Islamabad High Court. On 7 November, state representatives denied any knowledge of his whereabouts. On 17 December, the court's chief justice Sardar Mohammad Aslam reportedly said that "everyone knows where the missing people are", ordering that the doctor be brought to court forthwith. By year end, his whereabouts remained unknown. His lawyer said that the doctor may have been disappeared for treating "terrorists".

Violations in the course of counter-insurgency
Pakistani security forces deployed in the tribal areas bordering Pakistan and adjacent areas of the North West Frontier Province (Swat) killed and injured civilians during operations against tribal armed groups and Pakistani Taleban.

■ On 19 October during an operation against Pakistani and foreign fighters, fighter jets bombed a village in Swat. Local residents reported that 47 people, including many civilians, were killed.

The government's operations displaced hundreds of thousands of people. Many internally displaced persons remained without access to humanitarian assistance or adequate protection by the government. Some 20,000 Pakistanis crossed the border to seek refuge in Afghanistan.

Abuses by armed groups
Armed groups, many of them explicitly pro-Taleban, committed serious human rights abuses, including direct attacks on civilians, indiscriminate attacks, abduction, hostage-taking, torture and other ill-treatment, and killing captives.

■ In October, a Taleban suicide bomber killed more than 80 unarmed civilians and wounded almost 100 at a peace council in Orakzai Agency who were drawing up a strategy to decrease violence in the area.

Pakistani Taleban took dozens of hostages including an Afghan and an Iranian diplomat, a Pakistani and a Canadian journalist, and a Polish engineer. The Afghan diplomat was later released but the others remained missing.

In September, the Swat chapter of the Tehrik-e-Taliban Pakistan (the Pakistani Taleban) took several foreigners hostage to force the release of their 136 jailed associates.

Local Taleban unlawfully assumed judicial functions and "tried" and "convicted" people they accused of having transgressed Islamic law or spying for the government. Dozens of people were unlawfully killed after such "trials".

■ On 27 June, two Afghans were unlawfully killed in front of thousands of onlookers in Bajaur Agency after a council found them guilty of "spying" for US forces.

P

Violence against women and girls
Women and girls suffered human rights violations at the hands of the state and, in the absence of appropriate government action, in the community, including "honour" killings, forced marriages, rape and domestic violence. The Protection from Harassment at the Workplace Bill, approved by the cabinet in November, and the Domestic Violence (Prevention and Protection) Bill, submitted to the Ministry of Women Development in August, remained pending.

■ On 13 July, a girl, aged 16, and two women, aged 18 and 20, were reportedly abducted and taken in a car bearing a government number plate to Babakot,

Jaffarabad district, Balochistan province, where they were killed apparently for wanting to marry men of their choice. A post-mortem examination revealed that two of the young women had died of head injuries inflicted with a blunt weapon. The third body was not found. A Baloch senator defended the killing as "tribal custom"; locally influential figures reportedly hampered the police investigation.

Girls were also handed over in marriage to settle disputes.

■ In October, three girls aged between 12 and 14 years, were forced into marriage by a *jirga* (informal tribal council) in Drighpur, Shikarpur district, Sindh province, to settle a dispute over an "honour" killing which had taken place two months earlier. No one was arrested.

Threats by Pakistani Taleban prevented thousands of women from voting in the February elections.

Discrimination – religious minorities

The government failed to adequately protect religious minorities against widespread discrimination, harassment and targeted violence.

■ In September, two Ahmadi men, Abdul Manan Siddiqui, a doctor from Mirpurkhas, Sindh, and a 75-year-old trader, Sheikh Mohammad Yousaf from Nawabshah, Sindh, were shot dead by unknown persons days after a private TV channel had aired a contributor's call to kill apostates and blasphemers as a religious duty. No investigation was known to have been initiated.

Seventy-six people were charged with blasphemy in 25 registered cases, including 17 people charged under section 295C Pakistan Penal Code (PPC) which carries the death sentence for insulting the name of the prophet Muhammad.

■ In June, 16 Ahmadis were charged with blasphemy in Nankana Sadar, Punjab, for allegedly taking down a poster that negatively depicted their religious leader.

Children's rights

Recruitment of children by armed groups, trafficking of children, domestic violence against children, in particular girls, continued. According to the NGO Sahil, 992 children, 304 boys and 688 girls, were subjected to sexual abuse between January and June.

In July, authorities in Swat discovered Pakistani Taleban had recruited 26 boys aged between 13 and 18 for training.

Death penalty

At least 236 people were reportedly sentenced to death, mostly for murder. The total number of prisoners under sentence of death was at least 7,000.

On 21 June, Prime Minister Yousuf Raza Gilani announced that death sentences would be commuted to life imprisonment. However, President Zardari issued an ordinance in November that extended the death penalty to cyber crimes causing death.

At least 36 people were executed during the year, including 16 after the commutation announcement.

In December, Pakistan voted against a UN General Assembly resolution calling for a worldwide moratorium on executions.

Amnesty International reports

Pakistan: Repairing the damage – ensuring robust human rights safeguards (ASA 33/001/2008)

Pakistan: Denying the undeniable - Enforced disappearances in Pakistan (ASA 33/018/2008)

PALESTINIAN AUTHORITY

PALESTINIAN AUTHORITY

Head of state:	**Mahmoud Abbas**
Head of government:	**Salam Fayyad**
Death penalty:	**retentionist**
Population:	**4.1 million**
Life expectancy:	**72.9 years**
Under-5 mortality (m/f):	**22/17 per 1,000**
Adult literacy:	**92.4 per cent**

Inter-factional tension remained high between the West Bank-based Palestinian Authority (PA) caretaker government of Prime Minister Salam Fayyad, appointed by President Mahmoud Abbas of the Fatah party, and the Hamas de facto administration in the Gaza Strip. Both the PA security forces in the West Bank and Hamas security forces and militias in Gaza arbitrarily detained hundreds of members or sympathizers of rival factions without charge or trial and often tortured and otherwise ill-treated detainees. Both security

forces used excessive force against demonstrators. Hamas security forces in Gaza killed 24 members of armed clans. During the military offensive launched by Israeli forces on 27 December, Hamas forces and militias abducted political opponents and former detainees alleged to have "collaborated" with Israeli intelligence services; some were summarily killed, others were beaten or shot in the legs. The PA in the West Bank and Hamas in Gaza continued to clamp down on freedom of expression. Military courts in the West Bank and Gaza sentenced nine people to death; no executions were carried out. Palestinian armed groups in Gaza indiscriminately attacked towns and villages in southern Israel, killing seven Israeli civilians and two Palestinian civilians. Palestinian armed groups and individuals from the occupied West Bank, including East Jerusalem, killed 16 Israeli civilians.

Background

Reconciliation negotiations between the PA caretaker government and the Hamas de facto administration in Gaza, which were mediated by Egypt and aimed at forming a unity government, continued without reaching agreement. Most donor countries refused to provide aid to the Hamas de facto administration, but gave more than US$1.3 billion to the PA government in the West Bank with very limited aid allocated to emergency projects in Gaza. The Hamas de facto administration and Israel agreed a six-month ceasefire on 19 June, which broke down on 4 November after Israeli forces killed six Palestinian militants.

The Israeli government maintained a tight blockade of the Gaza Strip, a form of collective punishment of its 1.5 million population, for the continuing detention there of Israeli soldier Gilad Shalit. The inhabitants of Gaza became increasingly dependent on food, fuel and other goods smuggled into Gaza from Egypt through dangerous underground tunnels. At least 50 Palestinians were killed when tunnels collapsed. In October, the Hamas de facto administration took steps to regulate use of the tunnels. Conditions worsened further when Israeli forces launched the military offensive on 27 December in response to continued indiscriminate rocket attacks on population areas in southern Israel by Hamas and other Palestinian armed groups in Gaza.

Even before the December offensive, more than 1 million Palestinians faced deepening poverty, food insecurity and lack of access to adequate health care because of the Israeli blockade on Gaza and Israeli military checkpoints and barriers in the West Bank, including a 700km fence/wall (see Israel and the Occupied Palestinian Territories entry).

Arbitrary arrests and detentions

In the West Bank, PA security forces arrested hundreds of people, mostly Hamas supporters, and held them often without access to due legal process. More than 100 were detained after Hamas detained Fatah supporters in Gaza in July, but waves of arrests of Hamas sympathizers continued through 2008. Members of Fatah's armed groups were also held in prolonged detention without charge or trial at the request of the Israeli army.

In Gaza, security forces of the Hamas de facto administration detained hundreds of suspected supporters of Fatah, including more than 200 arrested after bomb attacks in July targeted Hamas members. The security forces were sometimes supported by Hamas' armed militia, the Izz al-Din al-Qassam Brigades. Such militia have no legal authority to arrest or detain people; those taken into their custody were handed over to the security forces or held by the Brigades in secret locations.

Both PA and Hamas forces rarely complied with Palestinian laws requiring that detentions be reviewed by a prosecutor within 24 hours and by a judge within 72 hours. Detainees' right to prompt access to legal counsel was routinely ignored. Most political detainees were released after a few days but some remained in detention for weeks or even months.

In both the West Bank and Gaza, detainees were allowed access to the International Committee of the Red Cross (ICRC) and the Palestinian Independent Commission for Human Rights (ICHR), but often only after 10 or more days. In December, Israeli forces bombed and destroyed all Gaza's prisons and detention centres, and most police stations. Some detainees were killed or injured in the bombardments, but most escaped unharmed.

Justice system

The judicial systems in the West Bank and Gaza remained highly dysfunctional. The PA continued to

P

forbid former members of the judiciary and security forces from working for the Hamas de facto administration in Gaza, and to pay them for not working. Hamas continued to use alternative prosecutors and judges who often lacked training and qualifications. Rulings made by the Palestinian High Court of Justice were frequently not implemented.

Torture and other ill-treatment

In the West Bank, detainees complained that they had been tortured or otherwise ill-treated by the PA's General Intelligence and Preventive Security services, apparently to make them confess involvement with Hamas' armed wing. Methods alleged included beatings, suspension, and forcing detainees to sit or stand for prolonged periods in painful positions (*shabeh*).

■ Majd al-Barghouthi, imam of a mosque in Kobar near Ramallah, was detained by the General Intelligence on 14 February and died eight days later. The PA stated that he had a heart attack, but fellow detainees said they had seen him being beaten and suspended by a chain from the ceiling of his cell. A fact-finding committee set up by members of the Palestinian Legislative Council found that Majd al-Barghouthi had been tortured; photographs of his body substantiated their findings.

In Gaza, allegations of severe beatings and other torture of detainees by Hamas forces and militias were widespread. After the Israeli military offensive began in December, Hamas forces and militias sharply increased their attacks on political opponents, former members of the security forces in the PA government and former detainees alleged to have "collaborated" with Israeli intelligence services. Some were summarily killed, others were shot in the legs or severely beaten.

■ Taleb Mohammed Abu Sitta, 72, was detained in al-Zawaida on 26 June following the arrest of his son for an alleged drugs offence. He was reported to have been severely beaten and taken the following morning to hospital in Deir al-Balah, where he was declared dead on arrival. The Interior Ministry announced an inquiry and several police officers were reported to have been suspended from duty, but no one was known to have been tried.

Neither the PA in the West Bank nor Hamas in Gaza took any credible measures to end impunity for

torture and other ill-treatment of detainees or for excessive and unwarranted use of force by security forces against demonstrators.

Freedom of expression

Both the PA in the West Bank and Hamas in Gaza suppressed freedom of expression, closing media outlets affiliated to or accused of supporting the rival party. Journalists were frequently detained, often several times and for long periods. At least 15 media workers were detained by the PA, which also closed media such as the pro-Hamas al-Aqsa TV station. Hamas suspended the distribution of newspapers such as *al-Ayyam* and *al-Hayat al-Jadida*, detaining and putting on trial their directors in Gaza.

■ PA security forces detained Mustafa Sabri, a freelance journalist and member of Qalqiliya municipal council affiliated to Hamas, at least three times during the year.

Excessive use of force

PA security forces in the West Bank used excessive force against demonstrators. For example, they fired live ammunition against demonstrators throwing stones in the village of Beit Furik near Nablus on 1 June, causing gunshot injuries to seven people, including two children.

Hamas security forces in Gaza frequently used excessive force against demonstrators and suspected opposition supporters attending public meetings.

■ Palestinian police and Hamas activists in civilian clothes used force to disperse a peaceful demonstration in Rafah commemorating the death of a Fatah activist in inter-factional fighting the previous year.

A committee of inquiry set up by the Interior Ministry of the Hamas de facto administration in Gaza into the killing of six demonstrators in November 2007 issued a report in April, but it was seriously flawed. The committee, which was not independent, concluded that Fatah supporters had carried out most of the shooting despite eyewitness testimony to the contrary and even though the people killed were Fatah supporters.

In August and September Hamas security forces in Gaza killed 24 members of armed clans linked to Fatah and Jaysh al-Islam (Army of Islam), including three children, when an attempt to arrest clan members turned into armed clashes. Several members of the Hamas security forces were killed by armed clan members.

Death penalty

In the West Bank, PA military courts sentenced four people, all civilians, to death after convicting them in summary trials of collaborating with Israeli intelligence. Two others, both security officers, were sentenced to death for murder. In Gaza, a Hamas military court sentenced one person to death for murder and two for collaborating with Israeli intelligence, after unfair trials. No executions were carried out.

Right to health

The dire situation caused by the Israeli blockade, which prevented hundreds of critically ill patients from leaving Gaza to obtain medical treatment unavailable in local hospitals (see Israel and the Occupied Palestinian Territories entry), was exacerbated by a strike of some 30 per cent of health workers in Gaza's hospitals and clinics. The strike, which lasted for the last four months of the year, was called by the Palestinian Union of Health Professionals in protest at the removal or transfer of health managers and hospital directors by the Hamas de facto administration in Gaza. Hamas claimed that the strike was politically motivated and carried out at the behest of the West Bank-based PA caretaker government. The strike in Gaza was supported by the West Bank-based PA Ministry of Health.

Abuses by armed groups

Palestinian armed groups in Gaza frequently launched indiscriminate rocket attacks against civilian areas in southern Israel. From the beginning of the year until the ceasefire in June, Palestinian armed groups in Gaza, including groups affiliated to Hamas and Fatah, fired more than 2,000 rockets and mortars against nearby Israeli towns and villages. These indiscriminate attacks killed seven Israeli and two Palestinian civilians, and wounded several other Israeli civilians. After the breakdown of the ceasefire in November, rocket attacks by Palestinian armed groups in Gaza against Israel resumed but did not result in further deaths of Israeli civilians until after the onset of the 27 December offensive by Israeli forces.

■ Roni Yihya was killed in Sapir College near Sderot in Israel and 10 others were injured on 27 February when Palestinian armed groups fired more than 50 "qassam" rockets and dozens of mortar rounds at the towns of Sderot and Ashkelon.

■ Malak Yunes al-Kafarneh, a three-year-old Palestinian girl, was killed on 1 March by a "qassam" rocket fired by an armed group towards Israel. The rocket fell short and hit her home in Beit Hanun, Gaza.

Palestinian armed groups and individuals from the occupied West Bank, including East Jerusalem, killed 16 Israeli civilians.

■ On 6 March an armed Palestinian killed eight students, including four children, in the library of a *yeshiva* (religious school) in Jerusalem. He was not known to be affiliated to any armed group, although several groups, including the previously unknown group Ahrar al-Jalil (Free People of Galilee), claimed responsibility.

Gilad Shalit, an Israeli soldier captured by Palestinian armed groups in June 2006, continued to be held in an unknown place in Gaza without access to the ICRC. His family received two letters from him and he reportedly received a letter from his family.

Violence against women and girls

At least three women were killed in alleged "honour killings" in the West Bank and Gaza.

■ In June Khouloud Mohammed al-Najjar was beaten to death in the southern Gaza Strip by members of her family who accused her of "immoral behaviour". Her father was detained.

■ In July the PA police in the West Bank town of Hebron said they had detained a man accused of killing his sister for "family honour". The police did not divulge the names of those involved.

Amnesty International visit/report

🚍 Amnesty International delegates visited the West Bank and Gaza in February-April.

▥ Occupied Palestinian Territories: Rival Palestinian factions must end crackdown on opponents (MDE 21/003/2008)

P

PAPUA NEW GUINEA

PAPUA NEW GUINEA

Head of state:	Queen Elizabeth II represented by Paulias Matane
Head of government:	Michael Somare
Death penalty:	abolitionist in practice
Population:	6.5 million
Life expectancy:	56.9 years
Under-5 mortality (m/f):	90/76 per 1,000
Adult literacy:	57.3 per cent

Women and girls suffered from widespread physical and sexual violence and those responsible were not brought to justice. Maternal mortality rates and HIV infection rates were high due to poor health services and infrastructure. A growing number of people were either assaulted or killed after being accused of sorcery.

Background

Violent crime continued unabated across the country. Police responded with excessive force against those in custody.

Violence against women and girls

Reports of rape and other sexual violence continued to rise. Police statistics revealed that there were 654 rape cases reported from January to October, compared with 526 cases during the same period last year. Few alleged perpetrators were held accountable because victims and witnesses were unwilling to come forward due to fear of violence by their husbands, other relatives and the police.

Women's rights

In November, the only woman parliamentarian and cabinet minister Carol Kidu together with the National Council of Women called on the government to allocate an additional eight national parliament seats to women by 2012, increasing the total number of seats from 109 to 117. As a temporary measure ahead of the 2012 elections, the cabinet endorsed the tabling of a motion in parliament to invoke a constitutional provision allowing for the nomination, rather than election, of three members to parliament. This would enable the nomination of three women as independent members in 2009.

In September, Prime Minister Michael Somare publicly announced his support for affirmative action to get more women into parliament.

Right to health

In July, Health Minister Sasa Sibe stated that despite the allocation of US$78 million for the health department, efforts to improve the health system were at a standstill. He blamed doctors and nurses for refusing to be posted to the rural areas, where the need for health services was greatest.

Maternal mortality

In July, the government acknowledged that the poor state of health services and facilities contributed to approximately 2,600 women dying yearly during childbirth.

HIV/AIDS

In January, the government submitted its country report on the UN Guidelines on AIDS to the UN General Assembly. The National Prevention Strategic Plan includes specific programmes and interventions to target high risk groups such as sex workers and men having sex with men.

In November, a report by the Papua New Guinea Independent Review Group on HIV highlighted that HIV infection rates had escalated. However, there were very few clinics in rural areas to deal with the rising epidemic.

Attacks on suspected sorcerers

There were numerous cases of violence, including killings of people accused of practising sorcery by relatives of the alleged victims. Police were ineffective in preventing the violence and killings in many provinces.

■ In March, two women in Goroka who were accused of sorcery over the death of a man, were assaulted and killed by relatives of the deceased before their bodies were thrown into a fire.

Forced evictions

In December, police forcibly evicted 400 people from Tete settlement in Port Moresby by bulldozing and burning their homes in response to the murder of a prominent businessman by suspects from the settlement. The settlers were forced to flee with their belongings. Government failed to provide any temporary accommodation, transportation or food for the evictees.

PARAGUAY

REPUBLIC OF PARAGUAY

Head of state and government:	**Fernando Lugo (replaced Nicanor Duarte Frutos in August)**
Death penalty:	**abolitionist for all crimes**
Population:	**6.2 million**
Life expectancy:	**71.3 years**
Under-5 mortality (m/f):	**43/32 per 1,000**
Adult literacy:	**93.5 per cent**

The Truth and Justice Commission published its report and recommendations, shedding light on human rights violations committed during the military government (1954-1989) and transition to democracy. Indigenous Peoples demanded government action to address continuing discrimination and poverty. Both Indigenous Peoples and *campesinos* (peasant farmers) voiced demands for the resolution of their land claims. Excessive use of force by police and armed civilian patrols was reported, including during disputes over land.

Background

In August, Fernando Lugo took office amid high expectations that his election marked a turning point in respect for human rights in Paraguay. President Lugo made a public apology to the victims of human rights violations under the military government of General Alfredo Stroessner, the first such statement by a Paraguayan head of state. However, he stopped short of accepting state responsibility for the violations. By the end of the year, a clear strategy for implementing electoral promises on land reform and addressing the many issues faced by Indigenous Peoples had yet to be set out.

Between August and the end of the year, Paraguay ratified several key international human rights treaties.

Indigenous Peoples' rights

The first National Survey of Indigenous Households conducted between May and June documented wide socio-economic disparities between Paraguay's Indigenous Peoples and the rest of the population. For example, it found that the illiteracy rate was nearly eight times higher among Indigenous Peoples (40.2 per cent) and that the average monthly income for Indigenous workers was less than two-thirds that of the rest of the population.

An official report published in September used government information to demonstrate that between 1989 and 2003, 19.3 per cent of Paraguay's land had been illegally allocated, favouring the allies of the former president, Alfredo Stroessner.

■ Paraguay failed to comply with an order of the Inter-American Court of Human Rights to return traditional territory to the Yakye Axa Indigenous community by the time the deadline expired in July. In November, President Lugo signed a bill to expropriate these lands; the bill was awaiting discussion in Congress at the end of the year.

Deforestation, soya plantations and the use of agro-chemicals continued to affect the livelihoods of Indigenous Peoples and *campesinos*. Government controls failed to halt deforestation by private companies and individuals. Officials estimated that 130,000 hectares of forest were being destroyed annually.

Torture and excessive use of force

Police used torture and excessive force during protests and during attacks against Paraguay's *campesino* population engaged in land claims.

■ In July, a group of approximately 65 *campesinos* camped near privately-owned land to which they believed they had a claim were attacked by police. The police raid in the town of San José, district of Horqueta, Concepción department, involved some 300 officials. Police reportedly opened fire on the camp, forcing the *campesinos* to lie face down on the floor. Police reportedly trod on them, beat them and threatened to burn them alive. Some *campesinos* were forced to eat earth by officers who taunted them that this was the quickest way that they would be able to own their own land. Several police also urinated on the *campesinos*.

■ In August a peaceful demonstration by approximately 60 people from the city of Villeta was violently broken up by approximately 25 riot police. The protesters were opposing the illegal dumping of rubbish less than 100m from their homes. Police fired rubber

P

bullets at demonstrators, beat them with truncheons and kicked them. Eleven members of the community, including a pregnant woman, sustained injuries as a result.

■ In December a presidential decree derogated a 2003 law that had allowed the creation of armed civilian patrols of "Neighbourhood Security Commissions". Many of these groups had been involved in violence and threats against *campesino* and Indigenous groups in isolated areas of the country.

Transitional justice

Nearly five years after it was established by law, the Truth and Justice Commission presented its conclusions and recommendations to the state in August. The Commission's final report was released publicly at the end of 2008.

The Commission's conclusions identified 20,090 direct victims of human rights violations during the period under investigation. These included 19,862 victims of arbitrary or illegal detention, 18,772 victims of torture, 59 victims of extrajudicial execution and 336 victims of enforced disappearance.

The Commission recommended that the Public Prosecutor and Procurator General investigate all cases further. It found that sexual violence had been employed as a repressive strategy, identifying cases of rape and sexual abuse by military and police officers committed against girls aged between 12 and 15. Through witness testimony, the Commission investigated violence against children, particularly in *campesino* communities. It also concluded that systematic and generalized violations against the Aché Indigenous Peoples in the 1970s may constitute a crime against humanity. The Commission investigated two cases related to sexual identity, but cited a lack of reliable evidence of wider repression against the lesbian, gay, bisexual and transgender population.

A new law passed in September enabled victims of detention on political grounds between 1954 and 1989 to seek reparations; those who were tortured or disappeared during that time were already eligible for reparations.

Amnesty International visits

🚍 Amnesty International delegates visited Paraguay and met with Indigenous communities, NGOs and government officials in September, November and December.

PERU

REPUBLIC OF PERU

Head of state and government:	Alan García Peréz
Death penalty:	abolitionist for ordinary crimes
Population:	28.2 million
Life expectancy:	70.7 years
Under-5 mortality (m/f):	30/26 per 1,000
Adult literacy:	87.9 per cent

Some progress was made in tackling impunity. However, legal representatives and others continued to receive threats and members of Congress presented proposals for amnesty laws for military and police personnel. Social protest, particularly at the failure of continuing economic growth to benefit the country's poor, increased.

Background

There were signs of growing intolerance by the government towards critics of its social, economic and environmental policies. Protests against some of these policies took place throughout the year and across the country; in some cases states of emergency were declared in affected provinces. Challapalca prison, which is situated over 4,600m above sea level, remained open despite statements by the Minister of Justice that it would be closed. The armed opposition group Shining Path (Sendero Luminoso) remained active in parts of the country and there were reports of armed confrontations with the military.

Right to health – maternal mortality

Some attempts were made to address gross inequality in access to maternal health services. However, Peru continued to have one of the highest maternal mortality rates in the region and lacked a national plan of action to address the problem. In a report published in December, the National Ombudsperson's Office recommended that the state co-ordinate and evaluate existing measures to reduce maternal mortality and update the national strategy for sexual and reproductive health as well as greatly increase monitoring of maternal mortality.

Human rights defenders and journalists

Government authorities attempted to discredit the work of human rights defenders. There was growing official intolerance of dissent in the face of heightened social protest and human rights defenders and journalists were threatened and harassed; some were attacked.

■ President García publicly accused the Association for Human Rights (Asociación Pro Derechos Humanos, APRODEH) of "treason to the fatherland" after APRODEH made a statement to the European Parliament that they did not believe the Túpac Amaru Revolutionary Movement (Movimiento Revolucionario Túpac Amaru, MRTA), an armed opposition group, was active. The European Parliament removed the MRTA from its list of terrorist organizations shortly afterwards. The Peruvian government immediately issued a decree withdrawing observer status in the National Council of Human Rights from the national coalition of human rights organizations (Coordinadora Nacional de Derechos Humanos) of which APRODEH is a member.

■ In March, 35 people working to ensure communities in Piura province had access to information and were adequately consulted about projected mining activities were accused of offences including acts of terrorism, incitement to commit violence, public order offences, illicit association, conspiracy to commit a crime, torture, assault, kidnapping, and criminal damage. Among the accused were members of human rights NGOs, community leaders and local officials. In October, some of the most serious charges were dropped owing to insufficient evidence. However, the prosecution lodged an appeal and proceedings regarding the remaining charges were continuing at the end of the year.

Impunity

Despite some advances, progress in bringing to justice those responsible for past human rights violations was slow. In August, five years after the publication of the final report of the Truth and Reconciliation Commission, the Commission's former president criticized the government's failure to implement any of the recommended reforms. Two separate bills proposing amnesties for police and military personnel implicated in human rights violations were presented to Congress in November.

■ Exhumations took place of the remains of 60 people killed by the military in the December 1984 massacre in Putis, Ayacucho department.

■ In August, a Lima court closed the case of the massacre of some 100 people in the island prison of El Frontón in 1986 on the grounds that the statute of limitations could be applied. The Constitutional Court was set to review the decision later in the year but finally rejected the right of the human rights organization who presented the appeal to do so.

■ The trial of former President Alberto Fujimori continued throughout 2008 and was expected to end in the first instance at the beginning of 2009.

■ In April, a court found three agents and the former head of the National Intelligence Service, retired General Julio Salazar Monroe, guilty of the 1992 killings and enforced disappearance of nine students and a professor from the Enrique Guzmán y Valle University for Education in Lima, known as La Cantuta. The three received 15-year prison sentences; General Salazar received a 35-year sentence.

■ In August the USA deported a former army officer wanted for his involvement in the massacre of 69 peasant farmers in Accomarca in August 1985. Another officer, already convicted in the USA in connection with the massacre, remained in prison in the USA awaiting the results of an extradition request.

Amnesty International visit

🚍 Amnesty International delegates visited Peru in July. Amnesty International attended the trial proceedings of former president Alberto Fujimori on a number of occasions during the year.

PHILIPPINES

REPUBLIC OF THE PHILIPPINES

Head of state and government:	Gloria Macapagal-Arroyo
Death penalty:	abolitionist for all crimes
Population:	89.7 million
Life expectancy:	71 years
Under-5 mortality (m/f):	32/21 per 1,000
Adult literacy:	92.6 per cent

Renewed armed conflict displaced more than 610,000 and killed over 100 civilians in Southern Philippines. Peace talks between the government and various armed groups stalled. The majority of extrajudicial killings and enforced disappearances remained unsolved. A culture of impunity continued to encourage vigilante killings. Indigenous Peoples (IPs) continued to struggle for land rights as the government failed to comply with its obligation to obtain IPs' free, prior and informed consent to development plans in their traditional territories. Cruel, inhuman and degrading conditions of detention persisted, and under-18s experienced abuse in juvenile detention centres.

Armed conflict – Mindanao

In August, heavy fighting erupted between government security forces and the Moro Islamic Liberation Front (MILF) after the Supreme Court issued a temporary restraining order on a previously signed Memorandum of Agreement on Ancestral Domain. The Memorandum widened the Autonomous Region for Muslim Mindanao and gave broader political and economic powers to Muslim leadership in the region.

Human rights abuses and breaches of international humanitarian law were committed by the government and the MILF during the renewed conflict. Over 610,000 people were displaced by the fighting; their situation was aggravated by floods, typhoons and reported cases of local government or the military blocking aid. Over 100 unarmed civilians were killed, some of them deliberately targeted and others indiscriminately attacked by MILF fighters. Over 500 houses were allegedly burned by both parties.

■ In August, the MILF killed at least 33 civilians and took more than 70 hostage including the elderly,

women and children, in an attack on civilians in Lanao del Norte province.

The MILF reportedly trained children as young as 13 for the Bangsamoro Islamic Armed Forces.

The Philippine military failed to protect civilians from MILF attacks, and killed several civilians in ground attacks and aerial bombings. Security forces allegedly tortured several Muslim civilians, resulting in at least two deaths, in their pursuit of MILF commanders.

The government armed militias. In August, the police announced that they would distribute 12,000 shotguns to "auxiliaries". Some local officials encouraged civilians to arm themselves for protection.

Enforced disappearances and extrajudicial executions

The national counter-insurgency policy did not differentiate between New People's Army (NPA) fighters, the military wing of the Communist Party of the Philippines (CPP), and activists in legal organizations. Allegations of enforced disappearances, extrajudicial executions and criminal cases brought against activists, political dissidents and NGO workers on what appeared to be spurious grounds continued.

In April, the UN Special Rapporteur on extrajudicial, summary or arbitrary executions submitted his report stating: "killings have eliminated civil society leaders, including human rights defenders, trade unionists and land reform advocates, intimidated a vast number of civil society actors, and narrowed the country's political discourse."

In November, the UN Human Rights Committee concluded that the government violated provisions in the International Covenant on Civil and Political Rights (ICCPR) in the 2003 murder of activists Eden Marcellana and Eddie Gumanoy, stating that failure to investigate the killings "amounted to a denial of justice".

Few effective investigations were conducted into allegations of enforced disappearances and extrajudicial executions, and conviction of those responsible was rare. Many cases were not brought to court due to a lack of evidence, often because witnesses feared reprisals. Out of the hundreds of cases that had been reported in previous years, only two were resolved and no high-ranking officials were prosecuted.

P

In a landmark ruling in July, a Regional Trial Court in Agusan del Sur province found Army Corporal Rodrigo Billones guilty of kidnapping and illegal detention of six individuals, suspected to be communist insurgents, in 2000. A military witness stated that the victims were tortured. Rodrigo Billones was sentenced to life imprisonment.

In September, Indigenous Peoples' rights activist and co-founder of group Cordillera Peoples' Alliance (CPA) James Balao was abducted by armed men claiming to be police officers. The CPA believed James Balao to be detained in an undisclosed security forces' facility.

In September, the Court of Appeals issued writs of amparo and habeas corpus to the families of disappeared students Sherlyn Cadapan and Karen Empeño, who had been abducted in 2006. The Court ordered the students' release, stating that the decision dealt with "a few misguided, self-righteous people who resort to the extrajudicial process of neutralizing those who disagree with the country's democratic system of government." However, the court did not permit inspection of military camps and facilities, and their whereabouts remained unknown.

In October, the Supreme Court upheld a Court of Appeals decision granting brothers Raymond and Reynaldo Manalo protection from harassment by security forces under a writ of amparo. The brothers were illegally detained and subjected to torture and other cruel, inhuman and degrading treatment by the military for 18 months before they escaped in 2007.

Freedom of expression

At least 11 journalists, mostly local radio commentators, were killed in separate incidents by unknown perpetrators. According to the Supreme Court Chief Justice, some 70 journalists were killed between 2001 and 2008, and of the cases filed on these killings, only one had been resolved, six were undergoing trial and 18 were under investigation.

Indigenous Peoples' rights

Despite legislative protection, Indigenous Peoples (IPs) struggled to realise their land rights and rights to determine the development of their own traditional territories and resources within them.

The government stepped up efforts to attract mining corporations to invest in the country's huge quantity of unexplored minerals – most of them within

IPs' traditional territories. In mining sites across the country, IPs were displaced and hundreds forcibly evicted. In many cases, no free, prior and informed consent was sought. In October, the Defence Secretary announced that the government will deploy more troops in mining areas and allow mining companies to create militias, to be trained and supervised by soldiers, to secure their mining interests against the NPA.

Prison conditions

Cruel, inhuman and degrading conditions persisted. Detention centres and prisons remained overcrowded and food was frequently spoiled.

Despite legislative and procedural safeguards, children in detention were held with adults in poor conditions and remained at risk of physical or sexual abuse.

Media highlighted discrimination in prisons, reporting as many as 6,000 special private cubicles, some reportedly with amenities such as large-sized bed and LCD TV, available to rich or influential prisoners.

POLAND

REPUBLIC OF POLAND
Head of state: Lech Kaczyński
Head of government: Donald Tusk
Death penalty: abolitionist for all crimes
Population: 38 million
Life expectancy: 75.2 years
Under-5 mortality (m/f): 8/7 per 1,000
Adult literacy: 99.8 per cent

An official investigation into the involvement of Poland in the secret detention programme led by the US Central Intelligence Agency (CIA) began after more detailed allegations emerged. Lesbian, gay, bisexual and transgender (LGBT) people continued to experience discrimination. Despite the re-establishment of a senior government post for gender equality and the introduction of new measures facilitating legal abortion, women's and girls' access to abortion services was restricted.

Counter-terror and security

The European Commission said in February that it was still awaiting response from Poland to charges that it hosted CIA prisons where al-Qa'ida suspects were questioned and guards used methods akin to torture.

In April, as a result of the UN Human Rights Council's Universal Periodic Review, Poland was urged to make public the findings of its investigations into the existence of CIA-operated secret detention centres in Poland, and to reply to the two communications sent by the European Commission requesting clarification of these allegations.

An investigation into the possible existence of CIA-run secret detention centres was opened in March by the District Prosecutor of Warsaw and was transferred to the Organized Crime Unit of the National Prosecutor's Office in June.

A letter on "CIA prisons in Poland", said to have been handed by former Deputy Prime Minister Roman Giertych to the incumbent Prime Minister about a secret memorandum issued by the Polish Intelligence Service in 2005, allegedly provided circumstantial evidence of a secret CIA detention centre on Polish soil between 2002 and 2005. The Prime Minister delivered the letter to the National Prosecutor on 1 September, which triggered a new official inquiry into the case by the National Prosecutor's Office. The inquiry remained confidential and the list of witnesses was kept secret. However, reports suggested that a number of officials had been questioned by the end of the year.

In October, the Prime Minister promised to relieve various individuals from their obligation to keep state secrets, as previously requested by the National Prosecutor. The Chair of the parliament also gave his permission for members of parliament to testify.

Discrimination

During the Universal Periodic Review in April, members of the Human Rights Council urged the Polish authorities to introduce comprehensive anti-discrimination legislation. The government declared that a new Act on Equal Treatment was expected to be adopted by the parliament in November. The draft Act, as consulted with NGOs, addresses discrimination based on gender, race, ethnic origin, nationality, religion, political views, disability, age, sexual orientation, and marital and family status.

Nevertheless, it only prohibits discrimination based on gender, race and ethnic origin when it comes to access to services, social welfare, health care and education. It does not ensure protection from multiple discrimination or discrimination through association.

■ In November, the Living Library, a project promoting diversity and rights of minorities initially planned to be held by human rights activists in Opole at the city-owned Cultural Centre, was banned by the Deputy Mayor without explanation. The project included the participation of representatives of the German and Romani minorities, refugees and migrants, people with physical and mental disabilities, and individual lesbians and gay men. The media reported that the Deputy Mayor opposed the participation of gay men and lesbians as "not acceptable" as they would "promote deviation". The Mayor publicly supported the decision of his Deputy. The University of Opole, independent from the local government, eventually hosted the project.

Violence against women and girls

In March, the Prime Minister appointed a senior government official for gender equality. The post, abolished by the previous government in 2005, was reintroduced as a result of lobbying by human rights bodies and NGOs. However, the role and powers of the post had not been made clear by the end of the year.

Refusal to provide abortion services

Denial of access to abortion for eligible women was raised during Poland's Universal Periodic Review by the UN Human Rights Council in April. This remained a concern despite a ruling in 2007 by the European Court of Human Rights that the government has the duty to establish effective mechanisms for ensuring that women have access to abortion where it is legal.

■ A 14-year-old girl from Lublin, identified in the media under the pseudonym Agata and as being pregnant as a result of rape, was subjected to delays in accessing a legal abortion. Hospitals in Lublin and Warsaw refused to perform the abortion, despite its lawfulness, and failed to refer her. According to media reports, there was a serious breach of Agata's right to medical confidentiality and she and her mother were not protected from direct and personal harassment by abortion opponents. Following the intervention of the Health Minister, Agata obtained an abortion four weeks after her initial request for the procedure and only one week before the end of the 12-week gestational limit on legal access to abortion.

P

Refugees and asylum-seekers

The law regarding refugees and asylum-seekers was amended in May, incorporating EU legislation. Subsidiary protection was introduced to protect individuals who do not qualify for refugee status but still face serious risk in their country of origin. The amendments also introduced detailed definitions of "a refugee", "persecution" and "persecutors".

In May, an integration programme was made available for people receiving subsidiary protection as well as for recognized refugees. However, asylum-seekers and recognized refugees continued to face difficulties accessing the labour market and health care, partly due to poor integration programme conditions.

Amnesty International visits/reports

🚌 Amnesty International delegates visited Poland in September and October.

📄 Oral statement on the outcome on Poland under the Universal Periodic Review (IOR 41/023/2008)

📄 Eastern Europe: Eighth session of the UN Human Rights Council, 2-20 June 2008: Review of the Czech Republic, Poland and Romania under the Universal Periodic Review – Amnesty International's reflections on the outcome (EUR 02/001/2008)

PORTUGAL

PORTUGUESE REPUBLIC

Head of state:	Aníbal António Cavaco Silva
Head of government:	José Sócrates Carvalho Pinto de Sousa
Death penalty:	abolitionist for all crimes
Population:	10.7 million
Life expectancy:	77.7 years
Under-5 mortality (m/f):	7/7 per 1,000
Adult literacy:	93.8 per cent

Allegations of torture and other ill-treatment and excessive use of force by law enforcement officials remained a concern. The prosecution of law enforcement officials implicated in two high-profile cases of torture and other ill-treatment proceeded slowly. Domestic violence continued to be a widespread problem, leading to numerous deaths.

Torture and other ill-treatment

There were continued allegations of ill-treatment by law enforcement officials. In February, the UN Committee against Torture expressed its concern about reports of torture and other ill-treatment in prisons and the excessive use of force, including the use of firearms, by law enforcement officials. It also expressed concern at the acquisition of Taser weapons by law enforcement agencies, stating that the pain such weapons inflict constituted a form of torture.

■ In October, the trial began of four police officers charged with torturing Leonor Cipriano in 2004 to obtain a confession that she had killed her daughter. Medical reports and photographs of Leonor Cipriano recorded extensive injuries after two days in police custody in Faro. Police officials said that she fell down a flight of stairs in the police station; however the Institute of Forensic Medicine stated that her injuries were not consistent with such an incident and were more in keeping with an assault. Leonor Cipriano said that she was punched, kicked, had a plastic bag placed over head, and was forced to kneel on glass ashtrays during interrogations. The trial was ongoing at the end of the year.

■ The Court of Appeal in Lisbon ordered a retrial in the case of Albino Libânio, who was assaulted by prison officers in Lisbon Prison in 2003. The Court granted a request by Albino Libânio's lawyers for the Portuguese state to be named as a defendant. The decision was made on the grounds that, as his injuries occurred while he was in the care of the prison system, the state should be held liable even if it was impossible to prove which prison officers were responsible for the attack. The original trial had recognized the injuries suffered by Albino Libânio but acquitted all seven prison officers of assault because of lack of evidence proving their responsibility. A new trial date had not been set at the end of the year.

Violence against women and girls

The Portuguese Association of Victim Support received 16,832 complaints concerning domestic violence in 2008, including seven murders. This represented an increase over the 14,534 complaints of domestic violence received in 2007.

According to statistics compiled by the NGO Women's Union, 48 people died as a result of domestic violence in the year to mid-November.

Racism

The Portuguese National Renewal Party provoked

P

controversy with an anti-immigration poster associating immigration with criminality and other social problems. The posters showed a white sheep kicking black sheep out of Portugal.

Counter-terror and security

The judicial investigation into suspected CIA rendition flights, opened in February 2007, was still ongoing at the end of the year. In January the UK-based NGO Reprieve stated that 700 prisoners had been illegally transferred to Guantánamo Bay "with Portuguese complicity" between 2002 and 2006, and at least 94 rendition flights had crossed Portuguese territory.

Information from the Ministry of Public Works given to Parliament in May stated that 56 CIA-operated flights originating from or heading to Guantánamo Bay passed through Portuguese territory between July 2005 and December 2007. No information was made public about the details of the passengers on these flights.

PUERTO RICO

COMMONWEALTH OF PUERTO RICO

Head of state:	George W. Bush
Head of government:	Aníbal Aceveda-Vilá
Death penalty:	abolitionist for all crimes
Population:	4 million
Life expectancy:	79 years
Under 5 mortality (m/f):	9/8 per 1,000

There were reports of police brutality against migrants and residents of poor neighbourhoods, as well as allegations of discrimination and racial profiling by police.

Ill-treatment by police

There were reports of police brutality against migrants from the Dominican Republic. In October, the Dominican Consulate in San Juan submitted a report to the Puerto Rican Senate stating that it received regular complaints of abuse and discriminatory treatment of Dominican migrants by the Puerto Rican police. The report outlined 15 recent cases of alleged police beatings. Migrant communities alleged that police officers regularly raided poor areas in search of undocumented migrants, whom they arbitrarily detained. The detainees were then handed over to the federal authorities for deportation, even though the Puerto Rican police had no powers to enforce immigration law. The Puerto Rico Police Department denied the allegations.

In July a grand jury indicted six San Juan Municipal Police Department officers for federal civil rights violations for beating a man to death in 2003, and with obstruction of justice for having tried to cover up their actions.

Discrimination

The UN Special Rapporteur on racism visited Puerto Rico during May and June, when he heard testimony about alleged racial profiling and police ill-treatment of migrants and residents of poor areas such as Villa Cañona in the town of Loíza. He also visited the site of the controversial Federal Bureau of Investigation (FBI) shooting of Puerto Rican independence activist Filiberto Ojeda Ríos in 2005. The Puerto Rico American Civil Liberties Union presented him with the preliminary findings of their inquiries into 42 unexplained prison deaths in Guerrero Prison in three years. The Special Rapporteur's report was due to be issued in 2009.

QATAR

STATE OF QATAR

Head of state:	Shaikh Hamad bin Khalifa al-Thani
Head of government:	Shaikh Hamad bin Jassim bin Jabr al-Thani
Death penalty:	retentionist
Population:	856,000
Life expectancy:	75 years
Under-5 mortality (m/f):	9/12 per 1,000
Adult literacy:	89 per cent

Hundreds of people were arbitrarily deprived of their nationality. Women continued to face discrimination and violence. Foreign migrant workers were exploited and abused, and inadequately protected under the law. At least 20 people were on death row but there were no executions.

Nationality rights

The government continued to deny Qatari nationality to hundreds of people who were consequently either denied employment opportunities, social security and health care, or were denied entry to Qatar. Most were members of al-Murra tribe, who were deprived of their nationality after a failed coup attempt in 1996 for which the authorities blamed some members of the tribe. They had no means of remedy before the courts.

■ Hamad Abdel Hadi Hamad Al-Hamran and members of his family continued to be denied entry to Qatar. They were stripped of their nationality after the 1996 coup attempt and sought exile in the United Arab Emirates where they continued to reside.

■ 'Abdul Hameed Hussain al-Mohammed, together with his six children and two brothers, were reported to have been stripped of their Qatari nationality and ordered to be deported in October 2002, after he and his two brothers were sentenced to prison terms. They were given no reasons and had no means to challenge the decision, which led to them being dismissed from their jobs, denied housing assistance and losing their employment rights. They remained in Qatar under threat of deportation.

Discrimination and violence against women

Women continued to face discrimination in law and in practice and were inadequately protected against violence within the family. In particular, family law discriminates against women, making it much easier for men to divorce than women, and placing women whose husbands leave them or who seek a divorce at a severe economic disadvantage.

In August, the government equalized the law on compensation which had previously set the level of compensation to be paid for the loss of a woman's life at half that of a man.

Migrants' rights

Foreign migrant workers, who make up a large proportion of Qatar's workforce, continued to be exposed to, and inadequately protected against, abuses and exploitation by employers. Women migrant domestic workers were particularly at risk of exploitation and abuses such as beatings, rape and other sexual violence. Some 20,000 workers were reported to have fled from their employers in 2007

alone due to delays in or non-payment of their wages, excessive hours and poor working conditions.

In June, the Consultative Council adopted draft legislation to improve migrant workers' conditions by requiring employers to allow rest days and three weeks' holiday a year or face fines or imprisonment. It had yet to be enacted.

Counter-terror and security

In May, the government acceded to the Gulf Cooperation Council Counter Terrorism Convention, 2004. This defines terrorism in very broad and vague terms, which could allow restriction or suppression of activities that constitute legitimate exercise of the rights to freedom of expression, association and assembly. Qatar's counter-terrorism laws are also overly broad and allow the authorities to detain suspects for up to six months without charge and for up to two years without trial on vaguely worded charges.

In July, the US authorities released Jarrallah al-Marri, a Qatari national, from Guantánamo Bay and returned him to Qatar. No charges were brought and he was released. His brother, Ali al-Marri, continued to be detained by the US authorities as an alleged enemy combatant.

Death penalty

At least 20 people were on death row, including 17 people sentenced in 2001 for involvement in the 1996 coup attempt, but there were no executions. Wabran al-Yami, a Saudi Arabian national sentenced in the coup attempt case, was released in July at the request of the Saudi Arabian Interior Minister and allowed to return to his country.

In December, Qatar voted against a UN General Assembly resolution calling for a worldwide moratorium on executions.

Amnesty International visits

🚌 An Amnesty International delegate visited Qatar in January and December.

ROMANIA

ROMANIA

Head of state:	Traian Băsescu
Head of government:	Emil Boc (replaced Călin Popescu-Tăriceanu in December)
Death penalty:	abolitionist for all crimes
Population:	21.3 million
Life expectancy:	71.9 years
Under-5 mortality (m/f):	20/15 per 1,000
Adult literacy:	97.3 per cent

There were further allegations that Romania was involved in the US-led secret detention and renditions programme, despite continued denials of any involvement by the government and the findings of a Senate commission of inquiry. There were reports of ill-treatment, excessive use of force and the unlawful use of firearms by law enforcement officials. Discrimination against Roma and lesbian, gay, bisexual and transgender (LGBT) people persisted.

Background

A progress report on Romania was published by the European Commission (EC) in July. This urged the Romanian authorities to improve the judicial system and to strengthen measures to tackle corruption, particularly at local government level.

Counter-terror and security

The authorities did not give satisfactory responses to repeated calls from the EC and others to clarify allegations about the use of Romanian territory in the US-led programme of renditions, secret detention and enforced disappearance.

In February 2008, a high-ranking Romanian official stated in a media interview that in 2004 and 2005 he had seen a black bus arrive five times in a secluded corner of the heavily guarded Mihail Kogălniceanu airport near Constanța. He said that parcels that looked like bundled-up prisoners were taken from the bus and loaded onto the jet, which then left for North Africa with its cargo and two US Central Intelligence Agency (CIA) agents on board. The official also said that US pilots routinely filed bogus flight plans, or none at all, and flew to undeclared destinations.

In February, the EC stated that Romania's response to a request by the EU Commissioner on Justice,

Freedom and Security for judicial inquiries into the existence of secret CIA detention centres on its territory was not complete. The EC again requested that Romania provide information on the possible transfer or detention of people suspected of involvement in terrorism. President Traian Băsescu declared he had no knowledge of any suspect packages being transferred at Mihail Kogălniceanu airport and noted that the airport was open to Romanian and foreign journalists.

The government repeatedly denied any involvement in US rendition and secret detention programmes. It noted that an investigation conducted by a Senate commission of inquiry during 2006 and 2007 had found no evidence of such involvement. The commission's report, much of which remained classified, concluded that "the accusations brought against Romania are groundless." The report was adopted by the Senate in April 2008.

In August, the Association for the Defence of Human Rights in Romania – the Helsinki Committee (APADOR-CH) filed a number of requests for information, including one to the Senate commission of inquiry. The commission responded in October that investigating the purpose of the flights entering Romania did not fall within its mandate which was "to investigate allegations regarding the existence of CIA detention centres on Romanian soil or of flights with planes hired by the CIA" on Romanian territory. As a result the commission had not requested and did not hold information about the purpose of the flights. It also stated that in May it had asked the competent authorities to consider declassifying certain information contained in its report; no decision had been made on this by the end of the year.

Torture, other ill-treatment and excessive use of force

Ill-treatment and excessive use of force by law enforcement officials continued to be reported. Many of the victims were members of the Romani community.

■ A Romani man, Ion Boacă, and his 15-year-old son alleged that they were injured when local police and gendarmerie officers entered their house in the village of Clejani, Giurgiu County, in August. The officers hit Ion Boacă in the face with a gun and fired a rubber bullet at his son. Two children, aged two and four, lost consciousness after police fired tear gas into the house.

■ On 4 March the European Court of Human Rights ruled that Romania had failed to conduct a proper investigation into allegations of police ill-treatment of Constantin Stoica. The 14-year-old Romani boy, who was represented by the NGOs European Roma Rights Centre and Romani CRISS, was injured during a clash between law enforcement officers and Roma outside a bar in Giulia in April 2001. He was knocked to the floor, beaten and kicked in the head by officers, despite telling them that he had recently undergone surgery on his head. Medical records following the attack stated that he was severely disabled as a result of the beating. The Court also found that the police officers' behaviour had clearly been motivated by racism.

In December 2008 the Council of Europe's Committee for the Prevention of Torture (CPT) published a report of its visit to Romania in June 2006. The report noted that a significant proportion of the detainees interviewed reported "excessive use of force by the police during their arrest or physical abuse during interrogations that followed."

The Romanian government failed to amend legislation on the use of firearms by law enforcement officials to bring it into line with relevant international standards.

■ The authorities failed to respond to the findings of an investigation by the UN Interim Administration Mission in Kosovo (UNMIK) into the deaths of two men and the serious injury of another during a demonstration on 10 February 2007 in Pristina, Kosovo. The UNMIK investigation had established that the deaths and injuries occurred as a result of the improper deployment of out-of-date rubber bullets by members of the Romanian Formed Police Unit. By the end of the year, no individual had been found responsible for the deaths; the investigation was continuing.

People with mental disabilities

A number of national and international NGOs, including Amnesty International, the Centre for Legal Resources and Save the Children-Romania, expressed continuing concern that the placement, living conditions and treatment of patients in many psychiatric wards and hospitals continued to violate international human rights standards.

The Romanian authorities acknowledged in May that measures to protect the rights of people with disabilities remained inadequate, that institutions and organizations caring for people with disabilities were seriously understaffed, and that staff lacked specialist training.

In its December report, the CPT expressed concern regarding the placement procedures and the legal status of people in psychiatric institutions and residential care centres. The Committee stressed that these institutions often operate with very limited funding and resources and that inadequate conditions and limited leisure and outdoor activities were reported. The Committee also reported cases of deaths related to severe malnutrition at the residential care centre at Nucet in 2004 and 2005 and urged the authorities to ensure that all deaths in psychiatric institutions and other social services of adults under 40, where a deadly disease had not been diagnosed, were investigated appropriately.

Discrimination

Roma

Discrimination against Roma, both by public officials and in society at large, remained widespread and entrenched. The Romanian authorities failed to take adequate measures to combat discrimination and stop violence against Roma.

In September, the High Court of Cassation and Justice ruled that the phrase "stinky gypsy", used by President Traian Băsescu when referring to a journalist in May 2007, was discriminatory. However, the Court did not apply any sanctions because the remark had been made during a private conversation.

Roma continued to be denied equal access to education, housing, health care and employment.

In its report to the UN Human Rights Council for the Universal Periodic Review in May, Romania acknowledged that Romani communities faced economic insecurity and were at particular risk of various forms of discrimination. The report also noted that Roma were subjected to policies which could in effect result in segregation, especially in the field of education.

■ On 2 October, Istvan Haller, a member of the National Council for Combating Discrimination, began a hunger strike over the persistent failure of the Romanian government to implement measures which had been promised in the wake of serious attacks on Roma communities in Hădăreni, Plăieşii de Sus and Casinul Nou in the early 1990s. At least five people were killed and 45 houses destroyed during mob violence. Hundreds of people were made homeless

R

while local authorities failed to intervene or actively participated in the attacks.

Following judgments by the European Court of Human Rights in 2005 and 2007 in these cases, the Romanian government undertook to initiate community development projects to improve living conditions and inter-ethnic relations. Measures included the creation of infrastructure, including houses for those whose homes had been destroyed, as well as anti-discrimination, educational and other social measures. However, the government failed to fulfil its commitments. Istvan Haller ended his hunger strike on 9 October following assurances by the government that it would not obstruct funding for the Hădăreni project, and a decision by the authorities to start the community development projects in Plăieşii de Sus and Casinul Nou.

Lesbian, gay, bisexual and transgender people

In its May Universal Periodic Review report to the UN Human Rights Council, the government acknowledged that LGBT people continued to face prejudice and discriminatory attitudes.

In February, an amendment by the Senate to the legal definition of the family effectively outlawed same-sex marriage. The amendment changed a 1953 law which referred to marriage "between spouses"; the new law defines marriage as "between a man and a woman".

On 24 May, around 200 LGBT rights activists marched through Bucharest in a heavily policed pride parade, defying efforts by religious and far-right groups to have the annual event banned.

Amnesty International visit/report

🚌 Amnesty International delegates visited Romania in October.

📓 Eastern Europe: Eighth session of the UN Human Rights Council, 2-20 June 2008: Review of the Czech Republic, Poland and Romania under the Universal Periodic Review – Amnesty International's reflections on the outcome (EUR 02/001/2008)

RUSSIAN FEDERATION

RUSSIAN FEDERATION

Head of state:	Dmitry Medvedev (replaced Vladimir Putin in May)
Head of government:	Vladimir Putin (replaced Viktor Zubkov in May)
Death penalty:	abolitionist in practice
Population:	141.8 million
Life expectancy:	65 years
Under-5 mortality (m/f):	24/18 per 1,000
Adult literacy:	99.4 per cent

The North Caucasus remained volatile and reports of human rights violations, including killings, enforced disappearances and torture, were frequent.

Russian armed forces were reported to have indiscriminately attacked civilian housing during the armed conflict between Russia and Georgia. They also failed to protect the civilian population in territories under de facto Russian control from human rights abuses committed by South Ossetian forces and militia.

The Law to Combat Extremism and legislation on libel and slander were used to stifle dissent and silence journalists and human rights activists. There were reports that criminal suspects were subjected to torture and other ill-treatment in order to extract confessions. Concerns continued about the failure to uphold fair trial standards.

Government officials spoke out against racism, but racist attacks continued to be reported on an almost daily basis.

The situation for those in Chechnya displaced by conflict remained insecure, as families were threatened with eviction from temporary accommodation.

Background

On 2 March Dmitry Medvedev was elected president. The OSCE declined to monitor the elections, citing restrictions on the monitoring process imposed by the Russian government. President Medvedev announced measures to address corruption. The United Russia party, headed in Chechnya by President Ramzan

Kadyrov, won an overwhelming majority in parliamentary elections in the Chechen Republic in October. In Ingushetia, President Murat Ziazikov was replaced by Yunus-Bek Evkurov in October.

Instability and violence continued to be reported in the North Caucasus, in particular in Chechnya, Ingushetia, Dagestan and Kabardino-Balkaria. Armed opposition groups were responsible for the deaths of dozens of police officers and local officials in Dagestan, Chechnya and Ingushetia. In November, 12 people were killed and many more injured in a bomb attack in Vladikavkaz in North Ossetia. In Chechnya a strict dress code was introduced. Women and girls not wearing headscarves faced expulsion from schools and universities or were prevented from entering government buildings.

After months of increased tension and low-level hostilities, tensions between Georgia and the breakaway region of South Ossetia erupted into an armed conflict in August which at its peak displaced more than 200,000 people. Russia later recognized South Ossetia and Abkhazia as independent states.

Insecurity in the North Caucasus

There were continuing reports of human rights violations – including arbitrary detention, torture and ill-treatment, and extrajudicial executions – by law enforcement officials in Chechnya, Dagestan and Ingushetia. There was ongoing concern that investigations into these violations were not effective, resulting in widespread impunity.

Independent journalists, media outlets and NGOs were targeted by the authorities for reporting about human rights violations. In June, the Parliamentary Assembly of the Council of Europe decided to continue monitoring the situation in the North Caucasus.

Ingushetia

Armed groups carried out numerous attacks, often fatal, against members of law enforcement agencies, including a failed attack on the republic's Minister of Internal Affairs. There were persistent reports of torture of detainees by law enforcement officials; at least one man was reported to have died as a result.

■ On 31 August, Magomed Evloev, a prominent opposition figure and owner of an independent website in Ingushetia, died of injuries sustained while in a police car; he had been detained by police at the airport upon arrival in Ingushetia. His death was initially categorized as caused by negligence; an appeal by his colleagues

and lawyer for it to be classified as murder was pending at the end of the year. In November a court in Ingushetia ruled that his detention had been unlawful.

Chechnya

A number of mass graves were found in Chechnya. However, the federal authorities blocked the construction of a forensic laboratory, which could have helped uncover the fate of victims of enforced disappearance.

In May, seven bodies were discovered in a mass grave on territory which had been under the control of the so-called "East" battalion of the Ministry of Defence.

About a dozen enforced disappearances were reported in Chechnya in 2008.

■ Makhmadsalors (or Makhmudsalors) Masaev was detained by men wearing camouflage on 3 August in Grozny. A month earlier a newspaper had published his account of his previous unlawful detention in 2006, reportedly in Tsenteroi in an area under the control of Ramzan Kadyrov, then Chechen Prime Minister. Makhmadsalors Masaev had also filed a complaint against his detention at that time and it was feared that his enforced disappearance may have been aimed at preventing his complaint from proceeding. His fate and whereabouts remained unknown at the end of the year.

In 2008 the European Court of Human Rights adopted judgments in more than 30 cases finding that the Russian authorities were in violation of the European Convention of Human Rights regarding the conduct of its forces in Chechnya or the failure to initiate prompt and effective investigations into enforced disappearances and deaths.

■ The European Court of Human Rights held the Russian authorities responsible for the presumed death of 15-year-old Aminat Dugayeva (Dugaeva) and her cousin, Kurbika Zinabdieyva (Zinabdieva), who have not been seen since they were taken from Kurbika Zinabdieyva's home by Russian soldiers in May 2003. The Court also regretted that the Russian authorities had not disclosed documents relating to the investigation and stated that the treatment of the relatives during the investigation had been inhuman and degrading.

Dozens of families of internally displaced people were threatened with eviction from temporary accommodation in Chechnya without being offered adequate alternative housing or compensation. There were also reports of families being evicted and their property destroyed because of alleged links with armed groups.

Dagestan

Armed opposition groups killed several high-ranking law enforcement officials. Several men accused of involvement with these armed groups were reportedly arbitrarily detained and tortured. Civilians were subjected to human rights violations during so-called counter-terrorism operations. One such operation lasted for about seven months during which time access to one village was partially blocked and villagers reportedly harassed by the military.

Kabardino-Balkaria

Preliminary hearings continued in the trial in Nalchik of 58 suspects accused of involvement in an attack on government buildings there in 2005. The health of several of the detainees reportedly deteriorated owing to the conditions in pre-trial detention. The Committee for the Prevention of Torture of the Council of Europe visited the detention facility between April and May. In September, a further three men were detained in Kabardino-Balkaria and accused of involvement in the 2005 attack. One of them claimed he had been tortured in order to extract a confession.

■ In February, the mother and brother of one of the suspects, Rasul Kudaev, who has been detained since 2005, were arbitrarily detained, their house was searched and documents relating to his detention were taken. According to his mother and lawyer, Rasul Kudaev, who had been previously detained by US forces in Guantánamo Bay between 2002 and 2004, suffered from chronic hepatitis for which adequate treatment was not provided.

Armed conflict with Georgia

Large-scale hostilities broke out in South Ossetia on the night of 7 August, resulting in a five-day war between Georgian and Russian forces in which over 600 people, more than half of them civilians, died. Russian forces rapidly pushed Georgian forces out of South Ossetia and further occupied areas of undisputed Georgian territory, referred to as the "buffer zone", until early October. By the end of the year the Georgian authorities reported that up to 25,000 internally displaced people from South Ossetia were unable to return, and faced long-term displacement.

Russian aerial and artillery attacks took place over 8 to 12 August. While most of the bombardments appeared to have targeted Georgian military positions outside of built-up areas, villages and towns were also hit amid reports that some attacks may have been indiscriminate, or directly targeted civilians and/or civilian infrastructure.

Russian forces also reportedly failed to take adequate action when militia groups loyal to the de facto South Ossetian authorities carried out large-scale pillaging and arson of several Georgian-majority settlements in South Ossetia, and threatened and abused the residents there. These settlements were under Russian military control at the time. There was also evidence that Russian forces had used cluster bombs during the fighting.

Following the five-day conflict between Georgia and Russia, a number of parliamentarians from the Council of Europe visited Russia in order to gather information about the humanitarian and human rights situation in the region. The Council of Europe's Secretary General and the Commissioner for Human Rights as well as the UN High Commissioner for Refugees also visited the region.

Human rights defenders

Human rights defenders, journalists and lawyers who spoke openly about human rights abuses faced threats and intimidation. The police appeared to be reluctant to investigate such threats and a climate of impunity for attacks on civil society activists prevailed.

■ In June, the Office of the Prosecutor General announced that it had finished its investigation into the killing of human rights journalist Anna Politkovskaya, who was shot dead in Moscow in October 2006. Three men accused of involvement in her murder went on trial in November; all denied the charges. A fourth detainee, a former member of the Federal Security Services who had initially been detained in connection with the murder, remained in detention on suspicion of another crime. The person suspected of shooting Anna Politkovskaya had not been detained by the end of the year and was believed to be in hiding abroad.

■ Four members of the human rights organization Memorial were detained on 17 June in Chechnya, while filming a building thought to have been used as a secret detention centre. The video footage was destroyed and the four were threatened.

■ On 25 July, Zurab Tsechoev, a member of the human rights organization Peace (Mashr) in Ingushetia, was taken from his home in Troitskaia, Ingushetia, by armed

R

men, thought to be federal law enforcement officials. He was found a couple of hours later in the street near Magas, the capital of Ingushetia, with serious injuries which required hospital treatment.

■ The home of human rights defender and anti-racism campaigner Dmitrii Kraiukhin in Orel in central Russia was the target of an arson attack in August. The authorities refused to open a criminal case. He had previously received a series of threats.

Freedom of expression

In a climate of growing intolerance towards independent views, several human rights defenders and supporters of opposition groups faced criminal charges for expressing dissenting opinions or criticizing government authorities.

■ In May, two organizers of an art exhibition in 2007 at the Sakharov Museum were charged with inciting hatred and enmity. Yurii Samodurov and Andrei Yerofeev faced criminal prosecution for organizing an exhibition entitled "Forbidden art 2006". The men were accused of displaying artwork intended to humiliate and insult the feelings of followers of the Christian Orthodox faith.

■ In February, human rights defender and head of the organization Movement for Human Rights, Lev Ponomarev, was charged with insulting Yurii Kalinin, the head of the Department for the implementation of punishment. In an interview, Lev Ponomarev had stated that he held Yurii Kalinin responsible for torture and ill-treatment in Russia's prison colonies.

Freedom of assembly and association

On 6 May, on the eve of the inauguration of President Medvedev, numerous people were detained for trying to participate in a peaceful demonstration against the government. The ban on the demonstration was later found to be unlawful by the Moscow Prosecutor's Office.

■ Oleg Kozlovskii, co-ordinator of the movement Defence (Oborona) was detained on his way to the demonstration and was given 13 days' administrative detention. He was acquitted in September by the Moscow City Court.

■ Charges against Ludmila Kuzmina, head of a branch of the NGO Voice (Golos), were dropped in March, a few days after the elections. She had been charged in 2007 with using unlicensed computer software. Her branch of Voice, which focuses on voters' rights, had

also faced closure for allegedly failing to comply with the law on NGOs.

In May, investigations under the Law to Combat Extremism were initiated against the head of an organization campaigning for lesbian, gay, bisexual and transgender rights in Tiumen, Siberia. Earlier, the organization had been denied registration, as its aims were considered to be directed towards reducing the population of the Russian Federation which might constitute a threat to national security. The investigation was believed to be continuing at the end of the year.

Torture and other ill-treatment

Torture and ill-treatment of detainees and prisoners were reported from throughout the Russian Federation. Methods detailed included beatings, electric shocks, suffocation with plastic bags and being forced to stay in painful positions for prolonged periods. There were also reports of rape in detention. Some detainees were denied necessary medical treatment.

A number of ethnic Ingush men were reported to have been abducted in Moscow in early September. One of them stated that he was ill-treated while held for several days in a secret detention centre in the Moscow region run by the Ministry of Defence. An investigation was opened and was continuing at the end of the year.

■ Sergei Liapin from Nizhnii Novgorod was detained in April as a suspect in connection with a spate of thefts; he strongly denied any involvement in the crimes. He stated that he was tortured in order to extract a confession. He said that police poured water over his body, applied electrodes to sensitive parts of the body, kicked and beat him. He was placed in a temporary holding cell overnight and was not transferred to hospital until the following day, by which time his condition had deteriorated.

In September, a law allowing public scrutiny of places of detention by selected individuals came into force. However, monitoring had not started by the end of the year.

Prisoners in several Russian prison colonies protested at their conditions of detention, which sometimes reportedly constituted inhuman or degrading treatment. Riots and hunger strikes were reported from several prison colonies in the Urals and the Volga Federal District. Prisoners complained about beatings and ill-treatment by prison officials and by other detainees and alleged that the prison

R

authorities refused them access to medical treatment. According to reports, four prisoners died after being beaten during transfer from one prison colony to another in Cheliabinsk region. Criminal charges were brought against several prison officials in connection with the deaths and the case was continuing at the end of the year.

Fear of *refoulement*

There were further attempts to extradite Uzbekistani nationals to Uzbekistan, where they would be at risk of torture and ill-treatment. In at least two cases the extradition was halted following an intervention from the European Court of Human Rights, but there was no general decision to suspend extraditions to Uzbekistan.

■ In April, the European Court of Human Rights ruled that 13 Central Asian businessmen should not be extradited to Uzbekistan. In the case of *Ismoilov and others v Russia*, the Court stated that it was persuaded that the applicants would be at a real risk of ill-treatment if returned to Uzbekistan.

Justice system

Trial procedures did not always meet international standards of fair trial and there were continuing concerns about lack of respect for the rule of law. In some cases with a political context, the treatment of suspects amounted to persecution. The right of suspects to legal representation during investigation was repeatedly violated.

In October, the former owner of the YUKOS oil company, Mikhail Khodorkovskii, was denied parole. He had served half of his eight-year sentence and so would normally have been eligible for early release. In the same month, he was held in a punishment cell for 12 days for giving an interview to a Russian writer. A court in Chita in Siberia later found this punishment, as well as two other punishments for alleged violations of the prison rules, to be unlawful. One of these punishments had been used as an argument against an early release. His pre-trial detention in connection with further charges of fraud was extended until February 2009 as was the pre-trial detention of one of his former colleagues, Platon Lebedev. In June, charges against both men were re-filed and they remained in Chita, where due to the great distance from Moscow, access to their lawyers and families was constrained.

Former vice-president of YUKOS, Vasilii Aleksanian, who had been held in pre-trial detention since April 2006, was transferred in February to a specialized hospital after worldwide protests against an earlier refusal by the authorities to grant him access to adequate medical treatment. His pre-trial detention was repeatedly extended during the year and he was only released on bail in late December, after a court decision. In an interview Vasilii Aleksanian, who was suffering from HIV/AIDS-related illnesses, claimed he had been offered medical treatment in exchange for statements incriminating the former head of YUKOS, Mikhail Khodorkovskii.

Discrimination – racism

According to Russian human rights organizations, at least 87 people died in the course of the year as a result of racially-motivated attacks. Government officials acknowledged that this was a serious problem and called for harsh punishments for those convicted of such crimes. However, no comprehensive plan to combat racism and racial discrimination had been put in place by the end of the year.

In July and August, the UN Committee on the Elimination of Racial Discrimination examined Russia's report under the UN Convention against Racism. In its concluding observations the Committee called on the Russian authorities to take appropriate action to tackle racially-motivated violence and racial discrimination by law enforcement officials.

■ In May, eight men were sentenced to between two years' and life imprisonment for their involvement in an explosion in 2006 in a Moscow market frequented by foreign traders. The explosion left 14 people dead and dozens injured.

■ In December, seven young people, several of them under 18, were sentenced to six to 20 years in prison for the killing of 20 people of non-Slavic appearance. Several of the killings had been filmed and distributed by the group on the internet.

Violence against women and girls

Violence against women in the family was widespread. While some government officials acknowledged the problem in public statements, government support for crisis centres and hotlines was totally inadequate. There were fewer than 20 shelters across the country for women fleeing domestic violence. No measures under Russian law specifically addressed violence against women in the family.

Amnesty International visits/reports

🚗 Amnesty International delegates visited several regions of the Russian Federation, including Ingushetia, North Ossetia and the Urals Federal District. Delegates were refused entry to the Chechen Republic in June.

📃 Russian Federation: Freedom limited – the right to freedom of expression in Russia (EUR 46/008/2008)

📃 Russian Federation: Human rights memorandum to President Medvedev (EUR 46/018/2008)

📃 Russian Federation: Submission to the UN Universal Periodic Review – Fourth session of the UPR Working Group of the Human Rights Council, February 2009 (EUR 46/026/2008)

RWANDA

REPUBLIC OF RWANDA

Head of state:	**Paul Kagame**
Head of government:	**Bernard Makuza**
Death penalty:	**abolitionist for all crimes**
Population:	**10 million**
Life expectancy:	**45.2 years**
Under-5 mortality (m/f):	**199/173 per 1,000**
Adult literacy:	**64.9 per cent**

The government continued to reform the judicial system, but the International Criminal Tribunal for Rwanda (ICTR) in Tanzania declined to transfer cases to Rwanda, citing fair trial concerns, especially protection of witnesses. Legislative elections reaffirmed the political dominance of the Rwandan Patriotic Front (RPF), the ruling political party. Freedom of expression was limited and civil society and the media were under close scrutiny by the government. Four former combatants of the Rwandan Patriotic Army (RPA), the armed wing of the political movement, were tried for murder in a military court. No other charges were brought against members of the RPA for crimes under international law committed before, during and after the genocide.

Background

The RPF continued to dominate all levels of political life in Rwanda, from the executive down to the local administration.

The government reacted with hostility to criticism. Donor governments were locked into a close relationship with the Rwandan authorities and did not for the most part challenge or criticize them openly, preferring a policy of soft diplomacy. Governments were however critical when a UN report found that Rwanda was supporting a rebel group in eastern Democratic Republic of the Congo, leading to a withdrawal of aid from the Netherlands and Sweden in December.

Significant economic growth was reported by the government in 2008. Donor governments provided considerable support; one development agency estimated that approximately 50 per cent of the national budget came from foreign aid. The same agency reported an overall reduction in poverty, including improvements in health and education. However, despite this overall reduction, the poor remained marginalized and inequalities between the urban elite and the rural poor reportedly grew.

Kigali showed signs of rapid urbanization, following the expropriation of land for urban reconstruction. Some Kigali residents complained that they had received inadequate compensation.

The National Assembly amended the Constitution to give former Presidents immunity from prosecution for life, including for crimes under international law. Another amendment reduced judge's tenure of office from life to four years, potentially compromising the independence of the judiciary.

Legislative elections in September were monitored by the EU Election Observation Mission to Rwanda, whose preliminary findings noted a lack of real political debate during the pre-election period and certain irregularities. The two main opposition parties, the Social Democratic Party and the Liberal Party, were allied to the RPF. Local election monitors stated that the voter turn-out of 98 per cent was indicative of coercion. They also stated that local results consistently gave the RPF well over 95 per cent, and that consolidated national results giving the RPF 78.9 per cent were deliberately lowered to lend the elections greater credibility.

The report of the Mucyo Commission, set up in 2006 by the Rwandan government to investigate the

R

role of France in the 1994 genocide, was published on 5 August 2008. The report alleged the involvement of 33 current and former French political and military figures in the genocide. The Prosecutor General stated on 15 November that the authorities were ready to indict 23 of those named. The Mucyo report followed an investigation instituted by a French judge into the shooting down in 1994 of a plane whose passengers included President Juvénal Habyarimana of Rwanda, President Cyprien Ntaryamira of Burundi and three French nationals. The French judge issued international arrest warrants on 17 November 2006 against nine leading members of the RPF for shooting down the plane. Rose Kabuye, Chief of Protocol for President Kagame, was arrested on 9 November 2008 in Frankfurt, Germany. She was transferred to France and charged with "complicity in murder in relation to terrorism".

Freedom of expression – the media

Freedom of expression remained severely limited. Journalists critical of the government were closely monitored by the authorities. Foreign journalists and Rwandan journalists working for foreign newspapers were prevented on several occasions from entering Rwanda or attending official events.

■ On 2 May, the editors of three newspapers were turned away from the World Media Celebration Day (a day to coincide with Press Freedom Day), by order of the Information Minister.

On 18 August, the Information Minister threatened to close the BBC and Voice of America broadcasts in national languages and accused the two broadcasters of lies and exaggeration.

Human rights defenders

Human rights work remained strictly controlled and limited by the government. There was little or no space for domestic human rights organizations critical of the government, and human rights defenders and other members of civil society generally applied self-censorship to avoid confrontation with the authorities.

■ Some election observers from a local NGO were prevented from carrying out their work by the authorities. The organization issued a public statement in September alleging that the election process was marred by irregularities.

Prisoner of conscience

Charles Ntakirutinka, a former government minister, remained in Kigali Central Prison, serving a 10-year sentence. He had been convicted, in an unfair trial, of inciting civil disobedience and association with criminal elements.

International justice

International Criminal Tribunal for Rwanda

The ICTR was to finish all first-instance trials by the end of 2008 and complete all work by 2010, according to UN Security Council Resolution 1503. This deadline became unfeasible, given the 28 detainees on trial and the nine accused awaiting trial. In July, the UN Security Council extended the terms of the Trial Chamber and its judges until 31 December 2009.

Four requests by the Rwandan Prosecutor General for cases to be transferred from the ICTR to Rwanda were rejected on the basis that the accused were at risk of being subjected to an unfair trial. The four decisions cited reports that defence witnesses inside and outside Rwanda risk being rejected by their community, mistreated, arrested, detained, beaten, tortured and in some cases killed. In this context, the presiding judges voiced concern that the accused would have limited ability to call defence witnesses to trial.

The 2007 transfer law abolished capital punishment and replaced it with life imprisonment in solitary confinement, commonly considered as a violation of Article 7 of the International Covenant of Civil and Political Rights. The ICTR decisions ruled that the application of life in solitary confinement as punishment would prevent the transfer of the cases to Rwanda. The Rwandan Parliament passed a law on 3 November to prohibit solitary confinement for transfer cases.

Criticism of universal jurisdiction

At the AU summit in June, President Kagame criticized abuse of the principles of universal jurisdiction in response to arrest warrants issued in France and Spain against leading RPF members. The AU summit called for an international regulatory body "to review and/or handle complaints or appeals arising out of abuse of the principle of universal jurisdiction" by states.

Genocide suspects living abroad

Judicial proceedings against genocide suspects took place in Belgium, Canada, France and the Netherlands. Extradition hearings against genocide suspects in Sweden, Germany and Norway were continuing. A genocide suspect was detained in Finland and it remained unclear whether he would be extradited to Rwanda. During the year, France refused an extradition request made by Rwanda. In the UK, the Home Secretary ruled that four genocide suspects in the UK should be extradited to Rwanda. The suspects all lodged appeals.

Justice system

At the end of December, Rwanda's prisons contained 59,532 people. Of these, 37,277 people had been accused of genocide and 22,321 of other offences. Most pre-trial detainees were being held on ordinary criminal charges, not genocide-related charges.

The international community supported the government in reforms of the justice system, including training judicial staff, training the Rwandan Bar Association and developing information management systems for prisons.

Gacaca proceedings

In October, an estimated 10,000 category one cases were pending before gacaca courts, whose procedures fail to meet international standards of fair trial. Category one cases involve the planners, organizers, instigators and supervisors of the genocide. Of these, at least 6,000 were rape cases which were transferred to category one in May 2008.

Gacaca trials were reportedly marred by false accusations and corruption. In addition, defence witnesses were reluctant to come forward because they feared that the authorities would level false accusations against them.

■ On 21 January, a gacaca judge in Karana sector was accused of trying to bribe a prosecution witness. The case was at the appeal stage and the accused had been sentenced to 27 years' imprisonment.

Impunity

War crimes and crimes against humanity committed by the RPF and RPA before, during and after the genocide remained largely unprosecuted.

■ In an isolated case, four former RPA officers were tried for the killing of 13 members of the Roman Catholic clergy in Kabgayi district in June 1994. The investigation was undertaken jointly by the Rwandan prosecution and the ICTR. On 24 October the Military Tribunal of Kigali sentenced two captains, who pleaded guilty, to eight years' imprisonment. The other two were acquitted.

Law on 'genocidal ideology'

A new law criminalizing "genocidal ideology", whose terms are vague and ambiguous, was promulgated on 1 October. The offence is punishable by 10 to 25 years' imprisonment. This law could potentially stifle freedom of expression, and restrict the ability of the accused to put forward a defence in criminal trials.

Rights of lesbian, gay, bisexual and transgender people

The government was hostile towards the lesbian, gay, bisexual and transgender (LGBT) community, whose members faced harassment and intimidation. In March, two female LGBT activists were accused of forging documents and detained for two weeks after attending a LGBT conference in Mozambique. They were subsequently released.

The National Assembly was considering an amendment to the Penal Code which would criminalize consensual same-sex sexual relationships.

SAINT KITTS AND NEVIS

SAINT KITTS AND NEVIS
Head of state: Queen Elizabeth II, represented by Cuthbert Montraville Sebastian
Head of government: Denzil L. Douglas
Death penalty: retentionist
Life expectancy: 70 years
Adult literacy: 97.8 per cent

A moratorium on executions ended and one man was executed in December.

Death penalty

Executions resumed after a 10-year moratorium. Charles Elroy Laplace was hanged on 19 December.

He had been sentenced to death on 30 March 2006 for the killing of his wife in 2004. According to a statement by the Prime Minister, a Notice of Appeal filed with the Court of Appeal was dismissed on 29 October 2008 because it was filed out of time. Concerns were raised as to whether all the avenues of appeal had been satisfactorily exhausted and whether the prisoner's right to apply for an amnesty, pardon or commutation of sentence had been respected.

When he announced the execution in the National Assembly, the Prime Minister defined capital punishment as a "deterrent among our people in taking another man's life". General public support for the resumption of executions increased in response to an upsurge in violent crime.

Press reports indicated that eight prisoners remained on the death row.

In December, Saint Kitts and Nevis voted against a UN General Assembly resolution calling for a worldwide moratorium on executions.

Amnesty International report

📄 St Kitts and Nevis: Execution is a shameless act (AMR 59/001/2008)

SAUDI ARABIA

KINGDOM OF SAUDI ARABIA
Head of state and government: **King Abdullah Bin 'Abdul 'Aziz Al-Saud**

Death penalty:	retentionist
Population:	25.3 million
Life expectancy:	72.2 years
Under-5 mortality (m/f):	26/17 per 1,000
Adult literacy:	82.9 per cent

Thousands of people continued to be detained without trial as terrorism suspects and hundreds more were arrested. In October, the government announced that more than 900 would be brought to trial. Human rights activists and peaceful critics of the government were detained or remained in prison, including prisoners of conscience. Freedom of expression, religion, association and assembly remained tightly restricted. Women continued to face severe discrimination in law and practice.

Migrant workers suffered exploitation and abuse with little possibility of redress. Refugees and asylum-seekers were not adequately protected. The administration of justice remained shrouded in secrecy and was summary in nature. Torture and other ill-treatment of detainees were widespread and systematic, and carried out with impunity. Flogging was used widely as a main and additional punishment. The death penalty continued to be used extensively and in a discriminatory manner against migrant workers from developing countries, women and poor people. At least 102 people were executed.

Background

The government increased its co-operation with UN human rights mechanisms. In January a government delegation appeared for the first time before the UN Committee considering Saudi Arabia's first ever report on its implementation of the Convention on the Elimination of All Forms of Discrimination against Women (CEDAW). In February, the UN Special Rapporteur on violence against women carried out a first ever visit to Saudi Arabia.

Prisoners of conscience

Human rights activists and peaceful critics of the state were arrested and imprisoned. Others detained in previous years remained in prison.

■ Dr Matrouk al-Faleh, an academic and human rights activist, was detained without charge or trial at al-Ha'ir Prison in Riyadh, and denied access to a lawyer, following his arrest in May. The authorities gave no reason for his arrest but it occurred shortly after he wrote an article criticizing the harsh conditions in which two brothers, Dr Abdullah al-Hamid and Issa al-Hamid, both prisoners of conscience, were being held in Buraida Prison. The al-Hamid brothers were serving six- and four-month prison terms respectively, imposed after they were convicted of "incitement to protest" in 2007 for supporting a peaceful protest outside Buraida Prison by relatives of untried political detainees. They were both released after completing their sentences.

■ Shaikh Nasser al-'Ulwan, arrested in 2004 or 2005 in Buraida reportedly for refusing to issue a *fatwa* (edict), continued to be detained without charge or trial or any effective means of redress. He was reported to have been held incommunicado and in solitary confinement for much of the time.

■ Prisoner of conscience Fouad Ahmad al-Farhan, an

internet blogger arrested in December 2007 apparently for criticizing the government, was held incommunicado at Dhahban Prison, Jeddah, until his release in April.

Counter-terror and security

The authorities invoked a wide range of repressive measures in the name of security and combating terrorism. The law prescribes harsh punishments for terrorism-related offences yet is vague and broadly drawn, encompassing the peaceful exercise of freedom of expression and other legitimate activities. This reality was exacerbated by a secretive judiciary which fostered impunity for perpetrators of human rights violations.

The authorities detained hundreds of people on security grounds, including people forcibly returned from Iraq, Pakistan and Yemen. Thousands of others detained in previous years remained in prison under conditions of virtual secrecy. Most had been held incommunicado for long periods for interrogation and denied access to lawyers, medical assistance and family visits for months or years. None had been allowed to challenge the legality of their detention. The government stated that many of the detainees were being held for "re-education". In April the authorities released 32 former inmates at Guantánamo Bay, who had been returned to Saudi Arabia by the US authorities in 2007 and detained; at least 24 others were still being held at the end of the year.

■ Eight Bahraini nationals were arrested on 28 February at a checkpoint during a short visit to Saudi Arabia. They were held incommunicado and in solitary confinement until 12 July, when they were released without charge or trial.

The tiny minority of security detainees brought to trial faced grossly unfair and secret proceedings. These included brief sessions before a panel of three inquisitors, who may not have been judges, who questioned detainees about confessions or other statements they had made under interrogation while held incommunicado. Those convicted reportedly were sentenced to flogging in addition to prison terms.

In October the government announced that a Special Criminal Court (SCC) was being established to try more than 900 detainees on capital charges, including murder and causing bomb explosions, but provided no other details. The defendants were expected to include eight men shown on Saudi Arabian television in 2007 "confessing" to planning terrorist attacks, a capital offence. All eight had been detained incommunicado for long periods and may have been tortured. Five are Saudi Arabian nationals: Abdullah and Ahmed Abdel Aziz al-Migrin, Khaled al-Kurdi, Mohamed Ali Hassan Zein and 'Amir Abdul Hamid Al-Sa'di; two are Chadian nationals, Ali Issa Umar and Khalid Ali Tahir; and one, Muhammad Fatehi Al-Sayyid, is an Egyptian national. It was unclear at the end of the year whether any trials before the SCC had started.

Some prisoners convicted of security offences continued to be held after serving their sentence.
■ Majed Nasser al-Shummari completed a three-year prison sentence in 2005 but remained in jail. He was convicted after a secret trial in Riyadh, during which he had no legal assistance, of charges related to a visit he had made to Afghanistan.

Violence and discrimination against women and girls

Women continued to face severe discrimination in law and practice and were inadequately protected against domestic and other violence despite greater government co-operation with international bodies concerned with women's rights. Among other concerns, women remained subordinate to men under family law, were denied equal employment opportunities with men, remained banned from driving vehicles or travelling alone, and Saudi Arabian women married to non-Saudi nationals, unlike Saudi Arabian men, could not pass on their nationality to their children.

Following her visit, the UN Special Rapporteur on violence against women noted progress in women's access to education but said she had received many complaints about discrimination and violence against women, including by the religious police.

The CEDAW Committee, reviewing Saudi Arabia's implementation of that treaty, expressed concern that the concept of male guardianship over women (mehrem), as applied, severely limited women's rights, notably in relation to marriage, divorce, child custody, inheritance, property ownership, and choices about residency, education and employment. It also noted a high incidence of domestic violence and lack of prosecutions. The government said that a law against domestic violence was being drafted.

S

In August, the National Human Rights Commission, an official body, urged the government to take measures to end the practice of child marriage. In September it announced that it was opening a women's branch in Riyadh to investigate abuses against women and children.

Migrants' rights

The rights of migrant workers were widely abused with impunity. Some workers staged protests over unpaid salaries, poor living and working conditions, and failure by employers to renew visas.

Many migrant domestic workers, mostly women, were kept in highly abusive conditions, being made to work up to 18 hours every day, in some cases for little or no pay. Domestic workers have no protection under Saudi Arabian labour law and have little possibility in practice of obtaining redress against abusive or exploitative employers.

■ In July airport officials were reported to have prevented the employer of Ela Adoul Madouky, an Indonesian domestic worker, from forcing her onto a flight to her home country because she was evidently ill and needed hospital treatment. Doctors said they had treated her earlier for severe malnutrition and external injuries, including burns and cuts. She said her employers had beaten her and given her only bread to eat.

Refugees and asylum-seekers

The authorities violated the rights of asylum-seekers and refugees. Some were held as virtual prisoners. Others were forcibly returned to countries where they were at risk of serious human rights violations.

■ Around 80 Iraqis remained in a fenced and guarded camp near Rafha; they had fled Iraq in 1991. None had been granted asylum or the chance to live a normal life in Saudi Arabia.

■ Some 28 Eritreans who sought asylum in Saudi Arabia in 2002 remained in detention near Jizan city. They continued to be denied access to the courts.

Torture and other ill-treatment

Torture and other ill-treatment continued to be widespread and committed with impunity. Commonly cited methods included severe beatings with sticks, electric shocks, suspension from the ceiling, punching, sleep deprivation and insults.

■ In March, three Chadian men – Muhammad Hamid Ibrahim Sulayman, Hassan Bashir and Muhammad Salih – were reported to have been convicted of theft and sentenced to have their right hands amputated on the basis of confessions allegedly made after they were beaten while held in prolonged incommunicado detention.

■ A former detainee held without charge in various prisons between 2003 and 2006 told Amnesty International in 2008 that he had been given electric shocks, held in solitary confinement for four months, and shackled for three weeks in a small cell without air conditioning during extremely hot weather.

Cruel, inhuman and degrading punishments

Flogging is mandatory for a number of offences and continued to be used frequently as a main and additional punishment by courts. Sentences of amputation were imposed for theft.

■ In January, following widespread campaigning locally and internationally, the flogging sentences imposed on a rape survivor referred to as the "girl from al-Qatif" and her male companion were dropped as a result of a royal pardon.

■ In February, Bilal Bin Muslih Bin Jabir al-Muwallad and Ahmad Hamid Muhammad Sabir, aged 15 and 13 respectively at the time of the crimes, were sentenced to receive 1,500 and 1,250 lashes. They were among seven males convicted of robberies and assaults in Madina; the five others were sentenced to death (see below). The case remained before the Court of Cassation in Makkah for review at the end of the year.

Death penalty

The death penalty continued to be applied extensively after summary and secret trials. Defendants are rarely allowed legal assistance and can be convicted solely on the basis of confessions obtained under duress or deception. As in previous years, capital punishment was used disproportionately against the poor, including many migrant workers from Asia and Africa, and women. In April, Amnesty International received secretly filmed footage of the public beheading of a Jordanian man convicted of drugs offences.

At least 102 men and women, 39 of them foreign nationals, were executed in 2008. Many were executed for non-violent offences, including drug offences, "sodomy", blasphemy and apostasy. Most executions were held in public.

In January, the parents of Moeid bin Hussein Hakami, who was beheaded in 2007, took the unusual and brave step of lodging a complaint with the authorities about the execution of their son. He was aged 13 at the time of the crime and was 16 when beheaded. The parents were not told in advance of his execution and, according to reports, they were not informed of his place of burial.

■ In February, five young men were sentenced to death in Madina for robberies and assaults, offences the judge deemed to amount to "corruption on earth". All had been held incommunicado after their arrest in 2004 and allegedly beaten to force them to confess. Two of them – Sultan Bin Sulayman Bin Muslim al-Muwallad, a Saudi Arabian national, and 'Issa Bin Muhammad 'Umar Muhammad, a Chadian national – were aged 17 at the time of the alleged offences.

■ In February, a court considered the appeal of Rizana Nafeek, a young Sri Lankan domestic worker, who was sentenced to death in 2007 for a murder committed when she was 17. The outcome of the appeal was not known.

■ In April, 17-year-old Sultan Kohail was sentenced to 200 lashes and one year in prison by a court without jurisdiction to impose the death penalty. The charge related to the death of a boy as a result of a schoolyard brawl. Following an appeal, the case was referred for retrial before another court, which had tried his elder brother on the same charge and sentenced him to death. This raised the possibility that Sultan Kohail could also be sentenced to death although he was under 18 at the time of the crime.

In December Saudi Arabia voted against a UN General Assembly resolution calling for a worldwide moratorium on executions.

Amnesty International visits/reports

🚗 Amnesty International again sought access to visit Saudi Arabia to investigate human rights, but the government did not permit this.

📑 Affront to justice: Death penalty in Saudi Arabia (MDE 23/027/2008)

📑 Saudi Arabia: Amnesty International Submission to the UN Universal Periodic Review (MDE 23/029/2008)

SENEGAL

REPUBLIC OF SENEGAL

Head of state:	Abdoulaye Wade
Head of government:	Cheikh Hadjibou Soumaré
Death penalty:	abolitionist for all crimes
Population:	12.7 million
Life expectancy:	62.3 years
Under-5 mortality (m/f):	120/108 per 1,000
Adult literacy:	39.3 per cent

The peace process in southern Casamance made no progress and civilians were sporadically attacked. Police cracked down on people demonstrating against high prices. Independent media and journalists were harassed and some journalists were detained. The long-awaited investigation in the case of former Chadian President Hissène Habré did not begin.

Background

Four years after the 2004 general peace accord, no progress was made in the peace process in southern Casamance where civilians continued to be victims of landmines and sporadic attacks by separatist fighters. In April, several leaders of the Democratic Forces of Casamance Movement (Mouvement des forces démocratiques de Casamance, MFDC) met in an attempt to reunify the separatist movement. By the end of the year divisions between the armed and civilian wings had not been overcome.

Excessive use of force

In December, security forces clamped down on demonstrators after protests over poor living conditions in the mining region of Kedougou (700km south east of Dakar) turned violent with government property and buildings being damaged and burned. Security forces used live bullets killing at least one person, Sinad Sidibé, and wounding several others. In the days following this protest, security forces arrested and tortured dozens of people who were still held without trial at the end of the year. Many others went into hiding to escape the wave of arrests launched by the security forces.

Freedom of assembly

In March, police officers broke up a banned demonstration against rising prices for basic

S

commodities such as rice, oil, milk and soap. Police used batons and tear gas to crack down on the demonstrators and they also assaulted journalists covering the demonstration. At least 24 people including two consumer group officials, Muammar Ndao and Jean-Pierre Dieng, as well as an opposition leader, Talla Sylla, were briefly arrested.

Freedom of expression

Independent media and individual journalists were targeted in an attempt to stifle freedom of expression and criticism of President Abdoulaye Wade.

■ In March, police raided a private television station after it transmitted images of police beating demonstrators during the protest against high prices.

■ In September, El Malick Seck, publisher of the daily newspaper *24 Heures Chrono*, was sentenced to three years' imprisonment after publishing an article implicating the Head of State in money-laundering. The newspaper was suspended for three months.

Abuses by armed group

Self-proclaimed members of the MFDC attacked and abducted civilians in Casamance, apparently to punish them for entering land they considered as their territory. The MFDC denied any involvement in these attacks.

■ In May, 16 villagers harvesting cashew nuts in Tampe, 15km east of Ziguinchor, Casamance's main city, were attacked by self-proclaimed MFDC members who tied their hands and sliced off their left ears.

Discrimination – lesbian, gay, bisexual and transgender people

Individuals faced arbitrary arrest, harassment and discrimination because of their suspected engagement in consensual same-sex sexual conduct.

■ In February, nine men and one woman were arrested following media condemnation of a party at which some of them were photographed. Commentaries subsequently posted online called for the men to be killed. As a consequence, several individuals had to flee the country.

■ In August, a Belgian national and his male Senegalese domestic helper were sentenced to two years' imprisonment for "homosexual marriage and acts against nature". Amnesty International considered them prisoners of conscience.

International justice – Hissène Habré

Despite the elimination of the last legal obstacles to a criminal investigation, the investigation of Hissène Habré's case did not begin during 2008.

In April, the National Assembly adopted a constitutional amendment introducing retrospective legislation for crimes against humanity, war crimes, genocide and torture which would permit the trial of the former Chadian head of state who was living in exile in Senegal. In May, a coordinating judge was appointed to organize the trial. On 16 September Chadian victims filed a further complaint. The Senegalese authorities claimed that there were no more obstacles to the trial except lack of funds, but took no further steps despite financial assistance from the European Union.

In August, Hissène Habré was sentenced to death in his absence in Chad. Human rights groups stressed that this conviction in Chad was based on different charges and should have no impact on the prosecution in Senegal.

Amnesty International report

▤ Senegal: Amnesty International Submission to the UN Universal Periodic Review (AFR 49/004/2008)

SERBIA

REPUBLIC OF SERBIA, INCLUDING KOSOVO

Head of state:	Boris Tadić
Head of government:	Mirko Cvetković (replaced Vojislav Koštunica in July)
Death penalty:	abolitionist for all crimes
Population:	9.9 million
Life expectancy:	73.6 years
Under-5 mortality (m/f):	14/13 per 1,000
Adult literacy:	96.4 per cent

Serbia made progress in arresting suspects indicted by the International Criminal Tribunal for the former Yugoslavia (Tribunal) and in prosecuting war crimes in domestic courts. Discrimination against minority communities and impunity for inter-ethnic violence continued in both Serbia and Kosovo. The UN Interim Administration Mission in Kosovo (UNMIK) failed to address impunity for human rights violations by the international community and for war crimes in Kosovo, including enforced disappearances and abductions. Few refugees voluntarily returned to Kosovo.

Background

In the absence of a decision by the UN Security Council on the Comprehensive Proposal for the Kosovo Status Settlement (Ahtisaari Plan), Kosovo unilaterally declared independence from Serbia in February. Kosovo's independence had been recognized by 53 states by the end of the year.

In April Serbia signed a Stabilization and Association Agreement with the EU, which in November indicated that Serbia might be granted candidate status in 2009, provided it continued co-operation with the Tribunal.

Major political divisions within the ruling coalition in Serbia, including over EU membership, precipitated elections in May. In July, after complex negotiations, President Tadić of the Democratic Party entered a coalition government with the Socialist Party of Serbia, formerly led by Slobodan Milošević.

In November, the International Court of Justice (ICJ) decided that it had jurisdiction over Croatia's motion to sue Serbia for genocide.

Final status of Kosovo

Following Kosovo's declaration of independence, protests took place across Serbia. Zoran Vujović, a Kosovo Serb, died in a fire at the US embassy in Belgrade that had been set alight during a mass demonstration. Over 200 attacks on ethnic Albanian property were reported, mainly in Vojvodina. Shops run by members of the Gorani community were vandalized. Few perpetrators were brought to justice.

In the predominantly Serbian north of Kosovo, following independence, Kosovo Serbs protested in sometimes violent demonstrations against UNMIK institutions, including border posts and the UNMIK court in north Mitrovica/ë, which was occupied by the Serbian judiciary in March. During an internally criticized UNMIK operation to regain the court, a Ukrainian UNMIK police officer was killed and 200 people severely injured. In the following months, Serb members of the Kosovo Police Service (KPS) resigned, and other public employees were urged to

leave their posts by the Belgrade government, which sought to establish parallel structures in Serbian areas of Kosovo.

In June, the Kosovo Assembly adopted a constitution which fails to establish effective human rights institutions or guarantee the rights of women and non-Serb minorities. It also passed legislation assuming legal control over competencies previously reserved to UNMIK, as set out in the Ahtisaari Plan. UNMIK remained in Kosovo under UN Security Council Resolution 1244/99, although it was unable to discharge its administrative functions.

In November, following negotiations with Pristina and Belgrade, the UN Security Council approved a "status-neutral" plan to reconfigure UNMIK. This enabled a European Security and Defence Policy mission (EULEX), envisaged in the Ahtisaari Plan and authorized by the EU in February, to take over in December responsibilities for international policing and the investigation and prosecution of outstanding war crimes. In northern municipalities where Serbia had opposed the EU mission's authority, police, justice and customs remained in theory under UNMIK jurisdiction. There were fears that this would result in the de facto partition of Kosovo.

The UN General Assembly in October approved Serbia's request for an advisory opinion of the ICJ on the lawfulness of Kosovo's unilateral declaration of independence.

International justice – International Criminal Tribunal for the former Yugoslavia

Former Bosnian Serb Security Chief Stojan Župljanin, indicted for genocide, crimes against humanity and war crimes in Bosnia and Herzegovina (BiH), was arrested in Pančevo in June.

In July former Bosnian Serb leader Radovan Karadžić was arrested in Belgrade, where he had been living under an assumed identity. He was subsequently transferred to the custody of the Tribunal. He faced charges of genocide and complicity in genocide, including the murder of over 7,000 Bosnian Muslim (Bosniak) men and boys in Srebrenica in 1995. He was also charged with extermination, murder, wilful killing, persecutions, deportation, inhumane acts and other crimes against non-Serb civilians in BiH between 1992 and 1995.

S

In April Ramush Haradinaj, former leader of the Kosovo Liberation Army (KLA) and former Prime Minister of Kosovo, and Idriz Balaj were acquitted of crimes against humanity and war crimes including cruel treatment, torture, rape, and murder of Albanians, Serbs and Roma in 1998. Lahi Brahimaj was convicted of cruel treatment and torture and sentenced to six years' imprisonment. The Trial Chamber of the Tribunal reported significant difficulties in obtaining evidence from the 100 prosecution witnesses, of whom 18 required subpoenas to appear, and 34 were granted protective measures. Two former government officials were convicted of contempt of court in December for attempting to influence a protected witness.

The trial continued of six senior Serbian political, police and military officials jointly indicted for crimes against humanity and violations of the laws and customs of war in Kosovo. Separate proceedings continued against Vojislav Šešelj, leader of the Serbian Radical Party, charged with the persecution and forcible deportation of non-Serbs in both Croatia and BiH.

Serbia

Justice system – war crimes

Prosecutions continued at the War Crimes Chamber at Belgrade District Court.

In June, in the first case transferred to Serbia from the Tribunal, three members of the Yellow Wasps paramilitary group were convicted of the torture and killing of at least 25 Bosniak civilians in the Zvornik area of BiH in 1992 and sentenced to 15, 13 and three years' imprisonment.

The Serbian Supreme Court in September upheld the appeals of two members of the Scorpions paramilitary group, convicted in April 2007 for the murder in 1995 of six civilians from Srebrenica, reducing one sentence from 20 to 15 years and ordering the retrial of another defendant sentenced to five years' imprisonment.

The trial opened in September of four members of the Scorpions paramilitary group indicted for the murder of 14 members of the Gashi family and the serious injury of five surviving children in Podujevo/ë in March 1999. Saša Cvjetan had been convicted of the offence in 2005.

In October, War Crimes Prosecutor Vladimir Vučković visited Albania to investigate allegations that more than 300 Serbs had been abducted by members of the KLA during 1999 and taken to Albania. The Albanian Chief Prosecutor refused him permission, citing an investigation conducted by the Tribunal which had not found evidence to substantiate claims that the Serbs had been transferred in order to remove and sell their organs.

In November closing statements were heard in the trial of 17 low-ranking soldiers charged with the murder of Croatian prisoners of war and civilians at Ovčara farm in Croatia in 1991. The Supreme Court had in 2006 overturned the previous conviction of 14 of the men.

The trial continued of eight former police officers for the murder of 48 ethnic Albanians, mostly from the same family in Suva Reka/Suharekë in Kosovo in March 1999. Over 100 witnesses had testified since proceedings opened in October 2006.

Proceedings continued against three police officers indicted for the murder of the three Bytiçi brothers, ethnic Albanians of US nationality, in Kosovo in July 1999.

Sandžak region

Disputes between political parties and rival Islamist groups continued to provoke violence in the Sandžak region, including the burning of a mosque near Novi Pazar.

The trial opened in January and continued throughout the year against 15 men from Sandžak believed to be of the Wahhabi faith indicted in September 2007 for conspiring against Serbia's security and constitutional order and the illegal possession of weapons and explosives.

Torture and other ill-treatment

There was no progress in investigations into the ill-treatment of detainees during a protest in Niš prison in December 2006; one detainee had died of his injuries. The NGO Leskovac Committee for Human Rights submitted two applications to the European Court of Human Rights in three torture-related cases. Allegations of ill-treatment of ethnic Albanian prisoners continued to be reported.

Reports of police ill-treatment continued, including of journalists and Roma. In November the UN Committee against Torture in their consideration of Serbia's report on its obligations under the Convention against Torture urged that the definition of torture in the criminal code be brought in line with that of the Convention, and that an independent oversight mechanism be established.

S

Unlawful killings

■ In August, six police officers were suspended for excessive use of force after Ranko Panić died of injuries sustained on 29 July during a demonstration in Belgrade opposing Radovan Karadžić's arrest. Investigations continued.

Discrimination – Roma

Serbia assumed the presidency of the Decade of Roma Inclusion in June, and announced priorities of legalizing Roma settlements and preventing discrimination in education, including in July introducing Romani as an elective language in schools. However, Roma remained excluded from employment in national and local government, and often faced evictions or other discrimination in relation to their right to adequate housing.

Roma in Bokeljska Street in Belgrade continued to protest against the demolition of their houses on land owned by the Adok company, which planned a new residential complex on the site. Residents in the Ovča suburb in Belgrade protested against the relocation into new apartments of Roma families from the Gazela settlement under the Belgrade highway bridge.

Human rights defenders

In February Nataša Kandić, director of the NGO Humanitarian Law Center, was threatened by leading politicians and in the media for attending the Kosovo Assembly's declaration of independence ceremony.

During October and November a media campaign against Sonja Biserko, director of the Helsinki Committee for Human Rights in Serbia, resulted in demonstrations outside the NGO's office. People were reported lying in wait outside Sonja Biserko's apartment after her personal details were published on the web. Campaigns against both women were characterized by misogynistic abuse.

Violence against women and girls

NGOs reported that proceedings to provide protection for victims of family violence were often delayed, and that such measures were often not imposed in cases of repeated violence. Prosecutors rarely initiated criminal proceeedings; when they did come to court judges failed to impose penalties provided by law.

Kosovo

Accountability – international community

Lack of accountability persisted for past human rights violations by UNMIK personnel against people in Kosovo. In October the EU agreed that US citizens participating in the EULEX mission would not be accountable to the EU for any human rights violations they might commit.

Sixty-two cases remained pending before the Human Rights Advisory Panel (HRAP), introduced in March 2006 to provide remedies for acts and omissions by UNMIK. In June HRAP declared admissible a complaint by the families of Mon Balaj and Arben Xheladini, killed by unidentified Romanian UNMIK police officers during a demonstration in February 2007, although the Special Representative of the UN Secretary-General challenged its admissibility. The HRAP delivered its first decision in November, finding that UNMIK police had failed to investigate the murder in 2000 of Remzije Canhasi.

In November Muhamed Biçi was awarded £2.4 million compensation by the UK Ministry of Defence, following civil proceedings in 2004 which decided that UK troops had in 1999 deliberately and unjustifiably caused him injury.

In their concluding observations in November on UNMIK's report on the implementation of the International Covenant on Economic, Social and Cultural Rights in Kosovo, the monitoring committee (CESCR) recommended that UNMIK include the treaty in the international law applicable in Kosovo.

The Kosovo Assembly again failed to appoint an ombudsperson; the mandate of the international ombudsperson expired in 2005.

Unfair trials

In February UNMIK suspended trial proceedings against Albin Kurti, leader of the NGO Vetëvendosje! (Self-Determination), who was indicted for organizing and participating in a demonstration in February 2007. The organization considered that the prosecution appeared to be politicized and proceedings before a panel of international judges demonstrated a lack of independence by the judiciary. Six lawyers had refused to represent Albin Kurti who sought the right to conduct his own defence.

Impunity – war crimes

UNMIK's remaining international prosecutors and judiciary made slow progress in addressing an estimated backlog of 1,560 war crimes cases. In August UNMIK said that proceedings were open in seven cases, only one of which was not an appeal or a retrial. According to UNMIK, international

S

prosecutors were also reportedly directing investigations in 47 cases. Measures for the protection of witnesses remained of concern.

Marko Simonović was indicted with three others in October for the murder in Pristina of four ethnic Albanians in June 1999.

In November the UN Secretary-General reported that the UNMIK Department of Justice had established guidelines to enable access to criminal files by EULEX prosecutors, who had repeatedly complained that war crimes files were not available.

Impunity remained for the majority of cases of enforced disappearances and abductions. Investigations were opened in six cases reported to UNMIK police by Amnesty International. Some 1,918 people remained unaccounted for, including Albanians, Serbs and members of other minorities. The Office of Missing Persons and Forensics performed 73 exhumations and recovered 53 sets of mortal remains. Some 437 exhumed bodies remained unidentified.

Inter-ethnic violence

Although the intensity and frequency of inter-ethnic violence declined after March, low-level intimidation and harassment of minorities continued. In October shots were fired towards six displaced Kosovo Serbs visiting their homes in Dvoran/e village, Suva Reka/Suharekë municipality; a Kosovo Albanian was later arrested. In November, Ali Kadriu, a displaced ethnic Albanian, was beaten by UNMIK police when he attempted to return to rebuild his house in Suvi Dol/Suhadoll in north Mitrovica/ë; he had previously been threatened by members of the Serbian community. Albanian shops were burned after an attack by ethnic Albanians on 29 December on a mixed ethnicity Kosovo Police Service patrol and the stabbing of a 16-year-old Serb boy on 30 December.

Impunity for past inter-ethnic violence prevailed. In July the OSCE reported that only 400 prosecutions had been brought in 1,400 cases reported to the police after the ethnic violence of March 2004, in which 19 people were killed and more than 900 injured. Trials were delayed when witnesses, including police officers, reportedly failed to attend court or provided conflicting statements; sentences imposed were inconsistent with the gravity of the offences.

In June Florim Ejupi was convicted of the bombing of the Niš Express bus near Podujevo/ë in February

2001, in which 11 Serbs were killed and 22 severely injured. He was sentenced to 40 years' imprisonment for murder, attempted murder, terrorism, causing general danger, racial and other discrimination and unlawful possession of explosive material.

No progress was made following the arrest in 2007 of an ethnic Albanian man suspected of involvement in the murder of 14 Serb men in Staro Gračko in July 1999; witness intimidation was reported.

Discrimination

Both Serbs and Albanians continued to suffer discrimination in areas where they were in a minority. The Law on Languages was inconsistently implemented and the 2004 Anti-Discrimination Law was not enforced. The government developed an action plan on measures recommended in 2005 by the Advisory Committee to the Framework Convention on the Protection of National Minorities. Members of non-Serb minority communities were excluded from consultations on the Kosovo Constitution.

Approximately a third of the Kosovo Roma, Ashkali and Egyptians reportedly lacked civil or habitual resident registration, which prevented them from repossessing their homes. Many children, in particular girls, did not enrol in school or frequently dropped out. Many families were unable to afford health care. Some 700 Roma remained displaced in camps in northern Mitrovica, some in locations where their health was seriously affected by lead contamination.

Refugees and internally displaced people – returns

Serbs and other non-Albanians did not flee Kosovo after the declaration of independence as feared, but few returns took place during the year. Some 445 internally displaced people returned to their homes; of whom 107 were Kosovo Serbs.

By the end of the year several EU member states had indicated that people under temporary protection would soon be forcibly returned to Kosovo. The OSCE reported that resources were not available for the integration of repatriated people: in September, in Klina/Kline municipality, for example, resources were not available to rebuild the house of a Romani couple forcibly returned from Germany.

Many other people were unable to return to their homes due to the backlog of 29,000 cases and 11,000 unimplemented decisions related to property claims originating from the 1999 war.

Violence against women and girls

A new Action Plan to Combat Trafficking in Human Beings was adopted in July. In November, 98 bars or clubs were considered to be involved in forced prostitution, although traffickers reportedly moved women to private homes and escort services to avoid detection. The KPS reported an increase in internally trafficked persons. Few perpetrators were prosecuted, yet trafficked women continued to be arrested for prostitution.

The CESCR in November noted the high incidence of domestic violence in Kosovo, low prosecution and conviction rates, and the lack of adequate victim assistance and protection.

Amnesty International reports

Kosovo (Serbia): The challenge to fix a failed UN justice mission (EUR 70/001/2008)

Serbia: Submission to the UN Universal Periodic Review (EUR 70/006/2008)

SIERRA LEONE

REPUBLIC OF SIERRA LEONE

Head of state and government:	Ernest Bai Koroma
Death penalty:	retentionist
Population:	6 million
Life expectancy:	41.8 years
Under-5 mortality (m/f):	290/264 per 1,000
Adult literacy:	34.8 per cent

The security situation was generally stable, despite violence before and after local elections in July. The trial of former Liberian President Charles Taylor resumed in January in The Hague. Two of the three trials on appeal before the Special Court for Sierra Leone were completed and one was due to be completed by the end of 2008. The Human Rights Commission of Sierra Leone released its first countrywide report. Little progress was made in implementing the recommendations of the Truth and Reconciliation Commission (TRC). Appeals for 11 people convicted of treason, 10 of whom had been sentenced to death, were upheld and all 11 were released in November.

Sierra Leone remained an extremely poor country, with maternal and infant mortality rates among the highest in the world. An estimated one in eight women died in childbirth and one in four children died before their fifth birthday.

Background

In February the President launched a Reproductive and Child Health Strategic Plan aimed at reducing maternal and child mortality rates by 30 per cent by 2010. Donors committed funds to addressing maternal mortality over the next 10 years.

The Human Rights Commission of Sierra Leone's first report released in July covered a range of human rights violations including police brutality and excessive use of force as well as numerous cases of prolonged detention without charge. The report had a particular focus on the rights of women and girls, highlighting high rates of both infant and maternal mortality as well as sexual and gender-based violence, including female genital mutilation.

Local council elections took place in July. Women candidates suffered harassment, including death and rape threats, from members of the community. Overall, 13 per cent of those contesting seats were women.

There were violent clashes between youths supporting the Sierra Leone People's Party (SLPP), the People's Movement for Democratic Change (PMDC) and the All People's Congress (APC) throughout the year. In January, four people were killed in such clashes in Port Loko and 11 houses were burned down. In June, July and August there was further political violence between the groups. In July, ahead of the elections, the army was deployed in Kenema district as a precautionary measure. Unrest was reported in various districts, as a result of which 71 candidates out of 1,324 withdrew.

The Anti-Corruption Act 2000 was replaced by a new Anti-Corruption Act 2008. In February a new national anti-corruption strategy was adopted by the government.

As part of this strategy, the Anti-Corruption Commission established a department of investigation, intelligence, and prosecution. Three senior public officials were charged with various offences under the new Act in November.

In January a Constitutional Review Commission was established by the government. It submitted 136

S

amendments to the 1991 Constitution, largely not human rights related, requiring approval by referendum.

In October the UN Peacebuilding Office (UNIPSIL) replaced the UN Integrated Office in Sierra Leone (UNIOSIL). Human rights and gender issues were to remain priorities for the office. In July the UN Peacebuilding Fund approved over US$17 million in social reform projects for Sierra Leone.

Special Court for Sierra Leone

The trial of Charles Taylor in The Hague resumed in January. He faced 11 counts of crimes against humanity and war crimes committed in Sierra Leone, including unlawful killings, rape and use of child soldiers. The prosecution case was completed by the end of the year.

In the cases against Revolutionary United Front (RUF) members Issa Sesay, Morris Kallon and Augustine Gbao, the defence cases were heard. Judgments had not been issued by the end of 2008.

In February the Appeals Chamber upheld the original sentences passed in the cases of Armed Forces Revolutionary Council (AFRC) members Alex Tamba Brima (50 years' imprisonment), Ibrahim Bazzy Kamara (45 years' imprisonment) and Santigie Borbor Kanu (45 years' imprisonment).

The case against Moinina Fofana and Allieu Kondewa, members of the Civil Defence Forces (CDF), concluded in May. Doubling their original sentences, the Appeals Chamber sentenced them to 15 and 20 years' imprisonment respectively.

Freedom of expression

Several journalists were harassed, and some arrested, during 2008.
■ In February Jonathan Leigh, managing editor of *The Independent Observer*, was arrested on libel charges and accused of defaming the Minister of Transport and Aviation. He was released on bail and later retracted the articles.
■ In March, Sylvia Blyden of *The Awareness Times* was arrested and accused of "ridiculing the President". She was released the same day.

In May, the authorities threatened *The New Vision* newspaper with legal action if the newspaper failed to retract stories deemed critical of the government.

In October, Emmanuel Saffa Abdulai, Director of the Society for Democratic Initiatives (SDI), and John

Baimba Sesay, the SDI's Information Officer, received death threats from an unknown caller every day for one month. They had published a report on press conditions in Sierra Leone. Staff of *The New Vision,* who printed the story in September, also received death threats.

Transitional justice

Despite a presidential promise in February to implement the TRC recommendations, little progress was made during the year. No steps were taken to create a TRC follow-up committee.

The mandate of the National Commission for Social Action, the agency in charge of reparations, was extended. It was given responsibility for overseeing the setting up of a Special Fund for War Victims. The Reparations Task Force was reconstituted as a Reparations Steering Committee and included one female NGO representative.

Police and security forces

Police brutality, excessive use of force and reported cases of sexual violence by police continued.
■ In August security personnel and police violently assaulted eight journalists who were covering meetings of the SLPP and APC, along with supporters of the two groups. An investigation was initiated after the SDI and the Sierra Leone Association of Journalists (SLAJ) called on the government to bring those responsible for the violence to justice, but by the end of the year no conclusive findings had been issued.

Justice system

Little progress was made in reducing excessive delays in hearing criminal cases and prolonged pre-trial detention due to repeated adjournments and remands in custody.
■ Eleven men convicted of treason who appealed against their conviction in January 2005 finally appeared in court in April 2008. It was then determined that there was no case against them, but they were only released in November.

Courts remain understaffed and underequipped with only 19 magistrates and 13 prosecution lawyers for the entire country.

Women's rights

The government approved a plan to implement the 2007 gender acts, namely the Domestic Violence Act, the Registration of Customary Marriage and Divorce Act and the Devolution of Estates Act. Copies of the gender acts were made available and training sessions took place throughout 2008 with women, traditional leaders and religious leaders. Despite the entry into force of the acts in 2007, high rates of sexual and gender-based violence and domestic violence continued to be reported. There was little progress in reducing the incidence of female genital mutilation.

Death penalty

In November, 10 men who had been on death row for treason were released after their convictions were overturned on appeal. The 10 were Lance Corporal Daniel Sandy, Private Issa Kanu, Captain Hindolo Trye, Alhajie Kamanda, Abdulia Taimu Tarawally, Richard Sellu Bockerie, Alhaji Mohamed Kondeh, Alhagie Kargbo, Ibrahim Koroma and Kai Mattia.

In May, three new death sentences were passed on Tahimu Sesay, Gibrilla Dumbuya and Mohamed Tarwalie. The three were convicted of beating a man to death.

At the end of 2008, there were 13 people on death row, of whom three were women.

In August, civil society groups unsuccessfully lobbied the Constitutional Review Commission to abolish the death penalty.

In December, Sierra Leone abstained on a UN General Assembly resolution calling for a worldwide moratorium on executions.

Amnesty International visit

🚐 Amnesty International delegates visited Sierra Leone in March/April.

SINGAPORE

REPUBLIC OF SINGAPORE

Head of state:	S. R. Nathan
Head of government:	Lee Hsien Loong
Death penalty:	retentionist
Population:	4.5 million
Life expectancy:	79.4 years
Under-5 mortality (m/f):	4/4 per 1,000
Adult literacy:	92.5 per cent

An easing of restrictions on freedom of assembly was overshadowed by heavy penalties and restrictive measures imposed on opposition activists, journalists and human rights defenders. Suspected Islamic militants remained detained without charge or trial under the Internal Security Act (ISA), amid concerns that some were at risk of torture and other ill-treatment during questioning. Foreign domestic workers continued to be excluded from legislation protecting the rights of foreign workers. Singapore rejected the UN General Assembly resolution calling for a moratorium on executions. At least five prisoners faced imminent execution, although the number of actual executions was unknown.

Repression of dissent

Defamation suits and restrictive measures continued against opposition activists, human rights defenders, foreign media and conscientious objectors. A climate of fear and self-censorship discouraged Singaporeans from fully participating in public affairs.

■ In September, the High Court ruled that the *Far Eastern Economic Review* magazine had defamed Prime Minister Lee Hsien Loong and Minister Mentor Lee Kuan Yew in an article about opposition leader Chee Soon Juan in 2006. The publisher was ordered to pay damages.

■ The *Wall Street Journal* Asia faced legal action for reporting that the judiciary was not independent.

■ In September, blogger Gopalan Nair was sentenced to three months in jail after criticizing a judge's handling of a case involving opposition leaders.

■ In October, Chee Soon Juan, who was already bankrupt, and activist Chee Siok Chin were ordered to pay S$610,000 (US$414,000) in defamation damages to government leaders. They were

S

subsequently sentenced to prison for contempt of court after criticizing the conduct of their trial. As bankrupts they were barred from seeking parliamentary seats or leaving the country without permission.

Freedom of expression and assembly

The government eased restrictions on public assembly (in one designated location), but continued imposing restrictions on media and peaceful demonstrations.

■ The film *One Nation Under Lee* was banned. The film depicted the former Prime Minister subjugating various government institutions.

■ Eighteen campaigners faced charges for holding unauthorized protest marches against the rising cost of living.

Migrants' rights

Singapore failed to provide basic protection for foreign domestic workers, such as a standard number of working hours and rest days, minimum wage and access to employment benefits. The Employment of Foreign Workers Act continued to exclude domestic workers.

Detention without trial

Some 23 suspected Islamist militants remained detained under the ISA. There were continued concerns about the risk of torture and other ill-treatment following arrest. Five detainees were released on restriction orders.

Death penalty

At least five people convicted of murder faced imminent execution.

The government did not provide comprehensive information about application of the death penalty, such as the number of executions and death sentences imposed and the nationality, age and background of those executed.

In February 2008, Singapore initiated and signed a statement of disassociation objecting to a UN General Assembly resolution calling for a worldwide moratorium on the use of the death penalty.

In December, Singapore voted against a second UN General Assembly resolution calling for a worldwide moratorium on executions.

Freedom of religion

Twenty-six Jehovah's Witnesses continued to be imprisoned for refusing compulsory military service. Five additional conscientious objectors were detained during the year.

SLOVAKIA

SLOVAK REPUBLIC

Head of state:	Ivan Gašparovič
Head of government:	Robert Fico
Death penalty:	abolitionist for all crimes
Population:	5.4 million
Life expectancy:	74.2 years
Under-5 mortality (m/f):	9/8 per 1,000

Roma continued to face discrimination in education, housing and health. The acceptance of diplomatic assurances against torture and other ill-treatment remained a cause of concern.

Political developments

In February, the European Parliament's Party of European Socialists lifted a ban on the senior coalition partner in the government of Slovakia, Direction – Social Democracy (Smer-SD), following a commitment by the Prime Minister to improve minority rights. After elections in June 2006, Smer-SD had formed a three-party coalition government with the Slovak National Party (SNS), and the People's Party-Movement for a Democratic Slovakia (LS-HZDS).

Discrimination – Roma
Education

The government publicized various measures to improve access to education for Romani children, but there was no practical commitment to reversing segregation in schools. The authorities continued to claim that the disproportionately high number of Romani children in special schools for children with mental disabilities was due to their socially disadvantaged background.

In March, the government adopted a five-year programme aimed at improving the lagging standards of living and education of its large Romani minority.

S

Measures outlined included compulsory nursery schooling for all five-year-olds by 2013, providing Romani language school books, and stricter rules governing placement of Romani children in special schools.

In May, the Slovak Parliament (National Council) passed the new Act on Upbringing and Education (the Schools Act), valid for the school year 2008/2009. The act prohibits all forms of discrimination, including segregation. A provision allowing temporary placement (*diagnostický pobyt*) of pupils at special schools after an inconclusive assessment, often leading to arbitrary placements, was removed from the law. In September the government abolished the motivational scholarships provision from its law on social assistance. The provision, weighted on pupils' performance, gave Romani parents a financial incentive to enrol their children at special schools. It will be replaced by a universal benefit, conditional on school attendance, for all pupils from families in material need.

However, the Schools Act does not include effective measures to eliminate the discrimination faced by Roma. International and national NGOs called for measures such as the compulsory provision of preparatory year classes and teaching assistants to be considered, and for a clear definition of the criteria and procedure for the placement of a child in special education.

The category of "socially disadvantaged children" remained in the list defining special educational needs in the Schools Act. Consequently, the association of social disadvantage with mental disability remained in practice.

◼ In Pavlovce nad Uhom, 99.5 per cent of the approximately 200 pupils at the special school were Roma. They constituted more than half of the Romani children attending primary school in the town. Following inspections in 2007, 17 pupils at the special school were formally acknowledged to have been wrongly assessed and were transferred to mainstream schools. Officially, children can only be placed in special schools after diagnosis of a mental disability and with full parental consent. However, many children had not been assessed at all and parental consent was often neither free nor informed. At the beginning of school year 2008/2009, the special primary school of Pavlovce nad Uhom continued in practice to be a segregated school.

Housing

In January, the Slovak Parliamentary Committee for Human Rights, Nationalities and the Status of Women adopted a resolution on forced evictions resulting from rent arrears, which disproportionately affect the Roma. Under the resolution, the government must undertake a range of measures to guarantee the right to protection against poverty and social exclusion, and to adequate housing.

In June, the Milan Šimečka Foundation published an evaluation of 57 social housing projects targeting inhabitants of Romani settlements. In 91 per cent of the localities studied, new housing maintained, and often increased, the existing geographic segregation of Romani beneficiaries.

Forced sterilization of Romani women

In February, the Regional Prosecutor's Office of Košice again halted the investigation into the case of alleged illegal sterilizations of three Romani women in eastern Slovakia in 1999, 2000 and 2002 respectively. The Prosecutor's Office considered that the sterilizations had been performed with the women's free and informed consent. The criminal investigation, begun in 2003, was halted three times but reopened following complaints to the Constitutional Court, which found that no effective investigation had taken place. In April a new complaint on behalf of the three women was filed with the Constitutional Court by the NGO Center for Civil and Human Rights, but was dismissed in July.

In July, the UN Committee on the Elimination of Discrimination against Women recommended that Slovakia "take all the necessary measures to ensure that complaints filed by Roma women on grounds of coerced sterilization are duly acknowledged and that victims of such practices are granted effective remedies".

Torture and other ill-treatment

◼ In March, Banská Bystrica Regional Court sentenced seven police officers for the ill-treatment and death of Karol Sendrei, a 51-year-old Romani man, while in police custody in 2001. Two of the officers, Ján K. and Miroslav S., were found principally responsible, and sentenced to eight and a half years each in prison on charges of torture and cruel conduct. Ladislav K., an officer who jumped on Karol Sendrei's chest, received seven years for the same offences. The officer on duty, Roman R., was sentenced to four years for torture. The court found that although he had not participated in the torture of Karol Sendrei, he had failed in his duty to prevent the incident. Three other officers received suspended sentences of one to two years. All of the defendants appealed their sentences to the Supreme Court.

Counter-terror and security
Non-refoulement
■ On 26 June, the Constitutional Court issued its decision in the case of Mustapha Labsi, an Algerian national held in Slovakia originally on the basis of an extradition request by Algeria. The Court concluded that the Supreme Court's decision of 22 January, allowing the extradition of Mustapha Labsi to Algeria, had violated his right to judicial protection and had failed to fully consider the human rights situation in Algeria.

The Court reaffirmed the absolute duty of the authorities not to return anyone to a country where they face a real risk of torture or other ill-treatment. Slovakia's obligation not to rely on diplomatic assurances was also implicit in the judgement's criticism of Regional and Supreme Court decisions.

The Supreme Court subsequently reconsidered Mustapha Labsi's case and ruled on 7 August that he could not be deported to Algeria where he faced serious human rights violations including torture and other ill-treatment. He was released but immediately detained again on the basis of a deportation order dating from 2006. Mustapha Labsi applied again for asylum, which was rejected on 6 October. An appeal against the rejection of his asylum application and a legal case against his detention were pending at the end of the year.

Amnesty International visits/reports
🚗 Amnesty International visited Slovakia in March and April.
📄 NGOs call on Slovakia on International Roma Day to address discrimination of Roma in education (EUR 72/003/2008)
📄 Slovakia: NGOs joint open letter on the occasion of the second reading of the draft new Schools Act at the Slovak National Council (EUR 72/004/2008)
📄 Slovakia: Constitutional Court upholds the absolute prohibition of torture (EUR 72/005/2008)
📄 A tale of two schools: Segregating Roma into special education in Slovakia (EUR 72/007/2008)
📄 Slovakia: Submission to the UN Universal Periodic Review – Fifth session of the UPR Working Group of the Human Rights Council, May 2009 (EUR 72/009/2008)

SLOVENIA
REPUBLIC OF SLOVENIA
Head of state:	Danilo Türk
Head of government:	Borut Pahor (replaced Janez Janša in November)
Death penalty:	abolitionist for all crimes
Population:	2 million
Life expectancy:	77.4 years
Under-5 mortality (m/f):	6/6 per 1,000
Adult literacy:	99.7 per cent

The rights of thousands of people who were removed from the registry of permanent residents in 1992 (known as the "erased") continued to be violated. Members of Romani communities continued to face discrimination, including in access to education.

Background
The Social Democrats won parliamentary elections in September, forming a coalition government in November which included members of the Social Democrats, the Zares Party, the Democratic Party of Pensioners of Slovenia and the Liberal Democracy of Slovenia. Borut Pahor, of the Social Democrats, was appointed Prime Minister.

Discrimination – the 'erased'
The authorities continued to fail to guarantee the rights of a group of permanent residents known as the "erased". A year after Slovenia's declaration of independence in 1991, more than 18,000 individuals were unlawfully removed from the registry of permanent residents. They were people originating from other former Yugoslav republics, many of them Roma, who had been living in Slovenia but had not acquired Slovenian citizenship after independence. The move was discriminatory as citizens of former Yugoslav republics were treated less favourably than other foreign nationals whose permanent residency status was granted automatically.

As a result of the "erasure", many permanent residents were forcibly expelled from Slovenia. Many others lost their jobs, were denied access to education and the right to a comprehensive healthcare service. The issue of the "erased" was the subject of much political debate in the run-up to the September parliamentary elections.

The Constitutional Committee of Parliament initiated a discussion on a draft constitutional law on the "erased". The draft law, which had been presented by the government in 2007, would maintain discriminatory treatment of the "erased". It would provide new legal grounds for discriminatory actions by the authorities, including the possibility of reversing individual decisions to restore permanent residency. It fails to restore the permanent residency status of the "erased", disclaims state responsibility for the "erasure" and explicitly excludes the possibility of reparations, including compensation for human rights violations suffered by the "erased".

Through the year deportation procedures were initiated against "erased" individuals, although deportations were not carried out.

The authorities failed to acknowledge the discriminatory nature of the "erasure", and did not implement two earlier Constitutional Court decisions which found the "erasure" illegal and anti-constitutional.

Discrimination – Roma

The authorities failed to conduct an independent and thorough evaluation of the so-called "Bršljin model", designed to enable pupils needing separate tuition to catch up and to return to mainstream classes. Despite the declared aim, the model could foster segregation as some of the catch-up classes were composed exclusively of Roma. The authorities failed to provide any evidence that Romani pupils in fact benefited from the catch-up classes.

The authorities also failed to submit plans on the development of the Bršljin model for public consultation, including with Roma communities. Amnesty International was granted access to specific information about the evaluation of the model only after having initiated an administrative complaint to the state commissioner for public information.

School curricula and teaching materials in Romani languages were not available to pupils during 2008, nor was Roma culture reflected in the teaching materials in a comprehensive way.

Amnesty International report

📄 Slovenia: Amnesty International's Briefing to the United Nations Human Rights Council 9th Session September 2008 (EUR 68/001/2008)

SOLOMON ISLANDS

SOLOMON ISLANDS

Head of state:	Queen Elizabeth II, represented by Nathaniel Waena
Head of government:	Derek Sikua
Death penalty:	abolitionist for all crimes
Population:	507,000
Life expectancy:	63 years
Under-5 mortality (m/f):	72/71 per 1,000
Adult literacy:	76.6 per cent

The growth of informal settlements in Honiara and surrounding areas reflects growing urban poverty. A lack of affordable housing options in the city, insufficient housing legislation, poor government planning and the failure to provide infrastructure has led to inadequate access to water, sanitation and health services for thousands of people living in informal settlements. Violence against women and girls remains prevalent.

Housing rights

There has been a rapid growth of informal settlements in Honiara, the capital, and the surrounding areas over the last 10 years. This is mainly due to increased rural to urban migration, poor town planning, including the absence of regulations preventing unsafe building, and a lack of legislation providing for security of tenure.

The government failed to provide adequate health care, clean water, sanitation and education to those living in the informal settlements, resulting in thousands of people without access to basic services. The government also failed to provide new low-cost housing in Honiara to alleviate overcrowding and address the lack of secure tenure.

In August, Honiara City Council acknowledged that the rise in informal settlements and the resultant overcrowding was a major cause of serious sanitation and health problems such as diarrhoea, dysentery and hook worm, which became further exacerbated by the lack of access to health services for those in many of the settlements.

Violence against women and girls

Reports of violence against women continued to rise. Seventy per cent of violence against women was

S

committed by the woman's partner, one of the highest rates of partner violence in the world, according to preliminary findings of a government-sponsored study carried out by the Secretariat of the Pacific Community, a regional intergovernmental organization.

In November, responding to the study, Prime Minister Derek Sikua committed the government to do all it could to effectively address gender-based violence. However, at the end of the year, no detailed plans on how the government planned to do this had been made public.

Death penalty

In December, despite being abolitionist for all crimes and guaranteeing the right to life in the Constitution, the Solomon Islands voted against a UN General Assembly resolution calling for a worldwide moratorium on executions.

SOMALIA

SOMALI REPUBLIC

Head of state of Transitional Federal Government:	**Adan Mohamed Nuur Madobe (replaced Abdullahi Yusuf Ahmed in December)**
Head of government of Transitional Federal Government:	**Nur Hassan Hussein**
Head of Somaliland Republic:	**Dahir Riyaale Kahin**
Death penalty:	**retentionist**
Population:	**9 million**
Life expectancy:	**47.1 years**
Under-5 mortality (m/f):	**196/186 per 1,000**

The interlinked human rights and humanitarian crises continued to worsen in 2008. Thousands more civilians were killed, bringing the total number of civilians killed as a result of armed conflict since January 2007 to more than 16,000. Transitional Federal Government (TFG) and Ethiopian armed forces fought against opposition clan-based groups and militias, most prominently al-Shabab ("youth") militias which emerged out of the former Islamic Courts Union (ICU). More than 1.2 million civilians were internally displaced in southern and central Somalia. At the end of the year an estimated 3.25

million people were dependent on emergency food aid, which was often disrupted due to widespread insecurity and impacted by insufficient contributions from donor governments. Humanitarian aid workers and local human rights defenders were increasingly targeted in threats and killings.

In the northwest, the self-declared Republic of Somaliland, whose independence was not recognized by international bodies, enjoyed relative peace and security until a series of suicide bomb attacks in the capital, Hargeisa, on 29 October. Simultaneous attacks were carried out in Bossaso in the semi-autonomous Puntland Region of Somalia in the northeast.

Background

Insurgent violence against the TFG, based in Baidoa, and allied Ethiopian forces, which began in December 2006, continued through 2008. Both insurgent attacks and the TFG and Ethiopian counter-insurgency operations resulted in massive and widespread human rights abuses against civilians. Abuses included arbitrary detention, rape and other forms of torture, and attacks on civilian populated areas which may have been indiscriminate and disproportionate. The TFG failed to establish governance structures, was unable to protect civilians in Mogadishu, and lost control of most of southern and central Somalia, including Kismayo and Beletweyne, and the ports of Merka and Barawa.

The Alliance for the Re-Liberation of Somalia (ARS), created in 2007 in Eritrea by former leaders of the ICU, former members of the Transitional Federal Parliament and other TFG opponents, split into two factions, one of which moved to Djibouti while the other remained in Eritrea. Both factions insisted on the withdrawal of Ethiopian troops from Somalia.

In May, the fifth reported US air strike on Somalia since early 2007 killed al-Shabab leader Aden Hashi Ayro in Dhusamareb in southern Somalia, in addition to an undetermined number of civilians, and destroyed civilian property.

After the replacement in late 2007 of Prime Minister Mohamed Gedi by Nur Hassan Hussein and the appointment of a new UN Special Representative to the Secretary-General, Ahmedou Ould-Abdallah, hope for progress in ending the conflict and consolidating governance emerged, despite ongoing

S

armed conflict. In April the TFG and ARS-Djibouti began negotiations. They signed a formal agreement in October, which included plans for a ceasefire, power-sharing and gradual Ethiopian troop withdrawal, which began in November. At the October meeting in Djibouti, TFG and ARS representatives also jointly called for a Commission of Inquiry into human rights abuses in Somalia.

Following a series of public confrontations and an unsuccessful attempt to oust the Prime Minister, President Abdullahi Yusuf resigned in December. Adan Mohamed Nuur Madobe, the Speaker of the Parliament, became Interim President.

Armed groups from Puntland and other regions of Somalia hijacked more than 40 ships off shore, including a Ukrainian vessel containing 33 armoured tanks and small arms. At least 15 ships and hundreds of crew members were still being held at the end of the year by pirates demanding large ransoms. The UN Security Council and the EU took action to improve counter-piracy operations.

By the end of 2008 almost equal numbers of Ugandan and Burundian peacekeepers brought the total AU peacekeeping force in Somalia (AMISOM) to some 3,200 out of 8,000 authorized by the AU and UN. Nigeria, Ghana and South Africa had not yet provided troops they had pledged to AMISOM. This force remained largely ineffective and without a mandate to protect civilians. As Ethiopian troops began to withdraw from Somalia, calls by the USA and other UN Security Council members for an eventual UN peacekeeping mission in Somalia continued.

All parties to the conflict in Somalia, as well as several neighbouring countries and other actors, reportedly committed violations of the UN arms embargo.

Armed conflict

Armed conflict of TFG forces and allied Ethiopian forces against insurgent al-Shabab and other militias continued to exact a heavy toll on civilians, with more than 16,000 civilians killed since January 2007. More than 1.2 million people were internally displaced in southern and central Somalia, with hundreds of thousands of refugees in neighbouring countries, including Kenya. All parties to the conflict violated international humanitarian law, committing war crimes including wilful killings of civilians, and

possible indiscriminate and disproportionate attacks on civilian populated areas. On 19 April Ethiopian forces conducted a raid on Mogadishu's Al Hidya mosque, killing 21 people and holding more than 40 children for days. While Ethiopian forces continued to be implicated in abuses against civilians, targeted attacks against humanitarian aid workers and local human rights defenders by al-Shabab and other militias markedly increased in 2008.

Freedom of expression

Human rights defenders, humanitarian aid workers and journalists remained at risk from attack by all parties to the conflict, most often by armed militias. They were regularly threatened, shot at, abducted and killed. More than 40 Somali human rights defenders and humanitarian workers were killed between January and September 2008 alone. Critics of any armed group faced extreme danger, despite mediation efforts by local clan elders and religious leaders.

Human rights defenders and representatives of civil society

Well-established civil society groups continued their work for human rights, development, peace and democratization despite high risks caused by conflict and lawlessness.

■ Two British teachers, Daud Hassan Ali and Rehana Ahmed, and two Kenyan teachers, Gilford Koech and Andrew Kibet, from the Hiran Community Education School in Beletweyne, were killed on 14 April during an attack by an al-Shabab militia.

■ Mohamed Hassan Kulmiye, a peace activist with the Centre for Research and Development, was killed on 22 June by unidentified gunmen in Beletweyne. He died after being shot in the head several times.

■ Ali Jama Bihi, a peace activist and mediator between Darod and Hawiye clan militias, was killed on 9 July. Two gunmen shot him as he came out of dawn prayers in Galkayo.

Insecurity – humanitarian aid workers

International and local humanitarian aid workers faced the worst violence against them since the early 1990s after the overthrow of the Siad Barre government. Perpetrators were often difficult to identify and survivors were often unwilling to report abuses out of fear of retaliation. Agencies were

S

reluctant to speak about the dire conditions they faced, out of fear of losing access to displaced people and other vulnerable populations in need of essential assistance.

■ Isse Abdulkadir Haji, an employee of the ZamZam Foundation, was killed on 7 January. He was shot dead in Yaaqshiid district in Mogadishu by unknown gunmen.

■ Victor Okumu, a surgeon, Damien Lehalle, a logistics officer, and Abdi Ali Bidhaan, their driver, were killed near Kismayo hospital on 28 January when a roadside bomb was detonated, apparently targeting their Médecins sans Frontières (MSF)-marked vehicle.

■ Ahmed Moalim Bario, director of the NGO Horn Relief, was killed on 17 May by masked gunmen as he arrived at his house in Kismayo.

■ Abdikarim Sheikh Ibrahim, Chairman of the Committee for the Assistance of Somali Orphans, was shot dead by armed men as he was travelling home from Bakara market in Mogadishu on 2 July.

■ Osman Ali Ahmed, head of the UN Development Programme (UNDP) in Somalia, was killed on 6 July. He was shot as he left a mosque in Mogadishu after evening prayers. His brother was also shot and wounded.

■ Abdulkadir Diad Mohamed, a World Food Programme (WFP) employee, and his driver were killed on 15 August in Dinsur in southern Somalia.

■ Four staff of the international NGO Action Contre la Faim and two pilots were abducted from Dhusamareb in southern Somalia by unidentified gunmen on 5 November.

■ Mohamed Osman, a programme officer for Mercy Corps, was killed in Jamame, Lower Juba, on 9 November.

Freedom of expression – journalists

While reported detentions of journalists decreased in 2008, as well as the duration of detentions, this appeared to be the result of a combination of factors, including a decreased capacity on the part of TFG authorities, including the National Security Agency, to make arrests, as well as increased self-censorship by journalists. Those journalists who remained active in Somalia continued to face intimidation, death threats and arbitrary detention by all parties to the conflict and armed bandits, although some attempts by Islamist groups to improve relations with the press were also reported. There were some 30 detentions of Somali journalists (lasting between four and 115 days), and they suffered more than 30 death threats, two killings and several injuries in 2008, with no means of bringing perpetrators to justice.

■ Abdikheyr Mohamed Jama, a presenter for Radio Galkayo, was shot in the mouth and critically wounded when he was attacked by gunmen in Puntland on 10 January.

■ Nasteh Dahir Farah, a BBC reporter and official of the National Union of Somali Journalists, was shot and killed on 7 June in Kismayo.

Refugees and internally displaced people

By late 2008 more than 1.2 million Somalis were internally displaced, including 870,000 since the start of 2007. Others, including members of minority groups, had been displaced for longer periods. Hundreds of thousands of internally displaced people continued to mass in the Afgooye Road corridor after fleeing Mogadishu.

In addition, by late 2008, hundreds of thousands of Somali refugees had sought safety (and some sought asylum) in Kenya, Djibouti, Somaliland and Yemen, among other locations. The Kenyan border remained officially closed to Somali refugees, but camps in Dadaab, across the border in Kenya, became severely overcrowded.

The situation of southern Somali displaced persons in Somaliland remained complicated as international agencies designated southern Somalis as internally displaced, while the government of Somaliland designated them refugees. Neither was able to provide adequate assistance to meet their basic needs.

Somali refugees and migrants who sought sea passage to Yemen faced dangerous conditions, and human traffickers were frequently reported to throw people overboard in order to elude Yemeni law enforcement authorities. Hundreds of Somalis and Ethiopians died in the Gulf of Aden while fleeing Somalia via Puntland.

Justice system and rule of law

Somalia had no effective national governance or functioning justice system. The UN Development Programme rule of law programme was unable to provide sufficient support for the effective establishment of detention facilities, courts and police capacity building. There was no discernible improvement in human rights conditions as a result of this programme, nor was there sufficient oversight.

Somaliland and Puntland authorities made a number of arrests following suicide bombings in October. A visiting human rights activist from southern Somalia and a prominent local journalist were arrested but released within days in Somaliland.

Death penalty and extrajudicial executions

Death sentences were reportedly carried out by those claiming local authority in Kismayo, including on 22 April when a man accused of murder was executed by shooting. Authorities of al-Shabab factions reportedly unlawfully killed several men accused of murder.

In Baidoa two men were executed without trial and a third killed in police custody on 26 November following a grenade attack that killed 10 people, including a TFG military officer.

■ Aisha Ibrahim Duholow, aged 13, was publicly stoned to death on 27 October by some 50 men in Kismayo. She was convicted of "adultery" by a *Sharia* court without legal defence after she reported to local authorities that she had been raped by three men. The men were not prosecuted.

Puntland authorities announced that they would apply the death penalty in cases of piracy in that region, but no executions were reported.

Somaliland

The Republic of Somaliland, which declared independence from Somalia in 1991, continued to seek international recognition. Although Somaliland government officials threatened to expel some 24 journalists who had fled from Mogadishu to the safety of Hargeisa in late 2007, that order was not carried out. It is estimated that Somaliland continued to host tens of thousands of displaced Somalis fleeing violence in southern and central Somalia.

The relative peace and security of Somaliland was disrupted in October by suicide bomb attacks on a UN compound, the President's residence and the Ethiopian trade mission in Hargeisa. More than 20 people were killed and more than 30 injured in the attacks.

National elections which were originally scheduled for 2008 were postponed until March 2009, with presidential elections scheduled before local elections.

The government of Somaliland maintained national

and regional security committees which reportedly carried out unlawful arrests and detentions. Human rights defenders continued to report incidents of government obstruction of civil society activities resulting in violations of freedom of expression and assembly.

Tensions over border areas, claimed by the semi-autonomous Puntland Region of Somalia, continued. Thousands of civilians from the disputed town of Las Anod remained displaced after extensive fighting between Somaliland and Puntland forces in late 2007, which ended in Somaliland control of the area.

Amnesty International reports

▤ Somalia: Journalists under attack (AFR 52/001/2008)
▤ Somalia: Routinely targeted: Attacks on civilians in Somalia (AFR 52/009/2008)
▤ Fatal Insecurity: Attacks on aid workers and rights defenders in Somalia (AFR 52/016/2008)
▤ Somalia (Somaliland/Puntland): Amnesty International condemns bomb attacks in Hargeisa and Bossaso (AFR 52/018/2008)
▤ Somalia: International Community must seize opportunity for accountability and justice (AFR 52/019/2008)
▤ Somalia/Ethiopia: Release children held in raid on Al Hidya mosque, 23 April 2008
▤ Somalia: Girl stoned was a child of 13, 31 October 2008

SOUTH AFRICA

REPUBLIC OF SOUTH AFRICA

Head of state and government:	**Kgalema Motlanthe (replaced Thabo Mbeki in September)**
Death penalty:	**abolitionist for all crimes**
Population:	**48.8 million**
Life expectancy:	**50.8 years**
Under-5 mortality (m/f):	**71/60 per 1,000**
Adult literacy:	**82.4 per cent**

S

The rights of refugees, asylum-seekers and migrants were violated on a large scale. Inadequate training of police and health care providers undermined efforts to address persistently high rates of violence against women. Barriers to non-discriminatory access to health services continued to affect the majority of people living with HIV for most of the year. Torture

and other ill-treatment by police, prison warders and private security guards continued to be reported and sometimes led to the deaths of detainees.

In an increasingly volatile political environment, the judiciary, and human rights bodies and defenders came under attack from national political figures. These tensions were also evident in the political responses to local campaigns to address deepening poverty and inequality, the shortage of adequate housing, threatened large-scale evictions arising from mining or development schemes, and the crisis over land claims.

Background

In September the National Executive Committee of the African National Congress (ANC) "recalled" Thabo Mbeki, leading to his resignation as President. ANC deputy president Kgalema Motlanthe became President following a parliamentary vote and appointed a new cabinet.

Earlier in September the Pietermaritzburg High Court had declared invalid the decision of the National Prosecuting Authority in late 2007 to institute fresh corruption charges against ANC president Jacob Zuma. The court did not rule on the merits of the prosecution case, but concluded that there had been a pattern of "political interference, pressure or influence" in the prosecution of this case. The Supreme Court of Appeal heard an appeal against the High Court decision in November, but had not issued its judgment by the end of the year.

These developments led to a major split within the ANC and the formation of a new political party, the Congress of the People (COPE), ahead of national elections in 2009. Incidents of violence, intimidation and threats were reported involving members of the ANC and COPE at public meetings and during municipal by-elections held in December.

In November a commission of inquiry, appointed by President Mbeki, to examine whether the National Director of Public Prosecutions, Vusi Pikoli, was fit to hold office reported to President Motlanthe. Vusi Pikoli had been suspended in 2007 by President Mbeki after obtaining a warrant to arrest the national commissioner of police on corruption charges. Although the commission's report concluded that the grounds for his suspension were without substance and that he should be restored to office, in December President Motlanthe decided to dismiss him and

referred the decision to parliament for final confirmation.

Refugees, asylum-seekers and migrants

In May more than 60 people were killed and over 600 injured in violent attacks against individuals, targeted because of their perceived nationality, ethnicity or migrant status. Tens of thousands of people were displaced from their homes and communities, particularly in areas in and around Johannesburg and Cape Town.

Preliminary inquiries highlighted contributing factors, including xenophobic sentiments, competition over jobs, housing and social services, and the impact of corruption. Official inquiries failed to clarify the role of criminality or of organized politically motivated elements behind the violence, or to assess fully the role and capacity of the police in response to it. In December the Consortium for Refugees and Migrants in South Africa issued an appeal to the South African Human Rights Commission to lead an investigation into the violence, expressing concern at government failure to bring to justice those responsible for the May attacks.

Government authorities, with the support of civil society organizations and humanitarian agencies, established "safety sites" for the internally displaced (IDPs). However, from July onwards, the authorities' response increasingly included actions contrary to their human rights obligations towards the displaced. Among other things, access to the sites by humanitarian, legal and other support organizations was sometimes obstructed; accelerated asylum procedures were implemented at the sites without sufficient procedural safeguards, resulting in rejection rates of over 95 per cent; and criminal charges, unlawful detention and threats of deportation were used against individuals who failed to co-operate with administrative procedures. Legal access to IDPs removed to the Lindela deportation facility was sometimes denied and breaches of the prohibition against *refoulement* occurred.

Essential services at the sites were reduced before conditions for safe and sustainable return to local communities were widely present. At the same time repatriation for people who fled conflict zones was not possible, and resettlement options were not available. While re-integration locally was successful in some areas, there were continuing sporadic incidents of

S

theft, assaults, rape and murder against IDPs using humanitarian assistance funds to re-integrate.

The political and humanitarian crisis in Zimbabwe led to the flight of thousands of Zimbabweans to South Africa, with 46,000 asylum applications between July and September alone. Towards the end of the year the Department of Home Affairs acknowledged that using the asylum system to screen out and deport economic migrants failed to address the crisis.

Violence against women and girls

High levels of violence against women continued to be reported.

According to police statistics, in the year ending March 2008, reported incidents of rape declined by 8.8 per cent. In June the Minister for Safety and Security told parliament that reporting figures underestimated the actual extent of crimes as many were not reported due to stigma and pressure from perpetrators. In the nine months prior to March 2008 there were 20,282 reported rapes of women, 16,068 reported rapes of children under 18, and 6,127 reported cases of indecent assault. The police reported a conviction rate of around 8 per cent for rape cases brought to the courts during this period.

From May, regulations under the new "Sexual Offences Act" began to be implemented, but there were gaps in training for police and health workers. Despite the regulations, some health care providers and police risked the health of rape survivors by insisting that they first lodge a criminal complaint before they could have access to emergency treatment including post-exposure prophylaxis (PEP) to reduce the risk of HIV transmission.

In August the Acting Commissioner of Police reported to Parliament that between July and December 2007 police recorded 50,497 incidents of domestic violence. Only a quarter led to criminal cases, because victims were reluctant to pursue charges because they were economically dependent on the perpetrators.

Women's access to legal remedies and protection continued to be restricted by lack of political commitment, insufficient budget and inadequate training of the police and provincial social services officials, and poor referral systems. Police informed Amnesty International in July that the heads of police stations in three provinces had been retrained, along with new recruits. However, in August the Acting National Commissioner of Police stated that the few trained officers were being undermined by other, untrained staff. The Independent Complaints Directorate (ICD) reported that many police stations were still failing to keep proper records as required under the Domestic Violence Act, and sometimes failed to assist women to open a case or to execute arrest warrants.

The number of domestic violence shelters rose from 39 in the early 2000s to nearly 100 in July 2008, according to national Department of Social Development officials. In August the National Shelter Movement was launched to address gaps in services for survivors. Severe problems remained, particularly for rural women with children.

In October a Court ruled as "arbitrary and illegitimate" the effective dismissal in 2001 by the Mpumalanga health department of a doctor involved in the provision of PEP to rape survivors.

Support organizations continued to report poor and prejudiced police response to cases of rape of lesbian women. In December South Africa did not sign the UN General Assembly statement on human rights, sexual orientation and sexual identity.

Right to health – people living with HIV and AIDS

An estimated 5.7 million people were living with HIV. In July the national Department of Health stated that 500,000 AIDS patients were receiving antiretroviral treatment (ART) at 409 accredited facilities. The numbers on ART had risen to 550,000, according to the new Minister of Health in October. There remained a wide treatment gap however. In June the government's progress report to the UN General Assembly Special Session on HIV and AIDS acknowledged that 58 per cent of those clinically needing ART were not receiving it. Severe staffing shortages in the public sector, disruptions in supply of the drugs, slow progress in decentralizing services for poor, rural communities, gender-based discrimination and poor political leadership contributed to this treatment gap. Some provinces, though, such as KwaZulu-Natal (KZN) and the Free State, increased the number of decentralized facilities accessible to patients unable to afford transport costs.

In February, after a long delay, the national

S

Department of Health issued revised guidelines on the use of dual therapy for the prevention of mother-to-child transmission of HIV (PMTCT). The provision of PMTCT treatment to HIV-positive pregnant women ranged from just over half in the Eastern Cape to 99 per cent in Western Cape province, where dual therapy had been offered since 2004 and transmission rates reduced to three per cent. Also in February a hospital doctor in KZN was subjected to disciplinary proceedings for having implemented dual therapy before its official rollout.

In July, the Director General of the Department of Health publicly criticized the Deputy Chairperson of the South African National AIDS Council, a representative of civil society, for advocating a rights-based approach to the growing crisis of tuberculosis (TB) and HIV co-infection and the emergence of multiple drug-resistant (MDR) forms of TB.

Civil society organizations campaigned for improved access to support grants for people living in poverty with HIV and TB, including MDR TB patients isolated in specialized facilities. In August the Ministry of Social Development announced increases to social assistance grants. The Department of Transport also began to implement a rural public transport strategy to improve access to health services.

From October, a revitalised national political leadership of the AIDS response and greater co-operation with civil society under the new Minister of Health also began to have an impact on some of the barriers to the right to health.

Torture and other ill-treatment

Torture and other ill-treatment by police, prison warders and private security guards continued to be reported and sometimes led to the deaths of detainees. Corroborated cases included the use of electric shock and suffocation torture and prolonged assaults with batons, fists and booted feet. In several cases police interrogators and prison warders attempted to conceal evidence relating to the cause of death. Crime suspects, injured by anti-crime vigilante groups, were sometimes denied emergency medical care while held in police custody, leading in one case, in December, to the death of a detainee.

■ S.N., a co-accused in a theft case, was assaulted by police in October when he went to report to the police station, as required under his bail conditions. He was pushed against a wall, punched, slapped and stamped on, while handcuffed and in leg-irons. He was threatened with being shot if he lodged a complaint. A medical examination revealed injuries consistent with his allegations.

■ Three Zimbabwean asylum-seekers were ill-treated by police officers in an immigration detention facility in Musina. They were handcuffed and forced to roll in urine while being assaulted with hosepipes and kicked. They were charged with malicious damage to property when they sought redress.

The ICD reported that between April 2007 and March 2008, it received 20 complaints of torture and 739 complaints of assault with intent to cause grievous bodily harm. In the same 12-month period it received 302 new reports of deaths in custody and 490 suspects fatally shot by police during investigations, an 87 per cent increase over the previous year. Continuing weaknesses in resources and legal powers of the ICD were highlighted in parliament. An NGO study showed that police implemented only half of their recommendations.

■ In April the Supreme Court of Appeal overturned two convictions and sentences for theft against Bongani Mthembu on the grounds that they were based on evidence extracted under torture from a witness.

In July the government made public a revised Combating of Torture Bill, following widespread criticism of the previous version in 2006, and concern expressed by a parliamentary committee in June at the government's lack of political will to implement treaty obligations. The new version, however, still had serious weaknesses, including a failure to make clear the absolute prohibition against torture.

Impunity

In December the Pretoria High Court ruled as unconstitutional, unlawful and invalid, the 2005 National Prosecution Policy on the prosecution of offences "emanating from conflicts of the past". The case had been brought by relatives of victims of extrajudicial executions and disappearances in the 1980s. The Court accepted that the policy would have the effect of allowing immunity against prosecution for individuals who had not co-operated with or had been denied amnesty by the Truth and Reconciliation Commission, even in circumstances where there was a well-founded case against them.

Amnesty International visits/reports

🚌 Amnesty International delegates visited South Africa in March, June/July and August/September.

📄 South Africa: "I am at the lowest end of all". Rural women living with HIV face human rights abuses in South Africa (AFR 53/001/2008)

📄 South Africa: Amnesty International calls on government to protect those at risk of "xenophobic" attack (AFR 53/007/2008)

📄 South Africa: Fear that closure of camps will result in human rights violations (AFR 53/010/2008)

📄 South Africa: "Talk for us please": Limited Options Facing Individuals Displaced by Xenophobic Violence (AFR 53/012/2008)

📄 South Africa: Survivors Still At Risk (AFR 53/015/2008)

📄 South Africa: No Transport, No Treatment (AFR 53/016/2008)

📄 South Africa: Nowhere To Shelter (AFR 53/017/2008)

📄 Oral statement on the outcome on South Africa under the Universal Periodic Review (IOR 41/024/2008)

📄 South Africa: Rural women the losers in HIV response, 18 March 2008

📄 South Africa: Displaced people should not be forcibly removed from temporary camps, 23 July 2008

SPAIN

KINGDOM OF SPAIN

Head of state:	King Juan Carlos I de Borbón
Head of government:	José Luis Rodríguez Zapatero
Death penalty:	abolitionist for all crimes
Population:	44.6 million
Life expectancy:	80.5 years
Under-5 mortality (m/f):	6/5 per 1,000

Torture and other ill-treatment by law enforcement officials were widely reported. There was continued use of incommunicado detention. The armed Basque group Euskadi Ta Askatasuna (ETA) continued its campaign of violence, claiming responsibility for killing four people. Efforts by the authorities to control migration in co-operation with the EU and certain African countries jeopardized the rights of migrants and asylum-seekers. A judicial investigation was opened and then closed into enforced disappearances during the 1936-39 civil war and the Franco dictatorship. On 12 December the government adopted its national action plan for human rights.

Torture and other ill-treatment

There were widespread allegations of widespread torture and other ill-treatment by law enforcement officials. In April the Constitutional Court reiterated the need for thorough and effective investigations into all such allegations. The UN Special Rapporteur on human rights and counter-terrorism expressed concern that allegations of torture and other ill-treatment continued and did not systematically result in prompt and thorough independent investigations. Some political and legal authorities continued to argue that allegations of ill-treatment by detainees held on terrorism charges were part of a strategy to discredit the state.

■ The judicial investigation continued into the death of Osamuyia Akpitaye, a Nigerian national who died in 2007 when being forcibly expelled from Spain. The investigating judge had charged the police officers involved with a "misdemeanour". However, following an appeal by the Public Prosecutor and the victim's family, the investigating court was ordered to lay a more serious charge against the police officers. At the end of the year the case was still under investigation.

■ The investigation into allegations of ill-treatment of detainees at Les Corts autonomous Catalan police station in Barcelona continued to progress slowly. In one incident, concealed camera footage from March 2007 showed police officers beating, kicking and insulting a detained man. Five officers were suspended from duty following the opening of a criminal inquiry, but on 16 January they returned to active duty while awaiting the outcome of the investigations. In June the Public Prosecutor formally presented charges against the officers of falsifying police documents and minor assault. The Prosecutor requested a sentence of four and a half years' imprisonment for the charge of falsifying documents and 15 months' imprisonment and a fine for degrading treatment and assault. At the end of the year the trial date had still not been set.

■ Almost three years after Mohammed Fahsi was allegedly tortured while being held incommunicado in January 2006, no criminal investigation into the allegations had been opened. Both the General Council of the Judiciary and the Madrid Public Prosecutor were asked to investigate; both replied that there were no grounds to do so.

■ On 5 January, two suspected members of ETA were detained and held incommunicado by Civil Guards in Mondragón (Guipuzcoa). Both were reportedly ill-

S

treated during arrest, with one subsequently admitted to San Sebastián hospital with two broken ribs and a punctured lung. An investigation into allegations of ill-treatment was opened immediately by Investigating Court No.1 of San Sebastián but had not concluded by the end of the year.

Refoulement

■ On 22 July Basel Ghalyoun was forcibly returned to Syria, despite concerns that he would be at risk of torture and arbitrary detention. On 17 July the Supreme Court had acquitted him of involvement in the 11 March 2004 bomb attack on commuter trains in Madrid, and he was released from prison. Upon his release he was immediately taken into police custody under an expulsion order, as his residence permit had expired while he was in prison. Neither he nor his lawyer had been aware of the expulsion order, and his lawyer was unable to submit an appeal against it before Basel Ghalyoun was expelled. He was arrested on arrival in Syria and held incommunicado at an undisclosed location.

■ On 31 December Murad Gasayev, a Russian citizen of Chechen origin, was extradited to Russia despite evidence that he would be at risk of an unfair trial and torture or other ill-treatment. The National Criminal Court approved the extradition request on the basis of "diplomatic assurances" from the Russian Public Prosecutor's office that the European Committee for the Prevention of Torture (CPT) would be allowed to visit Murad Gasayev in detention. The CPT informed the Spanish authorities that it would not accept this responsibility due to serious concerns over the reliability of such "diplomatic assurances". Despite this, the Spanish authorities extradited Murad Gasayev under the condition that the Spanish embassy in Moscow would be able to visit him.

Abuses by armed groups

ETA claimed responsibility for killing four people in 2008 and carrying out numerous bomb attacks. On 2 April the newspaper *Gara* published threats by ETA against members of the ruling Spanish Socialist Workers' Party, the Basque Nationalist Party and the public radio and television network in the Basque Country. Bomb attacks claimed by ETA on a Civil Guard barracks in May and at a military academy in September killed two officers.

■ On 7 March, two days before the national general elections, a former councillor from Spain's ruling Socialist Workers' Party was shot and killed in the Basque Country in an attack claimed by ETA. Isaías Carrasco was shot outside his home in Mondragón and declared dead in hospital.

■ On 3 December Ignacio Uría Mendizábal, joint owner of one of the construction companies involved in the high-speed train route connecting the Basque Country with Madrid, was shot dead. ETA claimed responsibility. In August, ETA had claimed responsibility for three bomb attacks on companies involved in the train construction works and issued threats against them.

Counter-terror and security

Both the UN Special Rapporteur on human rights and counter-terrorism and the Human Rights Committee expressed concern that the definition of terrorism in some articles of the Spanish Criminal Code could include acts that do not appropriately fall under this category. They also repeated the long-standing calls on Spain to abolish legislation authorizing incommunicado detention of people held on terrorism-related charges. Following the example set by the Basque and Catalan autonomous police forces, the national authorities announced that video cameras would be installed in the cells at the National Criminal Court where detainees are held incommunicado, as a precaution against torture and other ill-treatment. However, their use is not compulsory and must be requested by the investigating judge in each case.

The judicial investigation by the National Criminal Court continued into suspected rendition flights by CIA-operated aircraft and US military planes which stopped at Spanish military airports or crossed Spanish airspace. The government submitted information to the investigation regarding several flights to or from Guantánamo Bay between 2002 and 2007. In December top secret official documents from January 2002 were leaked to the press. These confirmed that the Spanish authorities at the time had knowingly authorized the use of Spanish military bases during the transfer of detainees to Guantánamo Bay, at the request of the US authorities.

■ On 5 March, the National Criminal Court cancelled the European detention orders it had issued in December 2007 for Omar Deghayes and Jamil El Banna, and abandoned criminal proceedings against them. The two men had returned to the UK in December 2007 following several years in US custody at Guantánamo Bay. They were both wanted by the Spanish authorities on terrorism-related charges. The two men had returned to the UK in December 2007 following several years in US custody at Guantánamo Bay. The National Criminal Court ordered that proceedings against Omar Deghayes and Jamil El Banna be abandoned. It stated that, although the Spanish investigation was initiated before the men's detention in Guantánamo Bay, any information later revealed in court which had any connection to their detention in Guantánamo Bay would be inadmissible as evidence and could contaminate proceedings. The Court also concluded that given the ill-health of the accused, it would be inhumane to continue proceedings. The Court noted that both men had suffered torture and other ill-treatment while detained for a prolonged period of time outside the rule of law in Guantánamo Bay.

Migrants, refugees and asylum-seekers

Large numbers of migrants and asylum-seekers continued to risk their lives travelling to Spain along dangerous sea and land routes, suffering abuse from criminal networks and state security forces along the way. Readmission agreements between Spain and numerous countries in north and west Africa did not take human rights guarantees into account adequately. Intense pressure by Spain and other EU countries to prevent irregular migration was believed to have been the cause of mass detentions and expulsions of potential irregular migrants in Mauritania.

Violence against women and girls

Three years after the introduction of the law against gender-based violence, women who had suffered such abuse continued to face obstacles in accessing legal and medical assistance in some parts of Spain. Women with irregular migrant status faced particular difficulties. In 2008, according to government statistics, 70 women were killed by their partner or former partner; 34 of the women were foreign nationals.
■ Sylvina Bassanni and her boyfriend Andrés Marzal were killed by her estranged husband on 10 April. In September 2006 she had told a court that she feared for her life as he had frequently threatened to kill her. He repeatedly breached a restraining order but no action was taken against him. Sylvina Bassanni made 28 further requests to the court for protection and investigation measures, all of which went unanswered or were refused. Six days after her death, her lawyer

received a letter from the court responding to her requests, some of them a year old, and stating that the Public Prosecutor had dropped its case against her husband.

Racism

Racist attacks by private individuals and cases of torture and other ill-treatment with a racist component committed by law enforcement officials continued to be reported. According to the EU's Fundamental Rights Agency, Spain is one of just five member states that do not publish official data on complaints and criminal proceedings related to racist offences.

Enforced disappearances

The procedural guidelines and mapping of graves required by the Law on Historic Memory, introduced in December 2007, had still not been developed by the end of the year. In October, an investigating judge of the National Criminal Court opened an investigation into an estimated 114,266 enforced disappearances that occurred during the civil war and early years of the Franco dictatorship. The Public Prosecutor appealed against the opening of the investigation, calling for the application of the 1977 Amnesty Law which granted amnesty for all crimes with a political connection committed up to 1977. He also stated that the statute of limitations for the alleged crimes had expired.

On 2 December, the National Criminal Court said that it was not competent to investigate crimes of this type and the investigation was closed. However, the investigating judge ruled that local courts were competent to investigate such crimes when they had been committed in their territorial jurisdiction and on 26 December he sent information to a number of local courts for further investigation on suspected cases of enforced disappearances and the illegal removal of 30,960 children from their families.

Amnesty International visits/reports

🚗 A high-level Amnesty International delegation visited Spain in June and Amnesty International delegates visited in October.
📄 Spain: Amnesty International calls for a thorough independent and impartial investigation to determine whether human rights were violated during the arrest of Igor Portu (EUR 41/001/2008)
📄 Spain: No pardon for torture! Four police officers convicted of illegal detention and ill-treatment have pardons confirmed by Supreme Court (EUR 41/003/2008)
📄 Spain: Briefing to the Human Rights Committee (EUR 41/012/2008)

S

Spain: Amnesty International condemns forcible return of Basel Ghalyoun to Syria (EUR 41/015/2008)

España: Ejercer la jurisdicción universal para acabar con la impunidad (EUR 41/017/2008)

Spain: Catalan autonomous government must take action against police officers convicted of torture (EUR 41/021/2008)

Spain: Amnesty International condemns killing of Ignacio Uría Mendizábal (EUR 41/022/2008)

SRI LANKA

DEMOCRATIC SOCIALIST REPUBLIC OF SRI LANKA
Head of state and government:	Mahinda Rajapaksa
Death penalty:	abolitionist in practice
Population:	19.4 million
Life expectancy:	71.6 years
Under-5 mortality (m/f):	14/12 per 1,000

Hundreds of thousands of civilians were displaced as a result of fighting in the north and east. By November, tens of thousands of families were trapped in the Wanni region without adequate food, shelter, sanitation and medical care as the government barred UN and other humanitarian staff. Government allied armed groups committed unlawful killings and enforced disappearances. The Liberation Tigers of Tamil Eelam (LTTE) deliberately targeted civilians in the south in a string of attacks throughout the year. The government failed to address impunity for past human rights violations, and continued to carry out enforced disappearances. The government arrested and detained increasing numbers of Tamils without charge. Human rights defenders and journalists across the country reported increased attacks including death threats.

Background
In January, the government formally withdrew from the 2002 Ceasefire Agreement with LTTE and the Sri Lanka Monitoring Mission departed. Independent accounts of the situation in conflict areas were rare as access by the media, the UN and humanitarian agencies was restricted.

Sri Lanka was not re-elected to the Human Rights Council in May 2008.

Armed conflict
In July, the conflict shifted to the north-eastern Wanni region, displacing over 300,000 people, mostly Tamils, including 30,000 children trapped between approaching Sri-Lankan security forces and LTTE, which imposed restrictions on their ability to leave and used them as an involuntary pool of recruits and labourers.

On 9 September, the government ordered the UN and NGOs to leave the Wanni region. However, from 29 September, the government did allow some international UN workers to accompany food convoys into the Wanni region but humanitarian access remained extremely limited. Due to these restrictions, displaced populations faced immense hardship including lack of shelter and restricted access to food and medicine. Tens of thousands of families were forced to live in the open during the rainy season in November.

The government also maintained the closure of the A9 highway, the only land route to the Jaffna Peninsula. The closure severely restricted access to humanitarian supplies by civilians living in Jaffna.

Violations by government-allied armed groups
The government increasingly used allied armed groups to carry out its counter-insurgency strategy. At the Human Rights Council session in June, the UN Special Rapporteur on extrajudicial, summary or arbitrary executions expressed concerns about the government relying extensively on paramilitary groups to maintain control in the East and, to a lesser extent in Jaffna, noting that there was evidence that these groups carried out extrajudicial executions.

The Tamil Makkal Vidulthalai Pulikal (TMVP), operating in the eastern provinces, continued to carry out unlawful killings, hostage-taking for ransoms, recruitment of child soldiers and enforced disappearances.

The Eelam People's Democratic Party (EPDP), operating in Jaffna Peninsula and the People's Liberation Organization of Tamil Eelam operating in Vavuniya District, were reportedly responsible for unlawful killings and enforced disappearances.

Abuses by the LTTE
The LTTE increasingly carried out targeted attacks on civilians. According to the International Committee of

the Red Cross, 180 civilians were killed and nearly 270 were injured in the first six weeks of 2008 in a series of attacks on civilian buses, railway stations and individuals in Colombo, Dambulla, Kebhitigollewa, Madhu, Okkampitiya and Welli Oya and Anuradhapura.

The LTTE imposed a strict pass system, hindering thousands of families from the Wanni region from moving to safer areas. They also sought to ensure that families returned to LTTE-controlled areas by forcing some family members to remain behind.

The LTTE punished those who resisted forced recruitment into the LTTE by holding them in detention centres. Child recruitment increased in LTTE-controlled areas of the Wanni region.

Enforced disappearances

Enforced disappearances continued to be part of a pattern of abuse apparently linked to the government's counter-insurgency strategy. Enforced disappearances were reported in the north and east as well as previously unaffected parts of the country including in Colombo and the south. Many enforced disappearances took place inside high-security zones and during curfew hours.

■ Sebastian Goodfellow, a driver for the aid agency Norwegian Refugee Council, was last seen on 15 May 2008. It is suspected that an armed group operating with the tacit support of government security forces abducted him.

In June and December, the UN Working Group on Enforced or Involuntary Disappearances expressed concern about the high number of recent cases of enforced disappearances.

Arbitrary arrests and detentions

The security forces in Colombo arrested an increasing number of Tamils under emergency regulations in cordon and search operations. Over 1,000 Tamils were in detention without charge; some have been in detention for several years. In September, the Police ordered all Tamils who had arrived from the north and east in the last five years to register with the authorities. Tamils holding National Identity Cards from the north and east were most likely to be arrested.

Impunity

Investigations into human rights violations by the military and police stalled and court cases did not proceed as witnesses refused to come forward for fear of reprisals.

In April, the International Independent Group of Eminent Persons tasked with overseeing the latest Presidential Commission of Inquiry (COI) into 16 cases of serious violations of human rights terminated their mission stating that the COI had not been able to investigate cases in an efficient and independent manner in accordance with international standards. The lack of a functioning witness protection system was highlighted by the COI.

In July, Sri Lanka rejected the recommendation made by at least 10 states during its Universal Periodic Review at the UN Human Rights Council to establish an independent human rights monitoring mechanism, in co-operation with the UN High Commissioner for Human Rights, despite a dysfunctional domestic criminal justice system.

■ On 7 October, Vinayagamoorthi Muralitharan, otherwise known as Karuna, was sworn into Parliament. As military commander of the TMVP, and previously as a military commander in the LTTE, Karuna is suspected of serious human rights abuses and war crimes, including the abduction of hundreds of teenagers to serve as child soldiers, and the torture, holding as hostage and killing of hundreds of civilians. There has been no official investigation into these allegations.

Human rights defenders and journalists

Journalists faced physical assaults, abductions, intimidation, harassment and being shot, by both government personnel and members of armed groups. Journalists and media workers in the north and east were particularly at risk. Since 2006, nine journalists and media workers have been killed in Jaffna.

■ On 23 May, Keith Noyar, editor of *Nation,* was abducted from his home in Colombo and returned the next day beaten. He has not spoken publicly about what happened during his abduction.

■ On 28 May, journalist Paranirupasingam Devakumar, aged 36, of Vaddukoddai, Jaffna, was hacked to death in Navanthurei by unidentified attackers while returning home to Jaffna town. Paranirupasingam Devakumar had been reporting on abuses by the EPDP; he was the last reporter to file television news based in Jaffna.

■ Journalist and prisoner of conscience Jayaprakash

S

Sittampalam Tissainayagam has been detained in Colombo since 7 March. He is believed to be held in connection with newspaper articles he wrote about the human rights situation in the Eastern Province. Although he was not initially charged with any offence, in August he was formally indicted in the Colombo High Court under terrorism legislation for inciting racial hatred. In December, the Supreme Court ruled that an alleged confession obtained while he was detained by the Terrorism Investigation Division was voluntary and admissible as evidence in his trial despite his claim that the confession was made following torture and other ill-treatment.

Human rights defenders continued to be attacked and threatened. Domestic human rights groups reported an increase in threats to their staff, particularly those working in the north and east.
■ On 27 September, human rights lawyer J.C. Weliamuna and his family survived a grenade attack on their home in Colombo.

Amnesty International visits/reports

🚗 No delegates were able to gain official permission to visit the country.

📑 Sri Lanka: Silencing Dissent (ASA 37/001/2008)

📑 Sri Lanka: Submission to the UN Universal Periodic Review – Second session of the UPR Working Group, 5–16 May 2008 (ASA 37/003/2008)

📑 Sri Lanka: Further information on arbitrary detention: Jayaprakash Sittampalam Tissainayagam (ASA 37/019/2008)

📑 Sri Lanka: LTTE, government endangering lives of tens of thousands of newly displaced around Wanni, 14 August 2008

📑 Sri Lanka: Karuna's presence in Parliament a travesty of justice, 7 October 2008

📑 Sri Lanka: Sri Lankan government must act now to protect 300,000 displaced, 19 November 2008

SUDAN

REPUBLIC OF SUDAN

Head of state and government:	Omar Hassan Ahmed Al Bashir
Death penalty:	retentionist
Population:	39.4
Life expectancy:	57.4 years
Under-5 mortality (m/f):	110/96 per 1,000
Adult literacy:	60.9 per cent

The conflict in Darfur continued unabated with an increase in attacks and violations of international humanitarian law by all parties to the conflict. An attack on Omdurman in May by a Darfur-based armed opposition group precipitated a wave of extrajudicial executions, arbitrary arrests and unlawful detentions, torture and other ill-treatment by the National Intelligence and Security Services (NISS) and the police, mainly targeting Darfuris and members of the Zaghawa ethnic group. Also in May, armed clashes in Abyei, on the border between northern and southern Sudan, led to the displacement of more than 50,000 people and the total destruction of the town. The Prosecutor of the International Criminal Court (ICC) applied for an arrest warrant to be issued against President Omar Al Bashir for war crimes, crimes against humanity and genocide.

The death penalty continued to be imposed, and courts passed death sentences on men, women and children under the age of 18. The security services imposed tight restrictions on the press and journalists.

Background

In January, the deployment of the UN-AU Hybrid Mission in Darfur (UNAMID) began, but by the end of the year only about half of the promised 26,000 peacekeeping force had arrived, and the force was also under-equipped.

The first census in more than 20 years took place in April. The census, one of the pillars of the Comprehensive Peace Agreement (CPA) that ended the decades-long conflict in South Sudan and a critical step towards a referendum on independence for South Sudan in 2011, was highly controversial. It did not allow the representation of all Sudanese communities, including Darfuris and Southerners.

On 10 May, a Darfur-based armed opposition group, the Justice and Equality Movement (JEM), took the Darfur conflict to Khartoum by launching an attack on the capital's twin city Omdurman. The attack was repulsed by Sudanese forces.

In June Djibril Yipènè Bassolé was appointed as the new joint UN-AU mediator for Darfur, replacing the UN and AU Special Envoys for Darfur, Jan Eliasson and Salim Ahmed Salim.

In July, the government adopted a new electoral law. The government also announced that the next presidential elections would be held in July 2009, another major step towards the referendum in 2011.

Sudan's parliament deliberated on the draft of a new Criminal Act that included crimes under international law, but was not enacted into law by the end of 2008.

In late October the President and the ruling National Congress Party (NCP) organized a gathering aimed at initiating a solution to the Darfur conflict. The so-called Sudan People's Initiative was highly controversial and was boycotted by 13 opposition groups. Its results were to pave the way for peace negotiations in Doha, proposed by Qatar. Negotiations were continuing at the end of 2008 to persuade the main armed opposition groups, such as the JEM, to attend.

International justice

On 14 July, ICC Prosecutor Luis Moreno Ocampo submitted to the ICC's pre-trial chamber an application for an arrest warrant to be issued against President Omar Al Bashir. The application includes 10 counts of war crimes, crimes against humanity and genocide that were allegedly carried out on President Al Bashir's "direct orders".

The announcement of the application coincided with an attack on UNAMID peacekeepers, putting the force on high alert and leading to the temporary relocation of non-essential staff from the UN and NGOs operating in Darfur.

The application triggered calls by states belonging to the AU, League of Arab States and the Organization of the Islamic Conference to defer the case under article 16 of the Rome Statute of the ICC.

In October the government announced that it had detained former Janjaweed leader Ali Kushayb, indicted by the ICC in 2007, pending his prosecution by a special court in El Geneina in West Darfur.

Despite an announcement that Ali Kushayb's trial would begin in October, the case had not started by the end of the year. There were unconfirmed reports that he remained free to travel between the Darfur states.

Ahmed Haroun, also indicted by the ICC in 2007, remained in his position as Minister of State for Humanitarian Affairs.

On 20 November, the Prosecutor applied for arrest warrants to be issued against three commanders of armed opposition groups operating in Darfur. The Prosecutor did not disclose their names. The commanders were accused of war crimes arising from an attack on the AU Mission in Sudan (AMIS) in December 2007 in which 12 peacekeepers were killed.

Armed conflict – Darfur

The conflict in Darfur intensified with an increase in attacks and violations of international humanitarian law by all parties to the conflict.

Attacks on villages noticeably increased in 2008, with between 270,000 and 300,000 people displaced during the year. Widespread human rights violations continued despite the deployment of UNAMID.

The UNAMID force was incapacitated by insufficient troop numbers and inadequate military equipment. With only 11,415 total uniformed personnel supported by 721 international civilian personnel, 1,393 local civilian staff and 246 UN Volunteers as of 31 October, UNAMID was not able to effectively discharge its mandate in Darfur. Its lack of attack helicopters and heavy ground transport undermined its ability to protect civilians and its own troops. In the course of the year, 17 members of the force were killed in various attacks. UNAMID was unable to intervene on a number of occasions where civilians in Darfur were under attack.

Attacks against humanitarian aid convoys peaked in 2008, leading to a reduction by half in the World Food Programme's aid delivery to Darfur. Eleven humanitarian staff members were killed between January and October. This sharp increase in the targeting of humanitarian workers, together with the hijacking of vehicles and abductions, limited the outreach activities of aid agencies and NGOs and their access to the most vulnerable communities in Darfur.
■ In January, the Sudanese Armed Forces tried to regain control of the northern corridor of West Darfur

S

from the JEM. The attempt resulted in attacks on the villages of Abu Suruj, Saraf Jidad, Silea and Sirba in West Darfur. The army, supported by the Janjaweed militia, resorted to aerial bombardments in support of their ground offensives. The entire area was inaccessible to humanitarian organizations and the UN from mid-December 2007 to March 2008. The attacks displaced an estimated 30,000 people, many to areas that were not easily accessible to aid agencies. The attacks were indiscriminate and the government's forces and security services looted and burned villages on their way. Damage to civilian property was widespread and at least 115 civilians were killed. In Sirba, several cases of rape were reported during and after the attacks.

■ On 25 August the NISS sought to enter Kalma camp in South Darfur to search for illegal weapons and drugs. Kalma camp is home to more than 90,000 internally displaced people (IDPs), the largest IDP camp in Darfur. When the inhabitants refused to allow the NISS to enter the camp, the NISS surrounded the camp, opened fire and reportedly shelled the camp. Access into and out of the camp was denied, including to the wounded and to humanitarian agencies. More than 47 civilians were killed. UNAMID did not intervene.

Violence against women and girls

Incidents of gender-based violence, including rape and other forms of sexual violence, continued.

The operations of a large number of international NGOs committed to addressing violence against women continued being restricted by the government. Interference by the government's Humanitarian Aid Commission, which monitors and co-ordinates humanitarian work in Darfur, was reported to have increased in 2008. Amnesty International also received credible reports that workers from organizations countering gender-based sexual violence were harassed by the NISS over the year.

In desperate attempts to free them from the conflict, women and their children continued to be sent by their husbands to the capital, where they ended up living in IDP camps around the city, often in extreme poverty.

Abyei, South Sudan

The implementation of the CPA was beset by problems between the NCP and the Sudan People's Liberation Movement (SPLM). Confrontations took place over issues such as the demarcation of the North-South border, the census, and returning southerners from Khartoum to South Sudan.

In the months leading to May, the forces of the Southern Sudanese Government and the Sudanese Armed Forces built up troops around Abyei, which lies in an oil-rich area on the border between the North and the South.

In May, the two forces clashed, resulting in the displacement of more than 50,000 people and the total destruction of the town.

On 8 June, the NCP and the SPLM reached the Abyei Roadmap Agreement to solve the Abyei crisis.

Arbitrary arrests and detentions

The JEM attack on Omdurman on 10 May, which was repulsed by government forces, caused more than 220 casualties, according to officials. Government forces then combed Omdurman, arresting and detaining any individual – man, woman or child – of Darfuri appearance, those suspected of supporting opposition groups, and especially Zaghawas. Hundreds of civilians were arrested in the aftermath, with reports of extrajudicial executions, torture and other forms of ill-treatment. Many people were held incommunicado in unofficial places of detention. The youngest victim of such detention was a nine-month-old infant who was held with his mother underground in a detention centre for two months. At least one individual died as a result of ill-treatment in detention during the first two weeks after the arrests.

In the aftermath of the attack, the government announced on national television that it was detaining in a social rehabilitation centre more than 80 children who had been arrested during the security crackdown on Omdurman. The government alleged that the children, some as young as 11, were found wearing uniforms and holding weapons. The children were reportedly ill-treated during the first days of their detention, but were allowed visits and were later released by the government.

Although many of the arrested individuals were released, many remained unaccounted for, their whereabouts and fate unknown.

Unfair trials – death penalty

Courts continued to hand down death sentences, including on women and children under the age of 18.

The 2004 Child Act was revised by the legal reform committee and was sent to the Cabinet of Ministers for further revision. The amended Act redefines a child as a person under 18 and raises the age of criminal responsibility to 18. However, pending its enactment, the 2004 Child Act remained in place, placing children under 18 at risk of degrading and inhuman punishments including the death penalty if they showed physical "signs of maturity" when they committed a criminal offence.

Following the JEM attack on Omdurman, the Chief Justice established five special counter-terrorism courts, in a first application of the Counter-Terrorism Act promulgated in 2001. The special courts initially took on the trials of 37 named individuals. More than 50 defendants appeared in front of these courts in June, July and August. A total of 109 individuals were eventually scheduled for trial before the special courts.

By the end of August, 50 individuals had been sentenced to death by these courts following unfair trials. The trials failed to meet international standards of fairness in a number of ways. Some defendants were only allowed to meet their lawyers for the first time after their trial had begun and others were convicted on the basis of confessions extracted under torture.

A number of lawyers, mainly members of the Darfur Bar Association, organized themselves into a defence committee and volunteered to defend many of those on trial before the special courts. These lawyers submitted an appeal to the Constitutional Court, contesting the constitutionality of the counter-terrorism courts. The appeal was rejected.

After the death sentences were passed, the lawyers appealed against the verdicts and sentences. The Special Court of Appeal had not ruled on the appeals by the end of 2008.

■ On 22 May, Al Tayeb Ali Ahmed Abdel Rahman was executed on the orders of the Constitutional Court, three hours after his family and lawyers were informed that he was going to be executed. Al Tayeb had been sentenced to death by a Special Court in El Fasher on 27 January 2004, following an unfair trial where he was not granted any legal representation. His death sentence was however confirmed by the Constitutional Court. A former member of the Sudan Liberation Army (SLA) (Mini Minawi faction), he had been convicted of taking part in SLA attacks, including an attack on El Fasher's airport in 2003. The Constitutional Court rejected an appeal submitted hours before his execution. Mini Minawi, by now a presidential adviser, called for an amnesty for Al Tayeb under the terms of the Darfur Peace Agreement, but this was disregarded.

In December Sudan voted against a UN General Assembly resolution calling for a worldwide moratorium on executions.

Freedom of expression – journalists

A clampdown by the security services on the press and journalists was the most severe since 2005, when the Interim National Constitution was adopted as part of the CPA's implementation, putting in place provisions to safeguard freedom of expression and freedom of the press.

The reintroduction of censorship measures against privately owned newspapers began in February. At the time, many local newspapers had reported on links between the Sudanese government and Chadian opposition groups that attacked the capital of Chad, N'Djamena. In retaliation, representatives of the NISS resumed a daily inspection of newspapers offices and printing houses. The JEM attack on Omdurman in May led to a further tightening of restrictions on the press. Journalists were widely targeted by the NISS; while some were intimidated and harassed, others were arrested and detained, especially in the aftermath of the attack.

The censorship measures that were reinstalled in February remained in place at the end of 2008. On 4 November, more than 100 journalists went on hunger strike for a day, in protest against the repression of the press and the government's continuing violation of freedom of expression. Three newspapers did not publish for three days in solidarity. They were censored for a day in response to their protest.

■ Al Ghali Yahya Shegifat, a journalist and president of the Association of Darfur Journalists, was arrested by the NISS in the aftermath of the May attack on Omdurman. He was held in incommunicado detention for more than two months during which he was continuously tortured. He was not given access to a lawyer and his family was not allowed to visit him or even informed of his whereabouts. He was not charged with any offence.

Human rights defenders

On 24 November, three prominent human rights defenders were arrested by the NISS in Khartoum. Amir Suleiman, Abdel Monim Elgak and Osman Humeida were arrested and tortured in custody before being released. Amnesty International considered the three individuals to be prisoners of conscience who were detained solely because of the

S

peaceful exercise of their rights to freedom of expression and association.

Amnesty International report

🗐 Sudan: Displaced in Darfur – a generation of anger (AFR 54/001/2008)

SURINAME

REPUBLIC OF SURINAME

Head of state and government:	**Runaldo Ronald Venetiaan**
Death penalty:	**abolitionist in practice**
Population:	**461,000**
Life expectancy:	**69.6 years**
Under-5 mortality:	**40/29 per 1,000**
Adult literacy:	**89.6 per cent**

The trial of those accused of carrying out extrajudicial executions in December 1982 continued. The Saramaka People's land rights remained unresolved.

Background

In July 2008 Suriname acceded to the Rome Statute of the International Criminal Court.

Land rights

In August, the Inter-American Court of Human Rights ruled on Suriname's request for an interpretation of a November 2007 judgment by the Court regarding logging and mining concessions on the territory of the Saramaka People.

The Saramaka People, are descendants of escaped African slaves who established settlements in Suriname's rainforest interior in the 17th and 18th centuries. The Court's judgment established that: "The State violated, to the detriment of the members of the Saramaka people, the right to property". By the end of the year Suriname had not complied with the Court's decisions made.

Impunity – trial developments

The trial of 25 people, including 17 former members of the armed forces, continued in the capital, Paramaribo. The men were accused of the extrajudicial execution of 13 civilians and two army

officers, who had been arrested in December 1982 on suspicion of organizing an attempted coup and held at the army barracks of Fort Zeelandia in Paramaribo.

One of the accused, former President Lieutenant Colonel Désiré (Desi) Delano Bouterse, announced on television at the time that the 15 detainees had been killed while trying to escape. Reports indicate that the victims showed signs of torture: smashed jaws, broken teeth, fractured limbs, and multiple bullet entry wounds in the face, chest or abdomen. The victims included journalists, lawyers, university lecturers, businessmen and a trade union leader.

The trial, which started in November 2007, was being held before a military court instead of an ordinary civilian court, despite the fact that all ordinary offences committed by military personnel, including human rights violations and crimes under international law, should be tried in civilian courts, according to ordinary criminal procedures. The charges against the accused do not include the crime of torture.

During the hearings in July and August, the defence challenged the impartiality of two judges, arguing a conflict of interest. In November, the court dismissed the objection of the defence regarding one of the judges. In December, the motion filed against the president of the military court, judge Cynthia Valstein-Montnor, was dismissed.

SWAZILAND

KINGDOM OF SWAZILAND

Head of state:	**King Mswati III**
Head of government:	**Barnabas Sibusiso Dlamini (replaced Absalom Themba Dlamini in October)**
Death penalty:	**abolitionist in practice**
Population:	**1.1 million**
Life expectancy:	**40.9**
Under-5 mortality (m/f):	**121/103 per 1,000**
Adult literacy:	**79.6 per cent**

Political violence and public protests led to a crackdown against critics of the government using the new Suppression of Terrorism Act. More than two-thirds of Swaziland's population lived in poverty and two-fifths required food aid. Women

and girls continued to be disproportionately affected by the country's HIV pandemic, and by sexual violence. Police continued to use excessive force against peaceful demonstrators and workers on strike. Torture, other ill-treatment and the unjustified use of lethal force by law enforcement officials were reported.

Background

The Suppression of Terrorism Act (STA) was signed into law by the King in August, after a parliamentary process involving little public input. The STA's broad definition of "terrorist act" fails to meet the requirements of legality. Offences created under the Act excessively restrict a wide range of human rights, including freedom of thought, conscience and religion; freedom of expression; freedom of association; and freedom of assembly. The STA limits the role of the courts and allows for seven days' incommunicado detention without charge or trial.

On 19 September national parliamentary elections were held, based on the traditional *tinkhundla* system. Electoral observers expressed concern about the credibility of the process; political parties were denied formal recognition and the right to participate in elections. Judgement was still pending in a case brought by the Coalition of Concerned Civic Organizations against their exclusion from voter education. Several large-scale protest demonstrations, led by the trade union movement, took place before the elections. Following the elections the King appointed a new government under Prime Minister Barnabas Sibusiso Dlamini.

Unfair trials

On 20 September, Musa Dlamini and South African national Jack Govender were killed while planting a bomb near one of the King's residences. A third man, South African national Amos Mbedzi, was injured and taken into custody. Amos Mbedzi was allegedly tortured and subsequently made a statement to a magistrate while still in police custody and without access to a lawyer. On 24 September he was charged under the Sedition and Subversive Activities Act, and on two other counts, and remanded to custody at Matsapha Maximum Prison. Subsequent remand hearings were conducted in the prison and not in open court. He was, however, given consular, legal and family access after his imprisonment.

On 15 November, the President of the opposition People's United Democratic Movement (PUDEMO), Mario Masuku, was arrested, detained and charged under the STA in connection with a speech he allegedly made at Musa Dlamini's funeral. The provision under which he was charged violated the principle of legality. In December the prosecution added an alternate sedition charge. His trial had not begun by the end of the year.

By the end of the year, 16 defendants charged in 2006 with treason had still not been brought to trial. The government had still not published by the end of 2008 the findings of a commission of inquiry into allegations that the 16 men were tortured in pre-trial custody.

Freedom of association, expression and assembly

On 14 November the Prime Minister declared four organizations to be "terrorist entities" under the STA: PUDEMO; the Swaziland Youth Congress (SWAYOCO); the South African-based Swaziland Solidarity Network (SSN); and the Swaziland People's Liberation Army (Umbane). The STA limits the role of the courts in reviewing banning orders.

In the following weeks the activities of civil society organizations and media workers were subjected to surveillance, harassment and disruption.

The police, using their powers under the STA, took in for lengthy interrogations other members of political parties and civil society organizations. They were released uncharged but warned that they would be subject to further interrogations and possible charges.

Police and security forces

Police and other security officials continued to use excessive force against criminal suspects and unarmed demonstrators including trade unionists, members of the unrecognized police union, striking women textile workers and political organizations.

There were persistent reports of criminal suspects being tortured, particularly at certain police stations. Investigations did not result in perpetrators being brought to justice.

■ On 8 August Musa Gamedze was shot in the back with a high velocity weapon by a game ranger in Mkhaya Game Reserve, owned by Big Game Parks, near his home in eSitjeni. A police investigation into his death did not lead to action against the alleged

S

perpetrator. The Game Act allows game rangers to use "reasonable force" to arrest suspected poachers and game rangers have immunity from prosecution for actions under the Act. Civil society organizations appealed for an end to impunity for game rangers and steps to address the inequalities and poverty forcing rural people into poaching game to survive.

Right to health – people living with HIV and AIDS

The prevalence of HIV remained high, particularly among women. The National Emergency Response Council on HIV/AIDS (NERCHA) noted that 34.6 per cent of young women attending antenatal clinics were HIV positive. UNAIDS/WHO estimated the prevalence among males aged 15 to 24 at 5.9 per cent and females at 22.6 per cent.

Only about 40 per cent of those needing life-saving antiretroviral therapy (ART) were actually receiving the treatment. However UNAIDS/WHO reported that the number of pregnant women living with HIV who received ART to prevent mother-to-child transmission had risen from under 600 in 2004 to 8,772, about three-fifths of those needing the treatment.

Over 40 per cent of Swaziland's population required food aid, and approximately 69 per cent of people were living on less than US$1 a day. Poverty and lack of food continued to impede the ability of people living with HIV and AIDS to access health services and adhere to treatment.

Violence against women and girls

In January the head of the police Domestic Violence, Sexual Offences and Child Abuse Department stated that the department had investigated over 700 cases of rape of children and over 460 cases of rape of women in the previous two years. In April UNICEF published a study on violence against girls and young women which found that one in three of the women interviewed suffered sexual abuse as a child and one in four had experienced physical violence. The victim knew the perpetrator in 75 per cent of cases. Less than half of the incidents were reported to the authorities.

The government failed to complete the reform of marriage and property laws. The Sexual Offences and Domestic Violence Bill, in draft since 2006, had still not been passed by the end of the year. The police complained that the delay in the passage of the

legislation prevented courts from using facilities to hear evidence from vulnerable witnesses in cases of sexual violence.

Death penalty

In December, Swaziland voted against a UN General Assembly resolution calling for a worldwide moratorium on executions.

Although the 2006 Constitution permits the use of capital punishment, no executions have been carried out since 1983. No new death sentences were imposed in 2008.

Two people remained under sentence of death.

SWEDEN

KINGDOM OF SWEDEN
Head of state:	King Carl XVI Gustaf
Head of government:	Fredrik Reinfeldt
Death penalty:	abolitionist for all crimes
Population:	9.2 million
Life expectancy:	80.5 years
Under-5 mortality (m/f):	4/4 per 1,000

Two victims of rendition were awarded compensation, although no decision was made on their applications for residence in Sweden. The level of protection given to asylum-seekers from Iraq was reduced. Relatively few cases of rape reported to the police resulted in a criminal trial.

Counter-terror and security

Ahmed Agiza and Mohammed El Zari were awarded around 3,160,000 Swedish kronor (€307,000) in compensation for the grave violations they suffered during and as a result of their unlawful deportation from Sweden to Egypt in December 2001. Both men were tortured while held incommunicado in Egypt. They had been denied access to a full and fair asylum determination process in Sweden, and were deported on the strength of worthless "diplomatic assurances" given by the Egyptian authorities.

Mohammed El Zari was released from prison in Egypt in October 2003, without ever having been charged. Ahmed Agiza remained in prison in Egypt, following an unfair trial before a military court. The Swedish government did not make a final decision on the appeals brought by both men against the rejection of their applications for residence permits in Sweden.

In June the UN Committee against Torture (CAT) called on Sweden to investigate in depth the reasons for the deportation of Mohammed El Zari and Ahmed Agiza and, if appropriate, prosecute those responsible.

■ In June, the Migration Board rejected an application for a residence permit from Adel Hakim, a refugee released from US custody in Guantánamo in May 2006. Adel Hakim, a Chinese national from the Uighur ethnic group, was transferred from Guantánamo along with four other Uighurs to Albania, which had agreed to offer the men protection. Adel Hakim applied for residence in Sweden during a visit in 2007, in part because his sister lives there. The Migration Board rejected his application on the grounds that he already had a right to reside in Albania. Adel Hakim remained in Sweden awaiting the outcome of an appeal.

Refugees and asylum-seekers

In June the CAT expressed concern that the detention of asylum-seekers before deportation was common, and regretted that Swedish law provides "no absolute limit on the length of time that an asylum-seeker can be detained".

Most new applications from Iraqi asylum-seekers were rejected after the Migration Board and the Migration Court of Appeal decided that there was no internal armed conflict in Iraq. Previously, the majority of asylum-seekers from Iraq had received some form of protection.

In February, the authorities in Sweden and Iraq reached an agreement on the forcible return to Iraq of rejected asylum-seekers. Prior to this, only Iraqi nationals who agreed to be returned were accepted by the Iraqi authorities.

The Swedish authorities continued to reject applications from Eritrean asylum-seekers. This exposed them to the risk of being returned to Eritrea, despite the UNHCR's recommendation that all states should halt forcible returns to Eritrea. At least one Eritrean national was forcibly returned from Sweden to Eritrea, in April.

In October, the CAT requested the temporary suspension of the planned deportation to Eritrea of another Eritrean national while it considered whether she would be at risk of torture if returned.

Violence against women and girls

Only an estimated 12 per cent of cases of rape reported to the police resulted in a trial. A lack of systematic independent research into, and analysis of, rape investigations and prosecution decisions in rape cases impeded efforts to strengthen the protection given to survivors of rape.

In June, the CAT expressed regret at the lack of national statistics on domestic violence and called on Sweden to increase efforts to prevent, combat and punish violence against women and children, including domestic violence and crimes committed against women and children in the name of honour.

Amnesty International report

State of denial: Europe's role in rendition and secret detention (EUR 01/003/2008)

SWITZERLAND

SWISS CONFEDERATION

Head of state and government:	Pascal Couchepin
Death penalty:	abolitionist for all crimes
Population:	7.5 million
Life expectancy:	81.3 years
Under-5 mortality (m/f):	6/5 per 1,000

Inadequate legislation failed to provide effective protection against discrimination. Allegations of racial discrimination, including ill-treatment, by law enforcement officials continued. Restrictive legislation violated the economic, social and cultural rights of asylum-seekers and irregular migrants.

Racism and discrimination

The UN Committee on the Elimination of Racial Discrimination (CERD) highlighted the continuing problem of discrimination in Switzerland, including the lack of adequate national and cantonal legislation prohibiting discrimination and the use of racial profiling by law enforcement agencies. The Committee also expressed concern at the continued discrimination against Roma, Sinti and Yenish communities, particularly in relation to housing and education. The Committee called for the

S

establishment of a national human rights institution. This recommendation was reiterated during examination of Switzerland in the Universal Periodic Review process of the UN Human Rights Council. The Review also called on Switzerland to take further measures against racism and discrimination.

Police and security forces

Allegations of ill-treatment by law enforcement officials continued. CERD expressed concern at excessive use of force by law enforcement officials, in particular against black people.

An independent inquiry was launched by the cantonal department of security following police interventions during a demonstration in Basel on 26 January. The results of the inquiry criticized the failure of the police to provide demonstrators who had been arrested with adequate information on the reasons for their detention; the lack of notification to family members of detainees, including parents in the case of detained minors; and mass arbitrary arrests. In Berne, a representative of the regional government was appointed as an observer by the Chief of Police to monitor the detention conditions of demonstrators arrested during a similar police intervention on 19 January. Her report raised similar concerns to those in Basel, as well as criticizing the lack of access to food and water of demonstrators detained by the police.

Migrants, refugees and asylum-seekers

Restrictive legislation continued to violate the economic, social and cultural rights of asylum-seekers and irregular migrants, many of whom experienced extreme poverty. CERD expressed concern that the legislation may be in violation of the Convention on the Elimination of All Forms of Racial Discrimination. Rejected asylum-seekers are excluded from the welfare system, resulting in marginalization and destitution.

On 18 March parliament adopted legislation authorizing the use of electro-shock weapons and police dogs during forcible expulsion of foreign nationals, which may violate Council of Europe standards on the proportionate use of force in such operations.

Violence against women and girls

Legislation introduced in 2007 to protect victims of domestic violence was inadequately implemented in some cantons. There was insufficient specialist training for police and no training for judges. Protection and counselling centres in some cantons were underfunded.

Switzerland signed the Council of Europe Convention on Action against Trafficking in Human Beings on 8 September.

Counter-terror and security

Applications for asylum in Switzerland were submitted by a lawyer acting on behalf of three detainees held at the US detention centre at Guantánamo Bay. The US authorities did not bring any charges against the three men, detained for over six years, and two of them had already been cleared for release. The men (nationals of Libya, Algeria and an ethnic Uighur man from China) were believed to be at risk of persecution if returned to their countries of origin. All three applications were rejected in November by the Federal Migration Office; appeals were submitted.

SYRIA

SYRIAN ARAB REPUBLIC
Head of state: Bashar al-Assad
Head of government: Muhammad Naji al-'Otri
Death penalty: retentionist
Population: 20.4 million
Life expectancy: 73.6 years
Under-5 mortality (m/f): 20/15 per 1,000
Adult literacy: 80.8 per cent

The state of emergency, in force since 1963, continued to give security forces sweeping powers of arrest and detention. Freedom of expression and association remained strictly controlled. Hundreds of people were arrested and hundreds of others remained imprisoned for political reasons, including prisoners of conscience and others sentenced after unfair trials. Torture and other ill-treatment were committed with impunity; seven deaths as a result were reported. Military Police were reported to have killed at least 17 detainees. Human rights defenders were harassed and persecuted. Members of the Kurdish minority faced

S

discrimination; many were effectively stateless and denied equal access to social and economic rights. Women were subject to discrimination and gender-based violence. Sixteen civilians were killed in a bomb explosion which state media attributed to an armed group.

Background

Diplomatic relations with France and the EU improved, and Syria and Lebanon agreed to re-establish diplomatic relations. The government engaged in new indirect talks with Israel.

On 26 October, US forces attacked a building in al-Sukkariyah near Syria's border with Iraq. The Syrian authorities said eight civilians were killed. A US military spokesman said an investigation was being carried out but its findings were not made public.

A report issued on 19 November by the International Atomic Energy Agency (IAEA) said it had not been able to establish the nature of a site in Syria destroyed by an Israeli attack in September 2007.

Political prisoners and prisoners of conscience

Hundreds of people were arrested for political reasons, including scores of prisoners of conscience. Hundreds of other political prisoners, including prisoners of conscience, remained imprisoned, including at least two detainees, Ziad Ramadan and Bahaa' Mustafa Joughel, held without trial since 2005. Scores faced trial before the Supreme State Security Court (SSSC), Criminal Court or Military Court, all of which failed to respect international standards for fair trials.

■ Kamal al-Labwani, a prisoner of conscience already serving a 12-year prison term, was sentenced to an additional three years by Damascus Military Court on 23 April, on charges of "broadcasting false or exaggerated news which could affect the morale of the country", on account of remarks he was alleged to have made in his prison cell.

■ In August, Nabil Khlioui and at least 12 other alleged Islamists, mostly from Deir al-Zour, were arrested. At least 10 of them remained in incommunicado detention without charge or trial at the end of the year.

■ On 15 August, Mesh'al al-Tammo was arrested because of his activities as spokesperson for the unauthorized Kurdish Future Current group. He was held incommunicado for 12 days and charged with "aiming to provoke civil war or sectarian fighting", "conspiracy" and three other charges commonly brought against Kurdish activists. If convicted, he could face the death penalty.

■ On 29 October, the Damascus Criminal Court convicted 12 pro-democracy activists of "weakening national sentiment" and "broadcasting false or exaggerated news which could affect the morale of the country". They each received 30-month prison sentences for their involvement in the Damascus Declaration for Democratic National Change, a coalition of unauthorized political parties, human rights organizations and pro-democracy activists from across the political spectrum. Dr Feda'a al-Horani, former prisoners of conscience Akram al-Bunni and Riad Seif, and nine others were arrested between 9 December 2007 and 30 January and were initially held incommunicado, during which at least eight of them were punched in the face, kicked and slapped, and forced to sign false confessions.

■ On 7 August, 'Aref Dalilah, a former university economist, was unexpectedly released under a presidential amnesty. He had served seven years of a 10-year prison term, much of it in solitary confinement, for his involvement in the so-called "Damascus Spring", a peaceful pro-democracy movement. He had been in increasingly poor health.

The UN Working Group on Arbitrary Detention announced in May that the detention of Mus'ab al-Hariri was arbitrary because his trial had failed substantially to meet international fair trial standards. He had been arrested when aged 15, held incommunicado for more than two years and reportedly tortured. He was then sentenced by the SSSC in June 2005 to six years in prison for belonging, despite no substantiating evidence, to the banned Muslim Brotherhood. Despite the Working Group's finding, the authorities took no steps to remedy the situation of Mus'ab al-Hariri.

Also in May the Working Group announced that it had found the imprisonment of Anwar al-Bunni, Michel Kilo and Mahmoud 'Issa to be arbitrary because they were convicted for legitimately exercising their right to freedom of expression and because their trials had substantially failed to meet international fair trial standards. Lawyer Anwar al-Bunni had been sentenced to a five-year prison term

S

in April 2007 for his legitimate work in defending human rights, while Michel Kilo and Mahmoud 'Issa had been sentenced to three years' imprisonment in May 2007 for their involvement in the Beirut-Damascus Declaration, a petition signed by some 300 Syrian and Lebanese nationals calling for the normalization of relations between their two countries. On 15 December, the Court of Appeal overturned its earlier decision in November to release Michel Kilo and Mahmoud 'Issa.

Also in May the Working Group declared that it had found the imprisonment of seven men to be arbitrary because they were convicted in a grossly unfair trial for legitimately exercising their right to freedom of expression. Maher Isber Ibrahim and Tareq al-Ghorani were sentenced to seven years' imprisonment and the five others to five-year prison terms in June 2007 for involvement in a youth discussion group and publishing pro-democracy articles on the internet.

Counter-terror and security

Individuals cleared of involvement in terrorist acts or who are related to individuals suspected of involvement in such acts were subjected to arbitrary and incommunicado detention.

■ Basel Ghalyoun, who was forcibly returned to Syria by the Spanish authorities after the Spanish Supreme Court acquitted him of involvement in the 2004 bomb attacks on trains in Madrid, was detained on arrival on 22 July. He remained held incommunicado at the end of the year.

■ Muhammad Zammar, a victim of suspected unlawful rendition to Syria by the US authorities, remained in prison serving a 12-year sentence imposed by the SSSC despite the UN Working Group's announcement in June 2007 that his detention was arbitrary.

■ Two women, Usra al-Hussein and Bayan Saleh 'Ali, were arrested on 31 July and 4 August respectively in al-'Otayba, east of Damascus, and were still held at the end of 2008. The authorities gave no reason for their arrest but some sources suggested that it was related to their efforts to communicate with an international organization regarding the detention conditions of Usra al-Hussein's husband, Jihad Diab, in the US military base at Guantánamo Bay.

Enforced disappearances and impunity

The fate of some 17,000 people, mostly Islamists who were victims of enforced disappearance in the late 1970s and early 1980s, and hundreds of Lebanese and Palestinians who were detained in Syria or abducted from Lebanon by Syrian forces or Lebanese and Palestinian militias, remained unknown. In August, the Lebanese and Syrian Presidents issued a joint statement pledging to examine the fate of people who disappeared in Syria and Lebanon.

■ In March, Milad Barakat, a Lebanese man imprisoned in Syria for 16 years, was returned to Lebanon, apparently in a traumatized state. Lebanese security officials had detained him in 1992 and handed him over to the Syrian authorities, who sentenced him to 15 years' imprisonment for fighting against the Syrian army.

On 30 September, the government issued Legislative Decree No. 69. This conferred immunity against prosecution to political security, police and customs officials for crimes committed on duty except in cases where a warrant was issued by the general leadership of the army and military forces.

Unlawful killings

Attacks were carried out by unidentified people. On 12 February, 'Imad Mughniyah, a suspected senior Lebanese Hizbullah commander, was killed by a car bomb in Damascus. On 2 August, Brigadier General Mohammad Suleiman, a senior security officer reported to be the IAEA's main Syrian interlocutor, was shot dead in Tartous.

A car bomb detonated on 27 September near a security forces' building in Damascus killed 17 people, including 16 civilians. State television broadcasted "confessions" of the alleged perpetrators on 6 November. They had not been brought to trial by the end of 2008.

Amid disturbances in Sednaya Military Prison near Damascus that started on 5 July, Military Police were reported to have killed at least 17 detainees and five other people. The circumstances of the violence and the fate of all prisoners there remained unclear, as the authorities did not announce whether they had investigated the killings, gave no details of the people killed or injured, and did not permit any visits to the prison or prisoners afterwards.

On 14 October, security officials opened fire on unarmed people in al-Mishrefeh, near Homs, killing Sami Ma'touq and Joni Suleiman. The Military Prosecutor announced an investigation but its outcome had not been made public by the end of the year. Unidentified individuals were reported to have tampered with evidence at the scene of the killings on 20 October, increasing concern that any investigation would be flawed.

Freedom of expression

Freedom of expression and all forms of media remained strictly controlled by the state. Punitive laws were used against those who expressed dissent.

■ Tariq Biasi, a blogger, was sentenced to three years' imprisonment by the SSSC on 11 May on charges of "weakening national sentiment" and "spreading false news". He had posted critical comments about the security services on a website. Arrested in July 2007, he was held in pre-trial detention for 10 months.

■ Habib Saleh, a pro-reform activist and former prisoner of conscience, was arrested in May and held incommunicado for three months, then brought to trial before the Damascus Criminal Court on charges including "weakening national sentiment" and "aiming to provoke civil war or sectarian fighting". The charges arose from articles on the internet calling for governmental reform and democracy. If convicted, he could face the death penalty.

■ Karim 'Arabji, a blogger, was being tried before the SSSC on the charge of "spreading false news". He was alleged to have moderated the internet youth forum www.akhawia.net. Following his arrest in June 2007, Karim 'Arabji was reported to have been held in prolonged incommunicado detention during which he was tortured and otherwise ill-treated.

■ It was reported on 8 December that Fu'ad Shurbaji, chief editor of a small private TV station, had been convicted of "slander" and "defamation" of a state media official and sentenced to three days' imprisonment.

Torture and other ill-treatment

Detainees continued to be tortured and otherwise ill-treated. Confessions extracted under duress were used as evidence in court. Seven deaths were reported to have occurred as a possible result of abuses in custody. The authorities took no action to investigate torture allegations.

Violence and discrimination against women

At least 29 women were reportedly killed in the name of "honour" and the perpetrators of such killings,

when prosecuted, continued to receive lenient sentences under the Penal Code. Women's rights defenders campaigned for better protection from gender-based violence and for an end to legal discrimination against women. In July, the authorities said that a committee was being formed to draft an anti-trafficking law.

Discrimination – Kurds

Members of the Kurdish minority, who comprise up to 10 per cent of the population, continued to suffer from identity-based discrimination, including restrictions on the use of the Kurdish language and culture. Tens of thousands of Syrian Kurds remained effectively stateless and so were denied equal access to social and economic rights.

On 10 September, the authorities issued Legislative Decree No. 49. This further restricted housing and property rights in border areas, including the pre-dominantly Kurdish-populated north-east border areas.

Human rights defenders

Human rights NGOs remained active although they were not officially authorized. Human rights defenders continued to face harassment. Lawyers Muhannad al-Hassani and Razan Zeitouneh were among at least 20 human rights defenders prevented from travelling abroad.

Death penalty

The death penalty remained in force for a wide range of offences. At least one person convicted of murder was executed and on 1 April seven others were sentenced to death for drug trafficking.

In December, Syria voted against a UN General Assembly resolution calling for a worldwide moratorium on executions.

Refugees and asylum-seekers

Syria continued to host around 1 million Iraqi refugees. Some Iraqi refugees were arrested and forcibly returned to Iraq for having incorrect residency or work permits or for being suspected of working with international organizations. Syria also hosted around 500,000 Palestinian refugees who are long-term residents. Tens of thousands of Syrians remained internally displaced due to Israel's continuing occupation of the Golan.

Ahwazi (Iranian Arab) asylum-seekers continued to

S

be at risk of forcible return to Iran.

■ On 27 September, Ma'soumeh Ka'bi and her five children aged between four and 14 were forcibly returned to Iran, where they were immediately detained.

Amnesty International visit/reports

🚌 An Amnesty International delegation visited Syria in February/March to look into the situation of Iraqi refugees and to gather information about human rights abuses in Iraq.

📄 Iraq: Rhetoric and reality – the Iraqi refugee crisis (MDE 14/011/2008)

📄 Syria: Repressing dissent – pro-democracy activists on trial in Syria (MDE 24/024/2008)

TAIWAN

TAIWAN

Head of state:	Ma Ying-jeou
	(replaced Chen Shui-bian in May)
Head of government:	Liu Chao-shiuan
	(replaced Chang Chun-hsiung in May)
Death penalty:	retentionist

At least eight people were sentenced to death but no executions took place. Restrictive laws continued to be used to limit freedom of expression and assembly. The recently revised Domestic Violence Prevention Act was not effectively implemented.

Death penalty

At least eight people were sentenced to death and an estimated 82 people remained on death row at the end of the year. No executions had been carried out since 26 December 2005.

In June, responding to a campaign for abolition, the President stressed the importance of public consensus and quoted a survey showing high levels of public support for the death penalty. On 9 August, the new Minister of Justice announced her intention to move towards abolition. A day later some ruling party legislators stated that they opposed the abolition of the death penalty as it acted as a deterrent.

Freedom of expression and assembly

In November, police barred entry to areas along the route of a quasi-official Chinese delegation to protesters carrying the Taiwanese flag, the Tibetan flag, or displaying anti-China slogans.

Following the delegation's visit, students staged a month of sit-ins across the country demanding an amendment to the Assembly and Parade Law which had been used by police to deny freedom of assembly. In December, the government proposed removing the requirement for prior police approval of demonstrations but maintained prior police notice and police powers to alter planned demonstration on national security and public interest grounds.

Violence against women and girls

The strengthened Domestic Violence Prevention Act failed to provide adequate protection for victims due to poor implementation. In June, a High Court judge revealed that it could take days to issue an emergency protection order, much longer than the four-hour limit required by law. Women's groups continued to criticize judges for lacking gender awareness.

Women continued to be trafficked into Taiwan. In November, the cabinet approved a draft Anti-Human Trafficking Law.

In November, the legislature passed a resolution calling on the Japanese government to apologize and issue reparations to the survivors of Japan's military sexual slavery system during the Second World War.

Refugees and asylum-seekers

Human rights organizations continued to campaign for enactment of legislation protecting refugees and a draft bill was being reviewed by the legislature.

Amnesty International report

📄 Taiwan: Police should avoid using excessive force at upcoming protests (ASA 38/001/2008)

TAJIKISTAN

REPUBLIC OF TAJIKISTAN

Head of state:	Imomali Rakhmon
Head of government:	Okil Okilov
Death penalty:	abolitionist in practice
Population:	6.8 million
Life expectancy:	66.3 years
Under-5 mortality (m/f):	81/72 per 1,000
Adult literacy:	99.5 per cent

The authorities failed to address the continuing serious problem of domestic and sexual violence. Members of religious minorities came under increasing pressure from the authorities. Hundreds of people were faced with forced evictions and displacement.

Background

The UN World Food Programme announced in August that it would deliver US$10 million worth of food to avert famine in the country. The decision was taken in the wake of one of the harshest winters in Central Asia in several decades. Tajikistan suffered severe energy shortages which crippled vital infrastructure and left most people with no heating or electricity and limited access to food. A subsequent drought and a locust infestation added to the hardships of one of the world's poorest countries.

Violence against women

Domestic and sexual violence against women remained a serious problem. In cases of domestic assault the police could only initiate an investigation if they received a written request by the victim. Many women did not submit written complaints because they feared reprisals from their partner or their partner's family. A draft law "On social and legal protection from domestic violence", in preparation for several years, had still not been presented to parliament. Poverty and unemployment affected women disproportionately and made them more vulnerable to human rights abuses. Unregistered marriages, polygamy and forced marriages were increasing. Suicides of women were reported to be on the rise.

Forced evictions

Authorities continued with forced evictions and displacement of people living in areas designated for urban regeneration. Affected residents claimed that they were offered no or inadequate financial compensation, nor suitable alternatives for resettlement. In the capital Dushanbe, the country's only synagogue was demolished in June. A Protestant Church was destroyed a month later.

■ April saw a rare small-scale peaceful demonstration by residents of a district in Dushanbe targeted for demolition. Police officers used force to disperse the demonstrators and detained 20 women protestors. They were released after giving assurances never again to participate in demonstrations.

Freedom of religion

A proposed restrictive new law on religion continued to be under discussion. Pending the new law's adoption no new applications for legal status by religious organizations were accepted. Two Protestant groups, Ehio Church and the Abundant Life Christian Centre, suspended for three months in October 2007, were unable to resume their activities. Another Protestant group lost its worship building in Dushanbe in August. This decision was appealed in October. Its senior pastor, a US citizen, was threatened by the authorities with removal of his visa.

■ In September a court in Dushanbe upheld the government's October 2007 decision to revoke the legal status of the Jehovah's Witnesses and to ban indefinitely all activities by the religious minority across the country. An appeal to the Supreme Court was pending at the end of the year.

Amnesty International visits/report

🚗 Amnesty International representatives visited Tajikistan in October and November.

📘 Central Asia: Summary of human rights concerns, March 2007-March 2008 (EUR 04/001/2008)

T

TANZANIA

UNITED REPUBLIC OF TANZANIA
Head of state:	Jakaya Kikwete
Head of government:	Mizengo Pinda (replaced Edward Lowassa in February)
Head of Zanzibar government:	Amani Abeid Karume
Death penalty:	abolitionist in practice
Population:	41.5 million
Life expectancy:	51 years
Under-5 mortality (m/f):	123/110 per 1,000
Adult literacy:	69.4 per cent

Despite economic growth, a significant part of Tanzania's population continued to live in poverty. Albino people were killed in some parts of the country and the government's response was inadequate. The right to freedom of expression came under attack. Reports of violence against women continued.

Background

Talks broke down between the ruling party, Chama Cha Mapinduzi (CCM) and the opposition, Civil United Front (CUF), regarding power-sharing and legal and electoral reform in semi-autonomous Zanzibar.

Discrimination – killings of albino people

As a direct result of discriminatory and harmful cultural practices, at least 28 albino people were murdered in what were believed to be ritual killings in different parts of the country, including Tabora, Arusha, Mara, Shilela and Shinyanga. These killings were allegedly driven by the belief that the body parts would make people rich when used in witchcraft practices. Some of the bodies were mutilated. The President condemned these killings and called for the arrest and prosecution of perpetrators and the central registration of all albino people in order to assure them of police protection. Police announced the arrest of 47 suspected perpetrators of the killings. However, by the end of 2008 there were no records of any prosecutions. The Tanzania Albino Society, a civil society group, criticized the lack of prosecutions, the slow rate of arrests of alleged perpetrators and the lack of a long-term comprehensive government plan aimed at preventing the killings.

Freedom of expression

The government withdrew the draft Media Services Bill, 2007, and stated that it would be redrafted. The Bill had been the subject of local and international criticism on grounds that, if passed into law, it would have severely restricted the right to freedom of expression. In October, local media civil society groups submitted a revised version to the government for consideration in the redrafting of the Bill. By the end of the year the redrafted version of the Bill had not been published.

■ In October the government ordered a three-month ban on the weekly *MwanaHALISI* newspaper for publishing a story identifying individuals allegedly trying to impede the President's efforts to stand for a second term in office. The Minister for Information cited provisions of the Newspaper Act which allows the government to order a newspaper to cease publication "if it is against public interest" or if it is "in the interests of peace and good order to do so". The Minister also announced plans to charge the paper's publisher and editor with sedition. By the end of the year the ban against the newspaper was still in force.

Violence against women and girls

Violence against women, including domestic violence, marital rape and early marriage of young girls, remained widespread. Female genital mutilation (FGM) continued to be practised in some rural areas. The government and a coalition of NGOs continued to campaign against FGM in the areas where it was prevalent. However, over 10 years since the enactment of the Sexual Offences (Special Provisions) Act (1998) outlawing FGM, the government's efforts to eradicate it remained inadequate. Implementation of the law was slow and perpetrators were rarely brought to justice. Local organizations working against the practice reported the continuation of a trend where girls and women over the age of 18 were still being forced to undergo FGM (even if they escaped it at a younger age), partly as a result of the failure in the 1998 law which only proscribes the practice for children under 18 years of age.

Prison conditions

Prison conditions – both on the mainland and in Zanzibar – continued to be harsh and inmates complained of inadequate food and poor medical services. A report by the Legal Human Rights Centre and Zanzibar Legal Services Centre, two local human rights organizations, found overcrowding of up to 193 per cent in mainland Tanzania and that this was mainly attributable to delays in disposing of cases in courts.

In a number of prisons children were held together with adult inmates, in breach of international standards.

Death penalty

Although there were no executions, courts continued to hand down death sentences. Despite the commutation of death sentences to life imprisonment in 2006, the government did not take formal steps to abolish the death penalty.

Amnesty International visit

🚗 An Amnesty International delegate visited mainland Tanzania in October.

THAILAND

KINGDOM OF THAILAND
Head of state: King Bhumibol Adulyadej
Head of government: **Abhisit Vejjajiva (replaced Acting Prime Minister Chaovarat Chanweerakul on 15 December, who replaced Somchai Wongsawat on 2 December, who replaced Samak Sundaravej in September, who replaced General Surayud Chulanont in January)**
Death penalty: retentionist
Population: 64.3 million
Life expectancy: 69.6 years
Under-5 mortality (m/f):   17/13 per 1,000
Adult literacy rates: 92.6 per cent

Insurgency continued in the south, where martial law and an emergency decree remained in force, and the official death toll since January 2004 reached 3,500. Security forces were responsible for human rights violations, including torture and arbitary arrest and detention. Armed insurgents also committed serious abuses, including deliberate attacks on civilians. In Bangkok, freedom of expression and assembly were curtailed by two emergency decrees issued after violent demonstrations, and restrictions on the media increased. The Act on Internal Security came into force with broad and vague application. The government forcibly returned several groups of Burmese and Lao Hmong asylum-seekers.

Background

The People Power Party, led by Prime Minister Samak Sundaravej, formed a coalition government in January. Both the party and its leader were aligned with deposed and exiled Prime Minister Thaksin Shinawatra. Anti-government protesters led by the People's Alliance for Democracy (PAD), took to the streets in May and forcibly occupied Government House and the Prime Minister's office in August. Samak Sundaravej was forced to resign the following month after the Constitutional Court ruled that he had violated conflict of interest rules. Violence erupted on a number of occasions between the PAD, pro-government demonstrators, and the police, resulting in several deaths and hundreds of injuries. In September, Somchai Wongsawat – former Prime Minister Thaksin Shinawatra's brother-in-law – became Prime Minister, leading to more demonstrations and violence, including several deaths. In late November, PAD occupied Bangkok's two international airports. In early December, Somchai Wongsawat was forced to step down after the Constitutional Court ruled that his party had violated electoral law. Abhisit Vejjajiva, leader of the opposition Democrat Party, became Prime Minister in December.

Abuses by armed groups

In January, a bomb set off by insurgents in a Yala Province market injured at least 44 people. In March, insurgents killed two people with a car bomb at the CS Pattani Hotel in Pattani Province, considered one of the safest hotels in the south. In Yala Province, 15 children were injured by bombs in March and April. Insurgents shot dead a 3-year-old boy and his father in Yala, and a nine-year-old girl, her young brother, and their father in Narathiwat. In September, insurgents shot dead a government official in Pattani before beheading him, the 41st person beheaded since January 2004. In November, two bombs on the same day in Narathiwat injured at least 75 people.

Arbitrary arrests and detentions

Security forces continued to arbitrarily arrest and detain young Malay-Muslim and politically active men

T

in the south, primarily for intelligence-gathering purposes. This was often carried out using lists of "suspects" compiled for this purpose, and through sweeping operations of Malay-Muslim villages.

Police and security forces

In January, a police captain and seven other members of the 41st Border Patrol Police unit were arrested for abuse of power, corruption, and police brutality in anti-drugs operations. They had allegedly abducted, framed, and tortured people in an attempt to extract confessions or ransom payments. In response, however, Police General Seriphisut Temiyavej, national police commissioner-general, threatened to take legal action against anyone who filed false complaints against police officers.

■ On 7 October, Angkana Pradubpanya-avut died from the impact of a tear gas canister fired directly at her chest by Thai riot police during a violent clash with anti-government PAD protesters in Bangkok. At least 440 others, including police, were injured in the violence.

Torture and other ill-treatment

Reports of torture and other ill-treatment by security services in counter-insurgency operations in the south increased. Detainees were reportedly subjected to torture and other ill-treatment in four southern provinces. Some died in custody.

■ A 42-year-old man from Pattani reported that three soldiers held him while another burned his foot with a lighter until it was out of fuel. Soldiers made him dig a hole and sit inside it as they filled it with dirt up to his neck.

■ A 22-year-old student from Narathiwat reported that he was drenched in water and had electric shocks applied to his feet.

No one had been held accountable for these acts at the end of the year.

Freedom of expression

The number of people charged with lèse-majesté, a law prohibiting any word or act which defames, insults, or threatens the royal family, increased substantially in 2008.

■ In January, a book that was critical of Thailand's 2006 military coup, and raised questions about the political role of the monarchy, was banned and its author placed under investigation.

■ In April, two Thais were charged for not standing up when the royal anthem was played at a cinema.

■ In July, a trade union leader was dismissed by her employer for appearing on television wearing a t-shirt deemed to be in violation of the law.

■ Between March and August, the Information and Communications Technology Ministry ordered internet service providers to block at least 340 websites because of content deemed insulting to the monarchy.

In November, the opposition party proposed shifting the burden of proof onto defendants in lèse-majesté cases.

In February, the government pressured a radio station to take a programme off the air after it contradicted controversial remarks made on CNN by then Prime Minister Samak about the 6 October 1976 uprising in Thailand.

In September, the government imposed an emergency decree in Bangkok for twelve days, severely restricting freedom of expression. The same decree was imposed for 13 days in November and December.

Impunity

In January, an independent committee found no evidence linking any government official to extrajudicial executions during former Prime Minister Thaksin's "war on drugs" in 2003. This was despite its objective of identifying people who might be brought to justice for such killings, and its findings that Thaksin's shoot-to-kill orders were widely implemented and that the Interior Ministry was ordered to issue a blacklist.

According to the report, of 2,819 people killed between February and April 2003 – 54 in shoot-outs with the police – only 1,370 were related to the drugs trade.

■ On 19 March, police from Rueso District police station and military personnel belonging to the 39th Special Task Force Unit in Narathiwat Province arrested Yapha Kaseng, an imam. He died in custody two days later. In December, a post-mortem inquest determined that he died as a result of his treatment in custody.

■ Impunity continued for those responsible for enforced disappearances, including that of Somchai Neelapaijit, a Muslim lawyer, in 2004.

T

Refugees and asylum-seekers

The authorities sent some 1,700 Lao Hmong people back to Laos, including an unknown number of forcibly returned asylum-seekers.

In February, the governor of Mae Hong Son Province refused permission for at least 20 members of Myanmar's "long-necked" Padaung ethnic group to leave Mae Hong Son Province on the basis that they were valuable tourist attractions, despite their being recognized as refugees and accepted for resettlement in other countries.

Legal, constitutional or institutional developments

The Act on Internal Security of 2008 came into force in February, giving the Thai military and security forces sweeping powers concerning internal security, including the power to "prevent, suppress, suspend, inhibit, and overcome or mitigate the situation". Its application to the insurgency in southern Thailand remained unclear.

The Anti-Human Trafficking Act of 2008 came into force in June.

Death penalty

At least three people were sentenced to death; no executions took place in 2008. In December, Thailand voted against a UN General Assembly resolution calling for a worldwide moratorium on executions.

Amnesty International visits

🚌 Amnesty International delegates visited southern Thailand in June and November.

TIMOR-LESTE

DEMOCRATIC REPUBLIC OF TIMOR-LESTE

Head of state:	José Manuel Ramos-Horta
Head of government:	Kay Rala Xanana Gusmão
Death penalty:	abolitionist for all crimes
Population:	1.2 million
Life expectancy:	59.7 years
Under-5 mortality (m/f):	90/89 per 1,000
Adult literacy:	50.1 per cent

The police and judiciary remained weak institutions. There were violent attacks on the President and the Prime Minister. Impunity for gross human rights violations committed during transition from Indonesian occupation in 1999 continued. The long-awaited report of the joint Indonesia and Timor-Leste Truth and Friendship Commission was delivered to the Timor-Leste and Indonesian governments. The UN had boycotted the Commission's investigation due to concerns about impunity. The number of internally displaced people living in camps after fleeing the violence in 2006 remained high.

Background

Those responsible for perpetrating human rights violations at the time of the independence referendum in 1999 and during violence in April/May 2006 continued to enjoy impunity.

The UN Integrated Mission in Timor-Leste (UNMIT) mandate was extended until early 2009. President José Ramos Horta called for the UNMIT to remain until at least 2012.

Police and security forces

The programme to rebuild the national police force continued. However, there were reports of human rights violations by both police and military personnel. Tensions between the two forces escalated when the police came temporarily under the authority of Timor-Leste's army following attacks on the President and Prime Minister. UN mentoring of the police force continued.

On 11 February, President José Ramos-Horta was shot three times during a raid on his home led by rebel soldier Major Alfredo Reinado. Major Reinado and the president's bodyguard were killed in the

T

ensuing gun battle. In a coordinated attack, the car in which Prime Minister Xanana Gusmão was travelling, and his home were also attacked but he escaped unharmed. Reinado had been charged with murder and was wanted by police for his leadership role in the 2006 violence. The President made a full recovery.

Impunity

The Commission of Truth and Friendship (CTF) report into the 1999 violence was officially submitted to the Timor-Leste government and the Indonesian government in July. It went further than expected in allocating institutional responsibility for gross human rights violations to pro-autonomy militia groups, Indonesia's military, civilian government and police. However, its mandate prevents the CTF from pursuing its own prosecutions, and it did not name individual violators. Concerns about impunity led the UN to boycott the CTF's investigations and instead resume prosecutions through the Serious Crime Unit, set up in conjunction with Timor-Leste prosecutors. By the end of the year, twenty cases had been submitted. The UN estimated that it could take three years to complete investigations into nearly 400 cases.

In May, the President reduced the sentences of numerous pro-Indonesian militia convicted of murder during the 1999 violence.

■ Militia leader Joni Marques' sentence was halved to 12 years. Originally set at 33 years, for crimes against humanity, his term had already been reduced by nine years in 2004.

■ In April, Indonesia's Supreme Court overturned on appeal the conviction and 10-year sentence of former militia leader Eurico Guterres for crimes against humanity in Timor-Leste. He was the only defendant out of the six originally found guilty whose conviction had been upheld and who was serving a prison sentence.

Internally displaced people

Approximately 40,000 people remained internally displaced. They continued to be in need of adequate food, shelter, clean water and sanitation and health care.

TOGO

TOGOLESE REPUBLIC
Head of state:	Faure Gnassingbé
Head of government:	Gilbert Fossoun Houngbo (replaced Komlan Mally in September)
Death penalty:	abolitionist in practice
Population:	6.8 million
Life expectancy:	57.8 years
Under-5 mortality (m/f):	134/116 per 1,000
Adult literacy:	53.2 per cent

Ill-treatment of detainees and inhuman prison conditions were reported. Freedom of expression was curtailed.

Background

In August, the body of Atsutse Kokouvi Agboboli, a former minister of communication and head of the political department of the Organization of African Unity, was found on a beach near the capital Lomé. The cause of death remained unclear.

International scrutiny

In January, the Special Rapporteur on torture noted in a report the commitment of the Togolese authorities to combat torture. However, in most police stations and gendarmerie posts visited, the Special Rapporteur found evidence of ill-treatment by law enforcement officials during interrogation of detainees, and beatings by prison guards as punishment.

The Special Rapporteur expressed concern that young people and children were at risk of corporal punishment while in detention and that prison conditions amounted to inhuman treatment.

In August, the UN and AU Special Rapporteurs on human rights defenders conducted a joint mission to Togo. During meetings the government acknowledged past human rights violations and said it would address them. Although the Rapporteurs acknowledged that the number of attacks and acts of intimidation against human rights defenders had fallen, they expressed concern about the stigmatization of human rights defenders who are seen as belonging to the political opposition. The Rapporteurs recommended that priority be given to ending impunity for violations against human rights defenders.

T

Freedom of expression

In July, the Togolese Coalition of Human Rights Defenders expressed concern about the abuse of power by the High Authority on Audiovisual and Communication (HAAC) and accused it of obstructing freedom of expression. The HAAC suspended radio stations and journalists considered critical of the authorities.

■ In January, Radio Victoire was pulled off the air for failing to comply with the HAAC's instruction to ban a foreign journalist from participating in a radio discussion on a sports programme which criticized the Togolese Confederation of Football.

■ In February, Daniel Lawson-Drackey, a journalist with Nana FM radio, was "indefinitely suspended" from the air by the HAAC after making comments critical of the authorities. The National Commission on Human Rights considered that this decision was "abusive and violates the right to information and the right to press freedom".

■ In July, the HAAC suspended the interactive programme of Radio Lumière, a station in Aného, southern Togo.

Impunity

In September, the representative of the UN High Commissioner for Human Rights submitted the final report on national consultations for a future Truth and Reconciliation Commission (TRC) to President Faure Gnassingbé. The consultations helped to gather the views of Togolese people on the nature and mandate of the TRC, established to shed light on political violence in Togo. The report called on the Togolese authorities to take appropriate steps to ensure the safety of witnesses, victims and alleged perpetrators.

No progress was reported in the examination of complaints lodged by victims of electoral violence in 2005.

TONGA

KINGDOM OF TONGA

Head of state:	King George Tupou V
Head of government:	Feleti Savele
Death penalty:	abolitionist in practice
Life expectancy:	72.8 years
Adult literacy:	98.9 per cent

The government established a Constitutional and Electoral Commission to propose a new system of government, which will see the devolution of the Monarch's governing powers. Freedom of expression was limited by the government on the eve of national elections. Women continued to be denied equal rights to ownership of land.

Legal developments

July saw the enactment of the Constitutional and Electoral Commission Act; King George Tupou V gave his consent soon afterwards. The Act provides for the establishment of a commission to make recommendations for a new system of government to be in place by 2010, with the possibility of the number of elected parliamentary representatives of the people (through universal suffrage) increasing from nine to 21 out of 30.

In August, a state of emergency giving extra powers to the security forces, which had been imposed in Nukualofa on a month-by-month basis following the riots of November 2006, was finally lifted.

Freedom of expression

On the eve of national elections in April, the government effectively censored coverage by reporters of the government-owned Tonga Broadcasting Corporation (TBC) of political programmes, and campaigns and prevented them from attending news conferences. The government also forced the TBC to remove a series of paid political announcements from its schedule, less than two weeks before elections. Censorship was lifted after the elections.

Women's rights

Women continued to be denied equal rights to ownership of land through the existing constitutional provisions.

T

TRINIDAD AND TOBAGO

REPUBLIC OF TRINIDAD AND TOBAGO
Head of state:	George Maxwell Richards
Head of government:	Patrick Manning
Death penalty:	retentionist
Population:	1.3 million
Life expectancy:	69.2 years
Under-5 mortality (m/f):	20/15 per 1,000
Adult literacy:	98.4 per cent

There were further reports of violations by the police, including unlawful killings and ill-treatment. Death sentences continued to be issued by the courts, but there were no executions.

Background

In September, the Prime Minister survived a motion of no confidence. According to the press, this was brought mainly in response to the rising crime rate and his alleged role in slowing down and frustrating an inquiry into the operations of the state-owned Urban Development Corporation of Trinidad and Tobago (UDeCOTT), which was suspected of corrupt practices.

According to press reports, there were 545 reported homicides in 2008, a rise of about 39 per cent over 2007.

The growing incidence of violent crime and the failure to bring police officers responsible for abuses to justice continued to undermine public confidence in the Trinidad and Tobago Police Service. In July, Acting Commissioner of Police James Philbert acknowledged that the Police Service owed the nation an apology for the poor quality of policing experienced by some sectors of society over the years.

Police and security forces

At least 40 people were reported to have been killed by police during the year. In most cases, the police officers involved in the killings claimed they acted in self-defence. However, in some cases, witness testimonies suggested the killings were unlawful.

■ On 8 October, Russel Samuel was shot by a police officer in La Canoa Road, Lower Santa Cruz. Residents who witnessed the shooting claimed that he was shot in the back while on his way to cut grass, thrown into a police vehicle and then allegedly shot three more times in the abdomen. Police officers claimed that Russel Samuel was caught brandishing a gun during a police operation and that he fired at them when ordered to drop the weapon. The incident sparked outrage among residents and led to protests. An investigation into the shooting was continuing at the end of the year.

Allegations of torture and other ill-treatment by members of the police and military were reported.

■ There were several allegations of beatings and unlawful arrests of residents following "operation lock-down" conducted by soldiers in Richplain, a neighbourhood of Diego Martin, in June. The legality of this operation was widely questioned as it was not clear under what powers the army was acting.

In its annual report, submitted to the Senate in April, the Police Complaints Authority recommended an amendment to the Police Complaints Authority Act 2006, in order to clarify its powers. No action had been taken by the end of the year.

Justice system

There were reports of shortages of judges and lawyers. Systematic intimidation and the frequent murder of witnesses, combined with a low detection rate for violent crime, contributed to the diminishing number of serious cases reaching trial. At least six state witnesses were reported to have been shot dead during the year, heightening concerns about the adequacy of the witness protection programme.

Death penalty

Ten people were sentenced to death.

In August, 52 prisoners had their death sentences commuted to life imprisonment by the High Court on the basis of a ruling by the UK-based Judicial Committee of the Privy Council that anyone sentenced to death who had spent more than five years on death row should not be executed.

In December, Trinidad and Tobago voted against a UN General Assembly resolution calling for a worldwide moratorium on executions.

T

TUNISIA

REPUBLIC OF TUNISIA

Head of state:	Zine El 'Abidine Ben 'Ali
Head of government:	Mohamed Ghannouchi
Death penalty:	abolitionist in practice
Population:	10.4 million
Life expectancy:	73.5 years
Under-5 mortality (m/f):	23/21 per 1,000
Adult literacy:	74.3 per cent

The security forces used excessive force in Gafsa against demonstrators, causing the deaths of two, and arrested and prosecuted at least 200 protesters, including human rights defenders and trade union leaders. The rights to freedom of expression, association and assembly were curtailed, and journalists, lawyers and human rights activists were prosecuted and harassed. There were reports of torture and other ill-treatment of detainees. At least 450 people were sentenced to prison terms following unfair trials on terrorism-related charges. The moratorium on executions was maintained.

Gafsa unrest

The south-east mining region of Gafsa was racked for months from January by protests against spiralling unemployment, poverty, rising living costs, and the recruitment practices of the Gafsa Phosphate Company, the main regional employer. In response, the authorities deployed security forces to Redeyef and other towns, who used excessive force when dispersing some protests, causing two deaths and many injuries. Hundreds of other protesters and people suspected of organizing or supporting the demonstrations were arrested and at least 200 were prosecuted. Some were convicted and sentenced to prison terms of up to 10 years.

■ Hafnaoui Maghzaoui was shot dead on 6 June when security forces used live ammunition to disperse protesters in Redeyef. Unofficial sources alleged that 26 others were injured; the authorities put the total at eight. One, Abdelkhalek Amaidi, died of his wounds in September. Eyewitnesses reported that the police opened fire without warning and that many of those wounded sustained bullet injuries to their backs and legs. The Minister of Justice expressed regret over the death of Hafnaoui Maghzaoui, but denied any wrongdoing by the security forces. He said an investigation was under way.

■ Adnan Hajji, Secretary General of the local office of the General Union of Tunisian Workers, was arrested in June. Along with 37 others whom the authorities accused of leading the protests, he was charged with setting up a criminal gang, belonging to a group that aims to damage property, and other offences. They appeared in court in December and 33 of them were sentenced to up to 10 years in prison; the other five were acquitted.

Legal and constitutional developments

The Constitution was amended in July to lower the voting age from 20 to 18 and to introduce exceptional provisions concerning the 2009 presidential elections. The exceptional provisions in effect bar from standing as candidates anyone other than elected political party leaders who have been in post for at least two years. In December the authorities announced draft amendments to the law on elections aiming to increase the seats of opposition parties in parliament and local councils from 37 to 50.

The Code of Criminal Procedure was amended in March. This strengthened procedural guarantees for detainees by requiring public prosecutors and investigating judges to give reasons when they authorize the extension for three days of the normal pre-arraignment period of police custody (*garde à vue*) of detainees. In June, new legislation brought the government-established Higher Council for Human Rights and Fundamental Liberties into conformity with the Paris Principles relating to national human rights institutions, with a view to enhancing its independence.

Counter-terror and security

Trials in alleged terrorism-related cases were unfair and mostly resulted in defendants being sentenced to long prison terms. Those tried included people arrested in Tunisia as well as Tunisians forcibly returned by other states, despite concerns that they would be at risk of torture. Often, convictions rested exclusively on "confessions" that defendants had made while held incommunicado in pre-trial detention and which they retracted in court, alleging that they had been obtained under torture. Investigating judges and courts routinely failed to investigate such allegations. Some 450 people were

T

sentenced on terrorism-related charges to prison terms during the year.

In June, the Italian authorities forcibly returned Sami Ben Khemais Essid to Tunisia despite fears for his safety. He was arrested on arrival as he had previously been sentenced, including by military courts, to prison terms totalling more than 100 years after being tried in his absence in several separate terrorism-related cases between 2000 and 2007. He challenged the sentences and in July and November was retried and sentenced in two separate cases to prison terms of eight and 11 years.

■ Ziad Fakraoui, who alleged that he had been tortured when held incommunicado at the Department of State Security in Tunis in 2005, was released in May but rearrested by state security officials on 25 June, two days after Amnesty International cited his case in a report on human rights violations in Tunisia. He was detained incommunicado for seven days before being taken before an investigating judge and charged with belonging to a terrorist organization and incitement to terrorism – the same charges on which he had been imprisoned following his arrest in 2005. He was acquitted of all charges and released on 25 November.

Political prisoners – releases

In November, 44 political prisoners were released conditionally to mark the 21st anniversary of President Ben Ali's accession to power. They included 21 prisoners serving long sentences after being convicted of belonging to Ennahda, a banned Islamist organization. The last of the Ennahda leaders to still be imprisoned, most had been held for more than 15 years. Some were reported to be in urgent need of medical treatment as a result of ill-treatment and harsh conditions, including prolonged solitary confinement.

Like other released political prisoners, they were reported to have been placed under "administrative control" orders imposed on most of them during their trial in 1992. This requires them to report frequently to specific police stations. Such restrictions limit their freedom of movement and make it difficult to obtain jobs and medical care. Sometimes, their immediate family members are also denied passports. Sadok Chourou, former head of Ennahda who was among those released in November, was rearrested at his home on 3 December. Three days later he was charged with "maintaining a banned organization" with reference to Ennahda, and sentenced to one year in prison.

Torture and other ill-treatment

There were new reports of torture and other ill-treatment in police stations and detention centres run by the State Security Department. Detainees were particularly at risk when they were being held incommunicado.

■ Jaber Tabbabi was detained on 5 June in connection with the Gafsa protests. Police tore off his clothes and struck him repeatedly while dragging him to a police station in Redeyef, where he alleges he was tortured. He was moved to a police station in Metlaoui, where he was blindfolded, placed in a contorted position and had a stick inserted into his rectum. A cut to his head required 16 stitches. He alleged that he was kept naked until he was taken before an investigating judge in the Gafsa Court of First Instance. The judge rejected his lawyer's request that he be medically examined for evidence of torture, but ordered his immediate release. He was released without charge on 9 June.

Freedom of expression

The government maintained tight restrictions on the media and several journalists were prosecuted on account of their professional activities, often on seemingly unrelated charges.

■ Fahem Boukadous, a journalist working for al-Hiwar Ettounsi, a Tunisian television channel, was charged with "belonging to a criminal association" and "spreading information liable to disrupt public order" because of his reporting on the Gafsa protests and human rights violations by the security forces. He went into hiding and was tried in his absence on 12 December together with 37 others (see above) and sentenced to six years in prison.

■ Naziha Rjiba was summoned by the Public Prosecutor in October and questioned about an article she had written for al-Mouatinoun, an opposition newspaper. The article accused the government of destroying the website of Kalima, an online news magazine she had set up with others following the authorities' refusal to grant it permission to publish in 1998. A few days earlier, the Interior Ministry had seized the entire issue of al-Mouatinoun in which her article had appeared.

T

Human rights defenders

Human rights activists and defenders were harassed and intimidated by the authorities, who subjected them to close and heavy surveillance, prevented the legal registration of human rights NGOs or obstructed their activities, and interfered with their communications by cutting telephone lines and internet connections.

■ In June, two lawyers and human rights defenders who had spoken about human rights violations in Tunisia at an Amnesty International press conference in Paris, were harassed by security officials when they returned to Tunis. Samir Dilou and Anouar Kousri were held briefly at the airport and told to report to the police, who questioned them about the press conference and accused them of circulating false information and damaging Tunisia's reputation. Samir Dilou was told that he should desist from such activities or he would face prosecution.

Violence against women

In September, Tunisia acceded to the UN Optional Protocol to the Convention on the Elimination of All Forms of Discrimination against Women. In November, the authorities introduced a free phone "hotline" for women victims of domestic violence.

Death penalty

The government maintained a de facto moratorium on executions but a number of prisoners remained on death row. In February, the Tunis Appeal Court commuted one of two death sentences imposed at the end of the so-called Soliman trial in December 2007 but confirmed the other. Imed Ben Amar's sentence was commuted to life imprisonment but the death sentence against Saber Ragoubi was confirmed.

In March 2008, a cross-party group of 25 members of parliament submitted a draft law proposing the abolition of the death penalty but it had still to be fully considered by the end of the year.

Amnesty International visit/reports

An Amnesty International delegate visited Tunisia in February to observe proceedings in the Soliman trial.

Tunisia: Court's decision to uphold death sentence a failure to redress injustice, 21 February 2008

In the name of security: Routine abuses in Tunisia (MDE 30/007/2008)

Tunisia: Open inquiry into killing of demonstrator against rising prices (MDE 30/008/2008)

Tunisia: Abuses continue despite official denial (MDE 30/010/2008)

Tunisia: Former political prisoners face harassment (MDE 30/012/2008)

Tunisia: Trial of trade union leaders a travesty of justice, 12 December 2008

TURKEY

REPUBLIC OF TURKEY

Head of state:	Abdullah Gül
Head of government:	Recep Tayyip Erdoğan
Death penalty:	abolitionist for all crimes
Population:	75.8 million
Life expectancy:	71.4 years
Under-5 mortality (m/f):	35/26 per 1,000
Adult literacy:	87.4 per cent

Human rights suffered in the context of political instability and military clashes. Reports of torture and other ill-treatment increased, while dissenting views were met with prosecution and intimidation. The right to freedom of peaceful assembly was denied, and law enforcement officials used excessive force to disperse demonstrations. Anti-terrorism legislation was also used to restrict freedom of expression. Unfair trials persisted especially for those prosecuted under anti-terrorism legislation, while barriers remained in bringing law enforcement officials to justice for human rights abuses. No progress was made in allowing the right to conscientious objection to military service. Forcible returns of refugees increased. Discrimination based on sexual orientation and gender identity persisted. Implementation of laws aimed at preventing violence against women and girls remained slow.

Background

Political tension and instability were heightened by polarizing legal battles, including at the Constitutional Court, and armed clashes between the Kurdistan Workers' Party (PKK) and the Turkish armed forces.

In legal cases that threatened the right to freedom of association, the ruling Justice and Development

T

Party (AKP) faced closure on the grounds that it was a focal point for anti-secular activities, as did the pro-Kurdish Democratic Society Party (DTP) on the grounds that it engaged in activities against the unity and integrity of the country. The Constitutional Court rejected the closure of the AKP in July; the case against the DTP was continuing at the end of the year.

In February parliament passed constitutional amendments aimed at withdrawing the ban on women wearing the Islamic headscarf at universities, but the Constitutional Court overturned the amendments in June on the grounds that they violated the secular principles of the state. However, the judgment did not adequately demonstrate the need for this limitation of freedom of religion and conscience based on the human rights of others.

In July, the indictment was issued in a groundbreaking prosecution against an alleged ultranationalist network, Ergenekon, with links to state institutions. Eighty-six people, including senior retired army officers, were charged with various offences relating to an alleged plot to violently overthrow the elected government through political assassinations and incitement of violence. The trial was continuing at the end of the year.

Armed clashes between the Turkish army and PKK continued and the use of temporary security zones in eastern and south-eastern provinces increased. Bomb attacks, often by unknown individuals or groups, killed and injured civilians. The army carried out military incursions into northern Iraq targeting PKK bases. In October, parliament authorized the armed forces to make further military interventions in northern Iraq.

In the context of the conflict, Turkish citizens of Kurdish origin faced increased hostility, including harassment, assaults and attacks on their property perpetrated by unknown individuals or groups. In September, such attacks took place over several days in Altınova province, western Turkey.

Freedom of expression

Human rights defenders, writers, journalists and others were unjustly prosecuted under unfair laws and subjected to arbitrary decisions by judges and prosecutors. Article 301 of the Penal Code was amended by parliament in April but remained an unfair limitation to freedom of expression. Investigations under Article 301 continued,

authorized by the Justice Minister as required by the amendments. Other articles and laws continued to be used to limit freedom of expression. Courts also acted disproportionately when shutting down websites on the basis of posted items.

People expressing dissenting views remained at risk, with individuals threatened with violence by unknown individuals or groups. Police bodyguards were provided in a number of cases.

■ In August, Minister of Justice Mehmet Ali Şahin gave permission for the prosecution of writer Temel Demirer under Article 301 for statements he made claiming state responsibility in the murder of journalist and human rights defender Hrant Dink in 2007.

■ Nine children, all members of the Diyarbakır Yenişehir Municipality Children's Choir, were prosecuted under Article 7/2 of the Anti-Terrorism Law for singing a Kurdish anthem among other songs at a cultural festival. They were acquitted at the first hearing, but an arrest warrant remained in force for the choir leader, Duygu Özge Bayar.

Human rights defenders

The work of human rights defenders was hampered by unjustified prosecutions, and some high-profile human rights defenders were subjected to regular criminal investigations. Human rights NGOs faced excessive administrative scrutiny of their work. Human rights defenders were threatened by unknown individuals or groups as a result of their work.

■ Orhan Kemal Cengiz received threats because of his legal work on behalf of the families of three men murdered in an attack on a Christian publishing house in Malatya in 2007. The authorities provided him with a bodyguard and investigated the threats.

■ In January, Ethem Açıkalın, head of the Adana branch of the Human Rights Association (İHD), was prosecuted under anti-terrorism legislation after attending a press conference about an alleged extrajudicial execution. In August, he and another İHD member, Hüseyin Beyaz, said that they were ill-treated by police while investigating the arrest of DTP members. Hüseyin Beyaz' arm was broken. An investigation was opened against Ethem Açıkalın and Hüseyin Beyaz for "resisting police officers".

Freedom of assembly

Some demonstrations were banned without legitimate reason and those held without permission, particularly in the Kurdish-populated south-eastern region, were dispersed with excessive force, often before peaceful methods had been tried. During clashes, police used plastic bullets and live ammunition, resulting in deaths and injuries. Demonstrators were arrested and ill-treated. In some cases, children were held in adult detention facilities. Allegations of ill-treatment by security forces during past demonstrations were not adequately investigated.

■ Traditional Newroz/Nevruz festivals after the 21 March equinox, which are celebrated especially by the Kurdish community, were refused authorization in south-eastern Turkey. Television footage showed law enforcement officials beating people after demonstrations went ahead without permission.

■ Law enforcement officials were filmed ill-treating 15-year-old C.E. during his arrest at a demonstration in Hakkari, but a prosecutor subsequently dismissed the complaint. C.E. was, however, prosecuted for his participation in the demonstration.

■ Permission for Labour Day demonstrations in Taksim square, Istanbul, was again refused on the unsubstantiated grounds that they would present a threat to security. Some 530 people were arrested for demonstrating without authorization on 1 May in Istanbul.

■ In October, demonstrations were held across southern and eastern provinces of Turkey to protest against the alleged ill-treatment of imprisoned PKK leader Abdullah Öcalan. Reportedly, more than a hundred children were charged with offences carrying prison sentences of more than 20 years in relation to the demonstrations. In addition, the Governor of the southern province of Adana threatened to withdraw benefits that allow access to health care and treatment from the families of children who participated in the demonstrations. The move, a form of collective punishment, threatened to violate the right of everyone to health and to an adequate standard of living, without discrimination. Adults and children involved in the sometimes violent confrontations with police were prosecuted under anti-terrorism laws.

Excessive use of force
Reports increased of police shooting people who allegedly failed to obey warnings to stop. In many cases it could not be established that a threat of death or serious injury necessitated the use of lethal force.

■ In November, 14-year-old Ahmet Yıldırım was shot by police officers at close range and paralysed from the waist down. Police stated that they had suspected Ahmet Yıldırım of stealing the motorcycle he was riding and fired at the tyres when he refused to stop. Eyewitnesses stated that no warning to stop was given.

Torture and other ill-treatment
Reports of torture and other ill-treatment rose during 2008, especially outside official places of detention but also in police stations and prisons. People accused of ordinary as well as politically motivated offences were vulnerable to ill-treatment. Counter-charges were often brought against individuals who said they had been ill-treated by law enforcement officials.

■ In October, Engin Çeber died in hospital after being detained in İstinye police station and Metris prison in Istanbul. An autopsy found that death was due to cerebral bleeding as a result of blunt trauma injuries consistent with those caused by blows to the head. Nineteen law enforcement officials were suspended from duty and an indictment was drawn up against 60 state officials, some facing torture charges. In the first such statement of its kind, the Justice Minister apologized to Engin Çeber's family and acknowledged that the death may have been due to torture.

Prison conditions
No progress was made in the implementation of a 2007 government circular aimed at improving the association time allowed to prisoners in high-security "F-type" prisons. Persistent allegations were made of ill-treatment in prisons and during transfer. Punishments, including solitary confinement, were arbitrarily imposed on prisoners. Small-group isolation remained a problem across the prison system for people accused or convicted of politically motivated offences.

■ In March, the report of the European Committee for the Prevention of Torture was published on the conditions of imprisonment of PKK leader Abdullah Öcalan recommending that he receive certain medical tests, that the material conditions of his detention be improved, and that the Turkish authorities take steps to increase his contact with the outside world.

Unfair trials
Protracted and unfair trials persisted, especially for those prosecuted under anti-terrorism legislation.

T

Convictions under anti-terrorism laws were often based on insubstantial or unreliable evidence.

■ In June, Murat Işıkırık was sentenced to seven years in prison for "membership of a terrorist organization" on the basis of evidence that he participated in the funeral of a PKK member and was pictured giving a "V for victory" sign.

■ In September, Selahattin Ökten was sentenced to life imprisonment for taking part in armed activities for the PKK. He was convicted on the basis of an insubstantial witness statement allegedly obtained under torture.

Impunity

Investigations into human rights violations by law enforcement officials remained flawed and prosecutions remained insufficient. Official human rights mechanisms were ineffective.

■ The trial continued of people accused of involvement with the 2007 murder of Hrant Dink. In a separate prosecution, eight members of the gendarmerie were charged with negligence based on their alleged failure to act on information that could have prevented the murder. A report published in July by the Parliamentary Human Rights Commission found that other state officials had been negligent in failing to prevent the murder.

■ In November, the Supreme Court of Appeals overturned the conviction of eight police officers for the death in custody of Alpaslan Yelden in 1999 in Izmir. The court found there was insufficient evidence that the officers participated in the torture.

■ In December prosecutors dismissed a case against police officers lodged by Mustafa Kükçe's family after his death in custody in June 2007. The prosecutor concluded that the death from cerebral bleeding could have been caused by a fall before he was taken into custody despite the last medical report while he was in detention finding injuries consistent with those inflicted by ill-treatment. The investigation also found that no record was made of Mustafa Kükçe's detention and that camera footage from the police station was not available due to the cameras being out of order.

Abuses by armed groups

Bomb attacks targeting civilians by unknown groups or individuals continued. In July, for example, 17 people died after a bomb exploded in the Güngören district of Istanbul.

■ In January, nine civilians died as a result of an apparent PKK attack targeting military personnel in Diyarbakır.

Prisoners of conscience – conscientious objectors

No civilian alternative to compulsory military service exists and promised legal reforms to prevent the repeated prosecution of conscientious objectors for evading military service were not introduced. Conscientious objectors were prosecuted and their supporters were also prosecuted under Article 318 of the Penal Code for "alienating the public from military service".

■ Halil Savda was re-imprisoned in March for his conscientious objection to military service. In June, he was additionally sentenced to five months in prison under Article 318 of the Penal Code after participating in a press conference held in support of Israeli conscientious objectors in 2006.

■ In June, conscientious objector Mehmet Bal was detained for evading military service. He said that he was repeatedly beaten in military custody.

Rights of lesbian, gay, bisexual and transgender people

Laws continued to be interpreted in ways that discriminated against people based on their sexual orientation and gender identity. Allegations persisted of violence by law enforcement officials against transgender people.

■ In May a local court in Istanbul ordered the closure of Lambda Istanbul, an organization that supports lesbian, gay, bisexual and transgender people, after the Istanbul Governor's Office complained that the organization's objectives were "against moral values and family structure".

■ A transgender person told Amnesty International that in February she was picked up on the street, taken to the Ankara Security Directorate and then insulted and beaten by police. She was released six hours later after paying a fine.

■ In July, Ahmet Yıldız was shot dead outside his apartment in Istanbul in what was suspected to be a gay "honour" crime. He had previously made a criminal complaint to prosecutors about threats made against him by relatives.

Refugees and asylum-seekers

There was an increase in forcible returns of refugees and asylum-seekers to countries where they were at risk of serious human rights violations. There were also reports of irregular deportations resulting in the death or injury of asylum-seekers.

■ A group of Uzbekistani refugees was twice forcibly returned to Iran, first in September and then in October. During the first forcible return, members of the group were said to have been beaten and threatened with rape unless they crossed back into Iran.

■ Four people drowned in April, according to UNHCR, when Turkish police forced a group of 18 refugees and asylum-seekers to cross a fast-flowing river on the Turkey-Iraq border.

Violence against women and girls

Laws and regulations designed to protect women and girls from violence were inadequately implemented. Insufficient funds and inaction by government departments undermined a 2006 circular from the Prime Minister aimed at combating domestic violence and preventing "honour" crimes. Limited progress was made in providing shelters for women survivors of violence to the extent stipulated by the 2004 Law on Municipalities – at least one shelter per settlement with a population of over 50,000.

Amnesty International visits/reports

🚐 Amnesty International delegates visited Turkey in February, March, April and May.

📄 Turkey: Memorandum to the Turkish Government (EUR 44/001/2008)

📄 Turkey: Bomb attacks condemned (EUR 44/014/2008)

📄 Turkey: Respect the rights and safety of demonstrators, 30 April 2008

📄 Turkey: Governor threatens to deprive demonstrators and their families of health care, 29 October 2008

TURKMENISTAN

TURKMENISTAN
Head of state and government: **Gurbanguly Berdymukhamedov**
Death penalty: **abolitionist for all crimes**
Population: **5 million**
Life expectancy: **62.6 years**
Under-5 mortality (m/f): **104/84 per 1,000**
Adult literacy: **98.8 per cent**

Independent journalists and their families were intimidated and prevented from carrying out their work. Several civil society activists were imprisoned after unfair trials and were held incommunicado. There was pervasive impunity for police, security services and other government authorities. Discrimination against ethnic minorities continued.

Background

Delegates from the EU visited the capital Ashgabad in April and again in June for the first of a series of "human rights dialogues" with the government. In April, pressure on human rights activists intensified, including on Turkmenistani activists in exile. Independent observers, such as the International Committee of the Red Cross (ICRC), continued to be denied access to prisoners and prisoners' families.

In September, a new Constitution was approved by the People's Council, which increased the President's power but was also said to broaden the role of parliament.

Repression of dissent

■ Social activist and possible prisoner of conscience Valeri Pal was sentenced to 12 years in prison in February for stealing property from his workplace. His supporters believe the case against him was fabricated to punish him for his contacts with human rights defenders abroad, and that the trial was unfair. He had a stroke in 2004, leaving him partially paralysed, and had other serious health concerns. In September, he suffered a heart attack in prison. Afterwards, his wife said that he had great difficulty speaking. There was serious concern about his access to medical treatment. Valeri Pal was released on 7 December from prison in the city of Mary under a presidential amnesty decree.

■ Former political dissident Gulgeldy Annaniyazov was sentenced to 11 years' imprisonment on 7 October after a closed trial before a court in Ashgabad. It was

T

not known under which provisions he had been charged. Gulgeldy Annaniyazov had left the country in 1999, and lived in Norway where he had been granted refugee status. He returned to Turkmenistan in June 2008 and was arrested on 24 June. He continued to be held incommunicado at the end of the year.

Enforced disappearance

■ The family of Boris Shikhmuradov, Minister of Foreign Affairs under former President Niyazov, has had no contact with him since late December 2002 and his whereabouts remained unknown. Boris Shikhmuradov was sentenced to 25 years' imprisonment in a closed trial earlier in December 2002. The People's Council increased his sentence the following day to life imprisonment.

Prisoners of conscience

■ Human rights defenders Annakurban Amanklychev and Sapardurdy Khadzhiev continued to serve seven-year prison terms for "illegal acquisition, possession or sale of ammunition or firearms" imposed in August 2006 following an unfair trial. They were both associated with the NGO Turkmenistan Helsinki Foundation. The Organization for Security and Co-operation in Europe (OSCE) reported in August 2006 that government sources had told the OSCE that Annakurban Amanklychev was detained for "illegal collection of information in order to encourage public dissatisfaction" and "transmitting materials to foreign citizens". Annakurban Amanklychev and Sapardurdy Khadzhiev were tried along with Ogulsapar Muradova, a correspondent with Radio Free Europe/Radio Liberty. She died in custody in disputed circumstances in September 2006.

Freedom of expression

The authorities increased access to the internet, but also took steps to more effectively block websites featuring articles about human rights violations and criticizing government policies.

In April the authorities launched a new wave of repression against independent civil society activists and journalists, intimidating individuals and their families. The authorities said they wished to identify contributors, some of whom used pseudonyms, to foreign media outlets and NGOs based outside the country. In November, all the mobile phones of Radio Free Europe/Radio Liberty contributors were blocked.

■ On 3 April Gurbansultan Achilova was summoned to the Ministry of National Security in Ashgabad. She was told she had to sign a letter stating that she would stop her work for Radio Free Europe/Radio Liberty until the authorities issued her with accreditation. The radio station attempted to confirm her accreditation without success. Without accreditation, Gurbansultan Achilova was liable to arrest if she continued working as a journalist.

■ Gurbandurdy Durdykuliev, a Radio Free Europe/Radio Liberty contributor, reported in May that since 2006 he had been visited by doctors of the psychiatric hospital of Balkan region and officers of the Ministry of National Security many times, urging him to go to the hospital for psychiatric check-ups. He had been forcibly confined in psychiatric hospitals from 2004 to 2006. In April 2008 his house was sprayed with intimidating graffiti, and burning bottles were thrown onto his veranda. He believed the intention was to discourage him from co-operating with Radio Free Europe/Radio Liberty and from complaining to the authorities about local social and economic problems.

During the year the Turkmen Initiative for Human Rights published a series of articles on its website accusing President Berdymukhamedov of nepotism. The website also carried reports and articles about human rights violations in Turkmenistan and provided a critical commentary on government policies and practices. The President reportedly ordered that access to this website be blocked in Turkmenistan and that those contributing to the website be identified.

Housing rights – '*propiska*'

"*Propiska*" – the system of registering the place of permanent residence – continued to restrict people's rights to access to housing, employment, social benefits, health care and education. The system had also become a breeding ground for corruption as many of its regulations could be bypassed by paying bribes. "*Propiska*" continued to be used by the authorities to deter people from moving around the country, especially to the capital, to find work. Moving without a "*propiska*" to live with another family member in order to share accommodation would result in the relative losing access to employment or social benefits such as pension payments. The threat of losing a "*propiska*" was used by the police and security services to prevent people complaining of ill-treatment by police.

Discrimination

Discrimination against ethnic minorities continued and was manifested clearly through restricted access to work and higher education. The policy of checking people's Turkmen origin up to the third generation continued, and meant that there were no members of ethnic minorities among ministers, directors or deputies of regional or district administrations. The three-generation check also applied to those applying to institutions of higher education. There were a few exceptional cases where members of ethnic minorities or people with a non-Turkmen relative were admitted to university, but this would reportedly only occur if a bribe was paid or the person was well connected.

Amnesty International reports

- Central Asia: Summary of Human Rights Concerns, March 2007–March 2008 (EUR 04/001/2008)
- Turkmenistan: No effective human rights reform (EUR 61/004/2008)

UGANDA

REPUBLIC OF UGANDA

Head of state and government:	Yoweri Kaguta Museveni
Death penalty:	retentionist
Population:	31.9 million
Life expectancy:	49.7 years
Under-5 mortality (m/f):	132/119 per 1,000
Adult literacy:	66.8 per cent

Security in the north increased after progress was made in peace talks between the government and the armed group, the Lord's Resistance Army (LRA), aimed at ending the 20-year conflict in northern Uganda. However, the final peace agreement was not signed by the end of 2008. The government continued to undermine freedom of expression and press freedom. Violence against women and girls persisted throughout the country. State security agents tortured or otherwise ill-treated detainees with impunity.

Background

A major corruption case remained pending. A former health minister, his two deputies and a government official faced criminal charges of embezzlement and abuse of office in connection with the Global Fund against HIV/AIDS, Tuberculosis and Malaria.

Armed conflict

The peace negotiations, which led to a number of agreements between the government and the LRA, were concluded but a final peace agreement was not signed by the end of 2008.

In February, the government and the LRA signed an Annex to the Agreement on Accountability and Reconciliation signed in June 2007. Under the terms of the Agreement and Annex, LRA leaders accused of crimes against humanity and war crimes would be tried by a Special Division of the High Court. The proposed framework fell short of a comprehensive plan to ensure that the truth is told, justice is done, and that reparation is provided for all the victims of the conflict. The arrest warrants issued in 2005 by the International Criminal Court for Joseph Kony, the LRA leader, and three LRA commanders remained in force, but were not executed by the Ugandan or regional governments.

In February, the parties signed an Agreement on Disarmament, Demobilization and Reintegration (DDR), committing both parties to an orderly DDR process in line with national policies and international standards. The agreement had significant flaws regarding victims' rights to measures to help them rebuild their lives.

Thousands of men, women and children who suffered abuses during the 20-year conflict in northern Uganda remained destitute and physically and mentally traumatized due to the government's failure to put in place a comprehensive reparations programme.

LRA forces outside Uganda were believed to have abducted hundreds of people during 2008, including children, and to have committed a number of other human rights abuses, including unlawful killings, in the Democratic Republic of the Congo (DRC), Southern Sudan and the Central Africa Republic. In December, Ugandan government armed forces participated in a joint operation with troops from South Sudan and the DRC in a military operation against the LRA.

Internally displaced people

By the end of 2008 over half (about 900,000) of the

U

internally displaced people (IDPs) in northern Uganda had left the IDP camps. Most moved to transit sites, smaller camps closer to their homes and some returned to their original villages. However, in Acholiland – the area most affected by the conflict – only 24 per cent of people reportedly returned to their villages of origin.

Right to health

In March, a report by the UN Special Rapporteur on the right to health noted that important right to health issues, such as sexual and reproductive health rights, were not fully captured in the government's policies. This neglect was evident in regular reports on cases of maternal mortality. Government health programmes aimed at prevention and treatment of HIV/AIDS left out certain categories of vulnerable people.

Trial of Kizza Besigye

The trial of opposition leader Dr Kizza Besigye and six others accused of treason remained pending in the High Court in Kampala. By the end of the year an application to the Constitutional Court challenging the continuation of the trial had not been decided.

Two cases of murder against Dr Besigye's six co-accused also remained pending. At the end of 2008 all six were free on bail.

Freedom of expression

Attacks on freedom of expression and press freedom continued.

In April the ruling National Resistance Movement party parliamentary caucus announced its support for a Bill which, if passed, could significantly hamper the right to freedom of expression in Uganda. The Bill had not been debated by the end of the year.

■ Two criminal cases in which five journalists working for *The Monitor* newspaper were charged with criminal libel and sedition in 2007 remained pending in court. The charges related to articles about the secret training of soldiers as policemen and the reinstatement of the Inspector General of Government onto the government payroll after retirement, in breach of public service regulations.

■ In April Andrew Mwenda, managing editor of *The Independent*, a bi-monthly news magazine, and two of the magazine's staff were arrested and interrogated in connection with a story about claims of torture at alleged secret government-run detention centres.

Police raided the magazine's offices and took away equipment. In May the three men were charged with sedition and "the publication of false news".

Freedom of assembly and association

In May the Constitutional Court ruled that section 32 of the Police Act amounted to an unjustified limitation on the rights to freedom of assembly and association in the Ugandan Constitution. The section gives unilateral powers to the Inspector General of Police (IGP) to prohibit any assembly or procession where he has reasonable grounds for believing that it was likely to cause a breach of the peace. The court decision did not deal with section 35 of the Police Act which empowers the Minister of Internal Affairs to declare any part of the country a gazetted area in which it is unlawful to demonstrate or convene an assembly of more than 25 people.

The government appealed against this decision to Uganda's highest court – the Supreme Court. The appeal was pending at the end of the year.

Refugees and asylum-seekers

From early August onwards, refugees and asylum-seekers fled from the DRC following a resurgence and escalation of fighting in eastern DRC. By mid-November more than 13,000 had arrived in Uganda.

According to UNHCR, the UN refugee agency, as of the end of October, Uganda hosted a total of more than 140,000 refugees, most of them from the Great Lakes and East and Horn of Africa regions. More than 48,000 were Congolese.

There was ongoing repatriation of Southern Sudan refugees back to Sudan, a process started in 2005.

A number of urban refugees and asylum-seekers, particularly from Ethiopia, Eritrea and DRC, complained of unlawful and arbitrary arrests, harassment and extortion by the police and other state security agencies.

Torture and other ill-treatment

Reports of torture and other ill-treatment committed by the police and other state security services, including in alleged secret detention centres, persisted. The Uganda Human Rights Commission's 10th annual report recorded that people held in detention facilities were still tortured to the extent of sustaining serious wounds. There were no prosecutions of alleged perpetrators of torture and other ill-treatment and a significant number of the Commission's compensation awards to victims of torture remained unpaid by the state.

Violence against women and girls

Violence against women and girls, including rape, marital rape, domestic violence, forced and early marriages, remained widespread in most parts of the country. Violence against women and girls was virtually never treated as a criminal offence. A number of proposed laws to address some forms of violence against women and girls remained pending. These included bills on Domestic Violence, Domestic Relations, Sexual Violence, and Trafficking in Persons.

Discrimination – lesbian, gay, bisexual and transgender people

There were continuing attacks on lesbian, gay, bisexual and transgender (LGBT) people and on human rights defenders working on LGBT rights.

In October, a government minister publicly labelled homosexuality and lesbianism a disease and declared that Uganda would seek to widen the scope of its legislation criminalizing homosexuality. In the month following the declaration, a number of LGBT activists and individuals were arrested and faced torture, including sexual assault, and other ill-treatment by police and security personnel while in detention.
■ In June, three LGBT human rights defenders were arbitrarily arrested and detained by police after distributing a press release to people attending a conference about HIV/AIDS policy implementation held in Kampala. They were charged with criminal trespass. The press release outlined the rights of LGBT people to treatment and prevention measures for HIV/AIDS.

Death penalty

Civilian courts continued to impose the death penalty but there were no executions. Military courts continued to hand down death sentences and order executions of soldiers in Uganda's armed forces; it was not clear whether there were any executions.

In December Uganda voted against a UN General Assembly resolution calling for a worldwide moratorium on executions.

Amnesty International visits/reports

🚍 Amnesty International delegates visited western Uganda in April and November and northern Uganda and Kampala in May and August.

📑 Uganda: Agreement and Annex on Accountability and Reconciliation fall short of a comprehensive plan to end impunity (AFR 59/001/2008)
📑 Uganda: Amnesty International condemns attacks against lesbian, gay, bisexual and transgender people (AFR 59/004/2008)
📑 Uganda: Amnesty International Concerns on the Regulation of Interception of Communications Bill, 2007 (AFR 59/005/2008)
📑 Uganda: Amnesty International says Anti-Privacy Bill should either be drastically amended or withdrawn (AFR 59/006/2008)
📑 Uganda: Left to their own devices: The continued suffering of victims of the conflict in northern Uganda and the need for reparations (AFR 59/009/2008)
📑 Uganda: Government cannot negotiate away International Criminal Court arrest warrants for LRA, 20 February 2008
📑 Uganda: Government miserably failing in care of victims of conflict, 17 November 2008

UKRAINE

UKRAINE	
Head of state:	Viktor Yushchenko
Head of government:	Yuliya Timoshenko
Death penalty:	abolitionist for all crimes
Population:	45.9 million
Life expectancy:	67.7 years
Under-5 mortality (m/f):	18/13 per 1,000
Adult literacy:	99.4 per cent

The authorities failed to respond adequately to rising racist attacks. Refugees and asylum-seekers were at risk of enforced return. Torture and other ill-treatment in police detention continued, and perpetrators of human rights violations enjoyed impunity.

Background

There was continuing political instability. After friction between members of the ruling coalition, President Viktor Yushchenko dissolved parliament on 8 October, and issued a decree proposing elections on 7 December. At the end of the year the validity of that decree was being contested in court. In April, NATO decided not to offer membership to Ukraine, but in December agreed to intensify co-operation, using the existing framework of the NATO-Ukraine Commission to review Ukraine's progress towards a Membership

U

Action Plan. In June Russian President Dmitry Medvedev warned Ukraine that there could be "serious consequences" if it joined NATO. An EU-Ukraine summit in September resulted in a framework for closer ties between Ukraine and the EU, but stopped short of offering the prospect of membership.

Racism

The alarming increase in violent racist attacks against foreigners resident in Ukraine, noted in recent years, continued. Inadequate provisions in the law, poor police responses, and a failure to acknowledge the gravity of racially motivated crimes led to virtual impunity for the perpetrators. Some officials demonstrated a lack of understanding of the seriousness of the issue, a lack of political will to tackle racism and a denial that the problem existed. In August, the terms of reference for an inter-ministerial working group to combat xenophobia and racial intolerance were approved by the Vice-Prime Minister, but it was not clear that this group had authority at a high enough level to be effective.

The European Commission against Racism and Intolerance recommended that Article 161 of the Criminal Code – one of only two articles that refer directly to racist crimes – should be amended to facilitate the prosecution of anyone who incites racial hatred, and that the scope of Article 161 should be extended to include all people under Ukrainian jurisdiction and not just citizens.

■ On 23 April, four young men, one of them a minor, were sentenced to 13 years' imprisonment each for the murder of Jeong Kwon Kang. Jeong Kwon Kang, a citizen of South Korea, was attacked in April 2007. The Consul of the Embassy of the Republic of Korea said that his attackers wore spiked boots and stamped on Jeong Kwon Kang's head "until his brains came out". According to the prosecutor's statement, one of the attackers stated that he wanted to kill Jeong Kwon Kang because of his nationality. Jeong Kwon Kang died on 17 May 2007 as a result of the severe head injuries he received during the attack. In May 2007, the four young men were charged with grievous bodily injury and hooliganism. In November 2007, after prolonged lobbying by the Embassy, the suspects were charged with murder and with "hatred aimed at humiliating the national honour and dignity of a person" under Article 161. However, the General Prosecutor's Office

appealed for the racist element of the charge to be dropped. It explained in a letter to the Embassy in October that Article 161 referred to the spreading of racial hatred, and the accused had not committed any acts that could be classified as propaganda, agitation or demonstration of racial hatred. The appeal was rejected by the Supreme Court.

■ In November 2006, Vyacheslav Manukyan, a Ukrainian of Armenian ethnic origin, had filed a civil suit against the police on the grounds that he had been subjected to discrimination. He was told by the police authorities that he was stopped frequently for document checks because his "characteristic appearance" made it necessary for them to check "the legality of his presence on the territory of Ukraine". On 27 March 2008 the Kharkiv District Administrative Court ruled that the police had acted "impartially, conscientiously and thoughtfully in accordance with the principle of equality before the law and avoiding any unfair discrimination". Vyacheslav Manukyan appealed against this decision, and on 29 July the Appeal Court declared that the police officer had failed to inform Vyacheslav Manukyan of his rights, but upheld the ruling of the first court that the behaviour of the police was not discriminatory. The Court ruled that the phrase "characteristic appearance" had not meant only ethnic origin but everything about his external appearance.

Refugees and asylum-seekers

The Ukrainian authorities continued to forcibly return asylum-seekers to countries where they would be at risk of serious human rights violations, and to disregard asylum procedures.

■ On 4 and 5 March 2008, the authorities forcibly returned 11 ethnic Tamil asylum-seekers to Sri Lanka where they were at risk of serious human rights violations including torture and other ill-treatment. All 11 asylum-seekers were registered with UNHCR, the UN refugee agency, in Kyiv, and six of them had applied to the Ukrainian authorities for refugee status. On 27 February the six applications were rejected by the Khmelnitskiy migration services for procedural reasons. They were not given the right to appeal.

Torture and other ill-treatment

Local human rights groups continued to receive complaints of torture and other ill-treatment in police detention centres and prisons. In 2008, the Kharkiv Human Rights Group registered 197 complaints of torture and ill-treatment; of these complaints 136 concerned ill-treatment by police and 49 by prison staff.

■ Sergei Ushakov, his wife Anna and his mother-in-law were detained by police in Frunzenskiy district in Kharkiv on 27 June in connection with the murder of Anatoliy Logvinenko on the night of 26/27 June. Sergei and Anna Ushakov were detained without access to a lawyer or any formal record of their detention. Anna Ushakova stated that she was threatened and beaten and forced to sign a statement implicating her husband in the murder. Sergei Ushakov also said he was beaten and forced to sign a confession. His lawyer observed that he had wounds on his wrists which did not seem consistent with the normal use of handcuffs. Anna Ushakov was released on 28 June, and Sergei Ushakov was released by the prosecutor on 1 July because of the absence of any proof linking him to the murder. Both complained about the ill-treatment on 1 July. However, while they were giving their testimony in the Deputy Prosecutor's office a group of policemen came into the office and forcibly took them back to the Frunzenskiy district police station. The couple described how they were again forced to sign false testimonies. Anna Ushakov was released the same day and Sergei Ushakov the following day. While they were in the police station both were concealed from the Prosecutor and at one point Sergei Ushakov was forced to leave the building through a window and was driven around Kharkiv for several hours to conceal his whereabouts. Sergei Ushakov was charged with murder on 4 July and was remanded in custody on 21 July. The case was continuing at the end of the year.

Impunity

On March 15, the Kyiv Court of Appeal sentenced Mykola Protasov to 13 years in prison and Oleksandr Popovych and Valeriy Kostenko to 12 years each for the murder of journalist Heorhiy Gongadze. Heorhiy Gongadze went missing on 16 September 2000 and his headless corpse was found two months later in a forest on Kyiv's outskirts. His widow, Myroslava Gongadze, stated that the organizers of the killing and those who ordered it should also be on trial. In June, the Parliamentary Assembly of the Council of Europe expressed concern that the investigation had been limited to bringing to justice only the perpetrators of the crime and that no progress had

been made in the investigation into the officials who ordered the murder. It called on the Ukrainian authorities to intensify their efforts to strengthen the independence of investigative bodies, in particular the prosecution service, and decided to resume consideration of the case.

■ In July, the General Prosecutor's Office again refused to open a criminal investigation into allegations that Aleksandr Rafalskiy had been tortured by police officers on several occasions in 2001. In a letter to Aleksandr Rafalskiy's parents, the Prosecutor General stated that there was no need to open an investigation into such "minor violations". Police detained Aleksandr Rafalskiy in Kyiv on 13 June 2001 in connection with a murder investigation. He stated that police officers beat him as they apprehended him and then subsequently in the police station on Vladimirska Street in Kyiv where they placed a black plastic bag over his head and tightened it around his neck with a belt, nearly suffocating him repeatedly. They then placed a gas mask on top of the bag on his face. On 16 July 2001, he was taken to the police cells at Stavishche in Kyiv region where electric wires were reportedly attached to various parts of his body and he was given electric shocks. On 30 June 2004, Aleksandr Rafalskiy was sentenced to life imprisonment for murder. All complaints to the authorities calling for an investigation into the allegations of torture were unsuccessful.

Amnesty International visits/report

🚗 Amnesty International delegates visited Ukraine in February, July and September.

📓 Ukraine: Government must act to stop racial discrimination (EUR 50/005/2008)

U

UNITED ARAB EMIRATES

UNITED ARAB EMIRATES
Head of state: Shaikh Khalifa bin Zayed Al-Nahyan
Head of government: Shaikh Mohammed bin Rashid
                            Al Maktoum
Death penalty: retentionist
Population: 4.5 million
Life expectancy: 78.3 years
Under-5 mortality (m/f):   9/9 per 1,000
Adult literacy: 88.7 per cent

Migrant workers were exploited and abused. Cases of torture and prolonged detention without trial were reported. Women continued to face legal and other discrimination. Access to certain websites was blocked. The authorities began to address the cases of stateless persons, or *bidoun*. One person was executed.

Migrant workers' rights

Cases were reported of debt bondage and ill-treatment of domestic workers, and of deaths of construction workers due to unsafe conditions in places of work and residence. Some migrant workers said that government obstacles inhibited them from lodging complaints against abusive employers, including state bodies.

Some protests by migrant workers against non-payment of wages, low pay and poor housing and other conditions caused damage to property and resulted in arrests and prosecutions.

In October, the government announced that it was creating an agency to monitor migrant workers' complaints and mediate labour disputes.

■ In February, a Dubai court sentenced about 45 Indian construction workers to six months' imprisonment followed by deportation in connection with protests in 2007.

■ In March, 30 people were arrested after around 1,500 labourers in Sharjah held protests demanding higher wages.

■ In July, over 3,000 mainly Indian workers in Ras al-Khaimah were detained after protesting about the poor quality of their food; some were charged with arson and rioting.

Arbitrary detention, torture and other ill-treatment

At least 20 people were arrested in Khor Fakkan in October in pre-dawn raids, and then detained incommunicado and denied access to lawyers. Some were reported to have been tortured or otherwise ill-treated.

■ Two Pakistani brothers were reported to have been detained in October and tortured, including with electric shocks.

Counter-terror and security

■ 'Abdullah al-Hamiri, a UAE national held at the US military base in Guantánamo Bay, was returned to the UAE in July. He was detained and remained held at the end of the year.

■ In December, US citizen Naji Hamdan was transferred to prison following months of incommunicado detention by Amn al-Dawla (State Security) officials in Abu Dhabi, during which he was said to have been tortured. His lawyers in the USA and his family believe that his arrest may have been requested by the US authorities.

Freedom of expression and association

In June the authorities announced plans to end prison sentences relating to journalism. A draft Press Code circulated in December would institute heavy fines for "insulting" specific members of government. The authorities blocked access to several websites considered critical of the UAE or because they were considered a threat to public morality.

■ Some 70-80 male teachers who had been transferred to other state jobs in November 2007 apparently because of their suspected Islamist views were not permitted to return to teaching. Many of their wives, who also worked in schools, were reported to have faced discrimination and been denied pay increases by the Ministry of Education.

■ On 31 December the authorities broke up a peaceful gathering intended to show solidarity with the people of Gaza. Permits are required for demonstrations but are rarely granted. One person was detained.

Discrimination and violence against women

Women continued to face legal and other discrimination.

■ A woman, a UAE national, who married a foreign

U

national abroad without her family's permission was detained for eight months when she returned to the UAE in November 2007, ill-treated in prison, and threatened with prosecution for adultery, a capital offence. She was then returned to a relative and eventually left the UAE.

Discrimination – *bidoun*

In April the authorities announced they had set up a body to register the thousands of *bidoun* in the country who do not have the identity papers that are required to access employment and state benefits.

International scrutiny

In December, following an assessment of the human rights situation in the UAE by the Working Group on the Universal Periodic Review, the government agreed to accede to the UN Convention against Torture; invite the UN Special Rapporteur on trafficking in persons, especially women and children, to visit the country; and address allegations of discriminatory treatment of migrant workers. The government rejected recommendations to implement a moratorium on the use of the death penalty; repeal legislation providing for corporal punishment; allow collective bargaining and the right to strike; and introduce legislation that would prohibit discrimination and ensure gender equality.

Death penalty

One man was executed in February in Ras al-Khaimah for murder.

In December the UAE abstained on a UN General Assembly resolution calling for a worldwide moratorium on executions.

Amnesty International report

United Arab Emirates: Submission to the UN Universal Periodic Review (MDE 25/006/2008)

UNITED KINGDOM

UNITED KINGDOM OF GREAT BRITAIN AND
NORTHERN IRELAND

Head of state:	Queen Elizabeth II
Head of government:	Gordon Brown
Death penalty:	abolitionist for all crimes
Population:	61 million
Life expectancy:	79 years
Under-5 mortality (m/f):	6/6 per 1,000

The government continued to attempt to return individuals to states where they would face a real risk of grave human rights violations on the strength of unenforceable "diplomatic assurances". Secrecy in the implementation of counter-terrorism measures led to unfair judicial proceedings. There were continued failures of accountability for past violations, including in relation to alleged state collusion in killings in Northern Ireland.

Counter-terror and security

Extension of pre-charge detention

In October, the House of Lords – the upper house of parliament – voted against proposals contained in the Counter-Terrorism Bill 2008, to give a government minister the power to extend from 28 to 42 days the period for which people suspected of terrorism-related offences could be detained by the police without being charged with an offence.

The government responded to the vote by withdrawing the proposals from the Counter-Terrorism Bill, and publishing a new piece of draft legislation containing similar proposals. The Home Secretary told Parliament that the government would ask it to pass this legislation in the future, "should the worst happen, and should a terrorist plot overtake us and threaten our current investigatory capabilities."

In October, before the vote in the House of Lords, the European Committee for the Prevention of Torture and Inhuman or Degrading Treatment or Punishment expressed its considerable concern over the existing provisions – and even more so over the possible new ones – regarding the permissible length of pre-charge detention in cases falling under the terrorism legislation.

U

Changes to coroners' inquests

In October, the government withdrew from the Counter-Terrorism Bill provisions which related to coroners' inquests, announcing its intention to re-introduce the proposals in forthcoming new legislation reforming the system of inquests more generally. These proposals, if passed, would have given a government minister the power to order that part or all of the evidence heard by a coroner's inquest should be heard in secret, in the absence of the family of the deceased person and their legal representatives, where the minister considered it in the public interest to do so.

Control orders

As of 10 December, there were 15 control orders in force under the Prevention of Terrorism Act 2005. These allow the government to impose restrictions of movement and association on people suspected of involvement in terrorism-related activity, if deemed necessary for the protection of the public.

In October the Court of Appeal of England and Wales decided four appeals from individuals subject to control orders. The individuals were referred to as A.F., A.M,, A.N. and A.E. In three of these cases – A.F., A.M. and A.N. – the High Court had ruled that the men had not been given a fair hearing; in the fourth, A.E., the High Court had ruled that the hearing was fair.

In each case the government had relied heavily on information which had not been disclosed to the individuals or their lawyers, and which had been heard in secret sessions of the court from which they were excluded.

The Court of Appeal ruled that there was arguably "no principle that a hearing will be unfair in the absence of open disclosure to the [controlled person] of an irreducible minimum of allegation or evidence"; but that, even if such a minimum of disclosure was required for fairness, this could "be met by disclosure of as little information as was provided [to A.F.]... which is very little indeed". The Court of Appeal ruled that the cases of A.F. and A.N. should be reconsidered by the High Court. It dismissed, on grounds which were kept entirely secret, the government's appeal against the High Court's decision, itself entirely secret, in A.M.; and upheld the High Court's ruling that A.E. had been given a fair hearing.

An appeal against aspects of these decisions to the UK's highest court – the Appellate Committee of the House of Lords (the Law Lords) – was pending at the end of the year. In July, the UN Human Rights Committee noted that control order hearings "in practice [deny] the person on whom the control order is served the direct opportunity to effectively challenge the allegations against him or her," and recommended that the UK should "ensure that the judicial procedure […] complies with the principle of equality of arms, which requires access by the concerned person and the legal counsel of his own choice to the evidence on which the control order is made."

Detention without trial

■ In February, the Court of Appeal of England and Wales ordered the Home Secretary to reconsider the government's decision to refuse to give any compensation to Lotfi Raissi.

On 21 September 2001 Lotfi Raissi, an Algerian national, was arrested in London for his alleged participation in the attacks on 11 September 2001 in the USA. He was subsequently detained for almost five months, on the basis of an extradition request from the US authorities. In April 2002 a judge dismissed the request, saying that there had been "no evidence whatsoever" to support the allegation that Lotfi Raissi was involved in terrorism.

In February 2007, the High Court had endorsed the Home Secretary's refusal to compensate Lotfi Raissi. The Court of Appeal overturned this decision, finding that the extradition proceedings had been "used as a device to circumvent the rule of English law".

By the end of the year no new decision on compensation had been reached.

Torture and other ill-treatment

Attempts continued to deport individuals alleged to pose a threat to national security to countries where they would be at real risk of grave human rights violations, including torture or other ill-treatment. The government continued to argue that "diplomatic assurances" – unenforceable promises from the countries to which these individuals were to be returned – were sufficient to reduce the risk they would face.

In April, the Court of Appeal of England and Wales ruled that the UK could not proceed with deportation in two cases involving diplomatic assurances.

In the case of two Libyan nationals, referred to as "A.S." and "D.D.", the Court of Appeal upheld the udgment of the Special Immigration Appeals Commission (SIAC), the tribunal which hears appeals against deportation on national security grounds, that he assurances obtained from the Libyan authorities were not sufficient to protect them from a real risk of torture or other ill-treatment.

In the case of Omar Othman (also known as Abu Qatada), a Jordanian national, the Court of Appeal found that the trial which he would face in Jordan – a trial in which SIAC said there was a high probability that evidence which may have been obtained by torture or inhuman or degrading treatment would be used against him – would amount to a flagrant violation of the right to a fair trial, and that the assurances given to the UK by Jordan would be no protection against this.

Following these decisions the Home Secretary announced that the government had "decided to discontinue deportation action in [the cases of D.D. and A.S.], and in the cases of 10 other Libyan nationals". At least five of those Libyan nationals were later made subject to control orders.

In October, the Law Lords heard an appeal by the government against the Court of Appeal's decision regarding Abu Qatada. At the same time they heard appeals by two Algerian nationals, referred to as "B.B." and "U.", against an earlier decision of the Court of Appeal which had upheld SIAC's conclusions that they could safely be returned to Algeria on the strength of assurances obtained from the Algerian authorities.

The Law Lords were asked to consider the reliability of diplomatic assurances and the fairness of SIAC's reliance on secret material.

By the end of the year, no judgment had been given in these appeals. The men facing deportation with assurances remained either in detention or subject to extremely strict bail conditions.

Renditions

In February, the Foreign Secretary announced that he had been informed by the USA that, contrary to repeated assurances, the USA had used the UK overseas territory of Diego Garcia on at least two occasions in 2002 for the purposes of transferring detainees in its programme of rendition and secret detention. The Foreign Secretary did not name the detainees involved.

■ Binyam Mohamed, an Ethiopian national formerly resident in the UK, remained in US custody at Guantánamo Bay, Cuba. In May, the Foreign Secretary told Parliament that "[UK] officials continue to discuss his case with the US", but that the USA was "not currently inclined to agree to our request for [his] release and return".

In October, a High Court hearing confirmed that an agent of the UK Security Service (MI5) had questioned Binyam Mohamed while he was detained in Pakistan in May 2002. The UK intelligence agencies had supplied information to the US authorities for use in the interrogation of Binyam Mohamed, in the knowledge that he was detained incommunicado and had been denied access to a lawyer. UK intelligence agents had continued to supply information for use in his interrogation even when it became clear that he was no longer detained in Pakistan but was in a third country, where US agents continued to have direct access to him.

The High Court found that in principle, the government should have disclosed to Binyam Mohamed's lawyers information in its possession which could support his claim to have been subjected to torture and other ill-treatment, on the grounds that "the relationship of the [UK] Government to the [US] authorities in connection with [Binyam Mohamed] was far beyond that of a bystander or witness to the alleged wrongdoing".

In October, the Home Secretary asked the Attorney General to investigate possible "criminal wrongdoing" by agents of the UK and USA in the treatment of Binyam Mohamed.

Guantánamo Bay

■ In March, a Spanish judge ruled that the physical and mental health of Jamil El Banna and Omar Deghayes, two UK residents returned to the UK from Guantánamo Bay in 2007, had been so severely damaged by their treatment during their years of detention that it would have been "impossible, even inhuman" to proceed with their extradition to stand trial in Spain.

By the end of the year, no decision had been made as to whether these two men, or a third man returned from Guantánamo at the same time, Abdennour Sameur, would have restored to them the indefinite leave to remain in the UK which they had enjoyed prior to their detention and transfer to Guantánamo.

Armed forces in Iraq

■ In March the Secretary of State for Defence admitted that "a substantive breach of Articles 2, right to life, and

U

3, prohibition of torture, of the European Convention on Human Rights" had taken place in the case of Baha Mousa, and that breaches of Article 3 had taken place in the treatment of a number of other individuals detained alongside him.

Baha Mousa died at a UK-run detention facility in Iraq in September 2003, having been tortured and ill-treated by UK troops over a period of 36 hours. A number of Iraqis detained alongside him were also tortured and ill-treated.

In May a public inquiry was announced into the case of Baha Mousa under the Inquiries Act 2005, legislation which has been criticized for failing to ensure that inquiries are fully independent. The terms of reference of the inquiry require it to "investigate and report on the circumstances surrounding the death of Baha Mousa and the treatment of those detained with him, [...], in particular where responsibility lay for approving the practice of conditioning detainees".

The inquiry opened in October.

Police and security forces

■ In December, the coroner's inquest ended into the death of Jean Charles de Menezes, a Brazilian man shot dead by police officers in London in 2005. The jury was unable, on the evidence it had heard, to conclude that the police officers who shot Jean Charles de Menezes had done so lawfully. The jury found that a number of failures in the police operation had caused or contributed to his death. The coroner had directed the jury that it could not return a verdict of unlawful killing. He did not consider that there was enough evidence for jury members to be sure beyond reasonable doubt that individual police officers had committed a criminal offence of murder or manslaughter.

Northern Ireland – collusion and political killings

In July the UN Human Rights Committee expressed concern that "a considerable time after murders (including of human rights defenders) in Northern Ireland have occurred, several inquiries into these murders have still not been established or concluded, and that those responsible for these deaths have not yet been prosecuted". The Committee was concerned that "even where inquiries have been established, [...] instead of being under the control of an independent

judge, several of these inquiries are conducted under the Inquiries Act 2005 which allows the government minister who established an inquiry to control important aspects of that inquiry".

■ By the end of the year, the UK authorities had still not instigated the promised independent public judicial inquiry into the 1989 killing of human rights lawyer Patrick Finucane. In July, the UK authorities insisted that "the only way such an inquiry could take place is under the Inquiries Act 2005". Serious concerns have been expressed by the family of Patrick Finucane and by human rights organizations, as well as by expert bodies of the UN, that any inquiry held under that Act would be insufficiently independent.

■ In April, full public hearings began as part of the inquiry (not held under the Inquiries Act 2005) into the 1999 killing of Rosemary Nelson, a human rights lawyer. To date no one has been charged in connection with the killing.

Refugees and asylum-seekers

In March, 60 rejected asylum-seekers were forcibly returned to Erbil in northern Iraq; in October, it was reported that a further 50 Iraqis had been returned to northern Iraq.

In March, the Asylum and Immigration Tribunal (AIT) gave its decision on an important test-case concerning humanitarian protection for asylum-seekers who have fled armed conflicts. The AIT ruled that, although there was an internal armed conflict in Iraq, the appellants in the case would not, just by virtue of being civilians, face a "serious and individual threat" if returned, and therefore were not entitled to protection under EU legislation known as the Qualification Directive. This decision would, if followed, result in even more Iraqi asylum-seekers being denied protection in the UK. By the end of the year an appeal against this decision was pending.

Trafficking in human beings

In December, the UK ratified the Council of Europe Convention on Action against Trafficking in Human Beings.

Children's rights

In October, the concluding observations of the UN Committee on the Rights of the Child in relation to the UK, stated that: "The Committee – while noting that child poverty has been reduced in the last years – is

U

concerned that poverty is a very serious problem affecting all parts of the United Kingdom, including the Overseas Territories, and that it is a particular concern in Northern Ireland, where over 20 per cent of children reportedly live in persistent poverty. Furthermore, the Committee is concerned that the Government's strategy is not sufficiently targeted at those groups of children in most severe poverty and that the standard of living of Traveller children is particularly poor." It went on to say: "The Committee would like to highlight that an adequate standard of living is essential for a child's physical, mental, spiritual, moral and social development and that child poverty also affects infant mortality rates, access to health and education as well as everyday quality of life of children."

Amnesty International visits/reports

🚌 Amnesty International delegates observed court proceedings in England throughout the year, including challenges to control orders, appeals against deportation with assurances, and part of the inquest into the death of Jean Charles de Menezes. Delegates also visited Northern Ireland.

📑 UK: Amnesty International's briefing on the Counter-Terrorism Bill 2008 (EUR 45/010/2008)

📑 UK: Briefing to the Human Rights Committee (EUR 45/011/2008)

📑 State of denial: Europe's role in rendition and secret detention (EUR 01/003/2008)

UNITED STATES OF AMERICA

UNITED STATES OF AMERICA

Head of state and government:	George W. Bush
Death penalty:	retentionist
Population:	308.8 million
Life expectancy:	77.9 years
Under-5 mortality (m/f):	8/8 per 1,000

The Pentagon announced the release from the US naval base in Guantánamo Bay, Cuba, of 22 non-US nationals held there, bringing the number held in the base at the end of the year to approximately 250. One detainee was transferred from secret CIA custody to Guantánamo in March. In June, the Supreme Court ruled that the Guantánamo detainees had the constitutional right to challenge the lawfulness of their detention in US federal courts. By the end of the year there had been rulings in the cases of only eight detainees contesting their detention as "enemy combatants" in habeas corpus petitions. The first two trials by military commission were held at Guantánamo and several others, some of which could potentially result in death sentences, remained pending at the end of the year.

There were continued reports of police brutality and ill-treatment in prisons, jails and immigration detention facilities. Dozens of people died after police used Tasers (electro-shock weapons) against them. The first successful prosecution in a US court for torture committed outside the USA took place in October. There were 37 executions during the year, the lowest annual total for 15 years.

Counter-terror and justice

Indefinite military detention without charge at Guantánamo of foreign nationals designated by the US administration as "enemy combatants" entered its seventh year.

In June, in *Boumediene v. Bush*, the Supreme Court rejected the government's arguments that the Guantánamo detainees, as non-US nationals held outside the sovereign territory of the USA, were beyond the reach of habeas corpus. The Court declared attempts to strip the detainees of their right to habeas corpus through the 2006 Military Commissions Act (MCA) unconstitutional. It dismissed as deficient the substitute scheme established by the administration and Congress to replace habeas corpus proceedings. That scheme consisted of Combatant Status Review Tribunals (CSRTs), panels of three military officers empowered to review the detainee's "enemy combatant" status, with limited judicial review of final CSRT decisions.

In November, following post-*Boumediene* habeas corpus proceedings, a federal judge ruled that five detainees were unlawfully held and ordered that they be released "forthwith". He concluded that a sixth man was lawfully detained as an "enemy combatant". The six men had been taken into US custody in Bosnia and Herzegovina in January 2002 and transferred to Guantánamo. Three of the five whose releases were ordered were returned to Bosnia and Herzegovina in December. In two more rulings in

U

December, the same federal judge found that two other Guantánamo detainees were lawfully held as "enemy combatants".

In October, a federal judge ordered the release into the USA of 17 Uighur men held without charge at Guantánamo since 2002. The government no longer considered them "enemy combatants", but the men could not be returned to China because of the serious risk that they would face torture and execution there. The government appealed against the release order, arguing that the government should be allowed to detain the Uighurs at Guantánamo while it sought the third country solution that had eluded it for years. Oral arguments were held in the Court of Appeals on 25 November. A decision was pending at the end of the year and the Uighurs remained in indefinite detention at Guantánamo.

Confirmation that the Central Intelligence Agency (CIA) was continuing to operate its secret detention programme came on 14 March when the Pentagon announced that Muhammad Rahim al-Afghani, an Afghan national, was being transferred from CIA custody to Guantánamo. The announcement did not reveal where or when Muhammad Rahim was taken into detention, where he had been held prior to the transfer, or if any other people were being held in the secret programme.

On 15 July, the Court of Appeals for the Fourth Circuit handed down its ruling in the case of Ali al-Marri, a Qatari national held in military custody in South Carolina since he was designated an "enemy combatant" in 2003 by President Bush. The Court held that Congress had authorized the President to detain Ali al-Marri as an "enemy combatant". This referred to the Authorization for Use of Military Force (AUMF), a resolution passed by Congress, in the immediate wake of the 9/11 attacks. Amnesty International reiterated its call for the AUMF to be revoked, citing the numerous ways in which the administration had abused this over-broad resolution. On a second question, the Court concluded that Ali al-Marri had not had been afforded sufficient process to challenge his designation as an "enemy combatant" and returned the case to the District Court for further proceedings. Ali al-Marri appealed to the US Supreme Court, which in December announced that it would hear his case. Oral argument in the case was pending at the end of the year.

Hundreds of people remained in US custody in Afghanistan and Iraq (see Afghanistan and Iraq entries).

Military commissions
The first two trials by military commission under the MCA were conducted. On 6 August, Yemeni national Salim Hamdan was convicted of "providing material support for terrorism", but was acquitted of "conspiracy". The following day, he was sentenced to five and a half years in prison; he had already spent more than five years in Guantánamo since he was first made eligible for trial in 2003. Salim Hamdan was transferred to Yemen on 25 November, a month before the end of his sentence, under an arrangement with the Yemeni authorities that he would serve the remainder in Yemeni custody.

On 3 November, Yemeni national Ali Hamza al-Bahlul was found guilty of "conspiracy", "solicitation" to commit various crimes under the MCA and "providing material support for terrorism" and sentenced to life imprisonment. Two detainees who were children when first taken into custody – Afghan national Mohammed Jawad and Canadian national Omar Khadr – were facing trial by military commission at the end of the year. Further evidence emerged during pre-trial hearings that they had been subjected to torture or other cruel, inhuman or degrading treatment in US custody.

Seven detainees who had been held for up to four years in the USA's secret detention programme before being transferred to Guantánamo in 2006 were charged under the MCA, with the government seeking the death penalty against all seven. In all but one case, the convening authority approved the charges as capital when referring them on for military commission trial. By the end of the year, no trial dates had been set for any of the seven.

Former 'enemy combatant' sentenced
In January, US national José Padilla was sentenced to more than 17 years in prison, following his conviction in 2007 of involvement in a broad terrorism-related conspiracy. He had been held for three and a half years without charge or trial in military custody as an "enemy combatant" and subjected to extreme isolation and other ill-treatment possibly amounting to torture. Troubling questions surrounding the fairness of his trial remained in relation to the presumption of innocence, right to a speedy trial and José Padilla's effective ability to assist in his defence.

Torture and other cruel, inhuman or degrading treatment

At a hearing in front of a Senate committee on 5 February, General Michael Hayden, Director of the CIA, confirmed that among other "enhanced" interrogation techniques, the CIA had used "waterboarding" – simulated drowning – against three detainees held in secret custody in 2002 and 2003. Amnesty International considers that this technique constitutes torture. The three detainees – Khalid Sheikh Mohammed, Abu Zubaydah and Abd al-Nashiri – remained at Guantánamo at the end of the year, in the classified conditions of Camp 7 with 13 other detainees previously held in the secret detention programme. The government continued to resist calls to release information about other techniques or conditions used in the secret programme, or the location of CIA detention facilities.

Conditions of detention, particularly the degree of isolation, in Guantánamo's Camp 5, 6 and 7, and their potential impact on the physical and psychological health of detainees already distressed by the indefinite nature of their detention, continued to cause serious concern.

In December, the Senate Armed Services Committee published a summary of its findings and conclusions on abuses against detainees in US custody in the "war on terror"; the rest of the report remained classified. The Committee found that in relation to the authorization of interrogation techniques, senior US government officials had "redefined the law to create the appearance of their legality", and had relied upon "deeply flawed interpretations of US and international law".

Torture and other ill-treatment

There were reports of ill-treatment by police and prison officers on the US mainland, often involving cruel use of restraints, or electro-shock weapons.

In October, former police officer John Burge was arrested and charged with perjury in a civil case in which he had denied knowledge of the abuse and torture of suspects. John Burge had been in charge of the Area 2 police station in Chicago where scores of black suspects had allegedly been tortured in the 1970s and 1980s. Although indisputable evidence of torture came to light through a subsequent inquiry, no officer had been prosecuted and John Burge was the first person to be charged indirectly in connection with the abuse.

Thousands of prisoners continued to be confined in long-term isolation in high security units where conditions sometimes amounted to cruel, inhuman or degrading treatment.

Réne González and Gerardo Hernández, two Cuban nationals serving prison sentences in the USA, continued to be refused visits with their wives who were denied temporary visas to enter the USA.

Electro-shock weapons

Fifty-nine people died after being shocked with Tasers, bringing to 346 the number of such deaths since 2001. Although these deaths were commonly attributed to factors such as drug intoxication, medical examiners concluded that Taser shocks caused or contributed to at least 50 deaths.

Many of those who died were subjected to multiple or prolonged shocks, were under the influence of drugs and/or had health or other problems which could have made them more susceptible to the adverse effects of such devices. Tasers were also frequently used against people who did not pose a serious threat. Amnesty International called on the US authorities to suspend the use of Conducted Energy Devices (CEDs) pending further studies or limit their use to situations where officers would otherwise be justified in using deadly force.

■ Seventeen-year-old Darryl Turner died in March when he was shocked after an argument in the store where he worked in North Carolina. A video-tape showed a police officer firing Taser darts into Darryl Turner's chest as the unarmed teenager stood with his arms by his side. The officer held the trigger down for 37 seconds and shocked him again after he had collapsed on the floor. Darryl Turner died at the scene. The coroner ruled the cause of death to be a fatal disturbance of the heart rhythm due to stress and the Taser shocks. The officer received a five-day suspension from duty.

In June the Justice Department published an interim report of its study of deaths following the use of CEDs such as Tasers. The report stated that, while there was no "conclusive medical evidence" of a high risk of direct adverse effects from such devices, "[m]any aspects of the safety of CED technology are not well-known". It noted that the risk of death or injury could be higher in certain populations, including children, the elderly, pregnant women and people with heart problems.

U

International justice

In October, Chuckie Taylor, son of former Liberian President Charles Taylor, was found guilty by a US court of torture and related crimes committed while he was head of the Liberian Anti-Terrorist Unit. This was the first conviction under the 1994 Torture Victim Protection Act.

Discrimination

In its concluding observations on the USA, published in May, the UN Committee on the Elimination of Racial Discrimination outlined a number of concerns, including in relation to law enforcement and to the persistent racial disparities in the criminal justice system. It called for an end to life imprisonment without the possibility of parole for children, which disproportionately impacted on racial and ethnic minorities.

The Committee expressed deep concern that racial, ethnic and national minorities, especially Latino and African American people, were "disproportionately concentrated in poor residential areas characterized by sub-standard housing conditions, limited employment opportunities, inadequate access to health care facilities, under-resourced schools and high exposure to crime and violence". It expressed regret that wide racial disparities continued to exist in the field of sexual and reproductive health and noted the high maternal and infant mortality rates among women and children belonging to racial, ethnic and national minorities, especially African Americans.

Right to health – maternal mortality

Marginalized and poor women were at higher risk of death and complications from pregnancy and childbirth, with the maternal mortality rate among African American women three times higher than that of white women. Although there was a lack of reliable national data, it was estimated that many deaths could have been prevented if the women had had better access to adequate health care. More than 46 million people in the USA had no health insurance, and it was common for people to delay or go without health care because of the cost.

Violence against women

Native American and Alaska Native women continued to experience disproportionately high levels of sexual violence and inadequate access to support and justice. There were some welcome measures to address this issue. For example, the US Senate passed the Indian Health Care Improvement Act in February, mandating the Indian Health Service to develop – in co-ordination with tribes, tribal organizations and the Office on Violence against Women in the Department of Justice – standardized policies and protocols for dealing with sexual assault. There were also hearings in Congress on the additional resources needed to tackle the problem. However, uniform protocols on dealing with sexual violence – as well as for comprehensive data collection about the incidence of sexual violence, responses by the authorities and the outcomes of cases referred for prosecution – were lacking.

Migrants' rights – conditions in detention

In March the UN Special Rapporteur on the human rights of migrants issued a report on his 2007 visit to the USA. He expressed concern, among other things, about the lack of due process for non-US citizens in deportation proceedings; indefinite and mandatory detention policies; and the inhumane conditions under which many immigration detainees, including asylum-seekers, were held.

In September, US Immigration and Customs Enforcement issued revised "performance based" national standards for the treatment of detained migrants, many of whom were held in local jails or private facilities. Migrants' rights organizations remained concerned about how effectively such standards, which were not binding, would be enforced.

■ In July, Mexican national Juana Villegas, who was nine months' pregnant, was arrested on minor charges and placed in immigration detention where she gave birth to a boy. She was shackled to a bed by her right ankle and wrist throughout her labour until shortly before delivery of the baby. She was shackled again about six hours after the birth.

Death penalty

Thirty-seven people were executed during the year, 18 of them in Texas. This brought to 1,136 the total number of prisoners executed since the US Supreme Court lifted a moratorium on the death penalty in 1976. The executions in 2008 represented the lowest annual judicial death toll in the USA since 2005; this was in part because executions were halted for seven months following the Supreme Court's announcement in September 2007 that it would consider a legal challenge to lethal injection.

In April, the Supreme Court upheld the lethal injection procedures in question and executions resumed the following month.

Mexican national José Medellín was executed in Texas on 5 August, in violation of the USA's treaty obligations and an order by the International Court of Justice (ICJ). José Medellín was never advised by local officials of his right as a detained foreign national to seek consular assistance, as required under the Vienna Convention on Consular Relations. In 2004, the ICJ ruled that the USA had violated its obligations under the Convention in the cases of José Medellín and 50 other Mexican nationals on death row in the USA. The ICJ ordered the USA to provide the necessary judicial "review and reconsideration" of the convictions and sentences. On 25 March 2008, the Supreme Court unanimously found that the ICJ's decision constituted "an international law obligation" but ruled that it was "not automatically binding domestic law" and that the authority for implementing it rested with the US Congress.

Four prisoners facing execution – John Spirko in Ohio, Samuel Crowe in Georgia, Percy Walton in Virginia, and Kevin Young in Oklahoma – had their death sentences commuted by acts of executive clemency. The reasons cited included serious mental illness, doubt about guilt, and disproportionate punishment. Four other prisoners were exonerated of crimes for which they had been sentenced to death. Each had spent more than a decade on death row. There had been more than 120 such cases since 1976.

On 12 November, the Maryland Commission on Capital Punishment voted to recommend abolition of the state's death penalty. The Commission's final report and recommendations were pending before the state legislature at the end of the year.

In December, the USA voted against a UN General Assembly resolution calling for a worldwide moratorium on executions.

Amnesty International visits/reports

🚌 Amnesty International delegates observed military commission proceedings in Guantánamo during the year.

📄 USA: "Less than lethal"? The use of stun weapons in US law enforcement (AMR 51/010/2008)

📄 USA: A case to answer. From Abu Ghraib to secret CIA custody: The case of Khaled al-Maqtari (AMR 51/013/2008)

📄 USA: In whose best interests? Omar Khadr, child "enemy combatant" facing military commission (AMR 51/028/2008)

📄 "The pointless and needless extinction of life": USA should now look beyond lethal injection issue to wider death penalty questions (AMR 51/031/2008)

📄 USA: Way of life, way of death. Capital charges referred against five former secret detainees (AMR 51/041/2008)

📄 USA: Where is the accountability? Health concern as charges against Mohamed al-Qahtani dismissed (AMR 51/042/2008)

📄 USA: Many words, no justice. Federal court divided on Ali al-Marri, mainland "enemy combatant" (AMR 51/087/2008)

📄 USA: From ill-treatment to unfair trial. The case of Mohammed Jawad, child "enemy combatant" (AMR 51/091/2008)

📄 USA: Indefinite detention by litigation. "Monstrous absurdity" continues as Uighurs remain in Guantánamo (AMR 51/136/2008)

📄 USA: Investigation, prosecution, remedy: Accountability for human rights violations in the "war on terror" (AMR 51/151/2008)

URUGUAY

EASTERN REPUBLIC OF URUGUAY

Head of state and government:	Tabaré Vázquez Rosas
Death penalty:	abolitionist for all crimes
Population:	3.4 million
Life expectancy:	75.9 years
Under-5 mortality (m/f):	17/14 per 1,000
Adult literacy:	96.8 per cent

Some progress was made in bringing perpetrators of past human rights violations to justice and efforts continued to overturn the Expiry Law. Several journalists were charged with libel after reporting on impunity for human rights violations.

Background

The 1986 Expiry Law remained in force. This grants members of the security forces immunity from prosecution for crimes committed during the military government (1973-1985). However, the Executive excluded some cases previously covered by the law, allowing investigations to progress.

In September, Uruguay ratified the International

U

Convention for the Protection of All Persons from Enforced Disappearance.

Justice system – impunity for past violations

Scores of former military officers were called to testify in the case against the former head of military government General Gregorio Álvarez (1981-1985) and Juan Larcebeau, a retired naval officer. Both men were accused of being co-authors of the enforced disappeances of more than 30 people. In October the Appeal Court changed the charge from enforced disappearances to "aggravated homicide".

The investigation continued into the 1976 abudction and enforced disappearance of 22 people returned to Uruguay from Argentina in a Uruguayan Air Force flight.

The investigation into the enforced disappearance of Maria Claudia García de Gelman, initially closed under the Expiry Law, was reopened in August. The move was prompted by a petition from her daughter, María Macarena, based on new evidence that she was on the 1976 Uruguayan Air Force flight. María Macarena was born in detention and raised in another family, unaware of her true identity.

Italy continued its efforts to prosecute Uruguayan military officers accused of abducting and torturing Uruguayan-Italian citizens in the context of Operation Condor, a joint plan by Southern Cone military governments in the 1970s and 1980s to eliminate opponents. One, Antranig Ohannessian, was arrested in Argentina in March, shortly before another, Jorge Tróccoli was released after Uruguay failed to request his extradition in time.

Freedom of expression – journalists

Several journalists were cleared of libel charges brought by former military officers named in their reports. In February a retired army major filed a suit against Roger Rodríguez of the newspaper *La República* for defamation and slander. The suit related to articles linking the retired major to the death of student Santiago Rodríguez Muela, who was shot dead in 1972 during an attack on a meeting of students, professors and parents at the Liceo N° 8 school in the capital, Montevideo. In April the court dismissed the case, but an appeal was pending at the end of the year.

Women's rights

In November President Tabaré Vázquez vetoed a bill on sexual and reproductive rights which had previously been approved by Congress. This bill would have allowed abortion in the first 12 weeks of pregnancy, and in cases of rape and when the woman's life is at risk. Less than a month earlier the UN Committee on the Elimination of Discrimination against Women had expressed concern at the high incidence of maternal mortality, the leading cause of which is the practice of unsafe abortion.

The Committee also criticized Uruguay for the absence of a direct and clear definition of discrimination against women in its legislation as well as discriminatory provisions in the penal code. A proposal to reform the penal code was submitted to the Senate in 2005.

UZBEKISTAN

REPUBLIC OF UZBEKISTAN

Head of state:	Islam Karimov
Head of government:	Shavkat Mirzioiev
Death penalty:	abolitionist
Population:	27.8 million
Life expectancy:	66.8 years
Under-5 mortality (m/f):	71/60 per 1,000
Adult literacy:	99.4 per cent

Conditional releases from prison of some human rights defenders, a number of legislative and judicial reforms, and increased dialogue on human rights between the government and the international community failed to lead to genuine and wide-reaching systemic reforms. The authorities persisted in their refusal to allow an independent, international investigation into mass killings in Andizhan in 2005.

There was little improvement in freedom of expression and assembly. Human rights defenders, activists and independent journalists continued to be targeted for their work. Widespread torture or other ill-treatment of detainees and prisoners, including human rights defenders and government critics, continued to be reported. The authorities failed to investigate such allegations effectively.

Several thousand people convicted of involvement with banned Islamist organizations continued to serve long prison terms in conditions that amounted to cruel, inhuman and degrading treatment. The authorities continued to actively seek the extradition of members or suspected members of banned Islamist parties or movements.

The death penalty was abolished.

Background

The harshest winter to hit Central Asia in several decades saw rare public demonstrations scattered throughout Uzbekistan protesting over cuts to domestic power supplies of gas and electricity.

A sustained campaign against the use of child labour in cotton fields by a coalition of international and Uzbekistani NGOs and activists successfully targeted major international clothing retailers. Several banned the sale of textiles made with Uzbekistani cotton or the use of such in their merchandise. In September, the Prime Minister enacted a National Action Plan to address concerns about the use of child labour after the government ratified the International Labour Organization's Worst Form of Child Labour Convention and its Minimum Age Convention in June and April respectively. Uzbekistan is one of the world's largest raw cotton exporters and income from cotton exports represents around 60 per cent of the state's hard currency earnings. School children had traditionally been used to help farmers meet strict collection quotas during the harvest season. They missed school, worked under harsh conditions and received little remuneration.

International scrutiny

Three years after the killing of hundreds of people in Andizhan, when security forces fired on mainly peaceful demonstrators, the authorities continued to refuse to allow an independent, international investigation into these events. They asserted that two rounds of expert talks held with representatives of the EU in December 2006 and April 2007 had addressed all the relevant issues. However, there was concern that these talks did not meet international standards for an effective, independent and impartial investigation and could not be substituted for them, and should therefore not be accepted by the EU as such.

The failure of the Uzbekistani authorities to allow an international independent investigation into these mass killings was the reason behind the original imposition of sanctions by the EU in 2005 – a visa ban on 12 officials, an arms embargo and a partial suspension of the Partnership and Co-operation Agreement. Following deliberations at the General Affairs and External Relations Council (GAERC) meeting in April, foreign ministers decided to continue the suspension of the visa ban started in November 2007 for another six months, with a review of the human rights situation in three months. Although certain benchmarks were included in the final April GAERC Conclusions, there was no mention of Andizhan or the demand for an international independent investigation.

In October the GAERC decided to lift the visa ban fully. The GAERC cited certain positive developments which had influenced its decision, including Uzbekistan's willingness to host an EU-Uzbekistan seminar on media freedom in Tashkent. However, no independent media from Uzbekistan or foreign journalists were allowed to attend the meeting. International NGOs which had participated at the invitation of the EU issued a joint public statement condemning the seminar as "a decoy designed to extract concessions at no cost to the authorities" which "should not be considered as evidence of any improvement in the country's 17-year policy of suppressing freedom of speech".

In March, a spokesperson for the International Committee of the Red Cross (ICRC) confirmed that an agreement had been reached with the government for the ICRC to resume prison visits under its mandate, for a trial period of six months.

In December the UN Human Rights Council reviewed Uzbekistan's human rights situation under the Universal Periodic Review mechanism.

Human rights defenders

The situation for human rights defenders and independent journalists continued to deteriorate despite assertions by the authorities that freedoms of expression and association were not restricted and that independent NGOs and civil society activists could function freely.

Some of the imprisoned human rights defenders were released under the terms of two separate amnesties; their releases were conditional. Among

U

those released in October was prisoner of conscience Dilmurod Mukhiddinov. However, at least 10 human rights defenders remained in prison in cruel, inhuman and degrading conditions, having been sentenced to long prison terms after unfair trials. They had limited access to relatives and legal representatives, and reportedly they had been tortured or otherwise ill-treated. Some were reported to be gravely ill in prison. At least two human rights activists were sentenced to long prison terms in October on charges they claimed were fabricated in order to punish them for their human rights activities. One of them, Akzam Turgunov, a member of the banned secular opposition party Erk, claimed that he was tortured in pre-trial detention.

Other human rights activists and journalists continued to be routinely monitored by uniformed or plain-clothed law enforcement officers, including by being summoned for police questioning or placed under house arrest. Human rights defenders and journalists reported being beaten and detained by law enforcement officers, or beaten by people suspected of working for the security forces. Relatives also reported being threatened and harassed by security forces.

■ In June, human rights defender Mutabar Tadzhibaeva was unexpectedly released from prison on health grounds. However, her release was conditional; her eight-year sentence imposed in March 2006 was commuted to a three-year suspended sentence. In May, Mutabar Tadzhibaeva was awarded the Martin Ennals Award for human rights defenders. She was granted permission to travel abroad in September and was able to attend the award ceremony in Switzerland in November.

■ In February prisoner of conscience Saidzhakhon Zainabitdinov was unexpectedly released under the terms of the December 2007 presidential amnesty. He was quoted in some news reports as saying that he had not expected to be released and that he had been treated well in prison. He later explained that he did not want to discuss his time in prison in order not to jeopardize the potential release under the amnesty of other human rights defenders. Saidzhakhon Zainabitdinov had been sentenced in January 2006 to seven years' imprisonment for his alleged participation in the Andizhan events.

■ Salidzhon Abdurakhmanov, a human rights activist and journalist writing for the independent Germany-based website uznews.net, was detained in June on suspicion of possessing illegal narcotics. Traffic police who stopped his car reportedly for a routine inspection claimed to have found opium and marijuana hidden in the boot. Salidzhon Abdurakhmanov categorically denied ever being in possession of narcotics or having used illegal substances. His brother, who was also acting as his legal representative, and supporters claimed that the charges were fabricated in order to punish Salidzhon Abdurakhmanov for his human rights and journalistic activities. The police conducted a search of Salidzhon Abdurakhmanov's home and office and confiscated his computer and technical equipment as well as books and papers and written materials. Medical tests ordered by the police investigating his arrest confirmed that Salidzhon Abdurakhmanov was not a user of narcotics. Examination of the journalist's electronic computer and hard copy files yielded no evidence of illegal activities or criminal links. However, in September Salidzhon Abdurakhmanov was sentenced to 10 years' imprisonment for possession of narcotics with intent to sell. An appeal court upheld his sentence in November. A further appeal to the Supreme Court of Uzbekistan was pending.

Freedom of expression

Pressure on international media and NGOs continued despite assertions to the contrary by the authorities. In May the authorities refused to register the work permit of the country director of Human Rights Watch. In June, a TV station denounced Uzbekistani staff of the international media organization Radio Liberty/Radio Free Europe as traitors to their country. The programme also gave personal details, including names and addresses, of local correspondents.

Freedom of religion

Protestant groups and Jehovah's Witnesses were also targeted in similar television programmes and newspaper articles, which depicted them as "destructive sects".

International organizations expressed concern about the government's violations of the right to religious freedom, not only of Christian Evangelical groups but also of Muslims worshipping in mosques outside state control.

U

Torture and other ill-treatment

Persistent allegations of widespread torture or other ill-treatment of detainees and prisoners continued. These reports stemmed not just from people suspected of membership of banned Islamic groups or of having committed terrorist offences but also from other groups, including human rights activists, journalists and former – often high-profile – members of the government and security forces. The failure by the relevant authorities to properly investigate such allegations remained a serious concern. In January, judicial supervision of arrest was introduced, transferring the power to sanction arrest from the prosecutor's office to the courts. These court procedures did not conform to fair trial standards and failed to give detainees the right to challenge their arrest or complain of any torture or other ill-treatment.

■ In August the daughter of imprisoned poet and regime critic Yusuf Dzhuma claimed that her father was routinely tortured and ill-treated in Yaslik prison camp. He said he was being singled out for beatings and ill-treatment because he was considered an enemy of the President by prison staff, and that he had been locked up in quarantined cells with prisoners suffering from tuberculosis.

Counter-terrorism and security

In the name of national security and the fight against terrorism, the Uzbekistani authorities continued to actively seek the extradition of members or suspected members of banned Islamic movements or Islamist parties, such as Hizb-ut-Tahrir and Akramia, from neighbouring countries as well as the Russian Federation. Most of the men forcibly returned to Uzbekistan were held incommunicado, thus increasing their risk of being tortured or otherwise ill-treated.

■ Authorities in the Russian Federation continued to ignore decisions by the European Court of Human Rights to halt deportations of Uzbekistani asylum-seekers pending examinations of their applications to the Court. In one such case, Abdugani Kamaliev was forcibly deported to Uzbekistan in November 2007 just days after being detained in the Russian Federation. In February, Abdugani Kamaliev's relatives reported that upon his return to Uzbekistan he was subjected to torture or other ill-treatment in the Namangan regional pre-trial detention facility. By March, he had been sentenced to 11 years' imprisonment.

■ In April the European Court of Human Rights ruled that the extradition of 12 refugees from Russia to Uzbekistan "would give rise to a violation of Article 3 [prohibition of torture] as they would face a serious risk of being subjected to torture or inhuman or degrading treatment there." The Court also stated that it was "not convinced by the Government's argument that they had an obligation under international law to co-operate in fighting terrorism and had a duty to extradite the applicants who were accused of terrorist activities, irrespective of a threat of ill-treatment in the receiving country." The Court also was "not persuaded that the assurances from the Uzbek authorities offered a reliable guarantee against the risk of ill-treatment" in this case. The 12 Uzbek men had been sought for their alleged participation in the Andizhan events.

Death penalty

A law replacing the death penalty with life imprisonment came into effect on 1 January, marking the formal abolition of the death penalty. On 23 December Uzbekistan acceded to the Second Optional Protocol to the International Covenant on Civil and Political Rights, aiming at the abolition of the death penalty. However, by the end of the year authorities had still not published statistics on the death penalty for previous years, including the number of sentences, executions and commutations. There was no list published of the total number of men on death row who had their sentences automatically commuted to life imprisonment. There was no progress on allowing relatives access to information on burial sites of executed prisoners. Also, there was no indication that old cases would be investigated where the accused or his relatives had alleged the use of torture in order to force a confession, nor was there any mention of possible compensation. The Supreme Court started reviewing death sentences pending at the time of abolition, and by mid-April it had commuted at least 17 death sentences to long prison terms of either 20 or 25 years.

Amnesty International reports

▤ Central Asia: Summary of Human Rights Concerns, March 2007-March 2008 (EUR 04/001/2008)

▤ Uzbekistan: Submission to the UN Universal Periodic Review (EUR 62/004/2008)

U

VENEZUELA

BOLIVARIAN REPUBLIC OF VENEZUELA
Head of state and government:	Hugo Chávez Frías
Death penalty:	abolitionist for all crimes
Population:	28.1 million
Life expectancy:	73.2 years
Under-5 mortality (m/f):	24/19 per 1,000
Adult literacy:	93 per cent

Attacks on journalists were widespread. Human rights defenders continued to suffer harassment. Prison conditions provoked hunger strikes in facilities across the country. Some significant steps were taken to implement the 2007 law on violence against women but there was a lack of commitment from many of the authorities responsible. Lack of arms control contributed to high levels of violence and public insecurity.

Background

On 31 July the enabling law that empowered President Hugo Chávez Frías to pass legislation by decree on a wide range of issues including public security and institutional reform came to an end with legislative power returning in its entirety to the National Assembly. During the 18 months the law was in force, President Chávez issued a total of 66 decrees covering a wide range of issues.

A law on national intelligence and security passed by presidential decree in May was withdrawn the following month following protests against several aspects of the law, including a provision that would have obliged people to inform on each other or face prosecution.

There were reports of physical attacks on journalists, by both security forces and by civilians. Public insecurity remained an issue, with high numbers of small arms in circulation, including within the prison system.

Local elections for mayors and governors took place in November. Implementation of anti-corruption orders against a number of public officials effectively prevented them from standing for election. The Supreme Court of Justice upheld the constitutionality of these orders in August.

In December, the Supreme Court ruled that a decision by the Inter-American Court of Human

Rights that three judges should be reinstated and compensated for their removal from their posts, was "unforceable". The judges had been dismissed in 2003. There was concern that the Supreme Court decision could undermine provisions in the Constitution guaranteeing the implementation of rulings by international bodies.

Violence against women and girls

Some advances, including the training of public prosecutors and the setting up of specialized tribunals, were reported during the year. However, some authorities with duties and responsibilities under the 2007 Law for the Right of Women to Live a Life Free from Violence – such as the Ministry of Health, the Ministry of Interior and Justice and regional authorities – failed to fulfil their obligations. At the end of the year there were still no shelters in most of the country and insufficient training had been put in place to enable police officers to implement the law effectively. In addition, perpetrators in cases preceding the 2007 law continued to enjoy impunity for their crimes.

■ Alexandra Hidalgo was kidnapped and subjected to a seven-hour ordeal during which she was raped and tortured by a group of men in May 2004. Only two of her attackers had been brought to trial by the end of 2008. She was not provided with adequate protection despite receiving anonymous threats and the fear of reprisals from her former husband, whom she accused of being among her attackers. Although an arrest warrant had been issued for her husband, he remained at liberty at the end of the year.

Human rights defenders

Government officials attempted to undermine legitimate human rights work by making unfounded accusations against human rights organizations.

Local human rights activists supporting the Yukpa Indigenous community who were involved in a dispute with local landowners over land rights in Machiques in the State of Zulia were harassed and detained in August. An official investigation was initiated following the death in July of the elderly father of Sabino Romero Izarra, one of the community leaders; he was allegedly beaten to death by armed men.

In September, two senior officials of the international NGO Human Rights Watch were expelled from the country following the launch of a report criticizing the government's human rights record.

■ Human rights defender José Luis Urbano was repeatedly threatened because of his work as President of the Foundation for the Defence of the Right to Education (Fundación Pro-Defensa del Derecho a la Educación). In May, the director of a school where he had exposed irregularities threatened him and called for him to be attacked. Also in May he received anonymous death threats by telephone. In September, state police tried to break into his sister's home, shouting threats against her brother. It is believed this was in reprisal for José Luis Urbano having reported harassment from a member of the same police force. Although the threats were reported to the authorities, it was not known if any investigations had been initiated by the end of the year.

Prison conditions
In February, the Inter-American Court of Human Rights ordered the authorities to implement measures to protect prisoners in Rodeo prison in the State of Miranda. Conditions in prisons led to a series of hunger strikes and other protests in jails throughout the country during 2008.

Police and security forces
In April, President Chávez approved a new Police Law which had been drafted by a National Police Reform Commission. Among the issues highlighted by the Commission were the need to control police use of guns and to devise and implement a code of police conduct.

The Attorney General's Office announced that it would create a designated investigation team in 2009 to look into more than 6,000 reported cases of extrajudicial executions in which people were killed in confrontations with police between 2000 and 2007.

Amnesty International visit/report
🚗 An Amnesty International delegation visited Venezuela in July to launch a report on violence against women in the family.
📄 "The law is there, let's use it" – Ending domestic violence in Venezuela (AMR 53/001/2008)

VIET NAM

SOCIALIST REPUBLIC OF VIET NAM

Head of state:	Nguyen Minh Triet
Head of government:	Nguyen Tan Dung
Death penalty status:	retentionist
Population:	88.5 million
Life expectancy:	73.7 years
Under-5 mortality (m/f):	26/29 per 1,000
Adult literacy:	90.3 per cent

A crackdown on dissidents continued with severe restrictions on freedom of expression, association and assembly. Political activists were arrested and detained; others remained in prison after being sentenced under national security legislation. Religious groups were discriminated against, including attacks against Catholics peacefully protesting over a land dispute with the state. More than 200 ethnic minority Montagnards fled to neighbouring Cambodia seeking asylum from persecution. The National Assembly rejected Government proposals to limit the scope of the death penalty.

Freedom of expression
At least 11 peaceful activists received prison sentences, bringing the number of dissidents imprisoned to 30 since a crackdown began in November 2006. Most were supporters of Bloc 8406, an internet-based pro-democracy movement, or other unauthorized groups calling for democracy and human rights. The majority were charged with offences under the national security section of the 1999 Penal Code which carried lengthy prison terms, with additional sentences of up to five years of house arrest on release. An unknown number of dissidents remained in pre-trial detention.

■ In January, Truong Quoc Huy was sentenced to six years' imprisonment plus three years' house arrest on release under Article 88 of the Penal Code, "conducting propaganda against the Socialist Republic of Viet Nam". He was first arrested in October 2005 and held without charge or trial until his release in August 2006; he was rearrested six weeks later after he publicly declared his support for Bloc 8406. Before both arrests he was active on an internet chat room site, discussing the political situation in Viet Nam.

V

In May, journalists Nguyen Viet Chien and Nguyen Van Hai were arrested. In October, both were found guilty of "abusing democratic freedoms to infringe upon the interests of the State…" for reporting since 2005 on a major corruption scandal involving officials from the Ministry of Transport. Nguyen Viet Chien was sentenced to two years' imprisonment. Nguyen Van Hai received a non-custodial sentence of two years' re-education after he confessed to the charges.

Freedom of assembly

Since December 2007, members of the Catholic Church in Ha Noi have protested in unprecedented numbers in support of the church's ownership of two pieces of land which the government claimed to be state-owned. In September, police violently broke up the mass peaceful protests. Several people were injured with batons and 20 people were hospitalized after tear gas was used. Intimidation and harassment of Catholics by security forces and state-sponsored gangs increased in the aftermath.

At least eight protesters arrested in late August were tried on 8 December for "causing public disorder" and "damaging property". They received non-custodial sentences.

In April, police arrested at least 14 people peacefully demonstrating when the Olympic Torch passed through Ho Chi Minh City; some were released after a few days. Those arrested included Nguyen Hoang Hai, a blogger known as Dieu Cay, who had written articles critical of China's foreign policies, and advocated for human rights in Viet Nam. He was sentenced to two and a half years' imprisonment in September for tax evasion, believed to be a politically motivated charge. At least nine dissidents were detained following Dieu Cay's trial, including writer Nguyen Xuan Nghia who had also been among those arrested in April. They remained in pre-trial detention, reportedly charged under Article 88 of the Penal Code.

Discrimination – religious and ethnic groups

Members of churches not sanctioned by the state continued to face threats, harassment, forced renunciation of their faith, arbitrary detention and imprisonment.
■ Venerable Thich Huyen Quang, 87, Supreme Patriarch of the banned Unified Buddhist Church of Viet Nam (UBCV), died in July while living under restrictions imposed by the authorities. He was a prisoner of conscience who has spent more than 30 years in prison or under house arrest. His deputy, Thich Quang Do, currently under de facto house arrest, became head of the UBCV.

Reports of harassment and ill-treatment of ethnic minority Montagnards in the Central Highlands continued. More than 200 sought asylum in neighbouring Cambodia. An unknown number of Montagnards were still serving lengthy prison sentences in connection with protests in 2001 and 2004.

Death penalty

In November, the Ministry of Justice proposed amendments to the Penal Code to reduce the number of capital offences from 29 to 12. However, the National Assembly rejected the proposal, insisting that the death penalty was necessary to combat serious widespread crime.

According to media sources, at least 19 executions were carried out, and 59 people were sentenced to death. The actual numbers were believed to be much higher.
■ Nguyen Minh Hung was released in June after spending more than five years in prison under a death sentence for drug trafficking. Nguyen Minh Hung was initially sentenced to death by the Tay Ninh Provincial People's Court in June 2004, but the Supreme People's Court (SPC) overturned the sentence and ordered further investigation. He was re-tried by the Tay Ninh court and sentenced to death for a second time. In April 2007, the SPC again asked for further investigation. The case was finally dropped due to lack of evidence. A witness in the case said she had lied when identifying Nguyen Minh Hung as an accomplice because of intense pressure from the police.

In December, Viet Nam abstained on a UN General Assembly resolution calling for a worldwide moratorium on executions.

Amnesty International reports

Viet Nam: Time to live up to human rights commitment (ASA 41/001/2008)

Viet Nam: Supreme Patriarch Thich Huyen Quang, a life committed to human rights (ASA 41/002/2008)

Connecting human rights in Viet Nam (ASA 41/003/2008)

YEMEN

REPUBLIC OF YEMEN

Head of state:	'Ali Abdullah Saleh
Head of government:	Ali Mohammed Megawar
Death penalty:	retentionist
Population:	23.1 million
Life expectancy:	61.5 years
Under-5 mortality (m/f):	83/72 per 1,000
Adult literacy:	54.1 per cent

Hundreds of political prisoners, including prisoners of conscience, were released. Some were freed after a presidential order announcing an end to armed clashes in the Sa'da region; others had been detained in connection with protests in the south. Hundreds of new arrests were made and an unknown number of people detained in previous years continued to be held. Dozens of prisoners were sentenced after unfair trials before the Specialized Criminal Court (SCC). The authorities failed to investigate possible extrajudicial executions and other killings by the security forces. Allegations of police brutality and torture or other ill-treatment were widespread. Sentences of flogging were imposed and carried out. At least 13 people were executed and hundreds of prisoners remained on death row, including minors.

Background

Several attacks were attributed to al-Qa'ida and its supporters, including a bomb attack in September near the US embassy in Sana'a which killed 16 people, including civilians. In December, a member of the minority Jewish community was killed in 'Amran Governorate and others received anonymous threats demanding that they convert to Islam or leave Yemen. Foreign tourists were also attacked: two Belgian tourists and two Yemenis accompanying them were killed in January. Two Japanese women and a German couple and their daughter were kidnapped and held briefly by members of tribes in protest against the detention of their relatives by the authorities.

In August the government announced an end to the armed clashes between the security forces and followers of the late Hussain Badr al-Din al-Huthi, a prominent cleric from the Shi'a Zaidi minority, which had taken place intermittently in Sa'da Governorate since 2004. Supporters of Hussain Badr al-Din al-Huthi also announced an end to hostilities. Hundreds of prisoners were then released by both sides, including people held before and after trial by the authorities and the security forces as well as government supporters taken prisoner by Hussain Badr al-Din al-Huthi's followers. It was not clear how many others remained unaccounted for. The President also ordered the release of prisoners, including prisoners of conscience, held in connection with peaceful protests that had occurred particularly in the south.

The government proposed negative changes to the Penal Code on corporal punishment, discrimination against women and the criminalization of criticism of religion. The government also proposed a Counter Terrorism Law and a Money Laundering and Financing of Terrorism Law, both of which define terrorism vaguely, would weaken safeguards for the protection of suspects, and contain no safeguards for the legitimate exercise of the rights to freedom of expression, association and assembly.

In July, the Committee on the Elimination of Discrimination against Women considered Yemen's sixth periodic report on implementation of the UN Women's Convention. It found that discrimination and violence against women and girls remained entrenched in the laws and traditions of society and urged the government to take all necessary measures to move towards the elimination of such discrimination by the time of its next periodic review, due in 2013.

Freedom of expression

Despite the releases of prisoners of conscience, hundreds of people were arrested in 2008 for peaceful protest because they were suspected of being supporters of Hussain Badr al-Din al-Huthi, supporters or members of al-Qa'ida, apostates or spies. Some were prisoners of conscience.

Y

■ Dr Mohamed al-Saqaf, a lawyer and university lecturer, was detained by National Security officials on 11 August in Sana'a as he was about to leave the country with his family on holiday. He was held at the Criminal Investigation prison for several days, then released on bail to face trial. He was charged with "undermining national unity" because he had criticized the government's repression of peaceful protest by retired soldiers in the south of the country. He was also acting as defence counsel for Hassan Ba'oom, a Socialist Party activist who had been repeatedly arrested and detained for short periods without charge or trial.

■ Haitham bin Sa'ad was reportedly arrested with four others in July in Hadhramout in connection with violent attacks in south-eastern Yemen. All five were suspected of being supporters of al-Qa'ida.

Prisoner releases

Prisoners of conscience were among the political prisoners released during the year.

■ Fahd al-Qirni, an artist sentenced to 18 months' imprisonment on charges of insulting the President after he satirized him and criticized the government's crackdown on protests in the south, was freed in September. He had been sentenced to 18 months' imprisonment and a fine.

Unfair trials

Scores of suspected spies and alleged supporters of Hussain Badr al-Din al-Huthi or al-Qa'ida were unfairly tried before the SCC, or had their sentences confirmed by the Appeal Specialized Court (ASC). Defence lawyers complained that they were not permitted full access to their clients' files, and defendants alleged that "confessions" they had made during lengthy pre-trial incommunicado detention had been obtained under torture or other ill-treatment.

■ In the so-called Sana'a Cell 2 case, 14 alleged supporters of Hussain Badr al-Din al-Huthi were convicted of violent offences and other crimes in connection with the civil unrest in Sa'da in 2007. Some received prison terms and one defendant was sentenced to death. Those convicted included journalist Abdul Karim al-Khaiwani, a prisoner of conscience sentenced to a six-year prison term; he was released in September under a presidential pardon.

■ Hamad 'Ali al-Dahouk and 'Abdul 'Aziz al-Hatbani were sentenced to death as spies in February. Both men were convicted of informing the Egyptian authorities that the governments of Saudi Arabia and Kuwait, with the knowledge of the Yemeni authorities, were financing armed groups in Yemen to mount attacks against foreign tourists in Egypt. In October the ASC confirmed the death sentence against Hamad 'Ali al-Dahouk but acquitted 'Abdul 'Aziz al-Hatbani. The case was due to be heard finally by the Supreme Court.

■ Three people charged with spying for Iran appeared before the SCC in October. They were reported to have been previously detained for two months, held incommunicado and beaten. They were connected to a legal Shi'a association in Aden which had operated openly for years. The trial was ongoing at the end of the year.

■ At least 37 alleged members or supporters of al-Qa'ida were tried before the SCC or had their appeals heard by the ASC. In February, Bashir Rawah Nnu'man was sentenced to five years' imprisonment for having false documents to travel to Iraq to participate in the conflict there. In October, the ASC upheld the convictions of 36 defendants sentenced by the SCC in November 2007; 33 received prison terms ranging from three to 15 years and three were sentenced to death in their absence. All had been convicted of belonging to an armed group and attacking oil installations.

Torture and other ill-treatment

Police brutality and torture of detainees held in connection with politically motivated acts or protests as well as ordinary criminal suspects were reported to be widespread and carried out with impunity. Confessions allegedly obtained under torture or other duress were accepted as evidence by the courts without being investigated adequately, if at all. Reported methods of torture included beating with sticks, punching, kicking, prolonged suspension by the wrists or ankles, burning with cigarettes, being stripped naked, denial of food and prompt access to medical help, and threats of sexual abuse.

■ Tawfiq al-Masouri, sentenced to death by the SCC in January for a murder committed when he was 17, was reportedly tortured while held incommunicado for three months by police in Sana'a. He said that he confessed as a result of torture, and a medical examination carried out at his lawyer's request found marks consistent with these allegations. However, no further investigation was known to have been undertaken by the authorities.

Cruel, inhuman and degrading punishments

Sentences of flogging were frequently carried out after being handed down by the courts for sexual and alcohol offences.

Unlawful killings

Several protesters were deliberately killed or died as a result of excessive use of force by the security forces during peaceful protests. No independent investigations were known to have been carried out and no one was brought to justice.

■ In May, Sheikh Yahya Muhammad Hassan al-Sawmali was reportedly beaten and then shot and left to die by soldiers at Tor al-Baha town in Lehj Governorate in the south. He was reported to have been unarmed and to have posed no threat to the soldiers. Several soldiers were reportedly arrested in connection with his death but there was no independent investigation and those responsible had not been brought to trial by the end of the year.

Refugees and asylum-seekers

The government said it was drafting a refugee law but provided no details. It was unclear if the proposed law would conform to international standards for the protection of refugees, which the authorities continued to violate. According to reports, in August at least eight people were forcibly returned to Saudi Arabia despite fears that they would be at risk of torture and execution.

Yemen hosted over 40,000 Somali refugees who survived the hazardous crossing of the Gulf of Aden; many others were believed to have drowned or been killed by people traffickers. Some 1,300 asylum-seekers, according to government statistics, were returned involuntarily to their countries. Among those at risk of forcible return was Mohamadain 'Abdel Hameed Haroun, a Sudanese national from the Darfur region, who would be at risk of torture and other ill-treatment if returned to Sudan.

Discrimination and violence against women

Women continued to face discrimination in law and practice and were inadequately protected against domestic and other violence.

In April, parliament reportedly endorsed legal amendments that benefited women in social security, retirement and holiday allowances. However, the government failed to address the wider problem of discrimination against women.

In a "shadow" report to the UN Committee on the Elimination of Discrimination against Women in advance of its July review of Yemen's application of the UN Women's Convention, Yemeni women's rights organizations highlighted various forms of discrimination and violence against women, including abuses such as marriage of girls as young as eight.

■ The case concluded against two police officers prosecuted for raping Anissa al-Shu'aybi in 2002 while she was detained in the Criminal Investigation Department in Sana'a. In April, the Court of First Instance in Sana'a acquitted one of the police officers but convicted the other, imposing a three-month suspended prison sentence. The court also awarded Anissa al-Shu'aybi compensation of 1 million Yemeni riyals (approximately US$5,000). Subsequently, the Appeal Court acquitted both police officers but upheld the compensation ruling.

Death penalty

At least 13 people were executed and hundreds of prisoners were on death row. Death row prisoners included individuals suffering from mental or other disabilities, and minors. Defendants with impaired hearing were sentenced after being denied interpretation facilities.

■ Walid Haykal, sentenced to death for a murder committed when he was 16, remained on death row. His sentence had exhausted all appeals and was awaiting ratification by the President.

Amnesty International visit/report

An Amnesty International delegate visited Yemen in January to attend a conference concerning Yemeni nationals in US custody at Guantánamo Bay and secret detention sites operated by the US government.

Yemen: Amnesty International submission to the UN Universal Periodic Review, May 2009 (MDE 31/012/2008)

Y

ZIMBABWE

REPUBLIC OF ZIMBABWE

Head of state and government:	**Robert Mugabe**
Death penalty:	**retentionist**
Population:	**13.5 million**
Life expectancy:	**40.9 years**
Under-5 mortality (m/f):	**100/86 per 1000**
Adult literacy:	**89.4 per cent**

The human rights situation in Zimbabwe deteriorated sharply in 2008 with an unprecedented wave of state-sponsored human rights violations, perpetrated mainly by security forces, war veterans and supporters of the Zimbabwe African National Union (ZANU-PF) after elections in March. At least 180 people died as a result; thousands were injured while tens of thousands were displaced in rural areas and had to seek refuge in urban centres. Many people were left in need of emergency shelter, food aid and medical treatment after they were targeted ahead of the run-off presidential election in June.

The economy continued to decline making it very hard for a large part of the population to access food, healthcare and education. According to the UN, more than five million people were in need of food aid by the end of 2008. Victims of the 2005 mass forced evictions continued to live in deplorable conditions.

Background

On 29 March the country held presidential, parliamentary and local government elections in an environment that was relatively peaceful compared to previous elections. The elections followed a year-long dialogue between ZANU-PF and the two formations of the Movement for Democratic Change (MDC), facilitated by the Southern African Development Community (SADC). The March elections saw ZANU-PF losing its majority in parliament for the first time since independence in 1980.

In the first round of the presidential election, Morgan Tsvangirai of the MDC obtained 47.8 per cent of the vote, Robert Mugabe of ZANU-PF obtained 43.2 per cent, while two independent candidates obtained less than 10 per cent combined. Morgan Tsvangirai withdrew from the second round of the election on 22 June, citing violence against his

supporters. However, the Zimbabwe Electoral Commission ruled that the election should go ahead on 27 June. The June election was widely condemned by independent local and regional election observers.

Efforts by SADC to find a political settlement between ZANU-PF and the two formations of the MDC resulted in a political agreement signed in September. However, negotiations to set up a unity government stalled over allocation of key government ministries including the Ministry of Home Affairs.

The economy continued to decline, making it increasingly difficult for most households to access food, healthcare and education. The humanitarian situation was compounded by a government directive in June to suspend all field operations of NGOs. In addition, food reserves were plundered to feed gangs of ZANU-PF supporters who established camps throughout the country to implement President Mugabe's violent election campaign in the run-up to the 27 June election.

Agriculture faced extreme uncertainty as the country experienced serious shortages of seed and fertilizer as the farming season approached. Health workers and teachers went on intermittent strikes over poor working conditions and low wages. There was a nationwide outbreak of cholera, due to lack of water treatment and uncollected waste, which resulted in more than 800 recorded deaths and 16,000 reported cases by the end of the year.

In December Zimbabwe voted against a UN General Assembly resolution calling for a worldwide moratorium on executions.

Impunity

The March elections were followed by a wave of human rights violations that resulted in at least 180 deaths, and at least 9,000 people injured from torture, beatings and other violations perpetrated mainly by security forces, war veterans and ZANU-PF supporters. There were also reports of inter-party clashes and retaliatory attacks by some supporters of the MDC. About 28,000 people were displaced from their homes in rural areas and went to urban areas to seek refuge and medical care.

The police were unable or unwilling to act against those responsible for instigating and committing human rights violations against people suspected of voting for the MDC in the 29 March elections.

Z

Repeated failure by the authorities to bring to justice people with links to ZANU-PF or members of the security forces allowed the violations to escalate.

Extrajudicial executions and unlawful killings

Dozens of MDC activists and supporters were killed after being abducted by state security agents, war veterans and other ZANU-PF supporters. Others died from injuries following beatings by security forces and ZANU-PF supporters.

■ Tonderai Ndira, an MDC activist, was abducted from his home in Mabvuku, Harare, on 14 May. About nine armed men in plain clothes, believed to be state security agents, forced him into a white Toyota truck and drove away. His decomposed body was reportedly found in Goromonzi a week later.

■ Joshua Bakacheza, an MDC driver from Mashonaland West province, and Tendai Chidziwo, an MDC activist, were abducted in Harare on 25 June by armed men in three unmarked trucks. Joshua Bakacheza and Tendai Chidziwo had been assisting the wife of Tonderai Ndira to move to another suburb. They were taken to a farm near Beatrice where they were tortured before being shot. Joshua Bakacheza's body was discovered on 5 July. Tendai Chidziwo, who was shot in the head, survived the shooting and was in a coma for about a week.

■ The body of Beta Chokururama, an MDC activist, was discovered in Goromonzi on 13 May. He had been abducted by people suspected to be state security agents earlier in May when he was on his way to Murewa. In April, he had been attacked by ZANU-PF supporters and both his legs were fractured.

Enforced disappearances

Prominent human rights defenders, political activists and their family members were abducted by groups of armed men believed to be working on behalf of or with the acquiescence of the Zimbabwean authorities. The abductions were conducted in broad daylight with total impunity.

Most of the missing people were found at various police stations in Harare on or around 23 December 2008 after they were reportedly handed over to the police by the men who abducted them, who were members of the security forces. The abducted men and women were then held in police detention. None of the abductors were arrested by the police.

Some of those abducted were tortured by their captors who tried to force them to implicate themselves or other activists in recruiting people for military training in Botswana or in bombing police stations and a railway line. All the detainees denied the charges.

By end of year all the detainees were still in detention and the authorities had failed to comply with court orders to release them. Police also failed to comply with orders to allow the detainees to seek medical treatment. Amnesty International considered all the detainees to be potential prisoners of conscience.

■ Fourteen members of the MDC and a two-year-old baby went missing in late October and early November after reportedly being arrested by police in Mashonaland West province and Chitungwiza town, near Harare. Despite earlier police denials the detainees were found detained at various police stations in Harare on or around 23 December. They were taken to court on 24 December and accused of recruiting people for military training in Botswana.

■ On 3 December, Jestina Mukoko, director of the Zimbabwe Peace Project (ZPP), a national human rights organization, was forcibly taken from her home in Norton, Harare. She was seized by about 12 men in plain clothes – some armed with handguns – who identified themselves as members of the Law and Order section of the Zimbabwe Republic Police. Police denied that they had arrested Jestina Mukoko and her whereabouts remained unknown until 23 December when she was found in police custody. She was taken to court on 24 December, accused of recruiting people for military training in Botswana, a charge she denied. At the end of the year, Jestina Mukoko remained in custody. Amnesty International considered Jestina Mukoko to be a prisoner of conscience.

■ Broderick Takawira and Pascal Gonzo, ZPP staff members, were seized at the organization's offices in Harare on 8 December. They were handed to police by their abductors on or around 23 December. At the end of the year, both remained in custody as prisoners of conscience.

■ On 5 December, at around midnight, Zacharia Nkomo, the brother of Harrison Nkomo – another leading human rights lawyer who was working on Jestina Mukoko's case – was abducted by four unidentified men in civilian clothes from his home in Rujeko, Masvingo. The men responsible for the

Z

abduction were travelling in two green-and-silver Toyota trucks. He was found in police custody around 23 December.

Torture and other ill-treatment

Torture and other ill-treatment of opposition supporters were widespread following the 29 March elections in Mashonaland, Midlands, Manicaland and Masvingo provinces. In most districts, war veterans, soldiers and local ZANU-PF leaders established makeshift torture camps. The camps were set up in tents, clearings within a community, classrooms or at the homes of ZANU-PF officials or displaced MDC activists.

Local people were forced to attend all-night meetings at these camps. They were made to watch their neighbours being beaten and warned that if they did not vote for ZANU-PF on 27 June they would face a similar fate. MDC supporters were forced to denounce the party and surrender all their party materials, including t-shirts and membership cards. Dozens of MDC supporters died after beatings at these camps. Local youths were forced to attend the camp meetings and participate in beatings.

■ Kingswell Muteta, a police officer, was fatally beaten by ZANU-PF supporters in Mudzi district on 17 July after visiting the family of his brother-in-law, a local MDC chairperson reportedly beaten to death by ZANU-PF supporters. Witnesses said that Kingswell Muteta confronted a group of ZANU-PF youths who were under the instruction of a senior police officer. The ZANU-PF youths took Kingswell Muteta to a camp near Kotwa and accused him of having gone to an "enemy's" home. He was beaten by about 20 youths. He sustained mainly soft tissue injuries on his buttocks, trunk and lower limbs. He was taken to hospital on 18 July and died of his injuries on 25 July.

Economic, social and cultural rights

Politically motivated violations of economic, social and cultural rights persisted throughout 2008 with violations of the right to food reported across the country. The government deliberately took actions to prevent suspected supporters of opposition parties from buying cheap maize sold by the state-controlled Grain Marketing Board. It also effectively blocked access to much needed food aid ahead of the 27 June presidential election run-off.

On 4 June, the Minister of Public Service, Labour and Social Welfare wrote to every NGO and Private Voluntary Organization (PVO) announcing a suspension of all field operations by humanitarian organizations. The Minister alleged that the organizations were in breach of their terms and conditions of registration, but gave no further details. The suspension worsened food insecurity in the country at a time when two million people were in dire need of food aid. The ban also severely disrupted the provision of health services such as anti-retrovirals for AIDS patients, tuberculosis treatment and medication and care for other chronic conditions. In June, UNICEF reported that the net effect of the suspension was that as many as 500,000 children were left with no access to health care, HIV/AIDS support, education assistance and food. Many of these children were orphans. The ban was lifted at the end of August.

Internally displaced people

The wave of state-sponsored violence after the March elections left at least 28,000 people displaced. Victims of violence moved to urban areas to seek refuge and medical care. Most had their homes destroyed and food stocks plundered or destroyed as a punishment for supporting opposition parties. The internally displaced were in dire need of emergency shelter, food and medical care. They also needed seed and fertilizer in order to produce food in the coming year.

■ On the morning of 25 April, police in Harare raided the offices of the MDC and arrested hundreds of internally displaced people, including children, who were sheltering there. About 215 of those arrested were taken to Harare Central police station. Among them were 35 children, the oldest of whom was 11. They were released after the MDC obtained an order from the High Court for their release on 28 April.

Freedom of expression

The authorities continued to restrict freedom expression. Several foreign and local media workers were arrested in the context of the elections.

■ On 8 May police in Harare arrested Davison Maruziva, editor of the privately owned weekly newspaper *The Standard*, over its publication of an opinion piece by Arthur Mutambara, leader of one of the MDC formations. He was charged with "publishing false statements prejudicial to the state and contempt

Z

of court". On 20 April, *The Standard* had published an article criticizing a High Court judgment dismissing an application by the MDC to compel the Zimbabwe Electoral Commission to release the delayed results of the 29 March presidential elections. Arthur Mutambara was arrested again over this article on 1 June.

Human rights defenders

Human rights defenders continued to face unlawful restrictions in carrying out their work.

■ On 25 April, police officers raided the Harare offices of the non-governmental Zimbabwe Election Support Network (ZESN), and took away files and documents. The home of Rindai Chipfunde-Vava, the ZESN national director, was also raided. On 28 April Rindai Chipfunde-Vava and the organization's chairperson, Noel Kututwa, were interrogated by police from the Law and Order section. From 28 to 30 April, Noel Kututwa and Rindai Chipfunde-Vava were ordered to report to Harare Central police station. Police also told ZESN to provide a list of the 11,000 local observers it had deployed during the 29 March election, names of board members, and sources of funding, including bank accounts.

■ Lovemore Matombo, President of the Zimbabwe Congress of Trade Unions (ZCTU), and Wellington Chibebe, Secretary General of the ZCTU, were arrested on 8 May on charges of "communicating falsehoods prejudicial to the state" following speeches made during May Day celebrations in Harare. On 12 May they appeared before a magistrate and were denied bail and initially remanded in custody until 23 May at Harare Central Remand Prison. However, after appealing they were granted bail by a High Court Judge on 19 May.

■ On 28 May, police in Harare arrested 14 members of the activist organization Women of Zimbabwe Arise (WOZA) during a peaceful march to the Zambian embassy to hand in a petition. The petition called on Zambia, which was then chair of SADC, to help bring an end to the state-sponsored violence. Leaders of the organization Jenni Williams and Magodonga Mahlangu were detained for 37 days at Chikurubi Female Prison, whilst the other 12 were detained for 17 days.

■ Jenni Williams and Magodonga Mahlangu were again arrested in Bulawayo on 16 October after participating in a demonstration highlighting the suffering of ordinary Zimbabweans. Police beat protesters while breaking up the peaceful protest. The two women were arrested together with seven other

WOZA activists who were released on the same day. However, Jenni Williams and Magodonga Mahlangu were denied bail and spent three weeks in Mlondolozi prison until they were granted bail by the High Court and released on 6 November.

■ In Harare on 27 October, 42 women taking part in a demonstration organized by the Women's Coalition of Zimbabwe (WCoZ) were arrested by police. Police used tear gas and baton sticks to break up the peaceful protest. Among those arrested was the National Coordinator of WCoZ, Netsai Mushonga. The women were released after being made to pay admission of guilt fines. The march was organized to draw attention to hunger in Zimbabwe and the repeated failure of regional leaders to find a solution.

■ On 11 November, 29 members of the National Constitutional Assembly (NCA) were arrested by police in Bulawayo, Gweru, Harare and Mutare after taking part in a protest over the worsening humanitarian situation and the need for a transitional government and a new constitution. On the same day the NCA's chairman, Dr Lovemore Madhuku, was detained for four hours at Harare Central police station. In Mutare, Stewart Muzambi, Never Mujokochi, Louis Dzinokuzara, Trust Zamba, Cynthia Chizaza, Catherine Chanza and three others were detained at Mutare Central police station and reportedly assaulted while in police custody. Police also used excessive force to break up the demonstrations. One of the eight people detained at Harare Central police station was denied access to medical treatment for a cut on his scalp. Some of the detainees were released after paying admission of guilt fines while those detained in Gweru were charged under the Public Order and Security Act.

Amnesty International visits/reports

🚃 Amnesty International delegates visited Zimbabwe in March and July/August. A mission planned for December was restricted to South Africa after the high-profile abductions of human rights defenders by people believed to be working on behalf of or with the acquiescence of the Zimbabwean authorities.

📄 Zimbabwe: A trail of violence after the ballot (AFR 46/014/2008)
📄 Zimbabwe: Time for accountability (AFR 46/028/2008)

Z

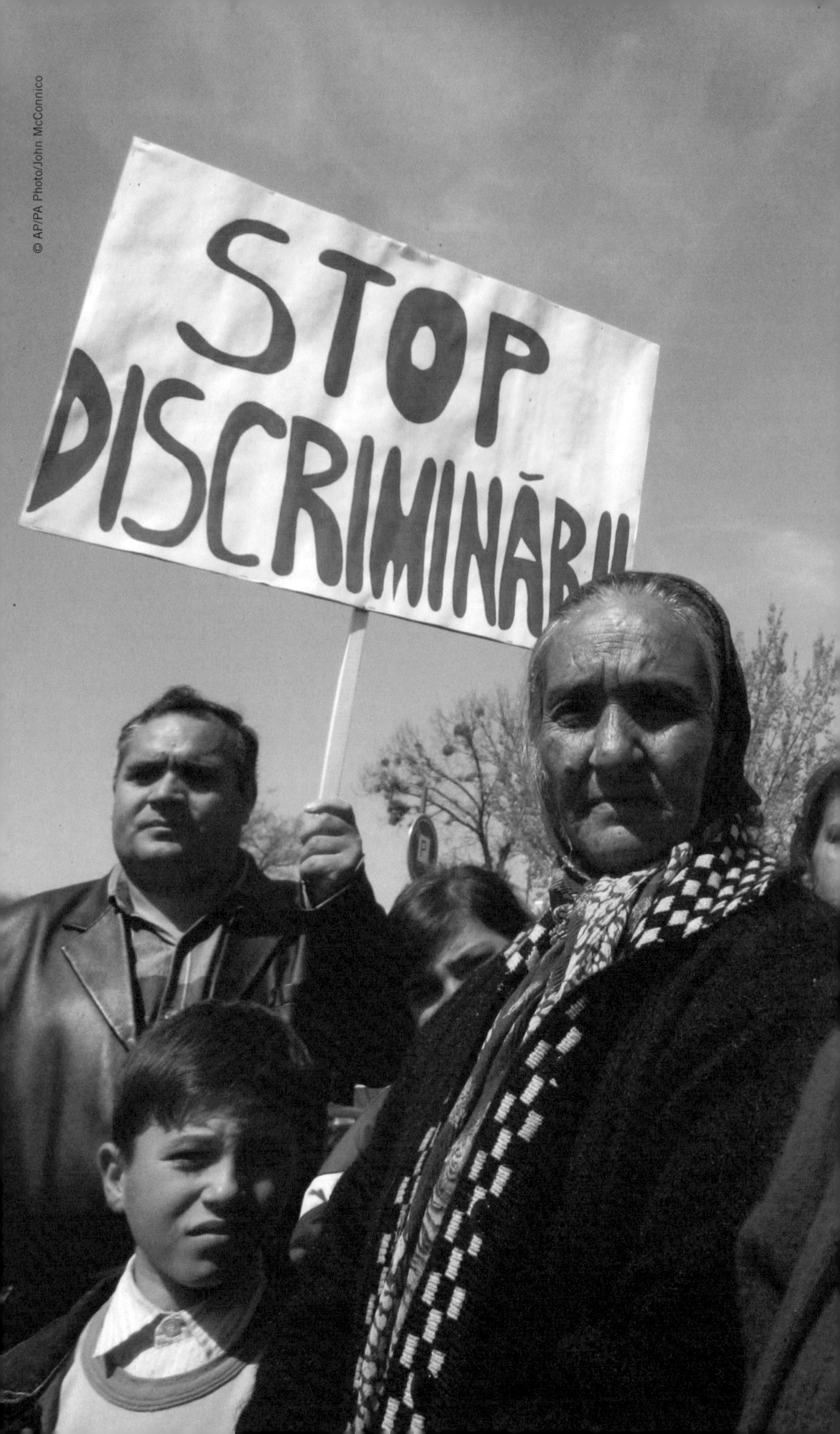
STOP
DISCRIMINĂRII

Roma march through the streets
of Chişinău, Moldova, on 8 April
2008 – International Roma Day.
Roma are among the most
discriminated against in Europe.

AMNESTY INTERNATIONAL REPORT 2009
PART THREE: SELECTED HUMAN RIGHTS TREATIES

Local residents search for survivors after a rockslide killed more than 100 people in Al-Duwayqah on the outskirts of Cairo, 6 September 2008. Millions of people live in informal settlements (ashwaiyyat) in Egypt, often without access to basic services.

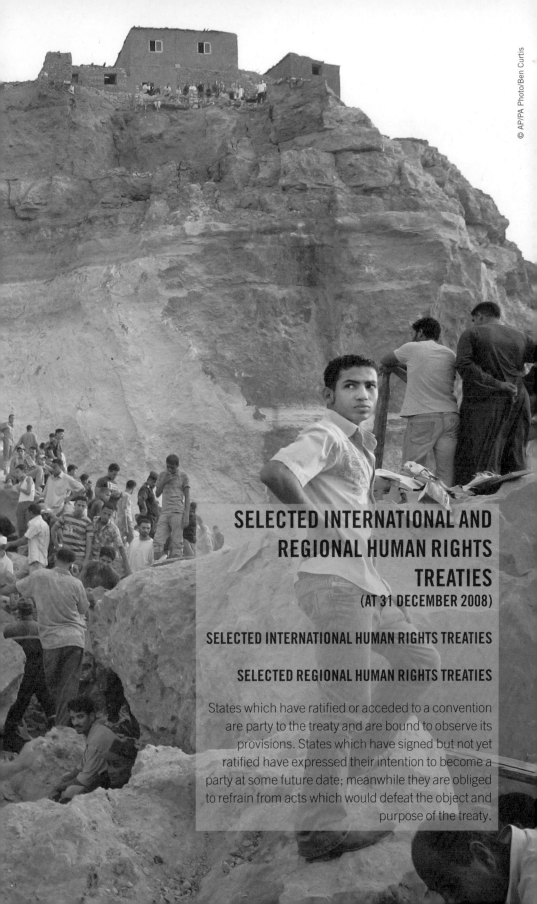

SELECTED INTERNATIONAL AND REGIONAL HUMAN RIGHTS TREATIES
(AT 31 DECEMBER 2008)

SELECTED INTERNATIONAL HUMAN RIGHTS TREATIES

SELECTED REGIONAL HUMAN RIGHTS TREATIES

States which have ratified or acceded to a convention are party to the treaty and are bound to observe its provisions. States which have signed but not yet ratified have expressed their intention to become a party at some future date; meanwhile they are obliged to refrain from acts which would defeat the object and purpose of the treaty.

	International Covenant on Civil and Political Rights (ICCPR)	(first) Optional Protocol to the ICCPR	Second Optional Protocol to the ICCPR, aiming at the abolition of the death penalty	International Covenant on Economic, Social and Cultural Rights	Convention on the Elimination of All Forms of Discrimination against Women (CEDAW)	Optional Protocol to CEDAW	Convention on the Rights of the Child (CRC)	Optional Protocol to the CRC on the involvement of chidren in armed conflict	International Convention on the Elimination of All Forms of Racial Discrimination	Convention against Torture and Other Cruel, Inhuman or Degrading Treatment or Punishment
Afghanistan	●			●	●		●	●	●	●28
Albania	●	●	●	●	●	●	●	◐	●	●
Algeria	●	●		●	●		●		●	●22
Andorra	●	●	●	●	●	●	●	●	●	●22
Angola	●	●		●	●	●	●	●	●	
Antigua and Barbuda					●	●	●		●	●
Argentina	●	●	◐	●	●	●	●	●	●	●22
Armenia	●	●		●	●	●	●	●	●	●
Australia	●	●	●	●	●	◐	●	●	●	●22
Austria	●	●	●	●	●	●	●	●	●	●22
Azerbaijan	●	●	●	●	●	●	●	●	●	●22
Bahamas	◐			◐	●		●		●	○
Bahrain	●			●	●		●		●	●
Bangladesh	●			●	●	●10	●		●	●
Barbados	●	●		●	●		●		●	
Belarus	●	●		●	●	●	●	●	●	●
Belgium	●	●	●	●	●	●	●	●	●	●22
Belize	●			○	●	●10	●	●	●	●
Benin	●	●		●	●	○	●	●	●	●
Bhutan					●		●	○	○	
Bolivia	●	●		●	●	●	●	●	●	●22
Bosnia and Herzegovina	●	●	●	●	●	●	●	●	●	●22
Botswana	●				●		●	●	●	●
Brazil	●			●	●	●	●	●	●	●22
Brunei Darussalam					●		●			
Bulgaria	●	●	●	●	●	●	●	●	●	●22
Burkina Faso	●	●		●	●	●	●	●	●	●
Burundi	●			●	●	○	●	◐	●	●22

Optional Protocol to the Convention against Torture	International Convention for the Protection of All Persons from Enforced Disappearance (not yet into force)	Convention relating to the Status of Refugees (1951)	Protocol relating to the Status of Refugees (1967)	Convention relating to the Status of Stateless Persons (1954)	Convention on the Reduction of Statelessness (1961)	International Convention on the Protection of the Rights of All Migrant Workers and Members of their Families	Rome Statute of the International Criminal Court	
		●	●				●	Afghanistan
●	●	●	●	●	●	●	●	Albania
	○	●	●	●		●	○	Algeria
							●	Andorra
		●	●				○	Angola
		●	●	●			●	Antigua and Barbuda
●	●	●	●	●		●	●	Argentina
●	○	●	●	●	●		○	Armenia
		●	●	●	●		●	Australia
○	○	●	●	◉	●		●	Austria
○	○	●	●	●	●	●		Azerbaijan
		●	●				○	Bahamas
							○	Bahrain
						○	○	Bangladesh
				●			●	Barbados
		●	●					Belarus
○	○	●	●	●			●	Belgium
		●	●	●		●	●	Belize
●		●	●			○	●	Benin
								Bhutan
●	◉	●	●	●	●	●	●	Bolivia
◉	○	●	●	●	●	●	●	Bosnia and Herzegovina
		●	●	●			●	Botswana
●	○	●	●	●	●		●	Brazil
								Brunei Darussalam
	○	●	●				●	Bulgaria
○	○	●	●			●	●	Burkina Faso
	○	●	●				●	Burundi

● state is a party

◉ state became party in 2008

○ signed but not yet ratified

○ signed in 2008, but not yet ratified

10 Declaration under Article 10 not recognizing the competence of the CEDAW Committee to undertake confidential inquiries into allegations of grave or systematic violations

22 Declaration under Article 22 recognizing the competence of the Committee against Torture (CAT) to consider individual complaints

28 Reservation under Article 28 not recognizing the competence of the CAT to undertake confidential inquiries into allegations of systematic torture if warranted

12 Declaration under Article 12(3) accepting the jurisdiction of the International Criminal Court (ICC) for crimes in its territory

124 Declaration under Article 124 not accepting the jurisdiction of the ICC over war crimes for seven years after ratification

* Signed the Rome Statute but have since formally declared their intention not to ratify

** Acceded in 1962 but in 1965 denounced the Convention; denunciation took effect on 2 April 1966

	International Covenant on Civil and Political Rights (ICCPR)	(first) Optional Protocol to the ICCPR	Second Optional Protocol to the ICCPR, aiming at the abolition of the death penalty	International Covenant on Economic, Social and Cultural Rights	Convention on the Elimination of All Forms of Discrimination against Women (CEDAW)	Optional Protocol to CEDAW	Convention on the Rights of the Child (CRC)	Optional Protocol to the CRC on the involvement of chidren in armed conflict	International Convention on the Elimination of All Forms of Racial Discrimination	Convention against Torture and Other Cruel, Inhuman or Degrading Treatment or Punishment
Cambodia	●	○		●	●	○	●	●	●	●
Cameroon	●	●		●	●	●	●	○	●	●[22]
Canada	●	●	●	●	●	●	●	●	●	●[22]
Cape Verde	●	●	●	●	●		●	●	●	●
Central African Republic	●	●		●	●		●		●	
Chad	●	●		●	●		●	●	●	●
Chile	●	●	◐	●	●	○	●	●	●	●[22]
China	○			●	●		●	◐	●	●[28]
Colombia	●	●	●	●	●	●[10]	●	●	●	●
Comoros	○			○	●		●		●	○
Congo (Republic of)	●	●		●	●	○	●		●	●
Cook Islands					●	●	●			
Costa Rica	●	●	●	●	●	●	●	●	●	●[22]
Côte d'Ivoire	●			●	●		●		●	●
Croatia	●	●	●	●	●	●	●	●	●	●[22]
Cuba	○			○	●	○	●	●	●	●[28]
Cyprus	●	●	●	●	●	●	●	○	●	●[22]
Czech Republic	●	●	●	●	●	●	●	●	●	●[22]
Democratic Republic of the Congo	●	●		●	●		●	●	●	●
Denmark	●	●	●	●	●	●	●	●	●	●[22]
Djibouti	●	●	●		●		●	○	○	●
Dominica	●			●	●		●	●		
Dominican Republic	●	●		●	●	●	●	○	●	○
Ecuador	●	●	●	●	●	●	●	●	●	●[22]
Egypt	●			●	●		●	●	●	●
El Salvador	●	●		●	●	○	●	●	●	●
Equatorial Guinea	●	●		●	●		●		●	●[28]
Eritrea	●			●	●		●	●	●	

Optional Protocol to the Convention against Torture	International Convention for the Protection of All Persons from Enforced Disappearance (not yet into force)	Convention relating to the Status of Refugees (1951)	Protocol relating to the Status of Refugees (1967)	Convention relating to the Status of Stateless Persons (1954)	Convention on the Reduction of Statelessness (1961)	International Convention on the Protection of the Rights of All Migrant Workers and Members of their Families	Rome Statute of the International Criminal Court	
●		●	●			○	●	Cambodia
		●	●				○	Cameroon
		●	●		●		●	Canada
	○		●			●	○	Cape Verde
		●	●				●	Central African Republic
	○	●	●	●	●		●	Chad
◐	○	●	●			●	○	Chile
		●	●					China
	○	●	●	○		●	●124	Colombia
	○					○	●	Comoros
○	○	●	●			○		Congo (Republic of)
							◐	Cook Islands
●	○	●	●	●	●		●	Costa Rica
		●	●				○12	Côte d'Ivoire
●	○	●	●	●			●	Croatia
	○							Cuba
○	○	●	●				●	Cyprus
●		●	●	●	●		○	Czech Republic
		●	●				●	Democratic Republic of the Congo
●	○	●	●	●	●		●	Denmark
		●	●				●	Djibouti
		●	●				●	Dominica
		●	●		○		●	Dominican Republic
○	○	●	●	●		●	●	Ecuador
		●	●			●	○	Egypt
		●	●	○		●		El Salvador
		●	●					Equatorial Guinea
							○	Eritrea

Legend:

● state is a party
◐ state became party in 2008
○ signed but not yet ratified
◌ signed in 2008, but not yet ratified

10 Declaration under Article 10 not recognizing the competence of the CEDAW Committee to undertake confidential inquiries into allegations of grave or systematic violations

22 Declaration under Article 22 recognizing the competence of the Committee against Torture (CAT) to consider individual complaints

28 Reservation under Article 28 not recognizing the competence of the CAT to undertake confidential inquiries into allegations of systematic torture if warranted

12 Declaration under Article 12(3) accepting the jurisdiction of the International Criminal Court (ICC) for crimes in its territory

124 Declaration under Article 124 not accepting the jurisdiction of the ICC over war crimes for seven years after ratification

* Signed the Rome Statute but have since formally declared their intention not to ratify

** Acceded in 1962 but in 1965 denounced the Convention; denunciation took effect on 2 April 1966

	International Covenant on Civil and Political Rights (ICCPR)	(first) Optional Protocol to the ICCPR	Second Optional Protocol to the ICCPR, aiming at the abolition of the death penalty	International Covenant on Economic, Social and Cultural Rights	Convention on the Elimination of All Forms of Discrimination against Women (CEDAW)	Optional Protocol to CEDAW	Convention on the Rights of the Child (CRC)	Optional Protocol to the CRC on the involvement of chidren in armed conflict	International Convention on the Elimination of All Forms of Racial Discrimination	Convention against Torture and Other Cruel, Inhuman or Degrading Treatment or Punishment
Estonia	●	●	●	●	●		●	○	●	●
Ethiopia	●			●	●		●		●	●
Fiji					●		●	○	●	
Finland	●	●	●	●	●	●	●	●	●	●[22]
France	●	●	●	●	●	●	●	●	●	●[22]
Gabon	●			●	●	●	●	○	●	●
Gambia	●	●		●	●		●	○	●	○
Georgia	●	●	●	●	●	●	●		●	●[22]
Germany	●	●	●	●	●	●	●	●	●	●[22]
Ghana	●	●		●	●	○	●	○	●	●[22]
Greece	●	●	●	●	●	●	●	●	●	●[22]
Grenada	●			●	●		●		○	
Guatemala	●	●		●	●	●	●	●	●	●[22]
Guinea	●	●		●	●		●		●	●
Guinea-Bissau	○	○	○	●	●	○	●	○	○	○
Guyana	●	●		●	●		●		●	●
Haiti	●				●		●	○	●	
Holy See							●	●	●	●
Honduras	●	●	●	●	●		●	●	●	●
Hungary	●	●	●	●	●	●	●	○	●	●[22]
Iceland	●	●	●	●	●	●	●	●	●	●[22]
India	●			●	●		●	●	●	○
Indonesia	●			●	●	○	●	○	●	●
Iran	●			●			●		●	
Iraq	●			●	●		●	●	●	
Ireland	●	●	●	●	●	●	●	●	●	●[22]
Israel	●			●	●		●	●	●	●[28]
Italy	●	●	●	●	●	●	●	●	●	●[22]

Optional Protocol to the Convention against Torture	International Convention for the Protection of All Persons from Enforced Disappearance (not yet into force)	Convention relating to the Status of Refugees (1951)	Protocol relating to the Status of Refugees (1967)	Convention relating to the Status of Stateless Persons (1954)	Convention on the Reduction of Statelessness (1961)	International Convention on the Protection of the Rights of All Migrant Workers and Members of their Families	Rome Statute of the International Criminal Court	
●		●	●				●	Estonia
		●	●					Ethiopia
		●	●	●			●	Fiji
○	○	●	●	●	◐		●	Finland
◐	◐	●	●	●	○		●124	France
○	○	●	●			○	●	Gabon
		●	●					Gambia
●		●	●				●	Georgia
◐	○	●	●	●	●		●	Germany
○	○	●	●			●	●	Ghana
	○	●	●	●			●	Greece
	○							Grenada
◐	○	●	●	●	●	●		Guatemala
○		●	●	●		●	●	Guinea
		●	●			○	○	Guinea-Bissau
						○	●	Guyana
	○	●	●				○	Haiti
		●	●	○				Holy See
●	◐	●	●	○		●	●	Honduras
		●	●	●			●	Hungary
○	○	●	●				●	Iceland
	○							India
						○		Indonesia
		●	●				○	Iran
								Iraq
○	○	●	●	●	●		●	Ireland
		●	●	●	○		○*	Israel
○	○	●	●	●			●	Italy

● state is a party
◐ state became party in 2008
○ signed but not yet ratified
○ signed in 2008, but not yet ratified

10 Declaration under Article 10 not recognizing the competence of the CEDAW Committee to undertake confidential inquiries into allegations of grave or systematic violations

22 Declaration under Article 22 recognizing the competence of the Committee against Torture (CAT) to consider individual complaints

28 Reservation under Article 28 not recognizing the competence of the CAT to undertake confidential inquiries into allegations of systematic torture if warranted

12 Declaration under Article 12(3) accepting the jurisdiction of the International Criminal Court (ICC) for crimes in its territory

124 Declaration under Article 124 not accepting the jurisdiction of the ICC over war crimes for seven years after ratification

* Signed the Rome Statute but have since formally declared their intention not to ratify

** Acceded in 1962 but in 1965 denounced the Convention; denunciation took effect on 2 April 1966

	International Covenant on Civil and Political Rights (ICCPR)	(first) Optional Protocol to the ICCPR	Second Optional Protocol to the ICCPR, aiming at the abolition of the death penalty	International Covenant on Economic, Social and Cultural Rights	Convention on the Elimination of All Forms of Discrimination against Women (CEDAW)	Optional Protocol to CEDAW	Convention on the Rights of the Child (CRC)	Optional Protocol to the CRC on the involvement of chidren in armed conflict	International Convention on the Elimination of All Forms of Racial Discrimination	Convention against Torture and Other Cruel, Inhuman or Degrading Treatment or Punishment
Jamaica	●			●	●		●	●	●	
Japan	●			●	●		●	●	●	●
Jordan	●			●	●		●	●	●	●
Kazakstan	●	○		●	●	●	●	●	●	●22
Kenya	●			●	●		●	●	●	●
Kiribati					●		●			
Korea (Democratic People's Republic of)	●			●	●		●			
Korea (Republic of)	●	●		●	●	●	●	●	●	●22
Kuwait	●			●	●		●	●	●	●28
Kyrgyzstan	●	●		●	●	●	●	●	●	●
Laos	○			●	●		●	●	●	
Latvia	●	●		●	●		●	●	●	●
Lebanon	●			●	●		●	○	●	●
Lesotho	●	●		●	●	●	●	●	●	●
Liberia	●	○	●	●	●	○	●	○	●	●
Libya	●	●		●	●	●	●	●	●	●
Liechtenstein	●	●	●	●	●	●	●	●	●	●22
Lithuania	●	●	●	●	●	●	●	●	●	●
Luxembourg	●	●	●	●	●	●	●	●	●	●22
Macedonia	●	●	●	●	●	●	●	●	●	●
Madagascar	●	●		●	●	○	●	●	●	●
Malawi	●	●		●	●	○	●	○	●	●
Malaysia					●		●			
Maldives	●	●		●	●	●	●	●	●	●
Mali	●	●		●	●	●	●	●	●	●
Malta	●	●	●	●	●		●	●	●	●22
Marshall Islands					●		●			
Mauritania	●			●	●		●		●	●28

Optional Protocol to the Convention against Torture	International Convention for the Protection of All Persons from Enforced Disappearance (not yet into force)	Convention relating to the Status of Refugees (1951)	Protocol relating to the Status of Refugees (1967)	Convention relating to the Status of Stateless Persons (1954)	Convention on the Reduction of Statelessness (1961)	International Convention on the Protection of the Rights of All Migrant Workers and Members of their Families	Rome Statute of the International Criminal Court	
		●	●			⬤	○	Jamaica
	○	●	●				●	Japan
							●	Jordan
⬤		●	●					Kazakstan
	○	●	●					Kenya
				●	●			Kiribati
								Korea (Democratic People's Republic of)
		●	●	●			●	Korea (Republic of)
							○	Kuwait
		●	●			●	○	Kyrgyzstan
	○							Laos
		●	●	●	●		●	Latvia
⬤	○							Lebanon
		●	●	●	●	●	●	Lesotho
●		●	●	●	●	○	●	Liberia
				●	●	●		Libya
●	○	●	●	○			●	Liechtenstein
	○	●	●	●			●	Lithuania
○	○	●	●	●			●	Luxembourg
○	○	●	●	●			●	Macedonia
○	○	●		**			⬤	Madagascar
	●	●					●	Malawi
								Malaysia
●	○							Maldives
●	○	●	●			●	●	Mali
●	○	●	●				●	Malta
							●	Marshall Islands
		●	●			●		Mauritania

● state is a party
⬤ state became party in 2008
○ signed but not yet ratified
○ signed in 2008, but not yet ratified

10 Declaration under Article 10 not recognizing the competence of the CEDAW Committee to undertake confidential inquiries into allegations of grave or systematic violations

22 Declaration under Article 22 recognizing the competence of the Committee against Torture (CAT) to consider individual complaints

28 Reservation under Article 28 not recognizing the competence of the CAT to undertake confidential inquiries into allegations of systematic torture if warranted

12 Declaration under Article 12(3) accepting the jurisdiction of the International Criminal Court (ICC) for crimes in its territory

124 Declaration under Article 124 not accepting the jurisdiction of the ICC over war crimes for seven years after ratification

* Signed the Rome Statute but have since formally declared their intention not to ratify

** Acceded in 1962 but in 1965 denounced the Convention; denunciation took effect on 2 April 1966

	International Covenant on Civil and Political Rights (ICCPR)	(first) Optional Protocol to the ICCPR	Second Optional Protocol to the ICCPR, aiming at the abolition of the death penalty	International Covenant on Economic, Social and Cultural Rights	Convention on the Elimination of All Forms of Discrimination against Women (CEDAW)	Optional Protocol to CEDAW	Convention on the Rights of the Child (CRC)	Optional Protocol to the CRC on the involvement of chidren in armed conflict	International Convention on the Elimination of All Forms of Racial Discrimination	Convention against Torture and Other Cruel, Inhuman or Degrading Treatment or Punishment
Mauritius	●	●		●	●	◐	●	○	●	●
Mexico	●	●	●	●	●	●	●	●	●	●22
Micronesia					●		●	○		
Moldova	●	◐	●	●	●	●	●	●	●	●
Monaco	●		●	●	●		●	●	●	●22
Mongolia	●	●		●	●	●	●	●	●	●
Montenegro	●	●	●	●	●	●	●	●	●	●22
Morocco	●			●	●		●	●	●	●22
Mozambique	●		●		●	◐	●	●	●	●
Myanmar					●		●			
Namibia	●	●	●	●	●	●	●	●	●	●
Nauru	○	○					●	○	○	○
Nepal	●	●	●	●	●	●	●	●	●	●
Netherlands	●	●	●	●	●	●	●	○	●	●22
New Zealand	●	●	●	●	●	●	●	●	●	●22
Nicaragua	●	●	○	●	●		●	●	●	●
Niger	●	●		●	●	●	●		●	●
Nigeria	●			●	●	●	●	○	●	●
Niue							●			
Norway	●	●	●	●	●	●	●	●	●	●22
Oman					●		●	●	●	
Pakistan	○			◐	●		●	○	●	○
Palau							●			
Panama	●	●	●	●	●	●	●	●	●	●
Papua New Guinea	◐			◐	●		●		●	
Paraguay	●	●	●	●	●	●	●	●	●	●22
Peru	●	●		●	●	●	●	●	●	●22
Philippines	●	●	●	●	●	●	●	●	●	●

Optional Protocol to the Convention against Torture	International Convention for the Protection of All Persons from Enforced Disappearance (not yet into force)	Convention relating to the Status of Refugees (1951)	Protocol relating to the Status of Refugees (1967)	Convention relating to the Status of Stateless Persons (1954)	Convention on the Reduction of Statelessness (1961)	International Convention on the Protection of the Rights of All Migrant Workers and Members of their Families	Rome Statute of the International Criminal Court	
●							●	Mauritius
●	◐	●	●	●		●	●	Mexico
								Micronesia
●	○	●	●				○	Moldova
	○	●					○	Monaco
	○						●	Mongolia
○	○	●	●	●		○	●	Montenegro
	○	●	●			●	○	Morocco
	○	●	●				○	Mozambique
								Myanmar
		●	●				●	Namibia
							●	Nauru
								Nepal
○	○	●	●	●	●		●	Netherlands
●		●	●		●		●	New Zealand
○		●	●			●		Nicaragua
	○	●	●		●		●	Niger
		●	●					Nigeria
								Niue
○	○	●	●	●	●		●	Norway
							○	Oman
								Pakistan
								Palau
	○	●	●				●	Panama
		●	●					Papua New Guinea
●	○	●	●			◐	●	Paraguay
●		●	●			●	●	Peru
		●	●	○		●	○	Philippines

● state is a party
◐ state became party in 2008
○ signed but not yet ratified
○ signed in 2008, but not yet ratified

10 Declaration under Article 10 not recognizing the competence of the CEDAW Committee to undertake confidential inquiries into allegations of grave or systematic violations

22 Declaration under Article 22 recognizing the competence of the Committee against Torture (CAT) to consider individual complaints

28 Reservation under Article 28 not recognizing the competence of the CAT to undertake confidential inquiries into allegations of systematic torture if warranted

12 Declaration under Article 12(3) accepting the jurisdiction of the International Criminal Court (ICC) for crimes in its territory

124 Declaration under Article 124 not accepting the jurisdiction of the ICC over war crimes for seven years after ratification

* Signed the Rome Statute but have since formally declared their intention not to ratify

** Acceded in 1962 but in 1965 denounced the Convention; denunciation took effect on 2 April 1966

	International Covenant on Civil and Political Rights (ICCPR)	(first) Optional Protocol to the ICCPR	Second Optional Protocol to the ICCPR, aiming at the abolition of the death penalty	International Covenant on Economic, Social and Cultural Rights	Convention on the Elimination of All Forms of Discrimination against Women (CEDAW)	Optional Protocol to CEDAW	Convention on the Rights of the Child (CRC)	Optional Protocol to the CRC on the involvement of chidren in armed conflict	International Convention on the Elimination of All Forms of Racial Discrimination	Convention against Torture and Other Cruel, Inhuman or Degrading Treatment or Punishment
Poland	●	●	○	●	●	●	●	●	●	●28 22
Portugal	●	●	●	●	●	●	●	●	●	●22
Qatar					●		●		●	●
Romania	●	●	●	●	●	●	●	●	●	●
Russian Federation	●	●		●	●	●	●	◓	●	●22
Rwanda	●		◓	●	●	◓	●	●	●	◓
Saint Kitts and Nevis					●	●	●		●	
Saint Lucia					●		●		●	
Saint Vincent and the Grenadines	●	●		●	●		●		●	●
Samoa	◓				●		●			
San Marino	●	●	●	●	●	●	●	○	●	●
Sao Tome and Principe	○	○	○	○	●	○	●		○	○
Saudi Arabia					●		●		●	●28
Senegal	●	●		●	●	●	●	●	●	●22
Serbia	●	●	●	●	●	●	●	●	●	●22
Seychelles	●	●	●	●	●	○	●	○	●	●22
Sierra Leone	●	●		●	●	○	●	●	●	●
Singapore					●		●	◓		
Slovakia	●	●	●	●	●	●	●	●	●	●22
Slovenia	●	●	●	●	●	●	●	●	●	●22
Solomon Islands				●	●	●	●			
Somalia	●	●		●			○	○	●	●
South Africa	●	●	●	○	●	●	●	○	●	●22
Spain	●	●	●	●	●	●	●	●	●	●22
Sri Lanka	●	●		●	●	●	●	●	●	●
Sudan	●			●			●	●	●	○
Suriname	●	●		●	●		●	○	●	
Swaziland	●			●	●		●		●	●

SELECTED TREATIES

INTERNATIONAL

Optional Protocol to the Convention against Torture	International Convention for the Protection of All Persons from Enforced Disappearance (not yet into force)	Convention relating to the Status of Refugees (1951)	Protocol relating to the Status of Refugees (1967)	Convention relating to the Status of Stateless Persons (1954)	Convention on the Reduction of Statelessness (1961)	International Convention on the Protection of the Rights of All Migrant Workers and Members of their Families	Rome Statute of the International Criminal Court	
●		●	●				●	Poland
○	○	●	●				●	Portugal
								Qatar
○	○	●	●	●	●		●	Romania
		●	●				○	Russian Federation
		●	●	●	●	◐		Rwanda
		●					●	Saint Kitts and Nevis
							○	Saint Lucia
		●	●	●			●	Saint Vincent and the Grenadines
	○	●	●				●	Samoa
							●	San Marino
		●	●			○	○	Sao Tome and Principe
								Saudi Arabia
●	◐	●	●	●	●	●	●	Senegal
●	○	●	●	●		○	●	Serbia
		●	●			●	○	Seychelles
○	○	●	●			○	●	Sierra Leone
								Singapore
	○	●	●	●	●		●	Slovakia
●	○	●	●	●			●	Slovenia
		●	●				○	Solomon Islands
		●	●					Somalia
○		●	●				●	South Africa
●	○	●	●	●			●	Spain
						●		Sri Lanka
		●	●				○*	Sudan
		●	●				◐	Suriname
	○	●	●	●	●			Swaziland

● state is a party
◐ state became party in 2008
○ signed but not yet ratified
◌ signed in 2008, but not yet ratified

10 Declaration under Article 10 not recognizing the competence of the CEDAW Committee to undertake confidential inquiries into allegations of grave or systematic violations

22 Declaration under Article 22 recognizing the competence of the Committee against Torture (CAT) to consider individual complaints

28 Reservation under Article 28 not recognizing the competence of the CAT to undertake confidential inquiries into allegations of systematic torture if warranted

12 Declaration under Article 12(3) accepting the jurisdiction of the International Criminal Court (ICC) for crimes in its territory

124 Declaration under Article 124 not accepting the jurisdiction of the ICC over war crimes for seven years after ratification

* Signed the Rome Statute but have since formally declared their intention not to ratify

** Acceded in 1962 but in 1965 denounced the Convention; denunciation took effect on 2 April 1966

	International Covenant on Civil and Political Rights (ICCPR)	(first) Optional Protocol to the ICCPR	Second Optional Protocol to the ICCPR, aiming at the abolition of the death penalty	International Covenant on Economic, Social and Cultural Rights	Convention on the Elimination of All Forms of Discrimination against Women (CEDAW)	Optional Protocol to CEDAW	Convention on the Rights of the Child (CRC)	Optional Protocol to the CRC on the involvement of chidren in armed conflict	International Convention on the Elimination of All Forms of Racial Discrimination	Convention against Torture and Other Cruel, Inhuman or Degrading Treatment or Punishment
Sweden	●	●	●	●	●	●	●	●	●	●[22]
Switzerland	●		●	●	●	◐	●	●	●	●[22]
Syria	●			●	●		●	●	●	●[28]
Tajikistan	●	●		●	●	○	●	●	●	●
Tanzania	●			●	●	●	●	●	●	
Thailand	●			●	●	●	●	●		●
Timor-Leste	●		●	●	●	●	●	●	●	●
Togo	●	●		●	●		●	●	●	●[22]
Tonga							●		●	
Trinidad and Tobago	●			●	●		●		●	
Tunisia	●			●	●	◐	●	●	●	●[22]
Turkey	●	●	●	●	●	●	●	●	●	●[22]
Turkmenistan	●	●	●	●	●		●	●	●	●
Tuvalu					●		●			
Uganda	◐	●		●	●		●	●	●	●
Ukraine	●	●	●	●	●	●	●	●	●	●
United Arab Emirates					●		●		●	
United Kingdom	●		●	●	●	●	●	●	●	●
United States of America	●			○	○		○	●	●	●
Uruguay	●	●	●	●	●	●	●	●	●	●[22]
Uzbekistan	●	●	◐	●	●		●	◐	●	●
Vanuatu	◐				●	●	●	●		
Venezuela	●	●	●	●	●	●	●	●	●	●[22]
Viet Nam	●			●	●		●	●	●	
Yemen	●			●	●		●	●	●	●
Zambia	●	●		●	●	○	●	○	●	●
Zimbabwe	●			●	●		●		●	

Optional Protocol to the Convention against Torture	International Convention for the Protection of All Persons from Enforced Disappearance (not yet into force)	Convention relating to the Status of Refugees (1951)	Protocol relating to the Status of Refugees (1967)	Convention relating to the Status of Stateless Persons (1954)	Convention on the Reduction of Statelessness (1961)	International Convention on the Protection of the Rights of All Migrant Workers and Members of their Families	Rome Statute of the International Criminal Court	
●	○	●	●	●	●		●	Sweden
○		●	●	●			●	Switzerland
						●	○	Syria
		●	●			●	●	Tajikistan
	○	●	●				●	Tanzania
							○	Thailand
○		●	●			●	●	Timor-Leste
○		●	●		○			Togo
								Tonga
		●	●	●			●	Trinidad and Tobago
	○	●	●	●	●			Tunisia
○		●	●			●		Turkey
		●	●					Turkmenistan
		●	●					Tuvalu
	○	●	●	●		●	●	Uganda
●		●	●				○	Ukraine
							○	United Arab Emirates
●		●	●	●	●		●	United Kingdom
			●				○*	United States of America
●	○	●	●	●	●	●	●	Uruguay
							○	Uzbekistan
	○							Vanuatu
	○		●				●	Venezuela
								Viet Nam
		●	●				○	Yemen
		●	●	●			●	Zambia
		●	●	●			○	Zimbabwe

● state is a party
● state became party in 2008
○ signed but not yet ratified
○ signed in 2008, but not yet ratified

10 Declaration under Article 10 not recognizing the competence of the CEDAW Committee to undertake confidential inquiries into allegations of grave or systematic violations

22 Declaration under Article 22 recognizing the competence of the Committee against Torture (CAT) to consider individual complaints

28 Reservation under Article 28 not recognizing the competence of the CAT to undertake confidential inquiries into allegations of systematic torture if warranted

12 Declaration under Article 12(3) accepting the jurisdiction of the International Criminal Court (ICC) for crimes in its territory

124 Declaration under Article 124 not accepting the jurisdiction of the ICC over war crimes for seven years after ratification

* Signed the Rome Statute but have since formally declared their intention not to ratify

** Acceded in 1962 but in 1965 denounced the Convention; denunciation took effect on 2 April 1966

	African Charter on Human and Peoples' Rights (1981)	Protocol to the African Charter on the Establishment of an African Court on Human and Peoples' Rights (1998)	African Charter on the Rights and Welfare of the Child (1990)	Convention Governing the Specific Aspects of Refugee Problems in Africa (1969)	Protocol to the African Charter on Human and Peoples' Rights on the Rights of Women in Africa (2003)
Algeria	●	●	●	●	○
Angola	●	○	●	●	○
Benin	●	○	●	●	●
Botswana	●	○	●	●	
Burkina Faso	●	●	●	●	●
Burundi	●	●	●	●	○
Cameroon	●	○	●	●	○
Cape Verde	●		●	●	●
Central African Republic	●	○	○	●	○
Chad	●	○	●	●	○
Comoros	●	●	●	●	●
Congo (Republic of)	●	○	●	●	○
Côte d'Ivoire	●	●	●	●	○
Democratic Republic of the Congo	●	○		●	○
Djibouti	●	○	○	○	●
Egypt	●	○	●	●	
Equatorial Guinea	●	○	●	●	○
Eritrea	●		●		
Ethiopia	●	○	●	●	○
Gabon	●	●	●	●	○
Gambia	●	●	●	●	●
Ghana	●	●	●	●	○
Guinea	●	○	●	●	○
Guinea-Bissau	●	○	◐	●	○
Kenya	●	●	●	●	○
Lesotho	●	●	●	●	●
Liberia	●	○	◐	●	◐
Libya	●	●	●	●	●
Madagascar	●	○	●	○	○

	African Charter on Human and Peoples' Rights (1981)	Protocol to the African Charter on the Establishment of an African Court on Human and Peoples' Rights (1998)	African Charter on the Rights and Welfare of the Child (1990)	Convention Governing the Specific Aspects of Refugee Problems in Africa (1969)	Protocol to the African Charter on Human and Peoples' Rights on the Rights of Women in Africa (2003)
Malawi	●	○	●	●	●
Mali	●	●	●	●	●
Mauritania	●	●	●	●	●
Mauritius	●	●	●	○	○
Mozambique	●	●	●	●	●
Namibia	●	○	●		●
Niger	●	●	●	●	○
Nigeria	●	●	●	●	●
Rwanda	●	●	●	●	●
Sahrawi Arab Democratic Republic	●		○		○
Sao Tome and Principe	●				
Senegal	●	●	●	●	●
Seychelles	●	○	●	●	●
Sierra Leone	●	○	●	●	○
Somalia	●	○	○	○	○
South Africa	●	●	●	●	●
Sudan	●	○	◐	●	○
Swaziland	●	○	○	●	○
Tanzania	●	●	●	●	●
Togo	●	●	●	●	●
Tunisia	●	●	○	●	
Uganda	●	●	●	●	○
Zambia	●	○	○	●	●
Zimbabwe	●	○	●	●	◐

SELECTED TREATIES
REGIONAL
AFRICAN UNION

● state is a party
◐ state became party in 2008
○ signed but not yet ratified
○ signed in 2008, but not yet ratified

This chart lists countries that were members of the African Union at the end of 2008.

	American Convention on Human Rights (1969)	Protocol to the American Convention on Human Rights to Abolish the Death Penalty (1990)	Additional Protocol to the American Convention on Human Rights in the Area of Economic, Social and Cultural Rights	Inter-American Convention to Prevent and Punish Torture (1985)	Inter-American Convention on Forced Disappearance of Persons (1994)	Inter-American Convention on the Prevention, Punishment and Eradication of Violence Against Women (1994)	Inter-American Convention on the Elimination of All Forms of Discrimination against Persons with Disabilities (1999)
Antigua and Barbuda						●	
Argentina	●62	◐	●	●	●	●	●
Bahamas						●	
Barbados	●62					●	
Belize						●	
Bolivia	●62		●	●	●	●	●
Brazil	●62	●	●	●	○	●	●
Canada							
Chile	●62	◐	○	●	○	●	●
Colombia	●62		●	●	●	●	●
Costa Rica	●62	●	●	●	●	●	●
Cuba*							
Dominica	●					●	○
Dominican Republic	●62		○	●		●	●
Ecuador	●62	●	●	●	●	●	●
El Salvador	●62		●	●		●	●
Grenada	●					●	
Guatemala	●62		●	●	●	●	●
Guyana						●	
Haiti	●62		○	○		●	○
Honduras	●62			○	●	●	
Jamaica	●					●	○
Mexico	●62	●	●	●	●	●	●
Nicaragua	●62	●	○	○	○	●	●
Panama	●62	●	●	●	●	●	●

	American Convention on Human Rights (1969)	Protocol to the American Convention on Human Rights to Abolish the Death Penalty (1990)	Additional Protocol to the American Convention on Human Rights in the Area of Economic, Social and Cultural Rights	Inter-American Convention to Prevent and Punish Torture (1985)	Inter-American Convention on Forced Disappearance of Persons (1994)	Inter-American Convention on the Prevention, Punishment and Eradication of Violence Against Women (1994)	Inter-American Convention on the Elimination of All Forms of Discrimination against Persons with Disabilities (1999)
Paraguay	●62	●	●	●	●	●	●
Peru	●62		●	●	●	●	●
St. Kitts and Nevis						●	
Saint Lucia						●	
St. Vincent and the Grenadines						●	
Suriname	●62		●	●		●	
Trinidad and Tobago						●	
United States of America	○						
Uruguay	●62	●	●	●	●	●	●
Venezuela	●62	●	○	●	●	●	●

● state is a party
● state became party in 2008
○ signed but not yet ratified
○ signed in 2008, but not yet ratified

This chart lists countries that were members of the Organization of American States at the end of 2008.

62 Countries making a Declaration under Article 62 recognize as binding the jurisdiction of the Inter-American Court of Human Rights (on all matters relating to the interpretation or application of the American Convention)

* In 1962 the VIII Meeting of Consultation of Ministers of Foreign Affairs decided to exclude Cuba from participating in the Inter-American system.

	European Convention for the Protection of Human Rights and Fundamental Freedoms (ECHR) (1950)	Protocol No. 6 to the ECHR concerning the abolition of the death penalty in times of peace (1983)	Protocol No. 12 to the ECHR concerning the general prohibition of discrimination (2000)	Protocol No. 13 to the ECHR concerning the abolition of the death penalty in all circumstances (2002)	Framework Convention on the Protection of National Minorities (1995)	Council of Europe Convention on Action against Trafficking in Human Beings	European Social Charter (revised) (1996)	Additional Protocol to the European Social Charter Providing for a System of Collective Complaints (1995)
Albania	●	●	●	●	●	●	●	
Andorra	●	●	◐	●		○	●	
Armenia	●	●	●	○	●	◐	●	
Austria	●	●	○	●	●		○*	○
Azerbaijan	●	●	○		●		●	
Belgium	●	●	○	●	○	○	●	●
Bosnia and Herzegovina	●	●	●	●	●	◐	◐	
Bulgaria	●	●		●	●	●	●	**
Croatia	●	●	●	●	●	●	*	●
Cyprus	●	●	●	●	●	●	●	●
Czech Republic	●	●	○	●	●		○*	○
Denmark	●	●		●	●	●	○*	○
Estonia	●	●	○		●		●	
Finland	●	●	●	●	●	○	●	●
France	●	●		●		◐	●	●
Georgia	●	●	●	●	●	●	●	
Germany	●	●	○	●	●	○	○*	
Greece	●	●	○	●	○	○	○*	●
Hungary	●	●	○	●	●	○	○*	○
Iceland	●	●	○	●	○	○	○*	
Ireland	●	●	○	●	●	○	●	●
Italy	●	●	○	○	●	○	●	●
Latvia	●	●	○	○	●	◐	○*	
Liechtenstein	●	●	○	●	●			
Lithuania	●	●		●	●	○	●	

	European Convention for the Protection of Human Rights and Fundamental Freedoms (ECHR) (1950)	Protocol No. 6 to the ECHR concerning the abolition of the death penalty in times of peace (1983)	Protocol No. 12 to the ECHR concerning the general prohibition of discrimination (2000)	Protocol No. 13 to the ECHR concerning the abolition of the death penalty in all circumstances (2002)	Framework Convention on the Protection of National Minorities (1995)	Council of Europe Convention on Action against Trafficking in Human Beings	European Social Charter (revised) (1996)	Additional Protocol to the European Social Charter Providing for a System of Collective Complaints (1995)
Luxembourg	●	●	●	●	○	○	○*	
Macedonia	●	●	●	●	●	○	*	
Malta	●	●		●	●	◐	●	
Moldova	●	●	○	●	●	●	●	
Monaco	●	●		●			○	
Montenegro	●	●	●	●	●	◐	○	
Netherlands	●	●	●	●	●	○	●	●
Norway	●	●	○	●	●	◐	●	●
Poland	●	●		○	●	◐	○*	
Portugal	●	●	○	●	●	◐	●	●
Romania	●	●	●	●	●	●	●	
Russian Federation	●	○	○		●		○	
San Marino	●	●	●	●	●	○	○	
Serbia	●	●	●	●	●	○	○	
Slovakia	●	●	○	●	●	●	○*	○
Slovenia	●	●	○	●	●	●	●	○**
Spain	●	●	◐	○	●	○	○*	
Sweden	●	●		●	●	○	●	●
Switzerland	●	●		●	●	○		
Turkey	●	●	○	●			●	
Ukraine	●	●	●	●	●	○	●	
United Kingdom	●	●		●	●	◐	○*	

● state is a party
◐ state became party in 2008
○ signed but not yet ratified
○ signed in 2008, but not yet ratified

This chart lists countries that were members of the Council of Europe at the end of 2008.

* State is a party to the European Social Charter of 1961, which is gradually being replaced by the European Social Charter (revised). The revised Charter embodies in one instrument all rights guaranteed by the Charter of 1961, its Additional Protocol of 1988 and adds new rights and amendments.
** Declaration under Article D of the European Social Charter (revised) recognizing the competence of the European Committee of Social Rights to consider collective complaints.

The Yakye Axa and Sawhoyamaxa have been living beside a highway in Paraguay for over 10 years. Despite court rulings in their favour, they are still waiting for their land claims to be resolved.

AMNESTY INTERNATIONAL REPORT 2009
PART FOUR

Ruins of a home destroyed by Cyclone Nargis. In May 2008, the cyclone devastated parts of southern Myanmar, affecting an estimated 2.4 million people.

AMNESTY INTERNATIONAL
SECTIONS

Algeria ❖ Amnesty International,
10, rue Mouloud ZADI (face au 113 rue
Didouche Mourad),
Alger Centre, 16004 Alger
email: amnestyalgeria@hotmail.com
www.amnestyalgeria.org

Argentina ❖ Amnistía Internacional,
Uruguay 775, 4°B,
C1015ABO Ciudad de Buenos Aires
email: contacto@amnesty.org.ar
www.amnesty.org.ar

Australia ❖ Amnesty International,
Locked Bag 23, Broadway NSW 2007
email: supporter@amnesty.org.au
www.amnesty.org.au

Austria ❖ Amnesty International,
Moeringgasse 10,
A-1150 Vienna
email: info@amnesty.at
www.amnesty.at

Belgium ❖
Amnesty International **(Flemish-speaking)**,
Kerkstraat 156, 2060 Antwerpen
email: amnesty@aivl.be
www.aivl.be
Amnesty International **(francophone)**,
Rue Berckmans 9, 1060 Bruxelles
email: aibf@aibf.be
www.aibf.be

Benin ❖ Amnesty International,
Carré 865, Immeuble François Gomez,
Quartier Aidjedo (une rue après le Centre d'Accueil
en venant de la BIBE),
Cotonou
email: amnestybenin@yahoo.fr

Bermuda ❖ Amnesty International,
PO Box HM 2136, Hamilton HM JX
email: aibda@ibl.bm

Canada ❖
Amnesty International **(English-speaking)**,
312 Laurier Avenue East, Ottawa,
Ontario, K1N 1H9
email: info@amnesty.ca
www.amnesty.ca
Amnistie Internationale **(francophone)**,
6250 boulevard Monk, Montréal,
Québec, H4E 3H7
www.amnistie.ca

Chile ❖ Amnistía Internacional,
Oficina Nacional, Huelén 164 - Planta Baja,
750-0617 Providencia, Santiago
email: info@amnistia.cl
www.amnistia.cl

Côte d'Ivoire ❖ Amnesty International,
04 BP 895, Abidjan 04
email: amnesty.ci@aviso.ci

Denmark ❖ Amnesty International,
Gammeltorv 8, 5 - 1457 Copenhagen K.
email: amnesty@amnesty.dk
www.amnesty.dk

Faroe Islands ❖ Amnesty International,
Hoydalsvegur 6, FO-100 Tórshavn
email: amnesty@amnesty.fo
www.amnesty.fo

Finland ❖ Amnesty International,
Ruoholahdenkatu 24, D 00180 Helsinki
email: amnesty@amnesty.fi
www.amnesty.fi

France ❖ Amnesty International,
76 boulevard de la Villette, 75940 Paris, Cédex 19
email: info@amnesty.fr
www.amnesty.fr

Germany ❖ Amnesty International,
Heerstrasse 178, 53111 Bonn
email: info@amnesty.de
www.amnesty.de

Greece ❖ Amnesty International,
Sina 30, 106 72 Athens
email: info@amnesty.org.gr
www.amnesty.org.gr

Hong Kong ❖ Amnesty International,
Unit D, 3/F, Best-O-Best Commercial Centre,
32-36 Ferry Street, Kowloon
email: admin-hk@amnesty.org.hk
www.amnesty.org.hk

Iceland ❖ Amnesty International,
Þingholtsstræti 27, 101 Reykjavík
email: amnesty@amnesty.is
www.amnesty.is

Ireland ❖ Amnesty International,
1st Floor, Ballast House,
18-21 Westmoreland St, Dublin 2
email: info@amnesty.ie
www.amnesty.ie

Israel ❖ Amnesty International,
PO Box 14179, Tel Aviv 61141
email: info@amnesty.org.il
www.amnesty.org.il

Italy ❖ Amnesty International,
Via Giovanni Battista De Rossi, 10,
00161 Roma
email: info@amnesty.it
www.amnesty.it

Japan ❖ Amnesty International,
4F Kyodo Bldg., 2-2 Kandanishiki-cho,
Chiyoda-ku,
Tokyo 101-0054
email: info@amnesty.or.jp
www.amnesty.or.jp

Korea (Republic of) ❖ Amnesty International,
Gwanghwamun PO Box 2045, Jongno-gu,
110-620 Seoul,
email: info@amnesty.or.kr
www.amnesty.or.kr

Luxembourg ❖ Amnesty International,
Boîte Postale 1914, 1019 Luxembourg
email: info@amnesty.lu
www.amnesty.lu

Mauritius ❖ Amnesty International,
BP 69, Rose-Hill
email: amnestymtius@intnet.mu

Mexico ❖ Amnistía Internacional,
Tajín No. 389, Col. Narvarte, Del. Benito Juárez,
CP 03020 Mexico DF
email: contacto@amnistia.org.mx
www.amnistia.org.mx

Morocco ❖ Amnesty International,
281 avenue Mohamed V,
Apt. 23, Escalier A,
Rabat
email: amorocco@sections.amnesty.org

Nepal ❖ Amnesty International,
PO Box 135, Amnesty Marga,
Basantanagar,
Balaju, Kathmandu
email: info@amnestynepal.org
www.amnestynepal.org

Netherlands ❖ Amnesty International,
Keizersgracht 177, 1016 DR Amsterdam
email: amnesty@amnesty.nl
www.amnesty.nl

New Zealand ❖ Amnesty International,
PO Box 5300, Wellesley Street, Auckland
email: info@amnesty.org.nz
www.amnesty.org.nz

Norway ❖ Amnesty International,
Tordenskioldsgate 6B,
0106 Oslo
email: info@amnesty.no
www.amnesty.no

Peru ❖ Amnistía Internacional,
Enrique Palacios 735-A, Miraflores, Lima 18
email: amnistia@amnestia.org.pe
www.amnistia.org.pe

Philippines ❖ Amnesty International,
18 A Marunong Street,
Barangay Central, Quezon City 1101
email: section@amnesty.org.ph
www.amnesty.org.ph

Poland ❖ Amnesty International,
ul. Piękna 66a, lokal 2, I piętro, 00-672, Warszawa
email: amnesty@amnesty.org.pl
www.amnesty.org.pl

Portugal ❖ Amnistia Internacional,
Av. Infante Santo, 42, 2°, 1350 - 179 Lisboa
email: aiportugal@amnistia-internacional.pt
www.amnistia-internacional.pt

Puerto Rico ❖ Amnistía Internacional,
Calle Robles 54, Suite 1, Río Piedras, 00925
email: amnistiapr@amnestypr.org
www.amnistiapr.org

Senegal ❖ Amnesty International,
303/GRD Sacré-coeur II, Résidence Arame SIGA,
BP 35269, Dakar Colobane
email: asenegal@sections.amnesty.org
www.amnesty.sn

Sierra Leone ❖ Amnesty International,
PMB 1021, 16 Pademba Road, Freetown
email: amnestysl@gmail.com

Slovenia ❖ Amnesty International,
Beethovnova 7, 1000 Ljubljana
email: amnesty@amnesty.si
www.amnesty.si

Spain ❖ Amnistía Internacional,
Fernando VI, 8, 1° izda, 28004 Madrid
email: info@es.amnesty.org
www.es.amnesty.org

Sweden ❖ Amnesty International,
PO Box 4719, 11692 Stockholm
email: info@amnesty.se
www.amnesty.se

Switzerland ❖ Amnesty International,
PO Box, CH-3001 Berne
email: info@amnesty.ch
www.amnesty.ch

Taiwan ❖ Amnesty International,
3F., No. 14, Lane 165, Sec. 1,
Sinsheng S. Rd, Da-an District,
Taipei City 106
email: amnesty.taiwan@gmail.com
www.amnesty.tw

Togo ❖ Amnesty International,
2322 avenue du RPT,
Quartier Casablanca,
BP 20013, Lomé
email: aitogo@cafe.tg

Tunisia ❖ Amnesty International,
67 rue Oum Kalthoum,
3ème étage, Escalier B,
1000 Tunis
email: admin-tn@amnesty.org

United Kingdom ❖ Amnesty International,
The Human Rights Action Centre,
17-25 New Inn Yard,
London EC2A 3EA
email: sct@amnesty.org.uk
www.amnesty.org.uk

United States of America ❖ Amnesty International,
5 Penn Plaza, 16th floor, New York,
NY 10001
email: admin-us@aiusa.org
www.amnestyusa.org

Uruguay ❖ Amnistía Internacional,
Wilson Ferreira Aldunate 1220,
CP 11.100,
Montevideo
email: oficina@amnistia.org.uy
www.amnistia.org.uy

Venezuela ❖ Amnistía Internacional,
Edificio Ateneo de Caracas, piso 6,
Plaza Morelos, Los Caobos,
Caracas 1010A
email: admin-ve@amnesty.org
www.amnistia.org.ve

AMNESTY INTERNATIONAL
STRUCTURES

Burkina Faso ❖ Amnesty International,
Rue 17.548, 08 BP 11344,
Ouagadougou 08
email: aiburkina@fasonet.bf

Czech Republic ❖ Amnesty International,
Provaznická 3, 110 00, Prague 1
email: amnesty@amnesty.cz
www.amnesty.cz

Hungary ❖ Amnesty International,
Rózsa u. 44, II/4, 1064 Budapest
email: info@amnesty.hu
www.amnesty.hu

Malaysia ❖ Amnesty International,
A-3-3A, 8 Avenue, Jalan Sungai Jernih,
8/1, Section 8, 46050, Petaling Jaya, Selangor
email: amnesty@tm.net.my
www.aimalaysia.org

Moldova ❖ Amnesty International,
PO Box 209, MD-2012 Chişinău
email: info@amnesty.md
www.amnesty.md

Mongolia ❖ Amnesty International,
PO Box 180, Ulaanbaatar 210648
email: aimncc@magicnet.mn
www.amnesty.mn

Paraguay ❖ Amnistía Internacional,
Tte. Zotti No. 352 casi Emilio Hassler,
Barrio Villa Morra, Asunción
email: ai-info@py.amnesty.org
www.py.amnesty.org

Turkey ❖ Amnesty International,
Abdülhakhamid Cd. No. 30/5, Talimhane,
Beyoğlu, Istanbul
email: posta@amnesty.org.tr
www.amnesty.org.tr

Ukraine ❖ Amnesty International,
vul. Kravchenko, 17, kv.108, Kiev
email: info@amnesty.org.ua
www.amnesty.org.ua

AMNESTY INTERNATIONAL
PRE-STRUCTURES

Croatia ❖ Amnesty International,
Praška 2/III, 10000 Zagreb
email: admin@amnesty.hr
www.amnesty.hr

Mali ❖ Amnesty International,
Badala Sema 1, Immeuble MUTEC
(Ex Jiguissèmè), Rue 84, porte 14, BP E 3885,
Badalabougou, Bamako
email: amnesty.mali@ikatelnet.net

Slovakia ❖ Amnesty International,
Karpatska 11, 811 05 Bratislava
email: amnesty@amnesty.sk
www.amnesty.sk

Thailand ❖ Amnesty International,
90/24 Lat Phrao Soi 1, Lat Yao, Chatuchak,
Bangkok 10900
email: info@amnesty.or.th
www.amnesty.or.th

AMNESTY INTERNATIONAL
SPECIAL PROJECTS

There are Amnesty International Special Projects in the following countries:

Brazil, Ecuador, Ghana, India, Kenya, South Africa, Zimbabwe.

AMNESTY INTERNATIONAL
GROUPS

There are also Amnesty International groups in:

Angola, Aruba, Bahamas, Bahrain, Barbados, Belarus, Bolivia, Botswana, Cameroon, Cape Verde, Chad, Colombia, Curaçao, Dominican Republic, Egypt, Estonia, Gambia, Guyana, Jamaica, Jordan, Kuwait, Kyrgyzstan, Lebanon, Liberia, Malta, Mozambique, Palestinian Authority, Pakistan, Russian Federation, Trinidad and Tobago, Uganda, Yemen, Zambia.

More information and contact details on both Amnesty International groups and Amnesty International Special Projects can be found online at www.amnesty.org.

AMNESTY INTERNATIONAL
OFFICES

International Secretariat (IS)
Amnesty International,
Peter Benenson House,
1 Easton Street,
London WC1X 0DW,
United Kingdom
email: amnestyis@amnesty.org
www.amnesty.org

ARABAI (Arabic translation unit)
c/o International Secretariat,
Peter Benenson House, 1 Easton Street,
London WC1X 0DW,
United Kingdom
email: arabai@amnesty.org
www.amnesty.org/ar

Éditions Francophones d'Amnesty International (EFAI)
47 rue de Paradis,
75010 Paris,
France
email: ai-efai@amnesty.org
www.amnesty.org/fr

Editorial Amnistía Internacional (EDAI)
Calle Valderribas, 13,
28007 Madrid, Spain
email: edai@edai.org
www.amnesty.org/es

European Union (EU) Office
Amnesty International,
Rue de Trèves 35, B-1040 Brussels,
Belgium
email: amnesty-eu@aieu.be
www.amnesty-eu.org

IS Beirut – Middle East and North Africa Regional Office
Amnesty International,
PO Box 13-5696, Chouran Beirut 1102 - 2060,
Lebanon
email: mena@amnesty.org

IS Dakar – Africa Human Rights Education Office
Amnesty International,
SICAP Sacré Coeur Pyrotechnie Extension,
Villa No. 25, BP 47582, Dakar,
Senegal
email: KGaglo@amnesty.org

IS Geneva – UN Representative Office
Amnesty International,
22 rue du Cendrier, 4ème étage, CH-1201 Geneva,
Switzerland
email: gvunpost@amnesty.org

IS Hong Kong – Asia Pacific Regional Office
Amnesty International,
16/F Siu On Centre, 188 Lockhart Rd, Wanchai,
Hong Kong
email: admin-ap@amnesty.org

IS Kampala – Africa Regional Office
Amnesty International,
Plot 20A Kawalya Kaggwa Close, PO Box 23966, Kampala,
Uganda
email: ai-aro@amnesty.org

IS Moscow – Russia Resource Centre
Amnesty International,
PO Box 212, Moscow 119019,
Russian Federation
email: msk@amnesty.org
www.amnesty.org.ru

IS New York – UN Representative Office
Amnesty International,
777 UN Plaza, 6th Floor, New York, NY 10017,
USA
email: aiunny@amnesty.org

IS Paris – Research Office
Amnesty International,
76 boulevard de la Villette, 75940 Paris, Cédex 19,
France
email: pro@amnesty.org

I WANT TO HELP

WHETHER IN A HIGH-PROFILE CONFLICT OR A FORGOTTEN CORNER OF THE GLOBE, **AMNESTY INTERNATIONAL** CAMPAIGNS FOR JUSTICE AND FREEDOM FOR ALL AND SEEKS TO GALVANIZE PUBLIC SUPPORT TO BUILD A BETTER WORLD

WHAT CAN YOU DO?

Activists around the world have shown that it is possible to resist the dangerous forces that are undermining human rights. Be part of this movement. Combat those who peddle fear and hate.

- Join Amnesty International and become part of a worldwide movement campaigning for an end to human rights violations. Help us make a difference.

- Make a donation to support Amnesty International's work.

Together we can make our voices heard.

I am interested in receiving further information on becoming a member of Amnesty International

name

address

country

email

I wish to make a donation to Amnesty International (donations will be taken in UK£, US$ or euros)

amount

please debit my: Visa ☐   Mastercard ☐

number ☐☐☐☐☐ ☐☐☐☐☐ ☐☐☐☐☐ ☐☐☐☐

expiry date

signature

Please return this form to the Amnesty International office in your country.
(See pages 396-399 for further details of Amnesty International offices worldwide.)
If there is not an Amnesty International office in your country, please return this form to the International Secretariat in London:
Peter Benenson House, 1 Easton Street, London WC1X 0DW, United Kingdom

www.amnesty.org

INDEX OF SELECTED TOPICS*

A

abuses by armed groups
(see also unlawful killings)

Afghanistan 56-7; Argentina 66; Brazil 87; Cambodia 95; Central African Republic 101; Chad 103, 105; Colombia 111, 112-13, 114; Congo, Republic of 115-16; Côte d'Ivoire 117, 118; Democratic Republic of the Congo 126, 127; Georgia 152; Iraq 177, 178; Israel 183-4; Lebanon 207; Macedonia 215; Nepal 241; Niger 246; Nigeria 247; Pakistan 252-3; Palestinian Authority 257; Senegal 282; Sierra Leone 287; Spain 302; Sri Lanka 304 -5; Thailand 321; Turkey 332

arbitrary arrests and detentions

Afghanistan 56; Angola 65; Armenia 67; Burkina Faso 91; Burundi 92-3; Cameroon 97-8; Central African Republic 102; Chad 103; China 107-8; Congo, Republic of 116; Democratic Republic of the Congo 127; Equatorial Guinea 137-8; France 149; Greece 156; Guinea 161; Haiti 164; Iraq 178; Israel 184; Korea, (Republic of) 201; Lebanon 208; Mauritania 222; Mexico 224; Mongolia 229-30; Morocco/Western Sahara 233; Niger 246; Pakistan 252; Palestinian Authority 255; Sri Lanka 305; Sudan 308; Switzerland 314; Thailand 321-2; Uganda 336; United Arab Emirates 34

armed conflict

Chad 103; Colombia 111-12; Democratic Republic of the Congo 125-6; Ethiopia 145; Georgia 152; India 169; Lebanon 207; Mali 220; Myanmar 237-8; Philippines 262; Russian Federation 272; Somalia 295; Sri Lanka 304; Sudan 307-8; Uganda 335

C

child soldiers

Chad 104; Colombia 111; Democratic Republic of the Congo 126-7; Nepal 241

children's rights

Haiti 163; Ireland 180-1; Pakistan 254; United Kingdom 344-5

counter-terror and security

Algeria 61; Australia 69; Belgium 79; Bosnia and Herzegovina 84; Canada 99; Egypt 133; France 149; Germany 153-4; Ireland 181; Italy 187, 187-8; Jordan 192; Kenya 198; Kuwait 202; Libya 212; Macedonia 216; Mauritania 222; Morocco/Western Sahara 233-4; New Zealand 243; Poland 264; Portugal 266; Qatar 267; Romania 268; Saudi Arabia 279; Slovakia 292; Spain 302-3; Sweden 312-13; Switzerland 314; Syria 316; Tunisia 327-8; United Arab Emirates 340; United Kingdom 341; United States of America 345-6; Uzbekistan 353

cruel, inhuman and degrading punishments
(see also torture and other ill-treatment)

Bulgaria 90; Burundi 92; Central African Republic 101; Cyprus 123; Democratic Republic of the Congo 127; Egypt 133; Eritrea 141; France 149; Germany 153; Iran 176; Korea (Republic of) 200; Malaysia 219; Philippines 263; Saudi Arabia 280; United States of America 346, 347; Yemen 359

D

death penalty

Afghanistan 56; Algeria 63; Argentina 66; Bahamas 72-3; Bahrain 74; Bangladesh 76; Belarus 78; Benin 80; Burkina Faso 91; Cameroon 98; Canada 100; Chad 104; China 108; Cuba 122; Democratic Republic of the Congo 128; Egypt 135; Ethiopia 145; Gambia 151; Ghana 155; Guatemala 159; Guinea 161; India 170; Indonesia 172; Iran 176; Iraq 177-8; Iraq - Kurdistan 180; Jamaica 190; Japan 190; Jordan 193-4; Kenya 198; Korea (Democratic People's Republic of) 200; Korea, (Republic of) 201; Kuwait 203; Laos 205; Latvia 206; Lebanon 209; Liberia 210; Malaysia 217, 219; Mali 220-1; Mauritania 223; Mongolia 230; Nigeria 249; Pakistan 254; Palestinian Authority 255-6, 257; Qatar 267; Saint Kitts and Nevis 277-8; Saudi Arabia 280-1; Sierra Leone 289; Singapore 290; Solomon Islands 294; Somalia 297; Sudan 308-9; Swaziland 312; Syria 317; Taiwan 318; Tanzania 321; Thailand 323; Trinidad and Tobago 326; Tunisia 329; Uganda 337; United Arab Emirates 341; United States of America 348-9; Uzbekistan 353; Viet Nam 356; Yemen 359

detention without trial
(see also arbitrary arrests and detentions)

Afghanistan 56; Algeria 61; Burundi 92-3; Cambodia 95-6; Democratic Republic of the Congo 127; Congo, Republic of 116; Egypt 133; Gambia 150; Japan 191; Jordan 192; Lebanon 207; Malaysia 218; Malta 221; Netherlands 242-3; Singapore 290; United Kingdom 342; United States of America 346

discrimination

Dominican Republic 130; Iran 174-5; Laos 205; Latvia 205; Malaysia 219; Namibia 239-40; Papua New Guinea 258; Puerto Rico 266; Russian Federation 274; Slovenia 292-3; Syria 317; Tanzania 320; United States of America 348; Viet Nam 356

discrimination – migrants

Dominican Republic 130; Estonia 142; Lithuania 213-14

discrimination – minorities

Arabs – Iran 174; Azerbaijanis – Iran 174; Baluchis – Iran 174; Bolivia 81; Bulgaria 89-90; Estonia 142; India 168, 169; Iran 174, 175; Ireland 181; Israel 184-5; Laos 205; Oman 251; Poland 264; Serbia 286; Turkmenistan 335; United Arab Emirates 341

discrimination – religion

Armenia 68; Egypt 135; Iran 175; Moldova 228-9; Pakistan 254; Viet Nam 356

discrimination – Roma

Bosnia and Herzegovina 84; Bulgaria 89-90; Croatia 120; Czech Republic 123-4; Hungary 166; Italy 186-7; Latvia 206; Lithuania 213-14; Macedonia 216; Montenegro 231; Romania 269-70; Serbia 285; Slovakia 290-1; Slovenia 293; Switzerland 313-14

discrimination – women
(see also violence against women and girls)

Afghanistan 57; Iran 173; Jordan 193; Lebanon 208; Morocco/Western Sahara 234; Namibia 239-40; Qatar 267; Saudi Arabia 279-80; Syria 317; United Arab Emirates 340-1; Yemen 359

E

enforced disappearances
Albania 59; Algeria 62-3; Argentina 66; Bosnia and Herzegovina 83-4; Chad 103; Croatia 119; Cyprus 122; Equatorial Guinea 138; Gambia 150; Korea (Democratic People's Republic of) 200; Montenegro 231; Morocco/Western Sahara 234; Nepal 241; Pakistan 252-3; Philippines 262-3; Slovenia 292-3; Spain 303; Sri Lanka 305; Syria 316; Turkmenistan 334; Zimbabwe 361-2

excessive use of force
Armenia 67; Bangladesh 75; Chad 103-4; Côte d'Ivoire 117; Estonia 142; Greece 156; Guinea 160-1; Korea, (Republic of) 200; Lebanon 208; Malaysia 218; Mali 220; Morocco/Western Sahara 233; Mozambique 235-6; Palestinian Authority 256-7; Paraguay 259-60; Romania 268-9; Senegal 281; Turkey 331

extrajudicial executions
Algeria 60; Bangladesh 75-6; Chad 104; Colombia 112; Nigeria 248; Philippines 262-3; Somalia 297; Zimbabwe 361

F

forced evictions
Angola 64; Argentina 66; Brazil 86; Cambodia 95; Chad 104; Equatorial Guinea 137; Guatemala 158-9; India 168-9; Israel 185; Italy 186; Kenya 197; Myanmar 237; Papua New Guinea 258-9; Tajikistan 319

freedom of assembly
Armenia 67; Bangladesh 75; Belarus 76-7; Bosnia and Herzegovina 84-5; Burundi 93; Cameroon 97-8; China – Hong Kong 109-10; Egypt 134; Jordan 192-3; Korea, (Republic of) 201; Kyrgyzstan 203; Russian Federation 273; Senegal 281-2; Singapore 290; Swaziland 311; Taiwan 318; Turkey 330-1; Uganda 336; Viet Nam 356

freedom of association
Argentina 66; Bangladesh 75; Congo (Republic of) 116; Cuba 121; Egypt 134; Iran 174; Jordan 192-3; Korea, (Republic of) 201; Libya 212; Nicaragua 245; Russian Federation 273; Swaziland 311; Uganda 336; United Arab Emirates 340

freedom of expression
(see also repression of dissent)
Bahrain 73-4; Bangladesh 75; Belarus 77; Burundi 93; Cambodia 95; China 108; China – Hong Kong 109-10; China – Macao 110; Congo (Republic of) 116; Cuba 121; Ecuador 132; Egypt 134; Equatorial Guinea 139; Ethiopia 144; Fiji 146; Finland 147; Georgia 153; Greece 158; Guinea-Bissau 162; Indonesia 171; Iran 174; Iraq – Kurdistan 180; Israel 185; Jordan 192-3; Kenya 198; Korea (Democratic People's Republic of) 200; Korea, (Republic of) 201; Kuwait 202; Malaysia 217-18; Moldova 228; Mongolia 230; Morocco/Western Sahara 232; Mozambique 236; Myanmar 238; Nicaragua 245; Niger 246; Nigeria 249-50; Oman 251; Palestinian Authority 256; Philippines 263; Russian Federation 273; Senegal 282; Sierra Leone 288; Singapore 290; Somalia 295; Swaziland 311; Syria 317; Taiwan 318; Tanzania 320; Thailand 322; Tonga 325; Turkey 330, 332; Turkmenistan 334; Uganda 336; United Arab Emirates 340; Uzbekistan 352; Viet Nam 355-6; Yemen 357-8; Zimbabwe 362-3

freedom of expression – internet
Armenia 68; China 108; Malaysia 217; Myanmar 238; Syria 317; Thailand 322; Turkmenistan 334

freedom of expression – journalists
Afghanistan 57; Algeria 61-2; Angola 65; Armenia 67-8; Azerbaijan 71; Belarus 77; Bolivia 81; Burundi 93; Cameroon 97; Central African Republic 101; Chad 104; China 108; Croatia 119-20; Dominican Republic 130; Eritrea 140; Gambia 151; Guinea 161; Korea, (Republic of) 201; Kuwait 202; Kyrgyzstan 204; Malawi 217; Mexico 224, 226; Montenegro 231; Mozambique 236; Nicaragua 244; Peru 260-1; Russian Federation 272-3; Rwanda 276; Somalia 296; Sri Lanka 305-6; Sudan 309; Tanzania 320; Togo 325; Tunisia 328; Uganda 336; Uruguay 350; Uzbekistan 352; Viet Nam 356; Zimbabwe 362-3

freedom of religion
Algeria 62; Azerbaijan 71-2; China 108; China – Xinjiang Uighur 109; Egypt 135; Eritrea 140; Indonesia 171; Iran 175; Kazakstan 195; Kyrgyzstan 203; Laos 204; Malaysia 219; Singapore 290; Tajikistan 319; Uzbekistan 352

H

health, right to (see also HIV/AIDS)
Afghanistan 57-8; Bulgaria 90-1; Burkina Faso 91; Czech Republic 124; Dominican Republic 129; Egypt 135-6; Haiti 163; Indonesia 172; Ireland 181; Kenya 197; Korea (Democratic People's Republic of) 199; Nicaragua 244; Palestinian Authority 257; Papua New Guinea 258; Peru 260; Poland 264; Romania 269; Slovakia 291; South Africa 299-300; Swaziland 312; Uganda 336; United States of America 348

HIV/AIDS
Dominican Republic 129; Papua New Guinea 258; South Africa 299-300; Swaziland 312

housing rights
(see also land rights)
Albania 60; Angola 64; Brazil 86; Czech Republic 124; Egypt 135; Equatorial Guinea 137; Ghana 155; Israel 185; Maldives 220; Nigeria 250; Slovakia 291; Solomon Islands 293; Turkmenistan 334

human rights defenders
Algeria 61-2; Angola 64-5; Armenia 68; Brazil 87; Cameroon 97; Central African Republic 101; Chad 105; China 107; Colombia 113-14; Democratic Republic of the Congo 127; Egypt 134; Estonia 142; Ethiopia 144-5; France 149-50; Guatemala 159; Honduras 164-5; India 169; Iran 173; Lebanon 208; Mexico 224-5; Peru 260-1; Russian Federation 272-3; Rwanda 276; Serbia 285; Somalia 295; Sri Lanka 305-6; Sudan 309-10; Syria 317; Tunisia 329; Turkey 330; Uzbekistan 351-2; Venezuela 354-5; Zimbabwe 363

I

impunity
Afghanistan 55-6; Algeria 62; Argentina 66; Armenia 68; Bangladesh 75-6; Benin 80; Bolivia 81-2; Burkina Faso 91; Burundi 94; Cambodia 95; Central African Republic 101; Chile

106; Colombia 111, 113; Democratic Republic of the Congo 127; El Salvador 136-7; France 148; Guatemala 159; Haiti 164; Honduras 165; India 170; Indonesia 171-2; Israel 185; Kenya 197; Lebanon 207; Liberia 210; Libya 212-13; Mexico 226; Moldova 228; Nepal 241; Peru 261; Russian Federation 271-2; Rwanda 277; Serbia 285-6; South Africa 300; Sri Lanka 305; Suriname 310; Syria 316; Thailand 322; Timor-Leste 324; Togo 325; Turkey 332; Ukraine 339; Uruguay 350; Zimbabwe 360-1

Indigenous peoples' rights
Argentina 66; Australia 69; Bangladesh 75; Bolivia 81; Brazil 86; Canada 99; Chile 106; El Salvador 136; Nicaragua 245; Paraguay 259; Philippines 263

internally displaced people
Afghanistan 58; Bosnia and Herzegovina 84; Chad 103, 104; Democratic Republic of the Congo 127; Georgia 152; Iraq 179; Kenya 196; Myanmar 238; Serbia 286; Somalia 296; Sudan 308; Timor-Leste 324; Uganda 335-6; Zimbabwe 362

international justice (see also justice system)
Bosnia and Herzegovina 82-3; Cambodia 95-6; Central African Republic 101; Croatia 118-19; Czech Republic 124-5; Democratic Republic of the Congo 127-8; Finland 147; Macedonia 215; Moldova 229; Montenegro 230; Rwanda 276-7; Senegal 282; Serbia 283-4, 285; Sudan 307; United States of America 348

international scrutiny
Bahrain 73; Burundi 94; Colombia 112, 114-15; Cuba 121; Georgia 153; Kenya 196; Korea, Democratic People's Republic of 200; Liberia 210; Malta 221; Myanmar 238-9; Nepal 241; Paraguay 260; Togo 324; Sierra Leone 288; United Arab Emirates 341; Uzbekistan 351

J

justice system
(see also international justice)
Afghanistan 55; Albania 58; Algeria 61; Austria 70; Bosnia and Herzegovina 83; Burundi 92; Chile 106; China 107; Croatia 119; Cuba 121-2; Egypt 133; Gambia 151; Ghana 155; Haiti 163-4; Iran 175; Israel 184; Jamaica 189-90; Jordan 192; Liberia 211; Macedonia 215; Malta 221; Mexico 224; Montenegro 230; Morocco/Western Sahara 234; Nicaragua 244; Nigeria 248-9; Palestinian Authority 255-6; Russian Federation 274; Rwanda 277; Serbia 284; Sierra Leone 287-8, 288; Somalia 296-7; Trinidad and Tobago 326; United Kingdom 342; United States of America 345-6; Uruguay 350

L

land rights
(see also housing rights)
Bangladesh 75; Guatemala 158-9; Liberia 210; Suriname 310

legal, constitutional or institutional developments
Albania 59; Armenia 67; Australia 69; Bahrain 73; Cambodia 96; Czech Republic 123; Egypt 132-3; France 149; Germany 155; Hungary 166; Ireland 181; Kazakhstan 194-5; Maldives 219-20; Mexico 227; Mongolia 230; Myanmar 238; Nepal 242;

Netherlands 243; New Zealand 244; Pakistan 252; Thailand 323; Tonga 325; Tunisia 327

lesbian, gay, bisexual and transgender people (rights of)
Belarus 77; Bosnia and Herzegovina 84-5; Bulgaria 90; Cameroon 98; Czech Republic 124; Egypt` 134-5; Gambia 151; Greece 158; Hungary 166-7; Jamaica 190; Latvia 206; Lithuania 214; Moldova 228; Morocco/Western Sahara 234; Nepal 242; Nigeria 250; Romania 270; Rwanda 277; Senegal 282; Turkey 332; Uganda 337

M

migrants' rights
Algeria 62; Austria 70; Bahamas 72; Belgium 79; Cyprus 122; Egypt 135; Estonia 142; France 148-9; Germany 154; Israel 185; Italy 187; Jordan 193; Korea (Democratic People's Republic of) 199; Korea (Republic of) 200-01; Kuwait 202; Latvia 206; Libya 213; Lithuania 213-4; Malaysia 218; Malta 221; Mauritania 223; Mexico 226-7; Morocco/Western Sahara 234; Netherlands 242-3; Qatar 267; Saudi Arabia 280; Singapore 290; South Africa 298-9; Spain 303; Switzerland 314; United Arab Emirates 340; United States of America 348

P

police and security forces
Afghanistan 56; Albania 59; Angola 64; Argentina 67; Australia 69; Austria 70; Bahamas 72; Belgium 79; Bosnia and Herzegovina 84; Brazil 87-8; Canada 99-100; Chile 106; China – Tibet 109; China – Hong Kong 110; Colombia 112; Côte d'Ivoire 118; Cyprus 123; Denmark 129; Dominican Republic 129-30; Ecuador 132; Egypt 133, 134; France 148, 149; Germany 153-4, 154; Guatemala 159; Haiti 164; Hungary 167; India 169-70; Indonesia 171; Iraq 178; Ireland 181; Italy 187-8; Jamaica 189; Jordan 192; Kazakhstan 194; Kenya 198; Kuwait 202; Libya 212; Macedonia 216; Mauritania 222; Mexico 225; Morocco/Western Sahara 233-4; Mozambique 235; Nepal 241; New Zealand 243; Pakistan 253; Poland 264; Puerto Rico 266; Portugal 266; Qatar 267; Romania 268; Saudi Arabia 279; Sierra Leone 288; Slovakia 292; Spain 302-3; Swaziland 311-12; Sweden 312-13; Switzerland 314; Syria 316; Thailand 322; Timor-Leste 323-4; Trinidad and Tobago 326; Tunisia 327-8; United Arab Emirates 340; United Kingdom 341, 344; Uzbekistan 353; Venezuela 355

political prisoners
Colombia 113; Eritrea 140; Ethiopia 143-4; Kenya 195-6; Malawi 217; Myanmar 237; Syria 315-16; Tunisia 328;

prison conditions
Albania 60; Algeria 61; Argentina 67; Benin 80; Burundi 92; Cameroon 98; Equatorial Guinea 138; Eritrea 141; Ethiopia 144; Ghana 155; Greece 157-8; Honduras 165-6; Ireland 181; Israel 184; Japan 191; Korea (Democratic People's Republic of) 199-200; Macedonia 215-16; Malawi 217; Mauritania 223; Namibia 240; Nigeria 249; Philippines 263; Tanzania 320-1; Turkey 331; United States of America 348; Venezuela 355

prisoners of conscience
Angola 65; Belarus 78; Cuba 121; Eritrea 140-1; Ethiopia 143-4; Finland 147; Israel 185; Mauritania 222; Mexico 225; Rwanda 276; Saudi Arabia 278-9; Syria 315-16, 317; Turkey 332; Turkmenistan 334; Uzbekistan 352; Yemen 357-8

R

racism
China – Hong Kong 110; Cyprus 122; Estonia 142; Italy 187; Latvia 206; Lithuania 213-14; Malta 221; Portugal 265-6; Russian Federation 274; Spain 303; Switzerland 313-14; Ukraine 338

refugees and asylum-seekers
Australia 69; Austria 70; Bahamas 72; Belgium 79; Bosnia and Herzegovina 84; Bulgaria 89; Burundi 94; Canada 99; Chad 104; China – Hong Kong 110; Congo (Republic of) 116; Cyprus 122; Democratic Republic of the Congo 127; Denmark 128-9; Egypt 135; Eritrea 140-1; Finland 147; France 148, 148-9; Germany 154; Greece 156-7; Iran 176; Iraq 179; Ireland 181; Israel 185; Italy 187; Japan 191; Jordan 193; Kazakstan 195; Kenya 197-8; Korea (Democratic People's Republic of) 199; Korea, (Republic of) 201; Kyrgyzstan 203-4; Lebanon 208; Libya 213; Macedonia 216; Malaysia 218; Malta 221; Montenegro 231; Morocco/Western Sahara 234; Netherlands 242-3; New Zealand 243; Poland 265; Romania 268; Russian Federation 274; Saudi Arabia 280; Serbia 286; Slovakia 292; Somalia 296; South Africa 298-9; Spain 302, 303; Sweden 313; Switzerland 314; Syria 317-18; Taiwan 318; Thailand 323; Turkey 333; Uganda 336; Ukraine 338; United Kingdom 344; Yemen 359

repression of dissent
(see also freedom of expression)
Georgia 152-3; Libya 211-12; Mongolia 229; Morocco/Western Sahara 232; Singapore 289-90; Turkmenistan 333-4

T

torture and other ill-treatment
Afghanistan 55; Albania 59-60; Algeria 61; Australia 69; Austria 70; Azerbaijan 72; Bahrain 73; Belgium 79; Bosnia and Herzegovina 84; Brazil 88; Bulgaria 90-1; Burundi 93; Central African Republic 101-02; China 108; Czech Republic 124; Democratic Republic of the Congo 127; Denmark 128-9; Egypt 133-4; Equatorial Guinea 138; Eritrea 141; Ethiopia 145; Fiji 146; Greece 157; Guinea 161; Iran 175-6; Iraq – Kurdistan 179; Israel 184; Italy 188; Jordan 192; Kazakstan 194; Latvia 206; Lebanon 207-8; Macedonia 215; Mali 220; Mauritania 223; Mexico 225-6; Moldova 227-8; Montenegro 231; Nepal 241; New Zealand 243; Niger 246; Nigeria 248; Pakistan 252; Palestinian Authority 256; Paraguay 259-60; Portugal 265; Romania 268-9; Russian Federation 273-4; Saudi Arabia 280; Serbia 284; Slovakia 291-2; South Africa 300; Spain 301-2; Syria 317; Thailand 322; Tunisia 328; Turkey 331; Uganda 336-7; Ukraine 338-9; United Arab Emirates 340; United Kingdom 342-3; United States of America 347; Uzbekistan 353; Yemen 358; Zimbabwe 362

trafficking in human beings
Albania 59; Dominican Republic 130; Greece 157; Guinea-Bissau 162; Haiti 163; Ireland 181-2; United Kingdom 344

U

unfair trials
Algeria 61; Belarus 77; Cameroon 98; China 107; Egypt 133; Equatorial Guinea 138-9; Iran 174-5; Iraq 178; Italy 188; Jordan 192; Liberia 210; Myanmar 238; Namibia 239; Rwanda 277; Serbia 285; Sudan 308-9; Swaziland 311; Turkey 331-2; Uganda 336; United States of America 346; Yemen 358

unlawful killings
(see also abuses by armed groups)
Bolivia 81; Burundi 92; Cameroon 97; Central African Republic 102; Democratic Republic of the Congo 126; Dominican Republic 130; France 148; Gambia 150; Ghana 155; Greece 156; Israel 183-4; Kenya 197; Mexico 225; Montenegro 231; Mozambique 235; Niger 246; Nigeria 248; Serbia 285; Sri Lanka 304; Syria 316-17; Yemen 359; Zimbabwe 361

V

violence against women and girls
Afghanistan 57; Albania 59; Algeria 63; Armenia 68; Australia 69; Bahamas 72; Burundi 93; Chad 104; China – Hong Kong 110; Colombia 114; Côte d'Ivoire 117-18; Croatia 120; Cyprus 122; Czech Republic 124; Democratic Republic of the Congo 126; Denmark 129; Dominican Republic 130; Ecuador 131-2; Egypt 134; El Salvador 137; Fiji 146; Finland 147; Ghana 155; Guatemala 159; Haiti 163; Honduras 165; Hungary 167; Iraq 179; Iraq – Kurdistan 180; Ireland 181; Jamaica 190; Japan 191; Jordan 193; Kenya 197; Korea, (Republic of) 201; Lebanon 208; Liberia 210-11; Lithuania 214; Macedonia 216; Mexico 226; Montenegro 231; Morocco/Western Sahara 234; Nepal 241-2; Nicaragua 245; Nigeria 249; Pakistan 253-4; Palestinian Authority 257; Papua New Guinea 258; Poland 264; Portugal 265; Qatar 267; Russian Federation 274-5; Saudi Arabia 279-80; Serbia 285, 287; Solomon Islands 293-4; South Africa 299; Spain 303; Sudan 308; Swaziland 312; Sweden 313; Switzerland 314; Syria 317; Taiwan 318; Tajikistan 319; Tanzania 320; Tunisia 329; Turkey 333; Uganda 337; United Arab Emirates 340-1; United States of America 348; Venezuela 354; Yemen 359

W

women's rights
(see also violence against women and girls)
Afghanistan 57; Brazil 88-9; Canada 99; Iran 173; Oman 251; Papua New Guinea 258; Sierra Leone 288-9; Tonga 325; Uruguay 350

workers' rights
Colombia 113-14; Ecuador 131; Greece 157; Guatemala 159; Honduras 165; United Arab Emirates 340

* This is an index of topics based around the subheadings that appear in the A-Z of country entries. It should be used by the reader only as a navigational tool, not as a statement of Amnesty International's human rights concerns in a particular country or territory.

Police used batons and tear gas to disperse an unauthorized demonstration against the rising cost of living in Dakar, Senegal, 30 March 2008. Demonstrations against social and economic conditions took place in many countries across Africa.